profession is eminent'   *Financial Times*

'Hughes could behave as badly as Byron or Shelley ever did … but the
characteristic that finally comes to distinguish him is a bloodied kind
of fortitude … biography,
sympathetic … movingly.
The fullest … *Independent*

'Bate has read this huge mass of material with a scholar's ability to date and arrange it ... This scrupulous and lucid biography makes [Hughes's life] all seem like muddle and self-deception, tormenting to himself and the many who loved him' *Guardian*

'Bate has written, capaciously, arrestingly, a kind of tragedy ... He reminds us Ted Hughes was a marvelous poet: firstly, then fitfully, and then in a blaze near the end, and that the greatness in the work draws power from sources deeper than myth' *New York Times Book Review*

'An incisive, humane and deeply absorbing account of Hughes's life and work' *New York Times*

'Bate's relaxed prose keeps everything moving anecdotally ... underpinning it all is a vast command of archival material ... He is also a sure guide to the genesis and reception of each of Hughes's major books' *Daily Telegraph*

'[Bate's] analysis of the poems and how they relate to Hughes's life is particularly illuminating' *Daily Mail*

'Fascinating' JOHN PRESTON, *Spectator*, Books of the Year

'Manages to illuminate the poet's lowering literary presence' CARL WILKINSON, *Financial Times*, Books of the Year

'An excellent biography: compulsively readable, elegantly assembled ... and sensitive to the many aspects of Hughes's grand and complicated character' *Wall Street Journal*

'An intelligent, even donnish work of criticism that connects the poems to the life' *Washington Post*

'Jonathan Bate is a dazzling scholar, and in *Ted Hughes* he sheds new light on the poet and his times ... Mr Bate embodies ... the touchstone of good biography: the complete sympathy of complete detachment'

SARA WHEELER, *Wall Street Journal*, Best Biographies of 2015

Ted Hughes

The Unauthorised Life

Jonathan Bate

WILLIAM
COLLINS

William Collins
An imprint of HarperCollins Publishers
1 London Bridge Street
London SE1 9GF
www.WilliamCollinsBooks.com

First published in Great Britain by William Collins in 2015
This paperback edition published in 2016

1

A catalogue record for this book is
available from the British Library.

ISBN 978-0-00-811821-1

Printed and bound in Great Britain by
Clays Ltd, St Ives plc

Contents

For Paula Jayne, again and always

And for Barrie and Deedee Wigmore,
because the shepherd's hut unlocked it

NOTE TO THE PAPERBACK EDITION

I am most grateful to Anne Donovan, Peter Fydler, Brenda Hedden, Carol Hughes and Rowland Wymer for pointing out a number of errors, ambiguities and contested memories, which have been addressed in this edition.

Jonathan Bate, January 2016

As an imaginative writer, my only capital is my own life

Ted Hughes (1992)

When you sit with your pen, every year of your life is right there, wired into the communication between your brain and your writing hand ... Maybe all poetry, insofar as it moves us and connects with us, is a revealing of something that the writer doesn't actually want to say but desperately needs to communicate, to be delivered of. Perhaps it's the need to keep it hidden that makes it poetic – makes it poetry. The writer daren't actually put it into words, so it leaks out obliquely, smuggled through analogies ... we're actually saying something we desperately need to share. The real mystery is this strange need. Why can't we just hide it and shut up? Why do we have to blab? Why do human beings need to confess? Maybe if you don't have that secret confession, you don't have a poem – don't even have a story.

Ted Hughes, interviewed for The Paris Review *(Spring 1995)*

Prologue

The Deposition

Q. Would you state your full name for the record?

A. Edward James Hughes.

Q. What is your residence address?

A. Court Green, North Tawton 11, England.

Q. Have you a business address?

A. That's it. I work from home.

Q. And what is your occupation, sir?

A. Writer.

The Yorkshire accent is unfamiliar. 'Eleven' is the stenographer's mishearing of 'Devon'. The date is 26 March 1986.

Q. And could you state your age for the record?

A. 55. I shall be 56 this year.

Q. Now, sir, were you at some time in your life married to a woman named Sylvia Plath?

A. Yes.

Q. Can you tell me when you first met her?

A. The 25th of February 1956.

Q. And where did you meet her?

A. Cambridge, England.

Q. And what were the circumstances of that meeting?

A. I met her at a party.

Q. Do you know what she was doing in England?

A. She was on a Fulbright scholarship.

Q. Do you know where she was from?

A. Did I know then?

Q. Yes.

A. I just knew she was American.

The details are established. Her home town was Wellesley, her college was Smith. And then:

> Q. Do you know whether or not she had been ill?
> A. She told me she had been ill later in the spring.
> Q. Did she tell you she had been mentally ill?
> A. She told me that she attempted to commit suicide.
> Q. Did she tell you the circumstances of her having done that?
> A. She only told me as an explanation of the scar on her cheek.
> Q. Let me see if I understand your answer. There was a scar on her cheek, is that correct?
> A. There was a big scar on her left cheek.[1]

The Deposition is being taken in the offices of Shapiro and Grace, attorneys, on Milk Street, Boston, before Josephine C. Aurelio, Registered Professional Reporter, a Notary Public within and for the Commonwealth of Massachusetts. Carolyn Grace, attorney, is acting on behalf of her client, Dr Jane V. Anderson, who is present in the room. Anderson is plaintiff in Civil Action number 82-0752-K, versus Avco Embassy Pictures Corporation and others, defendants. Edward James Hughes, writer, is one of the others.

He was a man who took astrology seriously. He believed in signs, auguries, meaningful coincidences. Often he would dream of something happening, only for it to happen subsequently. He lived by, and for, the power of words. His vocation was poetry, language wrought to its uttermost, words honed to their essence. The words of his poems – which he obsessively revised, refined, rewrote – are compacted, freighted with meaning, sometimes darkly opaque, sometimes cut like jewels of crystal clarity. He relished the resonance of names: Elmet, Moortown, the Duchy. He believed that houses held ghosts, strong forces, memories.

In Boston that March of 1986, walking familiar streets, he was flooded by memory. He and Sylvia had lived there some thirty years before, on:

Willow Street, poetical address.
Number nine, even better. It confirmed
We had to have it.[2]

Doubly poetical, in fact. There were the pastoral associations of willow: Hughes was haunted by the willow aslant the brook in Gertrude's account of Ophelia's suicide in *Hamlet*. More immediately, Hughes discovered that this had also once been the home of Robert Frost. Willow Street is just off Beacon Street, the heart of literary Boston. Here, a stone's throw from the Charles River, you would find the offices of publishers, both established (Little, Brown) and independent (the Beacon Press). At number 10½ stood the Boston Athenaeum, the library at the centre of the New England intellectual life that back in the nineteenth century had set the template for the nation's literature. For Ted Hughes, though, the name 'Beacon' was a call not only from the literary past but also from his Yorkshire home. His reading and his life came into conjunction. Which was something that seemed to happen to him again and again throughout his life.

The Yorkshire house, up on the hill, is called the Beacon. Square, rather squat, of dark-red brick, not the local gritstone that grounds those dwellings that seem truly to belong to the place. It stands, a little apart from its neighbours, on a long straight road at Heptonstall Slack, high above Hebden Bridge. It commands a sweeping view of hill and vale, down towards Lumb Bank, which would be another place of memory. This was the home of Ted Hughes's parents when they returned to the Yorkshire Moors and the Calder Valley while he was at Cambridge University. A return to their roots, away from the unlovely town of Mexborough, further south, though still in Yorkshire, in the industrial area between Rotherham and Sheffield. Mexborough Grammar had been the school that prepared Ted Hughes for the Cambridge entrance examination.

The move to the Beacon was a sign of upward mobility. Edward James Hughes, like his elder brother and sister Gerald and Olwyn, was born and raised in a cramped end-terrace dwelling in the village of Mytholmroyd. In Mexborough, they had lived behind and above the newspaper and tobacco shop where William and Edith Hughes made their living. It was a matter of pride that they were eventually able to buy a detached house with a name and a view, just as it was a matter of pride that their boy Ted had got into Cambridge. They were not to know that he would rise even higher: that the boy from the end-terrace near the mill would fish privately with Queen Elizabeth the Queen Mother, talk of shamanism with a man born to become king and, just days before he died, receive from the hands of the Queen her highest personal honour, the Order of Merit.

The Beacon became a house of memory. It was here that Ted brought his bride, Sylvia Plath, to meet his parents in 1956. It was from here that he took Sylvia – playing Heathcliff to her Cathy – on a day trip to Top Withens, the ruined farmhouse believed to be the original of Wuthering Heights. It was here that the family gathered on the day that Sylvia was buried, near the family plot, just down the road in Heptonstall graveyard. It was here that he came at moments of crisis in later relationships: when he was thinking of buying Lumb Bank and making a home there with Assia Wevill and when he found himself having to choose between two women in 1970. It was to here that he and his sister Olwyn brought back their mother ('Ma') in the last days of her life and here that he came after seeing her cold body in the Chapel of Rest down in Hebden Bridge.

And it was here that he sometimes fought with Sylvia. 'You claw the door,' he wrote in a poem called 'The Beacon'. The woman desperate to escape the house. Torrential Yorkshire rain crashes against the windowpanes. Inside the houses, on hillside and in valley, the lights of evening twinkle. 'The Beacon' gives a glimpse of Ted Hughes writing about domestic life. Yet it is also a poem of death, of graves and eternal silence. A beacon of memory, shining into the past. The memory of Sylvia among the Hugheses: chit-chat, telly, doing the dishes. Then a row, an explosion of anger. Sylvia, a trapped animal, brought fresh from the shining shore of the New World and confined in Yorkshire cold, Yorkshire grime, Yorkshire ways she does not really understand. She claws the door. Hughes at his most characteristic was a poet of claws and cages: Jaguar, Hawk and Crow. A poet who turns event and animal to myth.

Yet he was also a poet of deep tenderness, of restorative memory. If 'The Beacon' shines the light of memory into the past, there is another light that reaches forward with hope to the future, to redemption. In perhaps the greatest of his later poems, he calls it 'a spirit-beacon / Lit by the power of the salmon'. This other beacon is found in an epiphanic morning moment when he stands waist-deep in pure cold Alaskan river water with his beloved son Nicholas. Here the 'inner map' of wild salmon becomes the cartography of Hughes's own life: smoke-dimmed half-light of Calder Valley and wartime memory of 'the drumming drift' of Lancaster bombers. 'Drumming' had been one of Hughes's signature words ever since the 'drumming ploughland' of 'The Hawk in the Rain', title poem of his first volume.

The poem is called 'That Morning'.[3] Even a word as seemingly flat as 'that' is often full of resonance in Hughes: not any morning, but *that* morning, that magical, memorable, poetical, immortal morning. The poem ends with a redemptive couplet that rhymes with itself: 'So we stood, alive in the river of light / Among the creatures of light, creatures of light.'[4] It is a poem about life at its best not only because Hughes is doing something that he loves in a location that is utterly sublime, but above all because he is together ('*we* stood') with his only son, who lives on the other side of the world. It is a poem full of heart, of love. A few years later Ted would urge Nick to 'live like a mighty river'. 'The only calibration that counts', he wrote in a magnificent letter following another fishing trip, 'is how much heart people invest, how much they ignore their fears of being hurt or caught out or humiliated. And the only thing people regret is that they didn't live boldly enough, that they didn't invest enough heart, didn't love enough. Nothing else really counts at all.'[5]

The closing couplet of 'That Morning' is now inscribed on Ted Hughes's memorial stone in Poets' Corner. The national literary shrine in Westminster Abbey is indeed the place where England's last permanent, as opposed to fixed-term, Poet Laureate in one sense belongs. But his spirit was only at peace in moorland air or when casting his rod over water, so it is fitting that his ashes are not there in the Abbey. Their place of scattering is marked by another stone, far to the west of his England.

Ted Hughes is our poet of light, but also of darkness. Of fresh water but also of polluted places. Of living life to the full, but also of death. And among his creatures are those not only of light but also of violence. We must celebrate his 'dazzle of blessing' but we cannot write his life without being honest about the 'claw', without confronting what in 'That Morning' he calls the wrong thoughts that darken.

In view of Hughes's supernatural solicitings and given all the associations of the name Beacon, it was with grim satisfaction that, in the matter of Jane Anderson versus Avco Embassy Pictures and others, he found himself represented by Palmer and Dodge, working in conjunction with Peabody and Arnold, counsel for the lead defendant (Avco). These were two of Boston's oldest and most respected law firms. Both had their premises at the auspicious address of 1 Beacon Street.

It was there on the morning of Thursday 3 April 1986, a week after Ted had made his Deposition, that Alexander (Sandy) H. Pratt Jr, acting on behalf of the defendants, asked some questions of Dr Anderson. Mr Pratt: 'You felt, I take it, that Sylvia Plath wrote what she wrote in the book about the character Joan Gilling because she was hostile and angry towards you?'

Ms Grace: 'Objection.'

Mr Pratt told Jane Anderson that she could answer. She replied, hesitantly: 'I wouldn't say – I would say that one of the reasons that she wrote what she wrote was – again, this is a hypothesis – but that she had some angry feelings towards me.'

Why was she angry? Because, said Anderson, of what took place when she visited Sylvia Plath in Cambridge, England, on 4 June 1956.[6] That is to say, just over three months after Sylvia first met Ted Hughes 'at a party' and just twelve days before she married him in a swiftly arranged private ceremony in London. So what had happened at the meeting?

Sylvia Plath started talking in a very pressured way. That was my perception, that it was pressured. She said that she had met a man who was a poet, with whom she was very much in love. She went on to say that this person, whom she described as a very sadistic man, was someone she cared about a great deal and had entered into a relationship with. She also said that she thought she could manage him, manage his sadistic characteristics.

Q. Was she saying that he was sadistic towards her?
A. My recollection is she described him as someone who was very sadistic.[7]

Jane Anderson and Sylvia Plath had dated the same boys and had been fellow-patients in the McLean Hospital, New England's premier mental health facility. By the time of the Deposition, Anderson herself had become a psychoanalyst. On the basis of what she had seen of Plath during her treatment at McLean following a suicide attempt, it was her judgement that Plath had not worked through her own feelings of anger regarding her father. Jane had told Sylvia that she was not taking her psychotherapy sufficiently seriously. In the light of this earlier history, Anderson had grave doubts about the wisdom of Plath entering into a relationship with a 'very sadistic' man. She did not actually counsel Sylvia against going ahead with the relationship, but, thinking about it on the train back to London, she sensed that she had created anger in Plath precisely because Plath was herself anxious and ambivalent about committing herself to Hughes.

How did it come to pass that Hughes and Anderson found themselves making these Depositions over twenty years after Plath's suicide in the bitter London winter of 1963?

After the event, Ted Hughes's lawyer summed up the issue at stake: 'The plaintiff, Dr Jane Anderson, asserted that a character in the novel, *The Bell Jar*, and in the motion picture version was "of and concerning" herself, and that the portrayal of that character as a person with at least homosexual inclinations and suicidal inclinations defamed her and caused her substantial emotional anguish.'[8] Reporting the first day of the trial, which finally came to court nearly a year after the Depositions, the *New York Times* put the case more dramatically:

Literature, lesbianism, psychiatry, film making, television and video cassettes were all touched upon in United States District Court today as a $6 million libel suit opened here … The defendants include 14 companies and individuals, including Avco Embassy Pictures, which produced the 1979 film derived from the novel; CBS Inc., which broadcast it twice; Time–Life Films, the owner of Home Box Office, which played it nine times; Vestron Inc., which made and distributed a video cassette of the film, plus the director and screen writer of the film … At the defendants' table sat Ted Hughes, the poet laureate of England and a major defendant in the case.[9]

Many events in Ted Hughes's eventful life have a surreal quality about them, but none more than this: Her Majesty's Poet Laureate sits in a court room in the city of the Boston Tea Party, as defendant in a $6 million libel action against a film of a book that he did not write.

The full circumstances of the case, and its central significance in the Ted Hughes story, will be discussed later.[10] What is particularly fascinating about his Deposition is that it provided the occasion for one of Hughes's most forthright statements about what he considered to be the fallacy of biographical criticism. One reason why Jane Anderson had a good chance of winning her case, provided she could show that the character of Joan Gilling was indeed a 'portrait' of her, was that the first American edition of *The Bell Jar*, published posthumously in 1971, included a note by Lois Ames, who had been appointed by Ted and Olwyn Hughes as Sylvia Plath's 'official biographer'. The Ames note stated explicitly that 'the central themes of Sylvia Plath's early life are the basis for *The Bell Jar*' and that the reason she had published it under a pseudonym in England shortly before her death (and not attempted to publish it at all in the United States) was that it might cause pain 'to the many people close to her whose personalities she had distorted and lightly disguised in the book'.[11]

The name of Sylvia Plath has become synonymous with the idea of autobiographical or confessional literature. Teachers have a hard time persuading students that the character of Esther Greenwood in *The Bell Jar*, working as an intern at a New York fashion magazine, is not quite synonymous with Sylvia Plath working for *Mademoiselle* in June 1953 ('a queer, sultry summer, the summer they electrocuted the Rosenbergs').[12] Or, indeed, that her most famous and infamous poem 'Daddy' is not wholly 'about' Sylvia's relationship to her father Otto and her husband Ted – who habitually wore black, the colour of the poem.

'Do you remember disagreeing with any aspect of the biographical note?' Carolyn Grace asked Hughes. He had expected her to be a brisk, hard-edged feminist but found her more like a plump, slow-moving tapir, surprisingly sympathetic. After the Deposition was completed, they had a friendly chat – she told him that she had studied under the famous critic Yvor Winters, who had said how much he admired Ted's poetry. Hughes, with characteristic self-deprecation, assumed that she had misremembered and that the poet whom Winters really admired was his friend Thom Gunn. In the late Fifties, they had been the two rising stars, the twin angry young men in the English poetic firmament.

> A. I thought the whole thing was unnecessary.
> Q. What was unnecessary?
> A. Well, I thought by touching, attaching it so closely to Sylvia, it merely encouraged the general dilution that the book was about Silvia's life, it was a scenario from Silvia's life.

The court reporter is erratic in her spelling of Sylvia's name and has, in an almost Freudian slip, misheard 'delusion' as 'dilution'.

> Q. Which you disagreed with?
> A. Which I disagreed with.
> Q. What was the basis for your disagreement, sir, that the book was a scenario of Silvia's life?
> A. The turmoil that I've had to deal with since Sylvia died was of every one of her readers interpreting everything that she wrote as some sort of statement about her immediate life; in other words, trying to turn this symbolic artist, really [*brief gap in transcription*] That's why she's so famous, that's why she's a big poetic figure: because she's a great symbolic artist.

It is unfortunate that Hughes's exact words are lost to the record here, but it is clear what he was arguing: that Plath was a *symbolic* artist persistently misread as a *confessional* one. He went on to explain:

My struggle has been with the world of people who interpret, try to shift her whole work into her life as if somehow her life was more interesting and was more the subject matter of debate than what she wrote. So there's a constant effort to translate her works into her life.

> Q. And you object to that?
> A. It seems to me a great pity and wrong.[13]

At the time of the *Bell Jar* lawsuit, Ted Hughes was battling with Sylvia
Plath's biographers – as he battled for much of his life after her death.

Hughes was prepared for this line of questioning. The day before
making his Deposition he had phoned Aurelia Plath, Sylvia's mother.
By one of the coincidences typical of Hughes's life, Aurelia was
preparing to give a lecture in a high school later that week on the very
subject of *how non-autobiographical her daughter's novel was*. Aurelia was
ferociously bitter about the autobiographical elements in her daugh-
ter's work. People had accused her of destroying Sylvia and Ted's
marriage, simply on the basis of Plath's portrayal of her in the enraged
poem 'Medusa' in her posthumously published collection, *Ariel*:

> You steamed to me over the sea,
> Fat and red, a placenta
> Paralysing the kicking lovers.[14]

The conceit of the poem is that 'Medusa' is the name not only of the
monstrous gorgon in classical mythology but also of a species of jelly-
fish of which the Latin name is *Cnidaria Scypozoa Aurelia*. Mother as
love-murdering jellyfish: no wonder Aurelia wanted to play the
'non-autobiographical' card.

The trouble was, there had been a clause in paragraph 12 of the
agreement between the Avco Embassy Pictures Corporation and the
Sylvia Plath Estate (that is, Ted Hughes, represented by his agent,
Olwyn Hughes) prohibiting any publicity that referred to the film of
The Bell Jar as autobiographical. But somehow this clause had been
deleted, in an amendment signed by Ted. Letting this go through was
a fatal slip on Olwyn's part. That is why he felt vulnerable in the case,
despite the fact that he had in no sense authorised the offending
lesbian scenes in the movie. After the awkward fifteen-minute phone
call to Aurelia, he agonised with himself in his journal.

Nobody could deny that *The Bell Jar* was centred on Sylvia's break-
down and the trauma of her attempted suicide. Hughes accordingly
reasoned that he would have to argue that it was a *fictional* attempt to
take control of the experience in order to reshape it to a positive end.
By turning her suicidal impulse into art, Sylvia was seeking to save
herself from its recurrence in life: she was trying 'to change her fate,
to protect herself – from herself' but as an 'attempt to get the upper

hand of her split, her other personality, to defeat it, banish it, and, in the end, extinguish it' it was ultimately a failure.[15] The notion of the 'split' or 'other personality' in Plath was something to which Hughes returned again and again; it was also an obsession of Plath herself, already manifest in her 1955 undergraduate honours thesis at Smith, which was entitled 'The Magic Mirror: A Study of the Double in Two of Dostoevsky's Novels'. But these were deep matters, subtle distinctions that would not be easy to make in court. That night, Ted ate swordfish and went to bed early, readied for the encounter with Anderson's lawyer the following day. In the morning he awoke to the newspaper headline 'War with Ghaddafi'. His own literary-legal battle was about to begin.

Even as he was resisting the equation of art and life, Hughes was writing (though not publishing) poetry of unprecedented candour about his marriage to Sylvia. The Boston Deposition was a way-station on the road to *Birthday Letters*, the book about his marriage to Sylvia which he finally published in January 1998. In courtroom and hotel room, he followed Sylvia's example of turning life into art by transforming the saga of the *Bell Jar* lawsuit into a long poem, divided into forty-six sections, still unpublished today, called 'Trial'.

He wrote to his lawyer, to whom he had grown very close, directly after the trial: 'The whole 24 year chronic malaise of Sylvia's biographical problem seems to have come to some sort of crisis. I'd say the Trial forced it.'[16] Or rather, he added, the synchronicity of the trial and his dealings with Plath's biographers, of whom there were by that time no fewer than six.

Sylvia Plath's death was the turning point in Ted Hughes's life. And Plath's biographers were his perpetual bane. In a rough poetic draft written when a television documentary was being made about her life, he used the image of the film-makers 'crawling all over the church' and peering over Sylvia's 'ghostly shoulder'. For nearly thirty years, Hughes and his second wife Carol lived in Court Green, the house by the church in the village of North Tawton in Devon that Ted and Sylvia had found in 1961. Their home was, he wrote, Plath's mausoleum. The boom camera of the film-makers swung across the bottom of their garden. It was as if Ted and Carol were acting out the story of Sylvia on a movie set, their lives 'displaced' by her death.

The documentary crew crawled all over the yew tree in the neighbouring churchyard. Ted wryly suggests that if the moon were obligingly to come out and take part in the performance, they would crawl all over it. Both Moon and Yew Tree had been immortalised in Plath's October 1961 poem of that title: 'This is the light of the mind, cold and planetary. / The trees of the mind are black. The light is blue.' In the documentary, broadcast in 1988, Hughes's friend Al Alvarez, who played a critical part in the story of Sylvia's last months, argued that this poem was her breakthrough into greatness.[17]

Sylvia's biographers kept on writing, kept on crawling all over Ted. He compares them to maggots profiting at her death, inheritors of her craving for fame: 'This is the audience / Applauding your farewell show.'[18] Hughes was interested in both the theatricality and the symbolic meaning of Plath's moon and yew tree, whereas the biographers and film-makers worked from a crudely literal view of poetic inspiration. His distinction in the Deposition between the 'symbolic' and the autobiographical artist comes to the crux of the matter.

Having studied English Literature at school and university, and having continued to read in the great tradition of poetry all his life, he was well aware of the debates among the Romantics of the early nineteenth century. For William Wordsworth, all good poetry was 'the spontaneous overflow of powerful feelings'. Poetry was 'emotion recollected in tranquillity'. Wordsworth was the quintessential autobiographical writer, making his art out of his own memories and what he called 'the growth of the poet's mind'. His friend Samuel Taylor Coleridge, by contrast, though he also mused in verse in a deeply personal voice, argued that the greatest poetry was symbolic, that it embodied above all 'the translucence of the eternal through and in the temporal'. We might say that Wordsworth was essentially an *elegiac* poet, mourning and memorialising times past, whereas Coleridge was a *mythic* poet, turning his own experiences into symbolic narratives by way of such characters as the Ancient Mariner and the demonic Geraldine in 'Christabel'.

It might initially be thought that Plath was the Wordsworth (her autobiographical sequence *Ariel* being her version of Wordsworth's contributions to *Lyrical Ballads*) and Hughes the Coleridge (his Crow standing in for the Mariner and his figure of the Goddess for Geraldine). Ted Hughes certainly was as obsessed with Coleridge as he was with Shakespeare. But in another sense, Hughes was more of a Wordsworth: he was shaped by a rural northern childhood, by the experience of going to Cambridge, then abroad, then to London. He was the one who followed in Wordsworth's footsteps as Poet Laureate. Perhaps he was, as an admiring friend of his later years, manuscripts dealer Roy Davids, put it, 'Coleridge-cum-Wordsworth, and yourself'.[19]

Seamus Heaney, a more long-standing and even closer friend, began a lecture on Ted Hughes by describing how there was once a poet born in the north of his native country, 'a boy completely at home on the land and in the landscape, familiar with the fields and rivers of his district, living at eye level with the wild life and the domestic life'. This poet began his education in humble schools near his home, then went south to a great centre of learning. His work was deeply shaped by his reading in the literary canon but also by his memories 'of that first life in the unfashionable, non-literary world of his childhood'. Convinced of his own poetic destiny, he grew famous and mingled with the rich and the powerful, even to the point of becoming 'a favourite in the highest household of the land'. But the mark of his lowly beginning never left him: 'His reading voice was bewitching, and all who knew him remarked how his accent and bearing still retained strong traces of his north-country origins.'[20] Heaney then surprised his audience by revealing that this story contained all the received truths about the historical and creative life of Publius Virgilius Maro, better known as Virgil, the 'national poet' of ancient Rome. Of course his audience recognised that it was also the story of Hughes. What Heaney did not register at the time was that it is also the story of Wordsworth.[21]

Later in the talk, though, he did explicitly invoke Wordsworth. The context was a discussion of 'But I failed. Our marriage had failed,' the last line of 'Epiphany', a key poem in *Birthday Letters* in which Ted is offered a fox cub on Chalk Farm Bridge. The finality and simplicity of this conclusion, said Heaney, placed it among the most affecting lines in English poetry, alongside the end of Wordsworth's 'Michael' ('And never lifted up a single stone'). For Heaney, the whole of 'Epiphany' answered to Wordsworth's own requirements for poetry, as laid out in the 1800 preface to *Lyrical Ballads*: 'in particular his hope that he might take incidents and situations from common life and make them interesting by throwing over them a certain colouring of imagination and thereby tracing in them, "truly though not osten-tatiously, the primary laws of our nature'".[22]

One reason why Virgil and Wordsworth and, above all, Hughes meant so much to Heaney, whose signature collection of poetry was entitled *North*, is that their progression from humble rural origin to great fame and the highest social circles was also his own. He too is the poet described at the opening of the lecture. The transformation of the incidents of ordinary life through the colouring of imagination: this was the essence of Wordsworth, of Hughes and of Heaney.

There is a further similarity between Hughes and Wordsworth. Above all other major English poets they are the two who were most prolific, who revised their own work most heavily and who left the richest archives of manuscript drafts in which the student can recon-struct the workings of the poetic mind. Furthermore, they both wrote too much for the good of their own reputation. Sometimes they wrote with surpassing brilliance and at other times each became almost a parody of himself. Of what other poets does one find oneself saying so frequently 'How can someone so good be so bad?'

Indeed, what other major poet has been so easy to parody? In the late Sixties, the satirical magazine *Private Eye* began publishing the immortal lines of E. J. Thribb as an antidote to the dark Hughesian lyrics that filled the pages of the BBC's highbrow *Listener* magazine. The fictional poet, 'aged 17½', had no difficulty in impersonating the voice: crow, blood, mud, death, short line, break, no verb. Others followed, notably Wendy Cope, with her 'Budgie Finds His Voice *From* The Life and Songs of the Budgie *by Jake Strugnell*': 'darkness, blacker / Than an oil-slick … And the land froze / And the seas froze // "Who's a pretty boy, then?" Budgie cried.'[23] Cope has the affection that is the mark of the best parody, which cannot perhaps be said for Philip Larkin in a letter to Charles Monteith, his and Hughes's editor at Faber and Faber, upon being asked to contribute a poem for the Queen's Silver Jubilee, in which he mischievously and scatologically parodied the language of *Crow*.[24]

Larkin, with his grumpy self-abnegating pose, was Hughes's mighty opposite among the major English poets of the second half of the twentieth century. He liked to tease his rival over his reputed effect on women: 'How was Ilkley? I am sure you were as big a success there as here. I hope all these stories about young girls fainting in the aisles are not exaggerated.' And to rib him for his interest in astrology: 'Dear Ted, Thank you for taking the trouble to send my horoscope which I shall carefully preserve, though I don't know whether it is supposed to help me or frighten me; perhaps a bit of both. I never thought to ask what time of day I was born, and the information by now is gone beyond recall. I should guess about opening-time.'[25]

In order to be the object of strong parody, poetry must be memorable. What Larkin and Hughes had in common was the ability to write deeply memorable lines. Though none of Hughes's turns of phrase has become as famous as one or two of Larkin's, he is with Wordsworth and Tennyson in the very select company of Poet Laureates who have written line after line that passes the ultimate critical test of poetry, to be once read and never forgotten: 'His stride is wildernesses of freedom', 'It was as deep as England', 'a sudden sharp hot stink of fox', 'I am going to keep things like this', 'Your wife is dead'.[26]

The argument of this biography will be that Ted Hughes's poetic self was constantly torn between a *mythic or symbolic* and an *elegiac or confessional* tendency, between Coleridgean vision and Wordsworthian authenticity. His hostility to Plath's biographers was partly defensive – he wanted to protect his children and himself, to stave off the haunting memory of her death. But it was also based on the principle articulated in his Deposition: that it is a great pity and wrong to translate an artist's works into their life. And yet at the end of his career he finally published *Birthday Letters*, which became the fastest-selling volume in the history of English poetry precisely because it was a translation of his and Sylvia's shared life into a literary work. The tragedy of his career was that it took so long for the elegiac voice to be unlocked. But how could that have been otherwise, when the work and death of his own wife were turned before his very eyes into the twentieth century's principal myth of the fate of the confessional poet?

Hughes spoke repeatedly of the 'inner life'. And it is the story of his inner life that is told in the documents he preserved for posterity. However, as he observed in an early letter to Olwyn, the inner life is inextricable from the outer: 'Don't you think there's a deep correspondence between outer circumstances and inner? … the people we meet, what happens to us etc., *are* a dimension of the same and single complication of meanings and forces that our own selves are.'[27] His close friend Lucas Myers said that Hughes attended to and developed his inner life more fully than anyone he had ever known, save for advanced Buddhist practitioners. 'Poetry was the expression and the inner life was the substance.' But the context of Myers's remark was Hughes's material life:

> The first poem of Ted's I saw in draft and easily the least accomplished of any I have seen began 'Money, my enemy' and continued for six or seven lines that I do not recall. I think it doubtful that the poem survives. Before I met him, Ted had determined to devote his life to writing. 'Scribbling' was 'the one excuse.' Or 'the one justification.'
>
> But money was his enemy because generating it displaced the time and energy needed for the creation of poetry and the development of his inner life.[28]

The poem 'Money my enemy', written when Hughes was in his twenty-fifth year and eking out a living as a script reader for a film company, does in fact survive, because a manuscript of it was preserved by Olwyn. The poet represents his relationship to the world of money in the form of a great war. He imagines his own body cut into quarters, his brain carved up, his hands on the market with the heads of calves and the feet of pigs. Street dogs drag his gut, but his blood – mark of his true poetic vocation – sings of mercy and rest, cradled beneath the bare breast of a woman, satisfied with the food of love.[29]

Money was the enemy, but it cannot be neglected. Ted Hughes was perhaps the only major English poet of the twentieth century who, despite coming from humble origins, supported himself from his late twenties until his death almost entirely from his literary work. After a period of casual work upon graduating from Cambridge, and a brief university teaching stint in America, he never again had to take a day job as a librarian, teacher or bank clerk in the manner of other poets such as Larkin and Heaney, or for that matter T. S. Eliot.[30] His financial endurance was a heroic endeavour, albeit with moments of prodigality. The nitty-gritty of how it was sustained has to be part of the story of his literary life.

Ted Hughes wrote tens of thousands of pages of personal letters, only a small percentage of which have been published, sometimes in redacted form. He preserved intimate journals, appointment diaries, memorandum books, accounts of income and expenditure, annotations to his publishing contracts. The journals are of extraordinary value to the biographer. They were kept very private in Hughes's lifetime: Olwyn, his sister, agent, gatekeeper and confidante, did not even know that he kept a journal. It must be understood, though, that his diary-keeping was sporadic and erratic. The traces of his self-communion survive in fragmented and chaotic form. There is no equivalent of Sylvia Plath's bound journals of disciplined self-presentation. Ted's journal-style writings are scattered across a huge number of yellowing notebooks, torn jotter pads and thick sheaves of loose leaves.

The wealth and the chaos of his thoughts may be glimpsed from an account of just a very few items among the hundreds of boxes and folders of personal papers that were left in his home at his death. There was a box file inscribed 'Memory Books', containing prose notes on subjects ranging from Egyptian history and archaeological discoveries, to Hiroshima, to a book about Idi Amin called *Escape from Kampala*, to the Auschwitz survivor Primo Levi, to sagas, history, and notes for a metamorphic play on the Cromwells. Not to mention the Old Testament king Nebuchadnezzar, a park in West Glamorgan, and the German Romantic poet and short-story writer Bernd Heinrich Wilhelm von Kleist. Another box file, with 'WISE WORDS' written on it, contained dozens of prose fragments, diary entries from between 1970 and 1982, episodic passages that seem to be a draft for a first-person story, dreams involving Ted's children, quotations from books gathered for a planned but never finished 'Wisdom Book', photocopies of mind maps for classical subjects, and a drawing of a head with a cabbalistic legend. One could open a folder at random and find within it material as eclectic as a letter about a Ted Hughes impostor, an autograph translation of a poem by the Spanish dramatist Federico García Lorca, and a smoke-stained photocopy of a publicity questionnaire regarding the poet Laura Riding.

At the time of his death, he had already sold tens of thousands of pages of poetry and prose drafts, and many valuable notebooks, to the library of Emory University in America, but he retained a collection of twenty-two notebooks, mostly of pocket size, in which there were over 500 pages of poetry drafts and over 800 pages of autobiographical material, all mingled together. Again, he kept a thick buff-coloured quarto folder bulging with old partially used school exercise books, salvaged to save the cost of buying new notebooks. Here we find reading notes on the eighteenth-century English prophetess Joanna Southcott, the French Revolution, existentialism, China and anti-Semitism, together with thoughts on Sylvia Plath, memories of Frieda Hughes's birth, accounts of travels in America with Plath, of fishing with her in Yorkshire and going to London Zoo with the children. Precious personal memories are mingled with notes on Albert Camus, a stomach ache, yoga, ghosts, horoscopes, magic, Othello and Macbeth (both Shakespeare's villain and the poet George MacBeth, who was very involved with Ted's radio broadcasting), memories of a holiday in Egypt with his second wife, records of dreams in 1962, Scott of the Antarctic, and a visit in January 1964 to the weird woman at Orley House in Bideford. It was into this folder that he slipped an account of the last few days of Sylvia Plath's life, written within days of her death.

Another filing box was filled with loose sheets organised into roughly chronological sequence and amounting to nearly 500 pages of closely written manuscript prose: self-interrogation, descriptions of places and seasons, reflections on people, events and ideas. This was Hughes's preliminary attempt to put together a journal.[31] Given that he preserved it, the possibility of posthumous publication must have been on his mind.

Using all this raw material, it would be possible to write almost a day-by-day 'cradle to grave' account of his life. But the very wealth of the sources would make a comprehensive life immensely long and not a little tedious to all but the most loyal Hughes aficionados. Besides, certain portions of the archive will for some time remain closed for data protection and privacy reasons. The task of the literary biographer is not so much to enumerate all the available facts as to select those outer circumstances and transformative moments that shape the inner life in significant ways. To emphasise on the one hand the travails, such as the nightmare of the *Bell Jar* lawsuit, and on the other the joyful moments such as the mid-stream epiphany of 'That Morning'.[32]

In writing of the inner life, it is sometimes necessary to track a theme, criss-crossing through the years. Subjects such as Hughes's late work in the theatre, his curatorship of Sylvia Plath's posthumous works and his obsession with Shakespeare are best treated as stories of their own, rather than scattered gleanings that would all too easily disappear from sight if dispersed across many different chapters. This approach has the added advantage of breaking up the potentially deadening march of chronological fact-listing.

So, for instance, in the summer of 1975, Ted Hughes was farming in North Devon, revising his long poem *Gaudete*, corresponding and negotiating with his mother-in-law about excisions from Sylvia Plath's *Letters Home*, and reading an advance proof copy of *Millstone Grit*, a memoir of his native Calder Valley by Glyn Hughes (no relation). A strictly chronological biography would gather these four facts in a chapter on 1975. But the significance of the four facts is better demonstrated by placing them in separate strands of narrative: respectively, in chapters on 'Farmer Ted', 'The Elegiac Turn' in his poetic development, his 'Arraignment' by feminists and Plathians, and his own autobiographical 'Remembrance of Elmet' (the old name for the Calder district).

The biographer of Hughes faces the peculiar difficulty that he has been portrayed over and over again as Sylvia Plath's husband rather than his own self. In the United States he is known almost exclusively as 'Her Husband' (which happens to be the title of one of his own early poems). This has meant that his marriage to Sylvia is much the best-known part of his life. Because they were barely apart, day or night, from the summer of 1956 to the autumn of 1962, every biography of Sylvia – and they are legion – is in effect a joint life.[33] Furthermore, Olwyn Hughes contributed so much to Anne Stevenson's authorised *Bitter Fame: A Life of Sylvia Plath* (1989) that it became, as its prefatory Author's Note put it, 'almost a work of dual authorship'. *Bitter Fame* covered the first twenty-three years of Sylvia's life in just 70 pages, leaving nearly 300 for the seven years with Ted. It was a scrupulously detailed narrative of the marriage, checked for accuracy by Hughes himself. The marriage is also the subject of an entire book: Diane Middlebrook's sensitive and balanced *Her Husband* (2004). Elaine Feinstein, meanwhile, in the first biography of Hughes (2001), devoted 125 pages to the seven years from the meeting with Sylvia at that party in Cambridge to her suicide in London, but only 110 to the remaining thirty-five years of Ted's life. For this reason, my chapters on the years with Plath do not attempt a day-to-day record but focus instead on their joint writing life and on those moments that are caught in the rear-view-mirror perspective of the marriage in the published and unpublished *Birthday Letters* poems.

The cardinal rule is this: the work and how it came into being is what is worth writing about, what is to be respected. The life is invoked in order to illuminate the work; the biographical impulse must be at one with the literary-critical. The novelist Bernard Malamud's biographer puts it well: the first aim of an authentic life of a writer is 'to place the work above the life – but to show how the life worked very hard to turn itself into that achievement'. The second objective should be 'to show serious readers all that it means to be a serious writer, possessed of an almost religious sense of vocation – in terms of both the uses of and the costs to an ordinary human life'.[34] It was the assuredness of the sense of poetic vocation that most struck Seamus Heaney when he first met Ted Hughes: 'the certainty of the calling from a very early stage ... the parental relationship to writerly being is rarely so intimate'.[35]

In a journal entry written in 1956, Hughes quoted W. B. Yeats, an immensely significant poet for him: 'I wished for a system of thought that would leave my imagination free to create as it chose and yet make all that it created, or could create, part of one history, and that the soul's.'[36] Hughes's poetry was the history of his own soul.

Yeats also wrote, apropos of the question of what made Shakespeare Shakespeare, that 'The Greeks, a certain scholar has told me, considered that myths are the activities of the Daimons, and that the Daimons shape our characters and our lives. I have often had the fancy that there is some one myth for every man, which, if we but knew it, would make us understand all he did and thought.'[37] For Ted Hughes, who had a soul as capacious as that of any poet who has ever lived, there were many controlling myths. None, however, was more important or all-consuming than that of the figure whom he called the Goddess. He quoted this passage from Yeats as the epigraph to his longest (and itself almost all-consuming) prose work, *Shakespeare and the Goddess of Complete Being*.

Whether or not that book sees truly into the heart of Shakespeare, it unquestionably reaches to the core of Hughes's myth. His Daimon took the form of a woman and for that reason, if no other, women play a huge part in the story of his metamorphosis of life into art. It has accordingly been necessary to include a good deal of sensitive biographical material, but this material is presented in service to the poetry. His sister Olwyn said that Ted's problem, when it came to women, was that he didn't want to hurt anybody and ended up hurting everybody.[38] His friends always spoke of his immense kindness and generosity, but some of his actions were selfish in the extreme and the cause of great pain to people who loved him. I seek to explain and not to condemn. Plath's biographers have too often played the blame game. Instead of passing moral judgements, this book accepts, as Hughes put it in one of his *Birthday Letters* poems, that 'What happens in the heart simply happens.'[39] It is for the biographer to present the facts and for readers to draw their own conclusions.

There will be many biographies, but this is the first to mine the full riches of the archive and to tell as much as is currently permissible of the full story, as it was happening, and as it was remembered and reshaped in art, from the point of view of Ted Hughes. His life was, he acknowledged, the existential 'capital' for his work as an author. His published writings might be described as the 'authorised' version of the story, the life transformed and rendered *authorial*. His unpublished writings – drafts, sketches, abortive projects, journals, letters – are the place where he showed his workings. He kept them for posterity in their millions of words, most of which have now been made available to the public. The archive is where he is 'un-authored', turned back from 'Famous Poet' (the title of another of his early poems) to mortal being. Together with the memories of those who knew and loved him, the archive reveals that the way he lived his life was authorised not by social convention or by upbringing, but by his passions, his mental landscape and his unwavering sense of vocation. His was an unauthorised life and so is this.

1

'fastened into place'

Coming west from Halifax and Sowerby Bridge, along the narrow valley of the river Calder, you see Scout Rock to your left. North-facing, its dense wood and dark grey stone seem always shadowed. The Rock lowers over an industrial village called Mytholmroyd. Myth is going to be important, but so is the careful, dispassionate work of demythologising: the first syllable is pronounced as in 'my', not as in 'myth'. My-th'm-royd.[1] For Ted Hughes, it was 'my' place as much as a mythic place.

His childhood was dominated by this dark cliff, 'a wall of rock and steep woods half-way up the sky, just cleared by the winter sun'. This was the perpetual memory of his birthplace; his 'spiritual midwife', one of his 'godfathers'. It was 'the curtain and back-drop' to his child-hood existence: 'If a man's death is held in place by a stone, my birth was fastened into place by that rock, and for my first seven years it pressed its shape and various moods into my brain.'[2]

Young Ted kept away from Scout Rock. He belonged to the other side of the valley. Once, though, he climbed it with his elder brother, Gerald. They ascended through bracken and birch to a narrow path that braved the edge of the cliff. For six years, he had gazed up at the Rock – or rather, sensed its admonitory gaze upon him – but now, as if through the other end of the telescope, he was looking down on the place of his birth. He stuffed oak-apples into his pockets, observing their corky interior and dusty worm-holes. Some, he threw into space over the cliff.

Gerald, ten years older, lived to shoot. He told his little brother of how a wood pigeon had once been shot in one of the little self-seeding oaks up here on the Rock. It had set its wings 'and sailed out without a wing-beat stone dead into space to crash two miles away on the other side of the valley'.[3] He told, too, of a tramp who, waking from a snooze in the bracken, was mistaken for a fox by a farmer. Shot dead, his body rolled down the slope. A local myth, perhaps.

There was also the story of a family, relatives of the Hugheses, who had farmed the levels above the Rock for generations. Their house was black, as if made of 'old gravestones and worn-out horse-troughs'. One of them was last seen shooting rabbits near the edge. He 'took the plunge that the whole valley dreams about and fell to his death down the sheer face'. Thinking back, the adult Hughes regarded this death as 'a community peace-offering'.[4] The valley, he had heard, was notable for its suicides. He blamed the oppression cast by Scout Rock.

He wrote his essay about the Rock at a dark time. It was composed in 1963 as a broadcast for a BBC Home Service series called *Writers on Themselves*.[5] Broadcast three weeks earlier in the same series was a posthumous talk by Sylvia Plath (read by the actress June Tobin) entitled 'Ocean 1212-W'. The letter in which BBC producer Leonie Cohn suggested this title for the talk was possibly the last that Plath ever received.[6] Where the primal substance of Ted's childhood was rock, that of Sylvia's was water: 'My childhood landscape was not land but the end of land – the cold, salt, running hills of the Atlantic ... My final memory of the sea is of violence – a still, unhealthily yellow day in 1939, the sea molten, steely-slick, heaving at its leash like a broody animal, evil violets in its eye.'[7]

Though a suicide far from the Calder Valley preyed on Hughes's mind as he wrote of the Rock, there is no reason to doubt his memory of its force. Still, whenever writers make art out of the details of their childhood, a part of the reader wonders whether that was really how they felt at the time. Is the act of remembering at some level inventing the memory? William Wordsworth was the great exemplar of this phenomenon. He called his epic of the self a poem 'on the growth of the poet's mind'. And it was there that he pondered questions that we should always ask when reading Hughes's poetry of recollection. What does it mean to dissolve the boundary between the things which we perceive and the things which we have made? What is the relationship between the writing poet and the remembered self? Is a particular memory true because it is an accurate account of a past event or because it is constitutive of the rememberer's consciousness? Each member of a family remembers differently. Reading a draft of this chapter, Olwyn Hughes was angry: she did not recognise her own childhood, which in her memory was filled with light and laughter, happy family life and the absolute freedom of outdoor play. 'Hard task', writes Wordsworth, 'to analyse a soul.'[8]

Wordsworth, too, remembered a towering, shadowed rock as a force that supervised and admonished his childhood – the similarity of language in Hughes's 'The Rock' suggests a literary allusion as well as a personal memory. For Wordsworth, the overseer was a cliff face that loomed above him as he rowed a stolen boat across a lake. It cast a shadow of guilt and fear over his filial bond with nature. For Hughes, too, to speak of living in the shadow of the Rock was a way of externalising a darkness in his own heart.

From the Rock, young Ted could also see the arteries leading out to east and west. The railway, fast and slow lines in each direction. The station building was perched on a viaduct. Below, there was the largest goods yard in the West Riding of Yorkshire. Inward goods: wool from Yorkshire and cotton from the Lancashire ports. Outward: clothing and blankets from the mills and sewing shops. Corduroy and flannel, calico and moleskin; men's trousers in grey or fawn. New fashions: golf jackets, hiking shorts, blue and khaki shirts. The yard was also packed with boxes of chicks and eggs: overrunning the hillside above were chicken sheds belonging to Thornbers, pioneers of factory poultry farming.

Below the railway was the river Calder. A 'mytholm' is a meeting of streams. Just by the Co-op and the old Navvy Bridge, the Elphin Brook, darting down from the narrow gully of Cragg Vale, flows into the Calder. Beyond the river was the main road, the old cross-Pennine turnpike – rumbling lorries but some of the traffic still horse-drawn – that linked Halifax to Burnley, Yorkshire to Lancashire. The Calder Valley is on the cusp of the two great counties of northern industrial productivity, with their deep history of rivalry going back to the Wars of the Roses.

On the far side of the road – Ted's side – ran the Rochdale Canal, still in use for transporting goods, but only just. Now it was a place for the local children to fish for gudgeon and stickleback. Beyond the canal, a network of terraced houses clustered, back to back or back to earth, on the northern hillside. This was the Banksfield neighbourhood, where he and his family belonged. Some of the muck streets went vertically, others (including his own) ran horizontally, in parallel with the canal. The surrounding fields were dotted with smallholders' hen pens. Scattered above, where the fields sloped gently up to the moors, were farms. The path up the hill to the moor was always there as an escape from the blackened mills and terraces.

Down in the valley, Ted felt secure, if hemmed in. On top of the Rock that day in 1936 or '37, he was exposed. He looked down on a community that was closed in on itself. Nearly all the buildings were made of the distinctive local stone. Known as millstone grit ('a soul-grinding sandstone'),[9] it oxidises quickly, whatever the condition of the air. Add a century of factory smoke and acid rain. Then, as a tour guide will put it in one of Hughes's poems about his home valley, 'you will notice / How the walls are black'.[10] This was the cradle of the Industrial Revolution. Everywhere, blackened chimneys known as lumbs rose skyward from the mills.

On his side of the valley, the dark admonitory presence was not a rock but a building. A stone mass towered beside the Hughes family home: the Mount Zion Primitive Methodist Chapel. It was black, it blocked the moon, its façade was like the slab of a gravestone. It was his 'first world-direction'.[11]

Number 1 Aspinall Street stands at the end of the terrace. Now you walk in straight off the street; when Ted was a boy, before the road was tarmacked, there was a little front garden where vegetables were grown and the children could play. Go in through the front door and the steep stairs are immediately in front of you. The main room, about 14 feet by 14 feet, is to the left. From the front window the Hughes family could look straight up Jubilee Street to the fields.

There was a cosy little kitchen with a fireplace in the corner and a window looking out on the side wall of Mount Zion. According to Ted's poem about the chapel, the sun did not emerge from behind it until eleven in the morning. His sister Olwyn, however, recalls the kitchen being bathed in afternoon light. The poems have a tendency to take the darker view of things. By the same account, Olwyn always thought that Ted exaggerated the oppressive height and darkness of the Rock.

A tin bath was stored under the kitchen table. One day Mrs Edith Hughes woke from a dream in which she had bought a bath in

Mytholmroyd. She went straight to the shops, where she found one that was affordable because slightly damaged. The back door led to a ginnel, a passageway shared with the terraced row that stood back to back with Aspinall Street. The washing could be hung out here and the children, who spent most of their time playing in the street, could shelter from the rain. Which never seemed to stop.

The kitchen also had a door opening on some steps down to a little cellar, which had a chute where the coal was delivered, the coalman heaving sacks from his horse-drawn cart. Some of the terraces had to make do with a shared privy at the end of the row, but the Hughes family lived at the newer end of Aspinall Street, slightly superior, with the modern amenity of an indoor toilet at the top of the stairs.

Mother and father had the front bedroom and Olwyn the side one, with a window looking out on the chapel. Ted shared an attic room with Gerald. When he stood on the bed and peered out through the little skylight, the dark woods of Scout Rock gave the impression of being immediately outside the glass, pressing in upon him.

This was the house in which Edward James Hughes entered the world at twelve minutes past one in the morning on Sunday 17 August 1930. 'When he was born,' his mother Edith remembered, 'a bright star was shining through the bedroom window (the side bedroom window) he was a lovely plump baby and I felt very proud of him. Sunday was a wet day and Olwyn just could not understand this new comer.'[12]

Gerald, just a few weeks off his tenth birthday, lent a helping hand. Despite the rain, Edith's husband Billie went out for a spin in her brother Walter's car. Minnie, wife of another brother, Albert, who lived along the street at number 19, had offered to look after Olwyn, but she didn't that first day. A neighbour was called to take in the unsettled two-year-old.

As a teenager, Olwyn would develop a serious interest in astrology, which she shared with Ted. The conjunction of the stars mattered deeply to them.[13] He was born at what astrologers call 'solar midnight'. With knowledge of the exact time and place of his birth, a natal chart could be cast. He was born under the sign of Leo, the lion, which endowed him with a strong sense of self, the desire to shine. But because he was born at solar midnight, he would also need privacy and seclusion. His 'ascendant' sign was Cancer, bonding him to home and family. And Neptune, the maker of symbols and myths, was 'conjunct'. His horoscope, he explained, meant that he was 'fated to live more or less in the public eye, but as a fish does in air'.[14] Bound for fame, that is to say, but fearful of scrutiny.

Did he really believe that his fate was written in the stars? 'To an outsider,' he once observed in a book review, 'astrology is a procession of puerile absurdities, a Babel of gibberish.' He granted that many astrologers peddled rubbish and craziness. Others, he thought, did make sense. He did not know whether genuine astrology was an 'esoteric science' or an 'intuitive art'. That did not matter, so long as it worked: 'In a horoscope, cast according to any one of the systems, there are hundreds of factors to be reckoned with, each one interfering with all the others simultaneously, where only judgement of an intuitive sort is going to be able to move, let alone make sense.'[15] It is all too easy to select a few out of those hundreds of factors in order to make the horoscope say what you want it to say. Neptune is the sign of many things in addition to symbols and myths, but since Ted Hughes was obsessed with symbols and myths they are the aspect of ascendant Neptune that it seems right to highlight in his natal chart. By the time anyone is old enough to talk about their horoscope, their character is formed; at some level, they have themselves already written the narrative that is then 'discovered' in the horoscope. But there is comfort in the sense of discovery. For Ted, astrology, like poetry, was a way of giving order to the chaos of life.

'Intuitive' is the key word in Hughes's reflections on astrology. If the danger of a horoscope is that it is an encouragement to the abnegation of responsibility for one's own actions, a forgetting of Shakespeare's 'the fault, dear Brutus, is not in our stars, / But in ourselves', the value of a horoscope is its capacity to confirm one's best intuitions. The major superstitions – astrology, ghosts, faith-healing, the sixth sense whereby you somehow know that a person you love has died even though they are far away – are, Hughes thought, impressive because 'they are so old, so unkillable, and so few. If they are pure nonsense, why aren't there more of them?'[16]

His birth was formally registered in Hebden Bridge, the nearest large town. Father was recorded as William Henry Hughes, 'Journeyman Portable Building maker', that is to say a carpenter specialising in the assembly of sheds, prefabs and outbuildings. Mother was Edith Hughes, formerly Farrar.

William Hughes was born in 1894.[17] His father, John, was a fustian dyer, known as 'Crag Jack'. Family legend made him a local sage – 'solved people's problems, wrote their letters, closest friends the local Catholic and Wesleyan Ministers, though he spent a lot of time in pubs'.[18] Crag Jack was said to have been a great singer. He was a bit of a 'mystery man', who came to the Calder Valley from Manchester and, before that, Ireland. In the young Ted's imagination, he is perhaps a kind of bard or shaman, certainly a conduit of Celtic blood.

'Crag Jack's Apostasy' is one of the few early Hughes poems to mention his family directly. There Jack clears himself of the dark influence of the church that 'stooped' over his 'cradle'. He finds a god instead beneath the stone of the landscape.[19] Here Ted takes on Grandfather Jack's identity: the cradle stooped over by the dark church is clearly his own, shadowed by Mount Zion.

The story in the family was that Crag Jack died from pneumonia at the age of forty, leaving Willie Hughes a three-year-old orphan, together with his younger brother and elder sister. But there is a little misremembering or exaggeration here. The 1901 census records that John Hughes, aged forty-seven, and his wife Mary were living over a shop in King Street, Hebden Bridge, with their nineteen-year-old daughter, also called Mary, a 'Machinist Fustian', and the two boys, John aged eight (born Manchester) and Willie, seven (born Hebden Bridge), together with a young cousin called Elizabeth. Crag Jack died in 1903, closer to the age of fifty than forty. Willie was not three but nearly ten when he lost his father. Ted's widowed Granny Hughes kept on the King Street shop for many years. She died in her eighties.

Like her husband, she had been born in Manchester. Her father was apparently a major in the regular army, his surname also being Major. His station was Gibraltar, so family tradition knew him as 'Major Major of the Rock'. He married a short, dark-skinned, 'Arab looking' Spanish woman with, according to Ted, a 'high thin nose like Olwyn's'.[20] This association with Spain and a distant Rock, an outpost of empire overlooking the Mediterranean, gave Ted the idea that he might have some exotic Moorish blood in him. A touch of blackness, akin to that of Emily Brontë's Heathcliff, found on the streets of Liverpool?

It was the Farrar family, not the Hughes, who dominated Ted's childhood. In May 1920, Willie married Edith Farrar, who was five months pregnant with Gerald. There was a gap of eight years before Olwyn's birth. Ted was the youngest.

Farrar was a distinguished name, woven into the historical and spiritual fabric of English poetry. Edith's family traced their ancestry back to a certain William de Ferrers, who fought in the Battle of Hastings as William the Conqueror's Master of Horse. Later generations of Farrars became famous in Tudor and Stuart times. One of Ted's most prominent early poems was 'The Martyrdom of Bishop Farrar', telling of how his ancestor was 'Burned by Bloody Mary's men at Caermarthen'. It was a poem of fire and smoke, evocative of the tradition of Protestant brimstone sermons that still lived in the Mount Zion Primitive Methodist Chapel over the road. 'If I flinch from the pain of the burning,' said the bishop on being chained to the stake, 'believe not the doctrine that I have preached.'[21] A Stoic gene to prepare Ted for his travails?

Nicholas Farrar (1592–1637), a collateral descendant of the martyred bishop, was a scholar, courtier, businessman and religious thinker. In his own way, Ted Hughes would grow up to be all these things. Cambridge University was the making of Nicholas, but he also owed a debt to the New World in that his family was closely involved with the colonial projects of the Virginia Company. The seventeenth-century Farrars eventually settled in the rundown village of Little Gidding, not far from Cambridge, where they established a community of faith and contemplation. It was to Farrar that fellow-Cambridge poet George Herbert sent the manuscript of his poetry collection *The Temple* from his deathbed with the instruction that it should be either burnt or published. Farrar saw that it was published, with the result that Herbert's incomparably honest poetry of self-examination has remained in print ever since. As Hughes grew up, learning of his Farrar heritage, he could not have dreamed that a day would come when he too would be entrusted with seeing into print another poetry collection prepared at the moment of death, this one called *Ariel*. Like his Farrar ancestor, he had the responsibility of saving a loved one's confessional poetry for posterity. Decisions as to whether to burn or preserve literary manuscripts would trouble him throughout his adult life.

What he did come to know, as he began reading in the canon of English poetry as a teenager, was that T. S. Eliot, the most revered of living poets, took deep religious solace from the example of the Farrar family: his great wartime meditation on the cleansing fire of faith, his fourth *Quartet*, was called 'Little Gidding'. Eliot's language seeps into Hughes's own metaphysical lyric on his ancestor, 'Nicholas Ferrer' (Edith and her children were inconsistent in their spelling of the historic family name). Famously, in 'Little Gidding' Eliot began with spring in midwinter and ended with an epiphany of divine fire in the remote chapel deep in the English countryside. There is a catch of deep emotion in Hughes's voice as he speaks this phrase in his recorded reading of Eliot's poem. His own poem 'Nicholas Ferrer' is located in that same Little Gidding chapel, now 'oozing manure mud'. The speaker tracks Eliot's footsteps, past the same pigsty, in the same winter slant light. An 'estranged sun' echoes Eliot's 'brief sun' that flames the ice on what in retrospect seem very Hughesian ponds and ditches. Nicholas and his family had 'Englished for Elizabeth' but in Hughes's desolate modern November 'the fire of God / Is under the shut heart, under the grave sod'.[22]

Hughes's poem makes the death of Nicholas Farrar into a turning point in English history. It invokes the desecrating maw of Oliver Cromwell. The Little Gidding community was broken up by Puritans, who saw vestiges of Romish monasticism in their practices. Nicholas's books were burnt. For Hughes, influenced by the Anglo-Catholic Eliot's idea of a 'dissociation of sensibility' that fractured English culture and poetry at the time of the Civil War, Puritanism was the great enemy of those 'ancient occult loyalties' to a deeper, mysterious world that were embodied by such superstitions as astrology.

Ted's belief in a world beyond the normal came from his mother. Edith Farrar felt that the spirit world was in touch with her. Ever since childhood, she had often felt the sensation of a ghostly hand. One night in June 1944 she was woken by an ache in her shoulder. She got up and saw crosses flashing in the sky above St George's Chapel, which was across the road from their Mexborough home. She tried to wake William (whom she called Billie) to tell him that a terrible battle was going on somewhere and that thousands of boys were being killed. The next day the radio announced that the D–Day landings had begun early that morning.[23] Later, when she and her husband moved to the Beacon, she saw a shadow in the house. She learned that the previous owners had died and their daughter had sold the house and moved into Hebden Bridge. She told the shadow, who was the mother, where her daughter now lived. It never reappeared.[24]

Mr Farrar, from Hebden Bridge, was a power-loom 'tackler' – a supervisor, with responsibility for tackling mechanical problems with the looms. Tall and quiet, with black hair and a heavy black moustache, he was fond of reading, played the violin a little and had a gift for mending watches. His grandson Ted would be good with his hands. Grandma Farrar, Annie, was a farmer's daughter from Hathershelf, 'short and handsome with a deep voice and great vitality'. When they went to the local Wesleyan chapel, 'tears would roll down her cheeks under the veil she wore with her best hat', so moved was she by the sermon or the hymns. As well as regular chapel attendance, there were prayer meetings once a week in the evening. But on Sunday afternoons came the freedom of country walks and picnics at picturesque Hardcastle Crags. The Farrars had eight children, the eldest born in 1891, the youngest in 1908: Thomas, Walter, Miriam, Edith, Lily, Albert, Horace (who died as a baby) and Hilda. In May 1905, Lily died of pneumonia, aged just four and a half.

As she grew up, Edith got on especially well with Walter, who was both easygoing and strong-willed. He wasn't good at getting up in the morning. Soon he started work in the clothing trade, while taking evening classes to improve himself. Miriam and Edith left school at thirteen and went into the same trade, training to be machinists making corduroy trousers and moleskin jackets. Miriam was delicate. In June 1916, she caught cold and it turned to pneumonia and she died, aged nineteen.[25]

This was in the middle of the Great War. Walter had joined up by this time, along with some of the Church Lads Brigade. The whole village turned out to see them off, singing 'Fight the good fight' and 'God be with you till we meet again'. Just weeks after Miriam's death back home, Walter was wounded at High Wood on the Somme. He returned with a shattered leg that troubled him for the rest of his days. But it could have been worse: at first, he was reported killed in battle, only for the family to receive his Field Card saying 'I am wounded.'

Mrs Farrar shouted up the stairs, 'Get up all of you. He's alive! Alive alive!' Tom, who was in the Royal Engineers, came back gassed, broken by the death of many of his dearest friends.

Edith and her friends collected eggs and books to take to the wounded, the gassed and the shell-shocked in hospital. On the drizzly morning of 11 November 1918, she was working on army clothing when a male colleague tapped on the window, said, 'War's over,' and threw his cap in the air. A flag was hoisted over the factory and everybody was allowed home, but there was no rejoicing, only deep thankfulness that it was finally over. Thirty thousand local men had joined the Lancashire Fusiliers. Over 13,500 of them were killed.

Years later, Ted Hughes would write 'you could not fail to realize that the cataclysm had happened – to the population (in the First World War, where a single bad ten minutes in No Man's Land would wipe out a street or even a village), to the industry (the shift to the East in textile manufacture), and to the Methodism (the new age)'. As he grew up in Mytholmroyd in the Thirties, looking around him and hearing his family tell their stories, it dawned on him that he was living 'among the survivors, in the remains'.[26]

Edith's one joy at the end of the Great War was that Billie Hughes was safe. He was a Gallipoli survivor. The story went that he had been saved from a bullet by the paybook in his breast pocket. Edith first met him in 1916 when he was home on leave, having just won the Distinguished Conduct Medal but then broken his ankle playing football when resting behind the lines – he was always a great footballer, could have been a professional. After the war, they spent their courtship walking the hills and moors, and once a week went to a dance club. In 1920, they discovered that she was pregnant and they married on a pouring wet day. For two shillings and ninepence a week they rented a cottage in Charlestown, to the west of Hebden Bridge. It had a living room, kitchen, two bedrooms and an outside toilet. They scraped together the money for a suite of furniture and on their wedding day Mrs Farrar gave them a carpet and a sewing machine. Billie's mother was radiant on the wedding day, her white hair and fair skin set off by a mauve hat and veil.

Gerald's birth was traumatic. The newborn boy lay blue and stiff on the washstand, and the nurse cried, 'The baby is dead – fetch the doctor.' But Edith told her to shake and smack him, and before they knew it he was crying and the doctor arrived and said he would be fine. When he was two, Edith went back to work and young Gerald was looked after by Granny Hughes.

They were happy in their little cottage on the hillside above the railway, though Edith didn't like it when Billie went off for away football matches and did not return until very late at night. In 1927, they moved to Mytholmroyd, the other side of Hebden Bridge, buying the house in Aspinall Street. Now the Hughes family was truly among the Farrars: Uncle Albert, married to Minnie, was down the road at number 19 and Edith's mother, with teenage Hilda, just round the corner in Albert Street.

The other brothers were doing very well for themselves. In the year of Gerald's birth Uncle Walter, in partnership with a man called John Sutcliffe, started a clothing factory. When Sutcliffe left, Uncle Tom took over from him. Edith went to work for them. Walter marked and sometimes cut the cloth. He was very good at laying the heavy leather patterns for the trousers, then cutting out from the great long rolls of cloth. He was, his sister saw, 'the director in every sense of the word'. Tom was more subdued, still affected by the gas of the trenches; Edith was terrified that his mind would drift, costing him a finger on one of the great flashing blades of the cutting machines. He was often to be found sitting in the office next to his little sister Hilda, who did the paperwork.

It was not easy for Edith and Billie to see Tom and Walter in their detached houses on the outskirts of the village: Walter and his wife Alice at Southfield, a handsome villa set back from the Burnley Road, Tom and his wife Ivy at Throstle Bower, at the top of Foster Brook, up towards the moors. Having a house with a name instead of a number was a mark of upward mobility. In addition, the brothers had cars, the ultimate sign of affluence. None of the family liked Ivy Greenwood, who looked down on the Farrars, would not even acknowledge them and certainly never deigned to invite them up to her big house. Olwyn thinks that Ivy was jealous of the close family bond among the Farrars.

The brother who really struggled was Albert. Minnie was regarded as a good catch, but she pushed him hard, resentful that Tom and Walt were getting rich on the factory, while they couldn't keep up. Albert was a carpenter, like Billie Hughes. They both got work making prefabricated buildings. Albert would make wooden toys, to give to his nephews and nieces, or to sell: 'toy ducks / On wooden wheels, that went with clicks'.[27] One day he was knocked off his bike on the way to work and he was never the same after that.

Like all the Farrar children, Hilda left school at thirteen, but she took evening classes, learned shorthand, typing and bookkeeping, enabling her to become company secretary for her brothers. She married a much older man called Victor Bottomley, who had something to do with the motor trade. He turned out to be 'a wrong 'un',[28] and before long Annie Farrar was instructing her sons Tom and Walt to go and bring Hilda home, where she stayed with Minnie and Albert at 19 Aspinall Street (eventually Hilda and Grandma settled at number 13).

Walt had his sadness. His two elder children, Barbara and Edwin, were, as their cousin Vicky put it, 'witless'. Barbara seemed conscious that something was wrong with her as she struggled to learn to read. Edwin was in his own closed world. James, the only 'normal' son, died at the age of eleven.

When Gerald left school, he too went to work at Sutcliffe Farrar, which was located just beyond the Zion chapel. When the slump came in the early Thirties, men and women were laid off, or reduced to working two or three days a week. Billie had been working for his brothers-in-law but he was put on short time too, and in 1936 he got fed up, gave in his notice and went off with a friend to do building work for the government in South Wales. With no work at the factory, Gerald had taken to roaming the moors, leaving Edith miserable and alone with Olwyn and Ted, both under ten. She worked a little at the factory, sewing hooks and eyes on flannel trousers, and they had enough money to get by. They had paid off the house by then, food was reasonably cheap and Edith's sewing skills meant that clothes could be mended. Billie came home once a month and soon realised how much he was missing the children. They had come into a little money from Granny Hughes and with many people struggling through the Great Depression there were opportunities in small business. Billie decided he wanted a newsagent's. Eventually, they found one that was suitable. There was only one problem: it was 50 miles to the south-east, near Doncaster, in a 'dark dirty place'[29] called Mexborough.

They all went down in the removal van. When they arrived, Billie stood behind the counter of the new shop and the family walked in, trying to look confident. Then they went out and helped with the furniture. When the van left, Gerald sat down and cried.

2

Capturing Animals

Dumpy, bustling Moira Doolan was a powerhouse of ideas at the BBC in the early Sixties.[1] Middle-aged and unmarried, she spoke with an Irish lilt and was passionate about her work as Head of Schools Broadcasting. In January 1961 Ted Hughes wrote to her with an idea for a radio series. She invited him to lunch and they worked up his proposal. It eventually became *Listening and Writing*, a sequence of ten talks for the Home Service's daytime schools programming, broadcast between October 1961 and May 1964.[2] Nine of the ten, together with illustrative poems by Hughes and others, were published in a book, aimed at teachers and dedicated to his own English teachers, Pauline Mayne and John Edward Fisher. Entitled *Poetry in the Making*, it became a classroom *vade mecum* for a generation and indeed one of Hughes's bestselling books.[3]

In a brief introduction, he described the talks as the notes of a 'provisional teacher' and of his belief in the immeasurable 'latent talent for self-expression' in every child. The teacher's watchword should be for children – he was typically thinking of pupils between the ages of ten and fourteen – to write in such a way that they said what they *really* meant. With self-expression comes self-knowledge and 'perhaps, in one form or another, grace'.[4]

The series started from autobiography. The first talk, entitled 'Capturing Animals', began: 'There are all sorts of ways of capturing animals and birds and fish. I spent most of my time, up to the age of fifteen or so, trying out many of these ways, and when my enthusiasm began to wane, as it did gradually, I started to write poems.'[5] When the harvest was gathered in, little Ted would snatch mice from under the sheaves and put them in his pocket, more and more of them, until there were thirty or forty crawling around in the lining of his coat. He came to think that this was what poems were like: experiences captured and kept about the person.

He then explained that his earliest memory was of being three, placing little lead animals all the way round the fender of the fire in the front room, nose to tail. There was no greater treat than a trip to Halifax, where his mother or Aunt Hilda would buy him one of these creatures from Woolworth's. Then for his fourth birthday Hilda gave him a thick green-backed book about animals. He pored over it, read the descriptions over and over again, drew copies of the photographs of animals and birds. Sometimes he would place the lead figures on the fender and read their descriptions from the book: the words put together with the things, the poet in the making. When he discovered plasticine, the possibilities for his personal menagerie became infinite, bounded only by the limit of his huge imagination.

He confided to his listeners that his passion for wildlife came from his elder brother. Gerald was his hero. And his saviour. One Christmas Billie Hughes bought his boys a Hornby clockwork train set. It was laid out in the front room by the piano. Three-year-old Ted loaded his lead soldiers aboard and Gerald wound up the engine. But an excited Ted tripped on the fender and fell towards the fire. Gerald scooped him out, but not before his hands had been blistered. 'Fires can get up and bite you,' Ted would say in later years.[6]

But this is Gerald's memory. Olwyn's earliest recollections are of trotting out into the fields with her mother and baby Ted, then of Ted's two close friends, Derek Robertshaw and Brian Seymour, coming round every Saturday morning while the Hugheses were having breakfast, planning with Ted where they would go for the day and what animals they would find. They lived in the fields and they were never bored. As Olwyn remembered it, Gerald was always off with friends his own age. In Ted's adult writings, the bond between the two brothers has a mythic force which exaggerates their closeness.

It was just before his fifth birthday that he joined Gerald on a camping trip for the first time. They were to spend the night up by the stream in the woods known as Foster Clough. Edith told Gerald not to let Ted take his model boat, for fear that he would sail it in the stream and get soaked. Those two friends, Derek and Brian, came round with advice, then the brothers set off, stopping on the way to buy sweets from the shop just past Uncle Walt's factory. Watched by some very interested cows, they set up their tent and made a fire in a little clearing, fenced off with wire to keep the cattle out of the wood. Just before midnight, they heard their father's call. He had come to check on them and was taking Ted home because there was a bull among the cows, making them too frisky for comfort. Ted was very excited by the bull.

From then on, Ted would often accompany Gerald on to the moor. He scurried silently beside his brother, pretending to be a Red Indian hunter. He kept a tom-tom drum hidden in Redacre Wood, where, according to local lore, an Ancient Briton, buried spirit of land and nation, lay beneath a half-ton rock.[7] They loved the silence of the hills, shrouded in morning mist as they looked out over the valley below. They flew gliders and kites. Gerald taught Ted to identify all the different birds. The younger brother was fascinated by hawks and owls. Gerald shot rats, wood pigeon, rabbits and the occasional stoat, Ted acting as his retriever. Sometimes Gerald would let him have a go with the air rifle. Once the slug ricocheted back and gave him a bloody forehead, but they managed to keep the accident from their parents. They met an old-school gamekeeper called McKinley who regaled them with stories and sometimes paid them a shilling for a fat rabbit. They fished in the canal, using nets made from old curtains.

They poked around the site of a crashed plane – an RAF bomber on a training exercise had run into fog over Mytholmroyd – and salvaged bits of tubing for their own model planes. On the same site, they unearthed dozens of old lead bullets: it had been a firing range in the Great War.

In winter they sledged all the way down the fields above Jubilee Street. On snowy nights, they opened the skylight and listened to the shunting engines strain at the frozen trucks in the sidings. In summer, they would help out their uncles in the allotment or play tip cat in the fields with Uncle Albert – this was a game in which you balanced a block of wood on the end of a bat, then whacked it as far as you could send it. Occasionally, there was a special treat: a trip to the seaside, a first sight of big cats at Blackpool Zoo.

Olwyn did not join them on the hills, but she was there for family picnics at Hardcastle Crags and dips in the rocky pool on Cragg Vale. Mrs Hughes ('Mam' to Gerald, 'Ma' to Olwyn and Ted) was a great walker and swimmer. The children's love of nature came from her.

They all shared in the peace and magic of Redacre Wood, which seemed like their own private paradise.

The three siblings played in the open air around the Zion chapel. They stole gooseberries from a lady's garden up on the Banks. They gave a fright to a younger boy called Donald Crossley by tying him to a tree, spreading leaves around his feet and setting fire to them as they danced and whooped like Red Indians.

Time spent indoors meant model-making with Gerald or reading with bookish Olwyn. Ma wrote poems for them and made up tales. They all loved the one about Geraldine mouse, Olwyna mouse and Edwina mouse because it echoed their own adventures. Grandma Farrar was charmed when they went round and read her the words of Edward Thomas, the poet and countryman who had died in the war. It was Edith who also instilled a passion for poetry in Olwyn and Ted. Wordsworth was her favourite, as might be expected of a woman who loved walking and the beauties of nature.

The war haunted Ted and his father because it had decimated a generation of the Calder Valley's young men. The sorrow in the air of the valley came more from the war than from the decline of industry.

Gerald's earliest memory was of finding his father's sergeant's stripes in a drawer and wondering what they were. Billie Hughes brought two other relics back from the war: his Distinguished Conduct Medal and the shrapnel-peppered paybook that had been in his breast pocket at Gallipoli. He told the family that he was one of only seventeen men from the company to have survived. Olwyn had a pearl necklace, which she loved to play with. Her father explained that it had been taken from the body of a dead Turk. He would occasionally shout at night in his sleep, dreaming of the Turks charging towards his trench.

When Ted was four and Olwyn six, for half a year every Sunday morning their father stayed in bed and they came in with him and said, 'Tell us about the war.' He told them everything, in the goriest detail, including things not very suitable for a four-year-old boy. Dismembered bodies, arms sticking out of the mud. Ted either suppressed or forgot all this, later saying that his father never talked about the war. When he wrote his story 'The Wound' he told Olwyn that it was something he had dreamed. The moment he woke up, he wrote it down. But he forgot certain details, so he went back to sleep and dreamed it again, filling in the gaps. But Olwyn thought that part of it was taken from their father's memories of the war. The story includes a long walk to a palace: this was his father going up to the Front on the way to a particular sortie in which he, as Sergeant-Major, led a small group of men in a successful assault on a German machine-gun post. It was this walk up the line that Billie described so vividly in bed. He also talked about his time in the Dardanelles, but that mainly consisted of drinking tea and picking lice off his uniform. The Western Front was much more dramatic.[8]

Ted was formed by his outdoor life and his books, by his mother's stories and father's memories, but he was an attentive schoolboy at the Burnley Road Council School, bright, always asking questions. The headmaster gave a fearsome talk on the evils of alcohol. The message stuck. Ted grew up to love good wine, but always held his drink and never became addicted. Many writers have become alcoholics without bearing anguish remotely comparable to his.

A memory that became a foundational myth. In his fifties, Ted told his schoolfriend Donald Crossley that it was in Crimsworth Dene, camping under a little cliff on a patch of level ground beside what later became a council stone dump, that he had the dream that turned later into all his writing. It was a sacred place for him.[9]

It was sacred to Gerald as well: he told Donald that the memory of Crimsworth Dene sustained him through his service in the desert war. This secret valley, just north of Hebden Bridge, became in memory the spiritual home of the brothers.[10] Gerald remembered how they had pitched their two-man Bukta Wanderlust tent for the last time. Two days later the family moved to Mexborough and life was never the same again. He felt that they both spent the rest of their lives trying to recapture those early days in the happy valley, but they never did.

The site was recommended by Uncle Walter. It had been a favourite camping spot for him, Uncle Tom and their friends before the Great War. At the top of the valley, there was a pool and a waterfall, with an old packhorse bridge going over. This had long been a favoured picnicking place for locals. The Hughes family cherished an old photo taken there: it showed six young men in Sunday best, before the war.

There was a drystone wall along the slope above the clearing where the boys pitched their tent. On their second day, they found a dead fox there. It had been killed by a deadfall trap – a heavy rock or slab tilted at an angle and held up with a stick that when dislodged causes the slab to fall, crushing the animal beneath. That night Ted slept restlessly in the tent. He told Gerald of 'a vivid dream about an old lady and a fox cub that had been orphaned by the trap'.[11]

This was the dream that, according to Ted's letter to Donald Crossley nearly fifty years later, turned into all his writing. It was his first thought-fox. He told the tale himself in 'The Deadfall', a short story from the last decade of his life, written for a collection of ghost stories, published to celebrate the centenary of the National Trust and edited by one of his closest friends, the children's novelist Michael Morpurgo.[12] All the stories are set in houses or landscapes owned by the Trust, of which Crimsworth Dene was one.

In the story, it is Ted's first time in the secret valley, with its steep sides and overhanging woods. He immediately senses that it is the most magical place he has ever been to. The enclosed space means that every note of the thrush echoes through the valley and he feels compelled to speak in a whisper. At night, he can't stop thinking about the fox for which the trap has been set. The idea of the creature near by, in its den, 'maybe smelling our bacon', makes the place more mysterious than ever. On the second night he is woken by the dream of the old lady, calling him out of the tent. He follows her voice up the slope to the trap, where he finds a young fox, still alive but with tail and hind leg caught beneath the great slab of stone. He is choked by 'the overpowering smell of frightened fox'. He realises that the woman has brought him to the cub, wants him to free it. She has not gone to Gerald, because she knows that he would be likely to kill it. Summoning all his strength he manages to lift the corner of the slab – the cub snarling and hissing at him like a cat – just enough to set the animal free. It runs away and the old lady vanishes. But when he looks back at the deadfall there is something beneath it. At this moment, his brother wakes and calls him back to bed. It rains. In the morning, they go up to the deadfall and there is a big red fox, the bait (a dead wood pigeon) in its mouth.

According to the story, Gerald then digs a grave for the fox. As Ted helps him push the loose soil away, he feels what seems to be a knobbly pebble. When he looks at it closely, it turns out to be a little ivory fox, about an inch and a half long, 'most likely an Eskimo carving'. He treasures it all his days. He and Gerald conclude that the old lady in the dream was the ghost of the dead fox.

Hughes admits in the preface to his collected short stories that this version of the incident, prepared for Morpurgo's ghost collection, has 'a few adjustments to what I remember'. In Gerald's account, Ted's dream of the old lady comes the night after they have discovered the body, whereas in the story it is a premonition of the fox's death. Ted insisted on the reality of the memory, yet neither Gerald nor Olwyn has any recollection of the ivory fox.[13] It was only as an adult that Ted began collecting netsuke and Eskimo carvings of animals.

'The Deadfall' was the only short story of his later career. He had not written one for fifteen years. Morpurgo's invitation was an irresistible opportunity to round off his work in the genre. He gathered it together with his earlier stories and made it what he called the 'overture' to his writing.[14] The camping trip with Gerald in Crimsworth Dene, the dream of the freed fox and the ivory figure that symbolically transformed his lead animal toys into tokens of art came together as his retrospective narrative of creative beginning.

The radio talks for schools that were eventually published as *Poetry in the Making* give incomparable insight into Ted Hughes, poet in the making. As the boy Ted sculpted his plasticine animals, so the adult writer created poetic images of fox, bird and big cat. In the same way, Ted the teacher found the right voice to capture the attention of ten- to fourteen-year-olds – exactly as his own attention had been caught by Miss Mayne and Mr Fisher.

Early in the second talk, called 'Wind and Weather' (there was no shortage of either in the Calder Valley), he suggested that the best work of the best poets is written out of 'some especially affecting and individual experience'. Often, because of something in their nature, poets sense the same experience happening again and again. It was like that for him with his dreams, his premonitions and his foxes. A poet can, he argues, achieve greatness through variation on the theme of 'quite a limited and peculiar experience': 'Wordsworth's greatest poetry seems to be rooted in two or three rather similar experiences he had as a boy among the Cumberland mountains.'[15] Here

Wordsworth stands in for the speaker himself: the deadfall trap in Crimsworth Dene was Ted Hughes's equivalent of what Wordsworth called those 'spots of time' that, 'taking their date / From our first childhood', renovate us, nourish and repair our minds with poetry.[16]

At school, Ted was plagued with the idea that he had much better thoughts than he could ever get into words. He couldn't find the words, or the thoughts were 'too deep or too complicated for words'. How to capture those elusive, deep thoughts? He found the answer, he tells his schools audience in the talk called 'Learning to Think', not in the classroom but when fishing. Keeping still, staring at the float for hours on end: in such forms of meditation, all distractions and nagging doubts disappear. In concentrating upon that tiny point, he found a kind of bliss. He then applied this art of mindfulness to the act of writing. The fish that took the bait were those very thoughts that he had previously been unable to get into words. This mental fishing was the process of 'raid, or persuasion, or ambush, or dogged hunting, or surrender' that released what he called the 'inner life' – 'which is the world of final reality, the world of memory, emotion, imagination, intelligence, and natural common sense'.[17]

Though a fisherman all his life, Ted did not follow in Gerald's footsteps as a hunter, despite being an excellent shot. To judge from his sinister short story 'The Head', in which a brother's orgiastic killing of animals leads to him being hunted down himself, he was distinctly ambivalent about Gerald's obsessive hunting.[18] At the age of fifteen, Ted accused himself of disturbing the lives of animals. He began to look at them from their own point of view. That was when he started writing poems instead of killing creatures. He didn't begin with animal poems, but he recognised the analogy between poetry-writing and capturing animals: first the stirring that brings a peculiar thrill as you are frozen in concentration, then the emergence of 'the outline, the mass and colour and clean final form of it, the unique living reality of it in the midst of the general lifelessness'.[19] To create a poem was as if to hunt out a new species, to bring not a death but a new life outside one's own.

Like an animal, a living poem depends on its senses: words that live, Hughes insists, are those that belong directly to the senses or to the body's musculature. We can taste the word 'vinegar', touch 'prickle', smell 'tar' or 'onion'. 'Flick' and 'balance' seem to use their muscles.

'Tar' doesn't only smell: it is sticky to touch and moves like a beautiful black snake. Truly poetic words belong to all the senses at once, and to the body. Find the right word for the occasion and you will create a living poem. It is as if there is a sprite, a goblin, in the word, 'which is its life and its poetry, and it is this goblin which the poet has to have under control'.[20]

Poetry is made by capturing essences: of a landscape, a person, a creature. In one talk, Hughes suggests that 'beauty spots' – he was remembering his childhood places such as Hardcastle Crags and the view from the moors above Mytholmroyd – ease the mind because they reconnect us to the world in which our ancestors lived for 150 million years before the advent of civilisation (the number of years is a typical Ted exaggeration). Poignantly, given that the broadcast went out a year after her death, the example he quoted at the close of this talk was 'a description of walking on the moors above Wuthering Heights, in West Yorkshire, towards nightfall' – 'by the American poet, Sylvia Plath'.[21]

To capture people, you must find a memorable detail. 'An uncle of mine was a carpenter, and always making curious little toys and orna-ments out of wood.' This memory of Uncle Albert was all that was needed to create the character of 'Uncle Dan' in his children's poetry collection *Meet My Folks!*: 'He could make a helicopter out of string and beetle tops / Or any really useful thing you can't get in the shops.'[22] To invent a good poem, though, you shouldn't just transcribe your memories. You need to rearrange your relatives in imagination. 'Brother Bert' in *Meet My Folks!*, who keeps in his bedroom a menag-erie of every bizarre creature from Aardvark to Platypus to Bandicoot to 'Jungle-Cattypus', is an exaggerated version of Gerald (who never kept anything bigger than a hedgehog). But the line 'He used to go to school with a Mouse in his shirt', Hughes reassures his listeners, does not refer to Gerald: 'Somebody else did that.'[23] The somebody else was Ted. In the poem, he and Gerald have become one. It was a way of registering his affection for his brother. His feelings about his mother, he admits, were too deep and complicated to capture: she is the one absence from the feast of *Meet My Folks!*

Think yourself into the moment. Touch, smell and listen to the thing you are writing about. Turn yourself into it. Then you will have it. That, for Hughes, was the essence of poetry.

He ended that seminal opening talk 'Capturing Animals' with two personal examples. Late one snowy night in dreary lodgings in London, having suffered from writer's block for a year, he had an idea. He concentrated very hard and within a few minutes he had written his first 'animal' poem. It is about a fox but it is also about itself. The thought, the fox and the poem are one. In the 'midnight moment's forest', something is alive beside the solitary poet. He captures the movement, the scent, the bright eyes. The fox's paw print becomes the writing on the page. 'Brilliantly, concentratedly ... The page is printed': it is a captured animal.[24]

The second example was one of his 'prize catches': a pike in a pool at Mexborough.

Tarka, Rain Horse, Pike

They moved on 13 September 1938, four weeks after Ted's eighth birthday. They would stay for thirteen years to the day.[1] Olwyn cried for a fortnight and the cat moped beneath a bed upstairs. Ted seemed least affected by the move. He was always adaptable, ready for a new direction. He was immediately enrolled at the Schofield Street Junior School round the corner, getting to know the local boys, some of them shopkeepers' children, which is what he now was. His best mate was a lad called Swift, mother a greengrocer, father a miner. A neighbouring family had a brutal father, a miner who came home drunk, his face blackened from work. Ted befriended the redheaded daughter Brenda. On Saturday mornings he went to the local 'flea pit' cinema and watched Westerns.

The family's new address was 75 Main Street, Mexborough: a newsagent's in the centre of a busy mining town, where the bestselling paper was the *Sporting Life*, to be read daily before placing a bet on the horses. You went into the shop and diagonally to the right was a door to the downstairs living room. Edith and Billie had the front bedroom over the shop. Then there was a big bedroom to the right, over the living room. This had a double and a single bed. A door from here led to a smaller room over the kitchen. Beyond that, there was a room with just a bath. The loo was downstairs and outside. Ted played with his train set in the big bedroom. There was a garage behind, where Ted began keeping animals, notably rabbits and guinea pigs. He cried inconsolably when they died. It was not unknown for him to keep a hedgehog under the sofa in the living room.

Once again, they were overshadowed by a church: across the road stood the ugly red-brick edifice of the St George the Martyr Chapel of Ease to St John the Baptist Parish Church. Its clock had a loud tuneless chime. This was where, six years later, Edith would look out before dawn on D-Day and see crosses in the sky. It was within weeks of their moving to Mexborough that Prime Minister Neville Chamberlain returned from his meeting with Hitler in Munich and was heard on the radio speaking of 'peace for our time'.

The business went well. Billie ordered the magazines and the tobacco, and organised the paper rounds. He also took on a concession selling tickets for coach trips. Edith diversified the stock, ordering games, stationery and dress patterns. Gerald and Ted became paper-boys. Ted read all the comics and boys' magazines on the shelves before they were sold. Even his mature poetry would be shot through with a love of super-heroes and an element of zap, kerpow and kaboom.

In later years, Aunt Hilda and Cousin Vicky came down at Christmas. For the children, the whole shop was their Christmas present: each received a pillowcase stuffed with goods, toys, sweets, chocolate.

Gerald struggled to find work locally. He had a brief stint at a steel-works just outside Rotherham, but this was ended by an accident. Then he moved down to Barnet, just north of London, to train as a garage mechanic. He bought a motorbike and started roaring around the countryside, to the consternation of young Ted, who told him he should stick to pedal power. But Gerald's heart remained in the fields. His favoured reading was the *Gamekeeper* magazine and it was in answer to an advertisement there that he got a seasonal job as a second keeper on an estate in Devon. This involved rearing pheasants and locating them in the right places to be shot when the 1939 season opened. It was in Devon that he heard Prime Minister Chamberlain on the radio once again, this time announcing that the country was at war with Germany.

The war brought painful memories for Billie and Edith. For Gerald, it began a new life. He returned home at the end of the shooting season, remained there through the 'phoney war' and joined up in the summer of 1940. His skill with his hands and experience with engines meant that he was well suited for aircraft repair and maintenance in the RAF. From 1942 to 1944 he was posted to the desert war in North Africa. Gerald's absence meant that Olwyn and Ted clung close together, sometimes sharing a bed. One of his earliest unpublished poems, witty and affectionate, is called 'For Olwyn Each Evening'.[2]

For an adventurous boy such as Ted, there was a thrill in the sound of bombers overhead. Industrial Rotherham, just 6 miles along the river Don, was a target, as was Doncaster, 8 miles upstream. That meant blackouts at night and taped-up shop windows to prevent flying glass. A bomb fell on Mexborough railway station, but Main Street escaped.

Olwyn was a very clever girl. She got a scholarship to the local grammar school. Ted followed in her footsteps in 1941, also winning a county scholarship. Mexborough Grammar was the intellectual making of him. This was where his love of literature matured and began to intersect with his love of nature. In his first year he explored the school library and found Henry Williamson's *Tarka the Otter*. He took it out and kept it, on and off, for two years, until he knew it almost by heart. This became the first of the talismanic books that shaped his inner life.

Williamson's novel, first published in 1927, had become a bestseller and an acknowledged classic. Because it was written from an animal's point of view, yet unsentimental and at times extremely violent, English teachers found it especially good to recommend to boys of Ted's age. The combination of adventure (notably an extended hunting sequence), intricately observed natural history and heightened literary style truly caught Hughes's imagination at a formative moment in his early adolescence. What especially impressed him was the otteriness of the book, its rigorous refusal to anthropomorphise. Tarka, he explained in a *Sunday Times* colour supplement article in 1962, is not 'one of those little manikins in an animal skin who think and talk like men'.[3]

Hughes was enchanted. It was as if his own life in the fields and among the animals had been recreated in a book. This was the seeding of his poetic vocation. Among the set-piece descriptions that grabbed him was 'The Great Winter', which evoked six black stars and a great white one, 'flickering at their pitches' like six peregrines and a Greenland falcon, 'A dark speck falling, the *whish* of the grand stoop from two thousand feet heard half a mile away; red drops on a drift of snow'. The moon, 'white and cold', awaits 'the swoop of a new sun, the shock of starry talons to shatter the Icicle Spirit in a rain of fire'. Stories are written into the night sky: 'In the south strode Orion the Hunter, with Sirius the Dogstar baying green fire at his heels. At midnight Hunter and Hound were rushing bright in a glacial wind, hunting the false star-dwarfs of burnt-out suns, who had turned back into Darkness again.'[4] Here in embryo are the elements of Hughes's poetry: the violent forces of nature played out against a cosmic backdrop, figures of myth, creation and destruction, bird of prey, blood on snow, moon, stars, apocalyptic darkness.

When he moved to Devon, Ted got to know Henry Williamson. He sat at his feet and listened to his rambling memories.[5] In December 1977, he would deliver the address at a memorial service for the old writer, who had died on the very morning that the scene of Tarka's death was being filmed for the movie of the book – another of those synchronicities that so fascinated the superstitious Hughes. Speaking to the congregation in St Martin-in-the-Fields on Trafalgar Square, he explained what had inspired him when he found *Tarka* in the school library all those years before. His first encounter with the book was one of the great pieces of good fortune in his life: 'It entered into me and gave shape and words to my world, as no book has ever done since. In the confrontations of creature and creature, of creature and object, of creature and fate – he made me feel the pathos of actuality in the natural world.' This, he said, was a gift of only the greatest writers. Though Williamson did not write in verse, 'he was one of the truest English poets of his generation'.[6]

Williamson's writing was indeed a kind of prose-poetry. Chop up the lines of a passage such as the description of 'The Great Winter' and you would almost have a Hughes poem. After all, Hughes did sometimes draft in prose before finding the rhythms of verse: his translations of foreign-language poetry were often versifications of literal prose versions undertaken for him by his friends, while many of the unpublished drafts for *Birthday Letters* live in a hinterland between journal-writing and poetry.

Tarka the Otter also got him thinking about the role of typography in literature, something in which he would take a keen interest throughout his career, whether in collaborating with his sister and others on private presswork and hand printing, or in complaining to Faber and Faber about their choice of font for a particular poetry collection. When Tarka and the hounds go down to a watery death at the very close of the book, the diminuendo of the typesetting enacts their drowning:

and while they stood there silently, a great
bubble rose out of the depths, and broke, and as
they watched, another bubble shook to the
surface, and broke; and there was a
third bubble in the sea-going
waters, and nothing
more.

Williamson was a Devon writer through and through. *Tarka the Otter* vividly and exactly evokes the landscape of the valleys of the twin rivers Torridge and Taw that share a North Devon estuary. Shortly after Ted and Sylvia found the house called Court Green, he realised that he had landed upon another spiritual home. On the first day he went fishing on the Taw, at the beginning of the 1962 season, an otter leapt from a ditch and led him to the river. Unawares, Ted had walked into his own 'childhood dream', stumbled upon Tarka's two rivers.[7] Later, he would gain riparian rights on the Torridge, at the very spot where Tarka was born. And in the Eighties, when the twin rivers' otters and fish were threatened by pollution, he spent months and years fighting to save the aquatic life of the estuary.

Just as *Tarka the Otter* allowed Ted's readerly imagination to follow brother Gerald to Devon, so Williamson's war books, encountered later, would give him a way of comprehending his father's experience of the trenches. He regarded *The Patriot's Progress* (1930) in particular as one of the very finest of the many novels and memoirs that came out of the war. The incantatory quality of the prose, the transformation of the day-to-day realities of the soldier's life into something epic and biblical in cadence again shaped the tones and textures of his own writing: 'Their nailed boots bit the worn, grey road. Sprawling midday rest in the fields above the sunken valley road, while red-tabbed officers in long shiny brown boots and spurs cantered past on the stubble, the larks rising before them. But the sunshine ceased; and it rained, and rained, and rained. On the sixth day they rested.'[8]

John Bullock, the protagonist of Williamson's war novel, is a symbol of England. There is danger here. Disillusionment following the war brings temptation: the search for a strong leader who will clear up the mess, stiffen the national backbone and lead a patriotic march to a New Jerusalem. In the Thirties, Henry Williamson saw such a man in

Adolf Hitler. He attended the Nuremberg Rally in 1935 and was inspired by Hitler's charisma. He idolised Oswald Mosley and became a member of the British Union of Fascists. This would turn him into a pariah in the literary world.

Hughes did not shy away from Williamson's ugly politics. In his memorial address, he acknowledged that the stories of nature red in tooth and claw came from the same impulse as the fascism. That is to say, from a worship of natural energy that led to a fear (always close to rage) of 'inertia, disintegration of effort, wilful neglect, any sort of sloppiness or wasteful exploitation'. Williamson's 'keen feeling for a biological law – the biological struggle against entropy' sprouted into 'its social and political formulations, with all the attendant dangers of abstract language'. His worship of 'natural creativity' meant that 'he rejoiced in anybody who seemed able to make positive things happen, anybody who had a practical vision for repairing society, upgrading craftsmanship, nursing and improving the land'. This reverence for 'natural' as opposed to artificial life 'led him to imagine a society based on natural law, a hierarchic society, a society with a great visionary leader'.[9] The trajectory was very similar to that of D. H. Lawrence, whom Hughes would also come to admire. Such ideas, said Hughes, had 'strange bedfellows', but who was to say 'that the ideas, in themselves, were wrong?' Hughes himself shared exactly this vision of natural creativity and biological law. 'It all springs', he said, 'out of a simple poetic insight into the piety of the natural world, and a passionate concern to take care of it.' In this, Williamson was an ecowarrior before his time, 'a North American Indian sage among Englishmen'.[10] The lines of correspondence between Green thinking ('Back to the land!') and fascism ('Blood and soil!') are complex and troubling.[11] Hughes, though, was too canny and grounded, too suspicious of the 'abstract language' of ideology, to make the fatal move from biocentric vision to extreme right-wing politics.

In the schoolroom, the boys sat on one side and the girls on the other. On winter days, biscuits and little bottles of milk for morning break were thawed on the black iron stove that stood in the middle of the classroom.

Miss McLeod, Ted's first English teacher at Mexborough Grammar, praised his writing. His mother responded by buying him, second-hand, a library of classic poets. A children's encyclopedia introduced him to folktales and myths. Rudyard Kipling was the first poetic favourite: the lolloping rhythms, the voicing of animals and the fables of their origins ('How the Leopard Got his Spots'), the robust and conversational English working-class voices. Ted's teenage poems, which he was soon publishing in the school magazine, brought Kipling's style together with the substance of his Saturday-morning viewing of Westerns and jungle adventures. He rejoiced in imitating Kipling's 'pounding rhythms and rhymes': 'And the curling lips of the five gouged rips in the bark of the pine were the mark of the bear.'[12]

He also benefited from the attention of his next teacher. Sensitive to both praise and criticism, he showed her his Kiplingesque sagas. She pointed to a particular turn of phrase and said, 'This is really … interesting … It's real poetry.' What she had highlighted was 'a compound epithet concerning the hammer of a punt gun on an imaginary wildfowling hunt'. Young Ted pricked up his ears. This was an important moment.[13] Soon, this second English teacher, Pauline Mayne, would introduce him to more demanding fare: the sprung rhythms and compacted vocabulary of Gerard Manley Hopkins and the challenging obscurity of T. S. Eliot.

There were many happy returns at the end of the war. The towering figure of Gerald arrived on the doorstep in September 1945, to be greeted by a now tall and handsome fifteen-year-old who stared and then, with tears streaming down his face, called out, 'Mam, it's him, it's him!'[14] Ted picked up his big brother's kitbag and in they went for the reunion with Olwyn and their parents. At the grammar school, meanwhile, the masters were returning. Among them, coming out of the navy, where he had served on the North Atlantic convoys, was John Fisher, tall, with a long slim face and a copy of the Manchester *Guardian* tucked under his arm. Said to be the finest English teacher in Yorkshire, he put on plays, edited the school magazine – in 1947 the sub-editors were Olwyn Hughes and Edward Hughes – and taught poetry with a passion. He had the Bible, Shakespeare and classical mythology at his fingertips. He would sit on the edge of the desk and announce to the class that they were going to study Shakespeare, so they would all be bored to tears. But they never were. He brought wit and wordplay to the classroom, conjuring up Shakespeare's characters and moving seamlessly between close reading and historical context.

Whether it was Wordsworth (whom Fisher especially loved because he was raised on the Cumberland coast) or *Wuthering Heights* or the First World War poets, he brought the text to vivid life. He would gaze intently as he nurtured the class in the art of practical criticism, but then lighten the tone with some absurd remark ('The school is now anchored off the east coast of Madagascar').

'He used the blackboard to write up names, dates, always clearly scripted,' another pupil remembered. 'When marking homework-essays he would write generously long comments, often in red ink which did not signify censure. He had a clear, fluent, individual hand, a joy to read. But the nitty-gritty of his teaching was working with his students through discussion of the texts.'[15] Whether in catholicity of literary taste, in critical acumen, in firm-stroked handwriting or in the love of Beethoven, Fisher was an inspiration to the future poet, introducing him to Keats and Blake, Dante and Dylan Thomas. According to a fellow-pupil, Ted's appearance – the floppy fringe falling across the eyes – was modelled on that of his master.[16]

Under this tutelage, and with the academic achievements of Olwyn to spur him on, Ted continued to explore the school library. His next discovery was W. B. Yeats, whose work offered a perfect combination of mesmeric poetic rhythms with subject matter rich in folklore, myth and magic. He claimed (with characteristic exaggeration) to have learned the complete works by heart. His dreams became coloured by *The Wanderings of Oisin*. He was 'swallowed alive'. By a beautiful synthesis, the art of poetry, the natural world (his 'animal kingdom') and the world of myth and folktale 'became a single thing'. His own poetry 'jumped a whole notch in sophistication'.[17]

Olwyn added grist by introducing him to C. G. Jung's *Psychological Types*, with its divisions of the mind between sensation and intuition, thinking and feeling, extravert and introvert. Like Yeats, Hughes was beginning to develop a 'system', at once psychological, philosophical, poetical and not a little mystical. At the same time, Shakespeare, that most unsystematic of geniuses, was an infatuation. He read the complete works, going line by line through a battered copy of W. J. Craig's double-column, small-print Oxford edition, originally published in 1891. Then he went to the home of his girlfriend, Alice Wilson, and discovered that their edition included an additional play, *The Two Noble Kinsmen*, co-written by Shakespeare and John Fletcher.

Shakespeare's chief contribution, the first act, was written in verse of newly knotted complexity. Alice's mother loved classical music and, being rather better off, owned a gramophone, whereas the Hugheses only had the radio. Ted purchased recordings of Beethoven's symphonies and concertos, taking them round to play at the Wilsons' home.

Many of his contemporaries at the grammar school remembered him as a loner. But others recall him imposing his personality on the class, larking about (sometimes egotistically), dressing scruffily and writing vigorous reviews for the school magazine. He played a 'dark, brooding lighthouse keeper' in a play and wrote, cast and directed the sixth-form Christmas Revue 'containing surreal skits anticipating the humour of the Goon Show and Monty Python, in which, for example, cowboys entered saloons to order coffins in which to place their victims.' Mr Watkinson, the Headmaster, participated, 'dancing enthusiastically, in full gown and mortarboard mufti, with buckskin-clad sixth-form "squaws"'.[18] Above all, Ted was remembered for his size and strength. His sixth-form friend Alan Johnson, who came close to hurdling for Britain at the 1948 London Olympics, was convinced that Ted could have become a serious competitor in discus or shotput.

His academic results were more than satisfactory, though not outstanding. In July 1946, he got his School Certificate (the examination that later became O Levels, then GCSEs) in eight subjects: English Language was very good; English Literature, History, Geography, French and Physics all credits; Mathematics and Chemistry, passes. The following summer, he got a credit in Latin, a necessary prelude to the Higher School Certificate in Latin that was a prerequisite for entrance to the top universities.[19] And in the summer of 1948, he passed the Higher School Certificate (the equivalent of A Levels) in English Literature (good), Geography (distinction) and French (pass). Both he and Fisher were disappointed with the English result, but his teacher's strong support was enough to give him a shot at Cambridge.

Back in Mytholmroyd, there was a family tragedy in the summer of 1947. Uncle Albert's depression had been growing more severe. His only solace was his woodwork in the attic. One evening, his twenty-one-year-old daughter Glennys called for him to come downstairs for supper. There was no answer. She went up to find out what was going on and fell back down the stairs as she saw the chair that he had kicked away, the body hanging. Albert's wife ran for a neighbour, Harry Greenwood, who cut the rope.[20] Forty miles to the south, perhaps at the very moment when Albert hanged himself, his sister Edith let out a cry, as if she had received a 'hammer blow' on the nape of her neck.[21]

Throughout the war years, Ted spent every free hour in the fields and woods. Before leaving home, Gerald the huntsman had found a new domain. Ted inherited it, along with his brother's paper round. You went down Old Church Street to the edge of town and crossed a polluted river on a chain ferry, kept by an old man known as Limpy. On the other side, the road ran up the bank, over the railway, past an old pond and into the village of Old Denaby.

Ted came to regard all the land to the right of the railway and up to a place called Manor Farm as his own personal kingdom. He got to know it better than any place he would ever know. Apart from old Oats the farmer and his man, he never met a soul. In a mining town such as Mexborough during the war, nobody else was interested in nature for its own sake. His territory felt like deep country where he could stalk animals, watch, listen and shoot. He trapped mice, which he would then skin and cure, keeping them under the lid of his desk at school and selling them for a penny – or 'maybe tuppence for a good one'.[22] He got to know the local foxes, giving them personalities as if they were people. He practised discus-throwing in the fields. He joined the Denaby Wheelers, a cycling club with which he went on long-distance rides on a bike with drop handlebars.

The school magazine was named for the local rivers, *Don and Dearne*. In June 1946, Hughes's first published poem appeared there, along with a short story that vividly describes the gathering in of the harvest at Manor Farm and the shooting of the rabbits and hares that emerged from the corn. Thirteen years later, he would work this up into 'The Harvesting', one of a sequence of stories spinning off from his boyhood. In this expanded version, the tale is spiced with magic: the narrator goes woozy with sunstroke, aims his gun at the last hare in the field, then turns into a hare himself, wounded, pursued by hounds. Autobiography has been turned to myth, as the metamorphosis and the hunt of Shakespeare's *Venus and Adonis* are re-enacted in the landscape of Manor Farm.

The best known of his short stories, 'The Rain Horse' (1958), is also located at Old Denaby but again it diverges from its origin. The landscape – one particular copse especially – and the initial sighting of the horse come from a memory of being followed by a horse for about ten minutes near Manor Farm, but the animal's return and the sense of mystery and menace draw from elsewhere. The story combines an experience of his mother's, which, he alleges, was 'strangely repeated twice' in his own life, and 'an exactly similar experience that my brother had with a mad cow': 'On each occasion, the animal kept pretending to attack, or really did attack but kept shying off at the last moment. The cow really did attack, demolished several walls, and had to be shot.'[23] None of those incidents happened at Manor Farm. Yet the idea behind the story – that the natural world has a power that, once it grasps you, will never let you go, will gather you into a centrifuge of bond and violation – was something that he would also associate with Old Denaby.

He marked his memories of the war by those of another private kingdom, a little further out of town. Nearly fifty years later, he recollected a particular moment: 'I was looking up into a Holly Tree beside Crookhill Pond (Conisborough) where there was sometimes a tawny owl, and I thought: today is 4/4/44 and I shall never forget this moment. Now I orient all holocaust experiences, all 2nd world war events, by that fixed moment.'[24]

After the war Gerald left home again. He became a policeman in Nottingham. Then, one day when he was on point duty, he saw a hoarding with a sunny poster and the words 'Come to Australia'.[25] It was advertising a special scheme that provided a cheap (£10) one-way boat ticket on condition that the emigrant stayed and worked for at least two years. Those who went became known as 'Ten Pound Poms'. There was talk of his little brother following in his footsteps after doing a degree.

Ted had got to know a boy called John Wholey, who was in Olwyn's class. Though eighteen months apart in age, the two lads were alike in look and temperament: quiet, tall, thin, in love with fishing, shooting and the countryside. In Gerald's absence, John became a kind of substitute brother. His father was head gardener and gamekeeper on the Crookhill estate near Conisbrough, 3 miles east along the Don. The Wholeys lived in the keeper's lodge, remote from everywhere other than the big house, which was being used as a sanatorium for men with terminal tuberculosis. Sometimes, when walking in the grounds, Ted would loudly recite poetry to the bemused patients. 'Eh lad that were posh,' they would say.[26]

He introduced his girlfriend Alice to the Wholeys and she eventually married John. Ted, meanwhile, very much liked John's sister, Edna. He had regularly gone over to Crookhill on Saturdays. Now that he was older, he was allowed to go on Friday nights. 'Have you come for the weekend?' Mrs Wholey would ask. 'Yes, please,' said Ted. On one occasion, his parents accompanied him, in order to ensure that the arrangement was acceptable: 'If our Edward misbehaves send him home with a flea in his ear,' said his mother. He was soon one of the family. At their VE Day party, in the absence of fireworks, Ted and Johnny found some of keeper Wholey's cartridges and threw them on the bonfire. The explosion made the ladies jump and Mr Wholey angrily banned the boys from using guns for several weeks. In a way, this suited Ted. Something was changing in him, and he lost the urge to hunt and to kill. He rarely shot again. Trap and gun gave way to rod.

The usual pattern was homework first, then fishing. In winter, they made their own rods out of split canes. A nearby pond was stocked with perch, roach and pike. They caught frogs and spiked them on the barbed wire around the pond, but then they would be sorry, so they held animal funerals as atonement. Sometimes they went out without permission in a little rowing boat. Once Ted and Johnny threw in a hedgehog to see if it would swim, but were ashamed and fished it out again, and Ted wrapped it in his jumper and took it home, where they dried it on the kitchen range. Another time, Ted told Edna to close her eyes and he gently placed a dormouse in her cupped hands.

He found an injured owl by the roadside and brought it back to Crookhill. Mr Wholey let him keep it in one of the outbuildings on condition that he cared for it at weekends (the kind keeper looked after it himself during the week). Ted used to sit and talk to it for hours. Sometimes in the small hours of the morning, Mr Wholey would gently wake the boys and Edna so as to take them out to watch badgers at play, before returning for a hot drink and back to bed. Once, under a full moon, they watched hundreds of frogs cross the lane.

He always had a book in his pocket, together with pencil and paper. He would go out in the fields for hours. He and Edna roamed in the woods reciting Longfellow's *Hiawatha*, which she had to learn by heart for school. They walked, they talked, they dreamed. Ted would suddenly say 'Stand still and listen' and take from his pocket a crumpled page of poetry. They kept the ones that Edna liked best, stuffed others into holes in the tree trunks. He lay with his head on her lap and read to her. After John had left for National Service, Ted continued to go to Crookhill. He walked alone, high from reading verse aloud. 'I used to sit around in the woods, muttering through my books. I read the whole of *The Faerie Queene* like that. All of Milton. Lots more. It became sort of a hobby-habit.'[27]

His earliest surviving letter is to Edna, written when he was seventeen and she had gone off to train as a nurse. He wrote that there were things which held 'places of high wonder' in his imagination. Things that 'posterity may wonder at', things that when placed before the camera of everyday life 'invariably shattered the lens, burnt the film and slew the photographer'. 'I have seen', he went on, invoking the image of a caged animal that would become a recurring figure in his poetry, 'things which, when put on public view, slew the unlooking population by the thousand, melted the iron bars which encased it and leaping for freedom, reduced the room which contained it to general matchwood and lumber.'[28] Like the jaguar that he would conjure into poetry, Hughes came to hate being 'put on public view'. But in his imagination he melted the iron bars. Already he is imagining that it will be his vocation to create 'places of high wonder' for himself and for readers. Even as a schoolboy, writing half ironically and in full awareness of his own hubris, he wanted *posterity* to wonder at him. The same thought – voiced with self-mocking boyish arrogance – recurs in another letter to Edna in which he imagines himself as a great poet immortalised in a burial urn in Trafalgar Square.

His favourite fishing place on the Crookhill estate was a large pond, very deep in places. In the 'Capturing Animals' talk, he evoked the memory of seeing giant forms on the surface resembling railway sleepers. They were huge pike. His poem 'Pike', he said, captured not just a fish but 'the whole pond, including the monsters I never even hooked'.[29] The pond is as deep as England, deep as memory. It is at once his childhood, his unconscious and the spirit of place that made him who he was.

Throughout his life, he remained hooked by the mystique of the pike. They were, he said, 'fixed at some very active, deep level in my imaginative life'.[30] They filled his dreams. If he was feeling good about life, he would dream of giant pike that were also leopards, full of energy, connecting him to the vital forces of the universe. If he was feeling bad, he would dream that the pond of the pike was filled with concrete and bereft of fish. Nothing gave him more pleasure in the Seventies than fishing the loughs of Ireland with his teenage son Nicholas, plumbing the dark, mystic depths for what in a myth-heavy poem he called 'The Great Irish Pike'.[31]

At the end of 1968, he and Gerald drove to Mexborough to find the pond. The Wholeys' lodge was in ruins, its garden entirely over-grown. They went down to the pond and found that 'it had shrunk to an oily puddle about twenty feet across in a black basin of mud, with oil cans and rubbish'. Ted's son Nicky made a few half-hearted casts into the dank water. They felt low, despite the presence of Ted's name carved on a tree as a token of memory. As rain began to fall, Ted made one token cast himself, which he described as 'a ceremonial farewell', and there 'among the rubbish' he hooked 'a huge perch', one of the biggest he had ever caught: 'It was very weird, a complete dream.'[32]

Manor Farm is now a gastropub, the Crookhill estate a golf course, the pond of the pike shrunk by mud and reed. The magic landscape survives only in Hughes's writings.

4

Goddess

In order to get into Oxford or Cambridge University, you had to stay on at school for an extra term and take a special entrance exam. Ted Hughes duly won an exhibition: better than a mere place, but below a scholarship. Its value was £40 per year (a scholarship was £60), as much a matter of prestige as cash. His fees and a grant towards living expenses would be paid by the government; he was of that lucky first generation in which, thanks to grammar school and university grant, bright boys from very ordinary backgrounds had access to the best education without having to worry about money.

In later years, Ted liked to put about the myth that he got his place at Cambridge only because John Fisher sent the Master of the college a sheaf of his poems and a letter singing his praises as a budding writer, which led to his being admitted as a 'dark horse' despite failing the exam. But this would not have got him an exhibition and indeed in the Pembroke College archive there is a letter in which Fisher apologises for sending the poems, recognising that it might have been inappropriate to do so.[1] Hughes got a place to read English at Cambridge on his merits as a schoolboy literary critic.

But there was a hitch. At the end of his first year in the sixth form, the government had introduced a National Service Act. The army was not getting enough recruits – hardly surprising after the long years of war – so conscription was introduced for healthy males between the ages of seventeen and twenty-one. The Act was due to come into force on 1 January 1949. Just weeks before it did so, in the very month in which Hughes got his offer from Cambridge, the period of service was increased from twelve to eighteen months, in the light of the 'Emergency' in Malaya and the Berlin blockade that began the Cold War. There was a genuine fear that another major war might be on the way all too soon.

Boys with university places on offer were allowed to serve before or after taking their degree. Ted decided to get it out of the way and, following in Gerald's footsteps, applied for the Royal Air Force rather than the army. By the time his application had been processed and he had passed the medical, the eighteen-month period would have made it impossible for him to go up to Cambridge in the autumn of 1950. While he was still in uniform, the period of service was further extended, to two years, because of the outbreak of the Korean War.

He did not see active service. The RAF didn't really know what to do with its compulsory recruits. There was an awful lot of sitting around, which for Ted meant the opportunity to read and to write. For two years he would be identified as 'number 2449573 A.C. 2 Hughes E. J.' (the abbreviation stood for 'Aircraftman Second Class'). He sent witty, flirtatious and bored letters to Edna Wholey, first from Hut D35 of the RAF station at West Kirby on the Wirral, then from the Ops Section and after that from the Signals Section at RAF Patrington, near Hull in Yorkshire. His reports were of severe haircuts, rough and tumble in the barracks, dreadful food, pointless exercises, rain, rain and more rain, made bearable only by food parcels from home, the anticipation of the next '48' (two days' leave) and the quiet opportunity to read once he settled into his position as a flight plotter. He dated several local girls, none seriously, though he described one of them – Hilda Norris – as having 'eyes like a tiger'.[2]

Patrington was a radar station for ground-controlled interception, whereby fighter planes would be guided towards an incoming target. Since there was no immediate prospect of Russian bombers or missiles winging their way over Bridlington Bay to the Holderness marshes of the East Riding, the screen was usually blank and, especially when on night duty, Ted was free to deepen his knowledge of the psychology of Jung and the canon of English literature. Shakespeare, Yeats and Blake were his constant companions. Among prose-writers, he especially admired William Hazlitt, regarding his essays as a model of 'what-prose-ought-to-be'.[3] The influence tells on the lucid, muscular prose he wrote throughout his life. He also composed poems for Edna, including an 'epithalamium' for her marriage – though he expressed some displeasure at the idea of her being with another man. They were pals who flirted rather than true lovers. He writes of kissing her wrists, not her lips. But he felt possessive about their special bond with each other and with their secret Crookhill places.

The finest poem he wrote during his National Service was addressed to another girl, Jean Findlay, the great beauty of Mexborough Grammar School. Ted had wooed her with poetry when he was a sixth-former.[4] Now he saw her when he went home on leave. Walking back from a date, a love song formed in his head. On returning to duty – night watch, three o'clock on the morning of 13 June 1950, 'after slogging at stupidities' – he finished it in a two-minute heat of inspiration. It was the only early poem that he cared to preserve. Simply entitled 'Song', he included it (as a last-minute addition) in his first published volume, *The Hawk in the Rain*. He later said that it had a kind of 'natural music' that he never recaptured – or not at least until the more personal voice of his later poetry.[5] Influenced by the medieval traditions of courtly love in general and the early lyrics of Yeats in particular, it turns Jean Findlay into an icy or marbled lady, blessed by 'the tipped cup of the moon', caressed by the sea and kissed by the wind but unwilling to give herself to the poet. His heart has fallen 'all to pieces' at the thought of her.[6]

The all-male world of National Service was frustrating for young men of nineteen and twenty. Ted had a lot of time to turn Edna and Jean into creatures of his imagination. Thinking about them both, and writing poems inspired by them, made him reflect on ancient types. Was Edna in the woods an embodiment of woman as nurturing Mother Nature? And Jean the incarnation of desirable but dangerous Beauty?

His thinking about such dualities was shaped by his reading of Jung's *Psychological Types*, that book to which he had been introduced by his pathfinder Olwyn. She was now down in London, studying for an English Literature degree at Queen Mary College on the Mile End Road. She graduated in the summer of 1950 with a lower-second-class degree. As at school, she had not quite achieved her full academic potential: there was something prophetic in a sixth-form end-of-term report that read, 'Olwyn has done creditable work on the whole. But she must not allow herself to be distracted.'[7]

Jung's book divided human beings into two character types, introverted personalities who were highly subjective and absorbed in their own psychological processes, and extraverted personalities who were attuned to objects, to other people and to the external world. Jung treated this model as a key to all mythologies. His massive book worked through virtually the entire history of Western (and not a little Eastern) thought, dividing up ideas and writers according to extravert and introvert. Special value was attached to the inner life of the introvert, the type that was said to be typical of the creative artist.

Jung gave considerable space to a very distinctive exegesis of Carl Spitteler's allegorical prose poem *Prometheus and Epimetheus* (1881), making it the basis for the proposition that the mythical figure of Prometheus is both the exemplar of the creative artist and the archetypal introvert who surrenders himself entirely to his inner psychic function. Hughes took the model to heart: he told Olwyn of how he tried 'to inhibit all conscious thought and fantasy, so that my unconscious would compensate with an increased activity'.[8] His hope was that poetry would emerge directly from his unconscious, rather as Samuel Taylor Coleridge claimed that the vision of Kubla Khan came to him fully formed in a dream. For Ted, dreams would always be the taproot into the unconscious. Throughout his life, many of his journal entries consist of records of extraordinary dreams.

According to Jung, the union of opposites in the works of Spitteler took the form of the worship of women, a symbol for worship of the soul. In a move typical of Jung's development of Freud, it is suggested that the libido is originally attracted to woman in an erotic fashion, but then fastened on to a symbolic function that had something to do with the development of religion. As Ted would come to see it, the girl is replaced by the Goddess; the choice between two girls is transformed into a battle between two aspects of the Goddess.

Aircraftman Second Class E. J. Hughes finished his National Service and went home to prepare for university. His formal discharge was signed off later in the year, summarising his record as follows: enlisted, 27 October 1949; discharged from National Service 5 October 1951; 'Trade – Ground Wireless Mechanic – care and maintenance of transmitting and receiving gear'; 'Trade Proficiency – Good'; 'Character – Exceptional'; 'Bearing [the options being Very Smart, Smart or Untidy]: Smart'; 'Rank on discharge – L.A.C.' (Leading Aircraftman, one rank above entry level); '6' 2" fresh complexion, blue eyes, brown hair'.[9] His bearing was not always smart in later years, but transmitting on the radio would, in another way, become an important part of his life: in the early Sixties, his principal source of income was as a free-lance contributor to the British Broadcasting Corporation.

A letter dated 30 May 1951 arrived from the Awards Branch of the Ministry of Education, informing him that the University Supplemental Award offered to him in 1949, and postponed due to his National Service, was now being converted to a state scholarship, enabling him to study for his English degree at Pembroke College, Cambridge, with effect from the coming October. The award consisted of a grant to cover the whole or part of the tuition fees, together with a maintenance grant, its amount to be determined on the basis of parental income. A subsequent letter, following the financial assessment, informed Hughes that his university fees would be paid, and he would receive a grant of £218 per annum, in addition to the £40 exhibition that he had won from the college.

In the late summer, his father found a shop that would enable them to return to the Calder Valley. The family left Mexborough and moved to Woodlands Avenue at the Hebden Bridge end of Todmorden. Though on the other side of Hebden Bridge from Mytholmroyd, they were back in the family domain, once again on the north side of the valley. You went over a railway bridge and up on to the hillside. The road had a very respectable and rather suburban feel to it. One side of it was lined with Thirties houses, some semi-detached. The Hugheses were at number 4, opposite a big house called Stansfield Hall. It felt a rather indeterminate, in-between sort of place, but it was the home to which Ted would return in his university vacations.

As a 'going up' present before he left for Pembroke, his teacher John Fisher, to whom he owed so much, gave him a copy of Robert Graves's recently published *The White Goddess: A Historical Grammar of Poetic Myth*.[10] Reading it through the lens of Jung, Ted was engrossed. He saw in Graves a mature mirror of his own youthful self. 'Since the age of fifteen poetry has been my ruling passion,' began Graves. And so it had been for Hughes. Poetry is rooted in magic, the book claims; poets are in touch with a mysterious primeval magical potency. The poet is priest and judge, prophet and seer, 'in Welsh *derwydd*, or oak-seer, which is the probable derivation of "Druid"'. The truest poetry tunes in to ancient rhythms. Graves's very first example was the Welsh bardic *Cynghanedd* with its 'repetitive use of consonantal sequences with variants of vowels', as illustrated by the lines:

Billet spied
Bold sped,
Across field
Crows fled,
Aloft, wounded,
Left one dead.

Which sounds rather like a Ted Hughes poem.

Graves signs up to the belief of the Welsh poet Alun Lewis, who was killed in the Burma campaign, that the '*single* poetic theme' is Life and Death, 'the question of what survives of the beloved'. He then gives the Theme a capital letter and turns it into an ancient story that he finds played out in the myths and epic poems of every culture. It involved a battle between the God of the Waxing Year and the God of the Waning Year for the love of the 'capricious and all-powerful Threefold Goddess, their mother, bride and layer-out'. The poet identifies himself with the God of the Waxing Year and his Muse with the Goddess, while 'the rival is his blood-brother, his other self, his weird'. Graves's next paragraph haunted Hughes all his writing life:

> The Goddess is a lovely, slender woman with a hooked nose, deathly pale face, lips red as rowan-berries, startlingly blue eyes and long fair hair; she will suddenly transform herself into sow, mare, bitch, vixen, she-ass, weasel, serpent, owl, she-wolf, tigress, mermaid or loathsome hag ... The test of a poet's vision, one might say, is the accuracy of his portrayal of the White Goddess and of the island over which she rules.

Graves applied the term 'poet-laureateship' to the grounding of the Goddess in an island landscape and the role of the poet as the guardian of the spirit of both place and tribe. Hughes took this to heart. For better or for worse, in some of his richest poems and some of his poorest, till death parted him from Sylvia Plath and on until his own death, in health and in sickness brought on (he believed) by writing too much prose, Hughes married his imaginative vision to Graves's claim that 'a true poem is necessarily an invocation of the White Goddess, or Muse, the Mother of All Living, the ancient power of fright and lust – the female-spider or the queen-bee whose embrace is death'.[11]

Like Jung, Graves then went on to apply his system across cultures and ages. Hughes immersed himself in chapters with titles such as 'Fabulous Beasts', 'The Return of the Goddess' and 'The Roebuck in the Thicket' (a vital motif for the very first version of *Birthday Letters*). He took special pleasure in the Celtic material, which added Welsh traditions to the Irish myths he had already encountered in Yeats. Here was the ninefold Muse Cerridwen who was originally the Great Goddess in her poetic or incantatory character, who had a son who was also her lover, the Demon of the Waxing Year, before she was courted by the Thunder-god ('a rebellious Star-son infected by Eastern patriarchalism'), by whom she had twins, Merlin the magician and his sister Olwen. Ted lapped up all this and regurgitated much of it forty years later in his heftiest tome, *Shakespeare and the Goddess of Complete Being*. He once told Graves that *The White Goddess* was 'the chief holy book on poetic conscience'.[12]

All developed cultures, Graves suggests, eventually destroy the Goddess and replace her with a patriarchal sky god. 'This stage was not reached in England until the Commonwealth, since in mediaeval Catholicism the Virgin and Son – who took over the rites and honours of the Moon-woman and her Star-son – were of greater religious importance than God the Father.'[13] This idea chimed nicely with one of the tenets of certain prominent members of the English Faculty where Ted Hughes was now heading: that during the Civil War, just after the age of Shakespeare, a 'dissociation of sensibility' fractured English culture and society, and that it was the job of the poet to repair it.

In October 1951 he went up to Cambridge.

5

Burnt Fox

Cambridge is a city of water and history. Pembroke College, where Ted Hughes matriculated in the autumn of 1951, is at the top end of Trumpington Street, which leads out to the village where Chaucer's *Reeve's Tale* was set. Immediately outside the college was Fitzbillies bakery, which had served Chelsea buns to generations of students. Turn right and you are in King's Parade, dominated by the most glorious Gothic chapel in the world. Crossing the road from Pembroke, you pass the Pitt Building, which housed Cambridge University Press, the oldest publisher in the world. Then you are in Mill Lane, where gowned undergraduates attended lectures by such luminaries as Dr F. R. Leavis and (until his death in the year that Hughes went up) Ludwig Wittgenstein. In summer, you could hire a punt at Scudamore's Boatyard by the mill pond, beside which were two much-frequented and watery-named pubs, the Anchor and the Mill. From there, the river Cam meandered via Byron's Pool towards the village of Grantchester that had been immortalised by King's College student Rupert Brooke.

In Michaelmas term, when freshmen arrived, Cambridge was bitterly cold and shrouded in fog. According to student lore, the wind came straight off the Ural mountains. Ted wrapped himself in his Uncle Walt's Great War leather topcoat and fed all his change into the guttering gas fire in his room. But walking around town, among the colleges, there was something in the air that made everyone seem wide awake. He dressed in black, dying his own corduroy from the Sutcliffe Farrar factory. One contemporary said that he looked like a fisherman on a stormy night, while another – a jealous fellow-poet – remembered his 'smelly old corduroys and big flakes of dandruff in his greasy hair'.[1]

Ted Hughes and Evelyn Waugh could hardly have been more different as writers,[2] but they had one thing in common: the friends they made at university became friends for life. Ted's best friend in college was an Irishman called Terence McCaughey. They were supervision partners, which is to say that they had their weekly tutorial together in the room of the Pembroke College English Fellow, M. J. C. Hodgart, an authority on medieval ballads who also had a passion for James Joyce. McCaughey recalls how he and Ted bumped into each other in Heffers bookshop, where they were supposed to be buying set texts in their first or second week as freshmen. One book on the list was an anthology of *Fourteenth Century Verse and Prose*. Ted explained that he already had a copy, passed down to him by his sister, but that it was an older edition lacking the vocabulary list. He proposed selling this to McCaughey and buying himself a new one, complete with vocabulary, thus simultaneously getting a bargain and doing a favour.

They soon became fast friends, their Yorkshire and Irish accents contrasting with the self-entitled voices of the public schoolboys who lorded it over Cambridge. They shared a love of music, nature and words. They would spend their evenings in one or the other's room, reading poetry aloud or listening to Beethoven on 78rpm records. They went to the cinema together, especially enjoying the comedies of the Marx Brothers and Buster Keaton. Sometimes at dusk they walked along the Backs of the colleges or strolled on to Coe Fen, where, among the grazing cows, Ted blew mimic hootings to answering owls. They supplemented college food – which was no better than that of the National Service mess – with brown bread, cheese mixed with marmalade and, a particular Yorkshire delicacy, treacle sandwiches. Olwyn came to visit and Terence was amazed at the seriousness with which she and Ted discussed their friends in terms of horoscopic compatibility.

McCaughey went on to become a clergyman. They kept in touch by letter and occasionally visited each other. On Ted's last trip to Dublin, just four months before he died, Terence took him to the recently renovated University Church, built at Cardinal Newman's behest for the Catholic college. Quietly, Ted said, 'This fairly closely persuades me to become a Catholic or a Christian.'[3] But this was a sentiment felt in the moment: there was no subsequent deathbed conversion to orthodox faith.

About two-thirds of the Pembroke undergraduates were from public schools, one-third from grammar schools. Ted inevitably gravitated towards the latter group. Brian Cox was a typical example. Born in Grimsby into a frugal, lower-middle-class Methodist household, he grew up an avid reader, burying himself in the Grimsby public library after his mother died of tuberculosis when he was ten. After National Service, during which he wrote half a novel, he won a scholarship to Pembroke. With his friend Tony Dyson, another Pembroke man, he attended a term of Dr Leavis's classes but was disillusioned by the narrowness of his taste and the seeming puritanism of his critical method. Cox blamed Cambridge English for killing his own creativity and driving him to become a critic rather than an imaginative writer. Looking back on his time at college, he felt that he had learned more from his contemporaries than from the English Faculty: breakfast, lunch and dinner were taken in the college hall and the students who were 'in passionate love with literature' sat together, arguing 'over the long wooden tables about Shakespeare or Donne or Dickens meal by meal'.[4]

In his first year, Ted had to prepare for the 'Preliminary' examinations, which had to be passed but did not count towards the final degree. He took a medieval paper, in which his special delight was the anonymous alliterative poem *Sir Gawain and the Green Knight*, with its green giant carrying away his own chopped-off head, its seductive enchantress and wintry northern English landscapes (including a journey across 'the wilderness of Wirral' where Ted had begun his National Service). For the Shakespeare paper, *Richard III*, *Othello* and *Measure for Measure* were set texts, but with his voracious literary appetite he habitually woke at six in the morning and read a complete play by nine. The whole canon was at his command.

Then there was a compulsory language paper ('use of English' and translation from either French or Latin) and a paper offering, first, passages for detailed explanation and comment from the Metaphysical poets and Sir Thomas Browne's *Religio Medici*, and second, essay topics on seventeenth- and eighteenth-century authors. 'Swift is the only stylist,' he opined, the exemplar of 'clarity, precision, concisenesss and power'.[5] The Irish satirist taught Hughes the art of entering a word as if it were a world, of writing prose that is instantly accessible and memorable yet wild in imaginative reach. There was also a paper on literary criticism and, indeed, underlying all the work was the distinctive Cambridge method of practical criticism: close reading of the words on the page, dating of passages by their style, discrimination of good poetic writing from bad. In everything that he wrote, Hughes chose his words with care. He judged his own writing by the high standards instilled by John Fisher and reinforced by the Cambridge school of criticism. His letters to Olwyn are prose poems in themselves: 'Sometimes I think Cambridge wonderful, at others a ditch full of clear cold water where all the frogs have died. It is a bird without feathers; a purse without money; an old dry apple, or the gutters run pure claret.'[6]

In his second term, King George VI died and there was a sense of national excitement and new hope projected on to the young Queen. He exclaimed to Olwyn that they were the new Elizabethans, the first since the time of *Hamlet*; he wrote a masque in which the first Elizabeth met the second; he dared to dream that he might become the poetic soul of a new English Renaissance. His principal extra-curricular activity was the university Archery Club – a suitably Elizabethan sport.

Six feet two inches, dark and handsome, he cut a figure striding along King's Parade in his long dark coat. Reminiscing, he told of an occasion when an undergraduate called out, 'Ted, Ted,' ran up to him, shook his hand and said 'Thank you for saving England.' He had, he explained, been mistaken for Ted Dexter, the charismatic university cricket captain who made his Test debut while still an undergraduate. The two men did indeed share the same dark good looks. Whether or not there is embellishment in the telling,[7] the spirit of the tale is true: saving England by re-embodying the heady spirit of Elizabethan poetry was indeed our Ted's mission. He believed that a person's whole biography was visible in their walk.[8] All who knew him at Cambridge remembered the long coat and the confident stride, whereas his poetic ambition was, at least in his first year, kept under wraps.

The end of the academic year was marked by a May Ball, held in June. Ted was still in touch with Edna Wholey, who was now living with her husband in nearby Bedford. He had been to stay with them for a weekend and, though he confided to Olwyn that their company now bored him, he went over again and asked Edna to accompany him to the Ball. She declined, probably because her husband disapproved of the idea, but a visitor happened to present, a stunningly beautiful dark-haired Italian called Carina, niece of a Bedford celebrity, boxer and bit-part movie actor Tony Arpeno. So Ted asked her instead. Since they had never met before, everyone was rather startled when Carina accepted. Her parents booked a hotel room in Cambridge, waited up anxiously all through the night of the Ball and whisked her off to the station at dawn. A surviving photo from Ball night shows Ted with his trademark lock of hair falling over the eyes. He has the facial expression of a cat that got the cream.

Summer back home in Woodlands Avenue, Todmorden, was dull in comparison, with Gerald far away in Australia and Olwyn working in London. After graduating, she had taken a secretarial course at Pitman on the Bayswater Road in order to make herself employable. Ted set up a study for himself in the attic and prepared for his second year.

When he returned to Pembroke in the autumn, he had different accommodation. It was a good-sized first-floor room with large windows, tucked away in a building that had once been the Master's Lodge, reached via an opulent staircase and looking out over the Fellows' car park. He was screened from street-noise, but annoyed by a loud public schoolboy on the floor above. He took revenge by playing Beethoven far into the night.

Music was a serious passion. Olwyn moved to Paris that autumn to take up a secretarial job at the British Embassy, and he wrote to tell her of many a concert. His standards were high: at a recital by the legendary pianist Solomon (Cutner) there were some disappointingly slight encore pieces and then, in response to the cry 'More Beethoven!', a rendering of the *Waldstein* sonata which Ted did not consider up to scratch. He expressed a good deal more enthusiasm for his new academic supervisor, a graduate student called Eric Mottram, who was a poet and an enthusiast for avant-garde American poetry. 'I never knew anyone so forceful in his flow,' Ted told Olwyn. Supervisions were heated, argumentative, energising, extending well beyond the appointed hour's length.[9]

By day, Ted took charge of the reorganisation of the Archery Club. He kept a great bow in a corner of his room, and practised for hours. By virtue of representing the university against Oxford, he won a 'half-blue'. In the evenings, besides concerts, there were films and plays

– and the pub. The highlight of Michaelmas term was a poetry reading by Dylan Thomas, at the Cambridge Union under the auspices of the English Society. For the first time, Ted witnessed a charismatic poet in the flesh, holding an audience rapt with his word music. Afterwards, together with McCaughey and a couple of other friends, he followed Dylan Thomas and the society committee to the Eagle in Bene't Street so as to listen in on their conversation. Thomas and his acolytes spoke of filling Swansea Bay with beer. Elated, Ted and his friends then returned to Pembroke and burst into the room of Francis Holmes à Court, a literary-minded undergraduate of aristocratic pedigree (he subsequently succeeded his father, the 5th Baron Heytesbury). There they met another Welshman, a freshman called Daniel Huws who had been at school with Holmes à Court and had now come up to Peterhouse, just across the road. Ted, still high on the oxygen of Thomas's poetry, didn't really notice him, but the following year their respective circles of friends conjoined in the Anchor pub, with its dark-brown bar, table-football machine and, downstairs, benches by the landing-stage beside the punts waiting for hire.

In the Anchor, Ted was a brooding silent presence, content to let others make the conversational running. The most opinionated was Roger Owen, Liverpool Welsh, all politics and sociology. But when Ted spoke, everyone listened. He wasn't interested in politics but was an oracle on matters literary and was scathing about many of the dons in the English Faculty. Everyone in the group had a store of anecdotes, mostly mocking, about the lectures of Dr Leavis. Ted especially loathed the one on his beloved Yeats. In the Cambridge system, it was the weekly college supervision that counted. Lectures were an optional extra. Ted went to fewer and fewer as he progressed through his degree, but he thought well of both the theatrical Dadie Rylands and the sometime surrealist poet Hugh Sykes Davies on Shakespeare.

Towards the end of the pub evenings, much beer consumed, Terence McCaughey, with his seemingly inexhaustible repertoire of Irish ballads, led them in singing. Ted would eventually be cajoled into participation. 'He had a soft, light voice,' Huws recalled, 'with the slight tremolo which later characterized his reading voice.'[10] His party pieces were traditional numbers such as 'Eppie Morie' and Coleridge's favourite, the grand old ballad of 'Sir Patrick Spens'. Then they would all join in a round of 'Waltzing Matilda'.

Others who joined the Pembroke group at the Anchor were Fintan O'Connell and Joe Lyde, Northern Irish grammar school boys, one a Catholic and the other a Protestant. Lyde was loud and sometimes rude, a trumpeter and jazz pianist with the best band in Cambridge. A ladies' man, he would get to play in New Orleans, aggravate Sylvia Plath with his outlandish tales and brash words, and die young, of drink.

As for Ted's studies, there were supervisions on the Victorians and a special paper on Wordsworth and Coleridge, very much to his taste. Always able to read poetry with close attention, he jumped easily through the hoop of Cambridge practical criticism and achieved a 2.1 classification in Part I of the English Tripos, the honours examination at the end of the second year. Only nine candidates achieved first-class honours in English that year, and over 120 got a 2.2 or a Third. Ted and three of his Pembroke contemporaries were among the thirty 2.1s, outshining the four other Pembroke students, so this was a very creditable if not an outstanding performance.

The Cambridge degree is very flexible: it was perfectly possible to take one part of the Tripos in one subject and the other in something completely different. After Part I, half the Pembroke English students changed course. Ted's choice was Archaeology and Anthropology. He thus missed out on the paper that he would most have enjoyed had he stuck with English: the study of Tragedy from the ancient Greeks via Shakespeare and Racine to Ibsen, Chekhov and Yeats, a course in which Sylvia Plath would immerse herself a couple of years later.

Many times over the years Ted Hughes told the story of why he switched away from English. It was one of his party pieces, often used to introduce public readings of his best-known poem, 'The Thought-Fox' – though that poem was not written until well after he graduated. He was not always consistent in the details of the tale, so there may well be a characteristic element of invention, or at least embellishment, in the telling. But there is no doubting the centrality of the story to his personal myth.

A cornerstone of Cambridge undergraduate life is the 'essay crisis'. Terms are short, reading lists are long and extra-curricular distractions are legion. The essay for the weekly supervision is accordingly left to the last minute, written deep into the night. Ted sometimes wrote with great facility, especially if the subject was one of his passions, such as William Blake. But sometimes he could not get going on his essay. He'd stare at the blank page on his desk, write and rewrite an opening, cross it out, give up and go to bed.

One night when this happened, he dreamed that he was still at his desk, in his 'usual agonising frame of mind, trying to get one word to follow another'. The lamplight fell on the page. In the dream the door slowly opened. A head appeared in the dim light: at the height of a man but with the form of a fox. The creature descended the two or three steps down into the room. With its fox's head and 'long skinny fox's body', it stood upright, as tall as a wolf reared on its hind legs. The hands were those of a man: 'He had escaped from a fire – the smell of burning hair was strong, and his skin was charred and in places cracking, bleeding freshly through the splits.' The creature walked across the room to the desk, placed the paw that was a human hand on the page and spoke: 'Stop this – *you are destroying us*.' The burns were worst on the hand, and when the fox-man moved away there was a bloody print upon the page. The dream seemed so wholly real that Ted got up and examined his essay for the bloody mark. He determined forthwith to abandon his course in English Literature. In some versions of the story, he dreams again the following night. Either the fox returns and nods approvingly, or the creature returns in the variant form of a leopard, again standing erect.

In his fullest recounting of the story, Hughes says that the essay he was (not) writing was on Samuel Johnson, a personality he greatly liked. Johnson and Leavis are the only two English writers habitually referred to as 'Doctor' (the critic George Steiner once quipped that theirs were the only two honorary doctorates conferred by the Muses). Dr Johnson and Dr Leavis were archetypes of the critical spirit, so at this moment the former was standing in for the latter: 'I connected the fox's command to my own ideas about Eng. Lit. and the effect of the Cambridge blend of pseudo-critical terminology and social rancour on creative spirit, and from that moment abandoned my efforts to adapt myself.' Hughes explained that he had a considerable gift 'for Leavis-style dismantling of texts', indeed an almost 'sadistic' aptitude for it, but the procedure – surgical and objective, the antithesis of schoolmaster Fisher's spirit of 'husbandry and sympathetic coaching' – seemed to him both a 'foolish game' and inimical to the inner life.[11] The critical impulse cauterises the creative spirit.

Given his interest in folklore and comparative mythology, fostered by *The White Goddess*, Archaeology and Anthropology was an obvious choice for Part II of the Tripos. He was able to focus on the anthropological side. An added advantage of changing subject was that, in order to mug up his new discipline, he was encouraged to come into residence during the 'Long Vacation term' (an opportunity to study in Cambridge for part of the three-month summer break). This was an escape from the boredom of home. There were a demanding eight papers to prepare for. General Ethnology was an introduction to race, culture and environment, exploring different types of human economy in relation to habitat. Two papers on prehistory gave him an introduction to the archaeology of the Palaeolithic, Mesolithic and Neolithic Ages, and the 'origins of higher civilization'. Then there was Physical Anthropology: man's zoological position in relation to the animal world, a subject of considerable interest to Hughes. Social Anthropology was less attractive to him, but it was compensated for by a special paper in Comparative Ethnography that gave him the opportunity to read such classics as Margaret Mead's *Growing up in New Guinea* and Bronisław Malinowski's *Coral Gardens and their Magic*. The course was rounded off with an essay on a subject of the student's choice and a practical examination, 'being a test of the candidate's power of recognizing and describing bodily features and artifacts, ancient and modern, including those drawn from the culture or area specifically studied'.[12] Ted enjoyed identifying bones.

Promising as the prospect of such a course seemed, he quickly grew bored with the slog of factual learning. He attended very few lectures and instead borrowed the notes of his supervision partner. Pembroke did not have an 'Arch & Anth' don, so he was farmed out to St John's College, where he was supervised by Glyn Daniel, who later became a highly successful populariser of prehistory while writing Cambridge-based murder mysteries in his spare time. Ted spent most of his final year in the University Library, pursuing his own course of reading. Unlike the Bodleian in Oxford, the Cambridge UL housed most of its stock on open stacks, with an arcane classification system that led to serendipitous juxtapositions. It was perfect for browsing, for following one's nose, for the gathering of eclectic wisdom. Ted had a lust for free-range intellectual enquiry: he told a friend that he got an erection every time he entered the library.[13]

For his Finals, he leaned heavily on Graves's *White Goddess*, a book mistrusted by professional ethnographers, and he scraped a third-class result. Academically, he would have done better to stay with English Literature. Nevertheless, Mead's work gave him fascinating insights into alternative views of sex, marriage, the rearing of children and the supernatural, while Malinowski's 'ethnographic theory of the magical word'[14] could be read as an endorsement of his own attitude to the supernatural: its argument was that the magical spells of the Trobriand islanders had an essentially pragmatic function. Like all forms of language, they must be regarded as 'verbal acts' intended primarily not to communicate thought but to bring about practical effects. This was very much Hughes's view of the horoscope and the Ouija board (several of his contemporaries expressed some alarm at his attempts to conjure up the spirit world). Another set text – of which he would have got the gist, even if he didn't read it through – had the potential to contribute to his sense of modern civilisation's damaging alienation from nature: Ian Hogbin's *Experiments in Civilization* was a report on how the arrival of European culture severed a native community in the Solomon Islands from its ancient ways.

Cambridge had its own social anthropology. There were divides between the posh colleges and the more middling, between the hearties and the aesthetes, between the entitled public school crowd and the meritocratic grammar school boys. Cavalry twill and flamboyant hacking jackets were set against grey flannel trousers and tweed. Ted and his provincial friends, drinking in the Anchor, looked with a mixture of awe and scorn upon the metropolitan sophisticates who dominated the Union, the Amateur Dramatic Club and the student literary magazine *Granta*. Among the stars of their Cambridge were Peter Hall, future founder of the Royal Shakespeare Company and first artistic director of the National Theatre; Karl Miller, who would be literary editor of the *Spectator*, the *New Statesman* and the *Listener* and then found the *London Review of Books*; Thom Gunn of Trinity, regarded as the best student poet in Cambridge; and, most glamorous of all, Nick Tomalin, president of the Union and editor of *Granta*. Tomalin would marry a literary-minded Newnham College girl, Claire Delavenay, daughter of a French academic and an English composer. He became a journalist who was killed on the Golan Heights during the Yom Kippur War, she a leading biographer.

Ted published a couple of poems in *Granta*, hiding himself under the pseudonym Daniel Hearing. He also submitted work to new, smaller literary magazines. Peter Redgrove, something of a loner with unfashionably short hair and a leather jacket, set up *delta* explicitly to rival *Granta*. He took on Philip Hobsbaum, one of Leavis's Downing men, as an assistant editor. Hobsbaum, who could be malicious, recalls Hughes sidling up to him in that other pub, the Mill, where the preferred beverage was strong Merrydown cider. Ted muttered out of the corner of his mouth, 'I hear you and Redgrove are starting a poetry magazine. Here are some poems I'd like you to look at.' With that, 'he shuffled off to the gents':

> The wad of manuscript he had thrust at us was greasy and typed in grey characters, as though the ribbon in the typewriter had been used a great many times over a period of years, and never been changed. Redgrove looked at this dubiously, and uttered these memorable words: 'Ted's a nice chap, but I don't think we ought to publish his poems.'[15]

After Ted had graduated, *delta* did publish one of these poems. Entitled 'The Woman with Such High Heels She Looked Dangerous', it tells of a woman slick with makeup coaxing a man into the darkness and stabbing him: 'Men become wolves, but a wolf has become a woman.'[16]

The June 1954 issue of another little magazine, *Chequer*, appeared, in a bright yellow cover, in his final term. Daniel Huws, who had had a poem accepted there himself, was surprised to see Ted with a copy in his hands when he turned up in the Anchor one evening. Neither knew that the other wrote poetry. Ted quietly asked Dan his opinion of a poem by one Peter Crew. 'I wrote it,' he then explained.[17] Entitled 'Song of the Sorry Lovers', it features a couple in bed, a hyena laughing outside and a rousing of the 'animal faculties'.[18] Later that night, Hughes and Huws went to see Redgrove, who also had a poem in *Chequer*. There were six bottles of German wine in his room at Queens'. They got drunk, crashed a party on another staircase and Ted got into a fight and damaged his thumb. On another occasion, he received a police caution for being drunk and disorderly after an undergraduate escapade involving a purloined road sign.

He was growing in confidence. Stories about him began circulating in college. His final-year room was on the top floor of the eastern side of Pembroke's front court. He painted life-size pumas and what his bedmaker referred to as 'bacchanalian orgies' on the sloping ceiling. The Tutor, a benign classicist called Tony Camps, came to investigate. Ted suggested that the Tutor should lie down on the floor in order to appreciate the frescoes fully. He did so, then ordered whitewashing at Ted's expense. Camps noted in the Tutor's file that Hughes was often tipsy and that his manner had a bearish quality, but he still wrote him enthusiastic and affectionate job references.[19] An even better story was that a college porter informed the Tutor that Mr Hughes was entertaining a lady in his rooms. Camps went to investigate, knocking on the heavy old door. After a few moments, it opened slowly to reveal Mr Hughes 'stark naked with his arms outstretched like a cross'. Ted spoke: 'Crucify me.'[20]

As with most undergraduates, there was many an incident involving climbing into college at night. Gallingly for ex-National Service men, it was like being in the forces again: lock-up at 10 p.m., fines for staying out late (twopence, doubled to fourpence if it was after eleven), and no overnight female guests. All the Cambridge colleges were single-sex and many girls at Newnham and Girton, the only two female colleges, kept to themselves or were intimidatingly bluestocking. Outnumbering female students by fifteen to one, male undergraduates looked to the town, and in particular to the nurses training at Addenbrooke's Hospital on Trumpington Street, conveniently close to Pembroke. Ted started going out with a nurse called Liz Grattidge. Tall and blonde, from Manchester, she sat quietly in the Anchor, when she was free at weekends, 'smiling indulgently at the proceedings'.[21] Coming from a northern city of industrial grime and rain that was forever scudding in off the Pennines, she dreamed of making a new life in Australia – which she eventually did.

Ted was up for this. It would take him back to Gerald, who was now settled in Tullamarine, a suburb of Melbourne. He was married to a woman called Joan and sending home wafer-thin light-blue airmails filled with easy living and Australian light, perfect for painting (Gerald was showing a talent for watercolour). Just before sitting his Finals in May 1954, Ted surprised his mother and father with a letter. He had filled in emigration papers for Australia. Like Gerald, he would become a Ten Pound Pom. He told his parents that he was going to take a girl with him – she was up for anything. They would probably get married before going. He didn't mention her name, but explained that she was a nurse and that all his friends said that from certain angles she looked just like him (apart from the fact that she was blonde and he was dark). There was something comforting about the idea of marrying a nurse who was happy to submit to his will: 'I kick her around and everything goes as I please.'[22]

'a compact index of everything to follow'

After graduation, Ted treated himself to a trip to Paris. Olwyn had been working for various international organisations there and eventually settled into a job as a secretary–cum–translator for a theatre and film agency called Martonplay, where she would encounter such legendary figures as the Absurdist dramatist Eugène Ionesco. Ted had previously been on a motoring tour of Spain with Uncle Walt, but this was his first self-sufficient time abroad. At the end of his life he looked back at this young man in a Paris café, drinking claret and eating Gruyère cheese, experiencing their taste for the first time. Sophistication, cosmopolitanism, sensuality. A world away from Calder Valley and Cambridge fen. In a poem, he tried to recover the immersion and innocence of that moment, the sense of hope, of being on the threshold of a life not yet lived. The young man has no idea what is about to hit him: 'He could never imagine, and can't hear / The scream that approaches him.' A scream in the shape of a panther, a scream in 'the likeness of a girl'.[1]

He also had a wonderful holiday in Switzerland with his girlfriend Liz, whose sister lived out there. They rowed on the lakes, fished and walked. Their plans had slightly changed. He would go to Gerald in Australia, and get a job, while she went to Canada with her parents to visit her brother there, then she would return to the United Kingdom and join him 'down under' some time later.[2]

He kept his options open, applying not only for a passage to Australia but also for a postgraduate diploma in Education that would have qualified him as a teacher. Then he dreamed up one of his schemes: to make a fortune out of mink-farming. It would be an extension of the animal-trapping of his wanderings around Old Denaby. But Australia House informed him that mink would be out of the question down under. He contemplated Canada instead. Canada House told him that the climate for mink was much better in Britain. So for a while he would go back home and get some experience on a big mink farm. He made notes in his Collins Paragon pocket diary: '30 buckets for 1250 mink. In every 30, 4 buckets wheatmeal and bran or oatmeal etc., with grass-meal. 2 buckets milk and chemical feed.'[3] Before and after work, he could write poetry and – like the young Shakespeare – do a little poaching now that there were deer up on Hardcastle Crags.[4] Mink, though, did not inspire him into poetry in the manner of fox and fish, hawk and crow, or big cat.

Nor did he really want to return to Yorkshire. Friends and girlfriend were in the south. Over the course of the next year, he drifted. The passage to Australia came through, but he asked to defer it for a year. Dan Huws's father let him use a flat that he owned in Rugby Street in the Holborn district of London. Having made a little money doing casual work, Ted got into the habit of returning to Cambridge and reading in the University Library until the money ran out, at which point he would go back to London to earn some more. In Cambridge he stayed with his girlfriend Liz in her unheated ground-floor flat in Norwich Street, conveniently near the station and a favoured address for nurses and students in 'digs'. Most of his friends were still at the university. Terence McCaughey was pursuing graduate work in Celtic studies, while Dan Huws and the others were in their final undergraduate year.

At various times in the spring and summer terms of 1955 Ted slept on a camp bed in the room of a Queens' student called Michael Boddy or pitched his tent in the garden of St Botolph's Rectory, beside a converted chicken coop occupied by an American student who had placed an advertisement in the *Varsity* newspaper seeking accommodation, to which he had received a reply from the rector's widow asking 'whether you would be interested in a sleeping hut in my garden, which you could have rent free with free light and electric fire and radiator, in return for the stoking of two fires – an Aga cooking stove and a Sentry boiler'.[5]

Boddy of Queens' – a twenty-stone-plus trombonist, son of the Dean of Ripon – shared Hughes's love of country life and the writings of Henry Williamson. He was bemused when Ted took him on a tour of the occult section of the stacks of the University Library and intrigued by his advice on how to treat women. The theory was 'to build up the relationship gently stage by stage' so that the woman would be subjugated before she knew what was happening: 'First say "Bring me that cup." Then say, "Bring me that cup full of tea," until, I suppose, the woman was cooking a five-course meal, feeding the goldfish, walking the dog, and doing the laundry without argument.'[6] None of this was entirely serious: Ted was still playing the undergraduate. One night they commandeered a punt and stole along the Backs, Ted towering in the rear with the pole, until they reached St John's College, where Chinese geese grazed on the lawn. Boddy jumped out of the punt, caught one and broke its neck. Ted said that since it was dead it should be eaten, so the body was taken back to St Botolph's and boiled in a pot. It stunk out the kitchen and proved too tough to eat.[7] During exam season, Ted helped his friends prepare. He told Olwyn that Boddy wrote an entire set of answers on the basis of quotations he had selected. His gift of recall was coming in handy: he provided further assistance by recovering the argument of Shelley's *Defence of Poetry* from his recollection of a lesson at Mexborough Grammar.[8]

His horizon was becoming more cosmopolitan. Assorted Americans appeared in the Anchor crowd, among them the pot-bellied future critic Harold ('Hal') Bloom, who, like Ted, seemed to hold the whole of English literature within his prodigious memory. The two of them did not get on. Another new arrival was Danny Weissbort, who brought polyglot credentials. He was the son of Polish Jews who had arrived in Britain in the 1930s by way of Belgium. At home they spoke French and Danny answered them in English. He had come up to read History at Queens' while writing poetry under the influence of Dylan Thomas: 'I went up to Cambridge the year after Thomas died and I very much remember trying to write like him – and, of course, the idea of the poet as a bohemian wild boy was very attractive, even though I didn't really know what it all meant.'[9] The premature death of Thomas, in the Michaelmas term of Ted's third undergraduate year, had struck them all like a thunderbolt, though no one knew to what extent it could be attributed to his legendary drinking. After graduating, Weissbort went to work for a while in the family clothing factory (a similar path was open to Hughes), but then took up research on the subject of poetry in post-Stalinist Russia. He made a significant return to Hughes's life a decade later, when they launched the magazine *Modern Poetry in Translation*.

The American who had moved to the chicken coop in order to escape the constriction of college lock-up was Lucas ('Luke') Myers from Tennessee. He had been drawn to Downing College by the reputation of F. R. Leavis. In later years, he would become the correspondent to whom Ted opened his heart most fully. They were the same age; they had both done military service before university; they both began with English Literature and switched to Anthropology. And they both had vigorous relationships with attractive girlfriends. They enjoyed exchanging stories of their escapades, Luke telling of sex in the chicken coop and Ted describing how he had been in bed with Liz in her lodgings one morning when the landlady came in with tea. He dived under the covers and in answer to the question 'What's that lump down there?' Liz replied, 'That's Ted,' with the result that she was obliged to find new lodgings the same day. On another occasion, Ted came up from London for a party and the first thing he and Liz did was dive into an unoccupied bedroom. He felt remorse for 'violating hospitality'.[10]

Ted was getting a somewhat exaggerated reputation as a ladies' man. Myers recalled only a single one-night stand, but its circumstances had momentous consequences. It was the final week of the summer term, known in Cambridge as the Easter term, of 1955. A Peterhouse student, a friend of Dan Huws and his roommate David Ross, had invited a girl up from London for a few days. One night she was asleep in Dan's bed while he and Ross were out on the town with Ted and Luke. A porter observed two figures preparing to climb the wall back into college after hours. He thought he recognised the culprits, so went up to their rooms with another porter to check if the beds were indeed empty. They observed a trail of long yellow hair on Dan's pillow and a set of female underclothes draped over a chair. The girl was escorted out of college. The boys gallantly directed her across Coe Fen to the St Botolph's Rectory garden and then entered college to face their fate. Later, Ted and Luke returned to find the bed in the coop occupied by an attractive eighteen- or nineteen-year-old (this time clothed). With true Southern hospitality, Luke offered to sleep on the floor. But Ted and the girl decided that there was plenty of room in the tent, so Luke had his usual bed to himself. In the morning, the girl took him aside and said, 'Ted's so big and hot.'[11]

Huws, Ross and the student who had invited the girl in the first place were summoned before the Peterhouse authorities. Myers was implicated and his college informed. Ted's name was also given, but since he had graduated he was not under college jurisdiction. However, the University of Cambridge had an ancient right to exclude miscreants among their graduates from an area within a radius of 3 miles from Great St Mary's University Church. Peterhouse rusticated Huws and Ross, meaning that they had to leave the city for the remainder of the term (which was only a matter of days), while the boy who had issued the invitation was sent down permanently, thus losing the chance to get a degree. Downing decreed that Myers must move out of the debauched chicken coop and find other lodgings. The next term, the kindly widow allowed him to sleep in her dining room, so St Botolph's Rectory remained his home a little longer. As for Ted, he was summoned before a specially convened university committee. After returning to London, he was informed that he would indeed be prohibited from setting foot within the prescribed radius of Great St Mary's. He paid no attention. If he had done, he would probably never have met Sylvia Plath.

In the interim between trial and sentencing, Huws, Ross, Myers, Danny Weissbort and a medical student called Nathaniel ('Than') Minton met over wine in the ill-fated rooms in Peterhouse. It was then that David Ross announced that he wanted to start a new literary magazine. His father had generously agreed to put up some money. In the light of the recent misadventure, there was an obvious name for the new publication: *Saint Botolph's Review*. They would set to work on it when they returned after the Long Vacation.

In that summer of 1955 Ted took an outdoor job as an assistant rose-gardener at a nursery between Baldock and Hitchin. In the autumn, he was back in Rugby Street, putting out feelers at the BBC, winning the odd sum of cash in newspaper competitions, taking on more casual work, for instance £8 a week as a security guard in a girder factory. When he wasn't contemplating becoming a sailor on a North Sea trawler, he was dreaming up new money-making schemes: perhaps he could save up for five years to buy a house in Oxford or

Cambridge and let it to students and nurses at £3 per head per week, with a landlady accommodated gratis in the basement. Or maybe rent out a string of garages, or act as agent for the sale of Gerald's paintings, or teach English language in Spain or Hungary, where one could live cheaply.

The deferred offer to become a Ten Pound Pom lapsed. He did not want to commit to the other side of the world if there was any chance of making it in literary life at home. Philip Hobsbaum of *delta* had moved to London and revived the evenings of poetry reading that he had begun at Cambridge. He and his friends called themselves 'the Group'. Their first meeting was held on a wet October evening in Hobsbaum's bedsitter off the Edgware Road. Peter Redgrove was there, along with an Anglo-Argentinian poet who had also been at Cambridge, his American wife, a couple of aspiring actors, Hobsbaum's young fiancée and Ted, who read some poems that would soon appear in *Saint Botolph's Review*.[12] Over the following couple of years, Ted was a frequent, though not regular, presence at meetings of the Group, which was soon joined by the brilliantly inventive Australian Peter Porter and the talented Jamaican-born poet and artist Edward Lucie-Smith, an Oxford man.

Hobsbaum never forgot the power of Hughes's verse-speaking: 'One night he read Hopkins's "I wake and feel the fell of darkness, not day" in so vibrantly personal a manner that a young lady present took it to be a sonnet of his own recent composition.'[13] He also recited a large chunk of *Sir Gawain and the Green Knight* into Peter Redgrove's reel-to-reel tape recorder. A tape survives, now in the British Library, of an informal meeting of the Group and of Ted reciting some of his own poems as well as Yeats and Hopkins. His Yorkshire vowels are long but by today's standards he sounds quite posh, his lilting incantation learned from Dylan Thomas.[14]

Ted annoyed Hobsbaum's Rhodesian landlady by cooking a black pudding in her frying pan and singing ballads in the small hours of the morning, cajoling a shy, plain schoolteacher poet called Rosemary Joseph to join in. Rosemary later had a poem called 'Baking Day' published in an anthology of the work of the Group.[15] Hobsbaum believed that Ted portrayed her, with a change of profession though not of character, in the poem that was entitled 'Secretary' in his first book, *The Hawk in the Rain*.

'Secretary' first appeared, untitled, in *Saint Botolph's Review*. It is a cruel little poem about a nervous, demure young woman who would 'shriek' and run off in tears if touched by a man. Hughes imagines her scuttling 'down the gauntlet of lust / Like a clockwork mouse', darning and cooking for her family, then going to bed early with buttocks clenched tight against the force of youth and desire.[16] Hobsbaum's identification of this despised virgin with Rosemary Joseph should be treated with caution. As a student of F. R. Leavis, he should have remembered that one of the first lessons of practical criticism was to distinguish the speaker in a poem – the written 'I' – from the poet himself. The reader's business is to attend to the words on the page, to judge the authenticity of the feeling created by the verbal tone, the cadence and texture of the verse, not to suppose that the poem is a crude transcription of the writer's personal experience. Furthermore, as T. S. Eliot taught, all poems are as much engagements with previous poems, with the literary 'tradition', as they are expressions of the self. Hughes's 'Secretary' may have had one seed in his observation of a particular woman, or kind of woman, but it was also his reworking of the typist in her bedsit passively surrendering to the 'young man carbuncular' in Eliot's *The Waste Land*.

By the summer of 1955, Ted had broken up with Liz and was going out with a girl called Shirley who was reading English at Newnham. She was beautiful and clever, stronger and more interesting than Liz, though shy and quietly spoken. They were serious about each other. When she appeared leaning over the railings of the Mill bridge, Ted would leave his friends in the Anchor and go off with her.

Shirley was in her second year. She came from a suburban background in the north-west (her parents were both pharmacists), and had been to a mixed grammar school. At first she had been overawed by Cambridge, and most particularly by what seemed to her the supreme self-confidence of her fellow-undergraduates. Nevertheless, during her first year she had found some true friends at Newnham and come to feel more at ease.

What attracted Shirley to Ted initially was his unorthodox lifestyle, his residence in the orchard of St Botolph's Rectory, his poetry, his snatches of French picked up over his Paris summer the previous year ('Zut, alors,' he would say), his trademark black corduroy jacket – all part of a bohemian persona. He fried herrings in oatmeal for her; he taught her a betting system based on the form of three-year-old race-horses. He seemed rooted in reality – the antithesis of the rarefied and cerebral atmosphere of Cambridge. He made the conventionally ambitious men pale into insignificance. But what made her fall deeply in love with him was an intensity, a power, a sense of certainty, of sureness. He had a stillness, a watchfulness about him – not the watchfulness of a detached analytic observer; he was empathetic, he engaged with the world, but always retained an immutable inner 'self'. This, it seemed to her, encompassed but was more than his belief in his vocation as a poet. She thought it had been with him always. She grew to feel she had become part of that certainty, that 'self'. Later, when she had to accept that this was no longer true, the effect was devastating.

With her auburn hair and pale freckled skin, she was his Deirdre of the Sorrows, his ethereal Celtic girl. In the warm summer of 1955, Shirley stayed up for the Long Vacation term. She had a lovely room looking out on Newnham greenery. Ted came over from his gardening job, bearing armfuls of roses. He invited her to the Beacon for a week. She found his father quiet and withdrawn, his mother warm and properly maternal: she made them real homemade lemonade. While there, Shirley, in his mother's absence, made a disastrous attempt to cook Scotch eggs and left the kitchen a blackened mess. She feared that Ted's house-proud mother would be enraged, but Edith just laughed it off. Olwyn then arrived from Paris for a brief visit. Like Ted, she towered over her parents. Shirley felt more than a little intimidated by this striking, blonde Viking goddess. Olwyn shook her hand, turned it over, examined her palm and said: 'You have some very nasty moments coming.' Shirley was chilled by an antagonism she could not understand. When she and Olwyn had to share a bed, Shirley balanced herself precariously on the extreme edge for the whole night.

It was in his West Yorkshire home that Ted revealed his detailed knowledge of and passionate love for the natural world. He was truly himself there. When he took Shirley to Haworth Parsonage, she, who had always loved *Wuthering Heights*, felt that Ted, like Heathcliff, belonged to these moors. He himself was part of that landscape, elemental, unchangeable.

From Yorkshire they went over to Liverpool. Shirley's mother met them at the barrier at Lime Street station. They were both dressed in black, the uniform of rebellious youth. Her mother was shocked by Shirley's appearance, and said: 'You look as though you haven't slept for a week.' Shirley, of course, was secretly gratified by the remark. As they went down the avenue to her home, her mother walked a few paces ahead of them, not wanting the neighbours to associate her with this disreputable-looking pair. Shirley's father was not impressed with Ted's aspirations to be a poet. 'I suppose you would go out to work,' he said to his daughter, 'and he would stay at home writing poetry.' The following morning, Shirley, still in her nightdress, went into the guest room to bid Ted good morning. Her father saw her emerging, and Ted was asked to leave.

At the beginning of the Michaelmas term, Ted made a proposal: why didn't she leave Cambridge and everything else behind her and go to Spain with him? She was not quite enough of a bohemian to agree. Later in life she was to wonder how all their lives would have turned out if she had gone, but she also convinced herself that what was about to happen was meant to be – it would lead to the magnificent poetry of both Ted and Sylvia.

As for Shirley's appearance, Ted never forgot it. In an exquisite unpublished poem, the threads of memory are woven out of the 'bushed mass' of Shirley's densely tangled hair that overwhelmed her 'small-boned freckled / Irish face'. Her large green eyes were 'Startling and nearly too pretty' for her pretty and 'silent' face. 'Baffled and loving', she and Ted break out of themselves and into each other. A single strand of hair becomes his link, his bridge, to something he cannot forget, a world he never entered, a future that was not to be. Shirley offered him 'a great richness', but he was too young 'To recognize one of those offers / Life makes only once'.[17]

The poem was written many years later, as part of Hughes's long process of coming to terms with his marriage to Sylvia Plath and her death. He was always fascinated by the idea of the road not taken, the possible alternative life story. What if he *had* taken that passage to Australia? Or obeyed the command of the university Proctors and stayed away from the launch party of *Saint Botolph's Review*? Ireland – especially the west of Ireland, where W. B. Yeats had found his home – was always his land of lost content, the place to which he dreamed of escaping. If Shirley had accepted the invitation to Spain and then married him, his soul and body would have mingled with a child of Ireland.

Shirley was the inspiration for 'Fallgrief's Girlfriends', another of Ted's poems published in *Saint Botolph's Review*. The persona of Fallgrief, by this account a projection of Hughes himself, has a rather dim view of his girlfriends ('admiration's giddy mannequins / Lead every sense to motley') and of sexual congress ('insects couple as they murder each other') until he is changed by finding 'a woman with such wit and looks / He can brag of her in every company'.[18] He was proud of Shirley. But still he was marking time, waiting for his real life to begin. Just before his twenty-fifth birthday he wrote in his journal of how he still felt like an 'observer not yet called into the lists'. He sees himself as detached, idle, lacking in will, in need of some violent force to energise him and spark him into creative life.[19]

The living colossus in the pantheon of Ted Hughes and his contemporaries was Thomas Stearns Eliot. After Hughes became Poet Laureate, he delivered a lengthy toast in Eliot's memory on the occasion of the centenary of his birth. He wrote it up under the title *A Dancer to God*. Like his meditations on his other poetic heroes – Shakespeare, Coleridge, Yeats – this piece is a scarcely veiled manifesto for his own work. Its theme is 'the voice of Poetry as the voice of Eros', which is indeed the thrust of Hughes's own poetry. Eros: the primordial Greek god of desire, son of Aphrodite (Roman Cupid, son of Venus), embodiment of the madness of erotic love, and in Freud the term for the sex drive or life-force that is the opposite of the death drive (*Eros* versus *Thanatos*).

Even as a student, Ted was mapping out the argument that he later crystallised in what he called the 'unified field theory' of *A Dancer to God*.[20] He and his friends believed that the two great English-language poets of modern times were unquestionably W. B. Yeats and T. S. Eliot. Each of them was deeply responsive to 'the poetic Self – that other voice which in the earliest times came to the poet as a god, took possession of him, delivered the poem, then left him'. Yeats's dabbling in the supernatural, like Hughes's, though considered by many to be 'at best a wilful indulgence, at worst a little bit crazy', was of a piece with his belief in the magical spirit-force of the poetic self and with his attunement to Irish myth, legend and folklore. Yeats thus became the poet of the land and the spirit of place, the culmination of 'the complex of autochthonous traditions in these islands', the true Irish bard.[21]

Eliot, by contrast, was the poet of deracinated modernity. His 'unique position in the history of poetry' came from the fact that he was the first to see the 'desacralized landscape' of the world after the Great War, the first to give voice to 'a new terror: the meaningless'. *The Waste Land* announced a rupture in the history of the world: it shores against our ruin fragments of civilisation in a time broken not only by the mass slaughter of the trenches but also by Nietzsche's proclamation of the death of God and Freud's reinvention of the poetic or second self as the dark unconscious within instead of a quasi-divine Muse descending from above. Eliot's poetic career, Hughes suggests, followed a path from this new desolation to the redemption of *Four Quartets*, climaxing in the grace of the Farrar community at Little Gidding, 'the rose-windowed, many-petalled choreography of the dance before God in an English chapel'.[22] He also suggests that one of the key tensions in Eliot was that between the divine love embodied by Christ and the figure of 'Eros/Dionysus, the androgynous, protean daemon of biological existence and the repro-ductive cycle'.[23] Like many readers of Eliot, he links the imagery of desiccation and sterility in *The Waste Land* and elsewhere to some crisis of sexual frustration, to a failure of Eros concealed at the core of Eliot's inner life.

Hughes proposes that the richest revelation of the evolution of the poetic self in its hidden life often comes from a single early poem, 'either because the interfering ego is weakest then, or because these creative visions are very like conventional serial dreams, in that the first successful representation is likely to be a compact index of everything to follow'. In Eliot's case, the key was to be found in the early poem 'The Death of Saint Narcissus' ('Come in under the shadow of this gray rock, / And I will show you something differ-ent ...').[24] So which early Hughes poem is the 'compact index of everything to follow' in his writing career?

Eros is certainly a central feature of his early work. 'Bawdry Embraced' goes to it, with a vengeance:

> Great farmy whores, breasts bouncy more
> Like buttocks, and with buttocks like
> Two white sows jammed in a sty door,
> Are no dunghills for Bawdry's cock.[25]

But this is rollicking, playful stuff, not a hidden revelation of the inner self. Hughes himself clearly thought of 'The Thought-Fox' as his signature poem. It was written in 1955, sitting in bed at one o'clock in the morning after an evening in the flat of fellow-poet Thom Gunn.[26] But the point of his argument about the key early creative vision is that the 'interfering ego' has no say in its significance. So the poet himself is the last person to be in a position to identify the key early work. 'The Thought-Fox' is ruled out by the presence of Hughes's self, both in the poem and in his self-conscious mythologising of the poem when in public readings he linked it to the dream of the burnt fox.

Hughes was not a fox, he was a jaguar. An early manuscript draft of 'The Jaguar' survives: this is the poem that is a compact index of everything to follow. He began with a leopard, then crossed the word out. A leopard folding itself to sleep in the sun. No, he crosses it out again. Begin with the other animals: yawning ape, shrieking parrot, coiled boa-constrictor. And then the sleepers awake: excited children gather outside the cage of the pacing jaguar on a 'short fierce fuse' with eyes that drill as blood bangs inside its brain.[27] Voracious, violent and beautiful, the jaguar has embodied the raw force of nature for a million years. Now it is caged in our so-called 'civilisation'. Spinning on the ball of his heel, he stalks behind his bars like a prisoner serving a life sentence. This is the fate of the human spirit confined in dreary Fifties Britain. For Hughes, the role of the poet is to break the iron bars, to set free the spirit of the jaguar, to return humankind to its primal relationship with nature.

His later memory was of beginning the poem as he sat in a deep chair wearing his First World War greatcoat in the front room of Liz's flat in Norwich Street, Cambridge, on a freezing-cold morning in January 1955. He informed his American friend Ben Sonnenberg that the previous autumn he had had a temporary job doing the washing up in the cafeteria of London Zoo in Regent's Park. A particular jaguar was kept in a 'transit' cage near the kitchen window. He watched it going to and fro all day. He was reminded of seeing a jaguar in a very small cage on a family trip to Morecambe Zoo when he was about five and of how he had tried to model it in plasticine, clay and wax. Then he explained that in trying to describe the jaguar's snarl, he thought of a dog he had once seen trying to bite a fly that had landed on its nose. So in order to suggest the intensity of the jaguar's rage, he imagined that a fly had gone right up its nose. As he was writing a line to this effect, a bluebottle flew across the room in Norwich Street – which was very odd, given that it was midwinter and icy cold. It went straight up Ted's nostril. He took it out and pressed it into his precious volume of Shakespeare's complete works.[28]

'That's the magic of poetry,' Ted said to Sonnenberg, on telling him the story in London in the early Sixties.[29] He saw the incident as a classic example of what C. G. Jung called *synchronicity*, an idea that fascinated him. Jung and Hughes used the term for those moments of meaningful coincidence when the boundary between different worlds dissolves. A synchronicity is like a dream that offers a glimpse into an alternative reality.

Jung told of a patient who was locked in her own world, trapped in the self-created prison of her own mind. But then in a session of psychoanalysis she narrated a dream in which she was given a golden jewel in the shape of a scarab beetle. As she was recounting the dream, there was a tap on the window of Jung's consulting room. He opened the casement and in flew a gold-green scarabaeid rose-chafer beetle. He caught it in his hand, gave it to her and said, 'Here is your scarab.' Her defences were broken and she became open to treatment, with Jung reporting very satisfactory results.[30] For Jung, a synchronicity was a manifestation of an 'archetypal' pattern within what he called 'the collective unconscious'. The individual psyche comes into constellation with a deeper reality that transcends time and place. For Hughes, the same thing happens in the moment of red-hot poetic creativity. Poet and jaguar become as one.

The more mundane reality of the making of a poem is the craft of writing and rewriting. Ted wasn't satisfied with the ending of 'The Jaguar'. He continued working on the poem on a visit home to Yorkshire. The original manuscript has an additional stray line about the animal's eye being 'blind in fire'. The first published version ends with the jaguar staring out through the bars. Far from being completed in a white heat of inspiration, stimulated by a bluebottle in Liz's Norwich Street flat, it did not reach its perfected form for a long time.

A new issue of *Chequer* appeared in Cambridge with the date November 1954. Previously, Hughes had published there under a pseudonym. Now, having graduated, he put his real name to two poems. One of them was 'The Jaguar'. It was reprinted the following year in a collection of *Poetry from Cambridge 1952–4*, edited by Karl Miller. So was the first version actually written before he worked at the zoo? Was the story about the bluebottle an invented memory, a playful fantasy or even a self-conscious adaptation of Jung's story about the scarab beetle? Or was the poem a free translation of Rainer Maria Rilke's 'The Panther' rather than a memory of witnessing a real caged jaguar? The imagery is remarkably similar – the animal pacing endlessly behind its bars, then achieving a momentary vision of freedom. These questions cannot be answered with any certainty. Hughes was good at covering his tracks and laying false scents. And his belief in synchronicity and archetype would lead him to say that the details do not matter, provided the poem penetrates to the core of the reality embodied by the jaguar.

The young man drinking in the sensation of claret and Gruyère in that Paris café in 1954 sensed that there was more to life than anything he had yet found in Cambridge or London, in academic work or casual labour. He was ready to burst the bars, but didn't yet see how to do so. Something was needed to take his writing to another level. A stronger imagination was required in order to free the beast, to widen the horizon. In 1956, it came. A new ending, as powerful and sinuous as the jaguar's footfall: the 'stride' a wilderness of 'freedom', the 'world' rolling 'under the long thrust of his heel', the horizon coming 'Over the cage floor'.[31] In a scribbled note, Ted Hughes remembered the moment of achievement: 'Finished on Whitstead Lawn, Cambridge, with Sylvia.'[32]

Falcon Yard

Philip Hobsbaum was working for a television and film production company. He wrote a letter on his friend's behalf to the story editor at the film company J. Arthur Rank, which had studios at Pinewood in the London suburbs. Ted duly got a job reading dozens of novels, histories and biographies, summarising the plots with a view to their potential as movie scripts. Many of his treatments survive in his note-books: the Battle of Stalingrad, the Life of Robespierre, even James Joyce's *Ulysses*.[1] Summarising other people's work made him all the more eager to find a way of devoting himself to his own writing. He kept his complete Shakespeare in the drawer of his desk in the office and got it out when the supervisor wasn't around.

The movie people were not to his taste; he thought that they were all up their own or each other's 'arses'.[2] He lived for the weekends. Sometimes Shirley went down to London and stayed with him in Rugby Street. Ted, convinced that his talents lay only in poetry and that he had no aptitude for prose, suggested to her that he might give her some of the plot outlines he was reviewing at Pinewood for her to turn into narrative. They would part with a farewell drink at Dirty Dick's pub opposite Liverpool Street station before she got on the train to return to college. On other weekends, Ted would visit Cambridge and test Shirley's ability to identify brief quotations from Marlowe and Shakespeare. He recited Dylan Thomas to her, and gave her an inscribed copy of *Deaths and Entrances*. He also gave her a handwritten copy of a poem inspired by her, which was later included in *The Hawk in the Rain*.

Shirley began to detect a subtle change in their relationship, hard to pinpoint, but impossible not to feel. Two newly arrived blonde Americans were cutting a figure in Newnham. Shirley didn't get to know them, but she saw them weekly, waiting their turn, as she and her supervision partner left the room of Enid Welsford, author of the renowned study of *The Fool: His Social and Literary History*, who was taking them for the paper on the English Moralists. Shirley thought that they looked supremely all-American, so was surprised when Ted eyed them up and said that he thought they looked 'Swedish'.[3]

On Saturday 25 February 1956 a launch party was held for *Saint Botolph's Review*. During the day, the contributors and their friends sold copies on the streets and in cafés and pubs. Bert Wyatt-Brown, an American student at King's, sold a copy to a fellow-American Fulbright scholar from Newnham. She raced off on her bicycle, only to seek him out again a few hours later in order to ask him where she might meet these St Botolph's poets. She had been especially impressed by the work of Lucas Myers and Ted Hughes. If her very lightly fictionalised account of the day and night is to be believed, she crashed her bike into Bert in the market place, 'spilling oranges, figs, and a paper packet of pink-frosted cakes'.[4] He gave her an invitation to the launch party.[5]

They had hired a big upstairs room in Falcon Yard, just off Petty Cury in the centre of town. It belonged to the university Women's Union (female undergraduates were excluded from the bastion of the historic Union Society, where future politicians developed their debating skills). This was one of the few places in Cambridge where you could guarantee a party with more women than men. It had a polished floor for dancing and stained-glass windows as in a church. They hauled a piano up the stairs and Joe Lyde brought along his top-class jazz men. Luke Myers danced the 'hot-wild jitterbug'.[6] His recollection was that everybody was drunk except for Ted, who liked to stay in control.

The party was in full swing when the Newnham girl arrived, in the company of Hamish Stewart, a pale Canadian from Queens' College. She had left her essay on 'Passion as Destiny in Racine's Plays', with particular reference to *Phèdre*, half finished in her Smith Corona typewriter.[7] They were already drunk, having spent an hour slugging whisky in Miller's bar near his college. She was wearing a red hairband, red shoes and bright-red lipstick. Her fingernails were varnished in Applecart Red.[8] Her name was Sylvia Plath. She was one of the two

'Swedish-looking' girls who had caught Ted's eye. Bert Wyatt-Brown was dating the other one, who lodged in the same student house: Jane Baltzell (even more blonde and in several respects a rival). Bert introduced Sylvia to the men of the hour: Luke, with his 'dark sideburns and rumpled hair, black-and-white checked baggy pants and a loose swinging jacket'; Dan Huws, with whom she had a bone to pick because of his lukewarm review of the poems she had published in the student magazine *Broadsheet*; Than Minton, 'so small and dark one would have to sit down to talk to him'; Danny Weissbort with his curly hair; and David Ross, 'immaculate and dark'. They were all dark. She was exhilarated by this bohemian world of turtleneck sweaters and the jazz getting under her skin. She grabbed Myers from his girl-friend and danced with him, shouting about his poems, in particular his 'Sestina of the Norse Seaman', which took a highly complex poetic form and crashed through its rules and its line-endings.[9]

'Then', as she wrote in her diary when the morning finally came, 'the worst happened': 'That big, dark, hunky boy, the only one there huge enough for me, who had been hunching around over women, and whose name I had asked the minute I had come into the room, but no one told me, came over and was looking hard in my eyes and it was Ted Hughes.' She didn't know him, 'but she knew him by heart'.[10] Though she did not admit so much in her diary, she had come to look for him. Always obsessed with rivals and doubles, she was determined to take him off the Newnham girl she knew he was going out with. On arriving in the room, she noticed Shirley straight away: 'Pale, freckled, with no mouth but a pink dim distant rosebud, willowed reedy, wide-eyed to the streaming of his words … Silent, fawn-eyed. Clever.'[11] She too was a 'statue-worshipper', putting the dark poet on a pedestal.

Shouting to be heard above the band and the crowd, Sylvia enthused to Ted about his poems:

And he yelled back, colossal, in a voice that should have come from a Pole, 'You like?' and asking me if I wanted brandy, and me yelling yes and back into the next room past the smug shining blub face of dear Bert … and bang the door was shut and he was sloshing brandy into a glass and I was sloshing it at the place where my mouth was when I last knew about it.[12]

As if out on a moor in a high wind, they shouted about Dan's review of her poems, Ted flirtatiously suggesting that his mate had only said what he did because she was beautiful. He explained that he was working in London, earning ten pounds a week, and that he had 'obligations in the next room' – meaning Shirley, who was not happy. Neither was Hamish, who supposedly punched Ted before the evening was out, which is hardly surprising in view of what happened next:

> And I was stamping and he was stamping on the floor, and then he kissed me bang smash on the mouth and ripped my hairband off, my lovely red hairband scarf which has weathered the sun and much love, and whose like I shall never again find, and my favorite silver earrings: hah, I shall keep, he barked. And when he kissed my neck I bit him long and hard on the cheek, and when we came out of the room, blood was running down his face. His poem 'I did it, I.' Such violence, and I can see how women lie down for artists.[13]

For Sylvia, he was the 'one man in the room who was as big as his poems, huge, with hulk and dynamic chunk of words'. Both his spoken and his written words were 'strong and blasting like a high wind in steel girders'. She 'screamed' to herself, 'oh, to give myself crashing, fighting, to you'.[14] Her knees had gone 'jelly-weak' and 'the room of the party hung in her eyes like a death's-door camera-shot'.[15] When she bit him and tasted his salty blood, he 'shook her bang against the solid-grained substance of the wall' and her attempt at another bite closed on thin air.[16] Passion turned to embarrassment. She asked Hamish to take care of her – 'I have been rather lousy,' she explained.[17]

Shirley had entered the room at the moment of the kiss and the bite. Her friend and fellow-Newnham student Jean Gooder vividly recalled her figure framed in the doorway. Ted had his back to her as Sylvia came up to him, and his very height meant that Shirley did not see what happened.[18]

Ted had gone to the party with a sense of foreboding. He had cast the night's horoscope and found it predicting 'disastrous expense'. The launch was certainly not covered by the pitiful earnings of the magazine, but for Hughes it took the rest of his life to pay off the cost of that night:

> First sight. First snapshot isolated
> Unalterable, stilled in the camera's glare.
> Taller
> Than ever you were again. Swaying so slender
> It seemed your long, perfect, American legs
> Simply went on up.[19]

The camera will be a key metaphor in Ted's poems about Sylvia, an image of the gaze that fell upon their relationship. In this first snapshot, it is her bright confident American glamour and loudness that grab him and give him a glimpse of a very different world from that of Yorkshire Edna, Mancunian Liz and Liverpudlian Shirley.

His recall, in this *Birthday Letters* poem, may have been retrospectively shaped by the recollection of a famous photograph published in the *Varsity* student newspaper a couple of months later, in which 'Sylvia Plath, American Fulbright Scholar at Newnham, reviews May Week fashions'. In one of the accompanying illustrations she wears a halter-neck swimsuit that reveals long muscular legs, honed by bicycling around Cambridge. She sent a cutting to her mother, calling herself Betty Grable. In her journals, she would compare herself to Grable in one sentence and Thomas Mann in the next.[20] Glamour photography, movie stars, fashion, bright-red lipstick, sexually self-confident girls: in Fifties Cambridge, under grey skies and with memories of post-war rationing still alive, all these things were pure America. There was a vibrant but somewhat manic quality to them, as there was to this Fulbright scholar ('full' and 'bright' indeed). 'The pure products of America', wrote the poet William Carlos Williams, 'go crazy.'[21]

'You're all there,' Ted had said to her during their stamping dance. 'Aren't you?'[22] She found him big and he found her tall. From the start, each was turning the other into a figure from myth. But here we need to be careful: Ted's poem was written long after the moment. His memory was remade by subsequent events. It begins with astrological foreboding and ends with the knowledge, which he couldn't possibly have had at the time, that the encounter in Falcon Yard would 'brand' him for the rest of his life: his 'stupefied interrogation' of her 'blue headscarf' and 'the swelling ring-moat of tooth-marks' that would mark his 'face' for a 'month' and his inner self 'for good'. As the editor of Sylvia Plath's journals, Hughes knew perfectly well that the scarf was red. He turns it blue as a sign of the sorrow that was to come. He would finally close *Birthday Letters* with a poem called 'Red' that begins 'Red was your colour' and ends 'But the jewel you lost was blue.'[23]

What did he really think at the time? If he wrote a journal entry in the next few days, it is lost. Still, he could not but have been impressed and flattered that she knew his poems so well. She had quoted at him not only 'I did it, I', the punchline of 'Law in the Country of the Cats', his *Saint Botolph's Review* poem about male sexual rivals, but also an image from another poem that had carved itself upon her mind: 'most dear unscratchable diamond'.[24] It was in answer to this quotation that he had said 'You like?' It comes from 'The Casualty', one of the best of his early poems. This wasn't one of the new pieces released that very day in *Saint Botolph's*: it had been published in that other Cambridge magazine, *Chequer*, over a year before. Sylvia's memory of it is a mark of how Ted had impressed her on the page well before she met him in the flesh. It is also a mark of her critical acumen, for the two Hughes poems in the November 1955 issue of *Chequer* are much better than the four in the February 1956 *Saint Botolph's Review*.

'The Casualty', about the body of a shot-down airman in the burnt-out fuselage of his plane, crashed in the English countryside, is quintessential Hughes. It is his first war poem, inspired by a combined memory of the droning warplanes over Mexborough and the RAF bomber on a pre-war training exercise that had run into fog over Mytholmroyd, from the wreck of which he and Gerald had salvaged tubing for their own model planes. This yoking of Mexborough and Mytholmroyd readied him to bring together his own childhood experience of the Second World War and his father's traumatic survival of the First. In *The Hawk in the Rain*, he reprinted 'The Casualty' as the first of a sequence of war poems that ends the collection. There it is followed by 'Bayonet Charge', 'Griefs for Dead Soldiers', his finest Great War poem 'Six Young Men', 'Two Wise Generals' and 'The Ancient Heroes and the Bomber Pilot'.[25]

For Plath, it wasn't the military content of 'The Casualty' so much as the violent intensity of its language that bit into her spirit. An image that pierced her especially sharply was that of how the groans of the dying airman 'rip / The slum of weeds, leaves, barbed coils'. Drunk and dancing in Falcon Yard, she quoted the poem to its author and the 'rip' magically went from art to life, as he tore off her headband and earrings. From the outset, there was an electricity between them, a barbed coil of passion within. The latter image carries a hint of barbed wire and all its connotations of violence and the infliction of pain: 'Such violence, and I can see how women lie down for artists.'

Sylvia was sexually precocious and unusually adventurous for a Fifties girl. One reason why she was aroused by the hunk and heft, the 'flash of violent incredible action', in the poem about man standing up to man which she had read earlier that day, with its punch-up in the street and its cocky ending ('I did it, I'), is that she had a history of creating rivalry between men. During her final undergraduate months at Smith College the previous year she was coming to the end of a love affair with a gentle boy called Gordon Lameyer even as she was sleeping with a dangerously bohemian Yale student called Richard Sassoon. Over the summer she had a brief but sexually blazing liaison with Peter Davison, a New York editor working at a publishing house in Boston. Coming over to take up her Fulbright, she had a shipboard romance with another scholar aboard the *Queen Elizabeth*. Since her arrival in Cambridge on 1 October, she had flirted round many boys, made passionate love to Sassoon in Paris during the Christmas vacation and then been rejected by him after a huge row outside the Matisse Chapel near Nice.[26] She was ready for something new and big and preferably involving a fight.

After leaving Falcon Yard, she and Hamish stumbled around the foggy streets of Cambridge. She whispered Ted's name to the lamp-posts. She could not get out of her head how he had said her name, Sylvia, 'in a blasting wind which shot off in the desert' behind her eyes and his, and how 'his poems are clever and terrible and lovely'. Hamish tried to put her off by saying that he was the biggest seducer in Cambridge and that all the St Botolph's crowd were phoneys.

Then they found themselves surrounded by a group of undergraduates who were also out after college lock-up. The boys, reimagined in her journal as a symbolic group of potential boyfriends (or worshippers), were checking that she was all right, telling her how nice she smelt, asking to kiss her. Then Hamish was hoisting her over the railings into Queens', his college. A spike pierced her tight skirt, exposing her thighs, and another dug into her hand, creating stigmata that did not bleed because the air was freezing. Then she was lying on the floor of his room by the fire, with him on top of her. She liked his kisses on her mouth and his weight on her body, but she told him that he should scold her for her behaviour at the party. At two-thirty in the morning, he walked her back to Whitstead, the house on the other side of the river, at the far end of the Newnham playing fields, where she lodged with eleven other girls. Though she was pleased that Hamish had proved himself able to fight for her, it was Ted who now consumed her imagination. He entered her life as a rival to Sassoon: 'The one man since I've lived who could blast Richard.'[27]

Falling in love is often about place and placing yourself. Sylvia needed a proper Cambridge boyfriend in order to prove to herself that she had arrived in England and in English literature. Housemate Jane ('the blonde one') was content to go out with other American boys such as Bert. Though Sylvia would not have said no to handsome Luke from the Deep South, she sensed a fatal magnetism pulling her towards the huge man from the north of England. One of the attractions of Sassoon had been that he was collaterally descended from the First World War poet Siegfried Sassoon. One of the attractions of Davison had been that he was a literary publisher with British connections. Now she was on the brink of the thing itself: a great English poet. Her mind was steeped in the language of the English literature that had been her study for years. Her repeated use of the word 'blast' when writing about their first encounter and her image of them shouting passionately at each other as if in a high wind reveal where she is going: to a 'blasted heath' – the location of the opening of Shakespeare's most northern play – and more specifically to a Yorkshire moor. She is already, unconsciously, projecting herself as Cathy and Hughes as Heathcliff.

For Ted, thinking over and rewriting these events, again and again through the course of thirty-five years after her death, there was a fatalistic quality from the start. In their myth of themselves, Ted and Sylvia were Heathcliff and Cathy from the first instant, but in reality each of them spent the immediate aftermath of Falcon Yard in the company of another.

Ted had come to Cambridge that weekend to be with Shirley and to make love to her. He never wrote about what they said to each other that night. All she remembers is that she did not speak to Sylvia and that, though Ted was still attentive, she quickly became aware of a deliberate 'distancing' on his part. She returned to Falcon Yard the next day to search for an earring lent by a friend. She found the earring but knew that somehow she was losing Ted.

On the Monday, with Ted back at work in London, Sylvia Plath wrote 'a full-page poem about the dark forces of lust'. Its title was 'Pursuit'. 'It is not bad,' she told herself. 'It is dedicated to Ted Hughes.'[28] It began from a line in Racine's *Phèdre*, the play she was studying for the essay she had to write for the Tragedy paper that week: '*Dans le fond des forêts votre image me suit*' ('In the depth of the forests your image pursues me'). This was a line that haunted her. She believed that it captured the inextricable relationship between desire and death. It sprang her into a poem that she believed to be her best yet, one which offered 'a symbol of the terrible beauty of death, and the paradox that the more intensely one lives, the more one burns and consumes oneself'.[29]

> There is a panther stalks me down:
> One day I'll have my death of him;
> His greed has set the woods aflame,
> He prowls more lordly than the sun.[30]

Writing about the poem to her mother, Plath acknowledged the strong influence of Blake's 'Tyger, tyger' on its rhythms, its questions and its elemental force. When she first told her mother that she had written it, she acknowledged that it was directly inspired by the encounter in Falcon Yard with 'the only man I've met yet here who'd be strong enough to be equal with', but whom she would probably never see again.[31]

What she did not acknowledge, in either her journal or her letters, was that the most direct inspiration behind 'Pursuit' was the other poem that Hughes had published in *Chequer* a few months before: his compact index of everything to follow, 'The Jaguar'. Ted as panther, animal force, sexual marauder; Sylvia willing her own death of him. In mythologising their relationship from the start, she was in some sense creating the conditions for her own tragedy – and laying the ground for the posthumous dramatisation of her story, his story.

Now she knew what she wanted: 'a life of conflict, of balancing children, sonnets, love and dirty dishes; and banging banging an affirmation of life out on pianos and ski slopes and in bed in bed in bed'.[32] Ted proceeded in a more circumspect manner. All he said about the party was that 'it was very bright, and everything got smashed up'.[33] He was preoccupied with the approach of the final deadline on the option to take up the cheap passage to Australia.

Two weeks later he was back in Cambridge, staying with Luke. He came up on the bus from Victoria after work on the Friday and late that evening the two of them threw stones at what they thought was Sylvia's window. Bert told her the next day and she spent the weekend longing to hear the tread of the black panther on the stair, aching with desire for a new life. The boys tried again in the small hours of Sunday morning – mud as well as stones this time – but once again they got the wrong window.[34] Sylvia was in a little attic room, which she had tastefully decorated with art books artfully stacked or opened, a tea set of 'solid black pottery' and bright pillows on the couch.[35] The stones and earth could hardly have reached that high.

The next weekend, conscious that the Easter vacation was upon them, Ted asked Luke to ask Sylvia to come and see him in London. The timing was propitious. She was about to go to Paris, for another make-or-break visit with Sassoon. She called at 18 Rugby Street on the evening of Friday 23 March 1956, prior to her Channel crossing the following day.

18 Rugby Street

Rugby Street is in the Holborn district of central London, halfway between the elegant squares around the British Museum where the Bloomsbury Group once lived and the legal and financial district that spreads east and south from Gray's Inn. Among the local landmarks were the Great Ormond Street children's hospital, the old Foundling Hospital in Coram Fields, and the Lamb, a pub in Lamb's Conduit Street much frequented by poets. Rugby Street itself was a Georgian terrace that had seen better days. The freehold was owned by Rugby School and, with rent controls keeping the price of an apartment down to £2 per week, maintenance of the block was not a priority. Some of the houses were occupied by locals whose families had been there for generations. Others were divided into scruffy flats, occupied by bohemian types – graphic designers, actors, photographers, young men and women trying to make their way in what we now call the 'creative industries'. Number 18, where Ted was living in the flat belonging to Dan Huws's father, was lit by gas, had a single lavatory in the basement and the only water supply was a tap in a basin on the half-landing.[1] To Sylvia, raised on American plumbing and her mother's cleanliness, it was disgusting. But the occupant held irresistible allure.

She booked into a hotel in New Fetter Lane, the other side of Holborn, then met Ted for the evening. The following Monday morning, she wrote up her memories of the weekend: 'Arrived in Paris early Saturday evening exhausted from sleepless holocaust night with Ted in London … washed my battered face, smeared with a purple bruise from Ted and my neck raw and wounded too.'[2] Love-bites: for Plath, desire was always a purple bruise; for Hughes, poetry was the healing of a wound.

She called it her 'wild destructive London night'. She was anxious because Hughes's paunchy friend Michael Boddy had come up the stairs at one point, and he was a gossip, so all Cambridge would soon know 'that I am Ted's mistress or something equally absurd'.[3] She was also upset that once during their lovemaking he had called her Shirley instead of Sylvia.[4] She wanted to see him again, so that she could 'rip past' Shirley and prove her capacity to be as 'tender and wise' as Shirley was, while also being a better, fuller, wilder, more extreme lover. Regardless of Boddy's gossip, she wanted Ted's body and it was inextricable from his poetry: 'I lust for him, and in my mind I am ripped to bits by the words he welds and wields.'[5]

Ted shaped the night retrospectively, in a poem that he worked on for many years. It is a central pillar of *Birthday Letters*, though he nearly left it out, because it was too raw and was indiscreet in mentioning a third party who would enter their story later but whose posthumous privacy he wished to preserve. He begins by mythologising the house: as so often in his work, location is given symbolic force. '18 Rugby Street' is imagined as a stage-set and a Cretan labyrinth. Each of the four floors was the scene of the love-struggle of its inhabitant: a car-dealer who shared the basement with a caged bird and a mistress, a lovelorn Belgian girl (elsewhere he wrote that she was German) trapped in the ground-floor flat with a manic barking Alsatian which protected her from everything except her own oven in which she would one day gas herself.

His memories of the night were of waiting at his battered carpenter's bench that was both dining-table and work-desk; of Sylvia's breathless voice as she panted up the uncarpeted stairs with Luke (he could not remember how and when Luke excused himself and disappeared); of his sense of Sylvia as a great blue bird charged at high voltage, 'Fluorescent cobalt, a flare of aura'. He would always associate her with electricity, the positive pole being her innate energy and sex appeal, the negative that emotional volatility that took her to the darkest places and then the temporary cure that came from electro-convulsive therapy. Ted saw vulnerability in the temples above her bright brown and somewhat hooded eyes. In the theatre of her face, those temples were at first sight upstaged by her glamorous and fashionable bangs, but with knowledge of her history they elicited special tenderness because this was the place where the electrodes had been attached. The reference to her temples also evokes a place of worship, befitting this pagan goddess coming, with 'Sexual Dreams', from another world.

She recited the poem about the black panther that she had written for him. As she did so, he held her and kissed her and tried to keep her still. His poem then jump-cuts to their walk back to her hotel in New Fetter Lane. Opposite the entrance, there was a wartime bombsite on which some building work was being started. It was there that they 'clutched each other giddily' and took the plunge. She told him of the reason for her scar: her suicide attempt. In the poem of his memory, even as he is kissing her a part of him is sensing the danger and telling him to stay away. Something is being built, but there is also a bomb liable to explode. Somehow, she smuggled him into the hotel and they made love, her body 'slim and lithe and smooth as a fish'. For the first time in his life, he is making love to a girl who is not English, a girl who embodies the energy and hope of Shakespeare's 'brave new world', John Donne's 'my America, my newfound land'. 'Beautiful, beautiful America' has taken possession of him.[6]

Walking back to his flat at first light, he had an epiphany. His fullest account of that hour is excluded from '18 Rugby Street' but included in a version of *Birthday Letters* that he never published, a 4,000-line blank-verse autobiography of his relationship with Sylvia called 'Black Coat: Opus 131'. It was his equivalent of William Wordsworth's posthumously published autobiographical blank-verse epic, *The Prelude*. He tells of how he left her hotel and walked back across Holborn to his flat at about five o'clock in the morning. He felt himself 'floating / On air spilling in over the city / Off the Surrey gardens and orchards'. Then he heard 'London's hidden blackbirds and thrushes', 'a million singers', singing a blessing upon the 'sleeping millions'. It was like 'a high tide at dawn, the top of the tide, / Their dawn chorus awash through the whole city'. Meanwhile, his totemic birds, the crows, accompanied him at ground level.[7]

Like every young romantic after such an encounter, he is walking on air, every one of his senses refined, every detail of the moment etched in his memory for ever.

Back in Rugby Street, he penned a short letter and sent it for Sylvia to pick up at the American Express office in Paris. It had been a night, he wrote, consumed by the discovery of the smoothness of her body.

The memory of it went through him with the warming glow of brandy.[8] This could be described as his first 'birthday letter': the letter of the birth of their love. He asked her to come back to him, telling her that he would be in London till 14 April, and that if she did not come to him he would go to her in Cambridge.

In Paris, Sylvia poured her confusion into her diary. From one point of view, Ted was a diversion. She had got drunk at Falcon Yard and kissed (and bitten) him. She had got drunk in London and slept with him. That was that. Now it was time to give herself to Richard Sassoon, of whom she had written – after meeting Ted – 'I love that damn boy with all I've ever had in me and that's a hell of a lot.'[9] But on arriving in Paris, she discovered that Sassoon had gone south in order to avoid a confrontation with her. He needed time to make up his mind as to whether their long, passionate on–off relationship should turn to marriage or be finally ended. She was devastated. She had always been used to getting her own way with men: 'never before had a man gone off to leave me to cry after'.[10] She sat in the living room of the concierge of his apartment building on the rue Duvivier and wrote him a long, incoherent letter while the radio blared out 'Smile though your heart is breaking'.

Then she made a bad error. She wrote again to Sassoon, telling him about Ted. As Sassoon put it, she 'was going to start having an affair with a certain fellow so as to make me jealous and give me a mind to marry her, which I was unwilling to do just because of this imminent unfaithfulness'.[11] She cheered herself up with sightseeing and an afternoon in a hotel room with an Oxford student called Tony Gray. She juggled her options in her diary. To play it cool and wait for Ted to come to her? To go to him, for one night only, then go back to Sassoon? To play safe and marry her devoted friend Gordon Lameyer? Or even to join Ted in one of his hare-brained schemes, such as teaching English in Yugoslavia?

In the latter part of the Easter vacation, she travelled with Lameyer to Munich, Venice and Rome. Their relationship was disintegrating. Sassoon was giving no sign of returning. On Friday 13 April, her late father's birthday, Sylvia Plath boarded a plane in Rome, the ticket paid for by Lameyer. She had told Ted to expect her that night. In her possession was a prize: he had written her a poem. Though the first line read 'Ridiculous to call it love', it revealed that she had touched him to the quick, that he felt her absence as if it were a wound, that without her he was like a dying man, that 'Wherever you haunt earth, you are shaped and bright / As the true ghost of my loss.'[12] Even if this was a *jeu d'esprit*, a little act of seduction intended to bring her back to his bed for a second time, it is still an uncanny anticipation of the future haunting that would determine the course of his later life.

Sylvia wrote about their second night together in her incomplete novel 'Falcon Yard'. In the surviving draft, Ted is called Gerald – hardly a disguise – but her 'Character Notebook' for the novel calls him Leonard, a 'God-man, because spermy', a creator, 'Dionysiac', a Pan who has to be led into the mundane world of 'toast and nappies'.[13] 'What I need', she writes in the voice of Jess, the autobiographical protagonist, is 'a banging, blasting, ferocious love'. But a voice tells her that it will hurt. Her counter-voice replies, 'So what … better bleed.' She needs to stop being 'the Girl Who's Never Been Hurt'. She tells herself to get hurt and be glad of it, to take his desire 'even though he'll never love you but will use you and lunge on through you to the next one'. She determines to 'blast his other girls to hell and back'. After an encounter with another man on the bus from the airport, Jess heads for Rugby Street, 'blazing', 'letting the wet wind blow her hair back', only too glad to look wild because 'The recklessness came banging up in her: stronger and fiercer than she had ever known it'. She is greeted by the Ted character – his name now changed from Gerald to Ian – who observes that it is Friday the 13th as he takes her suitcase upstairs.

His voice, she notices this time, is 'UnBritish', almost 'Refugee Pole, mixed with something of Dylan Thomas: rich and mellow-noted: half sung'. They exchange small talk with Jim, the commercial artist from the flat upstairs – this is Jim Downer, with whom Ted was working at this time on an illustrated children's book called *Timmy the Tug*. The Sylvia character is pleased to be called 'Jess, not Judy', an allusion to the wound of Ted having called her Shirley not Sylvia when they were first making love back in March. Then he tells his dreams of white leopard, burnt fox and pike. He kisses her on the throat, loving the incredible smoothness – fish- or mermaid-like – of her skin. They openly discuss the violence of the first time:

'I went to Paris all scarred. Black and blue …'

'But you liked it?'

'Yes.'

'I was furious with myself. I don't know what happened to me ...'

She has it out with him about the wrong name being blurted out. He defuses the tension with an account of that moment of morning grace when he left her, the Wordsworthian epiphany that would be recaptured years later in 'Black Coat: Opus 131': 'I'll never forget it. When I came out into the streets, the air was all blue, like blue water, and the buildings were covered, just thick, with thrushes. Everything clear and blue. Not a sound. The air isn't like that in London at any other time.'

Then they read poetry to each other. First, her 'Conversation among the Ruins'. 'You love one-syllabled words, don't you?' he says, setting the template for their relationship by mingling literary criticism with love-talk, 'Squab, patch, crack. Violent.' She replies that she hates the abstraction of '-ation' words: 'I like words to sound what they say: bang crash. Not mince along in singsong iambic pentameter.' He responds by reading an old English ballad and his voice reaches to the core of her being: 'The way he took words, rounded, pitched them. It was holy. I will learn this by heart, she told herself ... part of her vibrating to the sound of his voice. I will learn it, and hear his voice every time, reading it.' She convinces herself that she will never forget the sound of his voice or a single syllable of the verse that passes his lips. Her bare arms 'go stippled with goose flesh', he tells her the poem is 'an altar to spill blood at', and the surviving fragment breaks off before they go to bed.[14]

'I can make more love the more I make love,' he said to her. 'The more he writes poems, the more he writes poems,' she was soon reporting to her mother.[15] Three days after the night in Rugby Street, Sylvia wrote in her diary of 'his big iron violent virile body, incredible tendernesses and rich voice which makes poems and quirked people and music'. He is a 'huge derrick-striding Ted'. He makes her feel safe but he makes her feel scared:

Consider yourself lucky to have been stabbed by him; never complain or be bitter or ask for more than normal human consideration as an integrated being. Let him go. Have the guts. Make him happy: cook, play, read ... keep other cups and flagons full – never accuse or nag – let him run, reap, rip – and glory in the temporary sun of his ruthless force.[16]

With Sylvia back in Cambridge for the summer term, Ted's problem was Shirley. His relationship with her came to a bitter end in an encounter that he recorded in several drafts of a poem that, sensitive to her privacy, he never published. It tells of how he turned up in Cambridge with a bottle of wine and two pounds of rump steak intended for a 'love-feast' with Sylvia at Whitstead. He went the long way round so as not to be seen outside Newnham College, only to turn the corner and see Shirley coming for him like 'an electrical storm', beautiful in her red-haired anger. He hid the wine and the parcel of meat in a privet hedge. He never forgot the pain of their exchange. He remembered her 'furious restraint' and 'her outraged under-whisper'. He 'refused' her and his memory is that as he did so he thrice denied that he had slept with Sylvia, even though he was only 50 yards from her door. The triple denial is an allusion to the disciple Peter denying his knowledge of Jesus; Shirley's memory, by contrast, is that Ted had always been true to himself and honest with her during their affair, and he was candid with her in their parting.

In Ted's colourful dramatisation of their blazing row, the wine bottle ('uncontrollable, bulbous / Priapic') rolls on to the pavement between them. It is as if even the world's inanimate objects are on the side of his new love. Shirley's green eyes fill with tears and she walks away across Newnham playing fields. He stands and watches her walk out of his life. It was as if she had turned not to the playing fields but the other way, into the road, 'And gone under a lorry'.[17] He never saw her again.

With the help of friends, she struggled through her last term at Cambridge and her final exams. She knew that nothing could change what had happened, but confronting her loss, accepting it, she found almost impossible. Ted had a deep and lasting impact on her life.

Both now free from serious relationships that might have led to marriage, Ted and Sylvia became inseparable. For much of the Easter term, he camped out on a mattress in a bare-boarded room on the top floor of Alexandra House, a soup-kitchen run by the Women's Voluntary Service just off Petty Cury. He found himself sharing a blanket with one of the volunteers, 'a lovely girl escaped freshly / From her husband'. For a month, they slept nightly in each other's arms, naked but never once making love. She tenderly traced her hands over the love-scratches that Sylvia had 'inscribed' across his back, while he 'never stirred a finger beyond/ Sisterly comforting'. Sometimes they were joined in the bed by a 'plump and pretty' friend of hers, who 'did all she could' to get Ted 'inside her' – without success.[18] Like a medieval knight lying between two naked temptresses, he was proving himself in the art of fidelity. He did not fail.

Cambridge is at its loveliest in the Easter term. According to Jane Baltzell, Sylvia's rival and housemate, one warm day Ted and Luke sat in a haystack in a field just outside town, drinking wine and making literary plans. Ted then walked to Whitstead with another bottle of wine, intending to share some of their dreams with Sylvia. She did not have a corkscrew, so Ted went down from her attic room to borrow one. The first door on which he knocked happened to be that of the resident don whose job it was to keep an eye on the Whitstead girls. Baltzell's version of the incident has the door opening and a face, 'framed in tight braids of dark hair', peering out. Ted asks if she has a corkscrew that he can borrow. Almost before she can reply that she 'most certainly has not' – she happened to be a teetotal Methodist – Ted loses patience, strikes 'the neck of the bottle off on her doorknob' and bolts back upstairs.[19] One never knows quite how much embellishment there is in the telling of such myth-making tales about Ted: Luke Myers was convinced that this story was pure invention, probably on the part of Sylvia.[20]

The lovers listened to Beethoven and Bartók in record shops. They went into the moonlight to find owls, and Sylvia immediately composed a poem called 'Metamorphosis'. They were both writing at an unprecedented rate, Sylvia being inspired by Ted to take on 'the vocabulary of woods and animals and earth' and creating poems for him in pastiche of his own style, such as an 'Ode for Ted' that begins:

> From under crunch of my man's boot
> green oat-sprouts jut;
> he names a lapwing, starts rabbits in a rout ...
> stalks red fox, shrewd stoat.[21]

They wandered the meadows around Grantchester, made love in the open air. Having at last found a man who loved food as much as she did, Sylvia cooked steak and trout on her single gas ring. Ted taught her – as he had once taught Shirley – how to cook herring roes and how to read horoscopes. He took her to 'the world's biggest circus'.[22] They shared improvised recipes:

> He stalked in the door yesterday with a packet of little pink shrimp and four fresh trout. I made a nectar of Shrimp Newburg with essence of butter, cream, sherry and cheese; had it on rice with the trout. It took us three hours to peel all the little tiny shrimp, and Ted just lay groaning by the hearth after the meal with utter delight, like a huge Goliath.[23]

They read and wrote and revised their poems in the garden of Whitstead, quoting swathes of Dylan Thomas and Shakespeare that Ted knew by heart. Each immediately became the other's best critic. He sharpened her style, made her feel she was writing from her truest and deepest self for the first time. She organised his poems, typed them up and began sending them to American periodicals. He taught her to punt on the Cam. She took him to a Fulbright reception in London, where they met the American ambassador and the dashing Duke of Edinburgh who, mistaking Ted for a student, asked him what he was doing, to which Ted replied that he was 'chaperoning Sylvia' and the Duke smiled and said, 'Ah, the idle rich.'[24]

She told of all this in effusive letters to her mother Aurelia. Otto Plath had died shortly after Sylvia's eighth birthday. He had gone to have his leg amputated as a result of gangrene, and died of an embolism while still in hospital. On being told the news, Sylvia had announced that she would never speak to God again. Mother and daughter were inevitably drawn intensely close by their loss. When Sylvia moved to England, her letters were a lifeline to her mother. She also kept in touch with her brother Warren, who was two and a half years younger than her. Ted, she wrote to tell him, was the one man worthy of becoming his brother-in-law, though he would benefit from Warren giving him some American-style training in how to buy himself a decent wardrobe.

Her Fulbright scholarship having been renewed for a second year, she arranged for her mother to visit England at the end of term. Aurelia arrived in London on Wednesday 13 June and the three of them went to a cheap but good German restaurant called Schmidt's, in honour of the Teutonic Plathian heritage. Sylvia was delighted that her mother and lover immediately hit it off. That night, Sylvia suggested to Ted that they should get married and he agreed.[25]

They rushed to make arrangements before Aurelia left town. This involved getting a special Archbishop's licence, tracking down a local vicar, buying new shoes and trousers for Ted, and spending the last of their money on gold wedding rings. The night before the wedding Ted dreamed that he had caught a pike from an enormous depth in the pond at Crookhill. As it rose to the surface, its head filled the entire lake. He backed away, straining to control it.[26]

By good fortune, Aurelia had in her luggage a pink wool knitted suit dress that she had never worn. Adorned with a pink hair ribbon and a pink rose from Ted, this served as a wedding dress. The hurried ceremony, conducted by a twinkle-eyed old clergyman who lived opposite Charles Dickens's house, took place at the church of St George the Martyr in Bloomsbury, just across the square from the offices of Faber and Faber, on 16 June 1956 ('Bloomsday', Ted noted – the date of the action of James Joyce's *Ulysses*). Ted wore his RAF tie and the corduroy jacket that he had three times dyed black. It rained. Aurelia was the only guest, so the curate was requisitioned as best man, delaying him from taking a busload of children to the zoo. 'All the prison animals had to be patient / While we married,' wrote Ted in *Birthday Letters*, where he turned the curate into a sexton, grimly foreshadowing Hamlet's macabre dialogue over Ophelia's grave. The vicar read an off-the-shelf printed marriage sermon entitled 'Unto Your Lives' End'.[27] Sylvia's eyes were like jewels, their brown glistening with tears of joy.[28]

Ted had told Olwyn that he had met a first-rate American female poet, 'a damned sight better than the run of good male', and that they were going to come to Paris in the summer.[29] But he didn't tell anyone in his family about the decision to marry. Sylvia, by contrast, poured out every detail in an ecstatic letter to her brother Warren. She explained that, because of the Newnham and Fulbright authorities, and the fact that Ted was probably about to go to Spain to get a job teaching English, the big wedding reception would be postponed for a second ceremony in Wellesley the following summer. For now, the official line was that they were engaged. The marriage was in keeping with their situation: 'private, personal, legal, true, but limited in its way'. She did not hesitate to write that she could now be addressed – Warren could take his pick – as Mrs Sylvia Hughes, Mrs Ted Hughes, Mrs Edward James Hughes, or 'Mrs E. J. Hughes (wife of the internationally renowned poet and genius)'.[30]

'Marriage is my medium'

They spent their wedding night in 18 Rugby Street. Ted then cleared his stuff from the flat and took it to Yorkshire. He still did not tell his parents that he was married. The story was that he would be off to Spain in search of work teaching English as a foreign language. Sylvia took the opportunity to show her mother round Cambridge. There was talk of a visit to the Beacon in early August so that the family could meet Sylvia and Aurelia, though this did not come off.[1]

They met up back in London and flew to Paris, with Aurelia. After a week's exhausting sightseeing, she went off on her European tour, while Ted and Sylvia stayed another week. They met up with Luke Myers, who had never seen either of them looking so happy. Ted was conscious that Sylvia's was an 'American' Paris of Impressionist paintings, chestnut trees and the shades of 'Hemingway, / Fitzgerald, Henry Miller, Gertrude Stein'. Also of the memory of her failed attempt to reconcile with Richard Sassoon just a couple of months earlier. His Paris, by contrast, was shaped by the memory of his earlier visit to Olwyn and the sense he had then of the shadows of the war – 'walls patched and scabbed with posters', the ghosts of SS men sitting in pavement cafés, the sense that the waiter serving you bitter coffee might have been a collaborator.[2]

Paris was proving too expensive, so they took a train to cheaper Spain, with nothing but a rucksack and Sylvia's typewriter. First stop was Madrid, where they attended a bullfight. Fascinated by the rituals and the blood, Ted wrote an enormously detailed account of it in a letter to his parents. Sylvia felt disgusted and sickened by the brutality, though recognised that the experience was good material for a story. 'I am glad that Ted and I both feel the same way,' she reported to her mother, 'full of sympathy for the bull.' The most satisfying moment was when 'one of the six beautiful, doomed bulls managed to gore a fat, cruel picador'.[3] He was lifted off his horse and carried away with blood spurting from his thigh. 'You could see great holes in him,' wrote Ted. 'Whether he died later or not I don't know.'[4]

From Madrid it was on to Benidorm, which was in the early stages of its transformation from fishing village to tourist resort. They began by lodging in a widow's house. There was no hot water or refrigerator and the dark kitchen cupboard was full of ants. They cooked – 'fresh sardines fried in oil, potato and onion tortillas, café con leche'[5] – on an ancient paraffin burner with a blue flame. Ted got sunburnt on the first day. Soon they moved to a rental house set back from the sea, away from the noise of the main hotels on the neon-lit tourist strip. They decided to stay all summer and write.

Sylvia filled her journal with detailed observations of fishermen, markets brimming with fresh food, and day excursions. Ted carried on with what he had started in Paris: a collection of fables for children, in the manner of Rudyard Kipling's *Just So Stories*. The first was called 'How the Donkey Became'. Myths of origin were a peculiar obsession throughout his writing career. He was very pleased with his narratives, though it would take several years before he found a publisher for them. He told Olwyn that Sylvia rated them, too: 'Sylvia is as fine a literary critic as I have met, and she thinks about my ordinary prose narrative style just as you do. But my fables she cries over and laughs all together.'[6]

He always remembered their big cool house and the hotels under construction in 'The moon-blanched, moon-trenched sea-town' where a 'hook of promontory' halved 'The two wings of beach'.[7] One of Ted and Sylvia's favourite devices was to apply the bleaching light cast by the moon as a filter upon their poetic lenses. They wrote all morning and bathed in the afternoons, 'played and shopped, maybe wrote again in the evenings'.[8] On some evenings, Ted worked to improve his Spanish while Sylvia translated Stendhal's *Le Rouge et le Noir* from the French. He tried to teach her the art of hypnosis, which gave her the idea of writing a story called 'The Hypnotising Husband'. She sketched in pen and ink, catching the outline of kitchen pots, an old stove, white-plastered tenements on the cliffs above the fishing bay, bowls of fruit, and her new husband in profile.[9]

Sylvia told her mother that they were utterly happy. She could not imagine how she had lived without him: 'I think he is the handsomest, most brilliant, creative, dear man in the world. My whole thought is for him, to make a comfortable place for him.'[10] She was just as effusive to her brother: 'He knows all about so many things: fishing, hunting, birds, animals, and is utterly dear … What a husband!'[11] Ted in turn told his brother in Australia that he had never been writing so well, that this 'American poetess' was the making of him.[12] In her journal, she described their writing table: 5 foot square, in the centre of the stone-tiled dining room, made of 'glossy dark polished wood', with a gap in the middle. At one end Ted sat 'in a squarely built grandfather chair with wicker back and seat':

> His realm was a welter of sheets of typing paper and ragged cardboard-covered notebooks; the sheets of scrap paper, scrawled across with his assertive blue-inked script, rounded, upright, flaired, were backs of reports on books, plays and movies written while at Pinewood studios; typed and re-written versions of poems, bordered with drawings of mice, ferrets and polar bears, spread out across his half of the table. A bottle of blue ink, perpetually open, rested on a stack of paper. Crumpled balls of used paper lay here and there, to be thrown into the large wooden crate placed for that purpose in the doorway. All papers and notebooks on this half of the table were tossed at angles, kitty-corner and impromptu.[13]

A cookbook rested open by his right elbow, where Sylvia had left it after reading out recipes for rabbit stew. These are the sort of conditions in which he would write for the rest of his life. On Sylvia's half of the table, by contrast, everything was neat, well ordered, carefully stacked. He wrote in longhand; she typed.

Though one would not guess it from the brightness of her journal-writing, if Ted is to be believed, Sylvia hated Spain. He said this in retrospect, on account of what he perceived as the darkening in the style of the poems that she wrote while they were there, of her reaction to the bullfight, and of a glimpse of her by moonlight walking alone by the sea in Alicante, looking out towards America like a lost soul. He loved Goya; she found something disturbing in the 'Goya funeral grin' of Spanish culture.[14]

A single brief shadow passed across their honeymoon summer under the Benidorm sun. Sylvia's fragmentary journal entry for 23 July speaks of 'The hurt going in, clean as a razor, and the dark blood welling'.[15] The first part of that day's diary is missing, apparently torn from her notebook. Years later, when her marriage to Ted was at rock-bottom, she allegedly told a friend that one afternoon he turned violent as they made love in the open air on a hillside. The – unverified – story went that his hands tightened around her neck and she nearly choked.[16]

After six hot weeks in Spain, they returned via Paris. Olwyn had been away on a conference when they passed through in July and this time she was away again, on holiday. They were, however, able to see Sylvia's brother Warren, who was about to take up a Fulbright himself. He took some photographs of the newlyweds, arm in arm. In the city, everything seemed rushed, and tiring, after their summer by the sea. Sylvia was ready to head north to 'Ted's wuthering-heights home'.[17]

The photographs were taken by a colleague from the trouser factory who was an enthusiastic amateur with a camera. In the most famous image, she holds with both hands the strong arm that is around her. His other hand is casually in his pocket. The light bounces off their white shirts on to their fresh faces and high cheekbones. He has just turned twenty-six and she is not quite twenty-four. They look impossibly beautiful, impossibly happy. In another snapshot, Edith is between them, proud of the son who has brought an American bride instead of going off to have a family in Australia. In a third, Sylvia is in the bosom of the family, sitting on a garden bench between Ted and Edith, with Uncle Walt and Bill Hughes standing behind.

On 2 September, she wrote to her mother, describing herself as 'a veritable convert to the Brontë clan', with warm woollen sweater, slacks, socks to her knees and a steaming cup of coffee, sitting in Ted's bedroom looking out over the beautiful landscape of moorland crisscrossed with drystone walls, as the wind whipped the rain against the side of the house and the coal fires glowed within.[18] On a never-to-be-forgotten day, Uncle Walt drove them over to Top Withens, the alleged original of Wuthering Heights. They had a picnic and walked over the moor to the 'lonely, deserted black-stone house, broken down, clinging to the windy side of a hill'.[19] Ted photographed her halfway up a tree, just by the ruin. She re-read *Wuthering Heights* and then on a day of freezing wind they hiked 10 miles over the moors to visit Top Withens again. They also went to the Brontë parsonage in Haworth, where they marvelled at Charlotte Brontë's little water-colours and the miniature books in which the sisters had written their earliest stories. Sylvia was full of hope and ambition. A poem 'unfurled' from her 'Like a loose frond of hair' from the nape of her neck, 'To be clipped and kept in a book'.[20] The moors and the Brontë connection would inspire two fine Plath poems, 'Two Views of Withens' and, later, 'Wuthering Heights'.[21]

Towards the end of September, they went down to London for a couple of days. Ted auditioned as a reader of modern poetry for the BBC's highbrow Third Programme (the station that a decade later was rebranded as Radio 3). At Sylvia's suggestion, he slipped in a couple of his own poems among selections from W. B. Yeats and Gerard Manley Hopkins. The producer, Donald Carne-Ross, sat with Sylvia in the listening room and murmured his approval of Ted's voice: 'Perfect, superb'.[22] There was the possibility of a programme about Yeats, if the commissioning committee agreed. He would be in touch.

In October, Sylvia had to return to Cambridge for her second year of study. Ted remained for a fortnight with his parents at the Beacon, then went back to Dan Huws's flat in Rugby Street. They still had not told the college authorities, or indeed the Fulbright Commission, about their marriage. Sylvia was unnecessarily worried about getting into trouble. So they were apart for a few weeks, one of the very few times that they were not together during the six years before the marriage broke down. They wrote each other love letters every day, alive with longing and playfulness and writing ideas and smart criti-cism of each other's work and dreamy plans for the future. Ted some-times took to typing instead of using his favoured black fountain pen, as if in homage to Sylvia's love of the new Olivetti typewriter she had bought in the month of their marriage. They were not averse to senti-mentality. 'Darling Dearest Sylvia kish puss ponk', Ted would begin, and he would end, 'I love you I love you, I love you I love you your Ted' or 'My kiss puss All my lovelovelovelovelovelovelovelovelove

lovelove from top to tow [*sic*]' – followed by a postscript with the promise that 'I shall see you Friday and we shall make up for all these interims.'[23]

His literary career was beginning to take off. Not least thanks to Sylvia's organisational skills, his poems were being sent out to magazines in both Britain and America, and some were being accepted. It made a difference that the submissions were neatly typewritten; one can guess from the American spellings who was responsible for that. News came from Carne-Ross of provisional acceptance of the Yeats programme. 'Darling darling Teddy,' wrote Sylvia, 'I read your letter over breakfast ... and fought and conquered a huge urge to ... leap up in the center of the table and shout: MY HUSBAND IS GOING TO READ OVER THE BBC! With appropriate whoopdedos. I AM SO PROUD.'[24] As it turned out, he was paid, but the Yeats readings were never broadcast. The first time Ted's voice was heard on the radio was on 14 April 1957, when a recording made on 24 October the previous year of him reading his poem 'The Martyrdom of Bishop Farrar' was included in an episode of a series called *The Poet's Voice*.

By the time he had done his recordings, the Governing Body of Newnham and the Fulbright Commission had been told about the marriage. Far from taking away Sylvia's scholarship or throwing her out, they congratulated her. The Fulbright took the view that the union was a boost to Anglo-American relations, which was their raison d'être. Ted was free to move to Cambridge. Mr and Mrs Hughes had found a ground-floor flat in Eltisley Avenue, in Newnham village, on the edge of the city, nicely placed between Sylvia's college and the green spaces of Grantchester Meadows. The rent was low (£4 per week) and they had a living room, dining room, cavernous kitchen and bedroom. Like many houses in west Cambridge, it was a single residence that had been divided into flats. This meant that they had to share a bathroom with the occupant of the flat upstairs; by a curious coincidence, that was George Sassoon, son of the First World War poet Siegfried, and thus a relative of Richard Sassoon (though Sylvia never mentioned him). Ted moved in first, with Sylvia following at the end of the academic term in December. She had sent a batch of their work to the prestigious American magazines the *New Yorker* and the *Atlantic Monthly*. All of hers had been rejected, but a poem of Ted's called 'The Hawk in the Storm' was accepted by Peter Davison, editor of the

Atlantic. Ted thought it was the worst of the poems that they had submitted.

In November, Olwyn stopped by for a weekend on the way back to Paris after a break with her parents in Yorkshire. Her first impression of Sylvia was of 'American-classic' clothes, good manners, blonde hair, fair skin, brown eyes ('deep, watchful and intelligent'), elegant limbs ('her best feature') and an attractively low-pitched voice ('deepening engagingly when she was amused'). She thought that her new sister-in-law was 'poised and controlled, with a hint of reserve or constraint'.[25] They went to Heffers bookshop and Sylvia bought an impressive pile of literary texts with her generous Fulbright book allowance. In the evening, Sylvia cooked a large dinner of roast beef, followed by straw-berries and cream. They drank wine. Sylvia thought Olwyn was 'start-lingly beautiful with amber-gold hair and eyes', but felt that she was 'quite selfish and squanders money on herself continually in extrava-gances of clothes and cigarettes, whilst she still owes Ted fifty pounds'.[26]

That same month, Sylvia spotted the announcement of a compe-tition for a best first book of poems. It came from the American publisher Harper Brothers, in conjunction with the Young Men's and Young Women's Hebrew Association of New York (YMYWHA), which had a renowned Poetry Center at its headquarters on 92nd Street. The judges were figures of immense distinction in the poetry world: W. H. Auden, Stephen Spender and the American Marianne Moore. Since Sylvia did not think she had quite enough good poems of her own to create a book, she and Ted selected what they thought were the best forty of Ted's. Six of them already had magazine acceptances. She typed them up and submitted them, with a renamed version of the *Atlantic* poem as the title piece: *The Hawk in the Rain*. He had for some time been intending to put together a collection of his poems, taking the title from a recurrent dream he had been having: 'A Hill of Leopards'.[27] The trouble was, he had not yet been inspired to write the poem that would go with the title. So he was happy to go with *Hawk* and to let his wife take the lead on the process. Sylvia was convinced that Ted would win the competition, and gain the prize of publication. She assured her mother that it was the best collection of any poet since W. B. Yeats and Dylan Thomas.[28]

Sylvia rounded up her year in a pre-Christmas letter to her dearest friend, Marty Brown, her sophomore roommate at Smith. She had found a husband who was 'the most magnificent man ever', a 'roaring hulking Yorkshireman' who had put the sound of a 'hurricane' in her ear at the Falcon Yard party. From that first instant, she 'just knew' that he was the one. She rescued him from a 'slum' in London, where he had told her that Dylan Thomas used to stay, and now they were writing 'like fury', each the other's best critic. He was 'a crack shot and fisherman, discus thrower and can read horoscopes like a professional'. He shot rabbits and she stewed them. They had nothing to their name but 'a wood coffee table, a travel rug and very sharp steak knife', but they wanted nothing more. They had each other. She loved that he was the only man she had ever met whom she could 'never boss' – she just knew that if she tried, 'he'd bash my head in'.[29]

They spent Christmas with Ted's family at the Beacon, all getting on well, then returned to Cambridge for the freezing-cold Lent term. Dorothea Krook, Sylvia's generous college supervisor, lent them a paraffin heater, at which Sylvia warmed her hands as she worked on an autobiographical novel about her Cambridge experiences. The 'greasy-grimed shelves' and 'tacky, dark walls' of 55 Eltisley 'confirmed' her 'idea of England': 'part / Nursing home, part morgue / For something partly dying, partly dead'.[30] The contrast between dirty, dying England and pristine, newborn America was a recurrent image in Ted's work. Sylvia cleaned the kitchen in a frenzy of scouring.

Ted brought in some income by getting a job as an English teacher at the Coleridge Secondary Modern School for Boys. The name had suitably inspiring literary connotations, but he found the work tiring. Because it was a school for boys who had failed to get into the more academic grammar schools, he worked across the curriculum, teaching basic Maths as well as English, History, Drama and Art. He brought the students' work home in the evening and read out samples to Sylvia as he was marking. It was not an easy school. Sylvia was only mildly exaggerating for comic effect when she told her friend Marty that his class consisted of 'a gang of 40 teddy-boys, teen-age, who carry chains and razors to school and can't remember their multiplication tables for 2 days running: a most moving, tragic and in many ways rewarding experience'. It took a lot out of Ted 'to maintain physical and emotional discipline (they still use the cane here!)'.[31] But the boys loved him, especially when he read out ballads and encouraged them to write their own. And still more when he made them stage little Elizabethan plays.

In February, three days before the anniversary of their first meeting at Falcon Yard, came winter cheer: Ted had won the competition. *The Hawk in the Rain* was going to be published in America. The distinction of the judging panel almost certainly assured English publication too. Ted told Olwyn that his first reaction on hearing the news was a tremendous sense of guilt – partly, though he did not say so, at the fact that he owed the breakthrough to Sylvia finding out about the competition, and yet it was his poems, not hers, that would be published. He went straight back to read the poems and immediately found all sorts of things he wanted to change. He was appalled at himself for letting Sylvia send them out 'in such an unfinished state'.[32] Sylvia had no such hesitation: the book was magnificent, Ted was a genius, the poems combined 'intellect and grace of complex form, with lyrical music, male vigor and vitality, and moral commitment and love and awe of the world'. He had everything and she was blissfully happy with him, happy indeed that *his* book had been accepted first. She rejoiced, she told Aurelia, that he was ahead of her: 'There is no question of rivalry, but only mutual joy and a sense of us doubling our prize-winning and creative output.'[33] She was proud to have been the one who had pushed Ted to make the selection and then typed up the poems.

Sylvia promptly sent a copy of the typescript to Faber and Faber, Britain's premier poetry publisher, mentioning the prize and the prospect of publication by Harper in America. Faber returned it with a curt note saying that they did not publish first volumes by American writers. With characteristic persistence, she sent it back, saying that Ted was actually English. They agreed to publish a UK edition. Mr T. S. Eliot himself very much liked the poems. Within a week of acceptance, Faber sent the poems in proof – well before Harper had set up the New York edition in type. Ted would, he proudly told his parents, be 'the first poet ever to publish his first book in both countries'.[34] Indeed, only Auden and Dylan Thomas had gone before him in having a volume of poems published simultaneously on both sides of the Atlantic.

More good news arrived from America: Sylvia was offered a teaching job at Smith, her old college. Ted would go too. Plans for language teaching in Spain or further afield were abandoned. To show her husband her own country was a much more exciting plan. In the better weather of Easter term, they walked on Grantchester Meadows, sometimes getting up early enough to watch the sun rise. One morning Sylvia sat on a stile and recited Chaucer to the cows: 'Whan that Aprille with his shoures soote / The droghte of March hath perced to the roote ...'.[35] Soon she was preparing for her final exams. Ted helped her to revise.

In May, he wrote to Gerald and Joan – they now had two children, Ashley and Brendon – saying that 'marriage is my medium'.[36] He and Sylvia worked and walked and repaired each other's writing. She was one of the best critics he had ever met and they understood each other's imagination 'perfectly'. She was 'the most responsive alert creature in the world'. They struck sparks, sitting by the river, just watching for water-voles, Sylvia thrilled when the little animals came close. Ted would let out a squeal in imitation of a rabbit, and out they would come. The sound was so realistic that once an owl flew down and tried to sit on his head.[37]

His visa and the necessary blood test were arranged. Before leaving Coleridge, he directed a school play and Sylvia attended, her only visit to his place of work. They would sail on 20 June, as soon as Sylvia had graduated. The plan was that they would be in New York for the launch of his book in August (in fact it appeared a couple of months later than that).

They went up to Yorkshire to say goodbye to the family. During this visit they happily corrected the Harper proofs of The Hawk in the Rain, but there was an embarrassing incident when Ted's old schoolteacher John Fisher and his wife Nancy drove up from Mexborough to see them. Olwyn, who was also over from Paris for a summer stay, remembered the visit as follows:

Sylvia was very 'gushy' when they arrived. This clearly disconcerted the Fishers, and possibly their inadequate response offended her. Well on in the afternoon, when the talk was deep in reminiscences, she suddenly rose and left the room. We heard the outside door open and banged shut. When she didn't return after about ten minutes, during which time Ted had become rather silent, he rose in turn and said he'd better go and see where she was. Quite a while later they returned, Sylvia rushing straight upstairs.[38]

For the family, this was a first glimpse of Sylvia's emotional volatility.

Then it was off to Southampton to cross the Atlantic on the *Queen Elizabeth*. The best thing about the crossing was the food: 'all included in the fare', 'steak, steak, steak – if you wish' (a real treat, in those years when post-war rationing was still a recent memory), 'Five courses to each meal and many choices of dish'.³⁹ For Sylvia, who always had a very hearty appetite, the only problem was the combination of this with the Atlantic swell. On one occasion she found herself 'kneeling on the floor of the little cabin under the electric light' with 'the vomit shooting out across the room from the rich dinner, the lobster and pecans and martinis'.⁴⁰ Landing in New York, a customs officer looked with suspicion at Sylvia's copy of *Lady Chatterley's Lover*. She had often joked that in Ted she had found her own gamekeeper.

'Ted is wonderful: how to get it down? All of a piece, smelling lovely as a baby, a hay field, strawberries under leaves, and smooth white, browning to tan, with his great lion head of hair erupting.'⁴¹ It was July 1957. Cape Cod. They had washed off the spiders and dust and coal-sludge and smeared windows of Eltisley Avenue, bathed and freshened themselves, rebaptised their marriage in the great salt tides of the Atlantic, under the summer sun.

Brother-in-law Warren drove them there a few days after a garden party at which Sylvia proudly introduced her handsome husband to more than seventy friends and family. Bicycles were strapped to the roof of the car. Aurelia's wedding present could not have been better judged: a summer rental of a cottage belonging to friends at Eastham, a short bike ride from Nauset Light and Coast Guard beaches. For seven magical weeks they could write, before heading inland for Sylvia to take up her position at Smith. It was a little wooden house in 'a Christmas tree forest',⁴² fully fitted out with squirrels on the roof and chipmunks under the floor. 'That's my first ever real chipmunk,' cried Ted. The little creature lodged in his memory as a 'midget Aboriginal American', a 'snapshot for life'. Especially as Sylvia would sometimes make a face like a chipmunk.⁴³

He recorded his first impressions of America in long, journal-like letters sent to his parents in Yorkshire, Gerald and Joan in Australia, and Olwyn in Paris. In comparison with dour, confined Fifties England, everything was large, opulent, brash. Even the robins were as big as thrushes. Sociability was compulsory. As was cleanliness, which he joked that he felt like reacting against: 'My natural instinct is to practise little private filthinesses – I spit, pea [*sic*] on shrubbery, etc, and have a strong desire to sleep on the floor – just to keep in contact with a world that isn't quite as glazed as this one.'[44] Wellesley seemed to him very suburban, so he was glad to return to nature on the Cape. He didn't like the way that things were homogenised and packaged. 'What a place America is,' he wrote to Olwyn. 'Everything is in cellophane. Everything is 10,000 miles from where it was plucked or made. The bread is in cellophane that is covered with such slogans as de-crapularised, re-energised, multi-cramulated, bleached, double-bleached, rebrowned, unsanforised, guaranteed no blasphemin. There is no such thing as bread. You cannot buy bread.'[45] What he liked was the kindness of everybody. Reading the literary reviews, which in England were 'bittermost gall to boil the heads and hearts of everyone', he was impressed by the tone of civility. The style was 'surprisingly honest, outspoken, but not venomous': 'They attack each other mercilessly – but openly.'[46] There was none of the sarcasm, the snide remarks, the backbiting that characterised the literary establishment back home.

Ted sat and wrote – or poised himself over a blank page – from seven in the morning until two in the afternoon. The poems weren't really coming, but his children's stories were exciting him. He hatched a grand plan to produce a great compendium – 5,000 fables, perhaps – which would bring together all the situations, characters and themes out of all the fairy tales and animal stories that he had ever read. And there weren't many that he hadn't read.

Then they would explore: sunbathing, swimming, fishing. Once, their little boat was swept out to sea and they were stranded on a reef until a motorboat rescued them. On another occasion, they went mussel-hunting at Rock Harbor, watching with fascination 'the weird spectacle of fiddler crabs in the mud-pools'.[47]

Sylvia started a new journal. She too was aching to fill a blank page. She would begin with short stories in which to work herself up towards a novel. She would aim for a 'jewel prose' akin to poetry. Little paragraphs. Vignettes. Memories of the cold, the food and the eccentricities of Cambridge. Then she would be ready for 'Novel: <u>FALCON YARD</u>: central image: <u>love, a falcon</u>, striking once and for all: blood sacrifice: falcon yard, central chapter of book: the irrefutable meeting and experience.' There would be an emblem out of the traditions of medieval courtly love: a lord and lady on horseback, smiling. A falcon on the wrist, not a hawk in the rain. The bird of prey tamed. She was struggling with writer's block, but was sustained by 'the endless deep love' in which she was living that second honeymoon summer. And by 'the unique and almost bottomless understanding of Ted'.[48]

As always, she had dark dreams, but there were joyful ones too: of Ted's rosy-cheeked mother holding a baby, with two older children by her side. Sylvia wondered whether this was a memory of a photograph of Ted and his elder siblings or a vision of the grandchildren that she would one day give to Edith.

Ted was teaching her the art of poetic economy. Choose something very particular: a pig, say, or a cow by moonlight. Describe with words that 'have an aura of mystic power'. Name the names of a quality: 'spindly, prickling, sleek, splayed, wan, luminous, bellied'.[49] Repeat the words aloud and the incantation will make them strong.

She felt that a new era had begun. After the months of exam-cramming, 'slovenly Eltisley living, tight budgeting, arranging of moving', she was becoming whole, stretching her writerly wings. Ted brought her cold orange juice to quench sleep-thirst and they exchanged dreams. In hers she was back at Newnham but this time surrounded by wild flowers instead of having her old bad dream about exams. In his, they walked a meadow in which there was a baby tiger and another tiger beyond a hedge. A tiger-man knocked at the door with a gun and Ted defended her, 'bluffing with an empty rifle'.[50]

Sylvia was reading Virginia Woolf, learning to write prose poetry, to follow the stream of consciousness and not worry about realistic detail. This was how she could turn 'Judith Greenwood', her autobiograph-ical character, into a symbolic figure. 'Make her enigmatic: who is that blond girl: she is a bitch: she is the white goddess. Make her a state-ment of the generation. Which is you.'[51] But was it possible to be both the eternal feminine of the White Goddess and the symbol of a new materialistic, carefree generation?

Before long, she would be blocked again. And then the anxiety would kick in, the jealousy of Ted's success. She wanted him to have it, she felt in her gut that he was the better poet and that he deserved it. The reason she could marry him and him alone was the knowledge that she would never have to restrain her own talent. With a lesser poet, she would have had to rein herself in so as not to emasculate him by overtaking him and becoming the successful one. With Ted, she told herself, however high she flew he would always be ahead. For all this, she could not but envy his prize, his winning of Mr T. S. Eliot's admiration, his forthcoming publication on both sides of the Atlantic.

Ted knew that 'the waters off beautiful Nauset' – a phrase from 'Daddy' that he quotes back in 'The Prism', his *Birthday Letters* poem about her grave – were the cradle of Sylvia's self. He kept her talis-manic stone in which, like a prism, he imagined seeing the Cape's 'salty globe of blue, its gull-sparkle, / Its path of surf-groomed sand'.[52] In the prism and in the Birthday Letter named from it, both her childhood – pre-depression, pre-suicide attempts – and their second honeymoon summer of 1957 were intact. Their sunlit seaside love was the antithesis of the snow-covered, windswept Brontë moors.

10

'So this is America'

With summer gone, they took up residence in the town of Northampton, on the banks of the Connecticut River in western Massachusetts. This was the location of Smith College, where Sylvia taught as an instructor for freshman English throughout the 1957–8 academic year. They lived in an apartment at 337 Elm Street, near a church, a high school and the green oasis of Childs Memorial Park. After a nervous first day, fastened in the straitjacket of a blue flannel suit that Ted remembered in a *Birthday Letters* poem, Sylvia threw herself into her teaching. Busy as she was preparing and taking classes, she continued to plan 'Falcon Yard', her Cambridge novel. Ted helped to steer her away from the superficial externals of her magazine-style prose, towards his own more inward territory. 'Place doesn't matter – it's the inner life: Ted & me,' she reminded herself in her journal.[1] But for Ted, place did matter. 'So this is America' was his memory of his thought on first making love to Sylvia.[2] Now he was in America with his American wife.

In her imagination, Sylvia was still in England. She planned short stories. One of them, 'Four Corners of a Windy House', sketched out in 'physical, rich, heavy-booted detail' their bracing hike across the moors to Top Withens:

blisters, grouse – picnic – honey soaking through brown paper bag – fear, aloneness – goal – cairn of black stones, small, contracted – their dream of each other, she & he … Strength – each alone – bracken, marsh – tea in deep cleft of valley – dark, cats – story of lost woman – match-flare of courage in the dark – moor sheep – bus-wait opposite spiritualists – ghosts & reality on moor … house: absolute reality, but clustered with ghosts – eternal paradox of identity.[3]

Before his eyes, Ted's life was being transformed into art through his wife's magical gift for words.

He, on the other hand, felt blocked. With Sylvia as the breadwinner, he was free to write full time, but the poems had dried up. He would sit for hours 'like a statue of a man writing'.[4] The only difference between him and an inanimate figure was that after a few hours a bead of sweat would drip down his forehead. For the first time, he was *trying to write* as opposed to writing down the words that just came to him. And it was the *trying* that proved the impediment. What was more, the fact of having published all the decent poems he had written meant that he had to move on to a new style. There would be no point in producing a second book that was just like the first – and it was on the basis of a second book that his long-term literary future would be judged. He cooked Sylvia both breakfast and lunch, but the life of idleness was not for him. He wandered around Northampton and was disconcerted by the Smith girls, who went around in gaggles, all looked like each other, and had a 'machined glaze of hyper-health'.[5] Later in the year, an encounter with some of them in Childs Memorial Park seems to have provoked an angry outburst from Sylvia.[6]

Ted sensed that, paradoxically, he would be more productive if he had less time on his hands. So he began to look for a job. The trouble was, there was nothing interesting for him to do in the dull town of Northampton. He made some enquiries about part-time work for the college radio station in nearby Amherst.

The Hawk in the Rain was published in London by Faber and Faber on 13 September 1957, at a price of ten shillings and sixpence, in an edition of 2,000 copies in a yellow dust jacket with narrow blue stripes, the title in blue and 'poems by Ted Hughes' in red.[7] The American edition appeared five days later, in a smaller edition, at a price of $2.75. A month later, Ted and Sylvia went to New York for a reading and launch party at the Poetry Center at the 92nd Street Y, which had been the country's leading venue for live poetry since 1939. Dylan Thomas's *Under Milk Wood* had had its premiere there.

Sylvia wrote to his parents afterwards, telling them that Ted had done a wonderful job, looking extremely handsome in his only suit (dark grey) and the golden yellow tie she had bought him in Spain for his birthday the previous year. She had persuaded him, much against his will, to have a haircut, so he looked like 'a Yorkshire god'. There were about 150 people in the audience, and he 'read beautifully'.[8] Some members of the audience bought the book beforehand and followed the poems on the page as he read. Afterwards, he signed autographs, using Sylvia's shoulder as a writing-desk. In the same letter, she thanked her in-laws for the mother-of-pearl earrings they had just sent her for her twenty-fifth birthday: these would go perfectly with the pink woollen dress that she had worn on her wedding day. She also told them that she had persuaded Ted to write an autobiographical children's story about a little boy who lived on the moors that he so loved.

Ted in turn wrote excitedly to Dan Huws, saying that the 92nd Street Y had been packed for his reading and that afterwards he was 'swamped by dowagers' who wanted to know why 'Bawdry Embraced' – those rollicking verses from their Cambridge days – had not been included in the book. The answer was that Marianne Moore had considered them 'too lewd' and insisted on the poem being dropped.[9] An assortment of 'maidenly creatures' asked him to sign their fresh copies of his slim volume. One of them took the book back after he had signed it, looked at him with wide eyes and said, 'And what I want to say is "Hurrah for you".'[10] This was his first full experience of the effect his poetry readings would have on females in the audience.

Reviews came more quickly in Britain than America. One of the first was by the distinguished Orcadian poet Edwin Muir in the *New Statesman*: 'Mr Ted Hughes is clearly a remarkable poet, and seems to be quite outside the current of his time.' His voice was very different, that was to say, from the urbane tones of the poets of the so-called Movement – the anti-romantic, anti-Dylan Thomas group, including Philip Larkin, Kingsley Amis and Donald Davie, whose work had been gathered the previous year in an anthology called *New Lines*. 'His distinguishing power is sensuous, verbal and imaginative; at his best the three are fused together,' Muir continued. 'His images have an admirable violence.' All in all, *The Hawk in the Rain* was 'A most surprising first book, and it leaves no doubt about Mr Hughes's powers.'[11] He said that Hughes's 'Jaguar' was better than Rilke's 'Panther', praise so high that Ted thought it would be more likely to provoke 'derision than curiosity'.[12]

The reviews that counted most were those in the *New York Times* and the London *Observer*. They appeared on the same day, 6 October.

The New York account was by a poet who would soon become a very good friend, W. S. Merwin. He could hardly have been more positive. The book's publication, he wrote, gave reviewers 'an opportunity to do what they are always saying they want to do: acclaim an exciting new writer'. The poems were more than promising. They were 'unmistakably a young man's poems', which accounted for 'some of their defects as well as some of their strength and brilliance', but 'Mr Hughes has the kind of talent that makes you wonder more than commonly where he will go from here, not because you can't guess but because you venture to hope.'[13]

Later in the autumn, they met Merwin. Ted found him impressively 'composed'. His English wife Dido was, according to Sylvia, 'very amusing, a sort of young Lady Bracknell'; to Ted, she seemed 'bumptious garrulous upper class'.[14] They were introduced through Jack Sweeney, director of the Woodberry Poetry Room in the student library at Harvard. Sweeney gave lively dinner-parties for local and visiting poets at his home on Beacon Street in Boston. Ted arrived with a limp and his foot in plaster, because he had fractured the fifth metatarsal in his right foot when jumping out of an armchair in the Elm Street apartment at a moment when his foot had gone to sleep. He was still limping when he struggled up the stairs some time later to the Merwins' fifth-floor apartment on West Cedar Street, for another dinner-party, at which Bill Merwin suggested that Ted and Sylvia should move back to England, because the opportunities for BBC broadcasting, together with newspaper and magazine reviewing, would give them much more time for their own writing than they would have staying in America, where the only way that poets could make a living was through distracting and debilitating university teaching. The Merwins were heading to London themselves.

In London, it was Al Alvarez, poetry editor of the *Observer*, who could make or break a young writer. He wrote poems himself – Ted thought they were 'very crabby little apples' – and he wasn't easy to please. His review dropped a lot of names in a manner that Ted considered 'undergraduatish' – D. H. Lawrence, Thom Gunn, Robert Lowell, Shakespeare's *Coriolanus* (from which he accused Hughes of stealing the word 'dispropertied').[15] Alvarez criticised some of the poems for being excessively 'literary' or having a 'misanthropic swagger', but said that half a dozen of them could only have been written by 'a real poet'.[16]

Alvarez's judgement was astute. Some of the poems in *The Hawk in the Rain* now read like period pieces. There is sometimes a clever literary allusiveness that does not feel real. And pieces such as 'Secretary' are unpleasantly misanthropic – or in this case, misogynist. Quite a lot of the poems are directly or indirectly about sex, viewed from a very masculine perspective. But there are indeed half a dozen pieces of true genius. Four of them are among the first five in the collection: 'The Hawk in the Rain', 'The Jaguar', 'The Thought-Fox' and 'The Horses'. The two other highlights are 'Wind', which begins with the memorable line 'This house has been far out at sea all night,'[17] and 'Six Young Men'. This was inspired by a photograph of a group of friends posing near the bridge at the top of Crimsworth Dene, that favourite spot of Ted's. They are all 'trimmed for a Sunday jaunt' some time just before the outbreak of war. The 'bilberried bank', 'thick tree' and 'black wall' were all still there, forty years on, but the young men were not. 'The celluloid of a photograph holds them.' The image is 'faded and ochre-tinged', yet the figures themselves are free from wrinkles. 'Though their cocked hats are not now fashionable, / Their shoes shine.' A shy smile is caught in one of the faces, another of the lads is chewing a piece of grass. One is shy, another 'ridiculous with cocky pride'. Little differences, but the same end: 'Six months after this picture they were all dead.'[18] The poem remains one of the two best retrospectives on the 'never such innocence again' motif of the beginning of the Great War, the other being Philip Larkin's 'MCMXIV', published a few years later in *The Whitsun Weddings*.

The hawk, the jaguar, the thought-fox and the horses all seem perfectly formed: animal images seamlessly entering the inner self of the poet. But Ted's notebooks reveal that all were struggled for, through draft after draft. So, for example, it was a tremendous trial to reach the shimmer of the line 'Steady as a hallucination on the streaming air' in the title poem:

~~As a hallucination in the avalanche of air untouched~~
~~As a hallucination in the heaving air buoyed~~
~~Like a hallucination in the swamping air to its sides~~
~~Like a hallucination the running air~~
~~Like a hallucination that the scene rides and it hangs~~
~~Like a hallucination that the scenes rides <vivid> through ...~~

After these six failed attempts, he got to 'Steady as a hallucination in the bursting sky', but still that was not quite right.[19] Again, it was a long time before he achieved 'The window is starless still; the clock ticks, / The page is printed' at the end of 'The Thought-Fox'. First he had to create and reject such variants as 'And the page where the prints have appeared' and 'The clock crowding and the whitening sky / Watch this page where the prints remain.'[20]

There were warning signs. Sylvia was exhausted by her duties at Smith. Ted told Olwyn that she was working twelve hours a day and cracking under the strain. Sometimes she would descend from the manic energy of her writing into days when she struggled to get out of bed, what with coughs and colds, fevers and flu, or sheer torpor. Christmas with Aurelia was marred by Sylvia suffering from viral pneumonia, exacerbated by her exhaustion from teaching and marking. In the new year, she told her head of department that she wanted to leave at the end of the academic session instead of accepting her option to stay on for a second year. Ted, meanwhile, got a similar teaching position for the semester over at the University of Massachusetts in Amherst.

He had to teach two classes three times a week on a 'Great Books' course. This meant mugging up on Milton's shorter poems, including *Samson Agonistes*, reading Goethe's *Faust* for the first time (opportune because he had been enthusing about Goethe and Nietzsche in a letter to Olwyn the previous autumn), getting advice from Sylvia about Dostoevsky's *Crime and Punishment* (they both heavily annotated their battered copy of the Penguin paperback of the English translation),[21] plunging into that quintessentially New England book, Thoreau's *Walden*, and going back to some of his favourite poetry – Wordsworth, Keats and Yeats. He also had to teach freshman English twice a week and a creative writing class in which he could do more or less what he liked. As a handsome young instructor with a relaxed teaching style, a rich English accent and a prizewinning first book of poems just published, he was an immediate hit with his students, especially the female ones. In the creative writing class, there were just eight of them, '3 beautiful, one brilliant & a very good person'.[22]

Back at Elm Street, despite all the preparation and marking, there was plenty of time for reading. Ted had some success in persuading Sylvia to share his Yeatsian occult interests, though these were more to

Olwyn's taste. He read through the *Journals of the Psychical Research Society* from the late nineteenth and early twentieth centuries and wrote to her of 'wonderful accounts of hypnoses, automatic writings, ghosts, double personalities etc'. He was delighted to find an anticipation of his own belief that the left side of the brain (in right-handed people) controlled 'all consciously-practised skills', whereas 'the subconscious, or something deeper, a world of spirits' was located in the right lobe.[23]

In April, Ted gave a poetry reading at Harvard. They drove down in the car they were borrowing from Warren Plath while he was away in Europe on his Fulbright scholarship. Sylvia's ex-lover, the poet and publisher Peter Davison, remembered the 'emphatic consonant-crunching of Hughes's voice' when he read.[24] The effect was to emphasise the nouns and underplay the verbs. As his poetry developed, Ted would often take the opportunity to omit some of the verbs altogether, even on paper. At a reception afterwards, they were introduced to several poets and writers. The literary scene in Cambridge and Boston was much more lively than that in Northampton and Amherst, so they felt justified in a plan they were hatching to move there in the summer.

Not that they had failed to find a few like-minded people during their teaching year. Several would remain particular friends: the poet Anthony Hecht was a member of the Smith faculty and the British poet and classical scholar Paul Roche was on a visiting fellowship, accompanied by his American wife Clarissa. Then in May 1958, they met the artist Leonard Baskin and his family. Eight years older than Ted, and with a comparably dark imagination, he taught printmaking and sculpture at Smith. 'How I love the Baskins,' Sylvia would write in her journal the following summer. They were 'a miracle of humanity and integrity, with no smarm'.[25] For Ted, too, Baskin would always remain the model of uncompromising artistic integrity. His volatile temper and forceful opinions were a necessary part of the package.

Sylvia's adoration of Ted and his poetry was undimmed. In March he did a public reading at the University of Massachusetts, coming on third, after two very inferior local poets. He 'shone', she wrote, 'the room dead-still for his reading'. Her eyes filled with tears and the hairs on her skin stood up like quills: 'I married a real poet, and my life is redeemed: to love, serve and create.'[26] When her own writing was going well, she dared to imagine that she might one day be 'The Poetess of America' as Ted would certainly be 'The Poet of England and her dominions'. She thought he was infallible in his suggestions for improvements in her poems, even down to the alteration of odd words such as 'marvelingly' instead of 'admiringly'.[27]

Just before the end of the semester, the mood suddenly changed. Their new friend Paul Roche, the visiting poet and classicist, had arranged a public reading of his new translation of Sophocles' *Oedipus the King*. Ted agreed to play the part of Creon, but he told Sylvia that he would prefer it if she did not attend. There had been no rehearsals and he did not have any confidence in the production. At the last minute, Sylvia did decide to go. She slipped into a seat at the back. For the first time, she didn't like the look of Ted: he appeared slovenly, 'his suit jacket wrinkled as if being pulled from behind, his pants hanging, unbelted, in great folds, his hair black and greasy' under the stage lights. Afterwards, he went backstage, frustrated with himself for agreeing to be inveigled into the evening. Paul Roche wondered whether he was grumpy because he thought he could have done a better job on the translation himself. With one finger, Ted banged out a tune on an old piano. It was probably a mistake not to have greeted Sylvia straight after the show: she was beginning to grow suspicious of Ted, not wanting to be apart from him for even an hour at a time. That semester there were rumours about all sorts of affairs going round the English Department. Something about his manner wasn't right. He wouldn't speak to her, but wouldn't leave. He had what she called an 'odd, lousy smile' of a kind she hadn't seen since Falcon Yard – was this the smile of the man who had taken Shirley to the party and ended up in a fierce embrace with Sylvia? In her journal she asked herself whether his behaviour could really be explained by his being 'ashamed of appearing on the platform in the company of lice'.[28]

The next day was the final day of teaching before the long summer break. Sylvia got a great round of applause from both her morning and her afternoon classes. Ted agreed that he would drive down to the Smith campus, return his library books and meet Sylvia to celebrate the end of term. He had time on his hands, since he had taught his last class at Amherst a day or two before. Sylvia had twenty minutes to spare before the afternoon class, so she went into the campus coffee shop. She noticed one of her male colleagues deep in flirtatious conversation with a very pretty undergraduate. This got her thinking about liaisons between professors and their students, which were not at all uncommon, especially in an English department at an all girls' college. After class, she went to look for Ted in the car park. Their car was there, but it was empty. Thinking he had gone to return his books, she drove it towards the library.

Suddenly she saw Ted, 'coming up the road from Paradise Pond where girls take their boys to neck on weekends'. He had a broad smile on his face and was – as Sylvia saw it – gazing into the 'uplifted doe-eyes of a strange girl with brownish hair, a large lipsticked grin, and bare thick legs in khaki Bermuda shorts'. When Sylvia appeared, the girl made a very hasty exit. Ted made no effort to introduce her. 'He thought her name was Sheila' (actually it was Susan).[29] Had he not once, Sylvia wrote in a bitter diary entry, thought that *her* name was Shirley? Everything seemed to fall into place: the unfamiliar smile, the excuses for returning home late. Suddenly, the God, the great poet, the only man she could ever want, was 'a liar and vain smiler'. They made up and made love, but afterwards, as he snorted and snored beside her, she lay awake, wondering, doubting. Why was his 'great inert heavy male flesh hanging down so much of the time'? Yes, there were 'such good fuckings' when they did make up, but why had he been sexually 'so weary, so slack all winter'? That had not been characteristic. Was he 'ageing or spending'? 'Fake. Sham ham. No explanations, only obfuscations': she was seeing again 'the vain, selfish face' she had first seen. The 'sweet and daily companion', the lovely 'Yorkshire Beacon boy', was gone. Now she could only think of his sulks, his selfishness, his greasy hair, the foul habits that she could not stand, obsessed as she was with personal hygiene (picking his nose, 'peeling off his nails and leaving them about'). Their marriage was over. She wouldn't slit her wrists in the bath or drive Warren's car into a tree or, to save expense, 'fill the garage at home with carbon monoxide', but, 'disabused of all faith', she would throw herself into her teaching and writing.[30]

Ted never published his side of the story, but many years later he did scribble a note about it. The 'big handsome girl' was in his creative writing class. She called herself 'Spring'. He had always found her very friendly, but she 'kept her distance'. He did feel a certain 'affinity' with her (having admitted this, he scored it out). He liked all his students in the little creative writing group. After his last class, this girl and her friend produced a bottle of red wine and three glasses, just as he was hurrying off to drive back from Amherst to Northampton. He excused himself and left them standing crestfallen. He did not expect ever to see any of his students again. By sheer coincidence, when he went to meet Sylvia on the Smith campus the following day, he bumped into the girl, coming out of the library with a bunch of other girls. So he walked with her for a few minutes. And that was when Sylvia appeared.[31] From his point of view, the encounter was entirely inno-cent and Sylvia's rage worryingly irrational.

They fought violently. There were 'snarls and bitings'. Sylvia ended up with a sprained thumb and Ted with 'bloody claw-marks' that lasted a week. At one point, she threw a glass across the room with all her might. Instead of breaking, it bounced back and hit her on the forehead. She saw stars for the first time.[32]

The fight cleared the air. They were intact. 'And nothing,' Sylvia wrote, 'no wishes for money, children, security, even total possession – nothing is worth jeopardizing what I have which is so much the angels might well envy it.'[33] If she could learn not to be over-dependent, not to require 'total possession', things would work out.

Reflecting on the incident when undergoing psychoanalysis six months later, she recognised that Ted was not habitually spending time with other women. There was no reason not to trust him. She had reacted so forcefully because the end of her exhausting teaching year was a big moment and she had wanted him to be there for her, and he wasn't. His absence, she reasoned, with the assistance of her analyst, must have made her think of her father, who had deserted her for ever by dying when she was eight. Insofar as he was 'a male presence' – though 'in no other way' – Ted was 'a substitute' for her father. 'Images of his faithlessness with women' accordingly echoed her father's deser-tion of her mother upon the call of 'Lady Death'.[34] Any act of male rejection or desertion, however temporary, would have an extreme effect because it would take her unconscious back to the primary trauma of Otto's sudden disappearance into death. This line of think-ing would crystallise in some of her later poems and give Ted lifelong food for reflection in both prose and verse.

That summer they had a week's holiday in New York and a fort-night revisiting Cape Cod, but otherwise they were in the apartment on Elm Street, writing. Or trying to write – they both suffered from bouts of block. In search of inspiration or relaxation, they took to experimenting with a Ouija board, conjuring up a spirit called Pan.

Two years after the whirlwind romance and the rushed wedding, the reality of married life was kicking in. 'We are amazingly compatible,' Sylvia reassured herself. 'But I must be myself – make myself and not let myself be made by him.' She was beginning to tire of his tendency to give mutually exclusive 'orders'. He would tell her to – or, to put it more moderately, suggest that she should – 'read ballads an hour, read Shakespeare an hour, read history an hour, think an hour'. But then he would say that no proper reading could be done in one-hour chunks; you had to read a book straight through to the end without distraction. There was an almost fanatical 'lack of balance and moderation' in his habits and his fads. He decided that, since he sat writing for much of the day, he should do some particular exercises for his back and his neck. They only made his neck stiffer, but that didn't stop him doing them.[35]

On the eve of Independence Day, they went for a walk and found a baby bird that had fallen out of its nest. Ted took it home and nursed it, just as he always used to care for injured fauna in his childhood. After a week, it became clear that the bird would not survive. Sylvia could not bear the thought of Ted strangling it, so he fixed their rubber bath hose to the gas jet on the cooker and taped the other end on the inside of a cardboard box. The bird was laid to rest, but unfortunately he removed it from the makeshift gas chamber prematurely and it lay gasping in his hand. Five minutes later, he took it to Sylvia, 'composed, perfect and beautiful in death'.[36]

In early September they moved to a tiny sixth-floor apartment at 9 Willow Street in the Beacon Hill district of Boston, with all its literary associations. Ted's poem named for the address evokes the claustrophobia they felt there, the sense that they were holding each other back instead of inspiring each other's work as they had done before. The main memory within the poem is a variant replay of the baby-bird incident. This time it is a sick bat that has fallen out of a tree on the nearby Common. In front of a bemused audience of passersby, he tries to restore it to its home and has his finger bitten for his pains. Then he remembers that American bats carry rabies, so he starts thinking of death.[37] His other *Birthday Letters* poems commemorating their residence in Willow Street are equally gloomy: visiting Marianne Moore, Sylvia devastated because the distinguished poet did not like her work; Sylvia and her 'panic bird'; the 'astringency' of the Charles River in a bitterly cold Boston winter.[38]

One day, looking over a letter from his wife to his parents before posting it, he misread the signing off as 'woe' instead of 'love'.[39] This seemed symbolic of the new mood in the marriage. Sometimes when his writing was not going well, he would while away the afternoon making a wolf mask. But that did nothing to keep the wolf from the door: the plan to live for a year off their savings, together with such casual literary earnings as they could muster, meant that they sometimes fought, because it wasn't always clear where the next month's dollars were coming from. They both sensed that the marriage had no future in America; Ted had not settled and Sylvia did not want to go back to teaching. There were days when they both suffered from 'black depression', relieved only by sporadic absorption in Beethoven piano sonatas.[40]

This was when she began seeing Dr Ruth Beuscher, her old psychoanalyst from McLean. Among her many worries was the fear that she was barren. Beuscher was a Freudian. She suggested that the main focus of their sessions should be Sylvia's 'Electra complex', the daughterly equivalent of the Oedipus complex. They explored the hatred that Sylvia had projected on to her mother following her father's death. That anger was by this time mixed up with a feeling that Aurelia was undermining the marriage by means of her constant complaints about Ted not having a proper job. 'I'll have my own husband, thank you,' Sylvia wrote in her diary, as if addressing her mother. 'You won't kill him the way you killed my father.' Ted had 'sex as strong as it comes'. He supported her in body and soul by feeding her bread and poems. She loved him and wanted to be always hugging him. She loved his work and the way he was always changing and making everything new. She loved the smell of him and the way their bodies fitted together as if they were 'made in the same body-shop to do just that'. She loved 'his warmth and his bigness and his being-there and his making and his jokes and his stories and what he reads and how he likes fishing and walks and pigs and foxes and little animals and is honest and not vain or fame-crazy'. 'And', she goes on, 'how he shows his gladness for what I cook him and joy for when I make something, a poem or a cake, and how he is troubled when I am unhappy and wants to do anything so I can fight out my soul-battles'.[41]

Life wasn't all bad. There was fresh fish. Luke Myers came through on a short visit, and they reminisced about Cambridge days. Ted and Sylvia were both getting poems accepted. Ted heard that he had won the Guinness Poetry Award (£300) for 'The Thought-Fox'. He received a treasured letter of congratulations from T. S. Eliot at Faber and Faber. The grand old man said how impressed he had been when he first read the typescript of the book and how delighted he was to have Ted on the Faber list.[42] And in Boston there was the proper literary scene that they craved: a reading by Truman Capote, dinner-parties with Robert Lowell, intense discussions about poetry at the apartment of poet Stanley Kunitz (Ted did most of the talking, Sylvia sitting quietly with a cup of tea), a meeting with the now old and rather deaf but still legendary Robert Frost. Ted loved hearing stories about one of his favourite poets, the very English Edward Thomas, who had been inspired by Frost to turn from prose to verse only a couple of years before his death on the Western Front.

Sylvia sat in on Lowell's poetry classes at Boston University, and he read both her work and Ted's. Lying on the bed in the Elm Street apartment earlier in the year, Ted had written a poem called 'Pike'. Lowell said it was a masterpiece.[43] Leonard Baskin admired it too, and reproduced 150 copies of it privately under his personal imprint, the Gehenna Press. This was Ted's first 'broadside'. The title was in red, the poem in black, and there was an illustrative woodcut by an artist friend of Baskin's, portraying two pike, one in black and the other in green. 'Pike' also appeared in a group of five immensely powerful Hughes poems in the summer 1959 issue of a magazine called *Audience: A Quarterly of Literature and the Arts*. The four others were 'Nicholas Ferrer', 'Thrushes', 'The Bull Moses' and 'The Voyage'. A couple of months earlier, another magazine had published 'Roosting Hawk', which he had written sitting at his work-table one morning in Willow Street. He told his parents that he was finding that the key to a creative day was an early night and an early start. He was hitting his stride and would soon have enough good poems for a second collection. He was also starting work on a play. They went to tea with Peter Davison in his apartment across the Charles River in Cambridge. He gave Ted a copy of Jung's *The Undiscovered Self,* which chimed perfectly with the ideas he was exploring. 'The Jung is splendid,' he told Davison in his thank-you letter, 'one of the basic notions of my play.'[44]

In January 1959 they acquired a tiger-striped kitten and called it Sappho. She was said to be a granddaughter of Thomas Mann's cat, a suitably literary pedigree. In April, Ted won a $5,000 award from the Guggenheim Foundation, in no small measure due to the support of Eliot. He wrote to thank him, signing off the letter with a dry allusion to the famous opening line of *The Waste Land*: 'I hope you are well, and enjoying April.'[45]

While living in the cramped Willow Street apartment, they were visited by Rollie McKenna, a diminutive Texan portrait photographer who was a genius with a Leica III camera fitted with a Japanese Nikkor screw lens of the kind used by *Life* magazine photographers in the Korean War. She had immortalised Dylan Thomas in two images, one with pout and cigarette, the other 'bound, Prometheus-like, in vine-tendrils (his idea), against the white wall of her house in America'.[46] Now she would capture Ted and Sylvia in images that would be published in the year of Plath's death in a book called *The Modern Poets: An American–British Anthology*, which included a real rarity in the form of a photograph of T. S. Eliot that he liked. The photograph of Ted, somewhat in Fifties Teddy-boy mode, shows him tanned, relaxed, leaning back, his tie artfully dishevelled but his hair for once swept back without the trademark lick over his forehead. His eyes melt the spectator. Ted and Sylvia were also photographed at work together: husband and wife as Team Poetry.

That spring saw the publication of *Life Studies*, Robert Lowell's first new volume for eight years. It was immediately recognised as a literary landmark. For one thing, it contained a distinctive mix of poetry and short prose memoirs. For another, in contrast to the intricate formality of Lowell's earlier work, the poems moved seamlessly between metrical regularity and free verse. The language had a new informality and the subject matter was frequently very personal.

A review in the *Nation* by the critic M. L. Rosenthal described the book as 'confessional'. The name stuck and Lowell, quite unintentionally, found himself labelled as the leader of a new school of American poetry. For Ted and Sylvia, it was exciting to be around Lowell at this time. Sylvia found in *Life Studies* a licence to write more direct poetic confessions of her own. Ted deeply admired the technical accomplishment, but was more sceptical about the personal content. 'He goes mad occasionally,' Ted told Danny Weissbort in a letter about Lowell, 'and the poems in his book, the main body of them, are written round a bout of madness, before and after. They are mainly Autobiographical.' At the heart of the collection was 'Waking in the Blue', Lowell's great poem about his period of confinement in a secure ward at the McLean mental hospital: 'We are all old-timers, / Each of us holds a locked razor.'[47] 'AutoBiography [sic]', Ted concluded his sermon inspired by *Life Studies*, was 'the only subject matter really left to Americans'. The thing about Americans was that their only real grounding was their selves and their family, 'Never a locality, or a community, or an organisation of ideas, or a private imagination'.[48] He was thinking about Sylvia as well as Lowell.

In a letter to Luke Myers written a couple of months later, he focused on a different aspect of contemporary American poetry, reflecting on William Carlos Williams's preoccupation with 'sexy girls, noble whores, the flower of poverty, tough straight talk' and describing E. E. Cummings (whom he considered a genius, a fool and a huckster) as 'one of the first symptoms and general encouragements of the modern literary syphilis – verseless, styleless, characterless all-inclusive undifferentiated yelling assertion of the Great simplifying burden-lifting God orgasm – whether by drug, negro, masked nympho or strange woman in the dark'.[49] His own recent poetry, by contrast, was combining a tough American assurance with the earth-grounded English eye of *Hawk*, without going into free form or confessional mode.

If there was a like-minded American poet, it certainly wasn't someone in the tradition of 'electronic noise' coming out of the suicidal Hart Crane, whom Lowell in *Life Studies* called the Shelley of his age. Rather, it was the Southern agrarian John Crowe Ransom. Behind every word of Ransom's poetry, Ted told Luke, repeating some of the Leavisite language of their Cambridge days, 'is a whole human being, alert, sensitive, reacting precisely and finely to his observations'. As for British poetry, it needed to get back to this kind of wholeness, the tight weave of 'the thick rope of human nature', which had been found in the old ballads, in Chaucer, Shakespeare, Webster, Blake, Wordsworth, Keats, the dialect poems of Burns, but virtually no one since. For a century and a half the English sensibility had got too hung up on 'the stereotype English voice' of the gentleman.[50] What was needed was a distinctly ungentlemanly tone and matter, a new poetry of working-class roots and rural rootedness. This is what he was developing in his new book, which was nearing completion. The name of D. H. Lawrence is strikingly absent from the genealogy outlined here: perhaps out of a certain 'anxiety of influence', Ted is suppressing the name of the writer who came immediately before him as a northern, working-class voice with a sensitivity to the raw forces of nature, an interest in myth and archetype, an unashamed openness of sexual energy, and a distinctly lubricious attitude to the female body (Lawrence was the poet who compared the 'wonderful moist conductivity' of a fig to a woman's genitals).[51]

Leonard Baskin agreed to consider doing a design for the cover of the new book. Ted gave him a lead by suggesting that the 'general drift' of the poems could be summed up as 'Man as an elaborately perfected intestine, or upright weasel'.[52] Ted proposed Baskin to Faber, but did not get the response he wanted; they went for a geometric dustwrapper design instead. In a separate development, though, Faber did accept 'a book of 8 poems for children', each of which was about a relative: a sister who was really a crow, an aunt devoured by a thistle, and so on. It was published under the title *Meet My Folks!*

Ted jokingly told Charles Monteith, his editor at Faber, that it was his own equivalent of Lowell's *Life Studies*, which had included intense poems of family memory and marital discord with such titles as 'My Last Afternoon with Uncle Devereux Winslow', 'Grandparents' and 'Man and Wife'. It would be a long time before Ted started publishing pieces about his family, let alone his marriage, in this 'confessional' voice.

Ted and Sylvia received a joint invitation to spend two months in the autumn at Yaddo, a rural retreat for writers in upstate New York. Though invited to apply, their proposals still had to be graded by the writers who were Yaddo's assessors (Richard Eberhart, John Cheever and Morton Zabel). Both applications received a good mix of As and Bs.[53] They were in.

They decided that, before taking up residence and then returning to England, they should set off to see America. They packed boxes for the journey, boxes in readiness for Yaddo and boxes for home. Ted wrote to his parents, telling them in great detail (complete with a little drawing) about the tent they had bought, discounted from $90 to $65. It had a sewn-in waterproof groundsheet, something unheard of in the camping days of his youth, and even a meshed window. Aurelia Plath bought them air mattresses that folded down to the size of pillowcases and thick puffy sleeping bags with zips all round (meaning that they could be joined together for cuddles on chilly nights in the wild). She threw in an assortment of other camping gadgets for good measure, and they had a trial night sleeping in the tent on the back lawn of her house in Elmwood Road, Wellesley. Ted pronounced it as comfortable a night as he had ever had. Any apprehensions that cleanliness-minded Sylvia would not be the camping type were swiftly dispelled. They said good-bye and off they went in Aurelia's car, on a ten-week road trip through mountain, prairie and desert, all the way to California and back.

First they headed for the Great Lakes, crossing the Canadian border into Ontario. They took snapshots of each other by the tent and the waterside. In the Algonquin Provincial Park, Sylvia looked happier than she had ever looked, as a deer took blueberries from her hand. Then they went west to Wisconsin, where they camped by Lake Superior in the field of a kindly Polish fisherman near a village with the wonderful name of Cornucopia. His daughter took them fishing, but there wasn't much in the way of catch, since lampreys had eaten nearly all the trout in the lake.

Then it was across the prairies, under big skies and through the Dakota Badlands. There were fierce electric storms, the earth was a sinister red. It was a place where seams of lignite ignited spontaneously, burning slowly for years or even centuries, turning the clay soil to brick shale. The land reeked of sulphur and tar. 'This is evil,' Ted remembered Sylvia saying. 'This is real evil.' There seemed to be some strange consonance between this America and the dark recesses of her mind. 'Maybe it's the earth,' she said, or 'Maybe it's ourselves.' The emptiness seemed to be sucking something out of them, the dark electricity within 'Frightening the earth, and frightening us'.[54] 'The Badlands', which went through dozens of drafts before reaching its final form in *Birthday Letters*, was one of his first poems in the loose style of a journal.

Stepping further westward, they crossed Montana. This was real cattle country, empty wilderness, not unlike the Yorkshire Moors, but with grass and richer soil, and without any valleys. At roadside cafés, you got 'steak the size of a plate, home-made berry pie piled with icecream, your coffee cup filled up as fast as you emptied it (for the price of just one cup)'.[55] This was the real America, the generous and friendly people real Americans. After a long drive southwards, they arrived at the Yellowstone National Park, which was becoming more famous than ever with the advent on television the previous year of the animated cartoon character Yogi Bear. Ted told his parents that it was like the Alps, but with bears. They counted nineteen on the road in the first 30 miles after entering the National Park. The bears would wander up to people's cars and stand on their hind legs, hoping for food. 'People get regularly mauled, trying to feed them,' Edith and Bill were informed.[56] On their first night in the park, Ted heard one sniffing round their tent, which was only 10 feet from a trash can.

On the second night they returned at dusk from a drive around the Grand Loop of the park, seeing the geysers and the hot pools, only to find a large black bear standing over their trash can. It lumbered off when it was caught in their headlights. They locked their food in the boot of the car and washed down the picnic table and benches. At 'the blue moonlit hour of quarter to three' Sylvia was woken from a dream in which their car was blown to pieces with a great crash. The crashing sound was real: her first thought was that a bear had smashed open the car with a great cuff and started eating the engine (a seed here for Ted's story about the metal-devouring Iron Man?). Ted, also woken by the crash, had the more prosaic thought that the bear had knocked their cooking pans off the picnic table. They lay listening to 'grunts, snuffles, clattering can lids'. Then there was 'a bumpity rolling noise as the bear bowled a tin' past their tent. Sylvia peered out of the tent screen and, 'not ten feet away', saw a huge bear 'guzzling at a tin'. In the morning they discovered that the noise was that of 'the black-and-gilt figured cookie tin' in which they kept their fruit and nut bars. Though they had secured most of their food in the boot, this had been on the back seat of the car inside Sylvia's closed red bag. The bear had smashed the car window, torn the bag open and found the tin, which it had also managed to open. The bag had also contained Ritz crackers and Hydrox cookies, which had been eaten, and a selection of postcards, which she found in the morning among the debris left from the visit. The top card, a picture of moose antlers, was turned upside down. And a postcard of a bear was face up on the ground with the paw print of an actual bear on it.[57]

Having consumed the contents of the cookie tin, the bear had gone away. Ted and Sylvia had lain awake, terrified that it might come back and rip its way into their tent. It did indeed return, just as dawn broke. Ted stood up and looked out of the window of the tent to see it slurping away at the oranges that they had left on the ledge behind the back seat of the car. 'It's the big brown one', he told Sylvia. They had heard that this was the nasty sort. Scared off by the sound of 'The Camp Ranger's car, doing the morning rounds', it ran away, tripped on a guy rope and nearly tumbled into Ted and Sylvia's tent.[58]

The story went around the camp. A Yellowstone regular told them to smear the tent with kerosene because bears hated the smell. Someone else suggested red pepper, but they decided that the best thing would be to move to a campsite higher up the hillside and not too close to any garbage cans. Ted appended a handwritten postscript to Sylvia's typewritten letter home: 'Well, I wanted to tell about the bear, but Sivvy's done that better than I even remembered it.'[59]

In the washroom, Sylvia told the story to another woman, who replied that the bears were particularly bad that year. On the Sunday night, just before Ted and Sylvia's arrival in the park, another woman had tried to scare one off with a flashlight and been mauled to death. This gave Sylvia the idea of, in Ted's later phrase, transforming their own 'dud scenario into a fiction'.[60] 'The Fifty-Ninth Bear' is one of her most effective short stories. It concerns a couple called Norton and Sadie. Norton was the surname of both a former boyfriend and the character in the television sitcom *The Honeymooners* whose vocal mannerisms inspired Yogi Bear.[61] Sadie was one of the names Sylvia thought of using for the autobiographical protagonist of 'Falcon Yard'. They count fifty-eight bears as they drive round the Grand Loop at Yellowstone. When they are woken in the night by the sound of another bear, Norton goes outside and sees the smashed car window. He waves a flashlight to scare the bear away, but is cuffed over the head and killed: 'It was the last bear, her bear, the fifty-ninth.' The sinister aspect of the story is that Norton's arrogance has in some sense made Sadie want him to die: in daydreams, he imagined himself as a widower, a hollow-cheeked, Hamletesque figure in somber suits, given to standing, abstracted, ravaged by casual winds, on lonely promontories and at the rail of ships, Sadie's slender, elegant white body embalmed, in a kind of bas relief, on the central tablet of his mind. It never occurred to Norton that his wife might outlive him. Her sensuousness, her pagan enthusiasms, her inability to argue in terms of anything but her immediate emotions – this was too flimsy, too gossamery a stuff to survive out from under the wings of his guardianship.[62]

Ted gave his own version of the story in the longest poem in *Birthday Letters*, also called 'The 59th Bear'. In the rear-view mirror of memory, he vividly revisited 'the off rear window of the car',

> Wrenched out – a star of shatter splayed
> From a single talon's leverage hold,
> A single claw forced into the hair-breadth odour
> Had ripped the whole sheet out. He'd leaned in
> And on claw hooks lifted out our larder.
> He'd left matted hairs. I glued them in my Shakespeare.[63]

Whereas Sylvia's story exits the husband to death, pursued by the fifty-ninth bear, Ted captures a trophy of the animal encounter and gives it to his Shakespeare. One may assume that he pasted the matted hairs somewhere near the famous stage direction in *The Winter's Tale*. He ended the poem by reflecting on Sylvia's short story, reading the bear as an image of the death that was hurtling towards her rather than her husband.

After leaving Yellowstone, they drove through the Grand Teton mountain range, stopping for photographs, then south to Salt Lake City and Big Cottonwood Canyon, where, as a reward after their immensely long drive, they treated themselves to a huge meal of Kentucky fried chicken, rolls and honey, potatoes and gravy. They swam in the great Salt Lake, discovering with amazement and delight that you really didn't sink, could almost sit up on the water as if in an armchair. Then it was across the desert into the sunset, passing into Nevada, where they stopped for the night to camp, Sylvia cooking the last of their Yellowstone trout, 'with corn niblets, a tomato and lettuce salad and milk'.[64] At last they reached California, camping near Lake Tahoe, then stopping in 'the lovely palm-tree shaded Capitol Park of Sacramento' – 'the site of the mine that started the gold rush' – in 114-degree heat.[65] They liked the holiday feel of California, the mix of mountains, forests, fertile farmland. Sylvia wrote of the lushness, Ted of the fruit.

At last they reached the sea, intending to camp at Stinson Beach State Park, just over 20 miles outside San Francisco. But their guide-book was out of date. The supposed campsite had been turned into a parking lot. Sylvia, desperately tired from yet another mammoth drive, was on the verge of tears. Ted suggested that they should try their luck in town. They had cold beer and fried chicken at a café and the gener-ous owner suggested that they park their car in his lot and sleep under the stars on the beach. For Sylvia, it was one of the best nights of her life, not least because she sensed new life quickening inside her. Her period was due and it had not yet come. Away from the stress of Smith, she had become pregnant early in the summer.

Ted did not quite share the sense of climax. He wrote several drafts of a poem about Stinson Beach under the title 'Early August 1959', but did not include it in *Birthday Letters*. 'We got to the Pacific,' he wrote. 'What was so symbolic about the Pacific?' Whatever it was, they had made it. But the sunset wasn't as spectacular as it should have been and it was foggy when they woke up in the morning. Still, they had 'kept to the programme of romance / Slept in our sleeping bags under the stars / Tried to live up to the setting'. He was then cheered when 'a phone-call from within sight of the sea' brought the news that Faber and Faber had accepted his second volume of poetry.[66] They were not sure about his proposed title 'The Feast of Lupercal', because there had been two recent novels of exactly that name (one of them a Faber bestseller), so he decided to call it 'Lupercalia' instead.[67]

They dipped into San Francisco to get the car window repaired. Then it was a beach camp halfway to Los Angeles, then a relaxing stay with Sylvia's Aunt Frieda in Pasadena. Her hot water and other amen-ities were much appreciated and her name, with its echo of D. H. Lawrence's feisty wife, gave them an idea for the baby, should it prove to be a girl. Their eastward journey began with the Mojave Desert and the Grand Canyon. At that grandest of all sights, 'America's Delphi', they sought a blessing on the baby in Sylvia's womb as a reward for their pilgrimage. Navajo dancers, standing on the rim of the greatest gorge in the world, beat a drum, sounding an echo that thirty years later Ted imagined he could hear, faintly, in the voice of his daughter.[68] The primitive power of the drumbeat would become a key resource in his theatre work. More prosaically, when they returned to the car their water-cooling bag, which had crossed the Mojave slung under the front bumper, had been stolen.

From the Grand Canyon they drove all the way across to New Orleans, then north to Tennessee to stay with Luke Myers's family. The gigantic trip ended with sightseeing in Washington DC and a stay with Sylvia's Uncle Frank near Philadelphia, before they at last returned home to the hot tubs and home baking of New England. Aurelia thought that they both looked tanned and well, but Sylvia was tired and worried about the pregnancy. She had a history of gynaeco-logical complications, so she still did not feel sure that there really was a baby growing inside her.

Yaddo is an artists' community located on a 400-acre estate in Saratoga Springs. It was founded in 1900 by a wealthy financier called Spencer Trask and his wife, Katrina, who wrote poetry herself. Left without immediate heirs by the deaths of their four young children, the Trasks decided to bequeath their palatial home to future generations of writers, composers, painters and other creative artists. Katrina had a vision of generations of talented men and women yet unborn walking the lawns of Yaddo, 'creating, creating, creating'. The idea was to nurture the creative process by providing an opportunity for artists to work without interruption in peaceful, green surroundings. The great American short-story writer John Cheever would write that the 'forty or so acres on which the principal buildings of Yaddo stand have seen more distinguished activity in the arts than any other piece of ground in the English-speaking community and perhaps the world'.[69]

When Ted and Sylvia arrived just after Labor Day, the main house had been closed for winter. They were given spacious rooms in the clapperboard West House, among the trees. Each of them had a sep-arate 'studio', Sylvia's on the top floor of the house and Ted's out in the woods – the perfect place for him. 'A regular little house to himself', Sylvia wrote to her mother, 'all glassed in and surrounded by pines, with a wood stove for the winter, a cot, and huge desk'.[70] A writing hut away from the main house would be his salvation at Court Green in later years. The chance to live together but work apart was exactly what they needed. Meals were taken care of and the food was very good, a welcome change from the campground cookery of the summer. Breakfast was available from eight till nine, lunchboxes were then collected and taken to each resident's studio, and in the evening they all gathered for dinner. Being a quiet season, there were only a dozen artists in residence, including painters, an interesting composer and a couple of other poets whose names were not familiar to them.

One of the painters, Howard Rogovin, did portraits of both Sylvia and Ted. For Sylvia, he set up his easel in the old greenhouse. To the sound of 'rain in the conifers', he painted Sylvia lifted out of herself 'In a flaming of oils', her 'lips exact'. But he also seemed to catch a shadow on her shoulder, a dark marauding 'doppelgänger'.[71] At one point, a graceful snake slid across the dusty floor of the hot greenhouse. Both this portrait and the one of Ted, which was said to be less successful, are lost.[72]

The composer was Chou Wen-chung, a United States immigrant from Shandong in China. A protégé of the radical experimentalist Edgar Varèse, he sought to integrate Eastern and Western classical (and modernist) musical traditions. They struck up a friendship and Ted began work on a libretto for him, for an oratorio based on the Tibetan Book of the Dead. The original title, *Bardo Thödol*, literally means 'Liberation through Hearing during the Intermediate State'. These 'intermediate states' included the dream state, the moment of death in which the clear light of reality is experienced, and the 'bardo of rebirth', which involved hallucinatory images of men and women erotically entwined. The project was never finished, but it took Ted into territory that he would make his own in almost all his later mythic works.[73]

His main project at Yaddo was his play (now lost, save for a few fragments), 'The House of Taurus'. Sylvia described it in a letter home written in early October: 'a symbolic drama based on the Euripides play *The Bacchae*, only set in a modern industrial community under a paternalistic ruler'.[74] She hoped that it would at least get a staged reading, but explained that she had not yet typed it up.

During the weeks at Yaddo Ted also revised one or two of the poems in his forthcoming 'Lupercalia' collection, but for poetic development it was more of a breakthrough moment for Sylvia. Before Yaddo, her verse had been highly accomplished but somehow brittle. A self-description in a journal entry of late 1955 was harsh but apt: 'Roget's trollop, parading words and tossing off bravado for an audience' (*Roget's Thesaurus* was the *vade mecum* of writers looking for unusual words for ordinary things).[75] Very few Plath poems written before Yaddo stick in the mind; almost all the hundred or so that Sylvia wrote thereafter sear themselves into the consciousness of the attentive reader. Years earlier, Plath had dreamed of gathering forces into a tight tense ball for the artistic leap. At Yaddo, she made that leap.

On 10 October 1959, she wrote in her journal: 'Feel oddly barren. My sickness is when words draw in their horns and the physical world refuses to be ordered, recreated, arranged and selected. When will I break into a new line of poetry? Feel trite.' It was certainly odd to feel barren when she was at last pregnant. Then on the 13th: 'Very depressed today. Unable to write a thing. Menacing gods. I feel outcast on a cold star.' Ted told her to 'get desperate'. On the night of the 21st, she felt 'animal solaces' as she lay with him, warm in bed. The next day, walking in the woods in the frosty morning light, she found the 'Ambitious seeds of a long poem made up of separate sections: Poem on her Birthday. To be a dwelling on madhouse, nature. The superb identity, selfhood of things. To be honest with what I know and have known. To be true to my own weirdnesses.'[76] Madhouse, nature, identity, self, weirdness: in 'Poem for a Birthday', Sylvia began for the first time to write poetry overtly about her suicide attempt, mental breakdown and electro-convulsive therapy, albeit refracted through a symbolic narrative of descent and rebirth.

Within a fortnight the sequence was 'miraculously' written. The title came from the fact that her birthday fell halfway through the process of composition. What was it that released the flow? The example of Lowell confronting his nervous breakdown in *Life Studies* was crucial. Ted, who was convinced that this was indeed the turning point in her poetic career, pointed to the influence of the poetry of Theodore Roethke, which she read in the Yaddo library (where she also renewed her acquaintance with the wonderfully confident and supple poetry of Elizabeth Bishop). Conversations with Ted about the death and rebirth structure of *Bardo Thödol* would also have played a part. But her journal offers other clues. It reveals that she was 'electrified' by the consonance between the imagery she was developing and the language of Jung's *Symbols of Transformation*, another book in the well-stocked Yaddo library. And a couple of days earlier, her creativity released by some breathing exercises that Ted taught her, she had written two poems that pleased her, one to 'Nicholas', the name they had chosen for their child if it proved to be a boy, and the other on 'the old father-worship subject'.[77] The father who had died when she was eight and the unborn child in her womb. She was on a cusp, about eighteen weeks pregnant. Did the baby quicken and give its first kick at this time? Before her stood tomorrow.

They returned to Wellesley just before Thanksgiving. Sylvia was now noticeably pregnant. Aurelia later remembered Ted working away in the upstairs bedroom while Sylvia 'sorted and packed the huge trunk' that they had set up in the breezeway. On the day they left, 'Sylvia was wearing her hair in a long braid down her back with a little red wool cap on her head.' She looked like a teenage girl going off to boarding school. As the train pulled out of the station, Ted shouted out, 'We'll be back in two years!'[78] He was looking forward to home, and English beer, having found the American variety 'unspeakable and unspewable'.[79]

On a clear blue day in March 1959, Ted and Sylvia had gone out from their little Willow Street apartment to Winthrop, the southernmost point of Boston's North Shore. In the morning, Sylvia had been with her psychoanalyst, probing further at her feelings about her dead father. It was time, they decided, for her to visit Otto Plath's grave in Winthrop for the first time. When they found it, she felt cheated by the plain and unassuming flat stone, tempted to dig him up in order to 'prove he existed and really was dead'.[80]

Then they walked over some rocks beside the ocean. The wind was bitter. Their feet got wet and they picked up shells with cold hands. Ted walked alone to the end of the bar, in his black coat, 'defining the distance of stones and stones humped out of the sea'.[81] Afterwards, Sylvia wrote a poem called 'Man in Black'. It was soon accepted by the *New Yorker*, one of her first big successes in getting her work into high-profile print. It catches the moment: the breakwaters absorbing the force of the sea, the March ice on the rock pools, 'And you' – Ted, that is – striding out across the white stones:

in your dead
Black coat, black shoes, and your
Black hair ...[82]

There he stands, a 'Fixed vortex' on the edge of the land, holding it all together, the stones, the air, Sylvia's life and her father's death. The line-break catapults the word 'dead' into double sense. At one level, Ted's coat is dead black in the sense of pitch black. At another level, it is black because black is the colour of death. Sylvia's black imagination has indeed dug Otto out of his grave – and reincarnated him in her husband.

That is how Ted read the poem. In *Birthday Letters*, he made a point of placing his reply-poem, which he called 'Black Coat', after the long journal-like poems about the road trip. In terms of strict chronology, it should have been before. But he wanted to make it into a sum-mation of their time in America. He places himself looking across the sea, ready for home. He remembers the moment in the Algonquin Provincial Park when he had photographed Sylvia feeding a wild deer with freshly picked blueberries. Something about the idea of a camera makes him uncomfortable. It is the same sensation as that provoked by the sinister image behind Sylvia's shoulder in the portrait that Howard Rogovin had painted in the Yaddo greenhouse. A shadow, a double, a whisper of death. He then imagines Sylvia taking a photograph of him. Perhaps she had brought a camera to snap her father's grave, or perhaps it is the metaphoric photograph of the poem 'Man in Black' that is entering her mind at this moment. Either way, he feels as if he has stepped 'Into the telescopic sights / Of the paparazzo sniper' nested in Sylvia's brown eyes. He feels as if she is pinning him with a 'double image', 'double exposure' (the name she would choose three years later for her lost novel about the disintegration of their marriage). He feels as if her dead father has just crawled out of the sea. He 'did not feel' Otto sliding into him as Sylvia's 'lenses tightened'.[83]

Or at least all this is what he thought he thought when, years later, he began to write the series of letter-poems that first took their overall title from the deer, then from the black coat, and finally from the poem that Sylvia had written at Yaddo, 'for a Birthday'.

11

Famous Poet

When I got here (having left in 1957 as a complete unknown)
I found myself really quite famous and was deluged by
invitations to do this, give readings, do that, meet so-and-so,
etc, and many doors were comfortably wide open that I had
never dreamed of being able to enter and places such as the
B.B.C., which I had been trying to penetrate for years,
suddenly received me as guest of honour.

(Ted Hughes to Aurelia and Warren Plath, December 1960)[1]

At Yaddo, Sylvia had a dream in which Marilyn Monroe appeared to her as 'a kind of fairy godmother', gave her an expert manicure and advice on hairdressers, invited her for Christmas and promised her 'a new flowering life'.[2] Dream Sylvia told Marilyn how much she and Arthur Miller meant to her and Ted: the dream couple. But perhaps because the new flowering life involved motherhood, Sylvia stopped imitating the Marilyn look. When Olwyn arrived to spend Christmas 1959 at the Beacon, the first thing she saw was Ted and Sylvia standing at the sitting-room door, waiting to welcome her. Sylvia's hair was mousy brown. Olwyn thought that she had stopped bleaching it (in fact, the last time she bleached it had been in 1954; thereafter, it was naturally lightened by sun-worship). Olwyn had not realised until that moment that she was not a natural blonde. Sylvia, she thought, had become less the 'good-looking girl' and more 'a contained individual'.[3]

On Boxing Day, Sylvia sat by a roaring coal fire in the little second parlour of the Beacon, digesting a light supper of creamed leftover turkey and mushrooms that she had made for the family, and wrote to her mother as the rain lashed against the triple window and a gale howled. This was what the weather had been like for the entire two weeks of their stay. She told Aurelia that to feel the Yorkshire weather she should 'reread Ted's poem "Wind": it's perfect'. Olwyn, she said, was 'very nice, a beautiful blonde, slim girl, my height and size, with yellow-green eyes and delicate, graceful bone structure'. Sylvia said that she liked Olwyn immensely and got on much better with her 'now that she's really accepted me as Ted's wife'.[4] Olwyn herself was not so sure. She thought that Sylvia overreacted to small incidents, such as some sharp words about a borrowed dressing-gown.

After the Christmas and New Year festivities, Ted and Sylvia went to London. They began in a bed-and-breakfast, then stayed in one of Daniel Huws's father's flats back at 18 Rugby Street, which had had a makeover since they had been away. There were now sinks in each flat and running water in their tiny kitchens. They threw themselves into house-hunting, looking in various parts of London before deciding on the Primrose Hill area near Regent's Park, where Bill Merwin and his posh English wife Dido had a lovely flat.

After one or two disappointments, such as a lovely furnished ground-floor flat that they were going to take until the landlord said 'no children', Dido pointed them in the direction of a third-floor flat in a five-storey house in Chalcot Square. The area was rather run-down, but beautifully placed close to both the park and the gentle green slope of Primrose Hill itself. The flat, which was in the process of being refurbished, was small, with only a single bedroom. They would have to furnish it themselves. But it was cheap – six guineas a week – and the shops, the zoo and the green spaces were all within walking distance, perfect for a young mother with a pram. The Merwins were near by and Dido was friendly with the local GP, Dr Horder. They registered with the practice and the obstetrician took on Sylvia. Home birth was the norm in those days.

They got their books and boxes from Yorkshire, negotiated with the workmen who were still sanding the floors and painting the walls, and were in by the beginning of February. Sylvia wrote 'You're', her bubbly poem to the baby in her womb. They decorated the walls of the living room with the Gehenna Press 'Pike', some Baskin prints and a greatly enlarged copy of an engraving of the great maternal goddess Isis from 'one of Ted's astrological books'.[5] The original print had been their 'lightest / Bit of luggage' when they drove round America.[6] Ted borrowed an old collapsible card-table from the Merwins and set it up in a small alcove in the hallway, intended as a place to hang coats. It was like a tiny cave – though the Merwins called it 'the Black Hole of Calcutta' – and he found he could concentrate there and get on with his radio play *The House of Aries* (not to be confused with 'The House of Taurus', which had stalled). He looked back on this cubbyhole as one of the best workspaces he ever had, though at the time he complained in the pub to Luke Myers that Sylvia was always inter-rupting him when he was trying to work there. One day he got so impatient that he decided to count the number of times she called out 'Ted' or 'Teddy'. The score reached 104 by lunchtime.[7]

Ten days after moving in, Sylvia signed a contract for her first book of poems, to be named *The Colossus* (the title of one of her best Yaddo poems) and dedicated to Ted, 'that paragon who has encouraged me through all my glooms about it'.[8] She proudly told her mother that the book had been accepted by the first British publisher to whom she sent the typescript, William Heinemann, whose list included Somerset Maugham, Evelyn Waugh and D. H. Lawrence. She and Ted celebrated with veal and mushrooms (her pregnancy craving?) at a little upstairs Italian restaurant in Soho. James Michie, her editor, told her that the book would be published in October, as close as they could make it to the date of her birthday, which struck her as a typical example of British kindness and pleased her greatly because of the centrality of 'Poem for a Birthday' to the collection.

Despite the advanced state of Sylvia's pregnancy, they started going to the theatre and the cinema with the Merwins. Ted did a poetry reading in Oxford and Sylvia was very impressed with the city and its colleges – it was much grander than Cambridge and they both had a pang that they had gone to the wrong university. Ted's sociability sometimes caused strain. On one occasion, Olwyn, over from Paris again, came to lunch with a friend, Janet Crosbie-Hill. Luke Myers was also there. Olwyn brought a cuddly toy, 'a bottle of best cham-pagne' to celebrate the upcoming birth and 'good French cologne' to cool Sylvia. She received no thanks, except from Ted. After lunch, Bill Merwin came round. Sylvia was charming to him, describing 'a rather beautiful flying dream full of lovely creatures', but Olwyn thought that she was insufferably rude in ignoring her friend Janet. Sylvia, in turn, thought that her wishes were being ignored: Olwyn and Janet smoked the whole time, and objected when she kept opening the window to get some fresh air into the tiny flat. There was talk of Merwin taking Ted and Sylvia for a spin in the country in his little sports car, but this did not happen, so there was 'a strained walk on Primrose Hill', during which Sylvia seemed very aggressive. Ted walked Olwyn and her friend the short distance to Chalk Farm Underground station. Olwyn asked him if he was aware how upsetting Sylvia's behaviour was, and he could only shrug.[9]

Towards the end of March, Ted received a telegram telling him that *The Hawk in the Rain* had won the Somerset Maugham Award, a prize of £500 to be spent on foreign travel. They planned to find a place in the sun as soon as the baby was old enough to go abroad.

Frieda Rebecca Hughes was born, five days after the due date, on 1 April 1960. In the early days, Ted sometimes called her Rebecca. The labour was remarkably brief for a first child (four and a half hours), with assistance from an Indian midwife, no doctor and no drugs, other than the lingering wooziness of the two sleeping pills Sylvia had taken the previous night – she had been so determined not to have the baby on April Fool's Day that she had convinced herself she wouldn't and therefore allowed herself to take the pills. Ted did what husbands were supposed to do (hand-holding, back-rubbing, kettle-boiling) and took some credit for the brevity of the labour. He had got into the habit of hypnotising Sylvia to make her relax and believe that she would have an easy, short labour. Since he had previously had a number of successes, such as making her believe that her period would begin on a particular day and be over in forty-eight hours, it stood to reason that his hypnotic arts had played a role.[10]

Ted immediately cast the baby's horoscope and sent it to Olwyn. It suggested that Frieda was going to be 'very bright', perhaps even 'too bright'. Sylvia added a postscript to the letter, addressing it 'Dearest Olwyn', agreeing that Ted's hypnosis had made the short labour possible, and saying that the baby had Hughes hands and a Plath nose.[11] The flat overflowed with flowers, telegrams and cards. Ted went out and bought daffodils, a lucky silver thimble for the baby and a 'pile of old *New Yorkers*' for Sylvia. He had correctly surmised that, to begin with, all she would be good for were the jokes and cartoons, then a few poems and short stories. But she was soon taking the baby out and about. At the age of seventeen days, Frieda was installed in her cot in a makeshift crèche on the grassy lawn outside the National Gallery overlooking Trafalgar Square as the 'Ban the Bomb!' marchers of the Campaign for Nuclear Disarmament arrived from Aldermaston. Sylvia was delighted that her daughter's first proper outing was to 'a protest against the insanity of world-annihilation'.[12] Bill Merwin had gone on the three-day march all the way from the Atomic Weapons Establishment in Berkshire. Ted and Dido watched the crowd from a different vantage point, the Albert Memorial. The threat of nuclear apocalypse hung as a shadow-image over many of his poems throughout the Sixties.

At the age of twenty-one days, Frieda was left for the first time with a Babyminder Service while her parents went to a cocktail party at Faber and Faber. The great T. S. Eliot was there, but they hardly spoke to him.

Ted and Faber had finally agreed on the title for his second collection: *Lupercal*. It came into the world exactly two weeks before Frieda. Ted explained his title to Olwyn. The feast of Lupercalia was a fertility rite in which 'various bachelors' ran naked through the streets of Rome, being splashed with goat and dog blood. Women who wanted to get pregnant stood in the way and held out their arms to be lashed with thongs wielded by the runners. This was supposed to make them fertile. Reading about it somehow made him think of God as 'devourer', 'mouth and gut', 'absolute power'.[13]

Nearly all the poems had been written on Cape Cod or in Elm Street or Willow Street, though 'Thrushes' went back to Eltisley Avenue days and 'Mayday on Holderness' was a late addition composed at Yaddo.[14] The rural England of his childhood was seen at a distance, through an American lens. There is a surviving early manuscript, entitled 'The Feast of Lupercal', with the return address Willow Street scratched out and replaced with 'c/o Plath, Elmwood Road, Wellesley, Mass, USA'. On the back of the poems, Ted scribbled notes about their origins.[15] These reveal that many of them were inspired by memories of the Manor Farm. So, for example, 'Sunstroke' recalls a field of grass being mown when he was nine, with men waiting in the four corners of the field to shoot the rabbits and foxes that emerged from the hay. The same scenario formed the basis of his short story

'The Harvesting', broadcast on the BBC (read by Ted himself) in December 1960.

Lupercal is alive with the apprehension of violence in places where readers would not normally expect to find it: 'Terrifying are the attent sleek thrushes on the lawn, / More coiled steel than living – a poised / Dark deadly eye' ('Thrushes'). 'Attent' is a brilliant choice of word, but there were false starts before he found it.[16] The originality of the language often comes from a trick learned from the Metaphysical poets he had studied at Cambridge: Dr Johnson had famously characterised their distinctive style as one in which 'the most heterogeneous ideas are yoked by violence together' and such yoking is exactly what Hughes achieves when moving from the watcher's envy of 'the single-mindedness of the thrushes' to the utter concentration of 'Mozart's brain' and then that of a 'shark's mouth'.[17]

This, without doubt, is Ted Hughes's best and most characteristic volume of poetry. All his trademark elements are there, more fully and finely honed than in his first book. His totemic beasts: hawk and fox in 'Crow Hill'; a photograph of 'the last wolf killed in Britain' in 'February'. His ability to imagine his way into the mind of an animal, whether bull ('The Bull Moses') or frog ('Bullfrog'). His love of water: 'An Otter' influenced by *Tarka*, the pike in the pond 'deep as England'.[18] His landscape: rock, sky and wind in 'Pennines in April'. His people: 'Dick Straightup', a real countryman from Heptonstall who, Ted explained in his manuscript notes, had died of pneumonia in the February before he wrote the poem (which he composed under the strong influence, in both form and content, of Edward Thomas's 'Lob'). 'I imagine the whole landscape – which he is now a part of,' Ted wrote of the old man, 'and I fancy that he has given up his human strength for the everlasting strength of the earth.'[19]

The subordination of humankind to the strength of the earth is one of the unifying themes of the volume. But, taken as a whole, *Lupercal*, with its closing poem 'Lupercalia' alluding to the rituals and the might of ancient Rome, is also alert to the rise and fall of empires, the capacity of humankind to destroy the earth in wars past and potentially future. He remembers the Great War in 'Wilfred Owen's Photographs'; 'A Retired Colonel' speaks from the heyday of the British Empire; a vestige of his father's experience of the Gallipoli disaster is summoned by the sea in 'Mayday on Holderness'; and the threat of nuclear warfare between America and Russia is the explicit starting point of 'A Woman Unconscious'.

The most famous poem in the collection – long a favourite of examination boards – is 'Hawk Roosting'. Spoken from the point of view of a bird of prey, holding Creation in its foot, contemplating its next kill ('No arguments assert my right … I am going to keep things like this'), it was glossed very simply by Hughes himself in his original notes on the collection: 'In this, I imagine the hawk speaking to himself. He is like a dictator, who thinks he is God and invincible.'[20] A few years later, telling the poet and BBC producer George MacBeth that 'Hawk Roosting' was the poem he wanted to read for a special edition of the radio programme *Poetry Now* to be recorded at the Edinburgh Festival, he said that if it was about violence, it was written to the text 'The truth kills everybody', and if the truth was 'ultimately, a totalitarian system' then his poem was indeed topical, but it wasn't to do with 'random, or civil or elemental violence'. Ultimately – though he doesn't explain how – it was 'about Peace'.[21] Interviewed many years later, he seemed to prevaricate between accepting and denying the reading of the hawk as a fascist, 'the symbol of some horrible genocidal dictator'. First he said, 'Actually what I had in mind is that in this hawk Nature is thinking. Simply Nature.' Then, in accordance with the way that his poetry developed from *Lupercal* through *Wodwo* to *Crow*, he invoked a Creation myth: 'It's not so simple maybe because Nature is no longer so simple. I intended some creator like the Jehovah in Job but more feminine. When Christianity kicked the devil out of Job what they actually kicked out was Nature' – now he is going into the argument of Graves's *White Goddess* (which he would further develop in his own *Shakespeare and the Goddess of Complete Being*) that the attack on the cult of Mary was the Reformation's banishment of the Goddess. Thereafter, Nature came to be regarded as 'the devil'. So the hawk has gone from being 'Isis, mother of the gods' to becoming 'Hitler's familiar spirit'.[22]

It is all very confusing, and becomes more so if one speculates about the unconscious influences on the poem, which was written during a morning sitting at the table in Willow Street. If Sylvia was beginning to think about her father's alleged sympathy for Hitler, is there something of Otto Plath in it? Does the proud roosting posture and the image of the strong talons evoke the American eagle, the national bird that Ted saw cut in stone on public buildings all around him during his time in New England? Were Cold War politics part of the story? Or is it better to follow the advice that Ted gave to so many of the schoolchildren who wrote to him over the years asking him to interpret his poems, and that the burnt-fox dream seemed to be giving him as he wrote his literary critical essay: don't look for too many symbols, or you might inadvertently kill the poem. The hawk roosting might just be a hawk roosting.

The reviews were ecstatic. Trendy society magazine *Queen* paved the way with a pre-publication puff under the heading 'The New Young Writers': 'Hughes is certainly among the most exciting poets writing in English today; like many of his contemporaries, he is attracted to themes of violence, but his treatment of these is often outstandingly striking and imaginative.'[23] The local paper in Yorkshire managed to time a feature for publication day, as if for the express purpose of making Ted's parents proud: it praised his powerful 'use of the elemental forces of his native Pennines', suggesting that 'in his best work he has concentrated the forces of nature into one image – a shrew, a stoat, an old man of Heptonstall, or even, in one hilarious piece of internal rhyming, into an old tomcat'.[24]

Then, on the baby's due date, came the important one: Alvarez in the *Observer*. The reservations he had expressed about *The Hawk in the Rain* were swept away. 'An Outstanding Young Poet' said the headline. 'Ted Hughes's first volume of poems was good but in some ways predictable. He was a Cambridge man and his work showed all the Cambridge influences' (Alvarez was an Oxford man). 'His second volume, *Lupercal*, is another matter entirely. There are no influences to sidetrack the critic, no hesitations to reassure him. Hughes has found his own voice, created his own artistic world and has emerged as a poet of the first importance.'[25]

More praise poured in over the following month, along with the congratulatory telegrams on fatherhood. According to the highbrow *Times Literary Supplement*, Ted's was (headline) 'The Renewing Voice' of English poetry, reacting against the 'sophisticated numbness' and 'neutral tone' of the Movement: 'Mr Hughes's second volume is startlingly better than his first. He is looking for the numinous, he is facing the terror of our contemporary world, and he finds, paradoxically, his central image of the numinous in the blind, instinctual thrust (in itself, in a way, an image of terror) of the animal and vegetable worlds.' The snowdrop was a conventional poetic image of 'pathetic and over-confident frailty', but in 'the most perfect short poem' in the book Hughes focused instead on the 'terrifying strength' that pushed the little flower's head through the hard winter soil. It was 'a remarkable achievement' to have made 'a narrow, vivid, rather obsessive range of images (images of blind but beautiful greed, terror, fierceness, lust for survival) seem so generally relevant to our contemporary world'.[26]

The distinguished poet Norman MacCaig came to a similar conclusion in the *Spectator*: it was as if the natural things in these poems 'become spokesmen for the hidden and violent beings that we partly are, to be regarded with a kind of rueful honesty as obeying the laws of their nature, however much we regret the redness of their tooth and claw'.[27] The *Daily Telegraph*'s poetry reviewer agreed: 'Toughness, we know, is suspect … But Ted Hughes's poems, *Lupercal*, which have been called violent, are in fact genuinely powerful, not self-consciously virile … Mr Hughes at 30 is to me the most strikingly original, technically masterful, poet of his generation.'[28]

Faber and Faber printed over 2,000 copies of *Lupercal*. They sold out by June, calling for a reprint of another 1,500. The American edition published by Harper at $3 in early August had a smaller print run, but the reviews were equally strong. The *New York Times* said that 'Like his patron priest, Faunus, Ted Hughes owns a "hair and bone wisdom" about husbandry, hunting and herding. Cows, pigs, cats, stoats, foxes, shrews, weasels, frogs, and wolves are his hedgerow familiars. And, like the old mid-winter fertility rites from which he draws the title of this second book, his poems revive us by their own brute vitality.'[29] And in *Harper's Magazine*, Stanley Kunitz, one of the poets Ted and Sylvia had met in Boston, wrote that *Lupercal* 'passes beyond all this pother of school and region and movement and vanguardism and coterie'. This 'second volume by Ted Hughes, a young Englishman lately resident in the United States, establishes him as one of the most exciting of living poets … These poems seem to be all process, and they are, running like the tide, or shooting thick as clover, until we discover, in a marvel of knowing, that they are completely things.'[30]

Alvarez summed up the general view, not just his own, when in the 'Books of the Year' round-up for the *Observer* he opined that *Lupercal* 'seems to me not only the best book of poems to appear for a long time but potentially one of the most important: a first true sign of thaw in the dreary freeze-up of contemporary poetry'.[31] One of the (less successful) poems in *The Hawk in the Rain* had been called 'Famous Poet'. Thanks to *Lupercal*, that is what Ted Hughes became in the course of his first year back in England.

Parenthood did not stop them going out. On 4 May, the Babyminder Service obliged again so that they could go to dinner with Eliot and his wife Valerie. The other guests were Stephen and Natasha Spender. Ted found Eliot whimsically amusing, but distant in his manner. He noticed a certain habit of looking down at the ground when talking. Old Possum only looked up 'to smile at his wife', his smile being like that 'of a person recovering from some serious operation'. Spender 'chattered so much' that he felt compelled to write Ted and Sylvia a letter of apology for having done so.[32] Ted was surprised by how much he liked Spender and by how thick Eliot's hands were. He was not surprised that all the talk, some of it indiscreet, was about the Bloomsbury Group and their acolytes. Eliot wrote afterwards to tell Ted that he had left his scarf behind. Either the newly famous poet was still nervous at the end of the evening with the world's most famous poet or he and Sylvia were rushing because the babyminder's time was almost up.

They resumed their theatregoing. Ted loathed Harold Pinter's much-praised *The Caretaker* at the Duchess Theatre. Some clever wit to begin with, but boring in the second half. Pinter's usual theme: 'the id emerging in some decrepit disgusting vindictive form and threatening the isolated dried-up ego'. The typically English assault on the ghastly English 'public school ego-kit, the do-it-yourself gentleman kit'.[33] He preferred *Roots* by Arnold Wesker, regarding it as a 'pepped-up' version of the kind of material found in the popular BBC radio soap opera *Mrs Dale's Diary*.[34]

On 23 June, there was another Faber and Faber cocktail party. This time Ted spoke to Eliot at length. He also met W. H. Auden for the first time, though 'scarcely spoke to him, since he was overpowered by the Blue-haired hostesses that seem to run those meetings'. Sylvia, relishing an evening of champagne instead of 'sour milk and diapers', engaged in conversation with Stephen Spender (drunk) and Louis

MacNeice – also drunk, and speaking, Ted told Olwyn, 'like a quick-fire car salesman'. Sylvia proudly reported to her mother that at one point Charles Monteith, Ted's editor, beckoned her out into the hall: 'There Ted stood, flanked by T. S. Eliot, W. H. Auden, Louis McNeice [*sic*] on the one hand and Stephen Spender on the other, having his photograph taken.' 'Three generations of Faber poets there,' said Monteith. 'Wonderful!'[35] Mark Gerson, one of London's leading portrait photographers, was the man behind the camera. He took a whole series of photos of the five poets.

Ted threw himself into radio plays, short stories and other broadcasts for the BBC, readings for schools, book-reviewing and all the drudgery of the freelance author's life. He also considered the possibility of trading in antique chairs. When he needed to get away from the cramped flat with the baby, he borrowed the Merwins' more capacious quarters (they had gone off to their farmhouse in France). In the summer Ted and Sylvia took a two-week holiday in Yorkshire, introducing the baby to the wider family. They went to the rather dingy seaside resort of Whitby with Ted's cousin Vicky.

Sylvia's first volume of poems, *The Colossus*, was published in the autumn. It meant a lot to them both that Ted wasn't the only one making an impression in literary London. It was an exciting time in the city, with a sense that the austere and stuffy Fifties were over – Sylvia attended the *Lady Chatterley* trial at the Old Bailey and was delighted by the verdict that D. H. Lawrence's novel was not obscene, for all the prosecuting counsel's infamous question to the jury as to whether it was the kind of book that one would wish one's wife or servants to read. She was beginning to get a little broadcasting work of her own.

They took the train to Yorkshire for Christmas. Edith moved the piano out of the sitting room so that there would be room for Frieda's playpen. But things went wrong when Sylvia and Olwyn had a bad quarrel. It began when Sylvia made a tart remark about a poet who was a friend of Olwyn's. 'I say, you're awfully critical, aren't you?' said Olwyn, who had – Sylvia alleges – been sniping ever since her arrival. Sylvia glared at her and drew Ted into the room, having whispered Olwyn's remark to him. Olwyn lost her temper and asked Sylvia why she was always so rude and selfish. She called her sister-in-law a 'nasty bitch', said that she had eaten too much Christmas dinner, and criticised her for not letting her stay in Chalcot Square the previous March – which would not have been very practical, given that the flat had one bedroom and Sylvia was eight months pregnant. She then referred to Sylvia as 'Miss Plath' (a jibe at her having published *The Colossus* under her maiden name?) and reminded her who was the true daughter of the house. Sylvia should stop treating the Beacon as if it were her own home; she was intolerant, selfish and immature. During the shouting match, Olwyn had been holding Frieda. She ended the row by saying, 'But we shouldn't talk like this over her sweet head.' Sylvia took her baby and went upstairs. She and Ted left early the next morning, sooner than planned. Olwyn would never see her sister-in-law again.

Olwyn Hughes hardly knew Sylvia Plath. 'I never either liked or disliked her. I didn't feel to <u>know</u> her,' she wrote, late in life.[36] They met just six times: for the weekend in Cambridge in the autumn of 1956, on summer holiday in Yorkshire the following year, over lunch in Chalcot Square in March 1960, and for three family Christmases at the Beacon, this being the last one. Arguments during family Christmas gatherings are not exactly unusual and in Chalcot Square it was understandable that Sylvia was irritated by Olwyn's smoking and the length of time she stayed in the tiny flat of her heavily pregnant hostess (though, from Olwyn and Ted's point of view, they needed a good catch-up because they hardly ever saw each other).

Olwyn's impression of Sylvia was formed almost entirely on the basis of hearsay from Ted and others, including some malicious witnesses, together with repeated readings, over the years after her death, of her poems, letters and journals. In truth, Olwyn was not a major first-hand witness. At the same time, she was one of only three people to have read Sylvia's last journals before one of them was destroyed and the other lost.[37] This meant that Olwyn felt qualified to opine about Sylvia's psychology. She spent nearly fifty years thinking, talking and writing about her. She bitterly regretted that their last meeting was so unpleasant, and this was her way of seeking justification and atonement.

Sylvia wrote to her mother, speculating about the reason for Olwyn's rage: it could only have been jealousy. Olwyn, she thought, was 'pathologically' close to Ted; they had even shared a bed as children. Perhaps this was why she had never married. There seemed –

says Sylvia, a year on from her own course of psychoanalysis – to be something horrifyingly 'Freudian' about the relationship, so little wonder that Olwyn did not like to see her brother now putting his wife and child first.[38]

Ted bottled up his feelings about the falling out between his wife and his sister. He delighted in his baby daughter, observing her standing up in her cot. His surviving personal journals begin at this point. As if in response to the new life embodied by Frieda, they are filled with observations of natural rebirth. On Christmas Eve at the Beacon, one of the earliest surviving entries, he noticed heather in flower, dandelions by a bus stop, the sun in the morning mist looking like a white disc suggestive of visionary apprehension, the line of the moor in radiant profile, 'limpid and smooth in undulations like the edge of ice held up and melting'. And he noticed birds: a little owl on his parents' washing pole, wrens, robins, a missel thrush and – a description that is a little prose poem in its own right – a magpie 'tossing himself up with powerful rising flirts' as it came up off the moor, 'then breasting like an arrowhead, plunging like a closed dart, then another flirt catching him, tossing him again, down the dropaway slope'.[39]

He observed people as acutely as landscapes and fauna. That Christmas, Ted noted that his parents lacked 'the ceremony and style' to be good present-givers. They preferred to hand over gifts discreetly, a few days early. This, he thought, showed a lack of poise. As often, he reached for a comparison in the terms of his own vocation: 'its equivalent in writing is a slovenly direct thrusting across of the facts without nuance, without relationship to larger patterns or permanence'. Olwyn, by contrast, gave with style but without show, always surprising the recipient and gracing the gift: 'the equivalent in writing would be an informal fresh true perfect style'.[40] He wrote about Frieda, aged eight months, being fascinated by shoes and cups. He perceived the family row as Olwyn attacking Sylvia, not vice versa. It reminded him of a similar attack Olwyn had made on Gerald's wife, Joan. 'In the animal world,' he noted, 'the attacker always wins.'[41]

Back in London, they went to the zoo – he had bought a season ticket and it became his regular outing with the pushchair – and he jotted down notes about the behaviour of elephants. Often he would walk alone on Primrose Hill and Hampstead Heath at dawn. Thus on 12 April 1961 at five in the morning he caught the moment through a lengthy diary description that began with 'faint marble of blue heaven in a sieved rippled glazing of cloud', came alive with a sea of blackbirds and the song of thrushes, then tracked his steps down to the Regent's Canal where the water was quivering 'as if the fish in it had first awakened, air beginning to spurt and shift on it'. In the park, his eye fell on a damp *Daily Express* on a bench, where he read of the first day of the trial of Adolf Eichmann in Jerusalem: the reality of history intruding upon the serenity of the morning. In their different ways, Ted and Sylvia were both trying to write poetry of the moment, to bridge their own concerns – for him, a hawk roosting or a pig destined for the oven; for her, a Germanic heritage and the oppression of domestic drudgery – with their consciousness of the momentous monstrosity of the recent past. Though they rarely admitted it in so many words, each of them shared the apprehension of Theodor Adorno that to write poetry after Auschwitz was to bear a heavy responsibility.

Minute observations and particular phrases in their journals gave both Ted and Sylvia the opportunity to try out phrases and raw material for potential inclusion in their poems. A good diary entry is like a good poem, a crafting of the world into words: 'wet dark blue pre-dawn push of slopping clouds', 'Daffodills [sic] blowing their dry zinc-green leaves seeming almost to boil'.[42] When Ted wrote in his journal of a chestnut tree with huge-sleeved Pierrot arms holding candles daintily, he was grasping at a moment's observation before it vanished, but there was always the possibility of such moments returning in a poem by one or other of them. By this time, they were becoming one soul. Within a few weeks of Sylvia writing the poem that begins 'The tulips are too excitable, it is winter here,' Ted was noting in his journal, 'The red tulips – hearts terrifyingly vivid terrible. Organs pulsing something red and uncontrollable … Tulips the colour of blooded yolks.'[43] They did not plagiarise each other; they achieved synchronicity of vision through their shared imagination and observation, their conversation, their healthy competition, their daily and nightly bond of love and work.

In January 1961, they recorded a joint interview for BBC radio, broadcast under the title *Two of a Kind: Poets in Partnership*. They were asked how they had met and how Ted had proposed. By writing poems to each other, Sylvia replied. 'The poems haven't really survived, the marriage overtook the poems,' interjected Ted.

Apart from their mutual dedications, interviewer Owen Leeming observed, their published poems appeared not to be to or about each other. Marriage freed them for other subjects, they explained, but, Sylvia added, 'I'd never be writing as I am and as much as I am without Ted's understanding and co-operation.' They liked the same things, lived at the same tempo, had the same rhythm in almost every way. 'Two people who are sympathetic to each other and who are right, who are compatible in this spiritual way, in fact make up one person,' said Ted, 'they make up one source of power which you can both use and you can draw out material in incredible detail from this single shared mind.'⁴⁴ Ted spoke of their telepathic union, Sylvia more practically of how Ted's love of animals sent her back to her own father's interest in bees, which gave her a new theme for her writing. They admitted that beneath, and in their poems, they had very different temperaments. But they spoke of their shared love of family. Sylvia envisioned a large house stocked with small children and small animals.

In February, there was a repeat incident of the kind that had spoiled the end of the semester at Smith. Ted went for the meeting with the BBC producer Moira Doolan that would lead to the commissioning of the broadcasts for schools that eventually became *Poetry in the Making*. He seemed to be out for far too long. Sylvia, pregnant again, and feeling vulnerable, began to have suspicions. She had spoken to Moira Doolan on the telephone when the appointment was being arranged and formed the impression that the lilting Irish voice must belong to a great and seductive beauty, which was far from the case. When Ted came home, he found that the manuscripts of his work in progress had been ripped to shreds and the pages torn from his trusty edition of the complete works of Shakespeare. His reaction on this occasion is not recorded, but long after Sylvia's death he admitted to his American editor, Fran McCullough, that sometimes when Sylvia was in a blind rage, all he could do was slap her, and that once 'she turned into his slap and got a black eye, and went to the doctor and told him Ted beat her regularly'.⁴⁵

A few days later, Sylvia miscarried her second baby and soon after that she had to return to hospital for an appendectomy. Her diary recorded Ted's visits to her bedside. One day he appeared in his familiar black coat, looking twice as tall as everyone else. She felt as 'excited and infinitely happy' as she had been in the first days of their courtship: 'His face which I daily live with seemed the most kind and beautiful in the world.'[46] Five days later she wrote, 'Ted is actually having a rougher time than I – poor love sounded quite squashed yesterday.' It was dawning on him just how tough housework and babycare could be: 'How do you do it all?' he asked. 'The Pooker' (their nickname for Frieda) 'makes an astonishing amount of pots to wash … She wets a lot.' He had no time to cook for himself, was forced to survive on bread. Hearing this, Sylvia felt very loved and needed.[47] Back home, she wrote to her Aunt Dotty, raving about Ted: he visited every day, each time bringing 'a pint of cream and a big steak sandwich', together with 'a glass bottle of freshly squeezed orange juice' (which did not come cheap in the early Sixties). She added that 'All the women in the hospital thought it was amazing he would take care of a baby so willingly and well and so do I!'[48]

Ted's tenderness when he visited her in hospital seemed to herald a rebirth of both their marriage and Sylvia's work – the New Yorker offered her a 'first refusal' contract for each new poem she wrote, and a couple of months later the prestigious publisher Alfred Knopf agreed to do an American edition of The Colossus, though they left out several pieces because it was judged that their similarity to certain poems by Theodore Roethke ran the risk of a plagiarism suit. In particular, the strange and disturbing 'Poem for a Birthday' was deemed to be too close to Roethke's 'The Lost Son'.

Shortly after this, in June, Ted won the Hawthornden Prize for Lupercal. This was the oldest and most distinguished literary prize in Britain, open to all genres, not just poetry. Previous winners had included Graham Greene, Evelyn Waugh, Robert Graves, Siegfried Sassoon and Henry Williamson. At the prize-giving, Ted and Sylvia met the author of the previous year's winning book, The Loneliness of the Long Distance Runner. Alan Sillitoe was the son of an illiterate Nottingham factory worker. His novels told of northern working-class life as it was, in tough, stripped-down prose. Though he did not like the term, he was one of the original 'angry young men'. He was married to Ruth Fainlight, an American poet of Sylvia's age. With so many similarities between them, the two couples quickly became fast friends.

In the summer of 1961 they decided to make up for their failure to fulfil the requirement of the Somerset Maugham Prize to travel abroad the previous year. They left little Frieda in Chalcot Square with Aurelia Plath, who had come over to see her granddaughter for the first time. In May they had bought their first car, a Morris Traveller, thanks principally to the proceeds of Ted's BBC work. His latest project was a play called 'The Calm', a modernised reworking of Shakespeare's *The Tempest* in which everybody stayed on the magical island, and the main characters – Prospero, Caliban, Ariel and even Caliban's witch-mother Sycorax – were all aspects of the same self.[49]

They took the Traveller on the ferry and drove down to stay with the Merwins in the Dordogne. Their stops on the journey included Berck-Plage, which inspired a long and dark poem by Sylvia, and Reims, where a gypsy punished Sylvia for not buying a trinket by coming up close to her face and saying 'Vous crèverez bientôt' – you will croak soon.[50] The visit to the Merwins was not a success. Sylvia, who was pregnant again, so always hungry, thought Dido was 'the world's best cook'. Dido found Sylvia lazy, greedy, obstreperous and altogether high maintenance. There were frequent 'scenes', which Ted found hard to cope with. On the way back, they stopped at Chartres; the detail remembered by Ted in *Birthday Letters* was Sylvia spending their last francs on a Breton jug for her mother. But he also sensed foreboding in the air (or was that only in retrospect?). It was around this time that friends such as Luke Myers began to hear – from others, never from Ted himself – stories of Sylvia's 'rages and passive aggression, with Ted standing by, apologetic and humiliated'.[51] After each such incident, Ted would always say a few words, 'not making any excuses – but simply to restore calm'.[52] Sylvia herself would never apologise; it was as if the offending behaviour were simply 'gone from her memory'.[53]

Relieved to be reunited with Frieda, they took Aurelia to Yorkshire, where she got on well with Ted's mother and Aunt Hilda. Back in London, she continued to look after Frieda while Ted and Sylvia drove the Morris Traveller to the West Country. They had decided to move to the country, confining their search to Devon and Cornwall. After rejecting eight houses, they found an old thatched house, being sold by a knight of the realm. Formerly a rectory and before that a manor house, it was located in a remote village called North Tawton, on the edge of Dartmoor. They both fell in love. The name of the house was Court Green.

12

The Grass Blade

On 26 August 1961, Olwyn's thirty-third birthday, Ted wrote to tell her that this was the day he was going to sign a contract and put down the deposit on a house. Thanks to a gift of £500 from his parents, an equivalent loan from Aurelia, and their savings of £2,000, they were able to buy it outright. He asked her to imagine 'a very ancient farm-house, white, with a steep thatch, adjoining a big thatched barn, along one side of a courtyard, 20 yards square, tightly cobbled with very tiny cobbles'.[1] The cobbles actually reached into the house, peppering the little passageway between the kitchen and the dining room. Round the courtyard, there was a store for apples, together with a stable and a woodshed. Beyond that, there was a self-contained thatched one-bedroom cottage that could eventually be done up as a guest house for mothers-in-law and others. The garden extended to more than 2 acres, with a vegetable patch, a 'prehistoric mound' and an orchard with about fifty apple trees, a mix of eaters and cookers, not to mention an assortment of currant and berry bushes. A sloping lawn led down to a row of cherry trees and there was a little greenhouse and even an overgrown tennis court.

Inside, the kitchen had a coal-burning Aga range and there was a small further kitchen beyond, with a pantry, a box room and steps to a wine-cellar. This was the old part of the house, dating, he reckoned, from the fifteenth century. Upstairs, it had a bathroom and two bedrooms. In the newer part, looking out on the garden, there were two living rooms, and a further three bedrooms above, not to mention a large attic. The house was well set back from the road. At the bottom of the garden, which was surrounded by thick hedges and tall trees, there was the churchyard, graced by mighty yew trees. Space, a garden, an orchard, a village, fishing near by: Ted and Sylvia had found their rural idyll.

They left London five days later, on a hot late-summer's day, their modest collection of furniture going down in a small removal van. Sylvia thought that the house was like a person, immediately responsive to sensitive touch. Her brother Warren was in Europe, so he came down to help them move in. He and Ted smoothed a great plank of elm and made it into Sylvia's first proper writing-table: the best possible housewarming present. The *Birthday Letters* poem 'The Table' plays on the retrospective irony that the particular cut was known as 'Coffin elm'.[2] Ted set up a study for himself in the quiet of the attic.

They erected bookcases and filled the shelves. They began the haphazard process of getting to know the village. Ted observed the bird life: the most whitely speckled starling he had ever seen nested over their bedroom and a family of goldfinches had their residence in the laburnum tree. He made it his business to catalogue all the plants in the overgrown garden. They planted a row of holly cuttings in the hope of making a hedge. They felt benignly watched by the three elm trees to one side, but oppressed by 'the black explosion of yew' in the graveyard beyond.[3]

In October, feeling strong in her pregnancy and inspired by her new surroundings, Sylvia wrote her superb poem 'The Moon and the Yew Tree'. The following month, she won a Eugene Saxton Grant of $2,000. Yet there was a darkness in her poetry. Ted proposed the subject of moon and yew tree as an exercise based on their observation of the full moon over the yew in the churchyard early one morning. Though Sylvia regarded the poem as an exercise, he read into it her troubled relationship with her mother (moon) and late father (yew). 'It depressed me greatly,' he wrote later. 'It's my suspicion that no poem can be a poem that is not a statement from the powers in control of our life, the ultimate suffering and decision in us. It seems to me that this is poetry's only real distinction from the literary forms that we call "not poetry".'[4]

Sylvia, who was always affected by the weather, struggled with the freezing cold of winter in the country before the days of affordable central heating, but that did not stop them from enjoying the best Christmas they had ever known, with all the trimmings of a big tree, piles of presents for Frieda, and a huge traditional dinner cooked by Sylvia. The new baby, to be called either Megan or Nicholas, was due on 11 January but, like Frieda, was late. Sylvia had been making cherry tarts, apple pie with the last of the autumn fruit from the orchard, and other supplies for Ted and Frieda to eat when she was recovering from the birth. Nicholas Farrar Hughes arrived in the world at five to midnight on 17 January 1962, weighing in at 9 pounds, in contrast to 'Frieda's ladylike 7 pounds'. This time Sylvia needed gas and air. A full moon beamed over the huge elm tree in the garden.[5] Ted drew his usual diagram of the horoscope at time of birth and sent it to Olwyn, seeking advice – there was a very odd set of conjunctions and he didn't know what to make of them.[6]

They took turns with the childcare. Sometimes Sylvia would sleep in the spare room, where she had given birth, so that Ted could have a good night's sleep in order to be fresh to look after Frieda the following day. He was still writing short stories and plays for the BBC. An interim project with Faber was a double selection of his poetry and that of his 'poet-twin' (Sylvia's phrase),[7] Thom Gunn. This came out in May, showcasing the best work of the two Young Turks of English poetry.

In March they decided to have both children baptised in the village church, even though they did not like the vicar, who preached a sermon heralding the H-bomb as the potential advent of the Second Coming and attacking 'stupid pacifists and humanists and "educated pagans" who feared being incinerated'.[8] Newly inaugurated President John F. Kennedy was adopting a hawkish attitude towards the Soviet Union. The world was looking a dangerous place, and it was time for poetry to reflect this.

In April Penguin Books published a paperback anthology with a brightly coloured abstract design on the cover. Entitled *The New Poetry*, it was the brainchild of Al Alvarez. A prefatory note explained that it was his personal selection of the British poetry of the previous decade 'that really matters'.[9] Alvarez also explained that, for reasons elaborated upon in his introduction, he had also included two Americans, John Berryman and Robert Lowell. The twelve-page introduction itself, provocatively entitled 'The New Poetry, *or* Beyond the Gentility Principle', outlined Alvarez's take – which was also Hughes's – on the course of twentieth-century poetry. The radical experimentation of T. S. Eliot and Ezra Pound had given way to the political poetry of the 1930s and then in the Forties the passionate

rhetoric of Dylan Thomas was a reaction against the cool intellectu-
alism of W. H. Auden. The Movement of the Fifties was, in turn, a
reaction against the 'wild, loose emotion' of Thomas.

At the heart of the Movement was the Larkin of 'Church-going',
which offered 'in concentrated form, the image of the post-war
Welfare State Englishman: shabby and not concerned with his
appearance; poor – he has a bike, not a car; gauche but full of agnostic
piety; underfed, underpaid, overtaxed, hopeless, bored, wry'. There
was, however, a certain undue 'gentility' about this incarnation of the
common man. Larkin and the Movement offered the lower-middle-
class equivalent of the upper-class, or Tory, ideal of Englishness that
was 'presented in its pure crystalline form by John Betjeman'.

Alvarez's manifesto proposed that what was needed now, at the
beginning of the Sixties, was a reaction against this. Precedents were
available, for example in the form of the First World War survivor,
Hughes's admired Robert Graves, and above all the working-class
D. H. Lawrence, the very antithesis of gentility. But the stakes were
higher than ever, as modern culture found itself forced to absorb the
reality of the concentration camps and the hydrogen bomb, not to
mention the Freudian understanding of the dark inner psyche and the
importance of the sexual libido. What Berryman and Lowell brought
from America was a willing nakedness in confronting their inner
selves. Eliot's cult of impersonality, itself a reaction against the self-
indulgence of late Romanticism, was no longer necessary. The new
poetry – for which Lowell's *Life Studies* was the flag-bearer – managed
to combine skill and intelligence with an openness to 'the quick of
experience, experience sometimes on the edge of disintegration and
breakdown'.

Alvarez exemplified the new poetry by contrasting Philip Larkin's
'At Grass' ('elegant and unpretentious and rather beautiful in its gentle
way') with Ted Hughes's 'A Dream of Horses': less controlled, techni-
cally speaking less good, but 'unquestionably *about* something; it is a
serious attempt to re-create and so clarify, unfalsified and in the
strongest imaginative terms possible, a powerful complex of emotions
and sensations'. Like so many of Hughes's poems, it had the quality of
a vivid dream that hinted at an inner life of fear and sensation. It
created a 'brute world' that was 'part physical, part state of mind'.
Cunningly, Alvarez talked up the power of Hughes by means of a

Childhood home now and then: (*below*) Mount Zion Primitive Methodist Chapel towering over 1 Aspinall Street, in the roof of which is the skylight of the attic bedroom from which Ted looked out on Scout Rock, and (*left*) 1 Aspinall Street as it is today

Ted as a schoolboy

Siblings: Gerald, Olwyn, Ted

Mirrored in the heart: Ted
photographed by Olwyn

Deep England overgrown:
the pond of the pike

During National Service:
mother and son

Family home in student
days and thereafter: the
Beacon as it is today

Sylvia Plath about to set off for
Smith College in 1950 (with mother
Aurelia and brother Warren)

Cambridge days: (*top right*) in June 1952, at
the May Ball with Carina; (*above*) graduation in
summer 1954; (*bottom right*) the first and only
edition of student poetry magazine *Saint Botolph's
Review*, at the launch party for which Ted first met
Sylvia on Saturday 25 February 1956

Honeymoon: (*left*) Sylvia and Ted photographed by Warren in Paris in 1956; (*below*) Ted drawn by Sylvia

Newly married: (*above*) Sylvia with typewriter on a Yorkshire drystone wall in September 1956; (*right*) studio portrait during residence in Eltisley Avenue, Cambridge, late in 1956

In the bosom of the family: Sylvia with Ted's family at the Beacon, William Hughes (*left*) and Uncle Walt (*right*) standing behind, Sylvia sitting next to Ted's mother

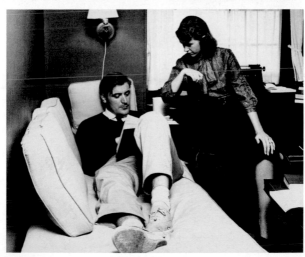

At work in the apartment on Willow Street, Boston, in 1958

On the rocks at Winthrop, after visiting Otto Plath's grave in May 1959

Boston literary life: Robert Lowell, who described Ted's poem 'Pike' as a masterpiece

Off to see America: Ted photographed by Sylvia, during a roadside picnic in Wisconsin in July 1959

poem that was far from his best. Though quoted in full in the intro-
duction, 'A Dream of Horses' did not make the cut of the Hughes
selection in the main body of the anthology. Alvarez was sufficiently
intimate with the work to offer what was as much a reading of the
superior poem 'The Horses' and the key short story 'The Rain Horse',
without actually mentioning them.

What he did mention was Hughes's literary antecedent: 'the strange,
savage horses which terrorize Ursula Brangwen at the end of *The
Rainbow*'. Dr F. R. Leavis, said Alvarez, had represented Eliot and
Lawrence as the warring and irreconcilable poles of modern literature.
The best modern poetry, exemplified above all by Hughes, could,
through its immunity to the English disease of gentility, creatively
reconcile those opposites by combining 'the new depth poetry, the
openness to experience, the psychological insight and integrity of
D. H. Lawrence ... with the technical skill and formal intelligence of
T. S. Eliot'.[10] The anthology duly included more poems by Ted Hughes
than anyone else, with Thom Gunn, seen once again as his poetic
brother-in-arms, coming a close second. The early Hughes classics
were all there: jaguar, thought-fox, roosting hawk, bull called Moses,
viewed pig, pike, pibroch and famous poet.

Ted was thrilled by his prime position in the anthology, and the
strength of its reception. Sylvia was neither represented in the selec-
tion nor mentioned in the introduction. Alvarez's behaviour, on read-
ing her new poems later in 1962 and discovering that more than
anyone else she embodied the essence of 'the new depth poetry',
pushing even beyond the spirit of Lowell's *Life Studies*, was partly
shaped by guilt at his realisation that he had overlooked her talent, by
hitherto regarding her – so ironically – as a genteel poet and as at best
midwife to her husband's genius rather than as the true genius of the
poetry of 'experience sometimes on the edge of disintegration and
breakdown'.

Ted and Sylvia were beginning to become part of the village commu-
nity. They had hardly met anyone before Christmas, but the local bank
manager invited them to his New Year's Eve party, where they met his
wife and their literary-minded and very pretty auburn-haired sixteen-
year-old daughter Nicola, on holiday from a posh boarding school in
Oxford called Headington. She loved literature and found the

Hugheses unbelievably glamorous and sophisticated in comparison with everybody else in the monochrome village community. When Ted heard that she was thinking of studying English at university, he offered to 'save' or educate her, suggesting that she could borrow some of their books.

She turned up in black stockings and a dark dress, her short hair neatly pulled with a dark ribbon. She raved in what Sylvia considered a 'cutely theatrical' way about Ted's latest play, which she had heard on the radio. She would have loved to play the 'romantic little-girl part' herself. She spoke breathlessly of her love of *Winnie the Pooh* and Ted decided to mature her taste by offering her Virginia Woolf's *Orlando*. Sylvia groaned and gave her the archetypal teenager novel, J. D. Salinger's *The Catcher in the Rye*. When Nicola brought it back, she said that she thought it had been a bit too long. She and Ted corresponded when she returned to school. He sent her an analysis of one of her set poems, Hopkins's 'The Windhover'. She came back at half-term, straight from the hairdresser. She wanted to lose some weight 'to have a nice shape'. Ted said that there was nothing wrong with her shape. They talked about films – she thought that *Seven Samurai* was boring. It happened to be Ted's favourite film, but he humoured her by agreeing. He did not, however, rise to her angling to be driven to the cinema in Exeter. Her role models, she said, were Brigitte Bardot and Lolita.[11]

In the Easter holidays, Nicola turned up at Court Green, offering to take Frieda for a walk. By ill fortune, Frieda had just been pecked by a crow and was feeling upset. Nicola asked if she could offer any other help, then announced that the family was moving to London – she wouldn't miss North Tawton but she would miss the literary company of Mr and Mrs Hughes. Sylvia's 'worries of N's increasing limpetlike clinging in the next 3 years' disappeared instantly. Ted wrote in a letter to a friend that he was relieved that they were no longer to be constantly pestered by the bank manager's mother and daughter.[12] But he seems to have enjoyed his conversations with young Nicola, sometimes going round to her house without Sylvia, who once said some sharp words when the two of them seemed to be talking a little too intimately under the laburnums outside Court Green.

Before leaving North Tawton, Nicola returned some gramophone records that had been borrowed and asked whether she could come over and listen to the Hughes's 'German linguaphone records'. At the thought of this, Sylvia 'seriously considered smashing up our old and ridiculous box victrola with an axe'.[13] The need passed, and she 'grew a little wiser'. Nicola, meanwhile, asked Ted if the girl in his poem 'Secretary' – the one about the sexually frustrated virgin – was a real person. 'So hopes begin,' Sylvia wrote dryly in her diary. Ted gave Nicola a fond farewell kiss the last time they saw her, together with copies of *The Hawk in the Rain* and his children's book, *Meet My Folks!*, with affectionate inscriptions.[14] She grew up to become a writer and journalist.

Sylvia's very funny notes on Nicola – there is no more than a glimmer of fear that Ted might have embarked on an affair with her had the family stayed in the village – survive among a set of vivid character sketches of village people, probably intended as material for a novel about her life in Devon that was to be entitled either 'Doubletake' or 'Double Exposure'. She had drafted about 130 pages.[15] Another of her vivid character sketches immortalises Major and Mrs Billyeald, and her father George Manly, ex-chief of the police in British Guiana. They named their tiny house on the Eggesford Road after the military compound there.[16]

The indomitable Bertha Billyeald was secretary of the Devon Beekeepers Association. Her father saw Ted gazing in admiration at the jaguar skin that was 'Splayed on the wall like a Picasso' – Ted's simile, in 'The Jaguar Skin', a poem intended for *Birthday Letters* but withdrawn at the last minute.[17] Old Manly told his daughter to tell Ted and Sylvia the story. A jaguar had been killing the local dogs. One night Bertha saw its shadow on the verandah. It was looking for the two dogs who slept with her for safety (their safety, not hers, interjected the husband). She went out to the verandah to shoot it, but as she got there, the screen collapsed and something came tumbling on to her. At first, she thought it was one of the dogs, but then she realised it was the jaguar itself. 'It must have got the shock of its life,' she said laconically.

The big cat bolted into the hen-house, a long low hutch. At this point, the Major took up the story, proudly telling Ted and Sylvia of how his wife had crawled in among the hysterical hens, felt for the jaguar with the muzzle of her rifle and shot it dead in the pitch dark. She went back to bed and dragged its body out in the morning. Ted then pulls back in his own narrative: they never met again, Sylvia died, the father died and Major Billyeald shot himself on his garden lawn. He wondered whatever happened to Bertha, with all her 'strength' and 'sweetness'.[18] Ten years later, Ted saw the jaguar skin 'In a local auction among the rubbish'. He had to buy it, no matter how high the bidding went. He forgot the cost, but remembered 'the strength, / The sweetness that went past so lightly'. The story mattered to him because the jaguar was his totemic beast, because Bertha Billyeald was the best of British, because the day that he and Sylvia went to tea with the Billyealds after a meeting of the Devon beekeepers at the home of local beekeeper Charlie Pollard was one of the last days they laughed happily together, and because the skin was a talisman giving afterlife to the dead.

The people Ted and Sylvia got to know best in North Tawton were their immediate neighbours in the little row of cottages between Court Green and the road. Percy and Rose Key were a Cockney couple, retired from London where they had run a pub (the other next-door neighbour was the booming-voiced widow of an old colonial tea-planter). In April, there was a great drama when Rose banged on the door of Court Green at lunchtime, asking Ted to hurry round because Percy had had a stroke. In their journals, both Ted and Sylvia recorded the ensuing scene, which involved a great to-do over false teeth. Over the next couple of months Ted went round almost daily to help Percy in and out of bed as his health declined further. He died at the end of June, when they comforted Rose and went to the funeral.

Through spring and summer 1962, guests descended on Court Green. A North Devon woman called Elizabeth Compton, who had written to them after the *Poets in Partnership* radio broadcast, came to tea, and Sylvia liked her. In April, there came an American actor and broadcaster called Marvin Kane, who was down to interview Sylvia, bringing his wife and children. Then Aunt Hilda and her daughter Vicky arrived for Easter, followed by a glamorous Swedish journalist called Siv Arb who interviewed Ted and took some lovely photographs of Sylvia and the children sitting among the daffodils in the garden. The moment is beautifully evoked in the *Birthday Letters* poem 'Perfect Light'. The Sillitoes, always friendly and helpful, came down from London. Sylvia read her poem 'Elm' and Ruth told her that it was extraordinary. The Sillitoes did sense tension and a certain distance between the Hugheses, but this could easily have been attributed to the strain of having two small children and the pressure of freelance work.[19] Baby Nicholas was not troublesome – Sylvia described him in a letter to the Baskins as 'dark, Farrarlike, like Ted, quiet and smiley and utterly lovable'[20] – but there was no relief from feeding, winding and nappies (diapers) to change.

More London visitors arrived on the third weekend in May, in the form of the couple to whom Ted and Sylvia had sub-let the flat in Chalcot Square. The lease was for three years and sub-letting was allowed; retaining the flat kept open the possibility of a return to London.

David Wevill was a rising poet, having considerable success in getting his work published. His wife Assia, three years older than Ted and eight years older than her husband, born Assia Gutmann, had a staggeringly beautiful face, but always complained that she did not have the body to match. In contrast to slender-limbed Sylvia, she was self-conscious of her broad hips and the thickness of her waist. She was nervous, of German-Jewish refugee origin, on her third marriage and now working in an advertising agency. On the Saturday, Ted and David drove out on to Dartmoor, taking little Frieda. They ran out of petrol, but managed to get home, thanks to the assistance of a passing army truck. While the men were out, Assia helped Sylvia weed onions in the vegetable garden. In the evening they all listened to a recording of Robert Lowell reading his great early poem, 'The Quaker Graveyard in Nantucket'. They talked about each other's poems. Sylvia left abruptly and went to bed. Despite calls for him to come up, Ted carried on talking to his guests until late.

The next day, Assia was helping to prepare Sunday lunch by peeling the potatoes in the kitchen, with Ted assisting. Sylvia and David were chatting outside. They could hear muffled voices. Sylvia touched David on the knee, said 'I'll be back' and headed for the kitchen. She did not return and was very quiet over lunch. The Wevills left as planned, in time to catch a slow Sunday train back to London. In the carriage, David asked Assia why Sylvia had changed from being so friendly to so silent and edgy. Assia said, 'Ted kissed me in the kitchen, and Sylvia saw it.'[21] David was shocked – he was not yet aware of any cracks in their marriage – but he did not press further, assuming (or hoping) that it was just a flirtation. Back at work in London, Assia said nothing of a kiss, but told her friend Suzette Macedo that she sensed that Sylvia had picked up a 'current of attraction' between her and Ted.[22] She told another friend that in the course of the weekend Ted had said that he hated Sylvia, that because of her he had not been able to write for four years, and that his only decent work in all that time, the poems in *Lupercal*, were written during the ten days she was in hospital for her appendectomy.[23] Since the last of these assertions is patently untrue (the *Lupercal* poems were written over a long period during Ted and Sylvia's residence in New England), the other claims are not necessarily to be trusted.

Assia's boss at the advertising agency claimed many years later that before leaving work on the Friday Assia had been showing off about the invitation to Devon and had said 'I'm going to seduce Ted!' The boss allegedly took the boast with a pinch of salt and muttered, 'I don't care what you do, as long as you come back on Monday in a better mood.'[24] At such a distance of time, it is impossible to know whether such an exchange ever took place and, if it did, whether Assia was joking or semi-serious. She did, after all, have a complicated marital history and something of a reputation as a seductress.

Ted's retrospective narrative in *Birthday Letters* offers little biographical help. It makes Assia into more of a mythical figure than a real woman. He creates an image of Sylvia being fascinated by the dark Germanic undercurrent in Assia's 'Kensington jeweller's elocution'. Then he turned her into a 'Black Forest wolf', a 'witch's daughter' out of the Brothers Grimm, a 'Lilith of abortions', a tissue of contradictions: one part Harrods, one part Hitler, as she helps Sylvia to weed the onions. The poem 'Dreamers' lays on such imagery to grotesque excess: 'An ex-Nazi Youth Sabra. Her father / Doctor to the Bolshoi Ballet' (which he indeed was), 'A German / Russian Israeli with the gaze of a demon / Between curtains of black Mongolian hair'. All this, the poem alleges in one of Hughes's most tasteless lines, makes Assia 'Slightly filthy with erotic mystery'. The poem also claims that while at Court Green Assia told of a dream about a giant pike, which made Sylvia 'astonished, maybe envious'.[25] David Wevill has no recollection of this. It is possible that Assia made up the dream, knowing that it would intrigue Ted – she had read his poems, and when she and David went round to the Chalcot Square flat to discuss the possibility of a sub-let, she would have seen the Gehenna Press Hughes Pike on the wall. But to suggest that she was putting out a line in order to catch a bigger poetic fish than her husband is to buy into the image of her as a ruthless seductress.

The day after the Wevills left, Sylvia wrote two poems. 'The Rabbit Catcher', according to Ted's *Birthday Letters* reply-poem with the same title, was inspired by a rabbit snare discovered by Ted on a recent clifftop walk. 'Without a word', Sylvia tore the snare out of the ground 'and threw it into the trees'.[26] Where Ted saw the countryman's heritage of living off the land, Sylvia saw only the cruel hands of the imagined trapper, a Lawrentian figure with hands closing round his mug of tea as they would close round the neck of the poor rabbit. There may also be a memory of Ted's hands on the hillside above Benidorm. The poem closes with a jump-cut to the idea of marriage as a trap, a form of suffocation:

> And we, too, had a relationship –
> Tight wires between us,
> Pegs too deep to uproot, and a mind like a ring
> Sliding shut on some quick thing,
> The constriction killing me also.[27]

The past tense and the images of closure suggest that something in the marriage had died at the sight of Ted and Assia in the kitchen the previous day.

The other poem written on 21 May 1962 was originally entitled 'Quarrel', then revised to 'Event'. It tells of a couple lying in bed by cold moonlight, back to back, as their baby cries for food. A rift has opened between them; they cannot meet each other's eyes (which is what Ruth Fainlight had noticed earlier in the month). 'Love cannot come here,' Sylvia wrote bleakly.[28]

There was no sense of guilt or embarrassment in Assia's thank-you letter to Sylvia for the weekend, which thoughtfully included a tapestry pattern in response to a passing remark from her hostess that needlework was something she was thinking of taking up. Shortly afterwards, Ted's family arrived at Court Green, complete with Uncle Walt. A visit from Aurelia, fresh from Warren's wedding in America (which Ted and Sylvia were not able to attend), then began in the third week of June and lasted for six weeks.

On 26 June, Ted and Sylvia, leaving the children with Aurelia, took the train to London to do some recordings for the BBC. During a break, Ted made an excursion from Broadcasting House to Assia's advertising agency in Mayfair. Unable to meet her, he left a note, which allegedly read, 'I have come to see you, despite all marriages.'[29] Assia seems to have wanted her husband to know that she was on the brink of an affair: she showed Ted's 'short declaration' to David, trying to get him to react.[30] He did not rise to it. It may be that she was trying to drop a hint because there was something else she really ought to have told him.

According to the novelist William Trevor, who also worked at the advertising agency, when Assia received Ted's note she looked out of the window of her office and saw a gardener mowing the lawn in the square below.[31] She went down and picked up a blade of freshly cut grass, which she posted to Ted at Court Green without any message. Presumably this was a clever joke. Since grass was Green, Court meant courtship. One might think that this story in William Trevor's memoir of Assia was a novelist's concoction, save that Ted corroborates it in a poem in his scarce and extremely expensive cycle of poems to Assia, *Capriccio*, which Trevor is most unlikely to have known: 'She sent him a blade of grass, but no word.'[32]

Sylvia found out about the affair before it had really started. On Monday 9 July, she returned to Court Green from a shopping trip in Exeter with her mother to hear the phone ringing. Sylvia got to it before Ted and realised from the embarrassed moment of silence at the other end that the call was not meant for her. Accounts vary as to whether it was Assia putting on a deep voice, or a male friend phoning on her behalf. Either way, it was clear that she and Ted were in, or at least on the brink of, a relationship. After the call, Sylvia ripped the telephone cord from its socket and there was an explosive row, Aurelia shielding the children. Ted left for London and Sylvia told her mother that he was having an affair.

Two days later, Sylvia wrote an anguished, angry poem called 'Words heard, by accident, over the phone'.[33] Ted's later poem 'Do not pick up the telephone' was, more obliquely, another answer to the call. 'A dead body will fall out of the telephone,' he writes: might everything have been different if neither of them had picked up the telephone that day? A line towards the end of the poem, 'You screech at the root of the house,' is a clear allusion to Sylvia's other poetic remaking of the fateful call, in 'Daddy': 'The black telephone's off at the root.'[34]

'Daddy' is a poem that yokes father and husband, under the influence of Sylvia's psychoanalytic journey. In Ted's case, a Freudian might well see a connection between the woman-trouble that began with the phone call and some lines in the original limited-circulation version of 'Do not pick up the telephone', which were cut from the mass-market reprint: 'Panties are hotting up their circle for somebody to burn in / Nipples are evangelising bringing a sword or at least a razor / Cunt is proclaiming heaven on earth.'[35]

The version of the poem that included these lines was in a group of four, published in a little literary magazine called *Ploughshares* in 1980. The others were the honeymoon remembrance 'You Hated Spain', which was later included in *Birthday Letters*; 'Lily', which, in Lawrentian mode, compares the look and feel of the inside of a lily to female genitalia; and 'A Dove', a poem of benediction that Hughes reprinted as the closing poem in both his volume of family elegies, *Wolfwatching*, and his summative 1995 *New Selected Poems*. Its two doves, 'Nearly uncontrollable love-weights', are simultaneously 'violently gone' and still present, 'coiled', 'bubbling molten', 'wobbling top-heavy / Into one and many'.[36] They are manifestations of the Hughesian Goddess, partly metamorphosed into the Holy Spirit, but perhaps also the spirits of Sylvia and Assia. In the contents list of *New Selected Poems*, the title 'A Dove' is placed on the page in such a way as to suggest that it is a coda to the sequence of 'Uncollected' Sylvia and Assia poems that are this volume's most remarkable feature.

The mini-cycle of four poems in *Ploughshares* was an epitome of both Hughes's myth and his life. In terms of his myth: initiation, infernal descent and rebirth. In terms of his life: the beginning of his marriage in Spain, the lily-imaged 'craving / Of cunt-flesh' which 'Hurt cannot open deep enough / To quench',[37] the end of his marriage with the telephone call, and the dove-imaged hope of redemption through cathartic poetry.

★

Shortly after the ill-fated phone call, Sylvia burnt a pile of Ted's manuscripts on a bonfire in the garden. In 'Burning the Letters', the incantatory poem that was companion to the act, she referred to the distinctive loops and jags of Ted's handwriting as 'spry hooks that bend and cringe', and proclaimed that the attic would be 'a good place' now that Ted was gone from Court Green.[38]

In London on 10 July, Ted went round to the Wevills' with four bottles of champagne. He said that it was his birthday, which it wasn't. Presumably he meant that it was the first day of his new life without Sylvia. When David went out to buy cigarettes, Ted told Assia that he was leaving Sylvia and that he wanted to see her, alone, the next day.[39]

She took the day off work, and Ted borrowed Al Alvarez's tiny flat. His memory of the occasion remained vivid for years: 'The first meeting at Al's flat: the Joan Baez records on – the strange bliss. The spicey suspicions: that she knew the place too well, that she had visited Al there.'[40] Reflecting on what he was doing, he recognised that what had really driven him into the affair was the quest for freedom and independence, the need to free himself from the 'bondage and tyranny' of marriage to Sylvia. Assia called herself the catalyst.

Their lovemaking was vigorous. Assia told her friend Nathaniel Tarn that Ted was 'very virile, "did things man does", <u>decides</u> etc. Everything D[avid] has stopped doing'. Ted stayed with Alvarez that night. Two days later, on Friday the 13th, he booked a hotel. (He was haunted by the significance of that date in relation to both Sylvia and Assia, making it the starting point of 'Capriccios', the opening poem of his elegy sequence for Assia.)[41] This time his lovemaking was 'so violent and animal' that he ruptured her. This turned Assia against him. She phoned her husband and told him that she was going to see Ted off at the station. David Wevill headed for Waterloo with a knife, turned back, went home and took eighteen sleeping pills. Assia returned home after midnight to find him 'lying so sweetly, so young (such contrast to fierce H. in bed)'. She woke him up, told him that Ted had raped her and called an ambulance so that he could have his stomach pumped in hospital. In the morning, David wrote a note to Ted: 'If you come near my wife again I will kill you. D.W.'[42]

Nathaniel Tarn, to whom Assia reported all this, described the next twist in telegraphic form: 'H. back in Devon. Wife has been having hysterics, child also. Wife had car crash. When A. tells H. over phone about D., he groans; says he was straightest man in the world etc. H. sends back table they had given him on S.'s orders. D. very tender and loving to Assia.' By the end of the month, Assia had told Ted that she did not want 'a slinky affair in London'. Her instinct was that Ted would probably stay with his wife.[43] He was indeed with Sylvia at this time: they fulfilled a commitment to give a joint poetry reading in North Wales, stopping on the way with Daniel Huws and his wife Helga, to whom Sylvia confided her marital woes. In early August, they said goodbye to Aurelia at Exeter station, with tension in the air. She would not see her daughter again.

Towards the end of August, Sylvia wrote to tell her mother that she was thinking of getting a legal separation. Ted was still seeing Assia in London during the week and only coming to Court Green at weekends. She felt degraded and she hated his lies. She was also concerned about financial support for the children.

In September, though, she decided to give the marriage another chance. To have any hope of rebuilding their relationship, they would need some space away from Devon and indeed the children. As so often when imagining an alternative life, Ted's thoughts turned to rural Ireland. They recalled an encounter of the previous summer. The Poetry Book Society, under the directorship of poet, novelist, biographer and Oxford don John Wain, was running a festival in London called Poetry at the Mermaid. Guinness the brewer had sponsored a dozen rising poets to write a piece on a subject of their own choice, for a modest fee. The best poem would then be awarded a Guinness Prize. For the brewer, it was a low-cost opportunity to run an advertising campaign under the slogan 'Thirst Prize'. Ted, along with Geoffrey Hill and Clifford Dyment, had read at one o'clock. He and Sylvia had then joined another of the poets, Richard Murphy, for a late lunch.

Murphy was in awe of *The Hawk in the Rain* and *Lupercal*. Sylvia did most of the talking. Ted was strong and silent, but came alive when the conversation turned to country life, fishing and the sea. Three years older than Ted, Murphy was a native of the west of Ireland. In 1959, a marriage just ended (following his wife's affair with the writer and politician Conor Cruise O'Brien), he had arrived at Inishbofin aboard a leaky sixty-year-old lugsail-rigged fishing and cargo boat with nothing but a box of books, a case of wine and a carton of orange juice. Determined to learn more about the sea, he bought and restored the *Ave Maria*, a fishing boat of the ancient kind known as a Galway hooker. The following year, based in the impoverished fishing village of Cleggan, he set himself up in a small business that involved taking tourists out into the Bay of Galway for a combination of sea angling and day trips to Inishbofin.

By the time of the Mermaid event, he had put together a volume of poems, many of them inspired by his adventures on the *Ave Maria*, called *Sailing to an Island*. The publisher Macmillan was looking at it. A few months later, Charles Monteith showed the manuscript to T. S. Eliot, who said 'yes', leading Murphy to withdraw it from Macmillan and become a Faber poet. Around this time, Murphy met Sylvia, but not Ted, for a second time: he was at a reception in the Goldsmiths' Hall in London, where she received a Guinness Prize for her poem 'Insomniac'. The following year, she was a judge for the same prize, and on Saturday 21 July 1962 she sent Murphy a letter tipping him off that he would soon be getting an official letter telling him that he was the next prizewinner. The letter went on to say that she and Ted desperately needed 'a boat and the sea and no squalling babies'.[44] Murphy invited them to stay in September, after the tourist season.

They arrived in Connemara on Thursday 13 September 1962, having taken a train to Galway and been driven the 60 miles to remote Cleggan. They planned to stay for a week of sailing and sea air. When Murphy asked them to sign the visitors' book of the *Ave Maria*, he could not help noticing that Ted put his address as 'Halifax, Yorkshire' and Sylvia hers as 'Court Green, North Tawton, Devon'. They slept in twin beds.

Murphy took them to Coole Park, home of W. B. Yeats's friend Lady Gregory, and then to Yeats's tumbledown tower at Ballylee. Ted and Sylvia said that they should steal apples from a moss-coated apple tree that had been planted in Yeats's time, perhaps by Yeats himself. They shook the branches. Murphy asked why they were doing this. 'When you come to a place like this you have to violate it,' said Ted in a 'voice of quiet intensity'.[45]

They did not criticise each other in front of Murphy. He never heard them quarrel. They spoke separately of their troubles. Sylvia was upset by Ted's lies; she wanted a legal separation. Ted never mentioned any fault in Sylvia, but he said that 'after six or seven years that had been marvellously creative for him, the marriage had become destructive, and he thought the best thing to do was to give it a rest by going to Spain for six months'.[46] He did indeed have Spanish plans, though not for a long stay.

Just three days after arriving, without saying goodbye to Murphy, Ted left. Sylvia explained that he had gone down to County Clare to fish with his friend the painter Barrie Cooke. She would meet up with him in Dublin later in the week. Left alone with Richard Murphy, Sylvia made a pass at him, which he rebuffed. Back at Court Green, she wrote him a very awkward letter, simultaneously thanking him for his hospitality, seeking his help in finding a place for her in Connemara, and withdrawing an invitation to Court Green on the grounds that Ted would not be there (the implication being that she had registered his desire not to have an affair with her). She had fallen in love with the west of Ireland and wanted to live there, with just the children. In early October, she wrote again, reiterating the plan. She said that the end of her marriage was proving good for her work: 'I am writing for the first time in years, a real self, long smothered. I get up at 4 a.m. when I wake, and it is black, and write till the babies wake.'[47]

Ted, it seemed, had not been serious about using Ireland as a real chance for a new beginning. By the end of the trip, he was acknowledging to Olwyn that a legal separation or even a divorce was on the cards. 'In her manner with other people she's changed extraordinarily,' he wrote of Sylvia, 'become much more as she was when I first knew her, and much more like her mother, whom I detest.' Olwyn had written some characteristically robust words, and now he agreed with her, hardening his heart against Sylvia: 'You're right, she'll have to grow up – it won't do her any harm.'[48] He had to attend to one or two things before going back to sort out arrangements at Court Green, he added.

One of those things was a clandestine holiday in Spain with Assia. Nathaniel Tarn was one of the first, and the very few, to know. On 1 October, he made one of his neat journal notes. Assia phoned him in the afternoon from work, 'very agitated to say that she spent the last 10 days of her trip with Hughes in Spain'. It had all been arranged before she had flown to Canada at the end of August to see her mother, who had breast cancer. 'She works wonderfully with Hughes,' she told Tarn, they were 'thinking of doing a film script together'. But should she inform David, or not? She and her husband were about to go to Germany together. Tarn sensed a ghastly inevitability about the whole unfolding drama. He replied that there was little he could do. The whole thing was 'like watching a Greek play'.[49]

13

'That Sunday Night'

Writing to happily married Gerald in Australia, Ted was evasive in describing his entanglement. He merely dropped a few hints about 'calamitous confrontations with all sorts of bogies' and the conflict between 'puritan tendencies' and the 'irregularities' that he needed in order to exist.[1] He particularly stressed the way in which fame had changed his life. He needed to get away from London to escape the pressures and demands that literary celebrity had placed upon him. Court Green was the creative haven that he required. But almost as soon as he was there, he was drawn back to London, not only for the necessity of BBC work and meetings with editors, but also because he could not help enjoying the adulation he received there.

Writing some time later to unmarried and much closer sibling Olwyn in Paris, he was more candid. The letter is undated, but it must have been written either around the same time as Sylvia's letter to her mother announcing that 'I am going to try to get a legal separation from Ted' (27 August 1962), or, more probably, immediately after Ted left Court Green 'with all his clothes and things' and Sylvia 'piled the children and two cats in the car' and drove to Cornwall to stay with the Kanes, the occasion that inspired the poem 'Lesbos' (16 October 1962).[2]

'Grave news,' he began his confession, 'Sylvia and I have decided to part ways, in spite of the obstacles.'[3] Something began to happen to him in 'April or so', he explained, deliberately not mentioning Assia's visit on the third weekend of May. Since then, the marriage, the house and Sylvia had all seemed like 'the dead-end of everything'. So he 'blew up – very mildly' (the kiss in the kitchen?) and then 'went on the spree' (the month of vigorous sex with Assia, presumably). But this was 'no substitute for the real thing', which was to go and live where he liked, 'working uninterruptedly', choosing his friends as he pleased and seeing them as often as he liked, and 'generally changing' himself 'without the terrible censorship of somebody like Sylvia' confining his 'every impulse and inclination'. The jaguar, in other words, was trapped in the cage of marriage.

Now he was making his bid for freedom. The cage was soul-destroying. They had been 'good for each other' in the first couple of years of their marriage, but then things had deteriorated until 'finally the mutual destruction has been too obvious and open to ignore'. He told Olwyn that during the previous two years the only decent things he had written were during the ten days when Sylvia was in hospital. This suggests that Assia may, after all, have been telling the truth when she informed Nat Tarn that Ted had said this to her during the week-end at Court Green – she just made the incorrect assumption that he was referring to *Lupercal*, since it was the only book he had published in the previous few years.

Village life in Devon, Ted went on, was like living in an old people's home. The 10,000 desires that he had repressed for six years 'in a gentlemanly considerate way' (for which the usual phrase would be 'out of marital fidelity') had 'suddenly appeared in full bloom, absolutely insatiable'. He would give Sylvia Court Green, the Morris Traveller and as much cash as he could send. The fewer his possessions, the better for his work. He would live in London till December, fulfilling his many reading engagements, then it would be off to Germany, Italy, wherever. He was beginning to write good poetry again. Sylvia had assisted in that by refusing him access to Court Green since he had become 'so sinful' (not strictly true – he was returning home at weekends). He wanted to break the mould of tedious, conventional English middle-class life. To be a kind of bohemian. The risk was that he would become a 'drifter', but he thought that he had the willpower and 'inner direction' to avoid this – besides, the need for cash would keep him working. Yes, his plan sounded like 'terrific egoism', but the alternative was – a phrase that reads with bitter irony in the light of subsequent events – 'suicide by wishi-washiness'. Sylvia would be 'O.K.', she was 'tough'. The only thing he says against her is that she 'made some terrible mistakes' and he 'let her make them'. He does not say what they are, but he was probably thinking of the outbursts of rage and the awkward incidents on social occasions. The loss of Frieda would be 'a problem'; as for Nick, being only a few months old, they hardly knew each other. He signed off by saying that he had written some film outlines – not mentioning that he and Assia were talking about collaborating on scripts. The letter does not mention Assia at all.

When a man has an affair, his classic defence is to say that there had long been cracks in the marriage anyway. A big part of the *Birthday Letters* project was an attempt to ask when things began to go wrong. Selection and retrospection, the rear-view-mirror perspective, meant that it was easy to highlight symbolic moments of foreboding – auguries and portents – from the start and all the way through. But some of the poems seek to pinpoint specific moments of crisis. Was there one as early as their first walk across the moors to 'Wuthering Heights', when they had seen an injured grouse and he had put it out of its misery with a crisp blow to the head, and she had been sorry for the poor bird and afraid of the ease with which, like Heathcliff, he could perform a casual act of violence? 'The Grouse' was not included in the published *Birthday Letters*, but probably should have been. It describes Sylvia 'shaking' and 'weeping, staring in horror', then verbally attacking Ted as if had done 'Something incredible, inconceivable'. The grouse was, for Sylvia, 'like the Rosenbergs' in the opening paragraph of *The Bell Jar*, with its foreshadowing of Sylvia's own electro-convulsive therapy:

> All the stupid murders of this earth
> Had moved into my hand to crush the eyebrows
> Of the heather-bird.[4]

Sylvia's reaction to the killing of the grouse echoes in Ted's mind with the later incident of the rabbit-catcher.

More plausibly: did the first crack appear at the time of the incident with the girl at Smith? Like 'The Grouse', the poem about this was excluded from the published version of *Birthday Letters*. It tells of how Ted was a little envious of the sexual freedom of his colleagues in the relaxed college world of the late Fifties. Sylvia was keeping him on a tight leash, suffocating him under her bell jar. He began to fight for air, to 'de-mesmerise' himself, to 'be normal'. This 'shattered no glass' – an allusion to the glass that Sylvia threw across the room at him, which so bizarrely refused to shatter but bounced back, hit her in the face and made her see stars. It did not shatter the glass, but it 'almost / Shattered' Sylvia. The poems tells of how his two pretty students arrived with their bottle of wine to celebrate the end of term, how he refused their offer, in the knowledge that Sylvia was 'waiting / Aggrieved', and of how 'They walked with me – till you saw them.' He 'could not understand' her 'frenzy'.[5] This was 'the first' in 'a series of lessons'. He humoured Sylvia, nursed her, spoiled her 'strange fits of possessive passion' (a neat twist on Wordsworth's 'strange fits of passion' in his 'Lucy' poem about his dead love). By doing all this, he 'cultivated a monster' or 'released a monster':'Yes, it was monstrous in you.'

So did the point of no return arrive when Sylvia's rages became uncontrollable – perhaps when she smashed the mahogany-topped table that was a Farrar family heirloom ('The Minotaur')? Or did it occur on the April evening in 1960, just after the birth of Frieda, when Ted walked over Chalk Farm Bridge, 'slightly light-headed / With the lack of sleep and the novelty', and was offered a fox cub for a pound and did not buy it? Was that the failed test?

> If I had grasped that whatever comes with a fox
> Is what tests a marriage and proves it a marriage –
> I would not have failed the test. Would you have failed it?
> But I failed. Our marriage had failed.[6]

As Heaney recognised, these lines have great poetic power. Biographically, however, this is nonsense: their marriage had not failed by the time of Frieda's birth. They were often blissfully happy in Chalcot Square. How could their marriage possibly have failed when eight months after this they wrote an ecstatic and hilarious joint Christmas card to Sylvia's undergraduate friend from Smith, Ann Davidow, in which Sylvia tells of how Ted 'got a wicked telegram from ABC television this morning (heaven knows how *they* knew where he was) asking him to appear as poet-of-the-year' (he refused) and Ted jokes about the three kings on the card holding caskets of 'petrol for their vespa', 'fuel of brandy' and cocaine, before signing off by saying that he would leave space for Sylvia to tell her 'how surpassingly indescribably dissectingly unearthingly collapsingly bisectingly beautiful her daughter is, because it is all true and needs to be told'?[7]

Symbolically, the failure of the fox–cub test is a retrospective version of the choice described in the letter to Olwyn. For Ted, ever since 'The Thought-Fox', a fox had meant the gift of poetry. The rejection of the fox cub signals that the choice to have children was a rejection of a life devoted wholly to poetry. It is the 'pram in the hall' argument.

Then again, could the crack in the marriage be dated to the time when Ted started suffering from fibrillations of the heart, while digging the garden at Court Green ('The Lodger')? Was that some kind of sign that his heart was not really in the marriage?

The most honest answer in *Birthday Letters* to the question of when and why it all went wrong is the poem called simply 'Error', which is filled with totemic images out of literary romance:

> I brought you to Devon. I brought you into my dreamland.
> I sleepwalked you
> Into my land of totems. Never-never land:
> The orchard in the West.

That was the beginning of the end: taking Sylvia away from the city, from the cocktail parties at Faber, the dinner-parties with Mr Eliot, the BBC, the theatre, the cinema and the art galleries, the buzz around the publication of her work. Trying to make her live his dream, burying her in the country, taking her to the 'vicarage rotting like a coffin, / Foundering under its weeds', where she would stare at her blank sheet of paper, silent at her typewriter, 'listening / To the leaking thatch drip, the murmur of rain, / And staring at that sunken church'.[8] That was the error.

Ted's imagining of a rural idyll came from the loveliest poem in the English language, Samuel Taylor Coleridge's 'Frost at Midnight', in which a poet in a peaceful cottage in a village in the West Country watches lovingly over his infant by moonlight as 'eave-drops' fall from the 'thatch'.[9] The line in 'Error' about the dank and depressing drip from the thatch of Court Green negatively rewrites this image in recognition that the idyll had turned into a nightmare. In sharp contrast to Coleridge's inspirational Nether Stowey, Mr and Mrs

Hughes's North Tawton has become a place where the entire world seems to come to an end in a field of bullocks 'Huddled behind gates, knee-deep in quag, / Under the huddled, rainy hills'.[10] Court Green: they thought it was paradise, but it had become hell.

Sylvia's own analysis of the reasons for the end of the marriage was expressed most clearly in letters to her dear friend and sophomore roommate Marty Brown, written in the last few weeks of her life. Her reasoning is remarkably similar to Ted's in his half-acknowledgement of the state of affairs in his letter to Gerald and his explicit account in the letter to Olwyn. First, there was the fact that fame had changed him: 'he lives just for himself without a care in the world in a Soho flat, flying to Spain on holiday and so on and universally adored. You have no notion how famous he is over here now.'[11] And secondly, there was his desire for freedom from family ties: 'Ted's suddenly decided he doesn't want any children, home, responsibility etc.'[12]

Soon after the break-up, she anticipated his poem 'Error': burial in the country was a dream for him, but a kind of death for her. To her friend Clarissa Roche, she wrote, 'I loved London life and did not want to leave – coming to the country was his idea, his "dream", as he said. I guess he thought we could live on potatoes and apples.'[13] And to her mother, 'I miss *brains*, hate this cow life, am dying to surround myself with intelligent, good people. I'll have a salon in London.'[14] Back amid the life and culture of the city in December 1962, she felt like kissing the paintings in the art galleries.

Though Assia may have been what a psychoanalyst would call the 'presenting problem', behind which there were deeper reasons for the breakdown of the marriage, had she not entered their lives Sylvia would not have thrown Ted out and he would not have stayed away. On the whole, a man does not leave his wife, home and two tiny children unless he has another woman's bed to go to. From the point of view of Ted's desire to live alone and do exactly what he pleased, it was advantageous that Assia was married to someone else. An affair was exciting and carried none of the drudgery or the compromises necessary when two people live together.

There is a degree of truth in Ted's claim that he had done his best work early in the marriage, though he should have said in the first three years, not the first two. *Lupercal*, the dazzling product of those years, was dispatched to Faber and Faber just after their third anniversary and just before they set off on their journey across America. By the time they were on the road in early July 1959, it was in the admiring hands of T. S. Eliot. Only one poem was added after Yaddo. But he did also write good poems in Chalcot Square and Court Green. They were not collected in book form until *Wodwo* of 1967. The main difficulty in 1960–2 was not so much the drying up of poetry as the need to write plays and stories, mainly for broadcast, because the BBC was the best source of income. It was also the case that Ted was distracted from his adult work by his children's writing. Sometimes, it wasn't clear to him whether a particular poem was for adults or children. His collection *The Earth-Owl and Other Moon-People*, sent to Faber and Faber just as he was leaving his marriage, was submitted as a children's book, moved to the adult list because some of its contents seemed rather grotesque and grown-up for children, then later returned to the roster of his children's works.

The uncomfortable truth was that, since her breakthrough at Yaddo, Sylvia's poetry had been getting better and better while Ted's had remained more or less the same. This was hard for him to admit, but perhaps a subliminal reason for his moving out. The great irony of the next four months was that he achieved very little by way of advance: he continued busily with radio plays, including one called *Difficulties of a Bridegroom*, an inauspicious title at this time in his life. Sylvia, on the other hand, launched into the best writing of her life, arguably (and certainly in Ted's opinion and Al Alvarez's) the best poetry by any woman since Emily Dickinson (whose work Ted was really discovering at the time).

The parting of the ways was supposed to help Ted with his work, but in fact it helped Sylvia. And, of course, it was her anger at his behaviour that fuelled her imagination. 12 October 1962, 'Daddy': the fascist brute, the boot in the face and the marital words 'I do' spoken to a 'model' of the father who is 'A man in black with a Meinkampf look'.[15] How could Ted not see himself as the 'man in black' to whom Sylvia said 'I do' on Bloomsday 1956 and who lived with him for 'Seven years, if you want to know'?

17 October 1962, 'The Jailor': 'My night sweats grease his breakfast plate ... I have been drugged and raped ... I wish him dead or away ... what would he / Do, do, do without me?'[16] 20 October 1962,

'Fever 103°': 'Greasing the bodies of adulterers / Like Hiroshima ash'.[17] 21 October 1962, 'Amnesiac': 'Name, house, car keys, / The little toy wife − / Erased, sigh, sigh … I am never, never, never coming home!'[18] 29 October 1962, 'Nick and the Candlestick': 'The pain / You wake to is not yours.'[19] Nick and Frieda were of course her prime concern. She kept herself cheerful through horseback riding and by writing to her mother about Nick cutting his first tooth, pushing around Frieda's building blocks as he learned to crawl.

She worried about money and raged about Ted in this regard, but there were many times when she felt as he did: that, for the sake of their art, it was better for them to be without each other. 'Living apart from Ted is wonderful − I am no longer in his shadow, and it is heaven to be liked for myself alone, knowing what I want.'[20] She voiced this feeling on one of her trips to London in early November. The Irish fantasy behind her, she was looking for a place in the city. A dream came true when she discovered that a flat was available in a house with a blue heritage plaque on the façade. It was in Fitzroy Road, just round the corner from Chalcot Square. She had noticed it when living in London before, and had fantasised about moving into it: the great W. B. Yeats had lived there as a child. Was it not a sign that, having been to his tower at Ballylee, now she had the opportunity to commune with his poetic spirit? At some level, she must also have hoped that the lure of the shade of his beloved Yeats might bring back Ted.

She was still thinking about divorce, urged on by various female friends. By coincidence, she was asked to review for the *New Statesman* a forthcoming book on *Lord Byron's Wife*. Her essay, filled with wit and praise, was published on 7 December 1962, under the headline 'Suffering Angel', three days before she moved with the children from Devon to London. The wronged but strong-minded wife of the handsome, famous, wildly promiscuous poet who has all London, and in particular all women, at his feet, and then the controversial, high-profile divorce case that brought exile and grief. Perhaps there was a lesson to be learned there. Divorce would have been an irreversible step. Perhaps she should wait it out. Various possibilities were opening up. She was seeing a lot of Al Alvarez. Ted invited her to bring the children for Christmas at the Beacon, but she declined. She offered herself to Alvarez on Christmas Eve instead.

After she moved to London in early December, it was much easier for Ted to see the children. Though he was giving everybody the Beacon as his postal address, he was spending most of his time in London. Initially, he had slept on the floors and sofas of friends. Then he was able to borrow a flat in Soho that Dido Merwin was selling for her mother. Then, some time after Sylvia moved to 23 Fitzroy Road, he found the little flat in Fitzrovia about which she would be so scathing in the letter to her college friend in which she also alluded to his holiday in Spain with Assia. The flat was a studio on Cleveland Street, north of Charlotte Street, just off the Tottenham Court Road, in a predominantly Greek and Cypriot area. It was 'spic' (clean), he told Olwyn, and well done up, a 'bit like a hotel room, big desk, ground floor, gas fire, one room', a little kitchen and a bigger bathroom than the one at Chalcot Square (a useful asset for lady guests). It had a phone.[21]

By the end of October, David and Assia were doing their best to repair their marriage. At least, he was. He would attentively open car doors and light cigarettes for her. They became 'very lovey-dovey, arm in arm all the time'.[22] They carried on through Christmas and into the New Year, pretending that nothing was happening. 'She has been seeing H. regularly,' Nathaniel Tarn noted early in January 1963, 'and D. knows it, though they have stopped talking about it.'[23] Tarn could not understand why Wevill had not kicked his wife out.

Ted Hughes was also seeing someone else.

Susan Alliston was born in London in 1937 and educated in a class of just four girls at Queen's Gate School in South Kensington. Her classmate Vanessa Redgrave remembered that they 'argued for hours over the meaning of T. S. Eliot and Ezra Pound, and the French symbolists that Sue was studying'.[24] At a young age, she married an American called Clem Moore, who by strange Hughesian coincidence had been Warren Plath's roommate at Harvard.[25] In the late Fifties, Sue began work as a secretary at Faber and Faber, also serving as a reader for other publishers. In May 1960, a poem of hers called 'St Martin's Lane, London' was published in America in the *Nation*.

Yes, and on the one hand were the jagged teeth of walls
And starred red paper screaming
Paper pasted with a host's eye
Screaming where it hung like flesh,
Torn away by a demolition plan
They felled the bricks and dust
Streamed about them,
Rose from the rubble – inevitable ghost
Haunting their mouths with grit …[26]

Ted Hughes read and admired this and enquired about the author. He was told by someone connected with Faber that it was by 'a gorgeous English girl with extraordinary hair'. Some time later, he met her in a lift at Faber and Faber. As he wrote in a brief introduction when he was hoping to get her poems published after her death: 'It was one of those faces you do not forget. She was tall, and seemed pale, with a shoulder-length dense mane of slightly crinkly hair the colour and seemingly almost the texture of that dark-bronzed fine wire on electrical transformers. It stood out thickly like the mane on an ancient Egyptian figure.' She spoke with 'comic flair and zest'. There was 'a disturbing blend of plangent resonance and aggressive edge' in her voice. She passionately plunged herself into 'situations and adventures and collisions'. Everything that she did, she did with her 'whole excitable body'.[27] She also had a dash of Welsh blood, which attracted him.

It was not until two years after reading the poem set in St Martin's Lane that he discovered she was its author. He got to know her among his circle of friends who drank in the Lamb in Lamb's Conduit Street, round the corner from Rugby Street. She had separated from Clem Moore and her constant companion was Tasha Hollis, daughter of White Russian émigré intellectuals. She too had recently separated from her husband. Hughes sensed that Sue 'was searching for a new direction': 'She talked a good deal about poetry and continually promised to show me poems. But she seemed to write rarely and with little confidence. She preferred to dance, to eat curry, to drink beer, and to wallow in talk about the peoples and politics of the world. She read a lot of anthropology and spoke of becoming an anthropologist.'[28] The latter interest was of course a Hughesian passion.

She eventually showed him a poem called 'Samurai', which astonished him with its power:

> Aïe – my head is severed
> By the sword of a samurai.
> Catch it before it falls! …
>
> I go down, down.
> A noble swipe, Jap!
> Carry my scalp.
> My hands, twitching, feel
> the three elegant arches of your feet.[29]

On the basis of poems such as this, Ted would one day write admiringly of the 'active, down-to-earth, almost aggressive streak' that gave vitality to Sue's work. Her poems were 'sinewy, intricate and real', with 'nimble penetration, nightmare, and a weird lucidity'. 'Even at their most abstract', he argued, they had 'the concreteness of an actual voice'. One senses that he is remembering her voice even as he writes this: 'Behind them we feel her rich insecurity, turmoil, a person plunged in the open world.'[30]

From 1956 until the summer of 1962, Ted Hughes and Sylvia Plath lived and worked together with utter loyalty and extreme intensity. They wrote joint letters to friends and families, they wrote poems and prose on the reverse side of sheets filled with drafts of the other's writing. They were inseparable. One of the reasons why there are so few letters between them is that they hardly ever spent a day or a night apart. Plath's temperament, exacerbated by her depression, made her possessive and jealous. It is hardly surprising that, having cut himself free by going to live a single life in London, and with Assia only available for hasty assignations, Ted enjoyed flirting with other attractive women among his circle of literary friends in the Lamb.

According to Susan Alliston's journal, her first conversation with Ted, other than the brief encounter in the lift at Faber, took place on 1 November 1962, a fortnight after he had packed his things and left Court Green. This was the moment when David Wevill was doing his best to re-woo Assia. The banter in the pub included an exchange in which Ted said, 'Marriage is not for me – nor you, I think.' Sue replied,

'Perhaps at forty,' a statement which takes on sad irony in the light of subsequent history.[31] Clearly Ted was signalling that, having just left an all-consuming marriage, not to mention two young children who still held his heart, he did not want to commit to anyone else. Assia, he told Susan some months later, was the most physically attractive person he had ever met (everyone who encountered Assia agreed upon her phenomenal sexual charisma). But he was unwilling to give himself wholly to her as he had to Sylvia. He needed the escape valve of other company.

For Ted Hughes, who was always Philip Larkin's mighty opposite, sexual freedom began in 1962, between the Chatterley trial and the Beatles' first single, 'Love Me Do'. For him, Sue Alliston and her flat-mate Tasha Hollis were embodiments of the bohemian life he was ready to embrace. Not feeling the loyalty towards the still-married Assia that he had for so long felt towards Sylvia, he was determined to enjoy the vitality of these equally beautiful but less intense and demanding young women. In January and early February, he saw as much of Sue as of Assia.

But he had not given up on Sylvia either. In early December, when she was in town making plans for Fitzroy Road, they went out to dinner with Eric White, the head of the Poetry Book Society, at a restaurant called L'Epicure in Dean Street. They ate beef stroganoff and got drunk on red wine. After saying goodbye to Eric at midnight, Ted and Sylvia walked round and round Soho Square, talking and talking. In 'Soho Square', a long poem about that night, drafted and redrafted on numerous occasions, but finally omitted from *Birthday Letters*, Ted read the moment as a precious opportunity: 'This was an invitation to the angel / Of reconciliation between us.'

Sylvia accused him of having an affair with Dido Merwin as well as Assia. Wasn't he living in her flat? He assured her that Dido was the last person he would take to bed. Then the floodgates opened. Sylvia's words of accusation 'stumbled' tipsily out, her defensive 'front' collapsing. Then her 'tears gushed', her face melted. It was like a bursting of the dam that had been holding everything in for months, a release of 'dreadful abandon' – *abandon*, such a potent word in the context of his departure from the marital home. She cried 'like a child who had become / The river-bed of infinite crying'. It was as if she had 'found the truth' and the truth was nothing but tears. He put his arm around her and tried to calm her. Her body crumpled under the support of his arm. He 'hung on', out of his depth. He could not 'check' her 'torrent of grief', could not 'escape it, or see any way out of it'. The railings and doorways of Soho Square spun dizzily past: in later years, he would go back and examine 'it all closely', note it 'detail by detail, blankly', like 'a murderer listening' for the ghost of his victim (one version of the poem was called 'The Ghost in Soho Square'). Everything that they 'had shared', the seven years since Falcon Yard, 'Came adrift in the flood' and poured over them, Sylvia crying in great waves, a 'drowning vision' of their 'whole life', the pair of them clinging to each other in the wreckage.[32]

The time reached two in the morning and Soho Square, in the middle of heaving London, was deserted. There wasn't even a police-man or a prostitute (the usual denizens of Soho) in sight. Ted took the plunge and invited Sylvia into Dido Merwin's mother's flat. He hoped that she might sleep. But the overwhelming flood of Sylvia's emotion could not be stopped. They had a night of blazing anger and sorrow, and perhaps love, much to the annoyance of the neighbours. Then came 'the bitter care', at the top of Sylvia's voice, the 'Volcanic' emotion that she could not control. The people in the flat beneath banged on the ceiling to no effect. The screaming went on, Ted rolling beneath it all,

> A boulder, insensate, irrelevant,
> While that tidal wave, that eruption
> From your childhood, swamped and buried our world.[33]

Emotionally, poetically, perhaps erotically, it was a climax. It was his chance to 'launch an ark', but he did not take it. They parted in the morning.

One cold December day, after Sylvia and the children had moved to the Yeats flat in London, Ted drove down to Court Green and back, braving the icy 200 miles each way on the A30, sliding at 'Twenty miles an hour' through 'The worst snow and freeze-up for fifteen years'. He dug potatoes from beneath snow and straw, gathered apples from the store in the courtyard. Victorias and fat Bramleys for cooking, Pig's Nose Pippins for eating. It was twilight by then. He crept through the house, feeling like a ghost or an intruder. He looked at each thing, as if for the last time: the living room, his and Sylvia's bedroom, which they had painted red, their books and 'white-painted bookshelves', a battered old desk he had bought for £6 and a 'horse-hair Victorian chair' that had been an even greater bargain (five shillings). The house was made 'newly precious' by the thought of Sylvia's 'lonely last weeks there'. How clean she had kept it, despite her sorrows. Court Green was like a sealed casket, from which the treasure was already lost. He said goodbye to the house and crawled back through the night, along the ice-treacherous A30. He took the bag of potatoes and the bag of apples to Fitzroy Road for Sylvia and the children.[34]

Ted Hughes said that he visited Sylvia Plath in Fitzroy Road almost daily in the last weeks of her life, taking the children for walks or to the zoo in the mornings, and talking to Sylvia, comforting her, in the evenings. Sylvia said that he came 'once a week like a kind of apocalyptic Santa Claus'.[35] The truth was somewhere between the two. When a marriage breaks down, the truth is usually somewhere between the two competing narratives of despair and blame, guilt and self-justification, confrontation and compromise. When only one partner is left to tell the story, it is more difficult to balance the narrative. There have been many tellings of the last days of Sylvia Plath. What follows is Ted's telling, in his makeshift journal, in the immediate aftermath.[36]

On Sunday 3 February, Sylvia called to ask him to go over and have lunch with her. He was supposed to be at the BBC for a recording. He told her he would get to Fitzroy Road at two o'clock in the afternoon. Because of retakes and so forth, he was forced to send a BBC messenger to tell her that he could not be there for another hour. He arrived at ten past three. She had cooked meatloaf. They had their 'pleasantest' and 'most friendly open time' since the break-up. Sylvia read her most recent poems aloud. Ted thought her voice was 'stronger, calmer'. She seemed 'more whole and in better shape than at any time since she came to London'. They 'planned', they 'conspired'. When he played with Frieda, 'she wept'. He 'held them both' and Sylvia wept. She continually repeated that sooner or later he would be bound to desire someone else, but he denied this completely. For the last few days he had been calling everybody Sylvia. He had been wanting 'to turn back but not knowing how to stay out of the old trap'. He told her that he wanted to take up their old life, 'but that it had to be different'. He 'couldn't be a prisoner'. He also told her that he thought she was 'strengthening in her independent life'. He was thrilled that her writing was taking off again. He gently suggested that her work was 'disabled' when she saw too much of him. It would not be good for her work if 'her centre of gravity' returned to him. She promised to visit him on Thursday night. He stayed till two o'clock in the morning.

On the Monday lunchtime, she telephoned. Her tone had changed completely. He had to swear to quit the country within a fortnight. He was 'ruining her life' by living in London. She could not stand hearing all the gossip about him. He asked who was gossiping. She refused to tell him. She was overwrought, all the rebuilding of the previous day having vanished. He told her that he could not possibly leave England. He was broke and where would he go? She made him promise. Finally he said he would go, but that he did not see how he could. Sounding 'terribly excited', she said that she wanted him 'never to see her again'. He promised to leave as soon as he could.

On the Wednesday, he saw Assia. She told him that Sylvia had told her friend Gerry Becker all about their affair and the end of the marriage. She was putting about a story that Ted had deserted her in Devon, and left her with no money. Ted wrote Sylvia a note to tell her that she must stop spreading lies. If necessary, he would threaten Becker with a solicitor's letter. He took the note round to Fitzroy Road. Sylvia begged him not to do anything drastic; she couldn't help what people said. But it was obvious to him that she had been spreading the rumours. They talked again about moving to Yorkshire and she kept asking him if he 'had faith in her', which seemed 'new and odd'.

The next morning she telephoned, 'freshly upset'. She came round to his little Cleveland Street flat for the first and last time. One moment she was telling him in no uncertain terms to leave England forthwith. The next she was telling him the exciting news that she had been asked to go on the prestigious radio programme *Critics on Sunday* (a weekly review of the latest offerings in the arts). Did he have faith that she would have the confidence to do it? They talked for a long time. He wondered if one reason she had come was in order to check out his flat. She noticed everything, even the fact that he had a new edition of Shakespeare. When she left in the afternoon, things were still in the air: was he to go abroad immediately or were the two of them to go to Yorkshire? Plans for reunion in one breath, demands for permanent separation in the next: it was this volatility and unpredictability that made Ted doubt whether he could go to back to life with Sylvia.

He wrote a poem about this Thursday visit, the last time he saw her face to face for any length of time. It was published in *Birthday Letters* as 'The Inscription'. It describes her contradictory demands – Yorkshire together versus abroad alone – and her inquisitive inspection of the flat. Its bed, its telephone ('she had that number'). But the main focus is on the edition of Shakespeare. In the poem, it is his old red Oxford edition, the one that she had partially shredded, back in the days when 'happiness' seemed 'invulnerable', when he was late coming back from his meeting with Moira Doolan of the BBC. Now the book is 'Resurrected'. What the poem does not say is that it was actually a different Shakespeare, a new one. Given to him by Assia, with a loving inscription. The poem also reports an exchange in the course of the conversation that always haunted him, because these were among their last words. The painful memory is distanced into the third person: 'Yes, yes. Tell me / We shall sit together this summer / Under the laburnum. Yes, he said, yes yes yes.'[37]

The next day, Friday, at about half past three in the afternoon a letter came from her. She had posted it that morning, thinking he would get it on Saturday, but the London post was so efficient that it arrived the day it was posted. 'It was a farewell love-letter, two sentences. She was going off into the country, and intended never to see me again. Very ambiguous.'

He went straight to Fitzroy Road. Sylvia was 'there alone, tidying the place up'. Ted was 'upset and crying': 'What did she mean, what the hell was going on?' Sylvia was 'very cool and hostile'. She 'Took the note, burned it carefully in the ash-tray' and told him 'to go'. He 'could not get her to talk'. She had a bag packed. It was a long time before he found out where she had gone. Later that evening, she returned to her friends, Gerry and Jill Becker, with whom she had been staying in order to get some help with the children. She remained with them all weekend, until Gerry took her and the children home to Fitzroy Road on the Sunday night.

Ted spent the weekend with Sue. On the Saturday night, Sylvia phoned him at his flat in Cleveland Street. Sue heard her voice. Early on the Sunday morning, she phoned again. She did not know that Sue was there with him. Sue wrote in her diary the next day:

> Ted leaned over the telephone, saying 'Yes, yes' – being non-committal, saying 'Take it easy Sylvie'. He came back to bed, turned his back, clasped his head in his arms, 'God, God', he said. And said how she seemed drugged or drunk and wanted him to take her away somewhere. 'But if I go back, I die', he said. And he starts talking about his family: the uncle forced to marry a cripple out of loyalty & also '£2000 on marriage the legacy is,' says her mother. The one who hanged himself. How they thought Sylvia like this a bit – grasping, destructive.[38]

Ted and Sue spent the Sunday together: 'That day – beautiful. All day freely an[d] lot in between and the need of company in the evening. The coffee drinking and then to Tasha and Aant [a Dutch friend] and then he reads my poems, edits "Hill behind Tunis" and we buy wine and go to David [Ross]'s and Gill [Preston]'s. And he tells his poems of moon animals and plants.'[39]

But they did not want another night of painful phone calls from Sylvia, so instead of returning to Cleveland Street, Ted took Sue to Dan Huws's spare flat in 18 Rugby Street. He was back in the very house where he had first spent a night with Sylvia, seven years earlier. Sue wrote in her diary that they 'slept like the dead, side by side on this narrow bed'. There was 'A great tendresse in the morning', by which she presumably meant gentle lovemaking. Then Ted drove her to work.

At four in the afternoon, her best friend Tasha called. Sue's ex-husband Clem had rung to say that Sylvia was dead. Various people had received telegrams from Ted saying 'Sylvia dead' and giving details of the funeral. It would be in Yorkshire in exactly a week's time. Sue sent a telegram to Ted, saying 'Sorry sorry sorry if I can do anything'. She rang Clem, but knew that it was wrong to probe. The following morning, she was frightened. She was worried that Ted might not be OK. She called Al Alvarez, who knew the news but had not seen him. Alvarez said that maybe they should all get together later in the week. Desperate to see Ted, she went round to Fitzroy Road for the first time. He wasn't there, but she noted that it was a 'nice house'. Later in the afternoon, he rang. He told her everything. She said that she would go to the funeral. 'She's free,' she said. 'Yes,' replied Ted, 'but O God.'[40] Than Minton, one of their friends, remembered her walking towards him as he stood on the corner of Lamb's Conduit Street near their favourite pub. She was screaming, 'Sylvia is dead, Sylvia is dead.'[41]

Thinking back on the phone call and the chain of events, the full truth dawned on Sue: 'We slept while she died in each others arms.'[42]

Ted parked his Morris Traveller on the north side of the Euston Road and walked over to Cleveland Street. Discoloured snow had been banked by the roadside for weeks. He went into his ground-floor flat, 'filled with snowlit light'. He lit his fire. He got out his paper and had just started to write when the phone rang, like 'a jabbing alarm of guilt'. He imagined that it had been ringing all night – Sylvia calling from the phone booth on the corner of Primrose Hill. This would probably be her again. The voice at the other end was, what: calm? quiet? – or crisp, yes, that was the tone. The voice of someone used to delivering bad news. It announced: 'Your wife is dead.'[43]

He walked the short distance to University College Hospital, where he went into the morgue and formally identified the body. Then he sent telegrams to everybody he could think of and a short letter to Olwyn in Paris, telling her that Sylvia had gassed herself at about six o'clock in the morning on Monday 11 February. 'She asked me for help, as she so often has,' he wrote. 'I was the only person who could have helped her, and the only person so jaded by her states and demands that I could not recognize when she really needed it.'[44]

Her GP, John Horder, who examined the body at 10.30 and then phoned Ted, concluded that the time of death was probably closer to four o'clock in the morning, the low point in the body's circadian rhythm. Sylvia had been ill with a virus and struggling with depression. Horder had recently prescribed her some new anti-depressants. He felt that she was responding well, apparently understanding her struggle against the suicidal depression and faithfully reporting any side-effects. But response to such drugs takes about two weeks. He was worried about her, and had arranged for a live-in nurse. She was the one who arrived for her first morning at 9 a.m. that Monday and discovered the body, and the children, who were cold but safe. Looking back, Horder came to the conclusion that Sylvia 'had reached the dangerous time when someone with suicidal tendencies is sufficiently roused from disabling lethargy to do something about it'.[45]

The coroner's inquest recorded a verdict of 'Carbon Monoxide Poisoning (domestic gas) whilst suffering from depression'.[46] Sylvia had taped up the kitchen and bedroom doors, and placed towels underneath, to stop the gas from spreading through the rest of the flat. Then she had placed her cheek on a kitchen cloth folded neatly on the floor of the oven and turned on the taps of the cooker. The bedroom window was wide open and she had left bread and milk by Frieda and Nick's high-sided cots.

Ted said farewell to Sylvia's body one more time, in the funeral parlour, where he was accompanied by Al Alvarez and another friend, the Australian painter Charles Blackman.[47] The following Sunday, Alvarez published four of her poems in the *Observer*, together with a brief announcement of her death. He described her as the most gifted woman poet of the age and wrote that the loss to literature was 'inestimable'.[48]

On the morning of Monday 18 February 1963, Jill Becker and her husband Gerry, with whom Sylvia had spent her last weekend, took the train to Yorkshire for the funeral. Aunt Hilda's daughter Vicky ferried them, and other mourners, from Hebden Bridge railway station up the hill to the dark stone village of Heptonstall. Over tea and sandwiches at the Beacon, Edith Hughes asked Jill about her friendship with Sylvia. 'We all loved her, you know,' said Edith. Bill Hughes was silent. There was a short service in the gloomy church a few hundred yards further up the hill from the house. 'For a few moments,' Jill Becker remembered, 'sunlight came through a stained-glass window, enriching the yellow in it.'[49] They followed the coffin out to the exposed graveyard on the hillside, with its view away to the moor. It had been the worst winter for a generation. Even down in London, pipes had frozen and snow had been banked in the street for weeks. The grave was 'a yellow trench in the snow, its banked-up mud the same colour as the stained glass'. When the rites were complete, they all walked away. 'I'll stay here alone for a while,' said Ted.[50]

They went to a private upper room in a pub in the village, about fourteen of them, mostly Ted's friends and relatives, though Warren

Plath and his wife Margaret had flown over from America. According to Jill Becker, at various times Ted said, 'Everybody hated her' ('I didn't,' Jill replied), 'It was either her or me,' 'She made me professional,' and 'I *told* her everything was going to be all right. I *said* that by summer we'd all be back together at Court Green' – which is indeed what he had said during that conversation in his Cleveland Street flat eleven days before.[51]

On the cover of one of the numerous recycled school exercise books filled with drafts towards the poetry sequence that was eventually published as *Birthday Letters*, Ted Hughes wrote the title 'That Sunday Night'.[52] Inside, there are just four poems. The first begins: 'What did happen that Sunday night? / Your last night?' It tells the story of Sylvia's farewell letter, how it arrived on the day that it was sent, thus throwing her plans, and of how she burnt it before his eyes. On the next page, the poem is redrafted and expanded. This time, he tells of how he spent the weekend following that last brief encounter in Fitzroy Road. The Saturday and Sunday represented a hiatus, a time taken out from the calendar of ordinary life, hours stolen from some other life. Into the gap came the drive of his love-life ('My numbed love-life'), in which he found himself pulled by the magnetic force of 'Two mad needles'. These compass-needles then become the sewing needles of 'two women', obsessively performing their own selves by sewing colourful tapestries made from his own 'nerves'. They are like classical Fates, Norns or perhaps *tricoteuses* at the guillotine of his reputation. They are, presumably, Assia Wevill and Susan Alliston. That weekend it was Susan.

He then tells of how, not knowing why, he took Susan to 18 Rugby Street and made love to her in 'our wedding bed' – a bed in which he had not lain since his wedding night with Sylvia. There is denial in the phrase 'not knowing why': it must have been to escape the telephone in Cleveland Street. The poem turns on the paradox that he was hiding from Sylvia in the very bed in which he had consummated his love for her. There is poetic licence here: on this occasion, he was actually in Dan Huws's father's other flat in the house. Later, Susan would live in 18 Rugby Street, and it would be from there that she would be taken to die, in the very same hospital where he had gone to formally identify Sylvia's cold body.

Some elements of 'That Sunday Night', or 'February 10th' as he called it in the exercise book's brief contents list, would eventually be worked into '18 Rugby Street', a last-minute addition to the type-script of *Birthday Letters* that he sent to Faber and Faber a year before his death. The bulk of it, with the final title 'Last Letter', would lie among Hughes's unpublished papers for more than ten years after his death. Only in 2010 would readers discover the words with which Dr Horder broke the news on the telephone when Ted was back in his Cleveland Street studio flat on the Monday morning. As published, the closing lines of the poem imagined the doctor's voice as a 'weapon' or perhaps 'a measured injection'. Just four words, spoken without emotion, penetrating deep into his ear: 'Your wife is dead.'[53]

The remainder of the 'That Sunday Night' exercise book contains 'The Gypsy', which did appear in *Birthday Letters* (the one about the ominous words spoken in Reims), the immensely moving 'Soho Square', and finally a short poem called 'Walking in the Snow Alone'. Although there was a telephone in Ted's flat in 110 Cleveland Street – which may have rung unanswered on the night of 10–11 February, because he was in Rugby Street – there was not one in Fitzroy Road. Sylvia had been phoning the Cleveland Street number all weekend. Ted did not know that some of the calls were from the Beckers' place. He assumed that, each time she called, Sylvia had to put on her long black coat and walk 'in the snow alone / Along Fitzroy Road'. She would have had to turn 'right down / Down Primrose Hill', cross the road and pass a sinister gateway 'At the North West corner of Primrose Hill' before reaching the telephone box. He could only assume that on her last night she had made that walk again, perhaps repeatedly, on the slippery pavement in the dark, in the depth of the coldest winter in living memory. It was 6 degrees below zero centigrade in London that Sunday night. The imagery, partially incorporated into the version of the scene that was eventually published in 'Last Letter', is some of Ted's most haunting:

> You walked it alone, over the packed snow,
> Between the barricades of snow
> Coarsened to dirty ice, with frozen slush,
> You walked it in your long black woollen coat –
> How many times?

> With your plait coiled up at the back of your head, you
>   walked it
> Alone. That is the point. I see you
> In the dark,
> Walking it – alone.[54]

That is what he saw in his imagination, and what he heard was the sound of the telephone ringing and ringing in the empty Cleveland Street studio flat as he and Sue slept in each other's arms in Rugby Street.[55]

Ted had been reading Sylvia's last poems. Al Alvarez had been publishing some of them. They both knew that her art underwent an extraordinary transformation into greatness in her last months. The separation had liberated her voice, not Ted's.

Early in 1963, he seems to have made a decision. At Yaddo, he had helped Sylvia to advance. Lowell's *Life Studies* and Roethke's example had helped too. But he had resisted 'confessional' poetry himself. The style was too American for him. Now, though, seeing what Sylvia was achieving by turning her own life, his own marriage, into poetry of such power, he thought again. Maybe it was time to follow her example, shattering as poems such as 'Daddy' were for him to read. Maybe he should write more directly about his own experience.

Three weeks before Sylvia's suicide, his radio play *Difficulties of a Bridegroom* had been broadcast on the BBC Third Programme. That same week, he wrote to Olwyn in Paris.[56] He enclosed two new poems. Though he called them mere 'bagatelles', they actually represented his own breakthrough into a new voice. A more personal voice: they were his first truly confessional poems, written under the influence of Sylvia. He worked at them repeatedly.

One of them was a poem of life, 'Frieda's Early Morning'. After numerous redrafts and extensive revision,[57] it was eventually published in *Wodwo* as 'Full Moon and Little Frieda'. It beautifully combines Ted's own experience as a watchful father with a voice learned from Sylvia's lovely mothering poems 'Morning Song' and 'Nick and the Candlestick'. 'Moon!' baby Frieda suddenly cries. 'Moon! Moon!' And 'The moon has stepped back like an artist gazing amazed at a work // That points at him amazed.'[58] As so often, Ted is at once personal and literary: even as he turns a real paternal experience into poetry, the image of father and infant and the first word 'moon' is a reprise of Coleridge carrying his little child out to greet the moon in 'The Nightingale: A Conversation Poem', a companion piece to 'Frost at Midnight'.

The other piece sent to Olwyn was a poem of death. It was called 'Uncle A'. It begins: 'My uncle made of catapult rubber hung by the neck'. It calls the family suicide 'A mystery'. It fondly remembers Uncle Albert being able to 'turn a somersault on a hearth-rug / Dangle his entire weight from any one finger and do pull-ups'. It ends: 'His wife sold all his clothes before he was buried.'[59]

Immediately after his very last conversation with Sylvia, the phone call when he was in bed with Sue Alliston on the morning of Sunday 10 February 1963, which he had ended by saying 'Take it easy Sylvie,' he had spoken to Sue of family troubles as well as marital ones. Uncle Albert, the subject of this poem, written just three weeks before, was still very much on his mind: 'The one who hanged himself'. The news of Sylvia's suicide came twenty-four hours after he had spoken of Albert to Sue.

It was more than twenty years before he published this poem, much expanded and revised as a tender elegy. It was called 'Uncle Albert's Suicide' in manuscript but 'Sacrifice' in print. In early 1963, Ted Hughes was on the brink of finding a quiet, touching, cathartic and elegiac voice by way of a poem about a family suicide. But how could he pursue such a line after Sylvia's suicide? How could he dare to trespass on the territory of the typescript of poems that she had left on her desk in 23 Fitzroy Road? His confessional voice would be silenced, or at least heavily disguised, for a full decade.

14

The Custodian

'Ariel' by Sylvia is in a class apart. She truly became the most
phenomenal genius just before she died. In English, there is
nothing quite so direct & naked & radiant – yet complicated &
mysterious at the same time. As you will see.

(Ted Hughes to János Csokits)[1]

The children were kept away from the funeral. Aunt Hilda remained
in London, looking after them. She stayed for a further month as Ted
settled into Fitzroy Road. Frieda was clearly delighted that Daddy had
returned. To begin with, the nanny, a Dorset girl called Jean, did very
well.

In the middle of March, Ted poured out his heart in a letter to
Aurelia. He said that he would never get over the shock of Sylvia's
death and did not want to. He had seen her bitter letters to his parents
and could only imagine the content of those to her mother. Aurelia
had to understand that it had always been a marriage of two people
'under the control of deep psychic abnormalities'. By the end, they
were literally driving each other mad. But Sylvia's madness then took
the form of insisting on a divorce, which was the last thing she really
wanted. The irony of her last days was that they had come to a point
where he had thought there was a serious prospect of giving the
marriage another chance. She had agreed not to divorce. They had
spoken of going away together. But now that she was dead he did not
want to be forgiven. If there was an eternity, he would be damned in
it: 'Sylvia was one of the greatest truest spirits alive, and in her last
months she became a great poet, and no other woman poet except
Emily Dickinson can begin to be compared with her.'[2]

That greatness was apparent from the black spring-loaded binder that Sylvia had left on her desk. When Sue Alliston and Ted's Cambridge friend David Ross came round, among Fitzroy Road's first visitors since the funeral, Ted read out some of the forty-one poems that it contained. Shivers went down Ross's spine. All three of them saw that Ted had in his hands something of a power far surpassing anything Plath had achieved before. There was no doubting the genius of the work. In response to a condolence letter from Robert Lowell, Ted wrote that Sylvia had written many 'marvellous' poems in the weeks leading up to her death. He typed out two of them, 'Sheep in Fog' and 'Words', for her mentor to see.[3] Publication was simply a question of time: how many of them should be released and how soon? He knew that Aurelia for one would be devastated by the anger of some of them.

Meanwhile, David Wevill flew to Canada, where his mother was dying of cancer. In her husband's absence, Assia started visiting Ted and the children when she finished work. To begin with, she still slept at home in Highbury. She did, however, take the opportunity to read Sylvia's last journal and her unfinished Devon novel. The portrayal of herself as an 'icy barren woman' and her husband as a weak-willed man called Goof-Hopper was not flattering. On 12 March, she went to lunch with Nathaniel Tarn and told him that she was now living in the flat in the Yeats house with Ted and the children, and that Sylvia's novel, which she hoped Ted would destroy, contained only 'saints and miserable sinners' – and a portrait of 'SP' herself, 'full of poems, kicks and kids'.[4]

She also shared with Tarn her dilemma in deciding between her husband and her lover. The 'anti-T.H.' case was, first, his 'voracious sexual appetite'; secondly, his 'superstitions about remarriage'; thirdly, his 'black moods'; fourthly, his 'lack of contact and showing his work' (David was always sharing his poetry drafts with her, creating a special intimacy); and fifthly, his 'puritanism' (which, unless it is intended to suggest stinginess, is hard to reconcile with the 'voracious sexual appetite'). The 'anti-D.W.' case was that 'sex is out now: D. is also a puritan and can't stand the idea of T.H. & A.'; that 'A. is pregnant by T.H. and D. appears to have known this'; and that 'D. will not work and make his living like a man.'[5] Tarn would have liked to reconcile the married couple, but saw that if their sex life had been poisoned and there was now going to be a child by Ted, then he would be fighting an uphill battle. Nine days later, Assia found an old Polish doctor in Maida Vale, who performed an abortion (illegal at the time). One of her colleagues at the advertising agency, Australian poet Peter Porter, was married to a nurse called Jannice. Assia asked her to visit Fitzroy Road, 'the ghost house', the following day, to check that she was not still haemorrhaging.[6]

Elizabeth Compton, whom Sylvia had befriended in Devon, also visited Ted in Fitzroy Road that month. She remembered him giving her a copy of *The Bell Jar*, just published and dedicated to her and her husband, and him saying, 'It doesn't fall to many men to murder a genius.' He told her how right it seemed that he was kept awake all night by the wolves howling in Regent's Park.[7]

At the end of the month, Ted told Assia that she would have to choose between him and her husband. She chose her husband and they went to Ireland together on his return from Canada. But they fought like cat and dog, and came to the conclusion that the best way forward would be a six-month trial separation. By early May, she was back with Ted, ensconced in Fitzroy Road but far from happy: 'I'm immersed now in the Hughes monumentality, hers and his.' She described herself as 'The weak mistress, forever in the burning shadows of their [Ted and Sylvia's] mysterious seven years', and castigated herself for the 'crazy compulsion' that drove her to leave her 'third and sweetest marriage' and condemn herself to 'this nightmare maze of miserable, censorious, middle-aged furies, and Sylvia, my predecessor, between our heads at night'. In her diary, she lamented that painful cystitis was interfering with her love-life and noted that Ted had taken to 'inspecting with pleasure' a bruise on her left breast.

Yet she watched him work with delight and awe. He would sit cross-legged, at an angle, too big for Sylvia's desk, mug of tea or sandwich in one hand and pen in the other, writing at speed, never getting a word wrong, 'His nostrils flared, his hair feathery, and leaping forward like a peacock's back train in reverse, swaying a little as he writes'.[8] Sylvia's ghost was everywhere: in Ted's dreams, in his preparation of her work for publication, in photographic form – Rollie McKenna's image from 1959 – when a copy of *The Modern Poets: An American–British Anthology* arrived in the post.

Ted, meanwhile, took Sue for a drink in the Lamb and told her that he was going to 'try with Assia'. He had never in his life found anyone so physically attractive. And there was a degree of creative collaboration in the film scripts they were plotting out. Assia was a rare person and they might save each other. Sue gamely said that his choice was 'a good thing', but she felt the rejection like the twist of a knife in a wound. She burnt Ted's hand with a match or a cigarette.[9]

Things got complicated when Aurelia announced that she was coming to see her grandchildren and visit her daughter's grave. Ted prevaricated. Should he sell Court Green and find a cheaper place in the North? Was it a good or bad idea to live close to his parents? Or should he make a completely fresh start somewhere far away – China, for instance? Perhaps he could sub-let the London flat. The nanny had not, after all, worked out: she was spending too much time out of town with her boyfriend. Having dispensed with her services, he took Assia and the children on a tour of the Lake District, keeping an on-the-road narrative of their encounters. Then they went to Yorkshire, so that Aunt Hilda could renew her assistance with childcare. Aurelia's awkward visit was successfully negotiated, with Assia being kept well out of the way. At the Beacon, in order not to offend the puritan sensibilities of his parents, Ted and Assia slept in separate bedrooms.

Court Green was being looked after by David and Elizabeth Compton. Ted sent them updates of his news, telling of how his parents were worried that the shame of Sylvia's death would prevent him from ever doing poetry readings in grammar schools again and have him permanently blackballed from getting a knighthood. Knowing that Sylvia had grown close to Elizabeth, he wrote movingly of his own sense of purposelessness without her: 'When somebody who has shared life with you as much as Sylvia shared it with me, dies, then life somehow dies, the gold standard of it is somehow converted into death, and it is a minute by minute effort to find any sense in life, or any value.' He had never understood Sylvia's 'wish to be with her father, as it appeared in her poems', but now, ironically, he was coming 'under the same law' – having his life determined, that was to say, by someone who was dead.[10]

In July he put Court Green on the market and an offer was agreed. On an impulse, he decided to put in an offer for a big house called Lumb Bank, down in the valley just below the Beacon. He described it with great enthusiasm in a letter to Gerald in Tullamarine. It was the original Heptonstall village manor house, secluded in a very private valley. The main house had a long frontage and a terrace, with the fields dropping steeply away to a stream at the bottom. There were three substantial living rooms and a long thin kitchen with a pantry. Some other rooms had been converted into a two-car garage with a self-contained flat above. There was a wonderful cellar with stone arches, as in a crypt. The bedrooms had window-seats and a view. There was a great stone barn and a coach house and a coachman's cottage (currently full of hens). The outside yard was carved into the hillside and there was a walled garden with fruit trees and traditional stone-socket beehives. Then there was another stone cottage, not to mention 17 acres of land – a dozen meadows and some fine woodland. He suggested that Gerald should come back to England so that they could share the place and start farming together.[11]

He reflected in his improvised journal on whether it would be possible to live in Heptonstall with Assia so soon after Sylvia's death. He told himself that Ma and Pa would get used to the scandal, if it was a scandal, but Aunt Hilda was the main problem: she was horrified by Assia, jealous, angry, panicked, afraid of what people would say, anxious about the effect on Ted's reputation and about whether Assia would drain him of cash and leave him bankrupt. She constantly sniped about Assia, 'with her 3 husbands, her gypsy looks' and her part in Sylvia's death.[12] The two women fought bitterly, Hilda convinced that she had the best interests of Ted and the children at heart. As for Lumb Bank, Hilda said that it would be nothing more than a white elephant. Could he deal with the local gossip by pretending that Assia was his housekeeper? Perhaps, but it was clear that Assia was never going to be one of the family. She had, he noted in his journal, like Sylvia before her, a 'great and final hatred of Olwyn'.[13] Or was it more that Olwyn had a hatred of any woman who came between her and Ted?

They went to an antique auction in Halifax. One of Ted's recurring schemes was to become an antiques dealer. He took it as a sign of his recovery from Sylvia's death that he was feeling once again his 'fever for pretty possessions'. With Sylvia, periodic retail therapy had a manic quality. With Assia, there was 'the temper of reality, as never with S.' Having known poverty, and knowing what she wanted, Assia was, he reassured himself, wary of unnecessary expenditure. He filled page after page of his journal with accounts of his dreams, sometimes mingled with details of his daytime life. So, for example, in August 1963: 'Letter from Pa to A[ssia]. Bewildered amusement rather than serious shock and dismay. Dreamed – for first time in 2 years – of Crookhill pond, catching big fish with flies that bit me.'[14]

When he really talked to himself in his journal, he reached his best resolutions with the recognition that what mattered most was giving a happy rural childhood to Frieda and Nick. But to be a good father was not enough. The self-communion by journal-writing was also a way of goading himself to live his own life: 'all it needs is action', he writes again and again.[15] Inaction – the overbearing sense of the impossibility of doing anything – is the prime mark of depression, and there is a powerful sense in which writing of all kinds was Hughes's way of staving off depression, private journal-writing being the most overt manifestation of this. Those entries that are most self-analytical seem to come at the moments when he is closest to fearing that he might share the depression of his Uncle Albert and of Sylvia.

For Ted's thirty-third birthday on 17 August, Assia gave him the stories of Thomas Mann in two volumes, inscribed with the words 'Love is not love until love's vulnerable', a quotation from a powerful love poem called 'The Dream' by the depressive Theodore Roethke, whose confessional voice Ted greatly admired.[16] He had died from a heart attack in a friend's swimming pool a few weeks before. By this time, Ted was thinking it would be better if Assia stayed in the London flat. He would see her when he came down to work and she could come to Heptonstall at the weekends. But then the sale of Court Green fell through and the price of Lumb Bank went up, so the plan changed again. What with family tensions and local gossip, Yorkshire wasn't working. In late September he took the children back to Court Green.

Ted stuck to the idea of a commuting relationship, but from Devon instead of Yorkshire. Olwyn left her job in Paris and moved to Court Green to help with the children. Hilda, ever the supportive aunt, assisted as they settled in. She wrote to reassure Aurelia that all was well: 'Frieda adjusts rapidly and is quite at home already, Nicky is not so easy and does not like to be put in his cot for some reason, but as soon as Ted holds him he is content. I shall not leave until he is quite used to his new surroundings.'[17] The trees were laden with fruit and they busied themselves making damson jam.

It would be two and a half years before Ted and Assia lived together again. Their relationship was largely conducted by correspondence. Ted spilled a great deal of ink reassuring her of his love and calming her down after quarrels and misunderstandings: 'My sweet Assia, sweetest, sweetnessest, sweetnesistest, your letter came this morning. Stop all your thoughts about manoeuvres – I don't like manoeuvres. If you just show me what you feel, nothing can go wrong. It's when you leave me to misinterpret, that things go wrong.'[18] By this time, Assia had moved back in with her husband. She was unashamed of loving both men, but jealous when she discovered that Ted had invited Sue Alliston and Tasha Hollis to spend Christmas at Court Green. Olwyn, who was tremendously fond of these two spirited divorced 'girls' (her term), remembers it as a Christmas of great warmth and liveliness. Luke Myers was also there, on a four-month stay in England, and Ted was always at his best in the company of his Cambridge friend. Olwyn had the short straw. All Sue and Tash wanted to do was sit around, talking with Ted. They were not interested in cooking or babies, so, despite having the flu, Olwyn had to do all the childcare. One evening Nick was crying and she took a long time to settle him. When she came down, Frieda was crying.'Has anyone fed her?' 'No.'[19]

Christmas was not Sue's only visit to Court Green. She went down for several weekends, both before and after. In early December, she had met Ted's sister-in-law Joan, who was over from Australia, and also staying for the weekend.[20]

Assia's reaction to the discovery that Ted was seeing Sue again was to say that the only revenge she could take would be to go to bed with any attractive man who asked, in order to hurt the sensation of him out of her body.[21] Pregnant again, she was feeling especially vulnerable at this time. She miscarried and was briefly hospitalised the following month. In his journal Ted made a brief reference to her miscarriage as he observed the sound of a curlew on a drystone wall, the smell of a stagnant pond and the sight of a rusted tractor. Was it part of his curse that both his first wife and Assia, whom some were already assuming was now his wife, had miscarried?

The desire to appease Assia led him to write about Sue with most uncharacteristic cruelty. 'As for that Sue – I've seen her for the last time if this upsets you. She must have gushed a great gush about Xmas & said & hinted Christ knows what but she's out.' If Sue started spreading rumours about their relationship he would 'never speak to her again'. He 'could kill' Sue and Tash for telling people that he was seeing them 'practically every weekend'. Then he let rip: 'And she'd stare at you with those horrible lobster eyes – for Christ' sake Assia Assia Assia – you're always telling me to believe you why don't you believe me. I love you & as far as I'm concerned no other women exist.'[22]

When he was in London three weeks later he had a blazing row with Sue, during which she hit him. She described it in her journal as 'an impossible and awful evening'. She drafted a letter of apology in which she opened her heart about the ups and downs of their relationship. 'One year ago, in the morning, Sylvia died,' wrote Sue in her journal a few days later, on 11 February 1964. She then described a nightmare that had come to her on the exact anniversary of the early morning when she had lain in Ted's arms as Sylvia was taking her own life. She starts talking to Sylvia: 'my poems – some of them modelled on yours … Sylvia, why didn't we meet? I am neither as extreme gifted nor as honest as you.' Ted, she said, had a 'stupid propensity to identify me with you'. He had said that Sue spoke as if she were married to him, as if she were the reincarnation of Sylvia. But she knew that she was not Sylvia, that they were 'completely different' in their personalities. 'I am nothing beside you,' she concludes. 'I wish you were alive.'[23]

Why did Ted find it so difficult to choose between Assia and Sue? One reason was that he glimpsed aspects of Sylvia in each of them but knew in his deepest self that neither of them was Sylvia. His infidelity to others was a form of fidelity to her. Another reason was that he had made himself so vulnerable by trying to share everything, exterior life and interior, with Sylvia that he could not imagine making himself so vulnerable again. His only self-defence was to split himself between two women.

Through all these twists and turns, he spent many hours writing. But he felt blocked. At the end of August 1963 he told Luke Myers that all he had managed since Sylvia's death were some 'stupid' book reviews, a radio play and one poem.[24] The latter was a skewed elegy for Sylvia. First it was called 'The Horrors of Music' and then 'Primrose Hill', before he finally settled on 'The Howling of Wolves'.[25] Lying in

Sylvia's bed in Fitzroy Road at night he heard the eerie call from the wolf enclosure at London Zoo. It was like the howl of pain in his own heart. There may also be a covert allusion to the unhappily apt coincidence of the coroner's inquest on Sylvia's death having taken place on 15 February, the date of the Roman festival of Lupercalia, with all its associations of Sylvia's part in the inspiration of his book named for that festival and the whole business of the Lupercal cave where Romulus and Remus, children of Rhea Silvia, were suckled by a she-wolf.[26] He revisited the memory of the wolves, making them more like benign guardians, in the poem 'Life after Death' in *Birthday Letters*, where Frieda and Nick become the Romulus and Remus orphans, 'Beside the corpse of their mother', nurtured by the wolves. The singing of the wolves was a kind of consolation:

> They wound us and enmeshed us
> In their wailing for you, their mourning for us,
> They wove us into their voices. We lay in your death,
> In the fallen snow, under fallen snow.[27]

The double sense in the 'wound' (both embrace and injury) is a stroke of genius.

He kept himself going with children's stories that connected him to Frieda and Nick. The first book he published after Sylvia's death was *How the Whale Became*, the series of sometimes surreal variations on Kipling's *Just So* stories that he had written all those years ago on his honeymoon in Benidorm. It received a rave review in the *New York Times* from the artist, fashion designer and millionaire Gloria Vanderbilt, in which she identified the essence of so much of Hughes's work for children: 'These 11 enchanting stories deserve to take their place among the classic fables. They come alive because they are rooted in the fundamental truth of the need for identity, and they illustrate the happiness that comes when we stop pretending to be something we are not and start being ourselves.'[28]

The next book, published in November 1963, was *The Earth-Owl and Other Moon-People*, a collection of poems with titles such as 'The Adaptable Mountain Dugong' and 'Moon-Nasturtiums'. The trade paper *British Book News* announced the volume laconically: 'This is a curious but enjoyable book. Mr Hughes, one of the most prominent of the younger generation of poets, has written twenty-three poems about the inhabitants of the Moon, most of whom, it appears, are vegetables.'[29] Both books were dedicated to Frieda and Nicholas. In 1964 there followed the comic verse narrative *Nessie the Mannerless Monster*. It was judged favourably by the novelist Robert Nye in the *Guardian* – 'Seemingly slap-happy, awkwardly off-rhyming, often very funny verse' – but the *Daily Telegraph* was mildly discomposed by its politics: 'The story is up-to-the-minute, with Nessie being used for "Ban the Bomb" processions before reaching her goal.'[30] On first seeing the illustrations, by Gerald Rose, as the book went into production, Ted had a curious dream: 'making love to the Queen on a carpet in the palace. – This assoc[iation] with the illustrations to Nessie which I saw yesterday, when Nessie, after eating Sir etc, lies on carpet.'[31]

As a widower with two very young children, it was entirely fitting that Ted should have been writing such things at this time. But it was not until 1967 that he produced a new volume of poetry for adults.[32] That was partly because of the devastation of his inner life as a result of Sylvia's death, but also because he had to spend a lot of time on money-making projects in order to support the children. He tried his hand at a number of film scripts, among them the story that eventually became *Gaudete*, as well as a farcical treatment concerning an American ornithologist in the Hebrides, and a collaboration with Assia (who was concurrently dramatising Turgenev's novel *First Love* as a screenplay) involving a Spanish beauty, a mob of prostitutes in Venice and an encounter with a beautiful art student at the Acropolis.

He was also feeling gloomy about the state of the nation. In the summer of 1963 the bestselling novelist Arthur Hailey made a brief return to England from Toronto, where he was living as an expatriate grown wealthy on his literary earnings. In the September issue of the magazine *Saturday Night* he published an article excoriating the old country as paralysed, miserable and class-ridden. The magazine received a torrent of outraged response: what right had Hailey to criticise his native land on the basis of one short visit? The editor fought back by inviting 'one of Britain's leading young literary lions' to read Hailey's article and write a response. The choice was Ted. His article, 'a pessimistic document, rooted in a depth of feeling conveyed by his exciting style', was published in the November issue, 'not to add fuel to the flame but to stir the hearts of those many readers who really do care about Britain's future'. It was entitled 'The Rat under the Bowler'.[33]

'Can anything definite be said about England and the English at present?' Hughes asked. First and foremost, Hailey was right about the importance of class. For most of the population, the working class, it was 'a bad place to be': 'They feel oppressed, cheated, exploited.' For the middle class, England was a place of 'goodish opportunities, enviable (they think) education, comfortable living, decent self-respect, all the amenities' – though with a certain uneasiness. As for the tiny ruling class, for them England was a paradise. These basic facts, Ted suggested, were insufficiently acknowledged because the lowest classes have very few spokesmen. When a lower-class boy managed to climb the ladder (usually via a grammar school education), he tended to become transformed and to lose his anger, his drive, his rooted memory of his origins. The 'angry young man' (Alan Sillitoe and David Storey in fiction, John Osborne and Arnold Wesker in the theatre) spoke up, 'but the rest of the country reads their books and plays as most people go to a museum, in amused incredulity'.

The other thing that Hailey was right about, Ted argued, was that the English were a drab race. He recalled his own incredulity at the sheer 'sooty grime' of England when he returned from America in 1960. He had originally thought it was confined to South Yorkshire but it seemed to have spread across the whole country. He was depressed by the 'funeral colour and antique design of the cars', the grubby clothes and café menus and house façades and newspapers. The perpetual rain and low dark cloud also depressed him 'after the vast, staggeringly brilliant skyscapes of America'.

The problem was, England had never recovered from the war. Come to think of it, it had never recovered from the Civil War: the country had been divided ever since the battle between Oliver Cromwell and the Crown. The monarchy had been restored in 1660, bringing back from France a 'hatred and contempt of the lower classes'. Ever since then, the downtrodden masses had been reduced to 'homicidal rage' – primal class hatred – which forever emerges 'two or three drinks down'. England is not really a democracy: 'the much boasted legal system is, in practice, just as in all other countries, highly adjustable, with different readings for richer or poorer'. The recent

Profumo scandal had revealed just how different life was within the 'establishment'.

'The Rat under the Bowler' was Ted's most explicitly political publication. It clearly positions him, at this point in his life, as a man of the left. How did this positioning relate to his poetic vocation? The answer to that question may come in a passage of the essay in which he argues that the key characteristic of the ruling class, cultivated in their 'big expensive Public Schools', was snobbery. All the qualities of the public school 'gentleman' were apparent from his manner of *speech*: 'The aloof, condescending superiority, the dry formality, the implicit contempt, the routine thought and extinction of feeling – above all, that pistol-shot, policing quality. It is a voice for a purpose, an instrument.' The purpose of a posh voice was to elicit 'instant obedience and fear'. This worked well enough when there was an empire – the function of the public school system had long been to mould the character of the men who would administer the colonies – but with the Empire having crumbled, things would have to change at home. He was not optimistic that they would.

Almost exactly a year after Hughes wrote this essay, the Labour Party won the October 1964 general election by the tiniest of majorities, bringing to an end thirteen years of Conservative rule. At 10 Downing Street, the plummy voice of Prime Minister Sir Alec Douglas-Home (formerly the Earl of Home) was replaced by the distinctively northern long vowels of Harold Wilson, a grammar school boy from the West Riding. A Yorkshire voice, like Ted's own. It was the beginning of the end of that upper-class manner of speech which he had nailed so decisively in the essay. There was change ahead, and possibly trouble. The rat was about to be released from beneath the bowler hat.

Listening to Ted's radio broadcasts – there were more than 300 of them in the course of his life – one notices that his voice becomes if anything more, not less, Yorkshire as he grows older. The longer he was away from the vowel sounds of his home valley, the more he held on to that voice as a way of grounding himself as a poet of the people. The great Caribbean poet Edward Kamau Brathwaite once wrote that he was liberated into writing poetry in his own dialect by hearing the cricket commentator John Arlott on the radio. Arlott's deep, musical Hampshire burr showed him that one did not have to speak 'BBC

English' – 'the Queen's English' – in order to have a poetic voice. In this sense Ted Hughes was the John Arlott of English poetry. Listen to the clipped tones of T. S. Eliot reading his *Four Quartets*, having turned himself into an English gentleman. Then listen to the long vowels of Ted reading the same poems ('cont – ai – ned in time future').[34] He was the man who democratised poetry by showing that you could publish with Eliot's Faber and Faber, and be heard on the BBC, while staying true to your own voice, your own people.

For much of 1964, when Assia was living with her husband David in Belsize Park, Ted sent her clandestine love letters addressed to a certain 'F. Wall Esq', supposedly a resident in one of the other flats into which their house was divided, but actually a private joke – he was the fly on the wall in her marital home. But most of the time he was in Court Green with Olwyn and the children. He loved fatherhood, what with the excitement of Frieda starting nursery school and Nicky enjoying full-on attention at home. But every now and then he dreamed of escape: he thought of just taking off for a couple of months, 'going to find the loneliest place' imaginable, perhaps 'in the Hebrides or Yugoslavia'.[35]

Ted's journal entries are dark at this time. On his thirty-fourth birthday he complained that he was tired. The previous night he had stayed up until four in the morning reading (and not being impressed by) Jung on *Sacred Marriage*. During the day he had worked on and off on his plays, had some precious moments making up stories for the children, and been to a soirée where there had been talk of politics and theatre. Now he was in reflective mode. The last twelve months had been 'the worst, most confused, most distracted, most superficial, least productive, most evasive, most desperate' of his life. He wished them good riddance and said that his only desire for the next year was to summon his willpower and to work. But the struggle went on. Three months later, he returned to the page and scrawled a parenthesis to the effect that the bad year was continuing.[36]

There was potent imaginative life in his dreams. A typical example has him wandering through a circular library, then handling a precious piece of porcelain in the shape of a woman's head. He catches his finger in a sharp lock of the figure's hair and is afraid he will break it. Then suddenly a woman is serving tea, among the shelves. He cups his hand to receive the sugar lumps and finds to his embarrassment that he is cupping her breasts, which are very small, while she explains that he will get tea only if he gives his name, because he is a visitor in the library, not the owner of it. After a series of further twists, in which a vulgar and pushy businessman enters the dream, he finds himself outside a wood, holding a shotgun. It is the wood at Old Denaby, that place of magic in his memory. Two other men are there, the business-man and the 'fop son' of the lord of the manor. They stand in for a mysterious 'other' who has shadowed him throughout the dream. He tries to shoot some birds, his aim difficult to steady in the high wind. Then he confronts the smouldering fragments of a crashed motorbike and the body of the rider, smashed up, legless, his head almost torn off. It is both the business entrepreneur and the fop, yet it is also neither of them. In another episode of the same dream – or was this another dream merging in his memory? – he is first a rabbit-catcher and then he is hunted by a boar. Analysing the dream, he saw the various figures – entrepreneur, fop, 'other' ('the mysterious element that wants a changeover') – as dimensions of his own self. The glaringly obvious thing he does not mention in his analysis is that the motorcyclist is manifestly Gerald and that a major aspect of the dream is what he would later call the theme of 'the rival brothers'.[37]

Sometimes the work of the night was less complicated: 'Extraordinarily vivid dream of Sylvia's return – ecstatic joy of her and me. Love, complete reality. In a hotel room. The next morning, I went to collect her in her room. Her bags were there, a meal that she had had in her room and not eaten – but she was not.' The next evening he described this as the most vivid dream experience of her that he had ever had. It had stayed with him all day.[38] A few weeks later, visit-ing his parents at the Beacon, he tried to find her spirit by walking to Top Withens in warm autumnal light. He noted every detail in his journal – streams, thorns, tumbling walls, grouse, waterfall noise – but everything seemed 'shadowy', so halfway up the hill he turned back.[39]

He also dreamed of flying. And of being able to make portraits in which all the poets could come alive, except – however hard he tried – for Shakespeare. He dreamed in bright colours.[40]

★

He continued to derive income from radio broadcasts, ranging from his talks aimed at schools to such projects as 'Dogs: A Scherzo', broadcast on the Third Programme a year and a day after Sylvia's death and described in the *Radio Times* as follows: 'Cases of possession by the spirit of an ancestor or of a historical personage have often been recorded. There is also possession by Heroic Fury and by the Furies. A small and seemingly irrelevant incident may be enough to start any of these. On the other hand, a large relevant incident may trigger off what is merely a case of possession by Dogs.'[41]

Like all freelance writers, he had to get used to irregular payments and keeping his own accounts as opposed to relying on a regular monthly pay cheque. His tally at this time is both precise in its recording of pounds, shillings and pence, and revealing in its ups and downs. May 1964: £133 8s 11d. June: £165 15s 8d. July: £428 18s 0d (including a £250 Arts Council grant). August: £122 9s 8d (plus £45 10s 0d rent for sub-let of 23 Fitzroy Road). September, down to £45 13s 6d. November was a good month: £634 14s 5d (including £172 for his radio play *The Wound*). The following February a bad one: £33 5s 6d. March 1965 was equally lean, redeemed only by £87 11s 6d for a broadcast of *The Wound* on German radio.[42]

Another project, with no earnings potential, was also keeping him busy at this time. Together with Cambridge friend Danny Weissbort, he started planning the launch of a magazine that would introduce English readers to *Modern Poetry in Translation*. He was becoming convinced that Eastern Europeans such as Zbigniew Herbert, Miroslav Holub, Czesław Miłosz and Vasko Popa, struggling under the pressure of Soviet occupation, were producing the most exciting new writing of the age. After lengthy planning, the first issue appeared in the autumn of 1965. Ted co-edited the first ten issues with Danny, choosing poems and contributing introductory editorials. The aim, he explained in the opening manifesto, was to honour the original poems by translating as closely as possible, but without pedantry: 'The type of translations we are seeking can be described as literal, though not literal in a strict or pedantic sense. Though this may seem at first suspect, it is more appropriate to define our criteria negatively as literalness can only be a deliberate tendency, not a dogma.'[43]

A steady stream of book reviews also occupied him. Just occasionally, there would be a title that provided him with inspiration as opposed to distraction. In the autumn of 1964, the *Listener* sent him the English translation of Mircea Eliade's *Shamanism: Archaic Techniques of Ecstasy*.[44] This became his bible on the subject of everything from sickness-initiation and dreams to the acquisition of shamanic powers to the descent into the underworld to 'Magical Flight' to 'The Three Cosmic Zones and the World Pillar'. It was as great an influence as *The White Goddess* in shaping the mythic and 'ecstatic' strand of his work. Eliade furnished him with a wealth of symbolic interpretations that resonated with his own poetic bestiary: 'The shaman encounters the funerary dog in the course of his descent to the underworld, as it is encountered by the deceased or by heroes undergoing an initiatory ordeal.' So much for the dog. As for the horse, it 'enables the shaman to fly through the air, to reach the heavens ... the horse is a mythical image of death and hence is incorporated into the ideologies and techniques of ecstasy'.[45]

All this was food for thought as he contemplated the images of infernal descent, the real and symbolic deaths, in Sylvia's poems, not to mention the ecstatic horse-ride of the title poem of her collection. He was pushing *Ariel* in the direction of Charles Monteith at Faber and Faber, having persuaded Heinemann, who had published *The Colossus* and *The Bell Jar*, not to exercise an option on her posthumous work.

Before the release of *Ariel* there was another editorial task. In November 1963 Faber agreed to publish a selected edition of Keith Douglas, regarded by Ted as the greatest English poet of the Second World War. He provided a fine introduction in which, without knowing it, he rehearsed his future writings about Sylvia. Douglas was cut off in his prime: killed in action during the Normandy invasion, aged just twenty-four. His poetry has an exceptional bluntness, an 'impatient, razor energy'. He developed rapidly during his brief nine-year poetic career, going at astonishing speed from 'virtuoso juvenilia' to a phase in which 'the picturesque or merely decorative side of his imagery disappears; his descriptive powers sharpen to realism'. He became a 'renovator of language', renewing 'the simplicity of ordinary talk' and 'infusing every word with a burning exploratory freshness of mind – partly impatience, partly exhilaration at speaking the forbidden thing, partly sheer casual ease of penetration'. Then in his maturity – a maturity achieved in a brief blaze of creativity in the months leading up to his death – he found the truth of the doomed man in the doomed body. His subject was 'the burning away of all human pretensions in the ray cast by death'. His late poem 'Simplify me when I'm Dead' was the consummation of his genius.[46] Every aspect of this account is as apt for Plath as it is for Douglas: from the early development to the peculiar death-ray quality to the culminating poem that envisions the poet's own end (as in Plath's 'Edge').

The Keith Douglas book was also important because it marked a turning point in Olwyn's life. She loved Ted so much that she had been prepared to give up her career for him. But residence at Court Green as substitute mother for her niece and nephew was dull indeed, in comparison to her life in Paris. She kept her professional self stimulated by taking an interest in the contractual side of her brother's publications. She happened to be opening the post one day in late 1963 and found herself looking at the contract from Faber and Faber for the Keith Douglas selection. Being familiar with contractual negotiations for film and stage work, thanks to her job at the Martonplay agency in Paris, she was astonished to see that Ted was to receive a one-off payment of £25 for making the selection and writing the introduction. Furthermore, Faber intended to recoup that sum by deducting it from the royalties payable to the fallen Douglas's widowed mother. Ted in turn was surprised to learn from his sister that contracts could actually be negotiated. Hitherto, simply grateful to be published, he had just signed whatever contract he was sent. He agreed, however, that he could do better with the Douglas book, so he asked Olwyn to negotiate the contract on his behalf and she achieved some improvements, not least for the widow. So began her career as his agent. During her time in Devon, she rounded up the novelist Jean Rhys, who lived near by, and a couple of other authors, who agreed that she could represent them too. For thirty years, Olwyn would go into battle on her brother's behalf with publishers, promoters and people requesting quotation rights. She earned a reputation as a fearsome, difficult gatekeeper and negotiator.

Olwyn also recognised the particular importance of Keith Douglas's poetry to both Ted and Sylvia. She thought back to a beautiful summer's day at the Beacon when Ted and Sylvia lay on a rug in the field beyond the low garden wall, engrossed in the edition of Douglas's collected poems that had been published in 1951: 'Two poets communing with a precursor whose work had many affinities with their own'. She always saw this 'as an image of Sylvia and Ted's central shared allegiance to poetry'. She reckoned that 'Douglas's skills and the presentiment of his death that haunted him must have deeply affected Sylvia'. Olwyn believed that his poem 'The Sea Bird', 'with its dazzling flight and doom', mirrored Sylvia's 'inmost fears and her own soaring achievement and end'.[47]

It was no coincidence that Hughes was preparing the *Ariel* manuscript for Faber at the same time as the Keith Douglas poems. Nor that this was also the moment when he wrote a review of Poet Laureate C. Day Lewis's edition of *The Collected Poems of Wilfred Owen*, another war poet whose slender body of work developed in astonishing leaps and bounds in the few months before his premature death, combining technical innovation with a sense of words as weapons and an 'extraordinary detachment from the agony' which allowed his work to reveal both 'immediate suffering and general implication, as nobody else did'. Nobody else before Douglas, before Plath, that is to say.[48]

In October 1963 he had released ten of Sylvia's late great poems, including 'Lady Lazarus', 'Thalidomide' and 'Daddy', to the magazine *Encounter*, introducing them with a brief eulogy signed 'T.H.' and ending with a poignant paragraph in which he wrote of how people who met Sylvia tended to be either 'alarmed or exhilarated by the intensity of her spirits'. 'Her affections were absolute,' he continued. 'Once she had set her mind to it, nothing was too much trouble for her.' Her every action was of a piece with 'the lovely firm complexity of design, the cleanly uncompromising thoroughness that shows in her language'. Above all, in 'spite of the prevailing doom evident in her poems, it is impossible that anybody could have been more in love with life, or more capable of happiness, than she was'.[49]

The *Encounter* selection was a bold harbinger of what was to come. Eighteen months later, on 11 March 1965, *Ariel* was published by Faber and Faber, in a yellow dust jacket printed in a bright pattern of blue, black and red. Ted was initially shocked by the design, but it grew on him. 'What an insane chance', he wrote to Richard Murphy on the eve of publication, 'to have private family struggles turned into best-selling literature of despair and martyrdom, probably a permanent cultural treasure.'[50] A further poignancy came from the way that the book seemed as much a part of him as of Sylvia: his other titles were promoted on the flap of the dust jacket and his name was on the copyright page.

The typescript of forty-one poems which Sylvia had left on her desk at the time of her death, with a dedication 'for Frieda and Nicholas', had four title pages. Below the clean one marked 'ARIEL and other poems by Sylvia Plath' were two others, in which she experimented with other titles: 'The Rival', then 'A Birthday Present', then 'Daddy'. It was clearly a work in progress, subject to revision. Ted had also read the nineteen poems that Sylvia had written after its completion, and he knew that they were some of her best. He was also aware that some of the poems in the typescript would have been very offensive to living people, such as the actor Marvin Kane and his wife Kathy, who were portrayed so savagely in 'Lesbos', and his own Uncle Walt, who was described in 'Stopped Dead' as 'pants factory Fatso, millionaire'.[51] He accordingly left out thirteen poems from Sylvia's prepared manuscript and added in ten others instead – 'Sheep in Fog', which he hugely admired, near the beginning of the collection and the remaining nine at the end. This meant that the book concluded not, as the typescript had done, with the uplifting promise of spring in 'Wintering', but with the death-ray of the poems of Sylvia's very last days, such as 'Contusion' ('The rest of the body is all washed out … The mirrors are sheeted') and 'Edge' ('The woman is perfected. / Her dead // Body wears the smile of accomplishment').[52]

Among the omissions were some poems that, if read autobiographically, did not reflect well on Ted himself, notably 'The Rabbit Catcher' ('It was a place of force') and 'The Jailor' ('I have been drugged and raped … Lever of his wet dreams').[53] When these editorial decisions became apparent upon his publication of Plath's collected poems in 1981, Hughes was vilified. The feminist line was that the husband was trying to control the posthumous voice of the woman for whose suicide he had been responsible. This argument was not entirely fair, given that he had already published some of the rejected poems, including 'The Jailor', in *Encounter*. The counter-argument would be that he and Sylvia had collaborated on each other's work and relied on each other's judgement during their marriage, and Ted was merely continuing this process after her death.[54]

Ted knew that there was more work to be done in securing Plath's permanent reputation. In about four years' time, he told Murphy, he would prepare a complete edition. For now, *Ariel* was enough to honour her memory and satisfy himself in his role of custodian of her work as well as her children. At publication time, he gave an interview to the *Guardian*, telling of how he and Sylvia were 'like two feet, each one using everything the other did'. Their partnership was all-absorbing; 'There was an unspoken unanimity in every criticism or judgment we made.'[55]

Prior to this, he wrote a detailed note introducing the volume in the *Bulletin* of the Poetry Book Society, which had made it a 'Spring Choice'. 'The truly miraculous thing about her', he wrote, 'will remain the fact that in two years, while she was almost fully occupied with children and house-keeping, she underwent a poetic development that has hardly any equal on record, for suddenness and completeness.' He dated the great leap forward to the birth of her first child and in this sense it was fitting that *Ariel* began with the wonderfully gentle 'Morning Song', written for baby Frieda. But he did not shy away from the toughness of the collection: 'She was most afraid that she might come to live outside her genius for love, which she also equated with courage, or "guts", to use her word.' *Ariel* had guts. It was unlike any other poetry. It *was* Sylvia. 'Everything she did was just like this, and this is just like her – but permanent.'[56]

He dispatched copies of the book to his friends and mentors. Richard Murphy was deeply moved and sent an elegy for Sylvia in return. In the covering letter with the copy sent to his old teacher John Fisher, Ted generously acknowledged a chain of influence: 'Nobody else writes like that or ever has done. If any of it is thanks to me, as it may be a little bit, then some of it is thanks to you.'[57] He then copied out a story by three-year-old Nick about a wolf who lived inside a giant mouse and drank its blood and drowned and was shot by a hunter and another wolf was then shot by a shark with a sun between its teeth and the second wolf was turned to ice and the mouse was turned to stone and a man came with a big sword and chopped its head off. Nick had recently met his Uncle Gerald, who had purchased two antique swords, one to leave at Court Green and the other to take back to Australia. Ted was hinting to John Fisher that Sylvia's, and his own, creative juices had flowed into the next generation.

*

Al Alvarez in the *Observer* hailed the publication of *Ariel* as a major literary event. His review was entitled 'Poetry in Extremis'.[58] It drew on a radio talk he had given on the BBC shortly after Sylvia's death. He had spoken there of the bravery of her writing, of the terrible unforgiving quality of 'Daddy', and of how the poems written in her last months tapped the 'roots of her own inner violence' ('violence', that word which was so often applied to Ted's work). 'Poetry of this order', he had ended the talk, 'is a murderous art.'[59]

Meanwhile in the *Spectator*, a magazine with especially influential book pages, *Ariel* was reviewed alongside Robert Lowell's latest poetry collection, *For the Union Dead*, under the headline 'Poets of the Dangerous Way'. The reviewer was none other than M. L. Rosenthal, who had coined the phrase 'confessional poetry' with regard to Lowell's *Life Studies*. For Rosenthal, the true confessional poet embodies the trauma of the age within their own psychological torment. 'If a poet is sensitive enough to the age and brave enough to face it directly,' he wrote, with regard to such poems as 'Daddy' and 'Fever 103°', 'it will kill him through the exacerbation of his awareness alone.'[60] The use of the male pronoun was unfortunate in the context of *Ariel*, but Rosenthal was astute in predicting that Plath's death would become the stuff of legend. Between them, Alvarez and Rosenthal established a connection, which has never been broken, between Plath's last poems and her suicide. The link was solidified in a review-essay of exceptional power by the brilliant young Cambridge critic George Steiner. Its title took a phrase from 'Lady Lazarus': 'Dying is an Art'.[61] Its content dwelt heavily on the Holocaust imagery of Sylvia's poetry – Steiner, of Viennese Jewish descent, wrestled throughout his writing life with the question of what it meant to create poetry 'after Auschwitz'.

The 3,000 copies of the first edition of *Ariel* sold out in less than a year. Hardback reprints followed, and in 1968 two paperback runs of 10,000 copies each. By the Seventies, the slim collection had come to be regarded as one of the century's most significant volumes of poetry, its impact on a par with that of T. S. Eliot's *The Waste Land*.

The first American edition appeared in the summer of 1966, with a foreword in which Plath's genius was hailed by no less a figure than Lowell himself. 'Her art's immortality is life's disintegration,' he wrote. In her 'last irresistible blaze', her 'appalling and triumphant fulfillment', she broke the bounds of tradition in poems that were 'playing Russian roulette with six cartridges in the cylinder'.[62] *Newsweek* picked up on that phrase for the title of its review, while *Time*, the other weekly magazine with a circulation in many millions, reprinted the whole of 'Daddy' and published a review entitled 'The Blood Jet is Poetry' (a line from 'Kindness'), which begins with the uncompromising sentence 'On a dank day in February 1963, a pretty young mother of two children was found in a London flat with her head in the oven and the gas jets wide open.'[63] For all that the majority of critics in the more highbrow outlets concentrated on the brilliance, but also the shocking quality, of the poems themselves, it was this image combined with the venom of 'Daddy' that laid the ground for the cult of Plath, what Ted called the Sylvia Plath fantasia.

Eight days before Faber and Faber ushered *Ariel* into the world, Assia Wevill gave birth to a daughter, Alexandra Tatiana Elise, to be known as Shura.[64] On the birth certificate, the father was named as Edward James Hughes, author, of Court Green, North Tawton, Devon.

The Iron Man

The day after St Valentine's in February 1965, Ted Hughes scribbled one of his journal notes. That day, as on so many days, he had struggled to clear a few hours for poetry writing. He had fought for fifteen years to get time for himself, but was still 'losing heavily'. The best moments were those when he was alone in the quiet, solid thatched house. Or when it was just him and the children. Did that mean that to be a writer one had to live alone? But how could he live alone when he was a father and when he so loved the company, the cooking and the lovemaking of women? He was beginning to feel that his words were slowly coming alive again, as they had not since Sylvia's death. But the Muse had not yet awakened. He was still processing his loss. Three nights after the second anniversary of her suicide he had a 'terrible grief dream about Sylvia, long and unending. In a house, large stone, on the moor's edge – the garden was also a cemetary [sic]'.[1]

The strain of what he described as his 'domestic game of chess'[2] was showing. Gerald, in England for an extended visit over the Christmas and New Year period, found his brother 'in a poor state, mentally and physically: he complained of feeling unwell, which was very unlike him'.[3] Ted was still close to Sue Alliston. He took Gerald to meet her in London. 'You met Joan,' Ted said. 'I like things to be symmetrical.' She found Gerald 'large and warm', but uncomfortable in the London literary environment. 'He uses bits of Ted's vocabulary, is uneasy with it, uses it like a new toy,' she noted in her journal. 'Tells stories at great length … He seemed somewhat simple at times – (not simple in a derogatory way) and very knowledgeable about archaeology and such things.'[4] Gerald told Sue that he was going back via Bombay and that he hoped to come to England again, but Australia was his home.

With Sue, there was a (relatively) pain-free transition from lovers to friends – 'OK,' she wrote, 'there's a lot Platonic in our relationship.'[5] The relationship with Assia was more complicated, especially after the birth of Shura. She told her friends that she was sure her daughter was Ted's. Olwyn's memory is that Ted told her that he could not be sure that he was Shura's father, but that he would treat her as if he were. Always jealous of anything that bound Ted more closely to another woman than her, Olwyn convinced herself that the baby girl had the facial features of David Wevill. Assia was still living with David, who undertook much of the baby care. Though emotionally absorbed in her newborn child, she was not the earth-mother type. Friends were impressed with David's fathering and somewhat startled when Assia took them aside and whispered that Shura was really Ted's.

They were engaged on a literary collaboration by correspondence. Like Sylvia before her, Assia was a talented artist. She and Ted worked on a book for which he would write poems and send them to her. She would then send back illustrations. The plan was to have a poem and a drawing for each card in a pack of playing cards. So, for example, for the three of hearts Assia drew three maidens dancing. The royal cards would each be a figure out of history, myth or the Bible. Queen Victoria was the Queen of Clubs, Nebuchadnezzar the King of Hearts, Don Juan the Knave of Hearts.[6] The title would be 'A Full House'. The scheme was eventually abandoned, though Ted revived a version of the idea many years later, giving the title to a cycle of poems in which the royal cards were made to represent Shakespearean characters.[7]

Financial prospects improved with the news that the German Embassy had established an annual three-month residency in Germany for an English poet, in honour of T. S. Eliot, and Charles Monteith had persuaded the awarding committee that Ted should be the first holder of the post, which would commence the following year. In his thank-you letter to Monteith, Ted mentioned that he was getting to work on a selection of Emily Dickinson's poetry for Faber. It was three years before this was published. He was deeply drawn to her vision of 'final reality, her own soul, the soul within the Universe', a nameless vision of something deep, holy, terrible, 'timeless, deathly, vast, intense'.[8] This is Emily as poetic big sister to Sylvia.

In June, leaving little Shura with the long-suffering David Wevill and a nanny, Assia accompanied Ted to the Festival dei Due Mondi

(Festival of the Two Worlds) in Spoleto, an ancient town on a foothill of the Apennine Mountains. Stephen Spender had asked Ted if he would like to travel with him, but Ted explained that he was going with 'a friend', so he would drive down in leisurely fashion and return via Germany, to improve his language before taking up his residency. Founded by the composer Gian Carlo Menotti in 1958, the annual Spoleto event had become one of the great arts festivals, in which Europe met the Americas and practitioners from every field of the creative arts came together in the Umbrian sunshine. The world's top poetic talent was there: the father of modernism, Ezra Pound, about to turn eighty, his face a map of trenched wrinkles, in Italian exile after his long imprisonment in an American mental hospital following his fascist collaboration in the war; Pablo Neruda from Chile, embodiment of communism at its most idealistic; Yevgeny Yevtushenko, Ted's contemporary, the rising star of Russian poetry, voice of the Khrushchev cultural thaw and now, in the more difficult era of the crackdown on dissent following the deposition of Khrushchev, agitating for the release of fellow-poet Joseph Brodsky from his sentence of hard labour in the far north. Pound spoke to no one. Assia, who enjoyed the food and the fact that the trip was expenses paid, said that old Ezra looked 'hand-dressed and about to die like a new magnolia'.[9] Ted described him as a 'resurrected Lazarus' with 'dead button eyes'. Neruda, meanwhile, 'read torrentially for about 25 minutes off a piece of paper about 3" by 4". Then he turned it over, and read on.'[10]

After Spoleto, Assia returned to her husband and her advertising job in London, where she was achieving considerable success. Ted went back to Court Green. He was beginning to think that it was time for them to live together. He desired and needed her. But there would have to be ground rules in order to protect their work. He proposed separate bedrooms, no sleeping together during the week, no visitors before seven in the evening, a banquet to usher in their lovemaking at the end of each five nights' abstinence, and 'Constant music'.

In order to prepare her for the dullness of life in the country, he then told her what a typical day in his life was like. Up at half past eight, to open the post and stare blankly at his correspondence for half an hour. Phone call from Doris Lessing who requires advice on her cottage. Ring builder and get price for new windows for Doris. Get down to work at ten o'clock. But it is not the proper work of poetry.

He has to type up his next talk for BBC Schools ('about how poetry is crime, and why theft is poetical, with poetical illustrations'). Write to Stephen Spender, who is on a grant committee. Write to Exeter University, returning a contract so that he could receive the fee for a poetry reading he has done. Write to the editor Donald Hall about the American edition of *Ariel*. At twelve-thirty, prepare a goat-meat stew for himself and the children. Go to post. Then to the bank and to pay for shoe repair. Take the cat to the vet 'to have its sore tail chopped off' (half an hour wasted in the waiting room). Return, put on the stew, start writing to Assia, fetch Frieda from nursery school. Look despairingly at pile of still-unanswered letters from Faber, Heinemann, the British Council, the Arts Council and others. At five-thirty, fetch the cat from the vet. Another day gone without any time for real writing. 'Tomorrow & tomorrow & tomorrow', he concludes in the vein of Macbeth's lament that life creeps on in petty pace from day to day to the last syllable of recorded time, a tale told by an idiot, full of sound and fury, signifying nothing.[11]

Later in the summer, he did a poetry reading on a miserably wet day at the Edinburgh Festival, then visited the Beacon on the way back south. Edith's health was in sharp decline. Ted feared that his parents could no longer cope on their own and would have to be moved down to Devon. Olwyn was getting restless. After the many months of childcare in the remote countryside, she wanted to go to London to start her literary agency. Ted came up with a scheme to move Edith and Bill into Court Green while he took the children to Ireland for a few months – with or without Assia and Shura. Richard Murphy offered his cottage in Cleggan, since he was off to America for a few months. Aurelia Plath was not pleased to hear that she would have to postpone her next visit to her grandchildren. 'Bomb #1 Dec 1965', she inscribed in thick black marker pen on the letter in which Ted broke the news.[12] The letter made no mention of Assia, let alone Shura.

Ireland was delayed by various complications, including William Hughes's attempts to sell his shop and a period when Edith was in hospital. By this time, Murphy had found a much better house than his own cottage: Doonreaghan in Cashel, a beautiful and remote area of Connemara on the far west coast. Ted so liked the sound of it that he started paying rent in December, even though it was far from certain exactly when he would be able to leave Devon and go there.

This time Ted did not want Elizabeth Compton to have access to Court Green. He suspected that she might be reporting back to Aurelia. So he asked some new friends to help his parents settle in. They were Trevor and Brenda Hedden, whom he had met through the Comptons. They lived 3 miles outside North Tawton at a place called Bondleigh, in open countryside. Trevor was studying as a mature student in Exeter, training to be a drama teacher. He felt that as a result of army service he had missed out on the chance to sow his youthful wild oats, so he was enjoying student life in the newly relaxed age of the Beatles, the Rolling Stones and the contraceptive pill. Brenda was nine years younger than Trevor and was influenced by his wider life experiences. She was a social worker who had studied psychodynamics. This sparked the interest of Ted, who had been fascinated by psychological theory ever since his youthful immersion in Jung.

In February 1966 Assia finally told David that she had made her choice. The marriage was over and she was going to live with Ted. She and Shura would go to Ireland with him. The night before they left, Ted went for a riverside walk alone. He clambered down an escarpment where the stream that he had been following joined the main river, and as he came down he saw salmon going upstream, leaping, shaking themselves in the air. On the riverbank he found himself 'completely covered with milt and spawn from these leaping salmon'.[13] From that night on, he claimed, his dreams were always of salmon instead of pike. Was Sylvia the devouring pike of the dream the night before their wedding and Assia a salmon running for home, drawing Ted to Ireland, the place where he always dreamed of finding peace?

Doonreaghan lived up to expectations. Light, spacious and well fitted, it nestled beneath a green hill and opened on a magnificent vista of the Atlantic. Ted could gaze across the ocean and imagine Sylvia's spirit looking back from the shoreline thousands of miles away on the other side. The bay was sheltered and the air surprisingly warm. Here, for a few sweet weeks, they finally became a family. Ted was at last writing what he truly wanted to write, instead of merely what he had to write to earn some cash. Assia sketched. To the children, it was paradise. Frieda, who had the luxury of her own bathroom, made a little house for the one toy she had brought, her puppet Percy Panda. Her painting and drawing, Ted told Aurelia in a happy letter, were growing 'like magic'.[14] Nick loved the outdoors, especially the seashore. Soon Ted was teaching him to fish. And both children were very excited to be sharing their home with a new little sister. They celebrated her first birthday and Ted wrote a poem for her.

They hoped to stay on longer, but the winter lease ran out at the end of March, so they moved up to Cleggan, where Richard Murphy had found them a farmhouse a mile down the road from his own cottage. They dined regularly with Murphy, and had visits from Barrie Cooke, artist and fisherman, and his wife. Ted was hatching his *Crow*, as well as gathering and polishing a range of his other work. He knew that Faber were waiting for a third book. He planned to take up the German award later in the year. While he was in Ireland, some further good news arrived: thanks to the Abraham Woursell Foundation of New York, Ted was offered a five-year bursary from the Philosophy Department of Vienna University, amounting to the equivalent of two-thirds of a professor's salary, a princely £1,500 per year (the equivalent of £25,000 or $38,000 in 2015). His sole duty would be to write poetry. Residence was not required. This was a much better prospect than commitment to a three-month residency in Germany.

The dream of making a permanent home in Ireland was ended by news from Court Green. Olwyn had finally had enough of domestic duties. She was off to London to start her agency. Edith's health was getting worse and worse, with frequent periods of being bedridden and several stays in the hospital in Exeter. Towards the end of May, Ted and Assia took all three children to Devon. By this time, Brenda Hedden had given up work in order to look after her daughter Harriet, who was born the previous month.

Now, for the first time, Assia was living in Sylvia's house. Bill and Edith accepted that Shura was Ted's child, but they could not stand Assia. Their constant complaint to Trevor and Brenda Hedden was that she had seduced Ted; because of her three previous marriages, they called him 'Edward the fourth'.[15] There was a perpetual bad atmosphere. As a veteran of the Great War, Bill Hughes had a visceral dislike of the Germans. He found Assia's upper-class English accent phoney in the extreme, and refused to speak to her. This was ironic, given her Jewish background: she, like him, was a survivor. Writing to her sister in Canada, Assia complained that Ted's father even averted his eyes when she put a plate of food in front of him. Sometimes they resorted to eating separately, Assia with Shura and Ted with his father, Frieda and Nick.

Visitors sometimes helped to relieve the tension in the house. Alan Sillitoe and his wife Ruth Fainlight were loyal as ever. Sylvia's journals had often been at their funniest and liveliest when she wrote – sometimes cruelly – about people. So too with Ted's. He was as hungry for human experience as he was for natural. On a day trip to Dartmoor with Assia and the Sillitoes (an outing marred by Frieda being car sick), he noted not only a lizard 'trickling down into a clump of heather' (the freshness of the description coming from the choice of verb), but also a 'bus-load of post-menopause women – hats like whipped cream walnuts, their fussy lavenders, pinks, lilacs and browns. Silver hair wiring and whiskering ... their faces anxious thoughtfulnesses'.[16]

Ted and Assia managed to escape for one brief return visit to Murphy in Cleggan, but most of the time they felt imprisoned by the demands of looking after Ted's parents as well as the children. Ted turned his back on the civil war in the house, spending most days working in his writing hut in the garden, or fishing or playing snooker with friends, or visiting the Heddens. Assia, who had a history of depression and suicide attempts, began voicing dark thoughts. She could not help comparing herself with Sylvia. She wallowed in the manuscript notebooks among the Plath papers and typed a bitter journal piece about her strong sense of Sylvia's 'repugnant live presence' – though elsewhere in her journal she wrote generously of Sylvia's great literary gifts.

Finding the phrase 'work at femininity' in one of Plath's lists of resolutions and things to buy ('including a bathrobe, slippers and nightgown'), Assia asked 'Were the elbows really sharp? the hands enormous and knuckled? or is this my imaginary shape-giving to the muscular brain, my envy of her splendid brilliance?'[17] She wrote a will and stole some pages of Plath manuscripts, which she sent to her sister with the information that they would fetch a good price if the time came when Shura had to be supported. She also wrote a cheque for over a thousand dollars, which would pay for an airfare to Canada and the initial expenses of looking after a little motherless child.[18]

She could equally well feel overwhelmed with passion for Ted. In one extraordinary journal entry, she wrote of how his generosity and affection were 'almost unsupportable'. His kindness and love reached such luxuriance that she would 'buckle over, speechless'. She imagined his writing hut smoking 'with the temperature of his presence in it'. She had 'huge fits of love and admiration for him'. But it was two parts that and one part 'memory of Ruthless'. And then she voiced a hymn to his beauty, manifestly imitating the style of the Sylvia journals in which she had been immersing herself:

> There he is in his white shirt scything in the glossy Rousseau jungle. In sweet sweat. There he is coming down the orchard in his plaid shirt carrying something. His superb legs and thighs – the beautiful Anatomical Man. One of God's best creations. Is God squandering him on me? He carries so many perfections that I would in all truth not begrudge him an affair or two with other women – as long as he remains loyal to me. I would suffer bitterly – but this in all truth is the only due thanks I could give him for all his grace. He ventures everything. His lovely, long risks of grasp. Sometimes little yaps of greed, but all accounted for. He is one of God's best creatures. Ever. Ever.[19]

*

In May 1967 Faber and Faber published the mysteriously entitled *Wodwo*. Though presented in their usual format for poetry, it was in fact an unusual hybrid work, with poetry at the beginning and end, and five short stories and Ted's 1962 radio play, *The Wound*, in the middle. Dedicated to his mother and father, perhaps in the expectation that Edith would not be around for many more years to have another work dedicated to her, it began with an author's note explaining that the stories and the play should be understood as 'notes, appendix and unversified episodes of the events behind the poems, or as chapters of a single adventure to which the poems are commentary and amplification'.[20] Either way, the book should be read as a unity. Following the contents list, there was an epigraph which explained the title (though only to readers versed in Middle English): 'Sumwhyle wyth wormeȝ he werreȝ, and wyth wolves als, / Sumwhyle wyth wodwos, þat woned in þe knarreʒ' – this is Sir Gawain, encountering an array of monsters as he crosses 'the wilderness of Wirral' in his quest for the Green Knight, in the poem that Hughes had especially admired when taking the medieval paper at Cambridge. The wodwo was a hairy wild man of the woods. In the title poem, written in early 1961 and printed as the last in the collection, he noses around – 'turning leaves over / Following a faint stain on the air to the river's edge' – like an adult version of one of the creatures in Ted's children's tales. He begins by asking who he is and where he belongs, concludes by deciding that he is 'the exact centre' of things, though he doesn't really know what or where his 'roots' are, so he'll just have to go on looking.[21]

Ted explained to his old schoolteacher John Fisher that *Wodwo* was a kind of completion of *The Hawk in the Rain* and *Lupercal*, the end of the first phase of his poetic career. He said that it had a hidden narrative but did not say what that narrative was. To János Csokits, an exiled Hungarian known to Olwyn from her Paris days and now broadcasting for Radio Free Europe, he was more forthcoming. Csokits had sent him a detailed critical analysis of what he saw as the strengths and weaknesses of the book. Ted sent a response. The collection was a 'transit camp' on the way to the next big thing (which was *Crow*). The poems were ordered not in chronology of composition but so as to suggest an 'undisturbed relationship with the outside natural world' being disrupted by a call 'from a subjective world'. The theme of the book, as of his own life 'from 1961–2 onwards', was 'this invitation or importuning of a subjective world, which I refuse'. 'The Rain Horse', the first story in the prose sequence in the middle of the book, was 'the record of the importuning, and the refusal'.[22] That 'refusal' led to a 'mental collapse into the condition of an animal'. The final short story, 'The Suitor', was written in January 1962, 'almost under dictation'. 'The Suitor is me,' he told Csokits, 'the man in the car is me, the girl is Sylvia, the Stranger is death, and the situation turns me into an animal – as Gog. Also, the girl is my spirit of light, my Ophelia.' The poems in the latter part of the book were 'poems after the event'. His overall feeling was that the book was too subjective. There was an awful lot of himself in it, which is probably why it was unsatisfactory. But he hoped that the ordering of the poems would lead him back to the 'objective world' where his talent really belonged.[23]

The 'event' he has in mind seems to be the moment of shamanic initiation that he had read about in Eliade. As with his discovery of Graves's *White Goddess*, Eliade gave him a context and a history for ideas that he had evolved, if inchoately, in his own thinking and writing. 'Both spontaneous vocation and the quest for initiation', he read in *Shamanism* in 1964, 'involve either a mysterious illness or a more or less symbolic ritual of mystical death, sometimes suggested by a dismemberment of the body and renewal of the organs.'[24] Having undergone this painful process, the shaman descends to the underworld and emerges as a healer and sage. Thus the 'poems after the event' in Part Three of *Wodwo* use a symbolic and quasi-mythological apparatus – Adam and Eve with the serpent, Gog, a rat and the wodwo – to penetrate a black inner world. This is the mode that anticipates the *Crow* poems on which he was continuing to work as *Wodwo* went through the production process at Faber.

Ted certainly thought he was wrestling with his shamanic destiny. But the other 'event' with which he was wrestling was Sylvia's death. The extraordinary thing about his account of the story 'The Suitor' is that it makes Sylvia into his 'Ophelia' – the girl who goes mad and kills herself because her Hamlet has rejected her – despite the fact that it was written well before his affair with Assia and its consequences.

The self-analysis of *Wodwo* prompted by János Csokits also hints at the struggle between Hughes's 'objective' and 'subjective' styles. By this account, the poems in Part One are 'objective' fresh looks at things in the world, in the style he had made his own in *The Hawk in the Rain* and *Lupercal*, whereas those in Part Three are more closely bound to his inner self. There is an element of truth in this. Among the poems in Part One are cleverly angled and innovatively worded responses to thistles (the first poem, and one of the best), crabs, grass flashed by wind, Beethoven's death mask, a bear and a jaguar – a 'second glance' at his totemic animal, written in front of the jaguar cage in the zoo in Regent's Park. Equally, Part Three is more subjective in the sense of using more autobiographical elements: not only the wolves heard from the zoo as he sat writing on Sylvia's bed in Fitzroy Road, but also little Frieda calling out 'Moon!' and his father sitting in his chair unable to forget the 'gunfire and mud' of the Western Front, 'Body buffeted wordless, estranged by long soaking / In the colours of mutilation'.[25]

It is not, however, the case that the objective and subjective voices of Hughes are neatly split between the different parts of the collection, nor that his 'brilliant physical particularity' is associated with one voice and his 'oracular rhetoric' with the other.[26] And although the title poem strongly suggested the idea of a quest for identity, no ordinary reader would be able to discern a narrative progression through *Wodwo*. The critics certainly didn't. 'What is this "single adventure"?' asked the poet Anthony Thwaite in some exasperation with respect to the author's note, as he reviewed the collection anonymously in the *Times Literary Supplement*.[27] Derwent May in the London *Times* thought that 'This wodwo haunting the countryside is a good, if whimsical, symbol for Mr Hughes as poet,' but he couldn't quite decide what the wodwo was questing for.[28] 'I'm not sure I properly understand Hughes,' wrote his old Cambridge contemporary C. B. Cox, in a review that astutely began from Ted's remark that 'when he first read D. H. Lawrence he felt as if he was reading his own autobiography'. *Wodwo* is full of Lawrentian language and includes an explicit homage in the form of 'Her Husband', a poem about a coal-blackened miner coming home to his wife.[29]

Elsewhere, Cox described the collection as undoubtedly the most important poetry book of the year.[30] An element of puzzlement did not stand in the way of critical acclaim. Typical plaudits were 'Hughes' poetry *is* the real thing,' 'the best British poet since Dylan Thomas', and, from Alvarez, 'he is the most powerful and original poet now writing in this country'.[31] The most insightful review, entitled 'As deep as England', was by the canny poet and critic Donald Davie, in the *Guardian*. He focused particularly on the short story 'Sunday', relating it to the 'remarkable poem' (unknown to him, one of the very few written after Sylvia's death) 'Song of a Rat'. 'The wolves which hunt through the boy narrator's mind,' Davie wrote of 'Sunday', 'the rats, the hawks, the otters and crabs – all the predatory and preyed-upon beasts which figure in the other poems – are projections of the predatory violence which is the only guise through which the English tradition is mediated to the poet through his war-shattered father.'[32]

Though Ted was well pleased with the reception of *Wodwo*, he was acutely conscious that almost all the poems in it had been written before Sylvia's death. The real test of his development would be the

Crow project – which kept growing but from which he kept being distracted.

Since Hughes was one of Faber and Faber's leading poets, and *Wodwo* was his first book for adults in seven years, his publishers mounted a strong publicity campaign. Together with the good reviews, this ensured that he was the centre of attention during the first Poetry International Festival in London in July 1967. The festival was indeed his brainchild, hatched in collaboration with the theatre director Patrick Garland. Since the previous autumn, Ted had been busy inviting major overseas poets, ranging from Lowell in America to Zbigniew Herbert in Poland to Israel's leading poet, Yehuda Amichai. The offer, laid out on Poetry Book Society notepaper, was not munificent: five pounds a day for the five days of the festival, up to fifty pounds for travel expenses and, if the funding could be scraped together, a further fee of perhaps forty pounds. Funding constraints meant that Ted had to scale back his ambitions. 'The Poetry Festival has lost a lot of feathers,' he told Richard Murphy. 'I was all set to cram London with geniuses, when John Lehmann etc [that is, the management board of the Poetry Book Society] decided I ought to be restrained – evidently. So the festival could only be five foreigners, five Americans, five English. It was those five English I was trying to avoid.'[33] It wasn't the particular English poets he objected to, but rather the fact that he did not want so many Anglophone voices. One of his main aims was to showcase the Eastern European poets whose work he and Danny Weissbort were publishing in their magazine *Modern Poetry in Translation*. He was disappointed that Herbert could not come, delighted when he made a late appearance in response to an urgent, pleading telegram.

The fifteen names lined up were impressive: from America, John Berryman, Anne Sexton, Allen Ginsberg and Anthony Hecht (a friend since New England days and a poet whose work Ted greatly admired); Pablo Neruda came all the way from Chile; Bella Akhmadulina from Russia; Hans Enzensberger from Germany; Yves Bonnefoy from Paris; Giuseppe Ungaretti from Italy; Yehuda Amichai from Israel; Hugh MacDiarmid from Scotland; and Patrick Kavanagh from Ireland. Eliot having died in 1965 (Ted was surprised how deeply he felt the loss), the three elder statesmen of English poetry were there: W. H. Auden, Stephen Spender and Robert Graves, who was now frail. The event was held in the brand-new 'brutalist' concrete Queen Elizabeth Hall and Purcell Room on the South Bank of the Thames. The programme was a success, though by no means on the scale of the more radical 'International Poetry Incarnation' that had been held at the Royal Albert Hall two summers before, when the wild man of San Francisco Ginsberg had appeared drunk on stage in front of an audience of 7,000, recited a very explicit poem about an orgy and been heckled for refusing to read his signature poem 'Howl'.[34]

Looking back on an exhausting five days, Ted felt that the whole thing had been almost too much of a poetry orgy, but very good 'dramatic entertainment'. Neruda and Bonnefoy read for far too long but Ginsberg kindly told Ted that the old professionals Spender and Auden had saved the day (this was on the one evening when he was absent).[35] Reflecting in his journal after the event, Ted expressed some regret at having got involved. Once he had started writing the letters of invitation, he had felt duty bound to follow through and effectively be the host. The Queen Elizabeth Hall had not really been a suitable space, the actor reading some of the translated poetry had not been very good, and so on. The whole process had taken an immense amount of time and emotional energy. Lessons would have to be learned if they were going to do it again. Renewal of his old friendship with Zbigniew Herbert and the start of a new one with Yehuda Amichai were the high points for Ted. He and Assia, who stayed with the Sillitoes for the duration of the festival, were much admired. A guest at one of the numerous parties during the week remembered the door opening and a couple emerging. She had never seen such beauty in her life. 'Who are these gorgeous people?' she asked Ruth Fainlight, who replied, 'Ted Hughes and Assia Wevill.'[36]

Back at Court Green, all was not well. Ted's mother was ill again and his father was continuing his 'cold war' with Assia. They talked about getting a nurse for Edith. The ideal would have been to find someone who could both mother his children and nurse his parents. Brenda Hedden was not a candidate for this role. In the summer of 1967, she gave birth to her second daughter, Judith. Assia visited with Ted, and gave a silver chain and a jewel box made of abalone.

It was a difficult summer for Ted. The day before visiting Brenda, he had driven Aurelia Plath to Exeter railway station at the end of a very uncomfortable visit to see the grandchildren, her first for two years. She had spent much of her time at Court Green talking with great bitterness about the effect of the publication of *Ariel* in the United States. Her life had become a 'torment', as she had to deal with endless correspondence about 'Daddy' and the humiliation of watching the critics publicly psychoanalysing her relationship with Sylvia. What Aurelia could not understand was how there seemed to be such venom in her daughter's poems and yet how when she had visited Sylvia at McLean she had been greeted with the words 'I don't hate you, it's not true, they tell me I hate you and I don't.' Aurelia reasoned that Sylvia must always have loved her because she asked her to come to England each year to visit her. Ted asked why she had not come for Christmas 1962.

Frieda and Nick saw that their grandmother had 'a heavy, terrifying will – which they respond to and yet see through at the same time'. They felt 'immense relief' at 'escaping her', though their response to her 'discipline and teaching' was also 'extremely energetic'. Ted concluded his journal note by summing up the paradox that was Aurelia Plath: 'She is a sweet, charitable, brave, very strong woman – but simply too pedagoguic [*sic*] in her insistence on the good, falsifying reality, protecting her charges from the wicked and the sorrowful and the <u>real</u>.'[37] One night later that week he dreamed of rats invading Court Green, then meditated in another journal note on a phrase used of people going to a mental hospital: 'to get sorted out'. Didn't dreams have the same function? And poems? Did poetry grow from neurosis but come to fruition as a form of healing? Could poetic experience be 'the vital, medical operation'? Was it in some sense 'the correction of God'?[38]

By now, he had met a teenage girl who lived near the village. She was called Carol, and was training to be a nurse. Her father was Jack Orchard, born not far away on a farm called Walson Barton near Bow in the summer of the Somme and raised to a farming life. Mrs Orchard was Welsh. Born Minnie Evans in Swansea, she had trained as a nurse in Devon. Carol was born in Crediton in March 1948 and was intending to tread in her mother's footsteps. She had an elder sister, Jean, who had just got married and would later join her new husband in running a local nursing home for the elderly. There was also a younger brother, Robert, who later became a parliamentary correspondent for the BBC while staging musicals in the summer recess.

Assia moved out. She had had enough, and was going to look for a job in London. A Pickfords van collected her belongings in mid-September. The children did not want her to go, Frieda saying so vociferously, Nick concurring but more silently. It was as if they were losing a second mother, and a sister (though in his journals Ted hardly ever mentions Shura). Ted's own feelings were a blank, the future a case of watching and waiting. He was taking comfort – stoicism, good sense, acceptance – from the essays of Montaigne. He was beginning to think that he should write more like Thomas Hardy than W. B. Yeats: instead of turning the real into an imagined world, life into myth and his inner self into a symbolic persona, he should ground his writing in reality, in experience: 'That is the weight behind his [Hardy's] poems – the real world, and especially the pathos of the past, of time passing. Even his tinpot love-plots have a kind of woman's magazine relevance – their triviality is awfully real.'[39] This was something he could also have learned from the 'woman's magazine' element of Sylvia writing, about which until this point he had always been sceptical. The *Birthday Letters* project would indeed entail a turn to a Hardyesque voice ('the pathos of the past' – his own past with Sylvia), but he was not yet ready for it while he was still working through his inner darkness in the mythic and apocalyptic voice of Crow.

In the same journal note, he recorded a dream of murderous rage about Olwyn. His unconscious was blaming his sister for the breakdown of his relationships with other women. And Assia's departure was also reminding him of the loss of Sylvia: 'dreamed: in bath – feeling somebody behind me, stunning shock, it was Sylvia, very young and happy'. That dream would play a part in 'The Offers', his greatest elegy for Sylvia, made public only in the week of his death.

There was a happy day soon after Assia's departure when Carol accompanied him and the children to Bideford Zoo. Where Ted saw only 'death-camp misery' in the face of the chimp behind bars and a 'greasy pool with a foul fish' for the seal to churn away in, Nick and Frieda loved their pretty, youthful companion, as she pointed out the parrots, the mynah bird, 'the spider monkey; the owl; the axolotl' (otherwise known as the Mexican salamander); 'the baby crocs; the brisk fox; the mountain lions'.[40]

Just before Christmas, Ted sent Luke Myers a letter with his news. *Wodwo* was out in the States (with slightly different content from the English version), his mother was rather better, Frieda and Nicholas were doing very well – Frieda, now seven and half, had started writing wonderfully imaginative poems. And, by a series of 'Napoleonic moves', he had got himself some 'qualified peace' in which to work. The main move, he explained, was Assia's back to London, where she had (Luke would be astonished to hear this) reconciled with Olwyn. 'Two local women come in to do the housework,' Ted added. That was true, but it was also the case that two other local women, Brenda and Carol, were now playing a big part in his life. His writing was at last going well. Crow was 'getting his feathers'. He was turning a play called *Vasco* into an opera libretto. And he was working on a version of Seneca's *Oedipus* for the director Peter Brook, to be staged at the National Theatre in the New Year. He was excited by the style he was finding, which was not so much verse as a new sort of hardened, compacted prose, written in chunks or 'gobbets'.[41]

Oedipus: not the famous Greek tragedy of Sophocles, but the little-known, more static and rhetorical Roman version of Seneca, dramatist of blood, ghost, revenge, explosive anger and stoic resilience. Ted explained to his Cambridge friend Peter Redgrove that the National Theatre had asked him to perform a light makeover on an existing translation by a Scotsman called David Turner, which had been broadcast on the radio by the BBC in Northern Ireland. But as he got deeper and deeper into the text, and worked with Peter Brook in the rehearsal room, it became a completely new version.[42]

Brook was at the height of his powers, the most highly regarded director in London. He had started directing for the Royal Shakespeare Company when he was only in his twenties and had conjured extraordinary performances out of Laurence Olivier in *Titus Andronicus* and Paul Scofield in *King Lear*. Then he had scandalised the British establishment but amazed the New York critics with his violent and sexually explicit production of Peter Weiss's *The Persecution and Assassination of Jean-Paul Marat as Performed by the Inmates of the Asylum of Charenton under the Direction of the Marquis de Sade* (known for convenience as the *Marat/Sade*). After this, there was his improvisatory-documentary anti-Vietnam agitprop evening, *US*, unprecedentedly political for the Royal Shakespeare Company.

In early January 1968, Ted asked Brook if he could be joined in the rehearsal room by a friend 'who helps a lot in these things'.[43] This was Assia. Ted was fascinated by the intensity of Brook's directing method. His rehearsals were 'like prolonged group-analysis of everybody concerned'. Ted, meanwhile, was working further on the 'abbreviated style' that seemed to him right for Seneca's muscular Latin. Director and cast made contributions to the evolution of the text. In the rehearsal room, Ted felt that he was drawing on a 'single battery of energy'. Brook was helping him to release the Oedipus story in its 'plainest, bluntest form' while at the same discovering 'ritual possibilities' in it. The great thing about the Seneca version was that it lacked the clear Hellenistic ethical imperative of Sophocles. These versions of the characters were even more 'primitive' than 'aboriginals'. They were 'a spider people, scuttling among hot stones'. Seneca's descriptive language somehow contained 'the raw dream of Oedipus, the basic, poetic, mythical substance of the fable'. The tragedy created an almost religious experience, 'the sacred, ritual progress under the marriage of love and death'.[44]

Ted was fascinated by the London theatre world, but repelled by some of the people in it. He did not like Kenneth Tynan, the National Theatre's flamboyant literary manager. When Tynan invited him to a dinner party, he declined. 'What a pity,' Tynan replied, 'Elizabeth Taylor is coming.' Ted, who regarded Taylor as the sexiest woman on the planet, was furious.

The production opened at the Old Vic on 19 March 1968 with the silver-tongued Sir John Gielgud as Oedipus and Irene Worth as Jocasta. She was fifty-one, fourteen years older than Ted, but still exceptionally attractive, with high cheekbones and dazzling eyes. She was as renowned as Ted for sexual charisma and the two of them shared several intimate evenings. She was a woman not easily discomposed, but on one occasion when he read out to her some of his still-unpublished *Crow* poems during a break in rehearsals, she had shaken with fear and pleaded with him not to write any more.[45]

As the audience entered the theatre, they saw actors in black roll-neck sweaters and casual trousers perched all over the auditorium, clinging to pillars every bit as though they were Hughesian crows.

They droned out a single note, then the players on stage turned over the cubes on which they were sitting and beat out a tattoo at ever-increasing pace. The drumming cut out and the play began. Throughout the performance, the actors would 'hiss, throb, vibrate and intone', interrupting the long Senecan speeches with 'group-sounds'.[46]

It was an evening of auguries, nightmares, priestly incantations, dark transgressions and a blighted land, with references to 'organs pulled bleeding alive from deep in the bodies of animals' and lines such as:

> my country rots / but it isn't the gods
> it is this / a son and a mother
> knotted and twisted together / a son and a mother
> a couple of vipers bodies twisting together
> blood flowing back together in the one sewer[47]

The script had lengthy blank spaces between phrases to help the actors with their rhythms and their pauses. Gielgud, used to flowing Shakespearean iambic pentameter, struggled a little with the fragmentary movement of such speeches as:

> birth / birthed / blood take this / open
> the earth bury it / bottom of the darkness
> under everything / I am not fit for the light
> Thebans your stones / now put a mountain on
> me / hack me to pieces / pile the plague fires
> on me / make me ashes / finish me / put me
> where I know nothing / I am the plague[48]

Two days before the opening night, Brook lined up the cast on stage and told them to go through the play at double speed, 'without moving a muscle, and with flat, uninflected voices like robots'. Ted said that it was the most astonishing theatrical experience of his life. The tension was so great that one of the actors collapsed and a stagehand sitting in the front row passed out. At the end, Hughes and Brook looked at each other with 'wild surmise'. It had been an 'amazing auditory experience', but they couldn't repeat it for the theatregoing public because 'it had only taken about 35 minutes and our audience wanted a night out'.

The next evening was the final dress rehearsal in the presence of Sir Laurence Olivier, director of the National Theatre, who had originally been going to direct the production but had fallen ill, which is why the job had been passed to Brook. At the finale, 'a spike was fixed in the middle of the stage, point upwards, and Jocasta killed herself by squatting on this and writhing downwards – a terrifying piece of acting by Irene Worth'. An enormous column draped in silk was then carried on, 'erected over the spike, and unveiled to reveal a giant golden phallus'. Olivier was so appalled that he said this effect had to be removed. Peter Brook 'exploded with such a shattering display of anger that Sir Laurence finally had to accept it'.[49] Ted described the end of the play as 'a sort of prodigious formal fuck and rebirth'. At the planning stage, he had suggested to Brook that a female figure should appear in the position of a 'Sheila-na-gig', a kind of ancient Irish stone carving of a woman with her knees more or less over her shoulders and her fingers pulling wide 'a very large cunt'. The Irish name, he explained, meant 'Woman of the Tits'. The giant phallus could perhaps, he thought, go up into the woman and then be seen on a 'sort of spider's web of veins, like the drapery of the placenta'.[50]

Irene Worth's Jocasta was indeed the highlight of the production. She reached an extraordinary emotional pitch as the character urged the second husband who is also her son to let go of the past:

> Oedipus / leave the dead alone / stop these
> diggings into the past / bringing my dead husband
> back to show his wounds and show himself still in
> death agony / leave him alone / hell cannot be
> opened safely / what can come out of it / only
> more pain and more misfortune / more confusion
> and more death[51]

The play ended with Oedipus speaking of:

> pestilence / ulcerous agony / blasting consumption
> plague terror / plague blackness / despair[52]

Then the chorus led him off to a rousing rendition of 'Yes, we have no bananas'.

Ted was proud and excited at the opening night at the historic Old Vic, which the National made its home prior to the construction of its own purpose-built theatre. He was a seasoned author of radio plays, but this was his debut work for the London stage. He scribbled a souvenir note on Assia's programme to the effect that she was the best sight on a very special night. She did not like the show, saying that it looked like 'an exhibit in the Greek Pavilion of Expo '67'. She was not impressed by the 'golden cubes, revolving searchlights' and costumes that looked like space suits. Her reaction to the phallus – which she described as 20 feet tall and pink, though it was actually 7 feet tall and golden – was to write 'Ugh' in her journal.[53] Some of the more traditional reviewers expressed either bemusement or disapproval at the whole thing, but the critic Ronald Bryden in the *Observer* said that Brook packed into one evening 'enough ideas to last an ordinary director a lifetime, once more proving himself light-years ahead of his nearest contemporaries, making most of what passes for avant garde nowadays look tamely nostalgic'.[54] Charles Marowitz, who had co-directed the RSC's famous 1964 'Theatre of Cruelty' season with Brook, but had now gone off to found his own Open Space Theatre Company, was more cynical: 'On a superficial plane, the production dazzles and seduces us with novelty, but a lingering dissatisfaction quickly banishes these virtues ... Brook is like the liaison between the true avant-garde and the bourgeois public and critics.'[55]

Brook greatly enjoyed working with Ted and invited him to join him on his new adventure of establishing an experimental, improvisatory, international theatre company in Paris.[56] It was, Ted excitedly told Gerald in an airmail letter, 'more or less an invitation to create' his own theatre, his 'own kind of play', with whatever actors he wanted, 'since any actor falls over to be directed by this Peter Brook'.[57]

Another plan was for Brook to return to his acclaimed Royal Shakespeare Company production of *King Lear*, starring Paul Scofield, and turn it into a film. It wouldn't be a film of the play like Laurence Olivier's *Hamlet* or *Richard III*, but rather an English equivalent of *Throne of Blood*, Akira Kurosawa's Japanese samurai adaptation of *Macbeth*, or perhaps Grigori Kozintsev's Russian *Hamlet*, with its script heavily truncated from a translation by Boris Pasternak. It would be 'a film of the story, using whatever in the text doesn't sound unreal in a film'. So, Ted told his old Shakespeare-loving schoolmaster John Fisher, with six exclamation marks, 'he wants me to rewrite the text'. He provided Fisher with a brief sample of how he was turning Shakespeare's words into something plainer and simpler. He laboured away at the task for several months. His archive includes a 'Draft Shooting Script' dated 9 September 1968.[58]

The problem was that, with Shakespeare, every word counts: 'take out one little nut' in one place and a wing will fall off, and the tail will begin to come loose because 'the whole thing is so intimately integrated'. If Ted is to be believed when reminiscing in a radio interview twenty-four years later, he was in the midst of his drafts when he had a dream in which there was a tremendous banging on the back door of Court Green. He opened it and 'there was Shakespeare himself, in all his Elizabethan gear, like that portrait of Gloriana – jewels, ruffs, and the rest of it'. He was 'boiling with rage', furious with Ted for 'tinkering with *King Lear*'. Shakespeare took Ted up into the great attic under Court Green's thatch and directed his own production of *Lear* 'as it should be put on, according to him'. This 'immense' performance filled the whole sky and unlocked 'the whole mythical background of the play'. The next morning, like Coleridge trying to recover his vision of Xanadu, Ted wrote down what he could remember of Shakespeare's interpretation of Shakespeare. But the real lesson of this dream – a reprise of the Cambridge one, with Shakespeare standing in for the burnt fox-man – was that he had to stop messing around with the play.

The Brook film was eventually released in 1971, with an orthodox (though truncated) script. But Ted hung on to his ideas about Shakespeare's substructure and developed them in an anthology of purple passages in 1969 and ultimately in his huge late book *Shakespeare and the Goddess of Complete Being*, which he described to Brook as his Shakespearean equivalent of the epic *Mahabharata* cycle.[59]

While *Oedipus* was in rehearsal, *The Iron Man*, Ted's latest children's book, was published. The American edition, published later in the year, was entitled *The Iron Giant*. This would prove to be Ted's bestselling and best-loved work. It firmly established his place as one of the world's leading children's authors as well as one of its most admired poets. The story begins under the influence of the great clifftop scene in *King Lear*, with a giant figure teetering on the edge and tumbling into a mighty fall down to the beach below. The broken man of iron is then reassembled by seagulls – they begin by picking up an eyeball, another nod to *Lear*. This is a version of the ritual 'dismemberment of the body and renewal of the organs' about which he had read in Eliade's *Shamanism*, and with which he had experimented in the film script that later became *Gaudete*.

The Iron Man then starts eating tractors, diggers and any other farm machinery made of iron. Not to mention chewing up barbed-wire fences (his equivalent of spaghetti). The figure who saves the farmers from this terrifying creature is a boy called Hogarth whom we first see fishing like a young Ted – or a young Wordsworth, since he blows mimic hootings to the owls and is frightened by the looming Iron Man in the exact same way that the boy Wordsworth feels awe and fear in the face of a rising cliff as he rows a borrowed boat across a lake. Like Ted and Gerald in Crimsworth Dene, Hogarth sets a trap for a fox. He catches the Iron Man instead and then, upon the giant's later re-emergence from the pit, leads him away from the farms to a scrap-metal yard. A giant space–bat–angel–dragon then lands on the earth. In the manner of H. G. Wells's *The War of the Worlds*, which Ted had so enjoyed reading when he was a schoolboy, humankind uses its assembled military might to try to destroy this monster from the stars, but to no avail (space flight was all the rage at this time, since it was the moment when the Americans were preparing to launch Apollo 8 towards the moon). The Iron Man saves the day when, out of gratitude to Hogarth, he fights on earth's behalf. He tames the space–bat–angel into singing the music of the spheres instead of waging cosmic war, with the result that human beings become peaceful, stop making weapons and live in global harmony.

In one sense, the story, published on the eve of the Prague Spring, is a dream of the end of the Cold War, an imagined realisation of the idealistic goals of the Campaign for Nuclear Disarmament. At a deeper level, the story gives vivid and compressed form to some of Hughes's key themes. When asked about its meaning, he said that his essential idea was 'to dramatise three centres of power'. Hogarth embodies 'the child's nature – the child's sense of himself'. The Iron Man is 'the giant Robot of Technology – terrifying and destructive, uncontrollable and inhuman, unless it is approached without fear, but with patience and good sense'. And the space–bat–angel–dragon is 'the infinitely mysterious life power that emerges from atoms, the biological psychic mystery of organic being'. This latter force is also 'terrifying and destructive, uncontrollable and inhuman, unless approached without fear but with firmness, superior courage, open-mindedness, cunning and kindness'. The story is 'a ritual by which the child and these two monstrous entities are brought into a single, inclusive, integrated pattern of behaviour and awareness in a shared life that is happy and peaceful'.[60]

But young readers do not need to know about this allegorical dimension. Frieda and Nick certainly didn't, as they listened in rapt attention to their father inventing the story for them at bedtime over five unforgettable nights.

'Then autobiographical things knocked it all to bits, as before'

When Ted was in London for the *Oedipus* rehearsals in early 1968, he told Assia that he wanted to mend their relationship. She asked him whether he still felt 'the animal thing between us'. Or did he just want her back in order to look after the children? She pleaded with him to open up to her again, as he had in their early days. 'I feel so full of love to you at your sweet best,' she wrote to him. 'I admire you and I am frightened at the power you have over me. No man has ever had this power over me as a woman.'[1]

Ted tried to probe at her feelings, sensing that what she really wanted was a home for Shura. He asked her to explain her intentions in detail, to describe afresh their 'real relationship', which had 'got buried in conveniences and necessaries'. What was she willing to do and what did she feel like doing? He suggested that if they were going to live together again back at Court Green, there would have to be some new rules. He proposed that they should each draw up a wish list, indicating how the relationship could be made to work from each party's point of view. He prepared what he half jokingly called a 'Draft Constitution: for suggestions and corrections'. Assia was invited to draw up a set of proposals of her own, and then they could compare notes and create a compromise. Ted described his own list as 'a row of horrors': children 'to be played with' and their clothes to be mended, bedtime routine to be supervised, German lessons 'two or three hours a week', no cooking for Ted 'except! In emergencies', at least one meal a week to be something new, some basic cooking lessons for Frieda as she approached her eighth birthday, 'a daily log to be kept of every expense and bill', general acceptance of his friends, no 'foolish battles over interior design' (which was to say, don't remove every last trace of Sylvia's taste), 8 a.m. as 'getting up time, no dressing gown mornings, no sleep during day unless emergency, and by agreement'.[2]

Assia began her counter-proposal with the words 'Teddy dear, forget the detail.' She did not return to Court Green. In April, she made a new will. She expressed a wish for her 'cadaver' to be buried in any rural churchyard where the vicar did not object (to burying a suicide, she meant). She instructed that a tombstone should be erected within six months of her death inscribed with nothing other than her name and dates of birth and death, and the epitaph 'Here lies a lover of unreason and an exile'. Then she set about her bequests: 'To Nicholas Farrar Hughes, since he is too young for possessions, I will all my most tender love. To Freida [sic] Rebecca Hughes, I will also my love and all the lace, ribbons and silks she can find, as well as a fine gold chain. To Ted Hughes, their father, I leave my no doubt welcome absence and my bitter contempt.'[3]

Her bitterness came from the fact that at the beginning of the month, his star sign in eclipse, Ted had vowed to make a final break with her. He interrogated himself, struggling to find the good, the human virtue, in the mess of torments and revelations to which his life had been reduced. How could he figure out the ABC of things? The A, the B and the C were Assia, Brenda and Carol.

Brenda and Trevor Hedden had separated. The parting was amicable. Brenda and her little girls moved 40 miles away to Welcombe on the Hartland peninsula, a lovely stretch of North Devon coastline. She explained to Trevor that she needed some space because Ted's intervention in their marriage had had a greater impact than she had anticipated when she had agreed to Trevor's – very Sixties – proposal that they should have an open marriage. Trevor then complained that when he had suggested she should have some occasional casual affairs, as he was doing, he had not meant that she should 'fall in love with them'.[4]

One of Ted's most beautiful unpublished love poems is for Brenda. It conjures into words their intimacy and unity, the depth of his love and the idea of her body, in three quintains of delicate repetition, variation and incantatory passion.[5] She had expressed apprehension about their relationship. She was always strongly drawn to him but sensed that if they continued it would drastically change her life and her relationship with Trevor, which had been sufficiently rewarding for a decade. The prospect was very unsettling. Ted returned a day later with the poem. He said that it was how he felt. After she had read it, she slowly crushed the paper within her hands, sensing that continued involvement with him would crush her, emotionally.[6] She loved him, but not because he was a poet. It was his personality and his intelligence that attracted her, but she knew that she was letting herself in for disruption and intricacy.

The young nurse who offered so much help with childcare was now also very much in the picture. With A in London, Ted moved between B and C on impulse, usually for a few days at a time, sometimes taking off in the night. Sometimes he was open about his unpredictable moods, suggesting to Brenda that it was better to share his secret life (as a mistress, that is to say) than to be part of his domestic life, fully exposed to his demons. He also admitted to her that he liked the fact that neither B nor C was literary. After the implosion of his lives with literary S and literary hopeful A, it would be better to keep his work and his entanglements apart. The particular attraction of B was that, unlike A, she was not haunted by rivalry with Sylvia. Brenda appreciated some of Sylvia's maternity clothes in 1965, but she never imagined herself stepping into Sylvia's shoes. He could accordingly be relaxed with regard to what he said about Sylvia, in a way that was never possible with Assia. He once confided to Brenda that he had asked Sylvia what she thought of his lovemaking ability. Sylvia indicated that he had a tendency to be too dominant.

Ted's only way of keeping going with the complications that he had created for himself was by continuing to write. He set himself a minimum of five pages a day. But he was struggling to maintain his resolution. He considered it ominous that his dream life had gone dead again.

There always seemed to be distractions and misadventures. One June day, driving out of Exeter, he bumped the car at some traffic lights. He crawled to a garage by the university. The radiator had burst and it would take till four-thirty to fix it. When he returned, he suddenly found himself pulled towards a police car and told to get in. A policewoman snarlingly asked him what he had done to those girls up in the university. He was taken to the station and interrogated. The mechanic at the garage had said that he had been away for an hour. A man in a white shirt and green trousers had been exposing himself to the female undergraduates. The police arranged for him to stand on the street while two girls were paraded past separately. Neither thought that he remotely resembled the flasher. The police did not apologise, though they had the grace to drive him back to the garage. Another afternoon wasted. Faced with major traumas of the kind that Ted faced again and again in his life, many people would vent their anger and frustration by becoming furious over minor incidents of this sort. It is a mark of Hughes's fortitude that he kept cool and saw the funny side.

As was the case for much of his life, he spent a lot of time going backwards and forwards between Devon and London. That summer he introduced the poet Michael Baldwin to the occult. He assumed that Baldwin would be interested because he practised hypnotism, which was banned from public performance, in clubs and at parties. Ted took him to a place that he called 'Watkins' bookshop' in an alleyway off St Martin's Lane. After lengthy browsing, he bought Baldwin a book called *The Magician: His Training and Work*. 'This is harmless,' he said. 'Solid, and harmless but very, very good. Keep it to yourself, read it critically and take from it what you will.' Behind the till stood Anna Madge, daughter of Kathleen Raine, poet, scholar of William Blake and expert on the Tarot, occult Neoplatonism, the gnostic tradition, the universal wisdom of the initiate and all such mysterious arts. Ted was a great admirer of Raine's writings and was very pleased, many years later, to propose her for the Queen's Gold Medal for Poetry. Late in life, he became a supporter of her Temenos Academy of Integral Studies, which fostered the arcane spiritual traditions and also won the support of Prince Charles.

Hughes and Baldwin remained friends for years. They were both dabblers as opposed to true initiates in the dark arts. 'We did not ever perform occultist ritual conjurations together,' Baldwin recalled, reassuringly, 'or join Peter Redgrove and Penelope, who had lain in a circle feet to the moon in order to conceive [their daughter] Zoe.' Baldwin remembered how Ted had shown him the letter from the Redgroves describing this ritual and said in mock horror, 'The child will be mad!' According to Baldwin, he then reflected for a moment and said, 'Should have been head to the moon anyway. You always rope the heifer head to the moon so the usual tides draw the bull's semen deep.'[7]

Despite his vow in April, by August Ted was seeing Assia again. He had assisted her with translations from the Hebrew of the selected poems of Yehuda Amichai. They were published under her maiden name Assia Gutmann on 11 July 1968, and received extremely favourable reviews. Assia's poems, which had more than a few touches of Ted, were praised as fine creations in their own right, not mere translations.[8] Before the end of the year, relations had been sufficiently repaired for Ted and Assia to participate jointly in a radio programme promoting the book. The broadcast was billed in the *Radio Times* as:

YEHUDA AMICHAI: Poems by an Israeli poet translated and introduced by ASSIA GUTMANN and read by TED HUGHES. Yehuda Amichai was born in Wurzburg in 1923, left Germany in 1937, and is now a citizen of Israel. During the 1950s he became the best known of the generation who freed Hebrew poetry from its traditions, and made it colloquial and supple enough to cope with the complexities of modern life.[9]

Assia provided spoken introductions and talked about Amichai's life, while Ted read a selection of the poems.

On 6 August 1968, Ted took Frieda and Nick to Heathrow in a taxi. They were off to see their grandmother Aurelia in America. The taxi took them to the wrong terminal, and he panicked that they might miss their flight. But it was delayed. While they were waiting, eight-year-old Frieda told her little brother Nicholas that Daddy ought to marry both Carol and Brenda, so they would have one mother each. He waved goodbye and watched the plane take off: 'Dropping skirts – motor-boat, nose-up, nearly horizontally before climb grips.'[10] Then he ate some foul food at the airport's Lyons café and took a bus to Clapham, where Assia now had a flat near the common. They made love. The next day, he was back at Heathrow with Assia and Shura. They took a BEA flight to Germany for a week's holiday. On the first day, they visited Beethoven's house in Bonn. For Ted, this was like paying homage at the shrine of a god. He noted down every detail: Beethoven's last piano, his viola, his three hearing aids, the manuscript of the Ninth Symphony. The rest of the week could only be an anticlimax after this, though they enjoyed sending Amichai a postcard from his birthplace. Ted was intrigued (and Assia horrified) by a conversation on the train from Frankfurt to Würzburg during which a retired SS man, living on his pension, told them of his adventures on Hitler's Russian campaign. Ted was prompted to write a death-camp poem for *Crow*. Assia noted in her journal that the trip was sometimes 'bleak with T's chemistry gone amok, an ugly impatient mood setting in', but that on other occasions he was delightful with Shura, rowing her on the Schluchsee in the Black Forest, buying her little wooden birds and playing imaginative games. Assia was delighted that their daughter was now calling Ted 'Daddy'.

Having said goodbye to Assia at the end of the holiday and returned to Court Green, he dreamed that Sylvia had returned to life. She hoped to see the children. A certain drug made it possible, so she spent a whole day with her old friends from Smith, and Frieda and Nick. She fell asleep at the end of the day and died again in her sleep.[11] In another version of the dream, Ted met her back at Smith, with all her college friends: 'She greatly surprised and pleased by the success of Ariel, knowing she was back only for a day. She dug a hole in the main path at Smith (one that doesn't exist) and there we buried her manuscript – the black book. It was her mother's decision to bring her back briefly in this way.' He wrote about the 'insanity' of the dream and its effect on him. He could not get over the strangeness of the sensation of 'her presence after so much death'.[12]

He gave Brenda a heart-shaped gold bracelet inscribed with their names, identical to one he had given to Assia. He also gave them both copies of an intimate and highly erotic poem that reads as if it were originally written for Sylvia. It was first published in July 1968 with the title 'Second Bedtime Story' and later reprinted in *Crow* as 'Lovesong'.[13] Brenda's copy is a typescript with her name written in giant capital letters across the page on top of the text. She recalls that at this point Ted's three loves were 'nicely spaced out', with Assia in London, Carol just outside North Tawton at Nichols Nymet, her family's large and handsome late-Georgian house, and herself in Welcombe. He had told her that 'after Sylvia, he no longer wanted to be dependent on one woman; he felt it was weakening and suffocating him'.[14] He left one of his lectures to himself on the subject of A, B and C on the kitchen table in Court Green. It came to the conclusion that the right balance was three.[15] But was he really enough of a God to maintain a trinity? He crisply summed up his dilemma in a journal entry: '3 beautiful women – all in love, and a separate life of joy visible with each, all possessed – but own soul lost.'[16] He also drafted a poem that began 'Which bed? Which bride? Which breast's comfort?'[17]

Assia was the one he took to a poetry reading in Dublin. The promising young Northern Irish poet Seamus Heaney was there. He remembered being mesmerised by her huge eyes. He had never met a woman with such sexual charisma. 'I think poets should be like bishops,' she said to him: 'they should have their own diocese and meet irregularly and formally.'[18] The next day they went up to Belfast for another reading. Afterwards, they went for a Chinese meal and Ted, ever the teacher, insisted that Seamus should use chopsticks for the first time in his life. Heaney had by this time published his very Hughesian first collection, *Death of a Naturalist*, which included his signature poem 'Digging', highly influenced by 'The Thought-Fox' in the way that it was a poem about the act of writing a poem. After the Chinese meal, they returned to the Heaneys' house in Ashley Avenue, where Ted and Assia and Seamus and his wife Marie drank poteen late into the night in the half-furnished front room: 'Marie singing Irish folk songs, Assia singing Israeli songs, Ted singing "The Brown and the Yellow Ale"'.[19]

The evening with the Heaneys was the beginning of one of the most important friendships of Ted's life. But Assia was close to despair by this time. 'The bottle-opener has left a small rosy map-lake on my wrist,' she had written to Ted the day before his birthday. 'Bring a postcard with you, and on it a short manifesto, and a razor-blade – and we'll celebrate your birthday so fabulously – there won't <u>ever</u> be another like it.' On 6 September 1968 she confided to her journal: 'It is only inevitable that the life I have lead [*sic*] should end like this. That I should be supplanted (<u>sub</u>-planted!) by others. I was endowed with too many minor qualities, but with neither the will nor huge intelligence to bring them a life of their own.'[20]

Late in life, looking back on his poetic development, Ted Hughes wrote that 'View of a Pig', 'Pike' and 'Hawk Roosting' were the most important poems in *Lupercal*, his second volume of poetry and the one where his distinctive poetic voice, with its 'broad inclusive concentration' on the facticity – the intractable condition – of the world, truly emerged. Writing 'Hawk Roosting' in particular was one of the best moments of his life. *Wodwo*, he went on, was the 'fall-out' from the 'Pig-pike-Hawk Roosting vein'. But the progression towards that collection was 'broken up by autobiographical events' – Sylvia's death meant that his poems of 1960 to 1962 were not published until 1967. The 'next conscious real step was Crow', in which he resimplified his language and broke it into a new form of 'lyrical-dramatic' narrative. But 'Then autobiographical things knocked it all to bits, as before'. His poetry came to an abrupt halt until, in the early Seventies, he started again with 'ABC language' in the 'diary pieces' that became *Moortown*, his farming book.[21] The autobiographical things to which he was referring here were the events of 1969. Hard as it may be to imagine, this was an even worse year than 1963. It was indeed the worst of his life.

In the autumn of 1968 his ailing mother had been taken back to Yorkshire by ambulance, his father following. Ted at last had Court Green to himself. Then in December Gerald, Joan and their children Ashley and Brendon, along with Joan's mother, came over from Australia. They spent a white Christmas at Court Green, meeting Carol for the first time. Gerald found her 'very attractive', shy but welcoming. His whole family took to her. Ted, Nick and Frieda then travelled north to the Beacon with Gerald and his entourage for a New Year's visit to their parents. There was a reunion with the extended Farrar family and it was on this occasion that Ted, Gerald and Nick drove down to Mexborough for the 'ceremonial farewell' to the pike pond at Crookhill.

The day after this, he wrote to Assia, talking about them finding a new place and moving back in together, with the three children. The perpetually on–off relationship appeared to be on again. The return visit to the Beacon seemed to have had the effect of drawing Ted back to A and to the North, far away from the complications of B and C in Devon. Charles Monteith at Faber had asked him to edit a selection of Emily Brontë's poems and this inevitably had him thinking again about Top Withens and the moors and Sylvia's snow-covered grave in Heptonstall.

On 18 March 1969 Ted went to Manchester to record a reading of his poetry for a television broadcast. He met Assia at the station. She had left Shura with her au pair. He was nervous. He had read and spoken on the radio dozens of times, but never done television before. He didn't want Assia in the room where the recording took place at Holly Royde College, so she waited in a corridor. She was annoyed not to be allowed into the monitoring van, where she would have been able to see how Ted looked on screen. He introduced and read eleven of his best poems, including 'The Thought-Fox', 'Wind', 'An Otter', 'Wodwo', 'Hawk Roosting', 'Six Young Men' and 'View of a Pig'. Assia was miserable at the meal after the recording, Ted stroking her shoulder to try to comfort her. They had a heart-to-heart in the dingy lounge of the Elm Hotel. Why could he not commit? 'It's Sylvia,' he said, 'it's because of her.'[22]

The next day, they drove to Yorkshire. Ted left Assia in, of all places, Haworth. He went to see his mother in hospital and spent the night at the Beacon with his father. That afternoon, Assia walked down the precipitous High Street towards the Brontë parsonage. The snow on the ground was hardening and deep. It felt, she wrote in her journal, like a town made of iron. She went to the local doctor's surgery and obtained a prescription for thirty-five Seconal sleeping pills. That night, feeling lonely, she read some of Zbigniew Herbert's poems. But it was cold and then the bedside light packed up. She lay in the dark, listening to the radio. First there was a programme on Radio 4 entitled *Exquisite Sister*. It told the story of Dorothy Wordsworth and how she had helped her brother with his poetry, how intimately she lived with him, but how she ended up, as Assia put it in her journal, 'mad and old'. The thought of a great poet and his intimacy with his sister inevitably brought to mind the strong influence that Olwyn always exercised over Ted. Then she turned over to Radio 3 and fell asleep listening to the Hollywood String Quartet playing Beethoven's late quartet in B flat major, Opus 130.[23]

But she had not taken the pills. She woke in good time in the morning. The Brontë parsonage had been closed to tourists the previous day. She tried again, but it was too early. Having asked the landlady at the pub where she was staying if she knew of any houses for sale, she strolled around the little town as the snow slowly thawed, wondering what it would be like to live there with Ted and the three children. He then arrived to pick her up and they spent the next two days house-hunting. They looked at places as far north as Hexham in Northumberland, where they saw a dower-house that was available for rent. It belonged, Ted later recalled, to 'Lord Whatsisname'. Assia was keen that his Lordship should know how important Ted was, which embarrassed him. They also saw a place called Green Farm, a lovely house available at low rent with salmon in a river close by. On the way back to Manchester, where they returned for Assia to get her train back to London, they inspected some less desirable properties. Assia had the feeling that by this time Ted was just playing along, that, as ever, he was not really serious about making a commitment. They said goodbye on the station platform and he headed off on the long journey down to Devon. 'Last embraces,' he would later scribble in a notebook, 'clear memory of her going off on the London train.'[24]

She phoned Court Green the next day, Sunday 23 March 1969. A friend of Olwyn's was staying. She picked up the phone. Assia assumed it was 'another woman'. Ted came in tired and it was several hours before he got the message that Assia had phoned.[25] He called back and tried to give her hope with regard to their future – there was talk of a house up for let in Barnstaple – but in a way that was insufficiently 'emphatic'.[26] Fatally, he misjudged the extent of her vulnerability. Her divorce from David Wevill had been finalised (he moved to Texas and started a new life). She had always been conscious that her body was not nearly so beautiful as her ravishing face; now she felt that she was losing her looks altogether, running to fat.[27] She no longer walked into a room and turned every head. If Ted was not going to give her hope, there was no future. In a small notebook, she wrote down his words: 'It was no good thinking they could live together in a house – it's because of Sylvia.' Then she wrote, 'I have no answer to that, so die soon … execute yourself and your little self efficiently.'[28]

That evening, a Mrs Jones in the neighbouring flat in the house in Clapham sensed the distinctive smell of gas. Some time later, Assia's au pair, Else, who had been to visit a friend, came home. Before leaving, she had checked that Shura, four years and three weeks old, was asleep in bed.

When Else opened the door, she was almost overcome by the gas fumes. Mrs Jones summoned a male neighbour from upstairs. He went into the kitchen of the darkened flat, switched on the light and saw the bodies of mother and child. He turned off the gas, opened the windows and called the police. Another neighbour, who happened to be a nurse, was called down. 'Mrs Wevill was lying on some blankets on the floor on her left side', she said in her police statement, 'and her daughter was lying on her back, with her face inclined towards her mother.' There was no pulse in either of them and the pupils were dilated. 'The little girl was much colder than her mother.'[29] It had not taken long for the fumes to overcome the sleeping child, whom her mother had carried into the kitchen. A post-mortem would reveal that Assia herself had taken whisky and the sleeping pills she had obtained in Haworth.

The police officer attending the scene found an envelope on the bedside which was addressed to Ted, together with another to Assia's father in Canada. As a result of this, Ted was contacted by the local police in Devon and asked to go to Southwark Mortuary to identify the bodies. He gave a statement to the police, explaining that he had met Assia seven years before, having known her husband David Wevill 'through the profession'. He and Assia had become 'very close friends, and eventually the friendship blossomed into love'. They 'became intimate, and there was a girl born of this union'.[30]

Ted took charge of the funeral arrangements, delaying the date so that there was time for Assia's father to fly over from Canada. Her sister Celia could not afford a ticket. At the end of March, Assia and Shura were cremated. Ted had managed to round up most of her friends. He asked Peter Porter and his wife Jannice to share the front taxi with him and Assia's father for the journey across the river to Lambeth Cemetery, where the brief funeral service took place. Porter thought that this was Ted's way of thanking Jannice for all the support she had given Assia, going back to her visit after the abortion in 1963 (five years later, Jannice killed herself, her husband believing that the example of Assia was in her mind). Colleagues from the advertising agency were also there. Edward Lucie-Smith remembered the tears pouring down Ted's face. Porter was haunted for the rest of his days by 'the memory of the two coffins waiting before the fire curtain, the one an adult coffin and the other a diminutive shape'.[31] Nathaniel Tarn thought it was wrong to have a Christian ceremony. There was no Hebrew Kaddish. He atoned for its absence in a lengthy verse requiem written soon afterwards and dedicated 'in memoriam Assia & Shura'. Here, as Ted would in poems written many years later, he used the fire of the crematorium to give 'these daughters of the people gone' back to their Jewish heritage:

> With lungs still full of gas
> with nostrils bruised by her last breath
> she lies oak-packaged on a pedestal
> beside her / in white cloth
> the child she took into the oven with her …
> We give her up now / to the lapping fire
> To Terezin / Auschwitz / and Buchenwald.[32]

After the cremation, Edward Lucie-Smith took Ted and Olwyn out to lunch with a group of Assia's friends. Among them was a jewel-maker called Pat Tormey. Afterwards, on the way back to Olwyn's flat (she was living in Hampstead at this time), Ted noticed an exquisite gold ring on Pat's finger. She had recently made it. Ted asked her for it because it seemed more right for Assia than any piece of jewellery he had ever given her. If she had been alive, he would have bought it without hesitation. It seemed uncanny that Pat had just made it and was wearing it. She willingly handed it over. 'I don't know what I shall do with it,' Ted wrote in thanks. 'When I saw it I thought I must bury it with her ashes and I think I shall.'[33] He repaid Tormey with a gift of one of his precious netsuke.

On 14 April 1969, Ted wrote to Celia Chaikin in Canada. He said what he could about the complications of his life with her sister. He cursed himself for not being more sympathetic in the final phone call – 'But I was exhausted, and nearly off my head with other distractions.' He mourned for Shura: 'the most wonderful little girl, full of fire'. And for Assia: 'my true wife and the best friend I ever had'.[34] Her memory was with him every minute of every day, every night.

He had no idea what his next move should be. On the same day, he wrote to Aurelia, saying that he planned to go to Ireland, where he would put the children in a famous Quaker school that had been recommended to him by friends who were professors at Trinity College Dublin. Ireland, as always, was the dream of escape and a fresh start. Leaving the children in Devon, he headed to Waterford to check out the school. From there, he drove north to County Kilkenny to stay overnight with Barrie Cooke, who had never seen him looking so terrible. He went on alone – one of his first days fully alone for many years – to Cashel in County Tipperary. Over a glass of brandy, looking out on the Rock of Cashel, associated in legend with St Patrick and the coming of Christianity to Ireland, he took out a spiral-bound shorthand notebook and began composing prose and poetry for the 'dead souls' of the women he had lost.

'Steady terrible pain', he wrote. 'How much remorse, how much sentimental pain at what I have missed, and am missing. Much much much more complicated. The face, the millionfold life, & Shura.' He dreamed of Assia every night. He castigated himself for their bitter misunderstandings. He began sketching a long poem about Orpheus and his attempt to recover his beloved Eurydice from the underworld. He turned into verse a recurring dream about being hauled into court and accused. With this second death, his sentence was doubled. He wrote of his prison, his desire to break out into the wilderness. 'I will get free. I summon the cunning fox / He will set me free. He will dig, / He will find freedom for me, find it, find it. / Fox, fox, in the wild open.' He blamed himself bitterly for the 'mistake' that 'cost two lives – three'. He wrote that he was not composing for readers, but for himself. He asked himself whether the 'momentary pleasure' of some stranger would one day 'pay' him for 'ruining' his own life 'and causing the deaths / of those I have loved best / and who loved me best, and who were my life'.[35] He did not consider this to be real poetry. He was only writing as a way of attempting to 'get out of the flames'.

He thought that he was at his nadir. He wrote to Peter Brook with an apology for his long silence, explaining that 'the most horrible thing has happened': 'In a fit of depression and a crush of wretched far-fetched coincidences Assia killed herself and our little four year old daughter.'[36] He included a note for Irene Worth, which is lost: it probably urged her not to feel any responsibility for Assia's jealousy of other women.

Then, before he could implement the plan to move back to Ireland with the children, there was bad news from Yorkshire.

On 13 May 1969, he was still wrestling with the dilemma of the choice between B and C, Brenda and Carol. He went to bed late and said a prayer for his mother, who was in hospital following a knee operation. At one o'clock in the morning he woke suddenly with a

sensation of 'awful horror'.[37] His immediate apprehension was that his
mother had died. Having banished the thought – she was supposed to
be convalescing – he managed to get back to sleep. He was up at 8.30
in the morning because some electricians were coming to work in
Court Green. He tinkered with some writing, and then at 10.15
Olwyn called. Edith had died in the night.

Later that day, he drove north with the children. Nicky had shown
no reaction, but as they got close to Yorkshire, Frieda, who had been
in tears for the first hour of the journey, said, 'My stomach is getting
very excited at meeting Grandad but I myself am getting sadder.' Bill
was quite lively when they arrived. The subject was not broached for
about a quarter of an hour. Then he said, 'Well this is a sudden
business,' and explained that Edith had been recovering well, expected
to be out of hospital soon, but had then suddenly developed breathing
problems.[38]

Ted had not written to his mother since Assia's death eight weeks
before, partly because he could not help blaming his parents, who had
been so horrible to her, for the downward spiral that led to her death.
His father had accordingly asked Olwyn what was wrong with Ted:
why had they not heard from him for so long? She told him the ter-
rible news, making him promise that he would not tell Edith while she
was still in hospital. But Bill couldn't keep the awful burden to himself.
He had no one else to tell, so he broke his word and told his wife. 'Well,
aren't you glad I told you?' he asked her, as she digested the appalling
reality of it. And she had replied, 'Well, – I'm not sure.' She was dead
within a few days. Ted convinced himself that the news of this second
suicide was responsible for her demise. As he told Aurelia Plath, 'I've no
doubt that the shock and the agitation was fatal, she reacted violently
to any news on that front, which is why I had not told her.'[39] His
mother's death seemed like a terrible requital for all the harsh words
that had passed between Assia and his family: 'A's death removed
Sylvia's to a great distance, swamped everything,' he wrote in his make-
shift journal. 'Now Ma's death has somewhat removed A's. Yet A's comes
back.' He struggled to grasp his own 'stupefaction in face of all this'.
'Must not go numb,' he told himself. 'Terribly tired.'[40] The writer must
never allow himself to go numb, but in the face of these successive
hammer blows Hughes was struggling not to go under. He said good-
bye to his mother's body in the chapel of rest in Hebden Bridge.

That summer, he spent a lot of time in London, leaving Nick and Frieda in Devon. He travelled up by train on 29 May. It was an unusually hot day and he couldn't help noticing the near-naked girls with long legs, strolling through the streets. He was flooded with erotic memories, then overwhelmed by the 'black dog' of depression, the sense of 'walking on air over a black gulf'. He thought one moment about the Neoplatonic philosophy of Jacob Böhme, the next about his multiple sexual entanglements. Then he noticed a hair on his pullover and realised that it was Assia's, a symbolic rope or 'hawser' mooring him to the memory of her.[41] Later in the summer, he scattered her ashes in a rural Kentish graveyard, doing what he could to fulfil her last wish for her body.

Nor could he escape the memory of Sylvia. On 13 July, he was staying with Olwyn in London. The second Poetry International Festival was under way, though this time he was not so centrally involved. While Olwyn took a siesta, he read through the proofs of an academic essay collection called *The Art of Sylvia Plath*. Reading about her poems brought everything back with absolute freshness and a sense of 'total recall'. 'To me,' he wrote, 'those poems open alphabet – every nuance, I know its whole history and connection, every phrase – its exact weight and angle.'[42]

With the memory of Sylvia thus freshened, he went in the late afternoon to visit Sue Alliston in University College Hospital. Back in 1967, inviting Zbigniew Herbert – who was very fond of Sue – to the first Poetry International, he had explained what had happened to her. She had enrolled for a degree in Anthropology, done well, and gone to North Africa to study the Bedouin. Ted imagined her 'setting out in her usual style – her long scarf ends dangling and her handbag swinging and colliding with things and her skirts in a swirl round her long, beautiful legs'.[43] The Bedouin chiefs tried to 'entangle her in marriage' – a nice irony, given her role in Ted's disentanglement from marriage. She returned after a few months with Hodgkin's disease, a lymphoma that had until recently been incurable, with a maximum life expectancy of five years. After several months of treatment, she had apparently responded, though she was painfully thin.[44] She and Ted had resumed their close friendship, now without a sexual element. But the remission was temporary. Now she was back in hospital, and dying.

It was the first time he had been in the hospital since going there for the formal identification of Sylvia's body in the mortuary. He went into the ward and saw Sue asleep, her tear-swollen face fallen sideways over a book. As he walked towards her, she woke in that half-amazed, half-alarmed manner that is familiar to anyone who has visited a dying loved one as they drift in and out of consciousness in a hospital bed. She said that she had been having such strange thoughts, strange dreams. She stared at Ted, composing her face, 'trying to remember'. She was utterly exhausted. He had brought cherries. She 'tries to eat some, then drink lime juice – later goes yellowy green, last 15 minutes she is wanting to vomit – I eventually go so she can vomit in private'. A little later, a nurse injects her and she notices Ted looking at her arm, that arm which was around him at the moment of Sylvia's death. She told him that she was tired of living alone. He said that she could recuperate in Court Green, his empty house. She wept, she talked emptily about work. He knew that it was to no avail: 'Very bad feeling about her. Kept seeing her dead. Felt her hopelessness & loneliness, her despair about future. I feel hollow and fake – since I betrayed her too, though not drastically.' She wanted love, 'somebody to live with and care for her'. He knew that he was the one person she really wanted. But it was too late for him to give her a home. 'Half-wave, half-smile. Farewell.'[45] This key journal entry gave him the raw material for one of the most important poems on his trajectory towards a personal voice.

As he walked to the Festival Hall for the poetry festival afterwards, the city seemed spectral and the river filthy. After the evening's readings, he went to a party but felt disengaged. Back at Olwyn's, he read the book about Sylvia deep into the night. He then returned to Devon, staying at Court Green with the children but also visiting Brenda in Welcombe. They fought and made up in the summer heat. His behaviour was becoming increasingly volatile.

At the end of the month, he was back in London, visiting Sue again, bearing roses and carnations. Into University College Hospital by the morgue entrance, with its memory of Sylvia. The antiseptic smell and polished floors. As soon as he saw Sue, he sensed that it was her last day: 'Her eyes huge in shrunken clay face. Her arms wasted and colourless, except for bruisemarks everywhere, and vein marks, skin tissue-thin.' It almost seemed as if one eye were trying to recognise him and the other did not care. She was too tired to speak, her mouth so numb that she could only mumble. With her wide eyes and inability to articulate, he couldn't help thinking of his mentally incapacitated niece Barbara. Sue didn't really register the flowers, so he gave them to a nurse who put them in a vase by the bed. Sue's hair was 'brushed to a tight crumpled dark material skullcap – that marvellous forest of auburn. Her pony face more so – sick, staring, like a sick animal.' She reached out to touch his leather jacket, did not have the strength to turn over, so he helped her. He found it hard to say anything. He kissed her and made to leave. The nurse told him that the bloods were not too bad, it was the 'strange awful drowsiness' that was puzzling the doctors. Perhaps, Ted mused, she wanted to die. Her dear friend Tasha Hollis had died, horribly, of alcoholism. What was there left for Sue to live for, all her lovers having fallen away? One death 'infects another', he wrote in his journal account of the terrible day. Tasha was some-how infected by 'the German girl' who took her own life in 18 Rugby Street. Then Tasha's death had infected Assia. Sue had reacted terribly on hearing of Assia's suicide. Now, with Tasha gone, Sue had no moti-vation to fight on. As he was speaking to the nurse, 'She waved an exhausted spread hand. I went back, kissed her again – left.'[46] He returned to Devon, and would not see her again.

On 7 August 1969, Ted and his father caught an early train to London. Ted put Bill on an onward train to Yorkshire, then met up with Olwyn and took a taxi to Golders Green Crematorium, where they attended Susan Alliston's funeral beneath a blue sky on a hot summer's day.

On an impulse on the day of his mother's funeral in May, he had bought the house that back in 1963 he had so nearly bought with Assia: Lumb Bank. He planned to close up Court Green, rid himself of all its associations. Frieda and Nick would be taken north, put in touch with their Yorkshire origins. Now he made his choice: it would be Brenda and her daughters that he would take with them. The two little girls would do something to fill the place left by Shura.

Frieda and Nick were sent on one of their summer visits to Aurelia in the States while their father prepared for the big move. By the autumn his new extended family was ensconced in Lumb Bank. 'It is very beautiful – marvellous house,' he told Richard Murphy, 'I'm pleased with all of it.' Ever mindful of Murphy's hospitality in Cleggan, he added that, despite this, he was still thinking of a place in Ireland: 'I need another pole – not Devon or London, out of England.'[47]

One piece of good news came during these bad times: Ted was awarded the 5 million lire City of Florence Prize for poetry, which was worth about £3,000. But as far as publications were concerned, 1969 was, understandably, an exceptionally lean year. There were only two works of any substance. The text of *Seneca's Oedipus* appeared from Faber in December: a showcase for Ted in mythic mode, a turmoil of violent passions but at a defensive distance from anything personal. Earlier in the year, he had published an essay in a very different voice, in the form of an introduction to an English translation of the selected poems of the Yugoslavian Vasko Popa. He described Popa as one of that 'generation of mid-European poets – Holub of Czechoslovakia, Herbert of Poland and Amichai of Germany/Israel are perhaps others of similar calibre – who were caught in mid-adolescence by the war' and who accordingly developed a new kind of poetry of survival which succeeded in yoking the suffering of the mid-century generation to 'their inner creative transcendence of it'. Ted recalled a remark of Czesław Miłosz, another of these poets, to the effect that 'when he lay in a doorway and watched the bullets lifting the cobbles out of the street beside him', he realised 'that most poetry is not equipped for a world where people actually do die'. 'But some is,' Ted replied, and Popa's was a supreme example.

The introduction then explores the characteristics of Popa's work, and its influence on Ted's own development quickly becomes apparent. Popa's poetry is a landscape in which 'heads, tongues, spirits, hands, flames, magically vitalized wandering objects, such as apples and moons, present themselves, animated with strange but strangely familiar destinies'. There is a 'surprising fusion of unlikely elements'; the 'sophisticated philosopher' is also 'a primitive, gnomic spellmaker'. A 'desolate view of the universe' is opened up by way of 'childlike simplicity and moody oddness'. 'The wide perspective of elemental and biological law is spelled out with folklore hieroglyphics and magical monsters.'[48] This account of Popa's poetic world was also a template for *Crow*. By the end of 1969, Ted had selected the poems to include in the published sequence and sent them to Leonard Baskin for illustration: 'Crow was your suggestion remember,' he wrote. 'Whether people like them or not, they are my masterpiece. Insofar as I can manage the likeness of a masterpiece.'[49]

A decade later, Ted updated his introduction for a new edition of Popa's *Collected Poems*. He noted a change of style in the late collection, *Raw Flesh* (1975). Though it included some overspill in the mythic vein from the earlier *Wolf-Salt* (the wolf was Popa's totemic beast), most of the poems were 'unlike anything Popa had published before: simple direct jottings evoking memories of the poet's childhood and youth, memories of the war years and the town of Vershats'. These poems were 'without mythical dimension', yet they still stretched their wings 'towards the wider legendary worlds of the other books, setting themselves into the bigger settings'.[50] Here Ted could just as well have been writing of his own change of style in the Seventies.

He anticipated his new direction in a letter written in the autumn of 1969 to Danny Weissbort, with whom he had worked so closely in bringing the Eastern European poets to English readers: 'I've decided I've been trying to write verse in completely the wrong way for some years. I've been excluding the real thing. I institutionalized the mode of one or two successes in 1962 – and got myself stuck on the board of management. So my best 7 years have passed in error and futile strife.' But of course they were the worst, not the best, seven years. Perhaps everyone in their thirties lived through a time of 'special chaos': 'you reap what the innocent eagerness of your twenties sowed, and before you can wise up'.[51] After the trauma of 1969, Ted was ready to wise up. For that to happen, he would need a stabilising female influence.

The Crow

One day, Ted Hughes looked at the sky and saw an aircraft crossing in one direction, a crow in the other. The plane drew his mind to Gerald and the receipt of airmail letters from the other side of the world. But what of the crow's flight? Would it be possible to see into that? To put aside the aircraft, the world, the sky, the self and to enter the full, the deep, 'crowiness' in the crow's flight: its 'ominous' quality, 'the bare-faced, bandit thing, the tattered beggarly gipsy thing, the caressing and shaping yet slightly clumsy gesture'. You could try to capture all that in words and still you might miss the crowiness, the essence – the 'inscape' as Gerard Manley Hopkins had it – of the way in which a knowledge of the human world might be derived in an instant from a glimpse of a crow's wing-beat, as it was derived by Shakespeare when Macbeth says 'Light thickens, and the crow / Makes wing to the rooky wood.' In seeing into the life of things, poets, probably always but certainly since the time of Wordsworth and the Romantics, have also been looking into their own selves, surveying their inner universe. When Ted Hughes writes about the crow's wing-beat, he says, echoing the language of Wordsworth, that the moment of its observation unlocks the doors 'of all those many mansions inside the head'. The words that he writes about the crow offer 'something of the inaudible music that moves us along in our bodies from moment to moment like water in a river'; they are 'the vital signature' of his own being. The long gestation of Hughes's writing about the crow was his struggle 'truly to possess his own experience, in other words to regain his genuine self'.

Human imagination, says Hughes, works in 'scenes, things, little stories and people's feelings'.[1] *Crow* is a series of scenes, a ragbag of things, a collection of dark little stories written over a period of years and given new and even more bitter meaning in retrospect as they displace into myth the raw cry of the barely imaginable feelings that are summoned by the book's spare dedication: 'In Memory of Assia and Shura'.

Nineteen-seventy was the year when the crow poems – or at least a selection of them – became a book. It was also a year of turmoil in his personal life. Just before Christmas 1969, leaving Brenda and her daughters in Yorkshire, he took his father, Frieda and Nick back south to Court Green for the holiday season. Then, in January, they returned to Lumb Bank, this time bringing Carol. But at the beginning of February, Ted changed his mind about living in what he called the Yorkshire battleground. So they all returned to Devon. Having deposited his own children at Court Green, he drove back to Yorkshire to collect Brenda and her children. He escorted them to a large farmhouse that he had rented for them on the North Devon coast and spent several days settling them in there. Over the coming months, he paid the rent for her to live in a succession of cottages. She was beginning to feel like a kept woman on a Yorkshire budget.

In March, he opened his heart in a letter to Assia's sister. Since the previous summer, he had been in a stupor and had done 'the most insane things'. Getting Lumb Bank, which he and Assia had come so close to buying, had been some kind of attempted atonement for her lonely death at a time when they had been searching for a house. Assia would have made Lumb Bank beautiful but in her absence it was merely bleak. The whole of England was bleak because of her absence, London 'unbearable'. Only a long journey far away would jolt him back to life. As it was, he was endlessly vacillating – going to and fro like a ping-pong ball – between schools for the children, between houses to live in, between north and south, between Brenda and Carol.[2]

Writing to Gerald from Court Green, he apologised for being out of touch, explaining that he had been trying to piece together his broken life. But he acknowledged that he perhaps didn't really know himself well enough to have done so more than provisionally. Nor were his planetary alignments encouraging. Still, he had come to a number of realisations. That Carol, who cared so well for the children, was the backbone of his survival. And that the purchase of Lumb Bank was an understandable impulse at the time of his mother's death ('ensuring my roots maybe'), but that it so stirred up the hornet's nest of family and memory that he now had a 'psychic horror of the place' and would do best to let it out for a couple of years and reconsider its future when his mind was more lucid. The other thing was that a house had come on the market near Bideford in North Devon. This was an area he loved because it was a pretty town with good schools, located near the sea and the estuary where he fished.

The house was to be auctioned in the summer, but the owners said that they would settle before then, for about £15,000. Two miles out of town, it was a beautiful Elizabethan manor house with a central tower, light rooms, a big dining hall, a walled garden with fruit trees and nearly 40 acres of sheltered hilly grazing land leading down to the sea. It was secluded along a private lane and surrounded by mature woodland. He sketched it for Gerald, pointing out the location of pastures, cedar tree and a badger sett. He told himself that he would never see another house like it. Built in the time of Shakespeare, this was his dream of England incarnate: the great hall in which to eat, the symbolic tower like that of Yeats, the surrounding landscape.

How to afford it? An American library had offered him £20,000 for Sylvia's manuscripts. But that money was rightfully the children's. He justified the temptation by saying that it would do them more good to live in such a wonderful home than to wait for an unknown amount of cash when they were grown up. But he didn't convince even himself with this argument. The better alternative would surely be for Gerald to come home and take a half-share in the house. He could keep bullocks and they could fish together: 'What the hell else are you going to do – you're 50 this year. I'm 40. What are we saving life up for? We could live here like barons – it's a kingdom.'[3] But Gerald had no intention of returning to the old country and its miserable weather.

Money was, as ever, the problem, given that Ted did not want to let go of Court Green (because of all the memories of Sylvia), or of Lumb Bank (because there would be a heavy tax hit if he sold it so soon after buying it), or of the manuscripts (his children's birthright). With Gerald unwilling to come in on the scheme, he turned to Aurelia, which proved to be a fatal mistake. Just before Easter, he wrote to tell her about the house and proposed that its purchase could be financed by the royalties on an American edition of *The Bell Jar*. Seven years earlier, the book would have seemed 'terribly raw and inflammatory', but now that 'Sylvia's eruption into American consciousness' was 'pretty well digested', the book would not be a bombshell at all – 'The poems were the bombshell.' Passages causing direct offence would naturally be quietly removed. If the book were not to be published soon, it would diminish in value until there came a point when it would be no more than 'a curiosity for students'. The children loved the house, he told Aurelia – what with the badgers and the lobsters under the rocks on the beach – and it was their immediate happiness that was paramount.[4]

Things did not work out as planned. A year later, Aurelia scribbled a bitter annotation on the fold of the wafer-thin airmail paper: 'Children said this was a "horrible house" and they didn't want to live there. Ted did send me $10,000 from the royalties (I protested the publication which Sylvia would not have allowed) and deposited $5,000 each in accounts for Frieda and Nick – Ted never bought the property!!!' The damage was done: Aurelia and, through her, several of Sylvia's biographers came to believe that Ted had opened the wound of *The Bell Jar* merely for the sake of a big house by the sea.

He was in no mood for new writing. The important task was to get those crows into print. Leonard Baskin, who had originally suggested the idea for a crow sequence, was commissioned to do the engravings for a de luxe edition on his Gehenna Press. For the trade edition, Ted identified 1 October as an astrologically auspicious date, though Faber missed this by eleven days. At the beginning of the year, the plan was to include forty-five poems. By Easter it was sixty.[5] The subtitle, *From the Life and Songs of the Crow*, was introduced in order to indicate that this was a selection, not the entire epic sequence.

To Ben Sonnenberg in New York he explained how, at the moment of Assia's death, when Crow was at 'the bottom of the inferno', the sequence had come to a halt. He had, he said, not written a word for a year. 'In piecing together the fragments of the beloved he himself is reduced to a scattered skeleton': this was as true of himself as of the Crow.[6]

He knew that the stakes for his reputation were very high. Setting aside private-press work, he had not published a volume of original poetry since *Wodwo* in 1967, and most of the poems there had been written before Sylvia's death. *Crow*, furthermore, had an immensely long gestation. It had begun from a request by Baskin to write a poem called 'The Anatomy of Crow' to go with a collection of his trademark Crow drawings – a request made just three weeks after Sylvia Plath's death, with the explicit intention of propelling Ted 'from despair to activity'.[7] A rendering called *Eat Crow* came first, in 1964, as 'part of a long waddling verse drama' based on Andreae's *The Chymical Wedding of Christian Rosenkreutz* (a Renaissance alchemical fantasia that Hughes considered to be 'a crucial seminal work – like *Parzival* or *The Tempest* – a tribal dream').[8] Then there was a plan for a folktale, initially for children, with the Crow in a similar role to that of the Raven in North American Indian tales. Hughes recalled making his first attempt before going to Ireland in 1965, then starting the sequence in earnest after his completion of the series of 'Skylarks' lyrics published in 1966[9] – a trajectory from an ascending bird long associated with lyric song to a descent into carrion. Things had started to flow on the trip along the Rhine with Assia, but had then been halted by the work of organising the first Poetry International Festival. A contract had been signed early in 1967. He had tried to grow the work into a saga, an epic poem, a creation myth, a counter-theology. He continued on and off, as his relationship with Assia imploded.

The Crow was many things and required many explanations. One of the most revealing was a gloss on the poem 'Crow on the Beach', in which he explained that the guiding metaphor of the sequence came from his reading of the 'Trickster' tale familiar from many different folk traditions. The Trickster – Ted knew a whole array of examples, from Loki in Norse sagas to the anthropologist Paul Radin's study of the 'Trickster Cycle of the Winnebago Indians' – is a part-god, part-human, part-animal figure who has some secret knowledge or power that is used to play tricks in order to disrupt the normal rules of nature and question the conventional behaviour of society. Though the intentions may be malicious, the outcome is ultimately valuable for humanity. The Trickster is cheater of death, hero and clown. He is both good and evil, affirmer and denier, destroyer and creator.[10] Trickster and sexuality, Ted alleges in his commentary, are 'connected by a hotline ... Trickster literature corresponds to the infantile, irresponsible naïvity [*sic*] of sexual love, as if it were founded on the immortal enterprise of the sperm.' The Crow, like the Trickster, has a kind of tragic joy, is 'repetitive and indestructible', a 'demon of phallic energy'. He makes fatal mistakes, indulges tragic flaws, but 'refuses to let sufferings or death detain him'. Never despairing, however low he falls, he 'rattles along on biological glee'.[11]

At the same time, he explained elsewhere, 'crow' is another word 'for the entrails, lungs, heart etc. – everything extracted from a beast when it is gutted. What is extracted, when this is done, is the vital organism of the creature – lacking only the brain and nerves.' At a profound and symbolic level, *Crow* is a skeletal autobiography: 'The Crow of a man, in other words, is the essential man – only minus his human looking vehicle, his bones and muscles.'[12] Ted Hughes was looking into the heart of his own darkness. The colour of the collection is the black of crow and death; the outlines are of blood, claw and bone.

God has a nightmare about a crow dragging him around. Crow is then born. He is questioned in an examination. His answers? The word 'death' is repeated, fifteen times, more. Then 'who is stronger than death? – Me, evidently.' The narrative proceeds with a series of poems reworking images of the Garden of Eden and our expulsion from it. A serpent plays a prominent part. There is a morbid wit: 'God crushed the apple and made cider.' At times the imagery is intensely violent or sexually charged. Of words as weapons: 'Crow turned the words into bombs – they blasted the bunker.'[13] Of laughter: 'People's arms and legs fly off and fly on again.'[14] And of lovers: 'In their entwined sleep they exchanged arms and legs ... In the morning they wore each other's faces.'[15] The journey extends via a river-crossing and strange encounters. Figures out of Greek mythology. A hyena and an elephant. Later, a white owl.

On numerous occasions, in letters, in published and unpublished notes, in broadcasts and at poetry readings, Hughes explicated the meanings of his sequence, told of how during his long tribulations Crow 'gradually develops some purpose in his life, which becomes a quest to find who created him': 'he's forever, through one clue and another, approaching his creator. And when he gets there, it always turns out that it's some female or other.' Some of these females seem human, but more often they are demons, serpents or versions of the Gravesian White Goddess. 'And so throughout his tribulations he's involved with all sorts of females' – which is something that Ted's friends noticed about him.[16]

The ways in which these females are represented can be startling. When God tries to teach Crow the word 'Love', Crow retches. 'And woman's vulva dropped over man's neck and tightened.'[17] In 'The Battle of Osfrontalis', words come 'in the likeness of a wreathed vagina pouring out Handel'. In 'Criminal Ballad', there is a 'woman of complete pain rolling in flame'. And in 'Truth Kills Everybody', Crow holds 'a screeching woman' by the throat.[18] But Hughes hastened to reassure a sceptical reviewer that these poems intended no violence against women. The violence was internal to Crow's psychology: the images are not of 'violence' *per se* but serve rather as metaphors of 'breakthrough' into self-knowledge. The poems are always grasping towards some dark mystery of the inner life: the creative tension out of which they are born is the incompatibility between the speaker's ostensible mentality and what Hughes calls 'the hidden thing' which fleetingly escapes. Like dreams, poems offer momentary glimpses of the inner mystery. The images in 'Truth Kills Everybody', he confided, 'are all from a series of dreams I once had, memorable to me for the shock they came with and the interpretation of them that presented itself'.[19]

Rarely has a volume of modern poetry had such a mixed reception as *Crow*. Al Alvarez set an authoritative, positive tone in a review in the *Observer* the day before publication. He said that the collection marked the end of Hughes's faith in animals, which is certainly true insofar as the sequence has little to do with the natural history of crows, little similarity with the earlier collections in which each animal poem stood in 'isolated perfection'. Alvarez compared Hughes's development to Freud's move from the pleasure principle to the death-drive after the First World War. The collection is described as an epic folktale in which 'The tone is harsh but sardonic and utterly controlled. The poet will not yield an inch to sentimentality.' The writing 'could easily slop over into melodrama', but it does not (in contrast to the less successful poems in *Wodwo*). Astutely, Alvarez identified the vivifying influence of Eastern European poetry, Vasco Popa especially: 'From him Hughes has learned to control his private horrors and make them public by subjecting them to arbitrary rules, as a psychotic child repeats and controls his terrors by turning them into play.' It is a collection, Alvarez concluded, 'equipped for life in a world where people do die'. 'With *Crow*, Hughes himself now joins the select band of survivor-poets whose work is adequate to the destructive reality we inhabit. I think he is the only British poet to have done so.'[20] The memory of the Holocaust, not fully grasped in Britain until the Sixties, and the anxieties of the Cold War, with its threat of nuclear annihilation, hang more heavily over the review than any intimations of Hughes's private life. The fear of real bombs is highlighted: there is no hint of the bombshell regarding Sylvia's death that Alvarez was priming even as he wrote the review.

Two poets admired by Hughes took a balanced view, admiring but more modest in praise than Alvarez. For Peter Porter, Hughes's achievement was 'to use legendary material as old as Gilgamesh or Eden and make it apply to modern genocides and the smaller disasters of individual human lives. The plot has disappeared and the poems in their isolation seem exaggeratedly misanthropic. The language is simpler than Hughes usually employs (the influence of folk legends) but it can still flower into violent eloquence.' The quality of the writing, Porter suggested, was by no means all good: 'Hughes has got stuck with a lot of traditional properties (emotive nouns, stale vocabulary, litanies, and catalogues) and for the first time he oversimplifies and coarsens some of his poems.' On the other hand, 'English poetry has found a new hero and nobody will be able to read or write verse now without the black shape of Crow falling across the page.'[21] And for Stephen Spender, 'By using his extraordinary gifts to project a state of consciousness which sees the destruction of the world behind everything, Hughes may well be speaking for what many of his contemporaries really do feel. Some of the most terrifying (and terrifyingly funny) passages in Crow give one the sense that this is the nightmare reality behind the American or world dream of salesmanship and television.' On the minus side, though, 'The defect of the poem, it seems to me, is that he tends to use the "end-of-civilization" situation – which is the contemporary one – as a metaphor for the whole of life.'[22]

Conservative critics did not hesitate to describe Crow as 'the assertion of a nihilistic violence'.[23] But fortunately for Ted, just as a rearguard action against the volume was being mounted in the English press early in 1971, the American edition was published to high acclaim. Newsweek said that 'Crow is one of those rare books of poetry that have the public impact of a major novel or a piece of super-journalism': 'Ted Hughes has created one of the most powerful mythic presences in contemporary poetry. Crow is the blackness of all of us, including the whiteness that was.'[24] And the influential *New York Times Book Review* trumpeted that 'this is no mere book of poems, but a wild yet cunning wail of anguish and resilience, at once contemporary, immediate, and as atavistic as the archaic myths it resembles', while astutely adding – without knowledge of the importance of the experience of Ted's father – that 'Among British poets, Hughes is the most haunted inheritor, from Wilfred Owen and Robert Graves, of the sensibility shaped by the appalling slaughter in World War I.'[25] In Boston, the *Christian Science Monitor* caught the humour as well as the darkness. 'Part of the fun', the reviewer suggested, was that, though the form was childlike and the topic often 'a myth of origin', the subject matter was 'anything but childlike'. It was a 'grim kind of fun': 'Black-humor poetry to be sure, but programmed to awaken man to what he is doing to his planet, warring, polluting, destroying its natural balance. Mr Hughes has a vision of what life on earth could be, and if he shows us its negative side, it is a stratagem to make us demand the positive.' Some commentators in England had hailed it 'as a work of genius, a seminal book which will change the direction of English poetry, a new *Waste Land* for the '70s'. Whatever the final critical reckoning might prove to be, *Crow* was a book 'too powerful to be ignored, too passionate to be overlooked; a marriage of primitive fantasy and sophisticated knowledge too rare to miss'.[26] The Eliotic comparison could not have pleased Ted more. He cut out the review and preserved it.

The retrospective judgement upon the collection has been equally mixed. For some readers, it represents Hughes at the height of his powers. So, for example, the experimental novelist Nicola Barker looked back from the vantage point of the Nineties and described the collection as 'a skinny Bible dedicated to life's stupid gory ugliness, but also a vindication, as joyous, as bubbly, as fizzy and nose-tickling as a glug of liver-salts'. Crow, she said, was a 'raddled, mangy, empty creature' who wasn't 'so much a bird as a smudge on the page, a blot of ink which links the collection of poems together, staggers between the poems and barks at them, eyes them up, tips his head, picks them apart, one by one … Hughes booked his ticket to immortality in 1970, and the way I see it, that ticket's not refundable' (despite, she meant, the weakness of some of the Laureate poems).[27] For others, though, the collection marked the beginning of a descent into poetic self-indulgence, misogyny and all too parodiable blackness. There are good critics who argued that Ted Hughes's best work was already behind him.

But perhaps the last word on the book's reception should be left to the local paper of Hughes's place of origin, the Mytholmroyd *Courier*: '*Crow* will hardly outsell the collected poems of Mrs Harold Wilson. But, with one flap of its monstrous black wing, it has swept Mytholmroyd-born Ted Hughes head and shoulders clear of the current generation of British poets, alike in reputation, daring and achievement.'[28]

Despite its distance from the versifying of the Prime Minister's wife, *Crow*, which cost twenty shillings (one pound), sold well. The first edition of 4,000 copies sold out within weeks; Faber brought out two further editions of the same quantity before the end of the year and two more the following year. Seven further poems were added to the 1972 reprint of another 4,000 copies (£1.40 in the new decimal currency). This too sold out. A further 5,000 copies were printed the next year and a paperback edition of 20,000 the year after that, with 20,000 more in 1976.[29]

There were also the usual Hughesian limited editions, beautifully crafted and intended for deep pockets. Olwyn established her own imprint, the Rainbow Press, at this time, though Ted was also collaborating with other fine printers. Following a number of broadsides early in the year ('A Crow Hymn' in March for three guineas, four further crows in August for £4), 150 copies of *A Few Crows*, at £5 signed or a guinea unsigned, were issued from the Rougemont Press in Exeter on the originally planned publication date of 1 October 1970. In April 1971 twelve further poems, 'excluded for personal reasons' from the public edition, were privately printed in Essex under the title *Crow Wakes*.[30] The title poem 'Crow Wakes' was extracted from *Eat Crow*, which appeared in full in 150 copies on Olwyn's Rainbow Press for the considerable sum of £16.80. And finally, in 1973, the project came full circle to its origins with a de luxe, hand-set limited edition of 400 copies of the full augmented collection illustrated with twelve drawings by Leonard Baskin. This also included three further poems, two that had first appeared in another of Olwyn's Rainbow Press limited editions, a selection of *Poems* by Ted and their friends Ruth Fainlight and Alan Sillitoe,[31] and one ('Crow's Song about Prospero and Sycorax') which had been published with a limited-edition text of the introduction to the selection of Shakespeare's verse that was his other major project at this time.[32] The price of the volume with the dozen clawed, hooded and visceral Baskin illustrations was £30. In the light of the rampant inflation of the Seventies, forty years on this equates to more than £300 per copy. A rare-book dealer might ask more than twice that sum for a second-hand copy.

The limited editions were not only about beauty, rarity and profit – which was not always substantial, given that the market was tiny and the production values of the highest, while the raw materials of fine-woven paper, bevelled boards and gold leaf for the spines did not come cheap. These special collections were also a form of catharsis, an opportunity to release poems of particular rawness to a very limited readership more interested in the look and value of a book than the inner life of the tormented Crow. So, for example, 'Crow's Song about England' appeared only in the Rainbow Press selection of Hughes, Fainlight and Sillitoe. It tells of a girl who 'tried to give her mouth' but found it 'snatched from her and her face slapped'. Then 'She tried to give her breasts / They were cut from her and canned'. And finally, 'She tried to give her cunt / It was produced in open court she was sentenced'.[33] This was the debased England of tabloid sex-crime headlines and a macabre national obsession with Myra Hindley and the Moors Murders. In the very month that this poem was published by Olwyn, Hughes blackly joked (or only half joked) that he had been put in the frame as a suspect in a high-profile Yorkshire sex crime. In October 1970 a twenty-three-year-old schoolteacher called Barbara Mayo, hitchhiking on the M1, had been picked up by a dark-haired man in a Morris 1000. He raped and strangled her. The 'Yorkshire Ripper' Peter Sutcliffe later became a suspect, though DNA evidence thirty years after the event pointed to another man who had by then emigrated to Canada. The photofit picture of the murderer did, unfortunately, bear a vague resemblance to Hughes, who had a Morris Traveller.

In the trade edition, Crow is always 'he', not an 'I'. He should not be mistaken for Ted Hughes. But a poet's persona is an essential part

of that poet's inner self. In the poem 'Crow Tries the Media', where
the verb in the title has a double sense, 'He wanted to sing about her'
but a 'tank had been parked on his voice'. He wants to 'sing to her soul
simply' but the media horde is waiting so he cannot release his inner
voice, with the result that 'her shape dimmed'.[34] This is the elegiac
voice, the desire to write about Sylvia struggling for release. Again,
Crow's 'Lovesong' is not only one of many battles with the maw of
the White Goddess but also an intensely felt yet oblique poem for
Sylvia:

> She bit him she gnawed him she sucked
> She wanted him complete inside her
> Safe and sure forever and ever.[35]

The bite cannot but be a memory of Falcon Yard, the complete and
all-consuming desire a recollection of Sylvia's strenuous and emotion-
ally demanding lovemaking.

Only in the very last line of the trade edition of *Crow* does the *he*
become a *me*, so allowing the open self to rest upon the page: 'Sit on
my finger, sing in my ear, O littleblood.'[36] And only behind the veil of
the limited edition does the mask slip and the 'I', the first-person
voice, emerge, hounded and broken, in an explosion, 'a bombcloud':
'I became smaller than water, I stained into the soilcrumble. / I became
smaller.'[37] He became smaller: Elizabeth Compton remembers that
Sylvia described Ted as having become a *little* man by virtue of his
affair with Assia.

These lines actually go back to the very beginning of the *Crow*
project: they belong to *Eat Crow* and were first published as early as
July 1965, under the enigmatic title 'X', in *Encounter* magazine – the
very place where such devastating poems as 'Daddy' and 'The Jailor'
had first appeared. The truth is that from the outset *Crow* was a means
of coming to terms, indirectly and 'through a symbol', with Sylvia's
death. But Hughes did not openly acknowledge this until the last year
of his life, after the publication of *Birthday Letters*.[38]

The Savage God

Just before Easter 1970, as he was preparing *Crow* for publication and wrestling with the choices in his personal life, Ted published a review in the *Spectator* of a book called *The Environmental Revolution*. This intervention heralded a highly important new direction in his work. The book was a history of the conservation movement by Max Nicholson, former director general of the government agency the Nature Conservancy. In his review, Hughes dates the modern awareness of impending ecological catastrophe to the publication in 1961 of *Silent Spring*, Rachel Carson's indictment of the effects of the pesticide DDT. He writes with authority about vanishing songbirds, the erosion of topsoil, the pollution of rivers and the threat to biodiversity presented by the monoculture of the Forestry Commission's conifer plantations.

But in typical Hughesian vein, he places the scientific facts in the context of a bigger picture, a story about Western man's increasing alienation from nature. Christianity, especially in its Reformed version, sees the earth as a heap of raw materials given by God to man for 'his exclusive use and profit'. It has no time for creepy-crawlies and almost as little respect for women: 'The subtly apotheosized misogyny of Reformed Christianity is proportionate to the fanatic rejection of Nature, and the result has been to exile man from Mother Nature – from both inner and outer nature.' Here Hughes pulls together several threads: the idea, derived from his Anthropology course at Cambridge, that human society has evolved from matriarchy to patriarchy; the narrative he had developed from *The White Goddess*, in which the fecund female earth goddess is displaced by quarrelsome male sky gods; and his reading, via Shakespeare and Milton as well as Graves, of the Reformation and its suppression of

the cult of the Virgin Mary. He finds hope in the stirring of ecolog-
ical consciousness, the emerging Green movement, since it represents
'something that was unthinkable only ten years ago, except as a poetic
dream: the re-emergence of Nature as the Great Goddess of mankind,
and the Mother of all life'.[1]

Along with some friends, he set about launching a magazine called
Your Environment, intended to alert the public to questions of conser-
vation – the disposal of nuclear waste, for example – by gathering all
the scientific evidence and making it accessible, though with more
rigour and detail than there was room for in the Sunday papers and in
debates on radio and television. For the rest of his life, Hughes pored
over research papers, clipped out news stories, wrote to politicians and
became involved in local environmental campaigns. His ecological
mission was of a piece with his poetic vision. In his essay on 'The
Environmental Revolution', he writes of the 'mental disintegration
and spiritual emptiness' that characterise 'the soul-state of our civi-
lization': this is the dark spirit of *Crow*. But he also writes of the true
(the 'mediumistic') artist's capacity to 'see a vision of the real Eden', to
release the spirit of Pan, to restore humankind to nature. 'While the
mice in the field are listening to the Universe, and moving in the body
of nature, where every living cell is sacred to every other, and all are
interdependent,' he rhapsodises, 'the Developer is peering at the field
through a visor, and behind him stands the whole army of madmen's
ideas, and shareholders, impatient to cash in the world.'[2] Poet and
conservationist, he believed, must unite and rise up against the spirit
of the Developer.

In the light of his personal relationships at this time, there is a certain
irony to his view that Christianity since the Reformation had shown
little respect for women. The year since the shattering deaths of 1969
had been chaotic, as he shuttled backwards and forwards between
Brenda and Carol, speaking words of commitment to them both but
in his darker moments confiding to friends that he might do better
without either of them. He had become a divided self. It was all very
confusing for the children. He was still moving restlessly between
Court Green, the North Devon coast and Olwyn's place in London
NW3. There were periods when he resorted to staying with friends,
in order to avoid facing his choice at home. In the early summer, he

stayed with the clergyman-scholar Moelwyn Merchant, then he went to Alan and Ruth Sillitoe.

A decision had to be made, if only to bring stability to the children. He called a family meeting and asked whether he should marry Carol or Brenda. 'Marry Carol,' said Nick and Frieda, who had long adored the pretty, kind, gentle young nurse. Frieda, aged ten, wanted Carol for her mother more than anything else on earth, so dearly did she love her.[3] Olwyn's reply was more worldly-wise: 'If you have to ask that question, you shouldn't marry either of them.'[4]

He listened to the children. In his journal he castigated himself for his dishonesty in relation to the two women, then wrote that he was convinced that the choice of C as opposed to B was the correct one. So 'full tangle with B' was to be 'suspended and pushed into a cupboard'.[5] Yet a mere three days after convincing himself of this, he was writing to Brenda again, addressing the letter to the house that he had rented for her and saying that he was missing their lovely times together and would be back in a few days.[6] In May, Brenda was the one whom he asked to move into Court Green. Over the following few months, she and Ted entertained several of his closest friends: the Sillitoes, the Heaneys and Peter Redgrove and his partner Penelope Shuttle. Seamus Heaney wrote a blessing for the house and its new chatelaine, but at times Ted's mood was dark. While Nick and Frieda were in America for a summer visit to their grandmother Aurelia, he went briefly to London, leaving Brenda and her little girls in Devon.

On 19 August 1970, two days after his fortieth birthday, in a register office ceremony as quiet as the first one, Ted Hughes married twenty-two-year-old Carol Orchard. As with his wedding to Sylvia, he did not hurry to tell family and friends that he was a married man.

A few days later he wrote from Danny Weissbort's house in London to Brenda at Court Green. He addressed her as his dear love, told her that a horrible thing had happened and that they urgently needed to meet. He returned to Court Green, made love to her and then told her that he had married Carol. He stayed for about a week, then went north, alone, to Lumb Bank. In the middle of September, he wrote to Brenda, telling her that in the circumstances it would be better if he did not return to Devon for the time being. By this time, she had decided that it was not appropriate to continue living in Court Green. She had found herself a job as a social worker in Sussex, far away to the east. But before her move, they would have a week together in Ireland. Once again, he was hoping to find some kind of root there. A friend wryly remarked that Brenda was the one who got the honeymoon, but that was not how it felt to her.

Court Green was closed up. Ted spent the next few months dodging about. In October, he was back in Yorkshire, writing to Brenda, who was by this time in rented accommodation in Lancing, Sussex. He complained that the children were running rather wild and that he would soon be down to fix a school and buy a house. His behaviour was becoming increasingly erratic. Visiting her in Lancing, as he sat waiting for her to come back from work, he sketched an imaginary animal, described it as Henry Williamson's Muse, and then dedicated it to the one he loved most in his wretched life. But, he complained, all she was interested in was conditions. Among the conditions he proposed was that she should not continue with her job in Brighton. He wrote her a cheque for a thousand pounds, the equivalent of her annual salary, but she gave it back, explaining that she needed to work. He signed himself 'from the loser', but, as Brenda perceived it, 'his ego then required him to concede nothing, so he continued "to the loser"'.[7]

After one of his visits, Brenda's Lancing landlady drew her aside and told her that she recognised her gentleman caller: it was someone very famous, wasn't it? Brenda asked her who she thought it was and she replied, 'Engelbert Humperdinck,' the pop star whose 'Release Me' was one of the biggest hits of the era and who hosted his own television show at the time.[8]

Ted set about making arrangements to rent a flat in Hove. Then he put in a successful offer to buy a house there.[9] He proposed that Brenda should live in the main part of it with her daughters, while he would be in a self-contained flat that would combine easy access to her with privacy in which to write. But then a telephone conversation with Olwyn revealed that something serious had happened. In late October, on the very day that contracts were to be exchanged, he pulled out of the house deal. He wrote to Brenda from London, saying that his life was in another horribly ironic mess, that he regarded himself with contempt, that the two of them had broken up their whole lives in order to have each other, but that it was not going to work. He had lost both himself and her, lost the love that was the most wonderful thing in his life (this kind of language is familiar from some of his letters to Assia). He would go to Ireland, put the children into school there, try to win back some self-respect.

Despite writing all this, he went back to Sussex for another try. But four weeks later, he was writing again, telling Brenda that she had shown him what he was. He could not go on living a dismantled life. He loved only her and he was horrified by his mismanagement of the situation. She had been his only chance for happiness and it was a horror to him that he had destroyed it. He would be out of England by the time she got the letter.

It is doubtful whether, after Sylvia, he would ever have found complete happiness with just one woman for any length of time. Part of the attraction of Brenda was that she did not necessarily want marriage. She had been there with Trevor and come out the other side. But a double life was never going to be an entirely satisfactory solution to the problem of the divided self. Over Christmas Ted took stock.

In the new year of 1971, Nick and Frieda were sent to Ibstock Place, a progressive boarding school in south-west London, a decision about which Ted later expressed qualms. To some of his friends, it seemed curious that he should have agonised over the question of which of his two women would be a better stepmother for the children, made his choice, and then within six months sent them off to boarding school, thus reducing parental care to a half-yearly responsibility.

With the children out of the way, he wondered about permanently leaving behind both Lumb Bank and Court Green in order to make a fresh start. Once again, he looked to Ireland for a home without the ghosts of the past. He wondered whether Carol would like to live there. But a trip to Waterford was not a success. He wrote to Brenda, telling her that he was a free man now that the children were in boarding school. Fulfilled at work in Sussex, she did not respond.

Before long, he and Carol were in Israel, in company with several other poets, for a reading tour organised by the British Council. Ted was deeply impressed both by the place, with its rugged beauty and profound history, and by the people, with their resilience in the face of their Arab neighbours. His friendship with Yehuda Amichai, which had begun in the time of Assia, grew stronger. It was built on their shared gifts for poetry, their bantering wit and the fortitude that enabled them to bounce back from adversity. Ted kept one of his vivid travel journals, noting the orange crush of the bazaars in Jerusalem, the abundance of Crusader crosses, the holy sites of the three Abrahamic religions, and the scorching heat. He could not face a visit to the Holocaust memorial (neither could fellow-poet Danny Abse, a Jew). This offended one of his hosts at the university.[10]

He then spent two weeks doing campus readings in America, with Richard Murphy and Tony White, an actor friend from Cambridge days, but without Carol. There was an especially memorable reading of *Crow* at the 92nd Street Y in Manhattan. He was delighted to meet up with old friends such as Luke Myers. And he was deeply taken with the energy of the new people whom he met, notably the writers Susan Schaeffer and Erica Jong. The former would become a close friend, though not a lover. The latter – who had something of Assia in her dark good looks – was soon to be author of the work of unashamed sexual liberation *Fear of Flying*. It was there that she coined the phrase 'zipless fuck', which, it has to be acknowledged, is what many women wanted when they met Ted Hughes. Her recollection of his charisma may stand for the experience of dozens of females, of all ages, who attended his readings:

> He was fiercely sexy, with a vampirish, warlock appeal. He hulked. He was tall and his shoulders were broad. His hair fell against his broad forehead. He had a square jaw and an intense gaze and he reeked of virility. Moreover, he knew how irresist-ible he was in the Heathcliff fashion, and he did the wildman-from-the-moors thing on me full force when we met. He was a born seducer and only my terror of Sylvia's ghost kept me from being seduced.[11]

She sat across a bar table with Ted and Luke while Ted 'put the poetic moves' on her. Knowing she would want a signed copy, he grabbed her *Crow* and sketched inside it a lascivious serpent entwining a Garden of Eden tree. 'To Erica, a beautiful Surprise,' he inscribed it. 'You could inhale the man's pheromones across the table,' she recalled, 'this stink of masculinity and musk that must have worked on countless girls.' His eyes 'held you in his gaze as if you were the only person on the planet'.

The only other man of such intensity whom Jong had met was the film director Ingmar Bergman, 'another born seducer – in the gloomy northern style'. She wondered whether 'these men from the cold and gloomy north' were 'so sexy because they taunt you with the promise of sex that can melt icebergs'? Or was it the intensity of their genius – that strongest of aphrodisiacs – which made so many women swoon?

Jong treasured the inscribed *Crow*. In retrospect she wished she had given in to his charms, though in another way she didn't, since by not consummating the flirtation she could keep Ted as her 'secret demon': 'My temperature rose and with it my panic. I taxied home to my husband on the West Side, my head full of the hottest fantasies. Of course we f— our brains out with me imagining Ted.'

The Heathcliff motif is by now familiar. Jong is smart: she gets that Ted is *playing* Heathcliff. But she still can't resist the fantasy. 'Secret demon' is the key phrase. Where Ted had his vision of the all-consuming White Goddess, Jong projects herself as, in the words of Coleridge's 'Kubla Khan', a poem with which Ted was obsessed, a 'woman wailing for her demon lover'. In her memoir, she goes on to note that after Ted's death 'dozens of women' (a bit of an exaggeration) came forward to claim that he was their secret lover. Some were telling the truth and others were fantasising, dreaming of submission to his charisma. In a typical Ted Hughes dream, there is an orgy in which he is offered first choice of partner.[12] For most men, this would be a fantasy of wish fulfilment. For Ted, it was but a stepped-up dramatisation of a reality that he knew and that caused him as much difficulty as pleasure. Once, a woman who met him at a party was so viscerally attracted to him that all she could do was go to the ladies' room and vomit.[13] The attention of women was, furthermore, a distraction from work. As he noted to fellow-author Peter Redgrove, the gift of poetry was something that a lot of women found very attractive with the effect that it could all too easily be converted 'into fucking, exclusively'.[14]

While in New York, he also had discussions about Sylvia's legacy with Fran McCullough, his publisher at Harper and Row. In Britain, *The Bell Jar* by 'Victoria Lucas', published a month before Sylvia's death, had been reissued in 1966 with the true author's name on the cover. At that time, Ted and Olwyn well understood that, for the sake of Aurelia's feelings, it should not be published in the United States. But there had been rumours that they might lose control of the right to withhold it. A curious provision in the copyright law of the United States meant that a work by a deceased US citizen published outside the country did not have protection at home for longer than seven years. Any unscrupulous publisher had only to get hold of a copy of the English edition, print their own and create a publishing sensation. What were the options, Olwyn asked Aurelia: to have no say in the novel's presentation and get no money, or to publish an authorised version with editorial control and make some money for the children? Put like this, it was a no-brainer: Aurelia agreed to publication, with dread in her heart.

As an exercise in damage control, a biographical essay was appended. This was written by Lois Ames, who had known Sylvia at Smith. She was the daughter of Elizabeth Ames, the director of Yaddo. In 1969 Ted and Olwyn had commissioned her to write Sylvia's official biography. The essay acknowledged *The Bell Jar*'s autobiographical content and sketched the outline of Sylvia's life, including her attempted and her actual suicide. In order to soften the blow of the novel's cruel portraits of real people, the essay included extracts from a letter written by Aurelia to Fran McCullough as the book was being prepared for publication. Here Aurelia explained that Sylvia had won an award to write a novel, but during the time she had been given to finish it she had undergone miscarriage, appendectomy and the birth of Nicholas. It was hardly surprising that the novel was a 'pot boiler'. Aurelia recalled Sylvia saying that she had merely thrown together events from her own life, 'fictionalizing to add color', with the intention of showing 'how isolated a person feels when he is suffering a breakdown': 'I've tried to picture my world and the people in it as seen through the distorting lens of a bell jar.' This, Aurelia explained, is why the reader should make allowances. 'Practically every character in *The Bell Jar* represents someone – often in caricature – whom Sylvia loved; each person had given freely of time, thought, affection, and, in one case, financial help during those agonizing six months of breakdown in 1953': the strain of the circumstances in which the novel was written had caused it to give the impression of harbouring 'the basest ingratitude', which is why Sylvia insisted to her brother Warren that it 'must never be published in the United States'. The duty of the sensitive reader was to understand about the distorting lens of the bell jar of depression, and not to jump to conclusions about the true character of either Sylvia or her friends and family.[15]

Like many a damage-limitation exercise, the inclusion of the biographical essay backfired. The novel was perceived as entirely auto-biographical. The fact of Sylvia's first attempted suicide, until then not widely known or discussed in America, became public knowledge. Sylvia's complicated life and relationships were reduced to two head-lines. Summer 1953: nervous breakdown and attempted suicide. Winter 1963: marital separation and successful suicide.

The Bell Jar was published in New York in February 1971. It went straight into the bestseller list, where it remained for twenty-four weeks. Over the next few months, extracts appeared in *McCall's* and *Cosmopolitan* magazines. There was a big Book Club edition and the following year a mass-market paperback, which was reprinted twenty-four times over the next seven years. The movie was optioned. The American paperback edition alone sold more than 3 million copies during Ted's lifetime.[16] He and his children made a lot of money from all this, but the exponential leap in Sylvia's fame would taint all his future visits to America. The country associated with her and with his youthful dreams of life and energy and youth and escape, with the summer on Cape Cod and the road trip and the intense creative flourishing of the weeks at Yaddo, would subsequently become a place of nightmare, of furious heckling women and cancelled poetry readings.

During his time in America, Carol went to Lumb Bank and packed up most of his books and manuscripts. He then returned home in time for the children's Easter holidays. He and Carol took Nick and Frieda on a chilly camping tour around the Scottish lakes. They went on the ferry to Stromness and Ted kept one of his vivid travel journals, describing memorable adventures, sublime landscapes, daily fishing and quirky encounters (though not, he regretted, with the Loch Ness monster). They drove back via the Lake District, where Ted's heart leapt up on seeing William Wordsworth's grave in Grasmere church-yard. Frieda and Nick rowed on the lake while their father fished with no success.

They arrived back at the Beacon in the evening. Ted's father greeted them with the news that there had been a fire at Lumb Bank. They drove down the hill. The electricity was off, so they went in by torchlight and were hit by the smell of fire the moment they opened the door. In the middle of the floor there was a heap of charred rubbish immediately below a 2-foot-wide hole in the ceiling. There were boxes of burnt papers and clothes. All the signs pointed to arson.

In the morning, they searched the house more fully. A curious selection of items, together with much of the bedding, had been removed. Two detectives arrived and took the details. One of them thought that the fire must have been set by local kids, but the other was convinced that there was personal malice in the case. The police were not given sufficient information to conclude an investigation. In a letter to Peter Redgrove, with whom he had not been in touch for some time, Ted told of the fire, explaining that by good fortune he had recently taken all his books down to Devon, so there was not much left in the house other than piles of manuscript drafts and other papers which he had not been able to face when clearing out. Because the house was damp and unventilated, the fire had smouldered, burning carpets and floorboards, instead of taking full hold. He told Redgrove that it did not seem coincidental that the arsonist's attention had been directed 'with nearly amusing exclusiveness at my writings, my private gods, my poetical stockpiles etc'.[17]

For Ted, the burning of manuscripts – including some of Sylvia's – was just one more disaster to add to the heap. But with typical resilience, he went on to take something positive from his year of 'very strange darknesses'. Since Assia's death 'the whole of my life so far, the world, all the great works, have undergone a simultaneous re-interpretation on an infinitely bigger scale than before': turning all that had happened to poetical account would give him imaginative work for the rest of his life. In the meantime, he expressed great satisfaction over Carol: 'She's from Devon, daughter of a farmer, half Welsh, very young, not very interested in literature but with perfect taste and judgement for what really counts in what she does read. Part gypsy – family name was Orchard, which is a West Country gypsy name. Exceedingly good for me.'[18]

Straight after Easter, Ted moved to Paris, where he resumed his working relationship with Peter Brook. It was a relief to be in a different country. In May, he made a brief visit to Court Green, then closed it up. He returned to Peter Brook, and Carol joined him in June. Paris had happy associations from his past, but the theatre work was arduous.

Brook was notorious for the demands, both physical and mental, that he placed upon everyone in his ensemble. In the three years since he and Ted had worked together on *Oedipus*, he had experimented on Shakespeare's *Tempest* in the abandoned railway-shed of the Roundhouse in Chalk Farm, staged a triumphant Chinese-circus-influenced 'white box' *Midsummer Night's Dream* for the Royal Shakespeare Company, completed the *King Lear* film, and got funding for a new International Centre for Theatre Research on the Rive Gauche in the concrete-slabbed Mobilier National off the rue Croulebarbe (a resonant street name for a director who had explored the 'theatre of cruelty').

The first task was to prepare material for a three-month residence in Persia that summer, climaxing in performances at the Shiraz-Persepolis Festival of Arts. Brook and Hughes were both fascinated by the myth of Prometheus, with its links between the gifts of fire and of artistic creativity, between freedom and imprisonment, light and darkness. But instead of simply staging, say, Aeschylus' *Prometheus Bound*, the company of actors from many different countries and theatrical traditions was tasked with creating a devised piece pulling together material from Aeschylus, Seneca's *Madness of Hercules*, passages of Spanish from Calderón's *Life is a Dream*, an Armenian play called *The Chained One*, Manichean myths, and the ancient Zoroastrian language of the Avesta. This then metamorphosed into a scheme for Hughes to write a new play in an invented language, to answer the challenge set by Brook in his manifesto for a new theatrical style, *The Empty Space*: 'Is there another language, just as exacting for the author as the language of words, a language of sounds – a language of word-as-part-of-movement … of word-as-contradiction, of word-shock or word-cry?'[19] That is to say, a primal language of the body. Food-loving Ted began with 'GR-' for 'eat', 'KR-' for 'devour' and 'ULL' for 'swallow'. He incorporated baby talk: MAMA (its meaning inferred from the sucking shape of the lips, he explained) and DADA, which he glossed, perhaps with half-conscious awareness of Plath's figurations of 'daddy', as 'that person over there, who doesn't give me food, is strange, and comes to represent the outside world'.[20] Soon, a destructive king emerged – KRogon – and a name for both the language and the play: *Orghast* (ORG and GHAST, 'the fire of being').

The best new words, Hughes said when interviewed about the project by Tom Stoppard for the *Times Literary Supplement*, were those that he 'fished out of the air', invented without conscious thought, his mind 'completely fixed on the thing or state' he wanted to express. These, he said, were sounds that tapped into the nervous system and the primal animal brain. Stoppard recognised that the aim was not to drop linguistic clues enabling listeners to pick up some discernible 'sense', but rather to create in a theatre audience 'the instinctive recognition of a "mental state" within a sound'. Inevitably, though, the invented words were inflected with what Ted called the 'North of England Anglo-Saxon–Norse pattern' of sound that was also present in much of his own verse.[21]

To begin with, the actors were given translations:

BULLORGA OMBOLOM FROR / SHARSAYA
    NULBULDA BRARG
darkness opens its womb / I hear chaos roar
IN OMBOLOM BULLORGA
in the womb of darkness
FREEASTAV OMBOLOM / NILD US GLITTALUGH
freeze her womb / rivets like stars
ASTA BEORBITTA / CLID OSTA BULLORGA
icy chains / lock up the mouth of darkness
IN OMBOLOM KHERN FIGYA GRUORD
in her womb I make my words iron.[22]

But eventually this was no longer necessary. Actors' bodies, diaphragms and vocal cords were inhabiting the new language.

In early June, Ted, Brook and the acting company flew into Tehran, walking into the terminal at Mehrabad airport under the blaze of TV lights – the state television service was sponsoring the visit to the tune of £60,000. They were driven out to a dusty desert hotel, owned by the Shah, in the foothills of the Alborz Mountains. One of the actors said that the landscape was like that of Spain. Another replied that it was more like limbo. In air-conditioned isolation, they felt disconnected from the culture they had hoped to explore. The hotel offered expensive and flavourless international cuisine, not local food. This didn't stop Ted from working his way through the menu, something, he confessed, that had been an ambition ever since his childhood of wartime rationing.

The work was coming together. Persian actors and musicians had joined the company. Several directors were involved and local poets drifted in. Ted elaborated upon the Orghast mythology. The entire story was to be imagined as taking place within the body of Prometheus chained on his rock, 'just as all languages originated in the physiology of man'. Different story elements and different sounds were assigned to different parts of the body: 'The figure of Krogon, a great bird of prey, squatted on the shoulders of Prometheus, blotting out the light – Orghast – which, however, was repeated inside him, in the womb, surrounded by fertile, female darkness.'[23] Ted drew a sketch to explain, all the time gesturing with his huge hands, which were ink-stained from invention and raw from a nervous skin complaint.

There was a White-Goddess type called Moa. Krogon withers under the light, croaks like Crow and is caged. Ted was asked what the vulture meant. Different things to different characters: 'To Krogon it is his prisoners, the earth, his own body, his bond with animal life on one hand, with spirit on the other; a compound crime he refuses to recognize, which is slowly dementing him.'[24] And so on, through the cast: a sickness at heart, a mysterious dilemma, suffering in time, the commitments of the body, the divided self, a hope for a cure, some ultimate reconciliation. Hughes was again wrestling with his own demons. Peter Brook wryly remarked that *Orghast* was turning into the most labyrinthine work since James Joyce's *Ulysses*.

Then it was time for reconnaissance of the 'found spaces' where the performances would take place. They bought sun-hats and were shipped by minibus into the desert, past camels, donkeys, eagles 'and an army camp ringed by barbed wire and mines'. At Persepolis, Brook led them up a mountain to the tomb of Artaxerxes II, carved into the rock, with a terrace in front of it and a sheer drop below. Ted climbed higher still, and eventually his giant figure loomed above the tomb, like 'a vulture in a Digger hat, speaking Orghast' and at that very moment 'a bluish hawk left its nest, in a hole by the carved sun'. Then they moved on to another site, a few miles out of Persepolis: Naqsh-e Rustam, a 200-foot wall of mountain out of which the cruciform tombs of Darius and Xerxes has been hollowed. A fire temple known as the Cube of Zoroaster stood opposite and vultures circled above. 'This is the dimension it requires,' said Ted.[25]

Back in the rehearsal room, there was more work to be done. To contrast with the epic and tragic scope of *Orghast*, Brook asked Ted to devise an improvised comedy of sexual competition and courtship. He based it on the scenario of *Difficulties of a Bridegroom*, the radio play which had been produced just before Sylvia's death, with its shy lover and his misadventures.[26] The surviving drafts include such stage directions as 'Hero wakes. He has had the most fantastic dream – rapturous description of a girl's visit etc, all that occurred.' Another girl is carried away by a King Kong figure. Before an ecstatic closing reunion, there is much sexual activity, including a game of strip poker with an invisible antagonist and a man falling in love with an empty box before some girls take out his heart as he sleeps.[27]

The final few rehearsals of *Orghast* took place on site. Under the vertical cliff of Naqsh-e Rustam they worked by the light of torches, the actors climbing on ladders amid swirling bats. Four oversized mottled vipers were killed in one night. Ted cut off their heads and skinned them.

And then the festival opened. The first performance took place just after sunset on Saturday 28 August 1971. Peter Brook gave his final words of advice to the actors: 'We are not setting out to teach the audience anything, do anything to them, explain anything, but, as we did at the village, to create a circle in which the impulse can go round.'[28] Hughes's working typescript survives. The scene was set at the tomb of Artaxerxes II or III, above the ruins of Persepolis. The cast was instructed to stand scattered on the platform below and on the hillside, with the audience seated on cushions on both sides of the platform: to one side of them, 'the carved face and entrance of the tomb'; to the other, 'the view out over Persepolis and the valley, south and west'. It began. The voice of 'LIGHT' was heard from above, repeatedly calling 'HOAN'. Then:

> MAN: (*from below platform*) GA-VE
> LIGHT: call HOAN
> MAN: GA-VE
> LIGHT: call (*continues under* MOA)
> MOA: (*from tomb*) GAVE

CHORUS: AMEM
MAN: GAVE
CHORUS: NEMEM
MOA: GAVE
CHORUS: UKHDHEM.[29]

The audience was for the most part absorbed but puzzled. At the end of the show, Ted and the rest of the company walked down a mountain path marked by bowls of fire. They partook of a buffet in the Harem Garden, then returned up the hill for a second performance by moonlight. A Yugoslav musician in the audience said that it was the most beautiful spectacle he had witnessed in a decade.

Questions were asked at the festival press conference. An English critic had misheard the opening cry of GA-VE as YAHWEH. This was good, said Brook, since *gaveh* meant both 'cow' and 'soul of man'. That was what they were trying to do: 'exploding atoms of sense'. A scholar of the Avestan language scornfully replied that 'cow' was *gav*, nothing to do with *gaveh*. A Persian chipped in: '*Gaveh* also means nonsense.' 'Even better,' replied Brook. A drama expert asked if his method was related to the 'poor theatre' of Jerzy Grotowski. No, the only model to which he was completely committed was the theatre of Shakespeare. Would there be a dictionary of the Orghast language? 'Where is the dictionary of music?' replied Ted. 'There is one – in your body. We use music only for itself, not for debate.'[30]

The performance at Persepolis, repeated in the presence of the Queen of Persia, was only Part I. They moved on to Naqsh-e Rustam for Part II. There, under the tomb of Xerxes, the White Goddess figure of Moa stood in a fissure that slashed the rock. Ted, who sometimes shared King Lear's dark view of women's genitals, named it Vulvig. Moa screamed her Orghast curses at the murderous Krogon to the sound of amplified drums. And so it went on, until as dawn broke over the rocky tomb a solitary figure with a cow, a bell tolling on its neck, chanted in Avestan and walked the length of the valley into the rising sun.

Carol joined Ted for some of the time, as did the children. After three months in this extraordinary environment, Ted returned to Devon, where he convinced himself that Court Green had been broken into, and some Plath papers stolen. His head was still full of

Iran and *Orghast*. He wrote enthusiastically to Luke Myers, telling him that the entire adventure was packed with mystery and excitement. Thanks to the actors, most notably Malick Bagayogo from Mali, who performed like a man possessed, he had fulfilled a dream and created 'the sort of cave-drama' he would never have thought possible: 'One of the performances was so completely stupefying the audience sat afterwards for 15 minutes in dead silence.'[31]

In the same letter, he asked Myers to try to get hold of an article that Alvarez had published in the *New American Review*. For some reason, Al was proving 'very cagey' about showing it to Ted. In November, it became obvious why. Alvarez was about to publish a book called *The Savage God* and he had been trailing it in the magazines and newspapers. The subtitle was *A Study of Suicide* and the prologue was a thirty-page essay about the last days of Sylvia Plath. An extract was published in the *Observer* and a second one announced as forthcoming.

Ted was devastated, not least by the ill timing. He had finally achieved a sense of equilibrium, with the children in a good school, Carol making a home, himself free of 'all entanglement' (that is, no more double life with Brenda) and thus free to work properly for the first time since 1966. All this was undone by Alvarez's unforgivable 're-invention of the inner life' of his marriage to Sylvia. The story was 'dynamite' for the children and 'insufferable' for Ted.[32]

He responded immediately. 'Dear Al,' he began, 'As a friend, please reconsider your writings, talks etc about Sylvia's suicide. It was enough before, without the details. Obviously you can't unwrite them, but I do ask you to set a quick limit on how far you popularize them.' Had he not thought about the effect on Ted, on Sylvia's family and above all on the children of his exhumation of her for the purposes of class-room discussion? Over 2,000 words long, the letter is among the most powerful that Ted ever wrote. At its centre is his concern for Frieda and Nick. 'For you', he says to Alvarez, Sylvia is 'a topic for intellectual discussion, a poetic/existential phenomenon'. A topic, moreover, spiced with macabre details that were not only little better than gossip, but also pressed into the service of a tendentious reading of her work and her death. For instance, Alvarez gave an exaggerated sense of the supposed poetic rivalry between Ted and Sylvia. For the family, Ted movingly wrote, Sylvia was not a literary-critical problem but a loved and still-mourned being: 'she is an atmosphere we breathe'. Above all, she was the lynchpin of Frieda's and Nick's sense of identity: 'they have made her very important, the more so because of her obvious absence throughout the mess I've made of replacing her these last years'. Their image of her – of what she did and was – would decide their lives: 'You know these things work out seriously. Yet you've defined their mother's pose – and set it up as the official final public version (the schools will make sure of that) – in an absolutely disastrous way.'[33]

Alvarez defended himself, saying that his interpretation of the events was a great deal more considerate than the stories doing the rounds in the cloud of feminist-inspired rumour. The piece was a tribute to Sylvia and it would be better for the children to see his sympathetic account than some of the other things that were circulating. He agreed to withdraw the second pre-publication extract, but the damage was done.

Ted had not told the children the true circumstances of their mother's death. He had let them assume that Sylvia had succumbed to pneumonia. Now there was the risk that they might hear it in the form of malicious school gossip culled from the papers. As a result of what Ted described as Alvarez's 'treachery', Nick and Frieda were brought home from Ibstock Place for a week, to be shielded from the story and told the truth. Ted even wondered if he might need to move them to another school, where they could start again with a degree of anonymity.[34]

Alvarez, of all people. What Ted knew but could not tell was that the memoir of Sylvia in *The Savage God* was a little economical with the truth. It presents a beautifully executed cameo of Alvarez's final encounter with Sylvia on Christmas Eve 1962, when she offered herself to him and he rejected her. But his account of their earlier evenings together is sparing. Ted and Olwyn knew rather more from what they had read in Sylvia's last journal before it was destroyed. 'Alvarez', she scribbled on her calendar for 29 October 1962: that was the night she read her latest poems to him and he thought they were extraordinary. A week later, on the day that she found Yeats's house in Fitzroy Road, she rushed round in a fever of excitement to tell Al. That evening, she noted in her journal with her usual acerbic wit, they were engaged in a certain activity when the telephone rang. She put her foot over his penis so that, as she phrased it, he was appropriately attired to receive the call.[35]

Ted asked himself who had the right to speak and who had the right to be hurt by the publication of intimate details of Sylvia's last days. He penned some bitter lines, seemingly intended for 'Black Coat: Opus 131', the autobiographical epic that he never published: 'Al hurt by my reaction to his account / Of S. death', the fragment begins. Who was Alvarez to claim 'perfect understanding' of these events? What was his compulsion to reveal 'That he too tended the final days / How he too performed on that stage / And shall now forever perform'?[36] Alvarez's performance extended beyond his revelation of the power of Sylvia's later voice, his eulogy in the *Observer* on the occasion of her death, and his vivid retrospect in *The Savage God*. Though Ted could not say so, it reached to the very heart of the story.

Sylvia, Olwyn reminded Alvarez in a letter written years later, 'was an all or nothing at all girl'.[37] For such a woman – especially one who was unusually sexually liberated for her time – an affair of her own was an obvious response to the discovery of her husband's extramarital liaison. She was hurt when Richard Murphy rejected her advances in Cleggan. Alvarez was the man to make up for it. He was the first to see the greatness of the poems liberated in her by her anger towards Ted. She hoped for a more sustained relationship with him. On Christmas Eve, preparing to see him again, she wrote 'a full page of tense instructions to herself' in her journal: 'to be patient, to be casual, not to show her feelings and scare [him] off'.[38] He was her opportunity to restore her self-esteem.

But Alvarez, manic-depressive himself, did not want the responsibility of a relationship with a manic-depressive genius with two young children and a husband who was having an affair. His own marriage to Ursula, granddaughter of D. H. Lawrence's wife Frieda, had disintegrated two years before. He had married her seven weeks after meeting her, a whirlwind romance of a similar duration to Ted and Sylvia's; he cheerfully admitted that an obsession with Lawrence was the main driver of his desire. More recently, his affair with the charismatic Australian Jill Neville had come to an end. He declined the opportunity of turning a dalliance into a relationship. Sylvia was rejected again.[39]

She sensed that she had lost her old sexual magic. As a result of the mental scar left by her father's sudden death when she was eight, she always reacted with extremity to the slightest hint of male rejection

– as witnessed by the incident with the girl at Smith. Alvarez's rejection may well have played its part in her suicide. It was hardly surprising that he did not admit as much in *The Savage God* and that his narrative focused instead on her parting from Ted.

But Ted could never write about this. It would have looked like self-exculpation and, besides, he was too loyal both to his friends and to the memory of Sylvia. Olwyn believes that one of the reasons why he burnt the last journal was so that Nick and Frieda could be spared the image of their mother being damaged further by other men.

And there was something else.

In Alvarez's autobiography, Assia Wevill is accorded a single hostile paragraph. He suggests that her affair with Ted would have blown itself out if Sylvia had been able to give her husband a little more space and time. He claims that Assia wanted Ted partly for the same reason that a host of other women wanted him: 'because he was gifted, subtle, handsome, manly'. Alvarez suggests that she also wanted Ted because 'he was Sylvia's husband and Sylvia was a woman to be reckoned with'. As an advertising copywriter and a translator of Hebrew poetry, Assia was enough of a writer to know that Sylvia was a much better writer. Alvarez accuses her of relentlessly badmouthing Sylvia's poetry after her death. He subscribes to the view that 'her only way of outdoing her dead rival was in the manner of her death'. In this interpretation, as Alvarez bluntly and rather clumsily phrases it, 'When her affair with Ted turned out to be just another affair, Assia gassed the child she and Ted had had together when she gassed herself.'[40]

At the time of Sylvia's death, a contemporary noted that Alvarez had a 'hangdog adoration of T.H.' and expressed the opinion that he was 'stuck in Freudianism like an American teenager'.[41] One does not have to share the Freudianism to see that in this sequence of his autobiography the pugnacious poker-playing boxer Alvarez is projecting on to Sylvia and Assia his own rivalry with Ted. The copywriter's sense of inferiority to the poet stands in for that of the critic. Alvarez could make or break a poet, but his own poetry was thin gruel.

According to Alvarez, Assia wanted Ted 'to add to her collection, because she saw herself as irresistible'. She was, he continues, 'a rapacious woman with a delicate, sultry face that seemed out of proportion with her heavy figure, and she made a pass at every man she met so automatically that it was hard to feel flattered'.[42] There is a

back-story to this pronouncement. In July 1962 Assia told her friend
Nat Tarn about her relationship with Alvarez, which she was keeping
from her husband. Alvarez had pleaded with her to abandon David
Wevill and go to America with him. She confided that she had by this
time grown sick of him, which was hardly surprising since she was
now with Ted. Alvarez was 'vermouth', she told Tarn in her sharply
witty way. When Assia told David about Ted's note inviting her to
begin an affair, what she was concealing was the fact that she was
already in very deep with another man.

Alvarez had not grown sick of her. He was in love with Assia to the
point of obsession. He 'cashed in' (Tarn's phrase) two weeks after the
terrible day when Ted ruptured Assia and she told her husband that
Ted had actually raped her, and David took an overdose of sleeping
pills. On 27 July 1962, Al Alvarez asked Assia Wevill to marry him.
She thought this was 'rather sweet' but of course she declined. She had
not yet decided to leave David and her head was full of Ted. Alvarez
took the sweetest revenge that was available to him. Nine days later,
he published a column of new poems in the *Observer*: first one by
Sylvia, then one by Ted, then, immediately underneath, a rather good
David Wevill poem about being a cuckold. Nat Tarn wryly described
this as 'A fine piece of family history'.[43]

Alvarez and Sylvia. Alvarez and Assia. Ted kept quiet about all this
all his life. And yet in 1971 Alvarez was the one who said that *he* was
hurt by Ted's reaction to *The Savage God*.

Farmer Ted

At daffodil time in 1972, Ted Hughes wrote one of his newsy letters to Gerald in Australia. He told of how he would try to sit in his writing hut in the garden of Court Green all day, only emerging in the evening. If the work went well enough, he could then reward himself with a day's fishing. But it had been nearly four years since he had been able to devote three consecutive days to his writing. Without complete absorption, he could not break through beyond *Crow*. Perhaps, though, he was making distractions for himself because he could not bear to face the past more directly. Money was a perennial concern: the house on the north coast of Devon, which he had hoped to buy for £15,000, had now tripled in value. A plan to buy a working farm faced the hurdle of ever-increasing prices. And he was convinced that inflation would only get worse: he took justifiable pride in his prophetic powers with regard to the broader economy, but was frustrated by his own sense of financial powerlessness.

Meanwhile, renovations were made to Court Green. A new Aga replaced Sylvia's old cooker. An ancient oak-beamed granite fireplace was exposed and the house filled with beautiful things. Ted contributed animal skulls and heads, kangaroo- and snakeskins sent by Gerald. He told his brother that Carol dreamed of wearing a coat made of red snake. Her father, Jack Orchard, tidied the orchard.

The old home was made new, but it remained the place associated with Sylvia, especially when the children were back for the holidays. They were pleased to acquire a pet badger, but Ted worried about them. Frieda seemed preternaturally adult, detached and insightful. She played at playing instead of playing as a child plays. Nicky had fads and obsessions; like his father, he was a great collector. Ted's own father was a continual worry: he was grumpy, still struggling with being a widower, didn't have a hobby and was altogether a model of how not to cope with retirement. The best plan, Ted told Gerald, would be to sell the Beacon and for Pa to live half the year in Australia and the other half in Devon. The cottage in the yard of Court Green could be renovated for him, though the burden of care would then have fallen upon Carol.[1] When Bill Hughes did come to stay, he slept in till lunchtime and spent much of the rest of the day in the pub.

A further distraction came in the form of a new collaboration with Peter Brook. Ted returned to the International Centre for Theatre Research in Paris in order to work on the script of a dramatisation of the medieval Persian tale *The Conference of the Birds*. Drafts survive in the Peter Brook Archive of sixty-two linked tales in verse, with casting. Among the titles are 'Exchanged Faces', 'The girl who wanted dawn's dress', 'The jealous wife', 'Sleeping Lover' and – at the close – 'Ariel in the Oak', featuring a bound and gagged female, the action to be played with long red material, a stick, two small bamboo canes, a box and a foam-rubber plug. Suffering is one of the great themes of the sequence. 'Do not ask for suffering,' Ted writes: a man asks what suffering is, his four sons kill each other, and a wise friend says, 'You asked for suffering, and look at you now: it has totally over-whelmed you.'[2]

Despite the money on offer, this time he decided not to accompany Brook and his actors on their three-month circuit of the tribes and villages of West Africa. Instead, he sank into what he called 'deep rural torpor', shaking off the literary life of London.[3] He complained that writing a hundred scenes for *The Conference of the Birds* had stopped him from writing anything else. In letters to friends he reiterated that he was hoping to collect his wits and go 'through the door that Crow opened' but was somehow blocked from taking the big next step.[4]

Unhappy about his failure to make a major poetic breakthrough, he distracted himself by becoming a farmer. He bought various parcels of land and started acquiring livestock. Then he purchased an old mill-house, used as a piggery, along with a stretch of riverbank. And in the summer of 1972, he succeeded in a bid for a complete working farm. It was at Moortown, 6 miles from North Tawton. Ninety-five acres for £22,000: a bargain. Ted reckoned they were lucky that a big estate had been auctioned off in parts the same day and that all the buyers had gone there. Jack Orchard, who had a lifetime of farming experience, took on the actual running of it, but Ted and Carol frequently got their hands dirty and bloody.

He kept a farming journal, making detailed notes that he turned into poems published first by Olwyn in a Rainbow Press limited edition under the title *Moortown Elegies* and later by Faber as *Moortown* and then *Moortown Diary*. The experience of working the land led him to reflect on hard winters, calving and lambing, birth and death, Devon bulls, foxhunting, the ulcerous infection of sheep known as orf. His material ranged from the brutal operation of dehorning cattle to the 'dawn inspiration' of two roe-deer glimpsed one snowy February morning. He was centring his self in North Devon, isolated, out of time, among old cob-walled farms 'hidden not only from the rest of England but even from each other, connected by the inexplicable, Devonshire, high-banked, deep-cut lanes that are more like a defence-maze of burrows'.[5] The verse of the farming poems is loose and infor-mal. Save for the line breaks, the writing is barely altered from its journal origins. Hughes thought of the project as akin to his trans-lation work, where he versified literal prose versions of the originals provided by others who knew the source language.

Where the poems are prosaic, some of the journal entries written at this time read like poems, consisting as they do of jotted images fuelled with the quick-fire short-line energy of Hughes's best verse: the isle of Lundy 'in vaporous violet sea', seagulls 'skimming' the 'swell', father-in-law Jack, 'naked to waist, shearing. / Cutting his finger', then 'wrapping' the sheep's 'oily fleeces'.[6] Strikingly, the journal brings his new wife and father-in-law to life, whereas the published verses anonymise them into 'she' and 'he'. The figures working the land in the poems have no personality.

Only two of the published diary poems stick in the reader's mind. One is the first journal entry that he turned to verse, 'February 17th' ('A lamb could not get born …'), an unforgettably vivid account – not for the squeamish – of an abortive birth in which Ted can save the mother sheep only by hacking off the head of the lamb. The other is 'Roe-deer', which shines with an epiphany in 'dawn-dirty light'. The two roe-deer happen momentarily into the poet's 'dimension' and so take him into their dimension, away from the 'ordinary' world where the poem begins and ends and the rest of the sequence remains. The deer are like ghosts, revenants from another world. The poem is dated

13 February 1973: a snowy dawn exactly ten years on from the week of Sylvia's death. The deer dip themselves through a hedge 'and upright they rode their legs / Away downhill over a snow-lonely field'.[7] Is he allowing himself a moment's imagined reversal in which the shades of Sylvia and Assia have found companionship in the Elysian Fields and he is the one left alone in the snow? It is not a coincidence that the first draft of the sequence that became *Birthday Letters* was entitled 'The Sorrows of the Deer'.

Scribbling in his notebooks kept him going as a writer. He noticed everything. So, for example, on a single day in August 1973: 'wet sloppy maroonish-grey clouds, against a clear blue sky' at dawn, a demonstration at a local farm and a neighbour who nearly drowned, the fat friend of a friend, salesmen offering drainage and plastic piping, salmon on the river Dart and the high tide in Bideford Bay, crab and crayfish in a pool, ragwort and twisted foxgloves, fallen rowanberries and the first blackberries of autumn, the writing method of the poet Paul Valéry, Nick cleaning his bee-boxes, high tea at Westward Ho!, daddy-longlegs everywhere, 'the hippies in the cottages' and the absence of swifts from the air.[8] Each detail had the potential to become an image in a poem, but none was enough to unlock the recesses of his consciousness.

At other times he used his journal to penetrate that self, to analyse his inner being. The problem of his existence was that there was 'always something in the way': every time he started on 'the vital journey' he was blocked by an intrusion from his 'outer life'. What was the solution? Perhaps by close *attention* to the world, he might sow some seeds for the inner journey. Perhaps he should loosen up, free himself to release his personal voice, ignore the sniggers of the anti-confessional poets of the Movement ('Even Larkin – he's a sniggerer'). You know, he tells himself, what the true goal should be: 'to hang on to the real life, at every point honour and nurse that'. Keep clear of 'the surrealist mask'. Don't cultivate a 'style'. Ensure that the writing is always 'a genuine investigation'.[9]

Self-exhortation of this kind came from the awareness that his more inward work had been in limbo since *Crow*. Early in 1974, he tried to galvanise himself by completing his translations of the Hungarian poet János Pilinszky, bringing from one mother-tongue to another the work of a writer deeply attuned to the power of words.

Conscripted into the retreating German army in 1944, Pilinszky had moved from prison camp to camp in Germany and Austria. The camps were a revelation to him of what King Lear calls unaccommodated man, humankind 'stripped of everything but the biological persistence of cells'. Pilinszky began to publish after the war and became widely admired in Budapest and beyond, though regarded with suspicion by the communist authorities. He said that he would like to write as if he had remained silent. This, said Hughes in the introduction to his translations, was 'a real thing', a raising of imaginative integrity to a price 'beyond what common words seem able to pay'.[10]

Because of his experience of the camps Pilinszky was somehow able to square the circle whereby the artist 'after Auschwitz' was compelled both to testify and to remain silent. For Ted, Pilinszky's poems achieved what the *Crow* project was striving towards: the revelation of a God of 'absences and negative attributes, quite comfortless', a God 'in whose creation the camps and modern physics are equally at home', a God who is 'the Truth', a truth discovered through 'naked, carnal, helpless' suffering but somehow touched by 'radiance'. In Pilinszky's love poems, 'he' and 'she' are separated from 'meaning and hope', as the human spirit is separated from consolation. Sexual love 'becomes a howl, or a dumbness groping for somebody – anybody – in the dazzling emptiness'. And yet there is no disgust. For all that 'the ultimate reality of total war has become natural law' and 'man has been reduced to the mere mechanism of his mutilated body', the language of poetry becomes redemptive: 'the symbols of the horror become the sacred symbols of a kind of worship'. The moment of near extinction becomes a moment of joy. The poetry reaches its most intense pitch when it achieves a stillness that is at the same time 'an ecstasy of affliction, a glare of inner exposure, a passivity of transfiguration'.[11] Pilinszky's direct witnessing of the camps gave an authenticity to his juxtaposition of love and war, of the personal and the political – no one could accuse him, as some accused Sylvia, of a tasteless appropriation of the dark matter of the Holocaust.

Hughes said of his translations that he had not turned Pilinszky's poems into his own poems, but rather that he had adapted himself to something that attracted him strongly. He had 'extended himself towards' a new voice rather than produced it 'out of himself'.[12] His translations are based on literal renderings by his friend János Csokits, who had by this time moved to London, where he was working on the Hungarian desk at the BBC. At a double distance from each poem's original moment of conception, Hughes finds a new mode of intensity without bombast. Some of the poems directly recall war and prisoners of war; others are dark intimations of erotic passion and loss with such titles as 'The Desert of Love'. Sometimes love is a war: 'I love you and nothing can console me ... Intimately you cleave to my body / and laugh. Savagely I hit you' ('Trapeze and Parallel Bars').

Hughes could not avoid being affected by the act of translating a group of poems in which the speaker aches for, yet also feels guilty about, his dead beloved. In particular, an eight-stanza lyric called 'What Underground Struggle' is uncannily close to his own contemporaneous dreams and later poems of being haunted by the ghost of Sylvia Plath. Since the lost love's departing – some unspecified aspect of her death makes the poet feel almost as if he has murdered her – the speaker cannot find his place anywhere: 'And I keep asking, "Though you are dead / are you still alive?"' The 'underground struggle' takes him down, down into fear of what might happen if the lost love is disinterred in the poet's dreams: 'I long for you, yet desperately / heap the earth over you.' He tastes 'the dirt / of a lurking hell'.[13]

The Pilinszky translations feel like an advance on Crow because of their stripped-down quality. By contrast, Hughes's original work at this time was going badly awry. He was publishing, but only in desultory fashion: a new Selected Poems; some short plays aimed partly at children (Orpheus and individual volumes of the group of dramas he had first collected with The Coming of the Kings, which was his homage to T. S. Eliot's 'Journey of the Magi'); the libretto of an opera called The Story of Vasco that was first performed by the Sadler's Wells Opera at the London Coliseum in March 1974, to baffled reviews.

The power of Orghast had come from its primal quality. The dramatic setting and forceful acting, together with the costumes and the music, were combined with the body-rich sounds of Hughes's invented language in such a way as to create the impression of an intense connection with the raw material of the Prometheus story, with its gift of fire, challenge to the gods and punishment in rock, chain and vulture gnawing at the liver. Myths are stories of the origins of those forces that make us most human – desire and loss, aspiration and transgression, bonds and the breaking of bonds, hope and fear, freedom and restraint, ego and other. As stories, they work especially well in the form of drama, where narrative is put into action and words are accompanied by visual images. The logical next step for Hughes would have been to dramatise *Crow* in the style of *Orghast*, but he chose instead to translate the core matter of *Orghast* from Persian stage to English page by writing a series of poems called *Prometheus on his Crag*.

The sequence was published by Olwyn's limited-edition Rainbow Press in November 1973. A slightly revised version reached a wider audience some years later in the portmanteau Faber collection *Moortown*. Lacking the narrative drive and visual effect provided by dramatic form, the effect falls flat. With language as the only available resource, Hughes overreaches and overwrites: 'a brain horoscoped cretaceous', 'two cosmic pythons, the Sea and the Sky', 'Babies were being dragged crying pitifully / Out of the wombs', 'A bitten-out gobbet of sun'. The sequence ends with Prometheus asking whether the vulture is his 'unborn half-self' or his 'anti-self', but the reader versed in Hughes cannot help feeling that the poetic voice has become a parody self, a rehash of the worst of *Crow* without the directness and clarity of the best of it.[14]

Similarly, if he had stuck with Brook's *Conference of the Birds* he could have produced something of great power, but instead he tried to create 'an alchemical cave drama' in a setting far from the tribal African environment that Brook saw as the project's natural home. He turned to another of his long-term collaborators, Leonard Baskin. *Cave Birds*, first published in 1975 in a Scolar Press limited edition, brought together Baskin drawings and Hughes poems of mythical, semi-mythical and real birds. At the Ilkley Literature Festival in May 1975, the drawings were projected on to a screen and the poems given a dramatised reading, produced by the poet and BBC man George MacBeth. This was broadcast on Radio 3 the following month, with Hughes himself providing a linking commentary. A revised and expanded collection of *Cave Birds* was published by Faber three years later, with more Baskin drawings. The whole project felt provisional and fragmented. The attempt to bring myth home to roost in Yorkshire was doomed: a projector in Ilkley somehow lacked the primal quality of the rocky tomb of Artaxerxes in the Persian desert at sunset. Once again, the language has all the agony and none of the ecstasy of the mythologised self: 'The scream / Vomited itself'; 'Spectral, gigantified / Protozoic, blood-eating'; 'olfactory X-ray … spread-fingered Efreet'; 'The baboon of panoply / Jumped at the sky-rump of a greasy rainbow'.[15]

Turning from pagan to Judaeo-Christian foundations, Hughes made a further projection into myth in the form of a sequence called *Adam and the Sacred Nine*, first published in part in 1976 and eventually included in *Moortown*. The *mise-en-scène* has a prostrate Adam, after the Fall, 'visited by nine birds who each in turn bring their gift of "how to live", for him to accept or reject'.[16] Looking back on the traumas of the previous decade, the Hughes of the early Seventies saw himself as a fallen Adam, having to make choices about both how to live and how to write. He had to choose between the literary world and rural life, between marital fidelity and his fierce libido, and in his writing between the way of myth and some other direction.

He collected old oak beams, Japanese netsuke and the skins of big cats. He wrote incessantly to Gerald about money. As ever, there were new get-rich-quick schemes – couldn't his brother come back to England and they could get a bigger farm or deal in classy antiques, or both? He worried about his father in Yorkshire. He worried about keeping the children together and getting them into a good secondary school. Nick flew through the entrance exam for progressive Bedales, but Frieda had to resit maths (she passed, thanks to extra tuition). He worried about his tax bills. Family troubles and money troubles came together when Olwyn separated from her alcoholic and sometimes violent partner Richard: Ted generously went halves with her on the purchase of a house in London, meaning he had to put the mill up for sale at the worst possible time, just as both the rural housing and the livestock markets were collapsing.

Some of the distractions were pleasurable, notably a holiday in Rome and Naples with Carol, recorded in bright journal snapshots. Then in November 1974, under the auspices of Poet Laureate Sir John Betjeman, he received the Queen's Gold Medal for Poetry and sent Frieda a long and very funny letter about his visit to Buckingham Palace with Carol: 'And there, far away across this great room, was a tiny person whom of course I recognized. Nobody else in the room

Faber poets: Louis MacNeice, Ted Hughes, T. S. Eliot, W. H. Auden, Stephen Spender in June 1960, the year of the publication of Ted's second collection of poetry, *Lupercal*

Court Green, North Tawton, discovered by Ted and Sylvia in 1961 (seen here photographed in 1972)

Family: (*top*) with baby Frieda in Knole Park, Kent, in 1960; (*middle*) Sylvia with Frieda and Nicholas among the daffodils at Court Green in 1962; (*bottom*) Ted with Frieda and Nicholas at Doonreaghan in 1966

Assia Wevill

Susan Alliston

Frieda on the doorstep of Court Green with Shura in push-chair

IN MEMORY
SYLVIA PLATH HUGHES
1932 — 1963
EVEN AMIDST FIERCE FLAMES
THE GOLDEN LOTUS CAN BE PLANTED

Lumb Bank, which Ted first tried to buy in 1963, and eventually bought in 1969, as it is today

Elm trees and Morris Traveller at Court Green

Seneca's Oedipus: Irene Worth as Jocasta and John Gielgud as Oedipus in the National Theatre production, directed by Peter Brook, at the Old Vic in 1968

Brenda Hedden in 1965

The Iron Man as rock musical: Ted at the Young Vic with Pete Townshend of The Who in 1993

at all. Just her. Then I saw Sir John seemed to have fallen asleep, with his chin sunk on his chest, so hastily I sank my chin too, and we presented the Queen with the tops of our heads.' Her Majesty told him that she particularly liked the *Lupercal* poem 'An Otter', so he told her all manner of bizarre stories about its origin.[17]

It was also in 1974 that he renovated Lumb Bank and leased it to the Arvon Foundation. This cost him two years' literary earnings and a great deal of stress with builders. The origins of Arvon, which became another of Ted's passions, went back to 1968 when two poet-teachers, John Moat and John Fairfax, came up with the idea of creating residential courses for aspiring poets, with a couple of experienced poets on hand to provide guidance. They received an offer to use a rural arts centre, owned by the progressive college Dartington, in the remote Torridge Valley in Devon. This was Hughes country and he agreed to give a reading on the last night of their first course. He listened to the young people's poems, sensed the thrill of transformation created by the course, and backed the plan to make it go on happening. The scheme gradually grew, finding a permanent home in an ancient thatched manor farmhouse with oak floors called Totleigh Barton. Arvon became a charitable foundation in 1972 and was now seeking a second home in the North. Though Ted never taught formally on the Arvon courses, he often dropped in on them and he devoted huge amounts of time to fundraising for the foundation.[18]

Farming and Arvon were typical examples of a pattern that would endure for the rest of Hughes's life: bursts of intense poetic creativity were brought to an end by the distraction of other passions. Some of these were literary: prose projects, most notably his work on Shakespeare; translations for the theatre; the preparation of Sylvia's works for publication; anthologies; support for young poets. Others belonged to the outdoors: the farm, the fishing trips, the environmental campaigns. Sometimes he was drawn away from his poetic vocation because he was too kind to say no when people asked him for help. More often, he threw himself into his extra-curricular passions because of his reluctance to complete and to publish the project that he knew in his deepest self he was destined to be remembered for, because it would be his own remembrance of Sylvia. 'The Sorrows of the Deer', 'Black Coat: Opus 131', *Birthday Letters*: whatever the title, whatever the length and the poetic form, that was the book he had to complete and to publish before he could take his work to a new plane. The only expiation would be for him to publish the poems: perhaps that would get Sylvia out of his system. But quite apart from the fact that Ted kept changing his mind about which poems should be published and which should not, he was wary of the glare of publicity that would fall upon Court Green in the event of publication.

Repress, distract, redirect: his new prize possession was a red bull called Sexton, bought in the summer of 1974, a time of terrible weather and national economic collapse. Contrarily, it was also a time when Ted discovered that his own finances weren't quite as bad as he thought. He got a recurrent virus, thought it was throat cancer and went to see a lawyer to get some advice on such matters as death duties. He was astonished to learn that his assets, adding together Sylvia's copyrights, his manuscripts, his houses and his land, were worth nearly half a million pounds (allowing for inflation, which was about to become rampant, that would be £4.5 million, or $7.5 million in 2015). He concluded that the best course would be to create a trust to give as much as possible to Nick and Frieda and to spend what he could of the rest while there was still time. The problem was, nearly all the assets were illiquid. So it was a relief to discover that it wasn't throat cancer after all.

As for poetry, something could be achieved by a return to bird and beast, flower and tree, nature sometimes burgeoning with green shoots and sometimes red in tooth and claw: the subject matter that had established his reputation. Back in 1968, he had written 'Five Autumn Songs for Children's Voices' to be performed by schoolchildren at the Harvest Festival in the village of Little Missenden. In 1974, he added five poems for each of the other seasons and published the sequence in a little private edition via Olwyn's Rainbow Press under the title *Spring Summer Autumn Winter*. He then added ten more poems and renamed the collection *Season Songs*. He dedicated it to Carol and published it with the Viking Press in New York in October 1975, in a handsome hardback with illustrations by Leonard Baskin and no indication of its origin as a work for children. Faber and Faber published the British edition the following spring, without the Baskin line drawings. The jacket quoted Hughes saying '*Season Songs* began as children's poems but they grew up.' When he read a selection on the radio he said that they were written as if 'within hearing of children'.[19] He was pushing at the boundary between his adult's and his children's poetry. The collection does not contain material to distress a child as 'February 17th' would, but there is a reasonable smattering of death and blood: this is nature as it is, not the soft pastoral of idealising poetic greenery.

'A March Calf' opens the first season, spring, delightfully:

> Right from the start he is dressed in his best – his blacks and
>   his whites.
> Little Fauntleroy – quiffed and glossy,
> A Sunday suit, a wedding natty get-up,
> Standing in dunged straw.[20]

And throughout the collection there are lovely details for the hearing of all ages: a 'spurt of daffodils' stiff as 'Guardsmen', birds and insects coming alive in April ('You just can't count everything that follows in a tumble / Like a whole circus tumbling through a hoop'), the children excited because the swifts have returned in May ('Look! They're back! Look!'), a harvest moon, an autumn chestnut splitting its 'padded cell'.[21] Yet for most of the time one gets the sense that Hughes is operating on autopilot, writing nature notes instead of penetrating to the forces behind nature and in himself. At times, too, he relies excessively upon the tricks and tones of the poets he admires: 'The crocuses are too naked' is derivative of Plath, 'Water-wobbling blue-sky-puddled October' of Hopkins.[22]

For some critics, *Season Songs* was merely a 'lovely collection of lyrics for children'. For others, it represented a true return to form: if *Crow* and *Cave Birds* were 'full of sub-Amerindian apocalyptic gibberish', then 'salvation came with *Season Songs*'.[23] Ted sometimes looked back on the collection as one of his favourites, but he also knew that he had to do something different, something more difficult. In December 1974, with only half-ironic self-deprecation, he described the collection as nothing more than 'a book of seasons' poems for senile children and infantile adults'.[24]

*

Nineteen-seventy-five. A typical letter to Gerald, Joan and their family in Australia. Ted thanks them for the python skin that has just arrived, then gives advice on how to test the quality of a tiger skin: tear it at the edge and if it rips in the manner of cardboard, avoid; whereas, however tatty it appears, if painful to tear it is good quality. He was also still hoping that his brother might send him the foot of an eagle. There was a new building on the farm at Moortown: great improvement. He had reached a decision on the kind of pedigree cow he wanted. The price was right, with a downturn in the livestock market, but with his usual bad luck he was out of money. Over the course of the previous year, Lumb Bank renovations had eaten up £20,000, the taxman another £9,000 – factoring in the oil-led inflation of the next few years, those two figures add up to the equivalent of more than a quarter of a million pounds ($400,000) at 2015 values. The other business for Gerald to consider was the need for their father to sell the Beacon and move to North Tawton. A perfectly sized and located, if overpriced, cottage had come up in the village. Ted drops a heavy hint that Gerald might like to assist.[25]

Farming was immensely hard work, but there was joy in physical labour. That summer he wrote to Frieda, now fifteen and still at Bedales. Having asked how her exams had been and whether she had raced through her answers, and before telling a story about Ginger-dandelion the cat and a 'great metropolis of mice' in the upper part of the orchard near the overgrown tennis court, he told her how the rain had come pouring down as they finished baling: 'we had a wild rush to get them in, bales into the landrover ... bales in the horse-box, bales into our ears, bales into the backs of our necks, bales in our boots, bales down our shirts. So we tottered home towering & trembling & tilting & toppling & teetering.'[26] Each of his letters to Frieda and Nick at boarding school is like a little story, vivid in observation, with love and tenderness spilling from the boundless energy of the prose.

Nineteen-seventy-six. The prognostication for the new year was good. As a Leo, Ted was a creature of the sun, which in July would transit Cancer, the house of his Muse and his doppelgänger. Saturn had hemmed him in, blocking sustained writing for two years, but now he was going to be free of that oppression. His plan was to put together all the bits and pieces he had drafted in the first years of his second marriage into a collection called *Clearing the Decks*. He hoped for an Arts Council bursary to assist with the process. Once the decks were cleared of both poetic patchwork and domestic obligation, he could get down to the real thing.[27]

Carol was busy lambing. The pipes and water-troughs froze. Ted wrote with his usual cheery advice to the children at boarding school – work hard and don't forget to take vitamin C and halibut oil[28] – while also bombarding newspapers and politicians with letters about the 'cod war' against Icelandic overfishing of the North Atlantic.

All that winter Ted had spent his days getting his hands dirty, being kept from his writing. Then a shadow fell. Six months earlier, his father-in-law Jack Orchard had been diagnosed with cancer of the bronchus. In mid-February, after long treatment and partial remission, the secondaries took him, suddenly. After the business of funeral, cremation and private committal came the realisation that the pastoral dream of farmer Ted had come to an abrupt end. Jack had been a father to Ted, a mentor in the art of tending land and beast.[29] They did not want to let an outsider run the farm. They decided to get rid of the livestock, but retain the land and sell the grass. Money was a serious concern, not least because Ted's lengthy dispute with the taxman, which mainly concerned his royalty earnings from *The Bell Jar*, was still rumbling on. He also arranged for a valuation of Lumb Bank, with a view to a sale – though that would have been a blow to the Arvon Foundation.

20

The Elegiac Turn

'I started again at the beginning'[1]

'Song', the earliest poem that Hughes wished to see preserved, written at three o'clock in the morning while on National Service in 1950, may be read in two ways. In its conscious origin, it was a love song for Jean Findlay. In the personal *mythos* that, he believed, spoke from his unconscious, it was his first encounter with the White Goddess. All his published collections from *The Hawk in the Rain* to *Prometheus on his Crag* sought to tap into the unconscious, to depersonalise and universalise his experience. Seeing the jaguar cage while he worked in the kitchens of the cafeteria at the zoo and hearing the howling of the wolves from the flat on Primrose Hill: these were occasions for literary inspiration, but the poems are not ostensibly about himself as a jaguar or the memory of Sylvia's suicide as a howl. Rather, jaguar and wolf are embodiments of natural forces that far transcend individual experience. So too, although *Crow* was dedicated to Assia's memory (and Shura's), Crow's temptress Eve is not in any direct sense a representation of Assia.

Ted Hughes became a poet under the influence of T. S. Eliot's insistence on the *impersonality* of great art. His reading of Jung and of Robert Graves's *The White Goddess* led him to cultivate a poetry of archetypes and myths, not of domestic minutiae and autobiographical recollection. The discovery of Robert Lowell's *Life Studies* with Sylvia in 1959 made him think again. But he shied away from a change of approach to his own poetry, regarding the new autobiographical or 'confessional' style as something distinctively American, Sylvia's domain and not his own. Hughes knew, as no one else upon earth did, exactly how closely the *Ariel* poems were elaborated from Sylvia's life and marriage: 'To me those poems open alphabet – every nuance, I know its whole history and connection, every phrase,' as he wrote in that journal entry in the summer of 1969.[2] But the inevitable consequence of *Ariel*'s publication was the opening to public scrutiny of his own private life, and in particular the circumstances leading to the end of the marriage and Plath's suicide. His resistance to autobiography in poetry was accordingly hardened.

In September 1962 he had written to Olwyn about the 'self-imposed curfew' he had placed upon the subjective voice in poetry.[3] There is a lot of himself in *Wodwo*, but he is there very indirectly. 'The Howling of Wolves', the only poem in that book to have been written in the flat in Fitzroy Road where Plath committed suicide, might be read as his first elegy in her memory, but there is nothing explicitly personal about it.

Steeped in the classics as he was, Ted took a Greek view of the origins of poetry. There was epic, the domain of myth, creation tales, heroes and descents to the underworld. The *Crow* project was his epic, reduced to craggy fragments. Then there was drama: the embodiment of myth on stage, as exemplified by the tragedians studied by Sylvia in Part II of the Cambridge English Tripos. For writers who wish to be 'impersonal', dramatic form is especially attractive. Shakespeare has often been held up as the ideal of the poet who brings to life all his different characters but never reveals his own self. Like T. S. Eliot in his later years, Hughes devoted much energy to the attempt to revive verse drama. There was, for example, the Yaddo project adapting the Tibetan Book of the Dead (*Bardo Thödol*) in verse as a libretto for the Chinese composer Chou Wen-chung. That story's dramatisation of 'the progress of the soul during the 49 days between death and rebirth'[4] was reworked, many years later, in *Cave Birds*. Another big project was the radio play *The Wound*, broadcast in 1962 and published five years later in *Wodwo*. It came to him, he claimed, in a dream as if it were a full-length film during the time he was working on *Bardo*. After this, he metamorphosed his verse drama based on Johann Valentin Andreae's *The Chymical Wedding of Christian Rosenkreutz* into *Difficulties of a Bridegroom*, the radio play broadcast in January 1963 and repeated on Sylvia's last Saturday night. Then there was *Eat Crow*, the early version of *Crow* in dramatic form. Radio was an excellent medium for symbolic dramas of this kind. Yet another of his early excursions in the field was *The House of Aries*, a tale of Freudian family romance set against a background of violent revolution, written in an array of different verse forms and broadcast on the Third Programme in November 1960.[5]

It was in this early 'dramatic' phase that Ted began work on what became his major Faber and Faber publication of the mid-Seventies: *Gaudete*. In the early Sixties, he developed a film script that began from the premise of the play he had begun at Yaddo, which is to say a drama of erotic intoxication and dismemberment loosely based on *The Bacchae* of Euripides. This was a period when the movies were the one place where a writer could make serious money. A detailed scenario was typed up by the end of January 1964.[6] Ted thought it beyond the scope of any English director. Ingmar Bergman would have been his ideal reader for it, but his Swedish contact, the literary editor Siv Arb, who had come to Court Green before Sylvia's death, sent it instead to Vilgot Sjöman, a director who later became famous for the sexually explicit avant-garde movie *I am Curious (Yellow)*. Sjöman was not interested, so Ted wondered instead about turning his idea into a novel. He then put it aside for several years.

His personal summary of the narrative went as follows: 'A nimble vicar organizes all the women in his parish – he is to father the saviour on one of them, so has to keep at it all the time with all of them, and has them hooked up in a witchy cult to promote the right sort of spirit.' He is then 'hunted down across the county by the husbands and shot in a lake' before being buried in his own church.[7] Were there ever to have been a pitch to a Hollywood producer (never a likely event), the strapline might have gone along the lines of 'orgiastic Bacchic women out of Greek tragedy meet naughty rural vicar out of the *News of the World*'. Ted had become an amused connoisseur of salacious red-top Sunday newspaper stories about the sexual misdemeanours of the English clergy.

'The subject was novel in 1964,' he later ruminated, 'charismatic priests, harem congregations, black magic or at least Old Religion magic in church precincts.'[8] By the early Seventies, he felt that he was in danger of missing the boat. Similar narratives were appearing else-where: in *The Magus* of John Fowles, in Peter Redgrove, and in the film *The Wicker Man*, based on *Ritual*, a horror novel by cult author David Pinner in which a puritanical policeman investigates the ritualistic

murder of a child in a secluded village in Cornwall, where he encoun-
ters mind-games, seduction and bloody pagan rites. Rather than revive
his own idea for a film or novel, in an attempt to break into genres
where he had no prior history of success, Ted reworked his treatment,
introduced a doppelgänger for the protagonist, and sent Charles
Monteith at Faber the resulting long poem, written in loose, almost
prosaic lines which Seamus Heaney would compare to the style of Walt
Whitman.[9] After more than a year's worth of revisions, a final version
was dispatched in May 1976. He was determined to stick by the title
Gaudete, despite – indeed, all the more because of – the folk band
Steeleye Span's recent top-twenty hit with their rendering of an early
church chant under the same title (Ted was awed by the voice of
Maddy Prior, their female lead singer). He told Monteith that the
subtitle ever since the original film treatment had always been (with
ironic intention) 'An English Idyll', though this was now dropped.[10]

Faber published *Gaudete* in May 1977, in an edition of 5,000 copies.
The *Guardian* reviewer likened the poem to being given a pair of
(D. H.) Lawrentian red trousers, which 'seem to have come from the
old Hammer Films wardrobe': 'There's toadstool in the sandwiches,
and they celebrate the ancient religion orgiastically in the basement
of the church, a lot of naked women in animal masks, and the vicar in
his antlers.' The review's overall verdict was not flattering: 'This ridic-
ulous hodge-podge could have made a campy horror-film, and indeed
started life as a scenario. The trouble is that Hughes wants it to be
taken much more seriously than that.' Nevertheless, 'Since Beauty,
asleep, is still beautiful, there are careless strokes of genius on most
pages, all at the level of rendering sensation.'[11]

For the Oxford critic Peter Conrad, the wonderful bestiary of the
early poems had turned to bestiality and the work was of interest only
'as a measure of Hughes's degradation'. The Jaguar had become a
Jaguar sports car and the thought-fox had been 'gutted and looped
around the neck of Maud the housekeeper as a fur wrap'. *Gaudete*,
Conrad suggests, revealed a poet who had become cynically material-
istic: 'Hughes the myth-maker betrays himself as a moneyed worldling,
adept in spotting the makes of cars and impressive in reciting the
brand-names of his instruments of death.'[12]

In the *Sunday Times* the poet and crime writer Julian Symons was
rather more favourably inclined, though ultimately baffled:

You might get an idea of *Gaudete* by imagining *Under Milk Wood* written by [Jacobean dramatists] Webster or Tourneur instead of by a chubby cheerful chappie of a Welsh verbal conjurer. Yet the effect is not at all depressing. Just as Webster's Flamineo and Bosola come through to us as superb comic monsters, so a lot of *Gaudete* is ferociously jocose, intentionally funny. It is a pity that the poem should be so obscure, not passage by passage but in its ultimate meaning.[13]

The American edition, published at the end of the year, provoked a very mixed response. Donald Hall in the *Washington Post* proclaimed it Hughes's best work, while other reviewers found its mixture of 'lust for women and loathing for women' repulsive, or railed against it as 'an obvious male fantasy rotted by unexplored misogyny in the de-humanization of the yearning women: "Already their eyes are glazed like young cattle. They are waiting for the first shiver of power."'[14]

Gaudete is indeed something of a puzzle: 200 pages long, a sexed-up Lawrentian *Under Milk Wood* with an epigraph out of the Parzival myth and a prefatory note explaining that the central character, an Anglican clergyman called the Reverend Nicholas Lumb, is a spirit double since the real Lumb has been abducted to the underworld (though in the epilogue he turns up in 'a straggly sparse village on the West Coast of Ireland'). It is written with an excellent eye for a filmic *mise-en-scène*. It is very good on male voyeurism. It is quite funny in the way that it turns the members of the Women's Institute into a horde of maenads. But it is troubling in its persistent linking of sex and violence:

> Inside Felicity a solid stone-hard core of honey-burning
>   sweetness has begun to melt
> And she knows this is oozing out all over her body
> And wetting her cheeks and trickling on her thighs.
> The sweetness is like the hot rough fur of the tiger as it
>   bulges and bristles into presence,
> A hot-throated opening flower of tiger, splitting all the leafy
>   seams of her body …
> Lumb is suddenly standing in front of her looking at her.
> He is holding something shaggy and terrible above her.

Felicity understands that she is a small anonymous creature
   which is now going to be killed.
She starts to cry, feeling the greatness and nobility of her
   role.
She starts to sing, adoring whatever the terrible lifted thing
   in front of her is,
Which needs all she can give, she knows it needs her,
She knows it is the love animal.[15]

And yet there are moments of aching beauty, as when, free from the
cage of his body, Lumb's spirit heads for the horizon:

He lopes out along a hogback
Through ungrazed grass
Toughened with buttercup and young thistles
Toward a hill-crown clump of beeches, black against the
   broad glare of sky,
Summit of power in the past.[16]

The young poet Simon Armitage was so mesmerised by the verse that
he forgot about his laundry and left it in the machine all night, as he
read into the small hours: 'What's so powerful about *Gaudete* is its
passion – that sensation, as if a line is writing itself in front of your own
eyes, which I'm sure is related to a feeling the author might have
experienced during the creation of the line itself.'[17] But the volume is
probably not the best starting point for those unacquainted with
Hughes's writing.

'It's like a play,' said Ted when interviewed about the poem, 'it
contains no author's comments. As far as interpretation goes – I leave
all options open.'[18] But when it came to biographical interpretation,
he closed the option with some dispatch:

Faas: Are critics aware of the extent to which the name
   Lumb is associated with your life? Your house in Yorkshire
   is called Lumb Bank.
HUGHES: It's a fairly common West Yorkshire name. It
   means chimney, the tall factory chimney.[19]

Interviewer Ekbert Faas, a German-born novelist and literary critic, did not respond by commenting on the choice of Lumb's Christian name, with its echo of Ted's ancestor the Reverend Nicholas Farrar. In the light of the Farrar family's unhappiness at Ted's dalliances on his return to Yorkshire after Sylvia's death, there is something a little provocative in the representation of Lumb as a man of irresistible sexual powers, running amok in a closed rural community.

The main body of *Gaudete* represents the extreme of that mode of Ted Hughes's poetry which focuses on the mythic, the dramatic and the shamanistic, which is hooked on the Goddess and explores the process of spiritual descent and regeneration. Yet shadowing the Lumb narrative is his second self: the autobiographical, the man who has loved and lusted after women ever since writing 'Song' under the influence of the beautiful Jean Findlay. It cannot be a coincidence that the environment in which the 'other', the authentic, Lumb appears in the epilogue is that of the Galway coast, where Ted went at the crisis point in his relationship with Sylvia and where he returned with Assia in the hope of making a new life.

Gaudete was published with an epilogue: a series of poems that are quite unlike the preceding narrative. This is a sequence of just over forty short lyrics in a style that feels very different from anything Hughes had published before. Within the fiction of the poem, they are associated with the 'real' Nicholas Lumb as opposed to the false messiah of his spirit double. In terms of poetic development, one might say that the Two Teds were split across the Two Lumbs: the mythic self in the main narrative, the confessional self in the epilogue poems.

He explained their origin to the enquiring Ekbert Faas. In 1973, he read a Penguin Classics anthology of South Indian *vacanas* or devotional lyrics in free-verse translations by A. K. Ramanujan, under the title *Speaking of Siva*. These little poems are addressed to a divinity – sometimes Siva, sometimes a nameless goddess – who is 'intensely personal, willing to share its ecstasies with animals and plants rather than with confederates of an organized religion'. But, 'rather than bestowing gifts of grace, prosperity or righteousness, the deity responds by annihilating the worshipper'.[20] This could be the White Goddess, with Ted himself as the worshipper.

He was very excited by Ramanujan's introduction to the anthology, which told of how the *vacana* was a form that combined homely images of everyday experience with 'the sense and idiom of the earth' as well as 'abstruse esoteric symbolism'. This made Ted prick up his ears. As did the idea that 'all the phases of love become metaphors for the phases of mystical union and alienation'. In some of these poems, the intervention of a transgressive divine force disrupts conventional family life, shatters traditional loyalties and causes marital breakdown. Ramanujan writes of a quasi-religious legitimation of fornication: 'The Lord is the Illicit Lover; he will break up the world of Karma and normal relationships, the husband's family that must necessarily be violated and trespassed against, if one should have anything to do with God.' This line of thinking cohered very well with the story of the Reverend Lumb's sexual profligacy breaking up a number of marriages. It may also have made Ted think about his own track record. But what most attracted him to the *vacana* was that the form squared the circle of being both depersonalised (tapping into the divine, the mythic, the archetypal patterns) and highly personal: 'They are uttered, not through a persona or mask, but directly in the person of the poet himself, in his native local dialect and idiom, using the tones and language of personal conversation or outcry.'[21] This was the poetic voice for which Hughes's inner self had been waiting.

Ramanujan's ruminations and translations were timely for Ted because he was growing anxious about his own mortality. He read *Speaking of Siva* in the period when he had been suffering from a chronically sore throat for a year and was worrying that it might be cancer. So he began to write his own *vacanas* as 'little prayers', attempts to make peace with himself before he met his maker.[22] Some of them went into a privately published volume, others became the epilogue to *Gaudete* (some appeared in both settings).

Another influence, he told Ekbert Faas, was his (always vivid) dreams, particularly his recurring adolescent nightmare of a plane crash over Mytholmroyd.[23] If he could begin by turning such memories into poetry, there might come a time when he could dare to release his dreams of Sylvia. Hughes told the critic Keith Sagar that the epilogue poems represented 'my furthest point, so far, some of them'. In a journal fragment dated 14 December 1974 he wrote, 'With Gaudete, I have broke some sound barrier. I mustn't let my momentum slack. I mustn't let my aim be deflected. I must now as never before step up the pressure, rip aside the web, smash up the shells.'[24]

Speaking of Siva had made him think more seriously than ever before of daring to speak in print of Sylvia.

In sum, the *Gaudete* epilogue poems mark the emergence of a new voice in the poetry of Ted Hughes: quiet, tender, elegiac. And autobiographical. To put it another way, this was the moment when Hughes began to shift his allegiance from the myths and archetypes of T. S. Eliot to the true voice of feeling exemplified by Thomas Hardy's poems in memory of his dead wife. When *Birthday Letters* was published near the end of Hughes's life, critics were amazed by the autobiographical candour of the collection and greeted it as the breaking of long silence. But this was not the case. Seamus Heaney remembers opening the issue of the *London Review of Books* dated 21 February 1980, reading 'The Earthenware Head' and saying to himself, 'Ah, he's begun.'[25] Ted had in fact begun to publish elegiacally with the *Gaudete* epilogue poems.

One of Hughes's acutest critics, William Scammell, delivered a lecture at the Cheltenham Literature Festival in 1997, which was published the following year in the magazine *Poetry Review*, together with a number of responses to *Birthday Letters*. Here Scammell noticed that the brief lyrics at the end of *Gaudete* were the place where 'for the first time [Hughes] publicly addresses Plath's suicide'.[26] He then quoted three beautiful poems from the heart of the sequence, 'Once I said lightly, / Even if the worst happens / We can't fall off the earth,' 'Waving goodbye, from your banked hospital bed', and 'I know well / You are not infallible.'

Hughes read the piece and wrote to Scammell on 1 May 1998. He made some slight corrections and explained that the epilogue poems were modelled on the *vacanas* of Tamil tradition and that, of the three mentioned in the lecture, the first was indeed 'related to SP', but the second was related to his mother, and the third 'to a close friend of mine Susan Alliston who died of Leukaemia'.[27] Yes, the journey towards the publication of *Birthday Letters* did begin at the end of *Gaudete*, but Hughes was not yet ready to write in detail about Plath's death. In 'Once I said lightly', he tempts fate with his words about the worst that can happen and is repaid when 'She fell into the earth / And I was devoured.'[28] But the two poems of explicit deathbed farewell are *not*, he corrects Scammell, about Sylvia. In that key journal entry in 1969, he had written 'A's death removed Sylvia's to a great distance, swamped everything. Now Ma's death has somewhat removed A's. Yet A's comes back.'[29] A similar sort of displacement is at work here. He could only proceed gradually towards the pain of Sylvia's death and Assia's. *Birthday Letters*, and indeed *Capriccio*, his Assia collection, lay in the future. He began with his mother and with Susan Alliston.

It was, then, with the deaths of those two other beloved women in the year 1969 that his elegiac voice first emerged. If his note to Scammell is to be believed, first there was a recollection of his mother knocking over a vase beside her hospital bed as he said goodbye to her for the last time. And then he turned into poetry the picture of the dying Sue Alliston, with her 'pony face' and once 'marvellous forest of auburn' now shrunk to 'a twist / As thin as a silk scarf' – that picture which he had sketched so precisely and tenderly in the journal entry written after returning from her bedside. Every detail is there: his lifting her hand for her as her chin sank to her chest 'With the sheer weariness / Of taking away from everybody' her 'envied beauty', her 'much-desired beauty', her 'hardly-used beauty', and the memory 'Of lifting away yourself / From yourself // And weeping with the ache of the effort'.[30]

'I know well' could truly have been titled 'Elegy for Susan'. At the same time, given that Ted's visits to her bedside in the summer of 1969 were his first return to University College Hospital since the day six years earlier when he had formally identified Sylvia's body in the morgue there, and given that he had been with Sue on the night of Sylvia's death, it was inevitable that the two women came together in his poetic imagination.

There was a similar coalescence in the poem that is allegedly about his mother's death. 'Waving goodbye, from your banked hospital bed' moves from ward to morgue and ends with the poet emerging 'In the glaring metropolis of cameras'. The chapel of rest in Hebden Bridge was hardly a metropolis alive with the flashbulbs of paparazzi. In imagination and memory, there is a jump-cut to Sylvia and an anticipation of the unwelcome glare of publicity in the years after Alvarez published *The Savage God*. The movement from Hebden Bridge to London is perhaps signalled by the line 'Like a pillar over Athens', suggestive of the caryatids that stand on the porch of St Pancras Church, on the Euston Road round the corner from University

College Hospital – and that also evoke the poem by Sylvia which Dan Huws mocked in their Cambridge days.

In the archive at Emory, there are a dozen manuscript drafts of 'Waving goodbye'.[31] In the original versions, Ted smiles and says goodbye to the dying woman in her hospital bed, then backs out and inadvertently walks into the morgue, where he bows and kisses a 'refrigerated glazed' temple. This is not his mother, but Sylvia. Other drafts reveal a shift from 'He' to 'I' that highlights the move into autobiography, together with images of hanging in space and time, or being in wrong time and space, that make the move to Sylvia more explicit. In the published text, the time–space jump is suppressed: Ted is not yet ready to go into print with explicit reference to Sylvia's dead body. The journey has begun, but the elegiac voice is still constricted.

Furthermore, consciously or unconsciously, he was still suppressing the importance of Susan Alliston. In his journal account of his last visit to her, he goes into University College Hospital by the morgue entrance. And there is a vase by the bedside as she raises her hand to wave goodbye for the last time. Those details are the key inspiration for the poem. The proximity in time of his mother's passing and Susan's brought the two deaths together. 'Waving goodbye' is not just the elegy for Edith Farrar that he claimed it was. It is also another love poem in memory of Susan. It is haunted by the thought of himself and Susan lying in each other's arms on the night that Sylvia died. And by the irony of its being in the same hospital that he said goodbye to them both – both so beautiful, once so alive, then dying so young – one on the ward in 1969 and the other in the morgue in 1963.

In the summer of 1978, a year after the appearance of *Gaudete*, a blackbound volume of poems called *Orts* was published by Olwyn's Rainbow Press, in an edition of 200 copies at a price of £50. Handsomely lodged in a black slip-case lined with flocked fabric, it had Italian mould-made 'laid' paper, with decorated Japanese endpapers, a drawing by Leonard Baskin, and distinctly opaque lyric content. 'Orts', from a Middle English word for food left by an animal, means the scraps or leavings that remain after a meal. The collection represented the offcuts from the outpouring of *vacanas* that were originally going to be published under the title 'Lumb's Remains' and a selection from which had become the Epilogue to *Gaudete*.

As in the epilogue poems, the voice is at once personal and impersonal, intimate and distancing. At one level, an unidentified speaker addresses either himself or an interlocutor who sometimes seems to be the Goddess. At another level, there is a clear movement towards the autobiographical. A poem about a bad meal in a restaurant or the awful food in a cafeteria on the M5 motorway must be drawn more from personal experience than ancient myth. An exquisite address to a female child collecting 'egg-pebbles' and 'tops of dandelions' is clearly to some extent about, or for, Frieda. The figure of Ophelia floating downstream to the underworld after her suicide cannot but evoke Sylvia. To anyone in the know, a final farewell wave on a station platform inevitably suggests the last glimpse of Assia. The biographer is also bound to ask whether there is an origin in experience as opposed to imagination for a litany of longing sickness for various women: the 'lecherous pallor' of one, the smooth fish-like flank of another (this was a favoured simile for Sylvia's body), the 'cool saliva' of another, the 'dirty feet in sandals' of another, the 'crazy yells and claws' of another. From a biographical point of view, it is also noteworthy that several of the *Orts* poems are about marriage as entrapment. A woman claws the door of a house: later, this poem will be explicitly linked to Sylvia. The phrase 'I do' – in such a context always redolent of 'Daddy' – is compared to the doomed charge of a hurt leopard. In another poem, the state of matrimony is compared to an obstinate tooth decaying 'In an imbecile's mouth'. In others, marriage is a life-sentence dished out by a judge or an analogous state to that of an animal imprisoned for life in a zoo.[32] The 'stuck in marriage' poem was first drafted in Ireland in the aftermath of Assia's death; the syntax is nicely ambiguous, so the phrase could refer to her marriage to David Wevill or Ted's own to Sylvia, or both: 'Then he met her, yes, he found her / Stuck in marriage like a decaying tooth.'[33]

Another volume appeared from the Rainbow Press a few months later. Printed as usual on handmade paper, but with sheets of a much larger size, this time there were 143 numbered copies bound in stiff vellum and priced at £140. A further set of twenty-six, lettered A to Z, was bound in full brown morocco with bevelled edges and the price jacked up to £175. This handsome volume was 'Dedicated to the memory of JACK ORCHARD'. It yoked the journal-like farming poems that Ted had written in the early Seventies to a series of elegies on his father-in-law.

The subsequent publishing history of this collection was complicated. A year later, Faber and Faber reprinted the sequence (slightly reordered) as 'Moortown', the opening section of the portmanteau volume called *Moortown*, a volume best described as an 'interim selected new poems'[34] – it also included *Prometheus on his Crag, Adam and the Sacred Nine* and a miscellany of short poems gathered under the title 'Earth-Numb'. A decade later, the farming poems were reprinted (with further slight reordering) as a standalone trade paperback entitled *Moortown Diary*. This 1989 edition added dates, prose notes and a preface.

From the point of view of Ted's poetic development, it was the final six poems in the Moortown sequence that had genuine significance. These were elegies in the true classical sense: poems in memory of a beloved and admired acquaintance who has passed away. *Crow* had been dedicated to the memory of Assia and Shura but was in no direct sense about them. Some of the epilogue poems in *Gaudete* – a volume that, tellingly, carried no dedication – were elegies for Sylvia, Sue and Edith, but they were not acknowledged as such. Now for the first time, albeit in a privately published collection, Hughes was openly advertising his move into the poetry of personal mourning.

The elegiac sextet begins with 'The day he died', written on Valentine's Day, the day after Jack died. It is a poem both moving and muscular, with earth as crisp as toast, 'snowdrops battered' and 'Thrushes spluttering'. There is a 'new emptiness' in the landscape, where the bright fields are as 'dazed' as the bereaved daughter and son-in-law who have been farming them. 'From now on the land / Will have to manage without him,' the poem declares. Ted already knew that he could not go on as a farmer without the manager of his land. The next three poems etch stark and vivid memories of rural life and labour, outlining the figure of Jack against his landscape and his community: putting up a wire fence, shearing 'an upturned sheep', standing stock still at an auction (like a poker-player, he gives nothing away and gets a bargain on a bullock). The final two elegies remember his hands: hands that tightened barbed wire, grasped bullocks by the nose, stripped down tractors, held cigarettes, hands that now 'lie folded, aloof from all they have done'. They are surprisingly 'slender hands', evocative of his mother's (and perhaps Ted's mother's), no longer in the motion of work but now folded in death's 'final strangeness of elegance'.[35]

The 1979 trade printing of *Moortown* once again carried the dedication 'To the memory of JACK ORCHARD'. Earlier that same year, Ted had published another collection with an equally telling dedication: 'Poems in memory of Edith Farrar'.[36] First father-in-law overtly remembered and memorialised, then mother. How long before it would be wife?

21

The Arraignment

One may as well begin with the book that Ted was reading in proof on the day when, for the first time since he had formally identified Sylvia's body in the morgue, he returned to University College Hospital to see the dying Sue Alliston. Published by Faber and Faber, *The Art of Sylvia Plath* reprinted the reviews of *Ariel* by Alvarez, Rosenthal and Steiner, together with a mix of critical essays, memoirs by acquaintances, an overview of the state of Plath's reputation, and a piece by Ted called 'Notes on the Chronological Order of Sylvia Plath's Poems'. This was his first substantial published essay on her work. It is where he wrote about 'The Moon and the Yew Tree' in terms of inner 'suffering and decision'. Implicitly, this is an acknowledgement that his own poetry – *Crow* in particular – was made out of his own inner torment.

The Art of Sylvia Plath went into print in January 1970. That same year, a rather more high-profile book appeared from the Viking Press in New York: *Sisterhood is Powerful*, subtitled *An Anthology of Writings from the Women's Liberation Movement*. That movement was in full stride. This was the era of Germaine Greer's *The Female Eunuch* and Kate Millett's *Sexual Politics*, of the burning of bras and the march to take back the night. The editor of *Sisterhood is Powerful* was Robin Morgan, who had been a leading figure in the campaign to disrupt the annual Miss America beauty pageant. She had written a ten-point protest called 'No More Miss America', point one being 'We Protest: *The Degrading Mindless-Boob-Girlie Symbol*'.[1] It was in 1970 that the movement came to prominence in Britain when the Miss World contest at the Royal Albert Hall was heckled by 'Women's Libbers' holding up placards, blowing whistles, and throwing smoke, stink and ink bombs on to the stage.

In *Sisterhood is Powerful*, Morgan coined the term 'herstory' to replace 'history'. The contents of the anthology included polemical essays with titles such as 'The invisible woman: psychological and sexual repression', 'Madison Avenue brainwashing: the facts', 'The politics of orgasm', 'Unfinished business: birth control and women's liberation', 'Sexual politics (in literature)', 'Double jeopardy: to be Black and female', 'Institutionalized oppression vs. the female', 'The politics of housework', 'The feminists vs. the institution of marriage' and 'Women against Daddy'. A few poems were included, among them one called 'Song of the fucked duck'. And sandwiched between an essay on the menopause and the SCUM (Society for Cutting Up Men) manifesto was Sylvia Plath's poem 'The Jailor'. If there was a single moment when Sylvia Plath was transformed from Fifties girl who loved lipstick and baking and *Mademoiselle* into icon of the oppressed woman brought to the edge and beyond by domestic drudgery, motherhood and male infidelity, but redeemed by the power of her poetic voice, this was it. Suddenly it became somehow symbolic that she had taken her own life in the year when the old myths about housewifery and a woman's place were exploded by Betty Friedan's *The Feminine Mystique*. For thousands of women, the *Ariel* poems became a venting of rage at, and a song of liberation from, 'The smog of cooking, the smog of hell'.[2]

This vision of her was compounded by Alvarez's account in *The Savage God*, in which he quoted from her note for a BBC reading that was never broadcast, where she spoke of writing the *Ariel* poems 'at about four in the morning – that still blue, almost eternal hour before the baby's cry, before the glassy music of the milkman, settling his bottles'.[3] The anti-Hughes backlash, stirred by images such as this, was beginning in earnest, even as he was continuing his curatorial work, preparing further selections of Sylvia's poems for publication under the titles *Crossing the Water* and *Winter Trees*. The first of these he described as a collection of transitional poems written between *The Colossus* and *Ariel*, the second as late poems written around the same time as those included in his text of *Ariel*. *Winter Trees*, he explained in an essay in the *Observer*, brought into print 'all but about six of the *Ariel* and after poems that were not in *Ariel*'.[4] He also gave Sylvia the private-press treatment at this time. Nineteen-seventy-one was the inaugural year of Olwyn's Rainbow Press, and two of its first four publications were *Crystal Gazer* (twenty-three Plath poems previously unpublished in book form) and *Lyonnesse* (a further twenty-one of Sylvia's poems). Each gave an initial high-price, finely bound, limited-circulation outing to poems that were published in trade form soon afterwards, a pattern that Ted and Olwyn would also use for the Rainbow Press fine editions of his own poems.[5]

On a rainy New York day in June 1972, Robin Morgan received a telephone call from her editor at Random House. She had just corrected the proofs of a volume of her verse called *Monster*. But now, she was told, the lawyers were going to have a look at one of the poems. Entitled 'Arraignment', it began as follows:

> I accuse
> Ted Hughes
> of what the entire British and American
> literary and critical establishment
> has been at great lengths to deny
> (without ever saying it in so many words, of course):
> the murder of Sylvia Plath.

Aside from the catchy opening rhyme, the language of the poem is prosaic. The content is anything but. The charge sheet is recited: 'mind-rape', 'body-rape', sexual unfaithfulness, the 'abduction and brainwashing' of Frieda and Nick, plagiarism of Plath's imagery, suppression of her last journals, financial exploitation by way of editing the poems, writing bad poetry himself, and, ultimately, not just metaphorical but real murder: 'if he's killed one wife, / he's killed two'. Morgan then names Assia (misspelling her married surname and incorrectly asserting that she was the woman in Plath's poem 'Lesbos'). She also names Shura and reveals that Assia took her with her. Playing on Assia's Jewishness and Sylvia's allusions to the Holocaust, made notorious by George Steiner's review of *Ariel*, she describes Ted as a 'one-man gynocidal movement'. She arraigns the male critical establishment, naming Alvarez, Steiner and Lowell. They are charged with aiding and abetting Hughes the 'legal executor' (a clever pun), with engaging in a conspiracy to celebrate Plath's genius while patronising her madness, diluting her rage and suppressing her (alleged) feminist politics. Robin Morgan then imagines a group of Hughes's female fans knocking at his door, liberating Frieda and Nick, cutting off his penis, stuffing it in his mouth, sewing his 'poetasting lips' around it and blowing out his brains. Meanwhile, the poems ends, 'Hughes, sue me.'[6]

Arthur Abelman, consulting counsel for Random House, feared that Ted might do just that. But could it be libel if the accusations were true, responded Morgan? And what about freedom of speech? Her female editor, Hilary Maddux, came under pressure from James Silberman, Random House's editor-in-chief. Did Morgan really wish to risk being injuncted, or poet and publisher being sued, just for the sake of one poem? Morgan brought in her own female attorney, Emily Goodman, who pointed out that the accusation of rape was surely not libellous since marital rape was not a crime (feminist campaigners were, of course, arguing that it should be). Morgan held firm over the summer. The poem was central to the politics of the book; if it were suppressed, she would withdraw the entire collection. A compromise was reached: a revised version would be included. Fifteen different attempts were made in the course of the summer. Eventually, in November, *Monster* appeared in print. 'How can / I accuse / Ted Hughes', it now began, before acknowledging that the accusation of rape 'could be conceived as metaphor, / and besides, it is permissible by law for a man to rape his wife, in body and in mind'. The story of Assia remains, as does the arraignment of Alvarez, Steiner and Lowell. At the close, 'Hughes, sue me' becomes a less brazen but still fierce (and intrusive) provocation: 'Hughes / has married again.'[7]

From Ted's point of view, even the revised version was actionable. But to sue in America would have been high risk. A lawsuit would not only cost a fortune; it would also draw massive attention to what might otherwise turn out to be a small-print-run volume of imperfect verse. Besides, anything that could be perceived as an attack on the First Amendment right of free speech would damage his reputation still further. He would stand a much better chance in Britain, where the libel law was stricter. And this was the place that mattered, the home of his family, his friends and his literary reputation. An agreement was reached with Random House: if the book were not distributed in Britain and the Commonwealth, he would not sue in the United States. However, cyclostyled or cheaply printed samizdat editions ('pirated' with the author's permission) began appearing in Canada, Australia and New Zealand. Some of them included both versions of 'Arraignment'. In November 1973, an 'English Feminist Edition', complete with images of Sylvia and her grave, appeared in women's centres and counter-culture bookshops, at considerable legal risk. Ted did not dignify or publicise it with a court action. But from this point on, he would be a marked man. Even some of his friends found themselves conflicted: Doris Lessing, revered in the women's movement as author of *The Golden Notebook*, wrote enigmatically that 'Since a great deal of effort has gone into trying to keep the Hughes scandals out of the limelight, it is a shame that Morgan's poem has provoked such emotional reaction.'[8]

Unsurprisingly, given Morgan's prominence in the movement, the poem made a considerable stir in feminist circles. Ted's hope that it might not be noticed proved vain: *Monster* sold 30,000 copies within six months of publication, a remarkable figure for a first volume of verse. Morgan's public readings played to packed houses across America. The Hughes name was vilified. Plath was turned into a martyr of a movement of which she was not really a part.

Ted was now in an impossible position. His inner voice was telling him that, having confronted Sylvia's death indirectly and mythically in *Crow*, his next poetic move should have been to face it openly in confessional and elegiac mode. Only then could his verse progress beyond the easy pieces of the Moortown diary poems and *Season Songs*. But to release his version of the story of his marriage would now inevitably look like a response to the arraignment, a laying of his defence before the court of public opinion. The voice of the defendant, however dignified, would only give the oxygen of publicity to the less restrained tones of the female prosecutors. Above all, he wanted to protect the feelings and the privacy of his wife and his children. He imposed upon himself a vow of silence that would endure for more than two decades: no published poems about Sylvia (unless sufficiently oblique to go under the radar of biographical reading). At the same time, he remained determined to honour Sylvia's legacy by continuing to curate her work and her posthumous reputation with all the care that he could muster.

★

Family mattered to Ted more than anything else other than writing. He wanted to be a good son as well as a good father. He worried about his own father, even as he was exasperated by him. He greatly admired the strength and the farming skills of his father-in-law. But he also had to contend with his first mother-in-law. Aurelia was bitterly hurt by the American publication of *The Bell Jar* in 1971. For the inside story of Sylvia's suicide attempt in the crawl space below the family home to have been shared with her friends and family, let alone with the media and the wider public, added deep insult to the injury of such poems as 'Daddy' and 'Medusa'. Soon after the novel's publication Aurelia had a heart attack.

During her convalescence, she made a proposal to Ted. There was clearly a huge appetite for Sylvia's work, so what about a collection of her letters? Sylvia was such a wonderful letter-writer, and so many of her letters home were full of joy. Would this not balance out *The Bell Jar* and create a more rounded picture? Aurelia's thinking, of course, was that to reveal Sylvia's openness and enthusiasm and eagerness to confide in her mother would shine a much more favourable light on the mother–daughter relationship. She set about gathering all the letters she could find and writing an interlinking commentary. The book would be like the 'life and letters' volumes with which great writers had been immortalised in Victorian times. She worked for two years, eventually producing a thousand pages of material, enough to fill two volumes.

In the summer of 1974 Ted Hughes lived a double life as farmer in collaboration with his father-in-law and literary editor in collaboration with his ex-mother-in-law. Three American women came to Court Green for extended visits. First there was Judith Kroll, who had recently completed a doctoral thesis on Plath, which Ted thought was full of amazing intuitions. He approved of Kroll's work not least because her argument was grounded in literary sources more than biographical events. In particular, the thesis suggested that Plath used psychoanalytical and mythological theories in order to create a controlling myth that underlay her poetry. Beginning from Sylvia's senior thesis at Smith on the figure of the 'double' in Dostoevsky, Kroll argued that her interior life was shaped by such sources as James Frazer's *The Golden Bough* and Jessie Weston's *From Ritual to Romance*, which had been so important to T. S. Eliot and the first generation of modernists and which introduced her to the figure of the Fisher King and the idea of a cycle of death, rebirth and transcendence.

Even more attractively from Ted's point of view, Kroll suggested that one of the keys to Plath's personal mythology was Graves's *The White Goddess* – to which he had introduced her. Furthermore, Kroll astutely perceived that both Ted and Sylvia had read Carl Gustav Jung and that another key to their shared poetic vision was the Jungian idea of the true inner self projecting its wound on to a false self embodied in an external hate figure:

> The actual process of individuation – the conscious coming-to-terms with one's inner centre (psychic nucleus) or Self – generally begins with a wounding of personality, and the suffering that accompanies it. This initial shock amounts to a sort of call, although it is often not recognised as such. On the contrary, the ego feels hampered in its will or desire and usually projects the obstruction onto something external. That is, the ego accuses God, the economic situation, or the boss, or the marriage partner of being responsible for whatever is obstructing it.[9]

The notion that the oppressive male figures in Sylvia's poetry were not so much Otto Plath and Ted Hughes as mythic archetypes, and that the speaker of her poems was more White Goddess than Aurelia Plath's daughter, promised to swing interpretation away from the biographical line that had been created by the influential early reviews of *Ariel* and above all by *The Bell Jar*. On the basis of Judith Kroll's doctoral dissertation, Ted and Olwyn had decided that she was the right person to help with the daunting task of preparing a scholarly edition of Sylvia's complete poems.

She stayed for several weeks. Ted discussed Plath's work in detail with her, showed her books that he and Sylvia had shared and even seems to have given her information, presumably derived from the lost last journal, that there was some kind of religious dimension to the crisis in the final weeks of her life.[10] And they started work on Sylvia's manuscript drafts, beginning by seeking to put all her surviving poems in chronological order, a task upon which – as was clear from his contribution to *The Art of Sylvia Plath* – Ted had been engaged for many years. In time, though, it became clear that Kroll's strong suit was critical interpretation, not the minutiae of textual bibliography and the investigation of manuscript drafts. Ted completed his work on the collected poems alone.

The second visitor in the summer of 1974 was Fran McCullough, who was preparing Aurelia's edition of the letters for Harper and Row in New York. Ted proposed various cuts, some in the interest of economy, others in that of privacy. McCullough relished her time at Court Green. Ted did not. He wrote in his journal of her paleness and 'monotone stillness', unflatteringly seeing in her 'Something resembling Sylvia as a zombie'.[11] After her departure, Ted continued wrangling with both her and Aurelia about what should and what should not be included. The process took a full further year. In January 1975, for example, Ted sent Aurelia one of many long lists of 'Notes for final cuts to letters'.

This document survives. Even as it proposed substantial cuts, it provided all sorts of fascinating biographical material not available elsewhere. Ted mentioned in passing that the true nature of his marriage to Sylvia would be revealed only 'when somebody produced her journals of the time and mine' – 'That could well be a long time coming,' he adds, but it is intriguing to overhear him mentioning that he kept a journal. Again, he revealed what she was reading at the time of her death: she was halfway through a re-reading of A. E. Ellis's *The Rack*, an extremely depressing book about the suicide of a young man in a tuberculosis sanatorium. Ted did not mention that it was published by Heinemann and edited by James Michie, who was also the in-house editor responsible for *The Colossus* and *The Bell Jar*. He went on to disagree with many of Aurelia's interpretations. 'Next point: "renouncing the subservient female role" sounds strange to me. One thing she never was, as I believe you know, was subservient.' Sylvia would never have allowed her cookery and homemaking to be described as 'subservient': 'She was "Laurentian" [*sic*], not "woman's lib".' And what on earth was this about her drying the dinner plates with her own 'dense hair'? 'As you probably remember, the washing up in our establishment was generally done by me, until maybe the last month of two.'[12]

The notes also suggest that Sylvia was exaggerating when she talked of snowdrifts 20 feet deep in the winter of 1962. He recalls the occasion when he drove down from London and back in a day in order to stock her up with home-grown potatoes and apples and two strings of their onions: yes, it had been snowing, but there were thousands of cars on the road. He also mentioned that in London in her final weeks she was not as lonely as some of her letters home made out: he visited her every other night and several times during the day and sometimes spent two or three evenings in succession in her company. When she wasn't seeing him, she was usually seeing somebody else.

Letters Home: Correspondence 1950–1963, 'selected and edited with commentary by Aurelia Schober Plath', was finally published in late 1975. The following year, it was reviewed in the *New York Review of Books* by Ted's Cambridge contemporary Karl Miller. His review essay, under the editorial title 'Sylvia Plath's Apotheosis', treated the letters alongside *Chapters in a Mythology: The Poetry of Sylvia Plath*, the book of Judith Kroll's thesis, and a biography by Edward Butscher called *Sylvia Plath: Method and Madness*. Like many an *NYRB* review, Miller's piece provoked some lively correspondence. A feminist writer called Mary Folliet had written a Morgan-influenced poem about Plath called 'Ten Years Cold'. She complained that Miller had quoted, as an example of the sort of thing Ted now had to put up with, her line 'Hughes has one more gassed out life on his mind.'[13] Olwyn also weighed in. She made some remarks about 'the lunatic fringe of Women's Lib', but what was really on her mind was the biography.

She explained that in 1969 Ted had signed the agreement with Lois Ames that appointed her Sylvia's official biographer. The contract stipulated delivery by 1975 and Ted had offered her exclusive assistance until 1977. Ames had been Ted's third Sylvia-researching visitor at Court Green in the summer of 1974. There had been a lot of talk about the journals, but very little progress towards the book. Olwyn pointed out in her *NYRB* letter that as a result of the exclusivity agreement, she had been unable to help Edward Butscher with his biography other than to correct the most egregious of his numerous factual errors. She had been unable to do anything about what she regarded as his naive belief in the inventions and exaggerations of unreliable witnesses, his 'outrageously dramatized versions of events' and his 'novelettishly sensationalized' portraits of just about everyone in Sylvia's life. She suggested that it was time for Lois Ames to throw in the towel and let someone else write 'a properly researched biography of Sylvia'.[14]

At the end of 1976, Ted told Dan Huws that he was having to waste so much time and emotional energy on this plethora of new Plath books that he was seriously considering getting the whole story of his first marriage off his chest by publishing his own account.[15] The first thing to do, though, was to publish the primary materials, so that readers did not have to rely on the second-hand and distorted perspective of biographers and critics. His selection of her short stories, under the title *Johnny Panic and the Bible of Dreams*, appeared in 1977. Four years later, his edition of the *Collected Poems* was finally published. There are few precedents – only Mary Shelley springs immediately to mind – for a creative artist taking on the academic role of textual editor of their dead spouse's works. The combination of personal knowledge and patient scholarship enabled Hughes to complete his arrangement of Plath's poems in chronological order. To the chagrin of some feminists, he took it upon himself to relegate her early work to the status of 'juvenilia', beginning the run of her mature poems in 1956 – the year of their first encounter at Falcon Yard. By Hughes's reckoning, Plath wrote 224 poems between 1956 and her death, her breakthrough into that uniqueness of voice which constitutes poetic greatness coming with the seven-part 'Poem for a Birthday' composed in late 1959 while they were in residence at Yaddo. The title of *Birthday Letters* is, among other things, a tribute to this turning point in Plath's career.

The year after *Collected Poems* came *The Journals of Sylvia Plath*, for which he was credited as consulting editor, along with Frances McCullough, and to which he contributed a brief foreword. He struggled to complete it, knowing it would be an important piece of work that would begin to reveal her poetry as 'the X-ray record of the history of a purely impersonal process', something akin to the paintings produced by Jung's psychiatric patients.[16] His foreword duly explained that, although he had been with her for six years 'and was rarely separated from her for more than two or three hours at a time', he never saw Sylvia 'show her real self to anybody – except, perhaps, in the last three months of her life'. That real self began to speak in her poetry at a moment in Yaddo when she 'recited three lines as she went through a doorway'. From that point on, she would 'throw off the artificial selves' of her earlier verse: 'It was as if a dumb person suddenly spoke.'

He developed this claim in a longer version of the foreword, published in his friend Ben Sonnenberg's magazine *Grand Street* contemporaneously with the appearance of the journals. Here he outlined his own version of the Judith Kroll argument about Sylvia's 'death–rebirth' cycle. His essay came to the conclusion that all her poems were in a sense 'by-products' of her 'real creation', which was 'that inner gestation and eventual birth of a new self-conquering self, to which her journal bears witness, and which proved itself so overwhelmingly in the *Ariel* poems of 1962'.[17]

But it was the end of the foreword that attracted the attention of Hughes's accusers. Ted explained that Sylvia's journals consisted of 'an assortment of notebooks and bunches of loose sheets'. His selection consisted of about one-third of the total sum of the manuscripts, which were held at Smith College. But two notebooks were absent from that collection. They were 'maroon-backed ledgers' similar to a surviving volume that covered 1957–9. They 'continued the record from late '59 to within three days of her death'. The first of them had 'disappeared'. The second contained entries for the final months of her life, 'and I destroyed it because I did not want her children to have to read it (in those days I regarded forgetfulness as an essential part of survival)'.[18] For anti-Hughesians this was another devastating indictment to add to the charge sheet: he had burnt the vital clue, destroyed the evidence, silenced Sylvia even as she was in the grave.

What was more, the edition was incomplete. There were extensive cuts, and two notebooks from the period August 1957 to November 1959 were excluded. It was Hughes's intention to keep them sealed until the fiftieth anniversary of Plath's death, probably because they contained such dark matter as some disturbing matricidal notes from the time of her psychoanalysis. As it was, he relented at the time of *Birthday Letters* and the unabridged journals were published just over a year after his death.

Soon after Edward Butscher had published *Method and Madness*, that first biography of Sylvia, he threw together a collection of essays entitled *Sylvia Plath: The Woman and the Work*. It included critical essays on her poetry, including distinguished work by the critic Marjorie Perloff and the novelist Joyce Carol Oates, together with a number of memoirs by people he had interviewed during his research for the

biography – lover Gordon Lameyer, fellow-*Mademoiselle* intern Laurie
Levy, Cambridge supervisor Dorothea Krook, fellow-Whitstead resi-
dent Jane Baltzell Kopp, and friends from later years, Clarissa Roche
and Elizabeth Compton (now Sigmund). It was a line-up that
entrenched the Plath narrative: carefree Smith girl with boyfriends
aplenty, crack-up following the New York summer, scholarship student
at Cambridge, deserted wife and mother in the bitter winter of
1962–3.

The thesis of the collection was that Plath was a writer in whom
there was a peculiarly close connection between the woman and the
work. 'Indeed', wrote Butscher in his preface, a little dramatically, 'a
poet's life and art have never appeared so intimately related before,
with the possible exception of Edgar Allan Poe's own horror tale.'[19]
The prize exhibit in support of this argument came from Gordon
Lameyer, who contributed not only his memoir but also an analytic
essay entitled 'The Double in Sylvia's Plath *The Bell Jar*'. The latter
began by noting the prevalence of mirrors and 'doubles' – psycholog-
ical projections of some aspect of the speaker – in Plath's poetry.
Picking up on Plath's own explanation, in her BBC interview, that the
poem 'Daddy' was to be imagined in the voice of a girl with an Electra
complex, Lameyer suggested that it was indeed 'spoken by the author's
evil double, resenting her father's death and consequent loss of love'.
He linked this idea to 'The Magic Mirror', Sylvia's 1954 Smith College
senior honours' thesis on the figure of the double in Dostoevsky, most
notably 'in the great study of parricide, *The Brothers Karamazov*'.
Dostoevsky's fiction, Lameyer suggested, gave Plath 'a deeper under-
standing of her own nervous breakdown, attempted suicide, and
recuperation' than she achieved from 'her limited psychoanalysis
at McLean'.[20] Lameyer's perceptive analysis of Plath's reading of
Dostoevsky provided a springboard into *The Bell Jar*, itself a novel full
of doubles. Towards the end of the essay, he referred to the biograph-
ical 'original' of one of them:

> The terrible irony of *The Bell Jar* is that the original of Joan
> Gilling, the double that Sylvia kills off so that Esther can live, is
> very much alive, and that it is Sylvia who has been successful in
> killing herself … The girl whom Sylvia knew in Wellesley and at
> Smith College and whom she felt had followed her to McLean

is actually very unlike the Joan Gilling who has lesbian leanings toward another inmate. In fact, Sylvia very much admired and liked the original girl. Was Sylvia, then, projecting her deepest fears onto the double of her heroine?[21]

Lameyer then stopped to think. Clearly there was a very strong case for the argument that one of those deep fears – the will to suicide – was a projection, that Joan's success in hanging herself was a proxy for Esther/Sylvia's failed suicide attempt. But, he asked himself, were the 'lesbian leanings' also a projection? His conclusion was that 'Sylvia was trying to free herself from certain negative attitudes that she recognized within herself, puritanical attitudes … which she projected in a perversion of sexual purity upon her double.' But then he hastened to inform the reader that this projection did not have a biographical origin:

> I knew her too well at the time of the incidents related in *The Bell Jar* ever to conclude that she had lesbian tendencies. Aside from the original of Buddy Willard, I am the only person, I believe, who has ever dated both Sylvia and the original of Joan Gilling. Although certainly neither girl was inclined towards lesbianism, Sylvia understood enough of the love–hate duality of rivals to suggest this characteristic in her artistic double.[22]

This is a very unusual moment in the history of literary analysis: the critic substantiates his argument on the grounds that he must be right since he has dated the two central female characters in the book he is writing about. In addition, Lameyer let slip the information that Dick Norton, the original of Buddy Willard, also dated both Sylvia and the original of Joan Gilling. The sharing not only of residential treatment at McLean but also of two boyfriends did indeed suggest that the two women were 'doubles'.

Just over a year after the publication of this essay, Avco Embassy Pictures released their film adaptation of *The Bell Jar*. It received dismal reviews, but had enough life to become a videocassette and to be shown on television. The screenplay took a fair a number of liberties with the novel. Plath's rigorously autobiographical account of the overdose and the crawl space beneath the deck of the family home were turned into a woozy dance in the basement followed by a collapse on the floor. And, in keeping with the tawdriness of late Seventies Hollywood, the novel's unrealised hints of lesbian desire in the character of Joan Gilling were fleshed into a scene where Joan kisses Esther's breasts as they kneel together in a field. She begs her friend to join her in a lovers' suicide pact, and it is Esther's rejection of this proposal that leads her to hang herself from a tree.

The 'very much alive' original of Joan Gilling was Jane Anderson. Like Sylvia, she was born in Wellesley. As girls, they went to the same junior high school and the same church. They both went to Smith. They both had intense relationships with Dick Norton as well as dating Gordon Lameyer. They both had complicated relationships with their fathers, though Sylvia's father was dead and Jane's alive. And they were fellow-inmates at McLean. Here, though, their paths diverged. Electro-convulsive therapy was remarkably effective for Sylvia, leading to her rapid discharge from the hospital, whereas Anderson was sucked in by the talking cure. She chastised Sylvia for not taking psychoanalysis seriously enough and she eventually became a psychoanalyst herself, engaging in private practice and teaching at Harvard. The explicitly lesbian scene in the film of *The Bell Jar* came as a shock to her. She began reading around the subject and alighted upon Lameyer's essay. In due course she would file a lawsuit that would engulf Ted Hughes.

22

Sunstruck Foxglove

In March 1976, just weeks after Jack Orchard died from cancer aged fifty-nine, Ted flew to Australia. He had been invited to the Antipodes' foremost literary gathering, the Adelaide Festival. With his father-in-law gone, it was an opportunity to take his own father to see brother Gerald. He rather hoped that Bill might stay on for a few months with Gerald and Joan, to relieve the pressure at home.

The trip proved to be another turning point in Ted's life. As on many occasions when he was travelling, he kept a more systematic journal than usual. After a stupefying train journey with watery food under a March sun, a wait at Reading station and a dreary taxi ride, he and his father arrived at Heathrow. They had asked for a seat with extra leg-room, so found themselves at the front by the toilets, which proved disruptive but sometimes amusing. Bill Hughes, who had never flown long haul before, was amazed at the size of the plane's wings. They stopped to refuel in the desert landscape of Bahrain where some 'incredibly black small ugly Arabs' came aboard to clean the plane.[1] They stopped again in Singapore, brilliantly lit and gaudy, a 'sinful Eastern city' with an unutterably boring airport, where the only relief in the hot wet air was the sight of 'Pretty Waitresses everywhere – Indonesians, Malays etc.' Then in a dazzling dawn they found themselves above the landmass of Australia, looking down on mountain forests, scattered homesteads, a tangle of dirt roads and periodic water-holes.

They arrived in a daze at Gerald and Joan's neat home in Tullamarine near Melbourne. Ted admired his brother's Japanese sword carefully stowed in a steel box in his den. He had earache from the flight. Then they were shown a telegram with more bad news: while they had been in the air, Uncle Walt had died. Walt, the patriarch of the family, in

many ways more of a father to Ted than his own father – memories of
that first journey abroad and of the visit to Top Withens with Sylvia.
To have been absent at the time of his death felt like another manifes-
tation of the curse upon Ted's life.

Later, from Gerald and Joan's seaside second home overlooking
miles of empty beach on the Mornington peninsula, they managed to
phone Aunt Hilda: Walt had eaten nothing for three weeks, then
finally asked for a bottle of whisky, which he drank through the night
in the front room while Hilda slept upstairs. When she came down in
the morning he was dead on the living-room floor, having laid himself
out with arms folded.

They reminisced and drank cold Australian beer. Ted peeled some
bark from an ancient gum tree as a keepsake of his visit, while Gerald
carved the name of his house on an ancient piece of tea-tree wood.[2]
Ted asked if there were foxes and Gerald showed him snake tracks. For
a fleeting moment, they were two boys in the wild once more. Then
Gerald drove his brother to the airport and Ted took a little plane to
Adelaide.

He liked the cleanness of the city, the lazy and innocent atmos-
phere, the extraordinary bird cries. Walking through empty streets and
parks in the early morning, he saw quail-crested doves, a grey-brown
and yellow thrush-like bird with a 'rear-eye corner like Groucho
Marx', budgerigars taking flight, and 'the giant rubber trees like acro-
batic elephants copulating'. Above all, the heat: being down under, he
did not have to wait for July to sense the transit of the sun into the
sign of his Muse. Something was stirring.

Fellow-poet Adrian Mitchell, who had been on the same plane
from London, had arrived in Adelaide a day before Ted, the time
agreed with the festival organisers. He was met at the airport by a
vivacious press officer in a white limousine with green-tinted
windows, hired to impress the visiting writers. Mitchell told her that
Hughes would be arriving the next day, since he was staying with his
brother in Melbourne. She thought that it was cheeky of him not to
arrive at the appointed hour, so she made a point of not fetching him
from the airport. Ted challenged her over this when he was standing
in the drinks queue at a barbecue hosted by the Writers' Week
Committee, sweltering in his heavy leather jacket. She said that she
would make it up to him by bringing him wine straight away. She

brought him four glasses, each with a different vintage. Telling him that he could not drink four glasses at once, she motioned to him to sit, where she joined him, unworried about the prospect of grass stains on her starched antique white dress. He asked her how she knew that he was a wine buff and she replied that she was psychic. He liked this.[3] Her name was Jill Barber.

The following day, she met him at the Hotel Australia in her role as press officer. She was discomposed when they were forced to confront a crowd of anti-Hughes 'libbers' bearing placards, so he let her rest in his room. That evening, at the gala opening of the festival, they drank champagne and left early. Jill tipsily drove the limousine over a cement bollard in the parking lot and Ted let himself go in raucous laughter. Back at the hotel, he mopped her brow with a wet flannel as she threw up the cheap champagne into his sink, then he tenderly unbuttoned and unzipped her, gazed admiringly at her body and made forceful love to her. He told her that she reminded him of a woman whom he had loved very much. The night after he made love to her, he had a strange dream in which he was taking the caps off the poison chimneys at Auschwitz.[4]

It was a heady week. Soon after his arrival, he had sat under the trees in 40-degree heat being interviewed by a female journalist in company with Don Dunstan, the premier of South Australia and a great contributor to the local arts scene. They talked about the importance of poetry, the joy of writing for children, the neglect of Zbigniew Herbert ('the greatest poet in the world', Ted affirmed), the high quality of contemporary Australian verse and finally the subject about which he was always reluctant to speak in public: Sylvia. Amid awkward pauses, his replies were terse:

Interviewer: Was it in [pause] comparative with your writing, sometimes better than your writing do you think?

Hughes: She was [pause] I think she was an extraordinary genius. But then I always thought that. And [pause] I don't think there's anybody like her [pause] like [pause] Those last poems are something unique in English literature.

Interviewer: Is it very difficult, the relationship of a creative man like you and a genius person like her?

Hughes: No.
Interviewer: Can you give to each other? I mean [tails off]
Hughes: Sure.
Interviewer: Did she have any great influence on you?
Hughes: Must have done.
Interviewer: You're not aware of it though?
Hughes: Not specifically. I might even have influenced her.[5]

Later, the same interviewer, Claudia Wright, spoke to Hughes at length in the studio, where he also read some of his poems for broadcast. He told of how he lived as a writer but how when that became too exhausting he took up farming simply in order to get away from dependence on writing. He was, however, still 'completely dependent on writing'. For what, she asked? 'Dependent for sanity,' he replied, before explaining that having another occupation meant that he was not entirely financially dependent on his words: 'You know that at the last crunch, you can eat a sheep, or you can kill a bullock, or [pause]. And besides, these beautiful animals occupy your whole time, or your thoughts. And the literary world fades away.' As ever, he was caught between the rural and the literary world. The conversation then turned to *Crow*. Wright waxed lyrical: 'half the beauty of listening to your poetry is watching you, your body and your hands and your face move with all the rhythms of the words'.

She drew him towards the poem 'Lovesong' and he explained that Crow voices 'dilemma questions, and they're all questions referring to his encounter with this – these females. So, they're all questions about a man and woman. They're questions about love.' The atmosphere in the studio became charged as the interview was interspersed with folk songs in the gorgeous voice of Hughes's admired Maddy Prior. 'Could you read something for me please?' asked Wright. 'I'll read you a rural poem, a little poem,' he replied. 'For a country girl,' she said, laughing.[6] After the interview they slept together.

Some of the big names had dropped out of the festival at the last minute, so Ted and Adrian Mitchell found themselves standing in for the legendary American writers Tennessee Williams and James Baldwin in a large sold-out lecture hall. The usual 'libbers' were in attendance. 'How is Sylvia Plath?' one woman asked. 'She's dead,' he replied. He read fifteen poems, including such favourites as 'The Thought-Fox' and 'Full Moon and Little Frieda' ('This is just a description of a little girl – a two-year-old girl – looking at a full moon. And "moon" being one of her first words – so she being very excited to use these words').[7] He then elaborated at his customary length on the meaning of the Crow narrative.

At the festival he was taken up by a group of young Australian poets. One in particular seemed to him a genuine talent. A. E. Housman once said that the mark of a true poem was that it would raise the bristles on a man's face, and Ted thought something similar about this young woman's work: it made his hair stand up. But the electricity also came from her beauty. She had an unusual face and the most haunting eyes he had ever seen.[8] In a letter to Richard Murphy, he remarked that she lived on a farm with a man who was quite a good poet – actually they lived in a suburb of Melbourne but had a retreat with a bush hut on it at Yerrinbool near Mittagong in the Southern Highlands. And though the husband was indeed a poet, he was, more significantly, one of Australia's finest painters, David Rankin.[9] Jennifer, the poet, was a free spirit, already on her second marriage and with a volume of verse called *Ritual Shift* about to be published. The Rankins were planning to travel to England. When they discovered that Ted lived in Devon, where David had been born, they asked him to arrange accommodation for them. He offered them his cottage on the farm at Moortown. The rumour around the festival was that the offer was made because an affair with Jennifer had already begun.

Bill Hughes did stay on with Gerald for a few weeks. Ted flew back via Perth, where he called Jill Barber from an airport payphone and said that he had fallen in love with her. Jack Orchard's death had released him from the self-imposed role of loyal son-in-law, faithful husband and toiling farmer. His psychological state, 'a close mesh of uncontrollable peculiarities and psychosomatic upsets', was in transition.[10] As the discovery of the poetic genre of *vacana* opened the way for the *Gaudete* epilogue poems, so the trip to Australia helped to unlock not only a new directness in his poetry but also a new freedom in his personal life.

*

Jill Barber flew to London. She stayed with friends in Putney. Timothy Dalton, a future James Bond, was also staying; Jill recalled that he liked her to see him wearing nothing but a towel. She moved on when renovations were complete in the flat that she had bought on the Fulham Road. As soon as he could escape from the country, Ted came to see her. He bundled her into his battered old Volvo and drove to Olwyn's house in Tufnell Park. There was some pretext about Jill having a contact with a potential Japanese purchaser for some of his manuscripts. But Olwyn immediately realised that she was meeting a new girlfriend. The awkward fact of Ted's marriage, which he had not previously mentioned, made itself apparent during this visit. Jill liked Olwyn and saw that she was Ted's London protector, as Carol was his protector in Devon: 'As for me, I was his ray of sunshine. He would carve up his life, half for me, maybe more than half in the beginning.' By Jill's account, Ted's excuse for falling in love with her was that his existence in Devon filled him with 'black electricity' and that his farm life was at odds with his literary and his 'inner' life.

Their love affair lasted for four years, intense in the first two, cooler thereafter. Jill was mesmerised by 'his feline eyes, deft hands and fabulous laugh', by the way that he listened intently to everything and 'could make people feel as if they had never lived before they met him'. He listened and heard everything. But she insists that she eventually broke off the relationship because she wanted a child before it was too late, and realised that Ted would never give her one. He had not been happy on the one occasion when she had a pregnancy scare.

In London, he did not keep the affair secret; to many of his friends, Jill's positive Antipodean energy was contagious. Like any other couple, they went to parties and literary events together. He helped her with contacts for the little magazine called *Mars* on which she was working as assistant editor. She was smart, sassy and quick-witted, but did not pretend to be an intellectual. She was very good at taking Ted out of his black moods and gently teasing his pretensions (though she shared his belief in a spirit world). They loved cooking and wine and laughter. Photographs taken in her flat show an exceptionally relaxed and happy Ted. He also became very close to her flatmate, a beautiful blonde American model and actress called Barbara Trentham, who later married John Cleese. Long evenings with two young women in a London flat inevitably reminded him of those few heady long-lost weeks with Sue Alliston and Tasha Hollis, both now so tragically dead.

Ted wrote some touching, if brief, love letters to Jill, but there are no references to her in the unrestricted pages of his journals, so we have only her account of what she meant to him. She loved to go barefoot and he called her his 'Gypsy Girl', giving her symbolic presents such as Egyptian beads. He liked making love to her out of doors, once on Dartmoor uncomfortably on a rock where, according to legend, consummation led to eternal union, another time under a hedgerow while they were on a northern motoring tour in Northumberland. He was serious enough about her to take her to Sylvia's grave at Heptonstall and to invite her to accompany him on fishing trips in Ireland.

The purpose of one of the Irish trips was for her to get to know the teenage Nick, who was uncomfortable around the woman who was obviously his father's girlfriend, though there was a glorious moment on 27 October 1977 when he caught a 24½-pound pike in Castle Lake, near Sixmilebridge, County Clare. Ted noted in his journal that this was a special day because it was Nick's mother's birthday. Sylvia would have been forty-five.

There was laughter on the holiday. Ted wrote in his journal about a redoubtable woman who would not let them fish in her lake. 'A fish can't piss in her lake but she knows about it,' said Jill.[11] She always saw the best in Ted, but did not approve when he left Nick alone in their tent while he came inside to make love to her in the bed-and-breakfast where she was staying. She was always conscious of the extreme vigour of his lovemaking ('He would walk through my front door after four-and-a-half hours in the car and want to have me on the floor of the hallway there and then'). For a time, she liked it when they fought. 'I was thrilled when he told me after one argument: "You're a bigger bitch than Sylvia."'[12]

When they first met, he complained to her, showing farm-calloused hands branded as if with stigmata, that he was suffering from writer's block and had written little of value since Assia's death. He sometimes called her his Muse and at a party he introduced her thus to no less a figure than Robert Graves, author of *The White Goddess*. He gave her each new book as it appeared. In her copy of *Season Songs*, he stuck an adhesive address label over the printed dedication 'FOR

CAROL', inscribed it by hand to her instead, describing her as his birthday beauty and calling her by the nickname 'Jillipops'. One or two London friends reckoned that Jill had Ted under her thumb. She did not seem to be in awe of him in the manner of a groupie. His letters to her are a mix of affection and playfulness. In one of them, he told her that he felt as if she had woken him up from a seven-year sleep. He then narrated two of his dreams. In one of them, he cast for a salmon and King Edward I (King Salmon as King Ted?) rose up from the riverbed and took him into his library. In the second dream, Jill made him laugh so much that she became angry and tried to drown herself in a bath of white wine, then emerged drunk to show him an Australian stone covered with hieroglyphics, which he sensed held the secret of his life, and she gave him the stone on condition that he treated her respectfully. He signed off the letter by saying how much he was missing kissing her ears.

Her part in his increased productivity in the late Seventies was perhaps less to do with her being an authentic Gravesian White Goddess than with her ability to relax him, to remove his inhibitions about revealing himself and having fun. Ted fell in love with places as much as women – Sylvia as embodiment of America, Brenda and Carol of Devon – and in this respect Jill the free spirit was the incarnation of the light and warmth, the youthful 'laid-back' atmosphere, of Australia.

Was Jill Barber a Muse in any profound sense? A lyric called 'Sunstruck Foxglove' begins with the speaker bending to touch a 'gypsy girl' who is waiting for him in a hedge. 'Her loose dress falls open', revealing 'the reptile under-speckle / Of her sunburned breasts'. She is 'Flushed, freckled with earth-fever, / Swollen lips parted, her eyes closing'. His head swims and they come together in the heat.[13] Allusions to origin, maternity and fecundity mark this as a White Goddess poem, but in the light of the nickname Gypsy Girl and the fact that Jill was notable for her freckles, there must also be a conscious or unconscious memory here of that afternoon of summer loving beneath a Northumberland hedge. This one poem at least belongs to her, and she was rather pleased when, many years after the end of the affair, the cover design for *New Selected Poems 1957–1994* was based upon a voluptuous image of a foxglove.

★

As agreed during the Adelaide Festival, Jennifer and David Rankin came to Devon. They spent their first night at Court Green. Ted told their young son that there was a ghost in the room where he was going to sleep. As always, he was wonderful with the children. Jennifer especially remembered a stormy winter's evening when they were all sitting around eating fish and chips out of newspaper. There was a lull in the conversation. Ted then turned to her daughter. 'Jessica, you are 5?' 'Yes.' 'Tell me something,' continued Ted. 'Can you remember when you were 3?' 'Of course,' said Jessica, disdainfully. 'Well!' said Ted, feverishly, almost on his hands and knees beside her. 'Then tell me! What was it like?!'[14]

The Rankins stayed all winter in a cottage rented to them by a friend of Ted's. Jill joined them there for Christmas. Jennifer and David remained in Devon, with time out for several trips to Europe, until the following autumn. David used a shed for a studio and took charge of the childcare, leaving Jennifer free to concentrate on her poetry. She also did a little tuition for Arvon on poetry weekends at Totleigh Barton. Their time in Devon was all about her – and Ted. Crucially, he helped her to find an English publisher. Her collection *Earth Hold* was placed towards the end of their stay. It was initially accepted by Chatto and Windus, but then the established poet D. J. Enright came along with a new manuscript and Jennifer's book, the newest on the list, was bumped off it. 'Great calamity-scenes', remembered a friend who was visiting them at the time. Then, on Ted's recommendation, Secker and Warburg took the poems. It was also his idea to pull off a Hughes–Baskin-type trick: admired Australian painter John Olsen was persuaded to provide illustrations, creating a large-format book that could make a splash. It duly appeared in 1978, with a puff from Ted praising it for introducing 'a new note' into English poetry, 'the note that tunes us in, somehow, to the bedrock of the ancient Australian landmass – that eerie, powerful presence which silences both aboriginal and white man'.[15]

He frequently visited the cottage and his relationship with Jennifer blossomed over poetry, laughter and clifftop walks around the Hartland peninsula. In her 'North Devon poem', unpublished in her lifetime, a charismatic, earth-holding Ted-like man kneels at the open door of the stove in the cottage and teaches her about coal-fires, 'His eyes / sudden pieces of sky in this winter kitchen'.[16]

In the year that *Earth Hold* was published in London, Jennifer, now back in Australia, was diagnosed with breast cancer. She was ravaged by intensive chemotherapy and died in early December 1979, a few days after her thirty-eighth birthday. During her illness, Ted wrote her many tender, moving letters.[17] After her death, he remembered her in a series of elegies in scattered publications, uncollected in his lifetime. In one she is a waif standing on the shore against the Pacific surf. In another she is lovesick: 'You barely touched the earth. You lived for love. / How many loves did you have?' And in the third, she is a lover of the desert, taken all too soon by 'boundless Tao'.[18] But his finest poem for her never appeared in print. It exists in ten manuscript drafts under the title 'For Jennifer, nothing has changed'. Here he remembers her on the Hartland cliffs by the 'insatiable Atlantic', then reflects on the utter loneliness of terminal illness, where even her poems seem to have deserted her, to have become survivors who are oddly reticent about the creator from whom they have turned away. For Jennifer herself, nothing has changed, but for Ted, and the others who have loved her, 'only one thing' had changed: the 'space' that she 'electrified' inside their heads. It had become 'a dark theatre', where her eyes, 'no longer interested in an audience', 'Brilliant, grave, silent heroines, alone', kept on 'rehearsing' everything that she was going through in her 'final days'.[19]

In September 1982, when Ted spent a week at the Hilton Hotel in Toronto, during the city's Harbourfront literary festival, the Australian poet and critic Judith Rodriguez met him on his way to an elevator after a session. 'I believe you knew Jennifer Rankin,' she found herself saying. 'What sort of person was she?' He looked at her balefully, said that 'She was the most nervous woman I have ever known,' and stepped into the lift.

Journalist and novelist the Honourable Emma Tennant, daughter of the second Baron Glenconner, was educated at St Paul's Girls' School, with childhood memories of the family's Gothic pile in the Scottish countryside. She had two marriages, both to writers, behind her. She had worked as a travel writer, been an assistant editor at *Vogue* and established herself as a novelist. In 1975, she launched a magazine called *Bananas*, attracting both new talent and established writers such as the great dystopian chronicler of modern times J. G. Ballard. At exactly the time Ted began his affair with Jill Barber, she called on Olwyn in the hope of getting some Hughes or even Plath material for the magazine. Her memoir *Burnt Diaries* offers a vivid picture of Olwyn and her terraced house in Chetwynd Road: the tall woman, once strikingly handsome, 'with her long, Spanish-looking face and quick flashes of charm under a harassed exterior'; the cluttered 'office' at the back of the house with 'raw materials of the Private Edition business', 'volumes of Plath and Hughes poems in slender tomes with names like Rainbow', 'sheaths [sheafs?] of thin paper looking desperately in need of salvaging', 'bills, some months old, for electricity and gas'.[20] Olwyn gave her an unpublished Plath short story called 'Day of Success'.

Some months later, there was a ring on the doorbell of Emma's house in Elgin Crescent, Notting Hill, in the small hours of the morning. It was her friend, the poet, biographer and translator Elaine Feinstein. 'Yevtushenko and Ted Hughes are here, can we come in for a drink?' They all sat on the floor while Yevgeny Yevtushenko beat out the rhythms of the poetry of the legendary Marina Tsvetaeva (which Feinstein had been translating). Ted was subdued, happy to prowl on the margin of the conversation. Soon afterwards, he and Emma met for a second time, at a party. As if in imitation of Sylvia at Falcon Yard, she forced a reluctant Ted to gyrate, despite his gruff claim 'I can't dance.' 'You're a fantastic woman,' he shouted over the music, before he was whisked away by his female entourage. Tennant clocked the presence of Jill Barber and sensed the younger woman's proprietorial aura.

She and Feinstein were then invited to teach on a weekend Arvon course down in Devon, where she registered the sweetness, loveliness and youth of Carol. Yevtushenko, who was staying at Court Green, picked them up and drove them over for Sunday lunch. Broad planks were propped up in the cobbled yard outside the thatched house, resembling up-ended coffins. 'I could make you a table, if you like,' said Ted, 'a work-table.' This was another echo of his life with Sylvia: the elm plank which he and Warren had made for her when they first moved to Court Green and which in Ted's imagination merged with the elm of her coffin as it was lowered into her Heptonstall grave. Emma Tennant left with a copy of Ted's Pilinszky translations, marked with a personal inscription in his 'black, barbed-wire handwriting'.

In the summer of 1977, now a year into his relationship with Jill, he invited Emma to lunch at Julie's Bar in Notting Hill. At the very least, she was hoping for a poem or story for *Bananas*. Alone with him for the first time, she found him magnificent. His face, 'like an Easter Island statue', seemed to dominate the room, as 'anger, certainty and pride' gave 'an unchanging air to his features' while, 'as if unwilled by himself, a smile, thin and nervous' played on his lips. He launched into tales of his 'love disasters': his being reported to the police following the M1 sex murder, the time he ran over a hare on the way to a girl-friend's house, picked up the body and read the future from its entrails in the girl's kitchen. He mesmerised her with his stories, including one about a woman who had taught him 'how to make the hairs on a person's neck stand up even if they are miles away'. Then they went to look at the peacocks strutting in Holland Park before going to his flat in Fortess Road, where they made love, unsatisfactorily. She was surprised by the paleness of his body.

Afterwards, he drove her back to Notting Hill. They passed the mansion block on Baker Street where Sue Alliston once had a flat: 'I knew a pretty woman of forty who lived there,' he said. 'She died.' When he dropped her off, he asked her if she knew of the habits of the greylag goose. 'They are faithful to their first mate, I may be,' he said, hesitating a moment, 'I may, after all, be a greylag goose.'

All these details are from Tennant's memoir *Burnt Diaries*. As a care-fully contrived work by a novelist, it is shaped with a degree of artistic licence. Did Ted really say 'I want you for no more than a year' before their second assignation (rougher and much more satisfying, she recalled), this time in a hotel in Bayswater? Did Emma really think of herself at the time as a 'sub-mistress', or was that witty term invented retrospectively in the act of writing the memoir? There is no reason to doubt, though, that he was more than half serious in proposing that they should go off together to Scotland – even as far as the Hebrides. As a scion of the Scottish aristocracy, the Honourable Emma was another person who embodied a place, in this instance a wild land-scape with fresh air and great fishing, far from the stultifying stuffiness of Anglo-Saxon society and the gossipy backbiting of literary London. This remained one of his unfulfilled dreams of a different life, another Frostian road not taken. He sent sporadic postcards between long silences as he visited schools to enthuse children about poetry, was knocked out with the flu on a trip to Paris, and went backwards and forwards between Devon and London. They occasionally met up again, but the sexual relationship petered out before it really got going.

Emma could never claim, as Jill did, that she effectively lived with Ted during his time in London in the late 'Seventies. As a writer, though, she was able to turn each meeting with him into vivid anecdote and imagery. His flat in Fortess Road, where they made love for the first time, is starkly drawn: furnished only with a Fifties-style basket chair, a large bed with rumpled sheets and 'piles of typescripts and notebooks everywhere, floor, chair and bed'. The seedy hotel room in Bayswater where they go for the second assignation has a 'pink nylon frilly lampshade on the mock-mahogany bedside table'. She alleges that in Regent's Park he once put his hands tightly round her neck, the gleam of the rabbit-catcher in his eye. She records that he never wanted to talk about Sylvia, but once when they saw a child with a baby fox on a lead in the park, he told of the incident on Chalk Farm Bridge. Again, on an autumn evening he looked out of the window, saw a girl walking past and said that she looked how Shura would have looked then, had she lived. Passing Sue Alliston's flat a second time, he said, 'All the women I have anything to do with seem to die.'

Ted was indeed superstitious in this regard, believing that any lover he made his Muse or White Goddess might then be taken from him. In this sense, he felt that he was doing his wife a great service by dedicating books to her but not actually writing poems about her. He also knew that he was doing her a disservice in his behaviour. Tennant claimed that Hughes referred to his home in Devon as a hospital, taking this as a cruel reference to Carol's nursing background. She was angry with herself for conniving at his infidelity. 'We did harm,' he once said to her on the phone after an evening party where Carol had unwittingly been in the same room as her husband's 'sub-mistress'. But Carol was unfazed. Her comment, looking back: 'I had been married to Ted long enough to be unmoved by the attentions frequently show-ered on him by the Emma Tennants of the world.' At the same time, Emma wondered what Ted was thinking of – or whether he knew what he was thinking of – when he wrote the story 'The Head', with its 'silent and illiterate' wife.

She tells of how he gave her books and she gave him a beautiful and expensive Mont Blanc pen. And of how she witnessed something of the drama of his life. On one occasion after lunch they left a plush restaurant in Notting Hill, aptly named La Pomme d'Amour. They walked towards Holland Park, where Ted's car was parked. Suddenly a man grabbed his arm. It was the schizophrenic homosexual poet Harry Fainlight, brother of Ted's friend Ruth. Emma recognised him because he had once turned up in the *Bananas* office in the hope of getting some of his work published. On that occasion, Harry had opened a black briefcase. It was empty save for a kitchen knife with a fearsomely long blade.

Ted managed to open his car door with his one free hand. He told Emma to get in the back (not easy, since the car only had two doors). According to Emma, Fainlight was 'literally foaming at the mouth'. Ted coolly told his lunch companion to open his battered old satchel, which was on the back seat, and get out a piece of paper. Meanwhile, he explained that Harry – now forcibly buckled into the front seat – had been stalking him, sleeping in his Devon barn for a year, then in a field, and now following him to London. A moment later he was holding Fainlight firmly by the shoulder as he got out a penknife, said 'Look at this,' and slit the sheet of paper diagonally 'into two identical halves'. He then released the now terrified-looking Fainlight, who 'shambled off aimlessly into the Holland Park crowd'. 'He won't trouble us again,' said Ted.

The story is probably exaggerated in order to dramatise Ted's quasi-occult powers, but it is absolutely true that mentally ill Harry Fainlight, who died alone in a field in 1982, did periodically stalk and send threatening letters to Ted, blaming him for Faber's rejection of his poems.[21] Ted, always protective of his friends and their loved ones (and Ruth Fainlight and Alan Sillitoe were among his closest friends), did his best to conceal all this, and would never have dreamed of reporting Harry to the police.

Elaine Feinstein told Emma Tennant that a poetry sequence in 'Earth-Numb' described all the women Ted had ever loved. The sequence begins 'I went into a worse chamber'. This led Emma to suppose that in the darker reaches of Ted's psyche – so scarred by Sylvia's death – all women were torturers and anything to do with women 'demanded a return form of torture'. If he could transform the women in his life into White Goddesses, creatures of myth and symbolic torturers, then why should she not transform him into an equally Gothic literary character for the purposes of her memoir? It would be a mistake to treat some of the stories in *Burnt Diaries* as reportage rather than quasi-mythic narrative. At the same time, Tennant understood many aspects of Hughes exceptionally well: his love of sea-bass, Dom Pérignon champagne and tall tales; his sometimes bonkers ideas about astrology and the occult; his use of ancient ideas and obscure literary sources as a way of explaining, even justifying, what most reasonable people would simply describe as bad behaviour.

Ted's affairs sometimes created difficulty for his friends. Most of his London friends were very good at not taking sides. Whatever they thought privately, they understood his need to have both a calm, well-managed house in Devon and a very different life in London. It is testimony to his capacity for friendship, and the loyalty he inspired, that he hardly ever lost a friend and that those who were close to him remained discreet, so that − although there were always rumours − much remained unknown outside his immediate circle until his death. Occasionally, though, there was tension, especially with Devon couples who were loyal to Ted and Carol as a couple.

The Baskins had moved to Devon so as to be close to Ted. On one occasion, Elaine Feinstein was visiting Court Green. Baskin offered to do a cover drawing for her latest volume of selected poems. She went to watch him at work. He drew 'a flat-faced woman with small mean eyes' and as he did so he began to ask questions about the affair with Jill Barber. Feinstein told him to ask Ted himself. 'You know all about it, don't you?' Baskin replied. 'Who is it? Has Olwyn arranged it?' Feinstein was stunned. Olwyn? 'She likes to involve herself,' Baskin went on. 'That witch! What does she do for Ted?'[22] Feinstein, who was one of the very small group of writers other than Ted whom Olwyn represented as an agent, defended his sister for the effort she put into arranging fees and contracts, promoting his work, running the Rainbow Press. Baskin was not satisfied. When Feinstein left, he dismissed her invitation to visit her in Cambridge, where she lived with her husband. Despite this, Baskin remained friends with Olwyn, though his letters to her contain some barbed remarks about Ted's extramarital life.

★

Ted Hughes was immensely generous in his championing of women writers, his assistance in getting such poets as Jennifer Rankin into print. But there was also a part of him that seems to have wanted to possess women writers. It is not always clear whether he succeeded. In contrast to those women who chose to advertise their affairs after his death, some subtle writers have been deliberately teasing. Angela Carter, brilliant and beautiful magic realist, hinted that there had been 'something' between her and Ted.[23] Edna O'Brien — sexually awakened Irish country girl and very much Ted's type — flirts delicately with the reader in her memoir. Early in the book she gives a hilarious account of a poetry evening at a suburban house in Dulwich around 1960 where 'the living Orpheus', 'the reincarnation of Heathcliff', is expected. The host has donned an orange velvet jacket and laid out suitably decadent yellow liqueur bottles with long yellow spires (totally empty — purely for show). A pair of Canadian lesbian poets turn up, then an earnest and bashful poet from Crystal Palace called Archie. But Orpheus Hughes proves a no-show and the evening dissolves into drunken, pretentious anticlimax.

Later, though, O'Brien tells of a vertiginous love affair that was written in the stars. At a party in Pall Mall she meets a man who emanates power and shares her love of Dylan Thomas. She leaves, weak-kneed, and soon he calls at her house and says what every woman yearns to hear: 'I will know you for a long time.'[24] From the high trapeze of the commencement of love, she descends to the mistress's familiar story of 'surprise meetings, cancelled meetings, devouring jealousies, the rapture and the ruptures of an affair'. She receives a phone call describing a party at which her lover is the principal guest, all the women swooning around him; she wanders the streets of Italy one summer, hoping vainly for a chance encounter, since she knows that he is on holiday there with his wife; they break off the affair and then start it again when they meet on a train, tossed from side to side at the place where two carriages join; she lives off 'emotional crumbs' until it comes to an end again. O'Brien emphatically does not identify the lover as Hughes, but the rollercoaster she describes is a fine evocation of what an affair with Hughes would have been like. Jill Barber recalls: 'When collecting material for Kristina Dusseldorp's literary magazine Mars, we were invited to Edna O'Brien's terraced house off the King's Road in Chelsea for tea.

She opened the door resplendent in a floaty kaftan, still very beauti-
ful. She was flirtatious with Ted and kept telling him about her erotic
dreams, asking for his interpretation of them. It was a distinct
come-on and I was not sure if he had invited me along to protect
him or to witness yet another woman desirous of taking him to
bed.'[25]

Other encounters, some of them friendships, others rather more,
some fleeting and casual, others felt in the heart, went below the radar
even of his close friends. They will remain private, perhaps for ever,
certainly for the time during which a number of archives, including
a significant part of Ted's own, remain closed.[26] Though he never
fully broke from Devon, he relished the personal freedom afforded by
reading tours, fishing trips and overseas travel. Seamus Heaney, remi-
niscing about his fellow-poet's times with Barrie Cooke on the rivers
and loughs of the west of Ireland, spoke with soft voice and twinkling
eye of 'trysts'.[27] And Ted always had an eye for the women he met
abroad. As late as April 1996, in Berlin for a reading, in his mid-sixties
and with his health failing, he wrote appreciatively in his journal of
the 'bewitching' allure of his guide Francesca, an 'Italian Madonna
model' with a 'caressing voice' and 'mercury mind'.[28]

All his life he loved women, but his reputation as a womaniser did
not endear him to Plathians. There is an irony to that: his infidelity in
later relationships was partly a function of his fidelity to the memory
of Sylvia. After the end of his first marriage, never again would he let
a woman possess the whole of him. Never again would he allow
himself to be fully caged. And it was when he was away from the cage,
in sight of new horizons, that he sometimes found it possible to speak
of Sylvia.

In November 1989 he was guest of honour at the second World
Poets Festival in Dhaka. He remained in Bangladesh for a week, fasci-
nated by the subcontinent, discovering the richness of Bengali
language and literature and the finer aspects of the local cuisine. He
and his hosts talked and joked. He ran through a selection of his
favourite set-piece stories. His account of 'the amazing island of
monkeys near Japan where they had an organized social life', his belief
in 'the aggressive nature of men through the ages', his rueful admission
of the failure of his farming career, the story of his rise from 'dairy
hand to the plumed and plum post of Poet Laureate', which gave him

'great liberty' in exchange for the small price of donning 'formal attire on rare occasions'.[29]

He gave an interview, in two sweltering sessions, one during a tea break at the festival venue and the other in his room at the Sonargaon Hotel. He was on excellent form, loquaciously offering some of the most cogent summaries of his work. With regard to that defining early poem, 'Hawk Roosting', he explained that the hawk represented the natural world, 'the whole biological kingdom' which was 'unaware of death'. Picking up on a powerful thought in a poem by Yeats, he remarked that 'only man knows of death, knows beforehand of death'. The hawk does not know that the death it inflicts on other beasts will one day come to it. 'In the early phases of writing it out,' he added, 'I had in my mind the notion of the Egyptian Horus, who was the hawk … who was the rising sun; so he was the sun in its positive phase, so he was the first original living energy in its positive phase. But that means a very destructive phase.' Then he turned to that strange hybrid volume, *Wodwo*, explaining that it was the product of his search for his own self in a modern Western world where people 'very easily lose touch with themselves'. Going on to *Crow*, he identified *The Conference of the Birds* and its quest-form as the model: Crow is a bird without any attribute other than 'the will to keep searching'.

In answer to a question about whether poetry has a role to play in society, he launched into his theory of poetry as 'the psychological component of the auto-immune system':

So you have the physical auto-immune system and in stress, in any stress, in any disaster, in any grief or mourning or just simply the stress of life, just the day-to-day biological response to the problems of your life, your immune system is in constant activity to repair the effect of this on your own body, on your own system. Your whole chemistry of your body is constantly under bombardment from external things, and your immune system is constantly repairing and renewing it. And that is a physical component of that which is actually a chemical process. But it seems to me that there is also a psychological component of it. And the psychological component is the strange business that we call Art.

He believed that poetry was 'simply the verbal form of that process'.

And did he think that the materialism and rationality of the modern West were crippling to the soul? 'Yes, I do, yes, yes, I would like to see the West completely injected by the East.' The West needs the spirit of the East because there was 'an easy acceptance throughout Eastern society that existence is based on spiritual things'. That was what had been lost in the West, which is why for all the material prosperity of the West, people were fundamentally miserable: 'they don't have the important thing, which is to be happy, and they know what they are lacking is something, some sort of spiritual foundation'.[30] The East was the place to find that foundation, or at the very least a resource to be used by the West in its reinvention. It was this sense of alienation from modernity and this yearning for the spirituality of the East that had by this time made the Poet Laureate into a guru for Prince Charles.

With his love of exotic travel, Ted took the opportunity to visit the Sundarbans in the hope of seeing a Bengal tiger. He also viewed with amazement the sixty-domed historic mosque at Bagerhat. And at Hiron Point, the southernmost point of Bangladesh, he looked out on the Bay of Bengal and wrote a delicate poem called 'Dreams Like Deer', in which he told of chaotic dreams spreading through the forest, meeting real tigers, and then a vision of the sea at dawn, looking like 'a bed of pink rose petals / Where somebody very beautiful had slept / A perfect sleep'.[31] The image of a deer, there in the simile of the poem's title, is one of his markers for the memory of Sylvia. She was very much on his mind at this time, as may be seen from another encounter on the trip.

Carolyne Wright was an attractive forty-year-old American poet in Dhaka on a two-year Fulbright fellowship, translating Bengali verse into English. She and Ted met during the mid-morning tea break on the first day of the festival, where he towered 'head and shoulders above the clusters of Bangladeshi journalists and the Thai and Indonesian and Bhutanese guest poets resplendent in their national dress'. Wright admired his broad-shouldered 'solid gravitas', writing later that 'in his dark woollen suit, he could have been a former American football player turned professor of English literature'. Ted fixed her with that 'warmth and focused concentration' that he gave to everyone he met, making them think they were the centre of his universe. 'It seems we're the only native English speakers here,' he said. This meeting with an American Fulbright Fellow unlocked something in him.

On the last day of the festival, the two poets, senior and junior, man and woman, leaned on the rail of the pleasure-launch *Rangapalli*, as it chugged along on the *noubihar*, the river cruise which was customary for guests of honour in Bangladesh. The conversation turned to accents and Ted said, as if from nowhere, 'that he had become very familiar with American English when he lived for two years in the United States with – and here he hesitated ever so slightly – "with, you know, my late wife, Sylvia"'. He then spoke, dreamily, of how the river landscape before them might have figured in her poetry. And as they stood at a distance from the other guests on the crowded launch, the floodgates opened and he spoke of Plath 'with respect, admiration, affection'. 'I've been writing my own version of events,' he continued, 'but it will be published posthumously. If people knew the full story, when they learn what really happened between us, they'll be surprised that it's so mundane, so ordinary.' With a poet's sensitivity, Wright understood 'that Hughes would go on living with Plath in the only way now possible – in words, in memory – perhaps to the end of his days':

> In his reserved, understated manner, he was making a profound expression of the undying nature of love – of his love and respect and sorrow for the brilliant and tormented poet-wife of his youth. In his words to me, as in the poems he was even then writing, he was seeking a resolution to his own and their children's loss and grief, some way of coming to terms with his beloved's abrupt, irreversible departure – from him, from her children, from herself. He seemed to seek no less than a reconciliation across the very boundary between life and death.[32]

Thanks to the presence of another woman, he seemed to recover Sylvia. It had occasionally happened with Brenda, as once when he returned to Court Green: 'I seemed to take a loop and recapture absolutely lost life, – coming up the path from the front gate, seeing toys on the lawn and the front door open, when I expected only the everlasting locked-up decayed gloom, of everything finished. Like dreams of S. returning.'[33] It happened again with a friend of Olwyn's, in a visionary moment immortalised in his achingly sad late poem 'The Offers'. And it happened here, during this peaceful moment in a beautiful alien place, with the Fulbright poet. 'But [he] who never felt that absoluteness of loss then found it again', he wrote in his journal on one such occasion, 'has missed the sweetest, strongest feeling in life.'[34]

Remembrance of Elmet

Emma Tennant tells a story, not recorded elsewhere, in which Ted Hughes recounts how his father once took off for London in order to have an affair with a pretty nurse, but got little further than King's Cross station before his pursuing wife caught him and marched him home.[1] On the Greek tragic principle of the sins of the fathers being visited upon – or replayed by – the children, this tale says something about Ted's feelings regarding the double life he was now living in Devon and London. The pretty nurse is clearly an inverted projection of his own guilt at his desire to escape the boredom of country life.

Like many men in their late forties, Ted spent a lot of time worrying about family and money. The investigation into the back taxes due on Sylvia's posthumous earnings was as interminable as a Dickensian legal case. By early 1977, the old tax inspector had died and the case was taken on by a fierce woman who rejoiced in the name of Mrs Skinner. 'Why does everything have to be so symbolic?' Ted asked Luke Myers when telling him of these woes.[2] Two and a half years later, he was still waiting for the assessment on the Plath earnings for the period between 1971 and 1975.

Carol was a worry. He wanted to sell the farm, but she didn't. He believed that she regarded its retention as a sign of faith in the future of their marriage. She was, he confided, not happy about his 'follies' (the term he always used when writing to Myers about his dalliances). Carol disputes these claims, insisting she was quite happy to sell the farm, being extremely busy supporting her bereaved mother – now all alone in a massive house with extensive grounds – and that she knew nothing of her husband 's 'follies' at that time. He did not want her to be wholly dependent on him, to devote herself merely to doing the books and bookings in relation to his literary career. Carol had been offered some work as a TV presenter on a new show in Plymouth. He dissuaded her from pursuing the opportunity, to her disappointment. Then Ted regretted doing so, thinking that she would have been very good at it. Then he supported her interest in becoming an acupuncturist, but nothing came of it.[3]

Frieda was a worry. When she left school, she spent all her time with the local bikers, tearing around the high-banked lanes of North Devon. On one occasion there was a chimney fire when she was at Court Green with her boyfriend, a handsome motorcyclist called Des. Ted came home from a happy Saturday's fishing at Slapton Ley to find fire engines in the lane outside, blue lights flashing on the house and the thatch soaked with water. He gave whisky to the firemen and ordered a barrel of beer that they drank when they came back a few hours later to check that all was damped down and to clear up some of the mess. Soon after this, Frieda left home and moved in with Des, who was a cowman living in tied accommodation on a big farm near Exeter. They married in the summer of 1979, Frieda aged just nineteen.

Nick was not a worry. The boy was doing superbly at Bedales, excelling in every endeavour from (non-motorised) cycle racing to academic work. The English and History teachers wanted him to do A Levels in Arts subjects. They had him writing wonderfully imaginative stories and poems. He was equally good when it came to practical skills such as carpentry and pottery. But his great love was the sciences and that was the direction in which he went for A Levels. He would secure straight-A grades and a place to read Zoology at the Queen's College, Oxford.

Father and son worked together composing Centaur type on an Albion hand printing press given to Nick by Olwyn and set up in an outhouse of Court Green. In the spring of 1979, they printed three of Ted's poems – 'Night Arrival of Sea-Trout', 'The Iron Wolf' and 'Puma' – each on a single sheet of thickly textured Italian paper, thirty signed copies only, proudly branded as coming from 'The Morrigu Press'. The Morrígu or Morrígan, meaning 'great queen' or 'phantom queen', was a goddess of battle in the ancient Ulster Cycle of mythical tales. She would sometimes appear in the form of a crow, flying above warriors as they went into battle, but she could also take the form of eel, wolf or cow. Sometimes she was imaged as triple goddess, three weird sisters. Robert Graves described her as a death goddess who often took the form of a raven and whom he linked to the figure of Morgan le Faye.[4] Ted's three poems for Nick's hand press metamorphose her into various characteristically Hughesian forms. As Iron Wolf with iron fate, she conjures up Ted's own grimmer histories. As puma sleeping in the sun, 'half-melted / in the sheet-flame silence', she opens 'one jewel' of an eye and there is a glimmer of the word that Ted habitually used for Sylvia's eyes and of the big cat poem in which she first wrote about him.

Printing was shared craft, but the greater bond was fishing. The passion passed from father to son, and would eventually lead to a distinguished academic career in the field of stream salmonid ecology.[5] Shared fishing trips became an annual treat. These often brought challenges. Jill's presence was an awkwardness in Ireland in the autumn of 1977. A week on a high-class stretch of the Dee in Scotland in April 1979 was marred by daily snow and no salmon (Nick half hoped for an invitation to fish on an even higher-class stretch at Balmoral with his school friend David Linley, son of Princess Margaret). Iceland that summer was full of natural beauty, but all the salmon runs were either too expensive or fully pre-booked. They had more success with sea-trout. Whenever Ted was cast down, Nick cheered him up with wise observations and funny stories. He also developed the art of cooking ingenious suppers with very limited ingredients. They made plans to venture further afield the following year: to Alaska, a place that would draw Nick back and hold him for the rest of his life.

Olwyn was a worry. For some time, she had been in an on–off relationship with a handsome Irishman called Richard Thomas, who had something of the look of Ted about him. He was a heavy drinker, who became violent when under the influence. Again and again, he would dry out, then lapse. By 1978 he was in hospital, critically ill with pancreatitis. He had been apart from Olwyn for some time, living with a teacher who was also an alcoholic. Olwyn heard that he was dying and went to say goodbye in hospital. Richard swore that he was going to get better, would never touch another drop, study at the Open University to become a History teacher. He had the Irish blarney as well as the good looks, and she was hooked. She discharged him from hospital and kept him financially while he began his degree. For nine months he kept off the booze. They travelled to Russia and Turkey, and for the first time Olwyn seemed to have found genuine happiness in a relationship with a man. On an impulse, they got married in June 1979, a few weeks before Frieda also tied the knot.

Things started to go wrong within a month. Richard tried to control Olwyn: what she could and what she couldn't do, no housework allowed, fury if a meal was not on the table at exactly the right time. He tried to stop her buying a house in Wales at a bargain price, simply because he didn't like the man from whom she was buying it – who happened to be an old boyfriend. It did not help when the New York comedian Marvin Cohen came to dinner and said, 'Where's that fire-eating Marxist Irish Nationalist that used to live here, that great fiery wonderful drinker? And who's this little quiet University student?' This provoked Richard to go and get a bottle of vodka. A week later, he went to an Open University residential course in Bath and came back after two days, blind drunk. After that, he did not stop. He took Olwyn's money, threatened her, pawned her jewels, shouted all night, smashed up her home. She was at her wits' end, so Ted went to stay with her. For two nights, nothing was seen of Richard. Then he appeared, drunk out of his mind. There was an evening of high drama, lasting into the small hours of the morning, when Richard gashed his wrists and disappeared, bloodily, into a taxi, presumably to go to the other woman in his life. By the end of the year, the marriage just six months old, Ted was helping Olwyn prepare her divorce papers.

Most of all, Ted's father was a worry. He was depressed, debilitated and difficult. He could not go on living on his own. Every time Ted left home – to go on a reading tour, to spend time in London with Jill, to pick up an OBE at Buckingham Palace in the summer of 1977 – there was the nagging anxiety about what Bill might do or fail to do. In May 1978, while Ted and Carol took a two-week holiday in Wales, they placed him in the private nursing home run by Carol's sister Jean. This was a success. Ted wrote to Gerald saying that their father would have to move in with one or other of them, or with Olwyn (which was hardly likely), or go into a horrible state-funded nursing home that would be little better than a prison for the dying. Unless the money could be found – a far from cheap £70 per week – to enable him to go permanently to Jean's, where he had fared so much better during his brief stay. Gerald did not rise to the bait and offer a financial contribution. Several months later Ted was still worrying about the impossibility of funding the nearly £4,000 a year it would take to secure a place for his father with his sister-in-law – he was terrified of how the sum would accumulate in the event of Bill staggering on for years.

As usual when faced with a financial challenge, Ted came up with various schemes. One of them was to professionalise his schedule of poetry readings for schools. Instead of going to them one at a time, he would do bigger events, creating a large audience by getting lots of different schools to send groups of sixth-formers along at £30 a time. Carol's brother Robert Orchard was recruited to organise the process. But then, after a hectic programme of readings and runnings about, Ted's body protested. In the middle of a reading at a Poetry Book Society event on the Isle of Wight he experienced agonising pain. He was laid up for a few weeks, and had to slow down when he went back on the road.

The freelance literary life meant constant juggling of priorities. His notebooks are filled with To Do lists. One typical February day, he listed the eight tasks in hand: completing his edition of Sylvia's *Collected Poems*; getting her manuscripts ready for Sotheby's to sell them; selecting the poems for an anthology on behalf of PEN, the organisation supporting oppressed writers; writing to Ted Cornish and two doctors, to fix a meeting in relation to plans for a book on Cornish's faith-healing (the doctors would monitor a selection of his patients to see if they really were getting better); completing a poetry anthology for children; writing to David Pease, the warm and energetic director of the Arvon Foundation (by now a great friend), to organise their poetry competition; and 'Write about ten letters, fending people off etc.'[6]

Some of these tasks would make him money. The manuscript experts Felix Pryor and Roy Davids had come down from Sotheby's and been very encouraging about the potential price that an American library or collector would pay for Sylvia's archive. Other tasks were associated with personal obsessions, notably his desire to write a biography of Ted Cornish. He tried to interest Prince Philip in Cornish's remarkable powers. And others were duties incumbent upon him as the country's leading missionary for the importance of poetry. The Arvon International Poetry Competition, which was Ted's idea, had great potential to raise the profile of as well as funds for the foundation, which was in severe financial difficulty.

He gave the competition a high profile by persuading three of the most distinguished poets of the day – Philip Larkin, Seamus Heaney and Charles Causley – to join him as judges. His letter to Larkin asking him to be a judge took the opportunity to offer congratulations on the recently published 'Aubade', a first venture back into print after long public silence. Larkin replied glumly that the act of writing the poem had staved off his fear of death for a few months but that it was creeping back. He in turn congratulated Ted on being 'our best/most popular/or whatever it was poet'.[7] Well over 30,000 people paid to enter the competition, providing much-needed income. The judges read every poem. Ted claimed that the whole process was so consuming that he wrote nothing for the next six months.[8]

It was interesting to observe Larkin (whose literary taste Ted described as 'spermicide')[9] and a pleasure to work with Heaney and Causley, a poet whose work he greatly admired. With his tongue only partly in his cheek, Ted said that the only submission he really liked among the thousands of entries was a thirty-five-page piece by Kenneth Bernard, founder of a movement called Theatre for the Ridiculous back in the late Sixties. The poem was a priapic celebration of a baboon in a nightclub having complicated and various sex with a beautiful woman. Ted was green with envy when he read it. He claimed that Larkin said that if it won he would dissociate himself from the prize, though in his notes on the short-listed poems Larkin actually described it as 'potentially funny and potentially lyrical and moving', though too long.[10] Causley thought that it was simply obscene. Heaney quite liked it.[11] The £5,000 first prize went to the young poet Andrew Motion, Ted's eventual successor as Poet Laureate, though not before a debacle in which the judges tried to change the rules and have six joint winners instead, at £1,000 each. This led the sponsor, the *Observer* newspaper, to threaten to withdraw the prize money and caused embarrassment to Ted's friend Melvyn Bragg, who was devoting a special edition of his television *South Bank Show* to the award.

The children's anthology was eventually published in 1982 under the title *The Rattle Bag* ('The Medicine Bag' was considered, but rejected). The origin of this project was a suggestion by Charles Monteith at Faber that Seamus and Marie Heaney – both teachers – should edit an anthology called *The Faber Book of Verse for Younger*

People. The project lay dormant because Marie was not keen, so in 1978 Monteith suggested that it should be a Heaney–Hughes collaboration. To begin with, they worked independently. Then they would compare selections. The process continued through 1980, in conjunction with the judging of the biennial Arvon poetry competition. The two poet-editors made a conscious decision to omit many of the canonical authors. The selection was deliberately personal, eclectic, intended for enjoyment rather than edification. The title, chosen at the last minute, nicely evoked the sense of the volume as a carnivalesque ragbag in which, as Heaney later put it, 'Gaelic charm and African oral poetry turned up alongside highly literary work by Elizabethan courtiers and contemporary Americans'. There were translations from Hungarian, Russian and modern Greek poets; 'Celtic monks and medieval hunters' were corralled alongside cosmopolitan high modernists and hippyish San Francisco beat poets.[12]

By self-denying ordinance, they did not include any of their own poems, but several of Plath's are there. Since the arrangement was alphabetical by title, to avoid the 'textbook' feel of chronological order, the final poem is, touchingly, 'You're', that loveliest of lyrics addressed to Frieda in the womb. Reviewers delighted at the book's success in restoring the 'thrill in reading' that was 'forfeited by most conventional anthologies'. This was that rare thing, a hugely varied collection of poems that had its reader 'laughing out loud, springing from his chair in delight, rushing to other books to supplement new discoveries, and beaming with remembered pleasure at odd moments of the day'.[13] Thanks to the respect in which Heaney and Hughes were held, especially among schoolteachers, the anthology was tremendously successful, with the paperback edition quickly selling out and being reprinted.

Ted's work for young people during this phase of his career also included a volume entitled *Moon-Bells* in a series published by Chatto and Windus called 'Poets for the Young'. This brought together a mix of new and previously published poems, mostly about animals and various moon-beings. Some were taken from *Earth-Moon*, a limited-edition sequence for the Rainbow Press, others from older collections. Confusingly, there is also a volume called *Moon-Whales and Other Moon Poems*, with drawings by Leonard Baskin and a dedication to Frieda and Nicholas, for the Viking Press in New York, which combines the complete contents of *Earth-Moon* and the much older collection of children's (or were they?) poems, *The Earth-Owl*. This (with some omissions) was republished in England by Faber more than a decade later. Each poem takes something from the earth – a whale, a lily, a wolf, a mirror, a theatre, an oak, haggis, a tulip, a nasturtium, a snail, a witch, a hyena, a foxglove, a clock, a walker, a bell, a hare, a bull, and more – and reimagines an inverted or surreal moon version of it.

Some of the poems are written in jogging rhyme: 'A man-hunt on the moon is full of horrible sights and sounds. / There are these foxes in red jackets, they are their own horses and hounds' ('A Moon Man-Hunt'). Others have the darkness of Hughes's poems for grown-ups. In the poem that gave the title to the Rainbow Press edition, a burning full moon rolls slowly towards a human out on a walk. It crushes boulders and dwelling-places as it goes. The man shuts his eyes against the glaring brightness, draws a dagger and stabs and stabs and stabs until 'The cry that quit the moon's wounds / Circled the earth'. The punctured moon shrinks to the size of a handkerchief, which the man picks up as a trophy which he carries 'Into moonless night'. Still others, such as 'Moon Marriage', begin in doggerel ('Marriage on the moon is rather strange. / It's nothing you can arrange') and end in a tone that, coming from Hughes, is to say the least pointed: 'On the moon it is all a matter of luck / Is marriage. / And the only offspring are poems.'[14]

Early in the Seventies, around the time he was determining to live in Devon rather than Yorkshire, Ted had suggested to Charles Monteith that he might write a series of poems memorialising his place of origin, accompanied by the landscape work of the distinguished photographer Fay Godwin. In 1970, she had been commissioned to take a new portrait photo of him as part of the publicity campaign for *Crow*. Ted usually loathed photo shoots, but he and Godwin hit it off. Her portrait became his preferred image for reproduction: brooding, looking straight down the camera, with lick of hair over forehead and leather jacket unzipped. With his hooked nose and cragged demeanour, there is something of the hawk or crow about him. They struck up a friendship and he suggested that she should create images of the Calder Valley that would stir him into poetry. She became excited by the scheme and fell in visual love with the area, taking dozens of photos. It was Ted who stalled on the project, feeling inner resistance to the idea of moving from simple evocation of place to 'auto-biography and history'. He didn't want to give away what he called his 'capital and the medicine bundle'.[15]

In the summer of 1976, helped by the release into elegy that had come with the poems in memory of Jack Orchard, he was ready. Then he heard news that Fay had been diagnosed with cancer. Once again, a woman to whom he had become close was in danger of slipping into death. In fact, she was treated successfully and went on to outlive Ted by seven years. But the prospect of losing her before he had done justice to her images gave him the added spur that he needed. He wrote her a long letter describing how he was getting to work on an 'episodic autobiography' that linked personal memory to the history of the place – its wildness, its centrality to the Industrial Revolution, its decline and the shadow of the First World War. A black history to match her stark black-and-white images of bleak landscapes, hard stone and blackened buildings.

He dug out his copy, received in uncorrected proof, of a book about the valley that had been published in 1975: *Millstone Grit* by Glyn Hughes.[16] It described the Calder Valley as 'the English Siberia', a place where the punished old have been left to die while the young go adventuring.[17] Glyn Hughes told of how the area created wealth in the nineteenth century for wars in the twentieth, how that wealth bene-fited London traders far more than the local people, how (as Karl Marx said) the only good that came of the Industrial Revolution was that it released the working class from 'the idiocy of rural life', how the Calder Valley was a place of broken walls and dead farms, a hilly enclave between two packed industrial areas, a man-made desert, yet with raw beauty. It had a particular grip upon Glyn Hughes, as it did upon Ted, 'because its arraignment against poisonous, dirty and ugly towns destructive of the human spirit, is a symbol of the human condition, balanced between the impulses of inspiration and destruction'.

The whole book is steeped in the mood of D. H. Lawrence, Ted-like in its account of how geology defines temperament ('dour'), prose-poetically evocative of millstone grit oxidising from its original orange and gold with glassy crystals of silica to the 'black, black, that makes your eyes ache everywhere in West Yorkshire, so that you think of dirt, no matter how clean and bright the day'. Houses back to back or back to earth, hanging on the edge of the valley. Houses now boarded up, clog factories slowly going broke, mills half demolished. Terraced rows where you hear the sounds of life next door. And the people: the Brontës, who were the first to give the region a literary consciousness; the fearsome Parson Grimshaw who went from Todmorden to Haworth, who once wore a horned mask to impersonate the Devil in order to frighten a young man into marrying a girl he had seduced, and who increased the congregation in the Methodist chapel at Haworth a hundredfold through the sheer theatricality of his fire-and-brimstone sermons; Billy Holt, self-taught writer and artist, also from Todmorden, who rode around Europe on a grey horse called Trigger bought from a rag-and-bone man. A little further afield was Saddleworth Moor, a place of 'violent conflicts that were, perhaps, as much products of that violent weather over the denuded uplands, as they were a product of social forces. And these conflicts were expressed, from time to time, in murders' – including the Moors Murders that Ted had gestured obliquely towards in 'Crow's Song about England'.

A few years later, Glyn Hughes turned Grimshaw's life into a novel called *Where I Used to Play on the Green*. Ted contributed an introduction linking the perverted parson to the Brontës and implicitly, by way of reference to 'sexual sacrifice', to his own Reverend Lumb. He noted that, like William Blake (whose poem 'The Garden of Love' gave the novel its title), Glyn Hughes saw the links between Puritanism and the factory, the psychosis of the minister passed to the millmaster. 'It is the story of a spiritual genocide, and the historical evidence for it is there, in the barren island bounded by Halifax, Todmorden, Colne and Keighley: the broken fragments of a cruel decalogue, tumbled about a giant graveyard.'[18] And yet Glyn Hughes's books – both *Millstone Grit* and the novel – are full of light, of glitter in the landscape created by pace in the writing.

All these aspects of Glyn Hughes's Calder Valley writing corresponded with Ted's feelings about the place. He was at last able to forge ahead with his collection, bringing together geology, meteorology, community, history and autobiography. People emerge as a product of place and weather. The spirit of Billy Holt is invoked. The poems are full of chills, hot food, clothes manufactured for money and employment but also worn for warmth. The moor becomes his mother. The child wanders on hillside and by water. Fishing for tiddlers, sheltering from a storm, throwing stones into the canal on the way to school, poaching, communing with birds, dreaming fearfully, meeting old men on the road, finding bones and thinking about ancient Britons. This is Ted as another Wordsworth, but a Wordsworth transported from the gentle bosom of the English Lake District to an edgier terrain.

By the spring of 1978, Ted was able to tell Gerald that the collection was nearly complete. *Remains of Elmet* was published by Faber and Faber a year later, in May 1979 (with the usual de luxe edition from the Rainbow Press a month before). Ted dedicated the poems to the memory of his mother. Fay Godwin dedicated the photographs to Ted. Immediately after the dedication page comes a poem, printed in italics, beginning:

> Six years into her posthumous life
> My uncle raises my Mother's face
> And says Yes he would love a cup of tea.[19]

For readers accustomed to the style of *Gaudete* and *Crow*, even that of the early poems, this feels like a new voice: quiet, matter-of-fact, above all deeply personal. Uncle Walt stands in for Edith as the repository of family memory, the connector that attaches Ted (in both senses of 'attach') to his 'inheritance'. Walt, now frail himself, holds the fragile, crumbling 'treasures' of the past; they must be captured and preserved before it is too late. The poem was written in 1975; the retention of the present tense for his voice when publishing it after his death the following year gives it added poignancy.

On turning the page, the reader finds a prefatory note that distances the poems from the personal. Here Hughes explains that the Calder Valley was 'the last ditch of Elmet, the last British Celtic kingdom to fall to the Angles'. It was a place of wilderness and outlaws, then 'the cradle for the Industrial Revolution in textiles', then a place of decay. Hughes notes that throughout his life he had watched the mills and chapels fall into disuse, the population – rooted and settled for centuries – change, the spirit of the place become elegiac. Godwin set out to capture that spirit in her photographs, he says, and it was the photographs that inspired the poems.

This depersonalisation is a screen. The first poem in the main body of the text is entitled 'Where the Mothers'. Godwin's photograph, on the page opposite, shows Abel Cross in Crimsworth Dene, a pair of stone markers associated with a local legend of rival brothers. Given the closeness of the spot to the place where Ted and Gerald camped, there can be no doubting the autobiographical resonance. So too with the second poem, 'Hardcastle Crags'. There is no explicit autobiographical reference, but Ted knew that this was his mother's favourite place, the site of family picnics and the walks with Olwyn and little Ted that first exposed him to the beauty of the natural world. The third poem, 'Lumb Chimney', inevitably, though again not explicitly, evokes Lumb Bank and the Reverend Lumb of *Gaudete*.

Then there is 'Open to Huge Light', printed immediately below a stark Godwin photograph of two bare trees at Top Withens. One of Hughes's most treasured possessions was another photograph, of Sylvia in one of these very trees, taken on the memorable day when Ted and his bride and Uncle Walt went in search of Wuthering Heights. Again, though, the personal association is not made explicit. Similarly, 'Football at Slack' contains but does not reveal the memory of his father's prowess as a soccer player.

'Crown Point Pensioners' has two old men – with 'Old faces, old roots. / Indigenous memories' – sitting, each with flat cap and favourite walking stick with polished knob, looking down on 'The map of their lives', reminiscing by way of the landmarks of the valley. What the poem does not say is that Crown Point is just a few yards up the road from the Beacon. The corresponding Godwin photograph was not actually taken at Crown Point (and it shows one old man, not two). Hughes is not so much turning the photographs into verse as using them as a springboard into his own memories. Crown Point is effectively a personal trig station, symbolically located between the Beacon, Lumb Bank and Heptonstall graveyard. At the end of the poem 'An America-bound jet, on its chalky thread, / Dozes in the dusty burning dome.'[20] The thread of memory is drawing him back to Sylvia.

Turn two leaves and there is a poem called 'Heptonstall'. Turn one more and there is a title that begins with a word that has occurred in only two poems in the previous hundred pages (and in these only glancingly, not flagged up in the title): 'You Claw the Door'. There is no doubting the identity of 'you': it is Sylvia, trapped in the Hughes family home. The image of the lights twinkling from the valley at night is borrowed from one of her poems remembering her time at the Beacon, 'Wuthering Heights'.[21] Like so many of Ted's most telling and powerful poems, this one has a complicated textual history. It first appeared in print the previous year in *Orts*, that privately published collection full of coded autobiographical musings not meant for public consumption. But in that first outing, Sylvia was veiled within a veil: here the poem was called 'Hathershelf', the alternative name of Scout Rock, the cliff that loomed over Ted's childhood home in Mytholmroyd. With that title, a reader in the biographical know might assume that it is Hughes himself – or a member of his immediate family – who is clawing the door.

In *Remains of Elmet*, the text of 'Hathershelf' is paired with an image of fallen leaves and tree roots – reaching tentacles on the surface of the earth – and, in the foreground, an oblong patch of compacted soil that looks somewhat like a freshly filled grave. But now the opening phrase has become the title: 'You Claw the Door'. The poem is deprived of the name that placed it in Mytholmroyd. Ted comes one step closer to the acknowledgement that the 'you' of his most personal poems is Sylvia more often than anyone else. When *Remains of Elmet* was revised some years later as *Elmet* the phrase 'You claw the door' was returned to the text and a new title introduced, locking the memory of Sylvia – and her nearby grave – into the house on Heptonstall Slack: 'The Beacon'.[22]

Steeped in the English literary tradition, the poem's ending – 'While the world rolls in rain / Like a stone inside surf' – echoes one of the greatest elegies in all literature, William Wordsworth's mysterious, lapidary 'A slumber did my spirit seal'. Wordsworth mourns for a dead girl called Lucy:

> No motion has she now, no force;
> She neither hears nor sees;
> Rolled round in earth's diurnal course,
> With rocks, and stones, and trees.

Hughes, always a poet of motion and force, converts Wordsworth's passive 'rolled' (Lucy's body beneath the earth) to an active 'rolls' (the world goes on). The tree is, as it were, moved out of the poem into the

Fay Godwin photograph, while the turf on Lucy's grave becomes 'surf', suggestive of the restorative power of water.

Turn the page again and the coded references to Sylvia multiply. The next poem in *Remains of Elmet* is a meditation on 'Emily Brontë' and her death: a Sylvia obsession. The one after that is called 'Haworth Parsonage'. It uses the resonantly Plathian image of electrocution for the suicidal depression of Bramwell Brontë – though here Hughes's memory is complicated by Assia's lonely day and night in Haworth in the last week of her life. The image of the parsonage as 'A house / Emptied and scarred black' echoes the language of her journal.[23]

Then comes 'Top Withens', enshrining the memory of the walk there with Walt. Next there is 'The Sluttiest Sheep in England', a deromanticised variation on Sylvia's 'Sheep in Fog', that poem about which Hughes the critic-editor of his wife wrote at enormous length. *Remains of Elmet* ends with a return to Hughes's mother, alluding to her dreams of angels. But the penultimate poem is called 'Heptonstall Cemetery'. It evokes wind slamming over the tops and then repeats the formulation 'You claw'. It ends with swans flying westward, low across a stormy sky, towards the Atlantic, tracing the same path as the American-bound plane over Crown Point. Ted knew well that swans, like greylag geese, mate for life and know the meaning of grief. Some bereaved swans stay alone for the rest of their lives, while others take flight and rejoin their flock. Between the wind and the swans comes an explicit sequence of namings:

> And Thomas and Walter and Edith
> Are living feathers
>
> Esther and Sylvia
> Living feathers.[24]

Here are Uncle Tom and Mother Edith joined in the family plot by Uncle Walt, who died while Ted was in Australia. And by Sylvia in double form, as both herself and as the Esther of *The Bell Jar*. Looking across the page, one sees a magnificent Fay Godwin photograph of radiant light and rising mist over a Yorkshire landscape with the silhouette of a church tower on the horizon. The list of photographic locations at the back of the book identifies it, needless to say, as

Heptonstall Old Church. The geographically and biographically alert reader will come to the realisation that the focal point of the image is Sylvia's grave. It is no coincidence that this is the image chosen for the front cover of the book. Nor that the back cover shows the two trees at Top Withens, one of which Sylvia had climbed on that never-to-be-forgotten day in 1956.

The recognition that 'You Claw the Door' is about Sylvia, and that her ghost inhabits so many of the poems in the second half of the book, raises the possibility that she is the 'you' mentioned twice in poems placed earlier in the collection, 'Churn-Milk Joan' and 'Bridestones'. The former, based on a stone above Mytholmroyd and the story of a rape and murder associated with it, ends with an image, reminiscent of Plath's 'The Rabbit Catcher', of screams and 'awful little death'.[25] The latter imagines a marriage mystically consecrated upon the moors and then a grave in which the dead bride, again like Wordsworth's Lucy, is rolled in earth's diurnal course:

> With the wreath of weather
> The wreath of hills
> The wreath of stars
> Upon your shoulders.[26]

Most of the reviews of *Remains of Elmet* were lukewarm. Godwin's starkly beautiful photographs garnered more praise than Hughes's chiselled poems, which critics tended to fault for 'a muscle-bound galvanism expressing itself in packed and tensile phrases listed down the page, often with no verb at all'.[27] The allusions to Sylvia went unnoticed.

A dozen years later, in the early Nineties, Ted told Faber and Faber that he was no longer satisfied with his existing *Selected Poems* but not yet ready for a new selection. And he certainly didn't want a *Collected*, which would be like a coffin. So how about republishing his poems in groups of three: *Hawk in the Rain*, *Lupercal* and *Wodwo* without the prose stories would make one trio, *Cave Birds*, *Remains of Elmet* and *River* (his next collection) another.[28] Faber knew that the first three books, his universally acknowledged masterpieces, still sold enough to be worth keeping in print as freestanding volumes, but they liked the idea of gathering together the latter trio and in 1993 they published *Three Books*: the Elmet, Cave Bird and River poems, though with many a variant (revisions, additions) from the earlier collections, and without any Fay Godwin photographs. Faber's marketing ploy was to explain that the three books were all 'central texts in Ted Hughes's output' and that by gathering them together, 'unadorned' (which is to say, without the cost of illustrations), 'each can now be read as part of a larger visionary enterprise, with family resemblances and shared concerns freshly accentuated'.[29] The argument works well enough for *Remains of Elmet* and *River*: when read together they form a diptych in which Yorkshire contrasts with Devon and ravaged community with restorative nature. But the arcane ritual of *Cave Birds* is a chasm, not a bridge. Where the first and third books brought Hughes's elegiac voice to a wide audience for the first time, the middle one feels like the last gasp of the tired, overworked mythic voice.

In several respects, the version of *Remains of Elmet* included in *Three Books* was significantly different from that published back in 1979. Most obviously, the absence of the photographs not only made it a normal – and affordable – pocket-sized paperback, it also marked the collection as being truly Ted's, the product of his rather than Godwin's vision and memory of the Calder Valley. His father was dead by this time, so it could now be dedicated to the memory of both his parents, not just his mother. Ted also took the opportunity to add an explanatory note, partly drawing on his introduction to Glyn Hughes's *Where I Used to Play on the Green*, in which he linked his own upbringing to the decline of the valley: the emptying chapels, the closing mills, the abandoned farms, the sense of 'living among the survivors, in the remains'.[30] The note gives context and added poignancy to some of the best poems in the collection, such as 'First, Mills', in which the land is gradually drained and quietened until at last all that is left is 'two minutes silence' (alluding to cenotaphs and Remembrance Day) 'In the childhood of earth'.[31]

There is also an increased personalisation. 'Hardcastle Crags', which was not explicitly about Hughes's mother, is replaced by 'Leaf Mould' from *Wolfwatching* (another intermediate collection), which vividly places her in this place that she loved. 'What's the first thing you think of?', a poem about Gerald and his model glider, first published casually in the *Spectator* in 1985, is now gathered into the family setting of the collection. 'Football at Slack' is brought nearer the beginning, in honour of Ted's footballer father. Above all, reordering of the sequence also makes the presence of Sylvia more apparent. 'Emily Brontë' and finally 'Heptonstall Cemetery', with its explicit naming of her, now form the climax of the collection.

And a new poem is added: 'Two Photographs of Top Withens'. In the original *Remains of Elmet*, precisely because of the presence of Godwin's photographs, Hughes avoided writing about photographs or even using the word in the poems. Now, in the absence of actual photographs, he conjures up the memory of two of them. One is Godwin's photo of a pair of trees by Top Withens, which had been on the back cover of *Remains of Elmet*. The other is that precious snapshot belonging to Ted: Wuthering Heights, ruined but with roof slabs still in place, and 'you' (Sylvia) smiling, halfway up one of the sycamore trees beside it. Emily Brontë is below the earth,

> But you smile in the branches – still in your twenties,
> Ear cocked for the great cries.
> 'We could buy this place and renovate it!'[32]

The 'great cries' are presumably those of Cathy and Heathcliff, calling their passion for each other across the moor.

The lovely thought of Ted and Sylvia restoring Wuthering Heights and making it their home is then modified by images of bleakness and horror, 'Mad heather and grass tugged by the mad / And empty wind'. No, Sylvia would have gone mad living on the moor. The only thing that endures in this bleak environment is stone. Even 'the spirit of the place', like that of Emily, is 'Hidden beneath stone'. By the end of the poem Walt, their guide, has gone into the earth too. But the trees remain, in the second photograph, and in them the camera-lens of Ted's poetic memory captures, if only for an instant, the 'ghost' of Sylvia.

24

The Fisher King

Wild Steelhead & Salmon: Do you bring that same intensity to
your fishing?
Hughes: I think now it's just focused on rivers and fishing. I
would never stop fishing because I do not want to lose what
goes with fishing [*pauses*] This last connection.
WS&S: To what?
Hughes: To this whole – to everything, I guess. The stuff of the
Earth. The whole of life.[1]

In the lead-up to Christmas 1979, Ted reflected in a letter to Gerald
and Joan, and another to Richard Murphy, on an exhausting year of
late nights, storms (both literal and emotional) and tiring, if rewarding,
fishing holidays with Nick. Despite the dislocated hip and the flu and
the exhaustion, his appetite for travel was unabated.[2] There were two
ways of witnessing the world, he would tell his brother in a later letter:
from a tent in the wild with his son and from an expensive hotel on
the tourist trail with his wife. Plans for 1980 were Mexico with Carol,
Alaska with Nick and perhaps Florida for some big fish with Barrie
Cooke. Ted was about to turn fifty and it was time, he thought, to do
exactly what he wanted before it was too late. The good news was that
on their return from Iceland Nick had helped him build a wonderful
new writing hut in the garden. He had cleared the decks of the Elmet
project and was in the right place for something new and important.
The Mexico visit, for a literary festival, was postponed and Florida
didn't happen, but Alaska did.

They had finally come up with the money to move his father into
his sister-in-law's nursing home, but Bill was becoming ever more
difficult, sometimes creating embarrassing scenes. Meanwhile,

following the break-up of her marriage, Olwyn moved out of Chetwynd Road and bought a house in Cambridge, near her friends Arnold and Elaine Feinstein. The sale of the Chetwynd Road house yielded a tidy profit, even though its basement flat was retained. On one occasion when Ted was in Cambridge, checking that Olwyn was coping, her ex-husband Richard turned up and voices were raised again. After more on–off dramas over the next two years, Olwyn moved back to north London and eventually took up residence in another terraced house in Chetwynd Road, where she would remain for the rest of Ted's life and well beyond.

William Hughes weakened rapidly after a fall, when he broke his hip. He may have had a minor stroke while under anaesthetic. His mind had been wandering for some time. He was moved to hospital and Ted would visit, sitting in silence. Early in 1981, Ted and Carol went to Yorkshire for the funeral of Uncle Walt's daughter Barbara, who had died in her early fifties, having always suffered from physical and mental-health problems. They stayed on for a few days after the funeral, especially enjoying the company of Anne Farrar, one of the daughters of Uncle Tom's only son David and his wife Rita. Ted told Gerald that she and her sister Ellen were both beauties and that Anne had great comic gifts – she had joined them for dinner with some old friends and had them all in fits of laughter until the small hours of the morning. Then on the Sunday, in rain and snow, they took their friend Roy Davids, the manuscripts man from Sotheby's, to the desolate ruins of Top Withens. They came down from the moors and were taking tea with Aunt Hilda when the telephone call came. Ted's father had died, in the nursing home owned by Carol's sister.

They hurried south. Looking at his father's body in an Exeter funeral parlour, Ted was reminded, he told Gerald, of 'a noble old Spaniard'.[3] He saw his father's body on 11 February, eighteen years to the day from the time when he had seen Sylvia in the morgue of University College Hospital. As with Sylvia, the body was taken north for a bleak February funeral in Heptonstall. The grave was next to Edith's, just along the row from Sylvia's. Olwyn and Hilda, Carol and Frieda threw in freesias, Ted 'a handful of wet, horrible Heptonstall soil'.[4]

The previous year, he had heard the news of the death of another father-figure, his inspirational English teacher John Fisher, whom he had visited and corresponded with ever since Cambridge days. The cause was lung cancer, which the doctors had been slow to diagnose. Ted was not so much bitter about their failure as troubled that Fisher had never managed to fulfil his hopes of new adventures in retirement: 'I think he died mainly of boredom – the depression of boredom, under the sulphur towers of that power station in Mexborough.'[5] There is something of a 'note to self' here: beware of staying in the countryside, where you might die of boredom. There were indeed many times – especially in this phase of his life – when Ted sensed that he was declining into depression himself. His writing, he told Than Minton, one of his old Cambridge friends, was his personal therapy: 'Without his unstoppable creative energy he could have collapsed into a state of chronic apathy.' A time would come when Ted was reduced to asking Minton for a supply of anti-depressants.[6]

Ted continued to talk to himself all through these years by stepping up his journal-keeping. He used it to work things out, to give himself a stock of raw material for future writing, and to remember experiences, people and places. The perpetual razor-sharp observations of the natural world are no surprise: the rise and fall of dippers by the bridge, Ginger the cat under an ash-pole at dusk, a flooded oak pot, the sense of wonder at watching a baby chestnut unfold. But the gift for character portrayal reveals another side of Ted, one that could have made him an extraordinary novelist. He writes with equal vivacity of casual acquaintances, whether a pretty girl sitting opposite him on a train to London or an accountant in his office with 'mauve shirt, orange pullover, freckled bald head and ginger remains of hair'. The journals are also filled with glorious set pieces, often involving food (and friends – especially the Baskins – arriving late and being provocative in conversation). People are turned into *characters*. In November 1979, he saw Dido Merwin for the first time in nine years. She is fresh from her final separation and divorce from Bill Merwin. Her face – epically lifted – comes up to meet him and they kiss. She gushes, she babbles, she tells of how she would lay her life down for a great artist, would 'sink in the vitamins' of his radiance. He cannot help admiring how well preserved she is at the age of sixty. Her voice and laughter are controlled tornadoes, her spirit is undimmed despite the 'soft kid-glove age-crumple' round her eyes.[7]

He experimented with the idea of turning his prose character sketches into poems. In the early Eighties he scribbled in manuscript a collection of light-hearted verse 'Portraits' of people he knew: Maurice Tibbles, wildlife photographer, who could equally well be compared to a ferret, a badger and a weasel; a seventy-eight-year-old thatcher who worked on the roof of Court Green; the great Peter Brook, with his eyes like a cold seagull, his small hands and his vision into the infinity of life and the infinity of death; Penelope Shuttle, Peter Redgrove's wife, with her 'ball-bearing oddity ideas'; Frieda's first husband, Des Dawe, the farm worker; Dido, with her facelift and her explosive laughter. In the same folder, he filed away some jokily schoolboyish verses about the women of literary history, beginning 'The Brontes / Ran over Hebden Moor without panties. / The wind blew on their triple bum / Till their toes went numb.'[8] These are lines that he might have done better to destroy than preserve.

With the 'Portraits' is a note in his journal-writing style about Wagner's *Tristan und Isolde* as an exploration of the 'exhaustive incursions of the sexual animal'. In sexual desire, we confront our deepest biological being, 'we taste our own roots, come to fullest flower'. This somehow makes the passion associated with death 'utterly desirable'. 'Passion', he concludes, 'is the only teacher – and so Death comes to be the only school.'[9]

Conscious of the march of the years, he wrote at length about physical illness: another bad hip episode after he fell when jumping overambitiously from a wall, the bad back that was almost inevitable when such a tall man had spent so many years bending over a page at his desk, Fisher's last illness, the long and difficult decline of his own father. His preoccupation with bodily decay and ill health was matched by an equal and opposite fascination with the skills of local faith-healer Ted Cornish. For Hughes himself, writing in his journal was a form of catharsis, perhaps indeed of faith-healing. Many of the entries read as if they were prayers, in the tradition of the harsh spiritual self-examinations of Dr Samuel Johnson. 'Forgive me for my mistakes: guide me and forgive me,' Hughes wrote in a characteristic passage, accusing himself of being cowardly and 'hospitable to evil', of coddling his disasters, pains and misfortunes as an old soldier would coddle his medals. 'No more of it,' he repeats three times. What he must do is 'reckon the reality of what occurred', 'trace out the cause and propa-

gation of it', and in so doing get beyond the idea that his life is so fated
that disaster will follow disaster.[10] The reckoning would have to come
through writing, first in journal form, then in poetry. Increasingly, the
journal entries themselves were written in loose blank verse. Fishing
trips in particular were often remembered thus.[11]

Journal-writing was also for speculation on such arcana as the arti-
ficial insemination of cattle, the interplay between the physical and the
psychic, and the four realms of 'psychedelic descent' (the 'sensory', the
'recollective-analytic', the 'symbolic' and the 'integral'). More
mundanely, it was an opportunity to record anecdotes, which Ted
loved. A typical example is a lengthy account of an evening in the
Fainlights' flat in London, where the conversation turned from Robert
Graves, senile and stricken by a stroke, to the story of Ruth's encoun-
ter at a remote petrol station in Finland with a 'gypsy madonna' in full
Romany regalia, to Yehuda Amichai's account of the great love of his
life, an American girl for whom he left his first wife, only to leave her,
though still in love with her, because she told him that she had so
much money that he could write all the time, a prospect he could not
endure.[12] The journal entries are always honest about the copious
consumption of alcohol on such occasions, and the morning
hangovers.

Above all else, the journals were in the literal sense an aide-mémoire.
'Remember' or 'Rem' or just 'R', he would write, before sketching
out an image, a moment. Thus, on flying into Mexico City in the
summer of 1982: 'Remember. Flying in after sunset – the soiled fleece
of cloud, bluish, lying over the mountains, below, solid and still and
below the light in which we still flew.' On the same visit, he fixed in
his memory every detail of the figurines and sculptures in the Museo
Nacional de Antropología. His lengthy journal of this trip, the second
half of which is written in verse, would make a lovely little book in its
own right.

The following year, as every year, there was day upon day of remem-
berings. His appetite for experience was insatiable. On any one day he
might remember a domestic detail ('Remember': an empty room, the
television on, Wimbledon being broadcast – 'school of brats' he calls
it, this being the John McEnroe era), a country walk (what was that
levelled place? 'Rem: … an old burial site; old tennis court?'), a field
of flowers ('Remember: … Iris and Ragged Robin. A marsh of Iris.

The playful bullocks come to push their heads at us'), an embrace ('Remember: Tricia's tight breasts, and life-jacket of plumpness when I kissed her') followed by a chance encounter ('Roger's sudden appearance in his woodland outfit, with binocs – been strolling in his trees, looking at birds').[13]

For the biographer, the journals are the most valuable of all sources because they provide an 'access all areas' pass to the inner life. They expose Ted at his most self-aware and self-critical, while at the same time they reveal his passions and his exultations in raw form. If anyone were to doubt the importance for Hughes of the Wordsworthian example, they would only have to turn to his journal for 30 April 1980 to have their questioning silenced. 'Remember,' Ted writes, 'Wordsworth's Dove Cottage: impressive.' The 'Deep clear atmosphere', the cool slabs of floor slate, the tiny house in which the rooms are somehow 'spacious' and 'sober'. A feeling of solidity to match that of Wordsworth's poetry. 'His ash-handled basket – for visitors' cards. His door on to the steep garden. The perfect guide. His skates.' Among Wordsworth's books, Ted examined his copy of Milton, with its 'testy reprovals' in the margin. Among the manuscripts, he pored over *The Prelude*, noting William's corrections of Dorothy's fair copy and then the 'endless correctings over the years'. And among the letters, three stood out: 'requests for money'.[14]

This is Wordsworth as he truly was, but also Wordsworth as Hughes. Court Green, like Dove Cottage, had a cool stone floor and a banked garden. Olwyn was a sister who helped her brother with his work. Requests for money jump out from dozens of Ted's letters. All that is missing is a direct reference to the fact that, as Wordsworth spent more than half his life revising his autobiographic epic *The Prelude*, so Hughes was by this time many years into an analogous project.

Hughes constantly sought measures for his own work in the achievements of other writers. On the next page of his journal, following the account of Dove Cottage and John Ruskin's equally atmospheric house, Brantwood on Coniston Water, he notes that while in Cumbria he has been reading the journal of the Italian poet Cesare Pavese and finding in it a model for a writer's 'talent for sexual embroilment, effectively recorded, convincing pain and desolation'.[15]

Just as his journal was especially detailed when he travelled, his letters about his travels resemble nothing so much as the great 'journal-letters' of John Keats to his brother and sister-in-law in America. He explained to his Cambridge friend Karl Miller, who was by this time editor of the *Listener* magazine, that the idea of his travel journals was to 'record every moment and detail just as it occurs'. This, he thought, would 'create an interesting kind of record'. As a poem captured a moment, a feeling, a thought, so this recording of impressions of a place would capture a sequence of details, a journey through a landscape and the passage of a life.[16] The letter to Miller was written on leaving for Alaska in June 1980. While he was away, Miller collected on Ted's behalf a prize from the Royal Society of Literature, awarded to *Moortown*. When Ted returned the following month, he told Miller that Alaska was the 'most fantastic land' he had ever been in.[17] Later in the summer he sent Barrie Cooke a detailed account of his fishing successes there. He loved the light, the atmosphere, the blue of the sky against the white of the snow, the clarity and the sound of the water, the sparseness of the population, the expanse of emptiness, the loyalty of the people to the place (they called America 'the outside'). He loved travelling by small plane and canoe rather than road. And he loved that Nick loved it too.

Three years later, he and his son went on another great fishing adventure, this time to Lake Victoria, where Nick was studying the Nile perch. Barrie Cooke was again treated to a journal-letter with all the details of huge 80-kilo perch and tiny dazzling silver omena (which resembled whitebait). Ted had an epiphany on an island on the lake. The group of fishermen there lived in mud huts with nothing but their nets and canoes. They sold their fish and lived off maize and sweet tea and chapatis. Spending a fortnight with them, Ted felt free of every care. To what avail were furniture and a clean carpet, polished shoes, appointment diaries and worries about money? These 'blacks' laughed and lived. They were happy 'because they didn't want anything'.[18] In both his unpublished journal of the trip and his published letters about it, Ted wrote prose of extraordinary vigour. In a single sentence of explosive energy he told of racing across the lake against another canoe under a thunderstorm at night. It was 'the most exciting half hour' of his life, with the lightning flashing in 'great vertical 15 second rivers of orange or blue or green', as if the sky were full of 'blazing thorns'. The swell poured into the boat, so one of the crew had to bail out for dear life as the others paddled and yelled, and the sail was 'like a giant map of the world in giant rips and holes', and the canoe was piled with huge fish, including two giants caught by Nick. Their eyes seemed to glare like 'orange torches' even though they had been dead for hours. They won the race and spent the rest of the evening decapitating the perch.[19]

Fishing was becoming more and more important to Ted. He told Luke Myers, the correspondent with whom he was most honest about his own failings, that it was 'a symbolic pursuit that swallows every impulse to folly in a primaeval stupor'.[20] Shakespeare's Leontes, in some lines of *The Winter's Tale* much admired by Ted, described extra-marital sex as fishing in a neighbour's pond. For Ted in the Eighties, by contrast, fishing was not a metaphor but a substitute for the 'follies' of the Seventies. He was moving in a new circle of acquaintances, among 'Colonels, Group Captains, one or two Lords, a newspaper owner who perpetually dines and relaxes with Cabinet Ministers'. They all gave him top-of-the-range fishing access. Before he knew it, he was a guest on the best salmon rivers. In the light of his humble origins this was in one way a most curious, indeed comical, develop-ment, but he found that his hosts all turned out to be 'very amusing, engaging chaps'.[21] Fishing in all its aspects became a complete obsession. He bought the finest rods and most intricate flies, purchased a small boat for fishing in the estuaries, and devoted himself to campaigns to eradicate the pollution of the Devon rivers, from where fish were vanishing at an alarming rate.

In August 1980, he told Gerald of a new project, which had in fact been brewing for a number of years. In 1976, Ted had directed a keen angler called Peter Keen to some of his sacred spots on the Taw and Torridge.[22] Keen had taken a large number of colour photographs of rivers and the life around rivers. Ted casually suggested that a selection of them, printed alongside a series of his river and fishing poems, would make an attractive book (Keen claimed that the collaboration was his idea). The project might do for Devon rivers what the collab-oration with Fay Godwin had done for the Calder Valley in *Remains of Elmet*. Keen took Ted's encouragement as a serious proposition, and pressurised him into making the project a reality. Ted was sceptical: with colour plates, it would be an expensive book. Anglers didn't read poetry, poetry readers didn't like expensive large-format volumes, and

Keen wasn't a major enough figure to appeal to photography connoisseurs. Did he really want to produce a coffee-table book, and only receive half the royalties?[23]

James MacGibbon of the Devon publisher David and Charles had expressed interest and by 1978 Olwyn, acting as usual as Ted's agent, was negotiating with him. Discussions foundered over American rights. There was talk of Faber taking over the project, but they could not make the numbers work: the production cost of colour photographs was very high. MacGibbon then moved to another publisher, James and James. He still wanted to be involved. Perhaps the solution to the high production cost would be to get sponsorship. One possibility would be a *Shell Book of the River*, on the model of other natural history works that the petrochemical giant Shell had bankrolled in the name of good public relations. Another possibility was British Gas. MacGibbon explained to Olwyn what the deal would be: 'the Corporation concerns itself with conservation when it comes to laying pipe lines across the country including under rivers and the book could be a subtle way of demonstrating their concern. They would however want to have two or three photographs illustrating their care of the landscape.'[24] Faber and Faber agreed to publish the book on condition that an arrangement was reached.

As the book went through production, Michael Wright of Faber and Faber found himself in the unusual position of negotiating with David Butler of the Public Relations Department at British Gas: 'As the theme of the intended photograph is presumably to underline the theme of re-landscaping after the submergence of gas pipes, I suppose plate 45 makes the point quite graphically.'[25] The whole process of choosing the photographs, waiting for Ted to have the right selection of poems, and negotiating with publishers and sponsors meant that the book was not ready until 1983. Even then, there was a further delay. Faber originally announced that *October Salmon: River Poems and Photographs* would be published in June, but it was not until September that the volume appeared, now entitled simply *River*. It cost £10, twice as much as the much thicker but unillustrated *New Selected Poems* that had appeared the previous year.

Two pictures were added late in the process, to give more credit to British Gas. They were described in the notes on the photographs at the back of the book. First, 'The Scottish Dee has been called "the river flowing out of Paradise". A British Gas pipeline crosses the Dee, unseen and unheard, at this point.' And then, 'A salmon, undisturbed by the large gas pipelines in the river bed, moves in a pool on the river Don. British Gas, in close consultation with river authorities, has crossed many rivers in bringing the pipeline southwards.' The image on the back cover of the book, which in the main body appeared beside Ted's poem 'August Evening', was given a similar description: 'On the river bed beneath the quietly flowing Aberdeenshire Don a high-pressure pipeline carries large quantities of North Sea gas – unseen and unheard – to the south.'[26]

There was, though, an unspoken pathos about Ted's association with the great scheme to bring North Sea gas across the land by pipeline. In 1966, the decision had been taken to convert Britain to natural gas, and a year later the first North Sea gas was brought ashore. There was then a ten-year national programme in which every appliance in the country was converted from the old toxic 'town gas' to run on the new carbon-monoxide-free natural supply. British Gas visited 13 million homes and factories, converting some 34 million individual appliances. The benefits of the great conversion were not just economic. Immediately after Assia Wevill had killed herself and Shura, F. W. Lucas, a service supervisor at the South Eastern Gas Board, visited the flat in Clapham and determined that there was no fault in the gas installation or appliances. He calculated that 'a normal healthy person would be expected to succumb to CO poisoning within one and a quarter hours'.[27] Principally as a result of conversion from town gas to natural gas, deaths in Britain by gas (either accidental or suicidal) fell from over 1,000 in the year that Sylvia was one of them to under 300 in 1970, when the supply to Clapham was converted, a year too late for Assia.

Many of the *River* poems are about life and death, struggle and rebirth, purification by water, but also the ache of loss. The leading image is that of the salmon run, the journey upstream to spawn. From the first poem, on obstetric procedures in a salmon farm, to the last, on salmon eggs, the volume teems with sperm and egg, intricately exploring the mechanics of breeding. Fish stock mattered to Hughes the angler. And the biology of salmon fascinated Ted the father of Nicholas Hughes, who was destined to become one of the world's leading experts on the subject. But at a deeper level, the story of the river and the cycles of aquatic life gave him an opportunity to come indirectly at his own feelings about those raw essentials of human life identified by T. S. Eliot's character called Sweeney: birth and copulation and death.

The first poem in the collection, 'The Morning before Christmas', ends with an image of a fox's paw print on a flood pond. Any such trace in Hughes is inevitably evocative of his signature poem, 'The Thought-Fox'. If there is a thought-fox, then there is also a Ted. The reader is thus alerted to the presence of a personal story beneath the stream-of-conscious reference. 'New Year', which appears opposite a photograph of a dead cock salmon, begins with the image of a Caesarean section. It moves swiftly from salmon redds (spawning nests) to hospital theatre, with surgeon at work, nurses busy in attendance, and the speaker of the poem – imaging himself as the husband of the woman on the operating table – pacing through the early hours of the day 'in the blue glare of the ward', empathetically feeling the anaesthetic, glimpsing 'the gouged patient sunk in her trough of coma'. She is like an exhausted fish. The 'ticking egg' has gone.[28] In the light of Hughes's several references to the fish-like smoothness of Sylvia Plath's body, there is a veiled memory here of her miscarriage. There may also be a glimmer of a more recent visiting of a similar hospital scene.

'*Only birth matters*,' says the river in 'Salmon Eggs', the closing poem.[29] But the shadow of death also falls upon the water. Much later, Ted explained the origin of 'October Salmon', his favourite poem in the collection, the one originally intended as the title piece:

> I had gone to visit my father who was very ill at the time and I stopped by a nearby salmon river. This was in the autumn, in the early 1980s. And from a bridge, I saw this one fish, a little cock salmon, lying motionless i[n] the clear shallow water – the only fish in a long pool that in October 1961, when I first walked there and counted the fish waiting to spawn in the gravels above and below, had held more than 100. I don't know if he'd spawned but, anyway, this was about him.[30]

These were the last words of one of Hughes's last interviews, published posthumously in the fishing magazine *Wild Steelhead and Salmon*.[31] The dying fish of 'October Salmon', resting after his 2,000-mile

journey home, 'stitched into the torn richness' of the world, is ineluc-
tably associated not only with a past when Sylvia was still alive and
Devon life a fresh dream, but also with the entropy of all things, and
with his dying father. The 'epic poise' of the salmon, held 'steady in his
wounds' and 'loyal to his doom', is also that of Bill Hughes.[32]

Even more notably personal is the delicate lyric 'Ophelia', trans-
planted from *Orts*. It appears opposite one of Keen's best photographs,
a series of silver ripples on a field of black (one of the few images that
shares the atmospheric artfulness of Fay Godwin's black-and-white
work for the *Elmet* project). 'There she goes,' Ted writes, evoking not
only John Everett Millais' famous painting of Ophelia floating down-
stream after her suicide, but also Plath's frequent imagery of dark
water, not least in 'Crossing the Water', the title poem of the selection
of her later poems that Ted had published in 1971. 'Darkfish', he calls
Ophelia, in an inspired coinage. With her 'finger to her lips', she goes
'Staringly into the afterworld'.[33]

Yet once more, the Plathian understory passed unnoticed by
reviewers, who for the most part greeted *River* with respect but with-
out ecstasy. The most enthusiastic response came from the poet
Christopher Reid, Ted's future editor at Faber and Faber, who opened
his *Sunday Times* review with high praise, describing Hughes as a 'great
poet, whose gift has suffered innumerable changes of fortune', some-
times losing itself in 'pretentious aridities', but who in this book has
returned to his best form and proved himself still to be 'the most
exciting English poet of our day'.[34]

River carried the logo of the Countryside Commission as well as
that of British Gas, so Ted felt that his conservationist credentials were
honoured. This was the period when he was becoming ever more
exercised about water pollution. In a letter written just after the book's
publication, he noted that twenty years earlier the Taw and Torridge
had produced a third of all the salmon caught in the West Country, but
by his calculation the catch on the Torridge in the last year was a mere
forty-three fish, whereas it used to be between 1,000 and 1,500. The
river had become 'a farm sewer'.[35] The *River* project proceeded in
tandem with Ted's involvement in a campaign against a new sewage
works at Bideford. Local anglers took the lead in forming the Torridge
Action Group. They planned legal action against the South West Water
Authority, and in September 1985 Ted spoke on their behalf at a

public inquiry. Marshalling an array of evidence ranging from charts showing the decline in catches over half a century to concerned reports from local doctors, he held the room in mesmerised silence as he commanded the room, speaking with all the clarity and allegorical force of his children's tales of how three-quarters of the visitors who came to the area for watersports left the estuary with stomach complaints:

> Bideford chemists prepare for the tourist season as if for a campaign. The chemist in Mill Street displays a window sign, advertising his cure for diarrhoea. And in spite of their con-ditioning the local population does not escape. In general, they complain of an endless grumbling epidemic of throat and chest complaints and stomach disorders … The effect of the estuary's pollution on the state of mind of the local residents is subjective and elusive. However, this depression is very real.[36]

Notwithstanding Ted's impressive intervention, when the public inquiry came to an end the Inspector approved the new 'fine screen-ing' sewage plant.

Like *Remains of Elmet*, *River* was revised extensively when a decade later Ted republished it without photographs in his *Three Books*. The poems are reordered: 'Salmon Eggs' goes from the end to the begin-ning (a better place for a poem about birth) and the sequence now comes to a climax with 'October Salmon' (the original title poem) and the epiphany of 'That Morning', which in the original collection had been buried at the midpoint, lacking the breathing-space it needed. Several fishing poems are added and, again consistently with the treat-ment of *Remains of Elmet*, some prose notes are appended. Here, Hughes dates his awareness of water pollution caused by silage all the way back to the river Don of his wartime childhood. The new version of *River* was published in full consciousness that environmental concerns had become ever more pressing in the decade since the book's first appearance. Ted's correspondence files in the intervening years overflow with gatherings of relevant scientific research and contributions to numerous anti-pollution campaigns. Among the new poems in the *Three Books* version is an ironic rewriting of Rudyard Kipling's 'If': 'If you have infected the sky' and if the earth has 'caught its disease off you', then you, modern Western man, disconnected from your mother earth, 'you are the virus'.[37] When he writes of earth rendered barren and water toxified, Hughes comes to resemble a cross between an Old Testament prophet crying in the wilderness and T. S. Eliot's wounded Fisher King, dangling his rod in the dull canal as he waits in vain for the sterile wasteland to be healed.

The Laureate

Taking stock at the end of 1981, Ted Hughes told Luke Myers that 'My doings touched a low low this last year, many things coming to an end, many mistakes coming to an end too I hope.' He looked back on the Seventies as a decade of 'estrangement' from himself, follies in his life and piddling about in his work. Nothing of 'the real thing' since *Crow*.[1] He had prepared a new *Selected Poems* as a kind of 'audit' of his progress to date, a clearing of the decks before the next big move forward. But the move would not come, not least because money worries meant that he was as ever being forced to accept trivial commissions and distracting commitments. Mercifully, the lengthy tax case arising from the huge royalties on *The Bell Jar* was finally settled. The large cheque, received via Sotheby's, for the sale of Sylvia's manuscripts to Smith, her old college, arrived just in time.

Other than *River*, his publications in the early Eighties were desultory. There was *Under the North Star*, a bestiary of poems for children, with illustrations by Baskin. Some of these, such as 'Puma' and 'The Iron Wolf', first printed on Ted and Nick's Morrigu Press, were by no means exclusively meant for – or easily understood by – young people. Around the same time he produced *A Primer of Birds*, also with Baskin, printed on the latter's Gehenna Press, the first twenty-five copies with signed and numbered Baskin prints for a cool £450 or $900 each. It includes some fine vignettes that would also appear in more accessible volumes. The 'Kingfisher' of *River* was first published here and the first swallow of spring, slipping through 'a fracture in the snow-sheet / Which is still our sky' and then 'Water-skiing out across a wind / That wrecks great flakes against windscreens', would be given a second flight in an expanded edition of *Season Songs* published in 1985.[2] But *A Primer of Birds* is a distinctly patchy little collection, with too many of the poems weighed down by excess Hughesian baggage: an evening thrush is not allowed to be heard in its own right, but is juxtaposed to the sound of a 'church craftsman' who is 'Switing idols, / Rough pre-Goidelic gods and goddesses, / Out of old bits of churchyard yew'.[3] It would have been a better poem if Hughes had simply listened to the thrush in the yew trees in the churchyard beside Court Green.

In the spring of 1982 Faber brought out a new *Selected Poems*, a well-judged selection from all his adult collections to date. Most of the *Gaudete* epilogue poems were there in their own right, but none of the main poem. There were poems from *Season Songs* and *Under the North Star*, those volumes on the borderline between children's and adult work. Two of the *River* poems, one of them being 'That Morning', were included even though the volume itself had not yet been published. The most startling inclusion, though one unobserved by reviewers, was 'You Hated Spain', which was appended to *Crow*, despite the fact that it was a poem about his honeymoon with Sylvia which had nothing to do with the life and songs of the Crow.

The year after the appearance of *River*, he published another children's book, *What is the Truth? A Farmyard Fable for the Young*, with drawings by Reg Lloyd, a painter, potter and printmaker who had previously done some limited-edition silk-screen prints with poems by Ted. The two of them 'found common ground in childhood memories of a shop bell ringing: Reg's parents had owned a draper's shop'.[4] *What is the Truth?*, developed from a farmyard-focused idea proposed by Michael Morpurgo and his wife, is like a gentle version of *Crow*. It begins with God saying that he will ask humankind a few simple questions. In their sleep, the people of the village, on which God and his Son are looking down by moonlight, will say what they truly know. Each then tells truly, in verse, of an animal that they know. Again, Hughes is coming at his central theme indirectly: the quest for the inner truth of things, and of self, which may be revealed first in dreams and then in art. The most moving poem in the collection is 'Bees', which turns on the image of a wedding and ends with a 'Priestly bee' that 'in a shower of petals, / Glues Bride and Groom together with honey'.[5] Beekeeper Sylvia would have loved this.

Throughout this time, he was writing essays and introductions, extremely variable in subject and tone, jobbing work one moment, private passions the next. He took on short pieces to give a leg-up to

fellow-writers, commissions for friends, opportunities to make a little
money for himself or for a worthwhile cause. He was equally happy
writing about the relative merits of Stoat's Tail and Silver Invicta flies
for an essay on the Rivers Taw and Torridge in a volume called *West
Country Fly Fishing* or offering a poem to a slim volume published in
memory of the radiantly beautiful and dazzlingly clever poet Frances
Horovitz, who died of cancer of the ear, aged forty-five, in October
1983 (Ted was a huge admirer of her work, and had hoped that his
friend Ted Cornish might cure her).[6] Typically, in the autumn of 1984
there appeared a poem on the river Nymet together with a polemic
on the decline of the otter in the rivers of the West Country due to
the pesticide dieldrin in the late Fifties and then the destruction of
their habitat under the policies of the Severn-Trent Water Authority.
This was published in a coffee-table volume extolling the natural
beauties of, and environmental threats to, *Britain: A World by Itself*
('Reflections on the landscape by eminent British writers'). Then a
few weeks later, in completely different vein, there appeared a long,
crabbed, inward-looking introduction to *The Complete Prints of Leonard
Baskin*, arguing that his forms were 'drawn from the hard core of
human pain'.[7] He determined to take from Baskin's work the lesson
that all art comes from a wound and the greater the pain the greater
the art, because art was simultaneously 'an anaesthetic and at the same
time a healing session drawing up the magical healing electrics'.[8]

Accolades did not especially interest him. In 1982 Exeter University
gave him an honorary doctorate and he wondered what such a thing
was for, other than raising a smile. It did not feel important in com-
parison to the real Ph.D. that was clearly going to be Nick's destiny
after graduating from Oxford. In 1984, Nicholas Hughes duly went to
the University of Alaska in Fairbanks to research the fish of the Yukon
river system. Ted described him proudly to Luke Myers: 6 foot 3½
inches (just taller than Ted himself, who was beginning to stoop with
age), immensely hard-working, very organised (far more so than Ted),
strong and fit (a weightlifter), funny and happy, but with a touch of the
Germanic quality of the Plaths. Frieda, meanwhile, had divorced her
farm boy Des and set up home with an insurance salesman, whom Ted
thought was a bit of a dodgy character. She now rejoiced in a superbly
voluptuous figure, was the image of her mother, and had the energy

of a rocket. She was writing surreal children's stories, making dresses and painting in a bold abstract style.

In contrast to his pride in his children, Ted was despairing about his own work. In this same letter to Myers, he acknowledged that it was a quiet time as far as his poetry was concerned. The events of 1963 and 1969 had been like 'giant steel doors shutting down over great parts of myself'.[9] He still had not emerged from his 'self-anaesthesia'. He worried that life wouldn't be long enough to wake up from it. He knew that what he had to do was break through into direct confrontation with those two terrible years. His dreams were telling him to look to his own past. In one of them, a lion licked his face under a new moon and led him into the landscape of his childhood – Mexborough, the pond at Crookhill, foundry lights over Sheffield and the earth burning, an open wound, an 'infernal crucible'. In a perfumed garden, he wept and mourned for his mother, half knowing that the real work of mourning was still to be done: germinations, gestation, but 'prohibited sources'.[10]

And there were poetic models available to him. He was trying to persuade Faber to publish more of the poetry of Yehuda Amichai, in which he found the honesty and integrity of 'the human being speaking like a human being about being a human being'.[11] Amichai's poetry, he said, opened him to his own life, enabled him to see his past freshly and to find richness at every turn. It freed him from his mental cage.

Then there was Seamus Heaney. Ted began to sense that he was being overtaken by the poet who had begun under his own strong influence. In the summer of 1984, Seamus had sent him his latest collection, *Station Island*, a volume that hit a new stride – some would see it as the apex of Heaney's achievement. 'Station Island itself must be what you've been pushing yourself towards. It obviously took some confronting,' wrote Ted in response. 'The passages where you tackle the greatest fright seem to me the most masterful successes. And I get the feel your real kingdom is in there – that's your way in & forward.'[12] The volume's title sequence, which Ted saw as the key, was a run of poems in which personal memory, elegy and myth were held in moving and measured equilibrium. Heaney mediates his personal and political development through a series of Irish encounters, at the climax with the imagined ghost of James Joyce. The publisher's blurb described the sequence as 'an autobiographical quest' concerning 'the growth of a poet's mind' – Wordsworth's description of the epic poem that was posthumously entitled *The Prelude*. Was this the moment for Ted to publish something similar, to release the ghost of Sylvia as Heaney had released his family ghosts?[13]

That summer, Ted combined literary festivals and fishing trips in the west of Ireland and the Orkneys. Sir John Betjeman, Poet Laureate since 1972, had died in May and the talk on the literary circuit inevitably turned to the appointment of his successor. Ted noted wryly that Philip Larkin had started signing himself 'P.L.' He would surely be regarded as the perfect choice, with his reassuring tone of voice, his occasional four-letter words to provide a dash of popular credibility, his loyal politics, and his mindset distinctly that of the little Englander.[14] Ted's personal preference was for Charles Causley, but over the coming months there was a general assumption that it would be P.L. for P.L. The whole thing seemed such a foregone conclusion that Ladbrokes the bookies stopped taking bets and Faber started reprinting Larkin's books.

In late November, Ted and Carol joined their friends Michael and Clare Morpurgo on a Nile cruise. This was relaxing for Ted after an exhausting two-week tour in which he had undertaken about twenty readings in the Midlands and the North – Oxford, Birmingham, Hull, Manchester, West Kirby on the Wirral. He had reached, he reckoned, some 6,000 sixth-formers. Morpurgo had become a friend after a meeting on the riverbank in Devon. Ted's children's books were an inspiration for his own, and the two wives got on famously. Ted and Carol were both giving assistance of various kinds to Farms for City Children, the charity established by the Morpurgos which gave urban children from all over the country the chance to spend a week living and working on a real farm in the heart of the Devon countryside.

Refreshed by fishing and sightseeing, impressed by a glimpse of a 6-foot-long crocodile-like Nile monitor[15] crawling into the reeds, but tired from the journey, they arrived back at Court Green to a huge pile of post. Sorting through it, Ted came across an envelope marked 'Confidential', with the return address 10 Downing Street. It was an enquiry as to whether he had received the Prime Minister's communication. Could he reply one way or the other, as a matter of urgency?

'Here we go,' he thought, 'how horrible.' Then he found the original letter from Margaret Thatcher: would he object to his name being put to Her Majesty the Queen for the position of Poet Laureate in Ordinary ('in ordinary?' he wrote to the Baskins with the written equivalent of a quizzical look).[16] He assumed, correctly, that Larkin must have refused. He felt as if he had fallen into a trap: whether he accepted or refused, demons would be raised. They had got back on a Friday, so he had the weekend to think about the pros and cons. He phoned Olwyn, who refrained from pressing him, merely remarking that acceptance would be good for his American sales. On the Monday, he phoned Downing Street and accepted.

The Palace issued a press release on Wednesday 19 December 1984: 'The Queen has been pleased to approve that Edward James Hughes be appointed Poet Laureate in Ordinary to Her Majesty in succession to the late Sir John Betjeman.' It helpfully explained that the Poet Laureate is a member of Her Majesty's Household, with annual remuneration of £70 plus a case of wine (actually a large quantity of sherry). Both salary and perk were unchanged since the time of John Dryden, the first official holder of the post back in the late seventeenth century. The announcement described Hughes as 'both author and poet'. It listed a clutch of his many awards: the Guinness Poetry Award in 1958, the John Simon Guggenheim Fellowship in 1959–60, the Somerset Maugham Award in 1960, the City of Florence Poetry Prize in 1969, the Premio Internazionale Taormina in 1973 and the Queen's Medal for Poetry the following year. The press welcomed the choice, noting how young Hughes was for the role and what a change he would be from Betjeman, to whom Larkin had seemed the natural successor. The London *Times* suggested that it was rather like a grim young crow replacing a cuddly old teddy bear. In America, with its dream of the backwoodsman going from a log cabin to the White House, there was particular emphasis on Ted's humble origins: son of a Yorkshire carpenter, former nightwatchman and rose gardener, and so forth. Plath's name was mentioned in most American reports of the appointment, but generally without rancour.

New Year brought vast numbers of congratulatory letters and considerable uncertainty as to what the role would entail – though it had been made clear that it was very much up to him to interpret his duties as he saw fit. He was especially pleased to hear from Larkin.[17]

Joking that he now considered himself a 'public convenience', Ted set about answering the deluge of requests to be the patron of this, the president of that, the guest of honour at such and such, a judge of so and so. Even gifts came with a price: someone sent him a package of lovely flies for salmon fishing, but only as bait to make him write a poem for the anniversary of the escape from Colditz.

He refused many such requests, but he took his royal duties very seriously. Two days after his appointment was announced, Prince Harry, younger son of Charles (Prince of Wales and Duke of Cornwall) and Diana, was baptised. Ted dashed off a 'Rain-Charm for the Duchy', with a subtitle that was soon mocked by the liberal metropolitan literary establishment: 'A Blessed, Devout Drench for the Christening of His Royal Highness Prince Harry'. It is in fact a very good poem, instantly achieving a standard he would never reach again in his Laureate work. Nineteen-eighty-four had been a year of drought. The poem begins with an image of the windscreen of Ted's Volvo 'frosted with dust'. A thunderstorm breaks and the rivers of the West Country are replenished. The water imagery befits the occasion of a baptism, the catalogue of river-names follows in a grand tradition of English royal poetry going back to Elizabethan times, and Hughes takes the opportunity to make a point about pollution ('the Okement, nudging her detergent bottles, tugging at her nylon stockings, starting to trundle her Pepsi-Cola cans').[18] The poem was published in the *Observer* newspaper just before Christmas. Its environmental message did not go unnoticed among local politicians in the West Country. Ted expressed pleasure that the Laureateship was clearly going to give him a public platform – but also relief that he had restrained himself from including some lines that were in the original draft of the poem, which, pre-Laureateship, he had intended for *River*: 'And the Torridge, that hospital sluice of all the doctored and scabby farms from Welcombe to Hatherlea to Torrington / Poor, bleached leper in her pit'.[19] It would not have done for his first official poem to have received a libel writ from an irate Devon farmer.

Two years earlier, he had written a poem for Prince William's birth, based on the royal child's 'very strange' horoscope and alluding to the White Goddess. He had not published it, out of respect for Poet Laureate Betjeman, but perhaps also because he recognised that it was not exactly his best poetic work: 'Sun, moon and all their family stand / Around a new-born babe, in England ... And a goddess, half-mother, half-coils, / The Serpent of Enigma, guarding the spoils.'[20] Now he sent handwritten copies of both princely poems to the Royal Household, to go into the private collections of the boys themselves.

In the summer of 1985 he published a pair of poems for the eighty-fifth birthday of the Queen Mother, one grandly mythical ('The Dream of the Lion') and the other, much more to her taste, about salmon. The best thing about the Laureateship was that his royal connection opened doors to some very high-class fishing. The pressure to perform in public at galas and fundraisers was a price worth paying for that. But he also needed to get away from the spotlight. In this regard, Nick's residence in Fairbanks was heaven-sent.

Some of Ted's happiest days in the first decade of his Laureateship were spent under big skies far from little England, with his son in Alaska or with fishing friends in British Columbia and the Yukon. The air was light there, he said, and he felt unencumbered, free in a way that he never could be at home.[21] The experience of fishing with Nick in Alaska was immortalised not only in the perfectly achieved *River* poem 'That Morning' but also in 'The Gulkana' (the name of a tributary of the glacial Copper River), a longer poem in the collection. It is an attempt to capture the feeling of the far north. The manuscript drafts ran to 150 pages. The climax of 'The Gulkana' has a similar feeling to 'That Morning' as it creates a sense of unity with nature achieved in the act of fishing:

> Word by word
> The voice of the river moved in me.
> It was like lovesickness.[22]

On such a river, his troubles with women were displaced by a greater love.

In 1986 he combined his visit to Nick with a poetry reading at the University of British Columbia, and for ten years thereafter he would return most years for a fortnight to an environment that rekindled his childhood self. He confided to his host that as boys he and Gerald had made a pact to emigrate to British Columbia. But of course Gerald had ended up in Australia and Ted in Devon. Now he had arrived, albeit transiently, at their original destination.

Ehor Boyanowsky, criminal psychologist and professor at Simon Fraser University, author of academic papers on violence and aggression, was Ted's host. In his memoir of his days 'in the wild with Ted Hughes', he sets the scene for their first expedition up the Dean River, 52 degrees north and 126 west, legendary among fishermen as the best place in the world for 'that most glamorous of fish' (Ted's phrase), *Oncorhynchus mykiss*, the steelhead, or seagoing rainbow-trout, which could weigh up to 55 pounds and grow to almost 4 feet in length:

> The river hisses against the oars and lashes at the inflatable raft, trying to force our craft downstream through the rapids into a looming logjam. Hunkered down on the pontoon, Ted looks around, feeling the river's power; he drinks in the spicy aroma of the great cedars, and his face is wet from the spray, his gaze filled with the sweep of muscular granite cliffs shouldering the banks and the undulating horizon of glacier-topped peaks upstream and down.[23]

First he tries with a 'dry fly' – intended to bring the mighty but elusive steelhead to the surface, catch him on the fly, gain the full sensation. 'Like making love with the lights on' is how Boyanowsky puts it. No luck, though the seed is sown for a poem called 'Be a Dry-Fly Purist' that will be included in the second edition of *River*. Ted then puts on 'a sinking tip line' and a 'Squamish Poacher' fly. He casts his 'powerful fifteen-foot Bruce and Walker rod' upon the water: 'Turning off the lights, are we, Ehor?' 'Afraid so, better sex in the dark than none at all.' And on the third cast comes the reward: 'Thank you, Ehor, thank you for bringing me to my first steelhead. She is surpassingly beautiful. Thank you.'[24] The fish is gently returned to the water, as, according to local custom, steelhead always should be, for fear of alienating the spirit of the mighty river.

Boyanowsky and his friends made Ted keep the logbook of the week's fishing. The highs and lows of great catches and near misses. The evening meals of steak béarnaise, baked potatoes and magnums of unnamed red wine. The grizzlies strolling through the camp. The log gave him raw material for a new poem called 'The Bear', which he included in the revised version of *River* in *Three Books*: first a storm, then the 'ecstasy' of mountain and river embodied in the steelhead. These lines are an especially striking manifestation of the way in which fishing could stand in for sex in Ted's later years:

> This actually was the love-act that had brought them
> Out of everywhere, squirming and leaping,
> And that had brought us too – besotted voyeurs –
> Trying to hook ourselves into it.
> And all the giddy orgasm of the river
> Quaking under our feet –

And then the sight of a bear that salutes and vanishes, 'a scapegoat, an offering'.[25]

His second trip to British Columbia was combined with an arts festival in Victoria, where he was delayed by a ruptured appendix. But that did not stop him joining his new friends, and Nick, who had come down from Fairbanks, on the Thompson River. Father and son shot chukars (a kind of partridge) together, one of the few times Ted had picked up a rifle since his early days with Gerald. As he got to know Ehor Boyanowsky and his fishing companions, Ted relaxed and began to tell stories. For instance, of the time when he and Nick were fishing for pike on an Irish lough and the locals started asking probing questions, and the next thing they knew they were hauling up a heavy object from the depths. Just as they discovered that it was a 'heavy burlap bag', they realised that they were being watched through binoculars from the shoreline. They had stumbled upon an IRA arms cache and needed to make a quick getaway.[26]

At night in the wilderness, by the crackle and flicker of the campfire, he opened his heart. Who were his favourite artists? Bosch, Goya and Cranach. What cause was closest to his heart? The environment – 'If it were up to me alone, I would give all my money to Greenpeace.'[27] Why did he marry Sylvia? 'Because she was beautiful, passionate, a genius and I loved her.'[28]

And why did he marry Carol? He met a 'local lad named Orchard' while fishing, who told of his teenage sister. Later she would occasionally help out with the children, who took to her straight away. So did his mother: 'Marry that girl. She is one in a million.' But she was just a girl, he told his mother, and so much younger than him. He thought no more of the idea for a time. Then Olwyn came down to Devon and they all went out to a dinner party. Carol was invited. The girl seemed a little overcome by the loud banter, the wine, the company. She said little. Olwyn said, 'And what do you have to say for yourself?' At that point, Carol 'fainted dead away right at the table'. Ted gathered her into his arms and took her out into the garden for some fresh air: 'I set her on the grass in the moonlight and stroked her forehead and, gazing at her, her long black hair, pale skin and lovely features in repose, I fell in love with her.' The fishermen loved this story, not caring whether it was 'true or apocryphal'.[29] Ehor proposed a toast to Carol. 'My true salvation,' said Ted.[30]

When Ehor visited Devon, he found Carol to be a wonderful cook but rather a formidable presence. His memory is that she took one look at the cameras slung over his shoulder and told him that he should not take photographs at Court Green. The house was not what he expected: it seemed 'too tidy and stylish to be Ted's'. But then Ted summoned him into a long dark room 'replete with papers, fishing gear and more papers and books stacked and strewn as far as the eye can see'. Ted's world: 'chaos on an epic scale'. This was where Ted was gathering material for the projected but unfinished *Faber Book of Fishing* on which he and Ehor were collaborating. Then Ted showed his guest the writing hut in the garden – a single room with a lamp and a big desk, raised on stilts on the ancient mound, looking for all the world like a large Wendy house or low-level treehouse. 'This is where I work,' Ted explained, 'away from the phone and family and friends.' Big books could only be finished in such a place, otherwise 'the tendrils reach out and surround you and drag you away, every day, as certain as the seasons come and go'.[31]

Much as Ted's friends adored him, they acknowledged that the marriage was not easy for Carol. There was nothing in her farming and nursing background to prepare her for marriage at the age of twenty-two to a famous poet almost twice her age, a man of prodigious energy and capacious sexual appetite, with a restless desire for new experience, a fierce but cranky intelligence that frequently veered into fads and eccentric diversions, and an unwavering creative mission centred in the conviction that he would by the time of his death be, as Keats put it, 'among the English poets'. The gaze of press and public, consequent upon his dead first wife's fame, created great strain. As did the poet's enduring memory of that first wife. Not to mention the presence of a stepdaughter who was the absolute image of her mother.

What could she do, friends such as Ehor asked themselves? Feed him well, keep a clean house (though he wouldn't really have cared if it had been dirty), maintain the financial accounts (she was good at this), make the garden beautiful (she was very good, and very fulfilled, when it came to this), be an exemplary hostess when required (she was always beautifully dressed, with impeccable hair and makeup), avoid asking too many questions about his extra-curricular activities. For Ted, Court Green as remade by Carol was the place of stability and homeliness; he worked off his excesses in London and on his reading tours and fishing trips.

Ehor Boyanowsky once confided in Ted at a difficult time, when his wife was having an affair. Ted wrote back with words of kindness, comfort and advice: he could understand the wife's point of view because he too had experienced sexual obsession leading to infidelity. He explained that on two occasions he had been 'out of control' yet 'remaining during and forever after in love with – for him – a person infinitely more significant'. On the first occasion, when married to Sylvia, 'he experienced total separation and loss'. On the second, when married to Carol, the response was, he presumed, 'total forgiveness'.[32]

In the mountains of British Columbia, by the mighty Dean River, far from all such worries, Ted and his Canadian fishing friends marvelled at the aurora borealis. Back in Vancouver they toured the strip clubs. 'They are so much more elegant and feminine than I recall from my youth in England, in the army,' Ted allegedly remarked of the graceful naked pole-dancers. 'Nor did they [the dancers of his youth] remove all their clothing. Amazing.'[33]

In February 1986 Ted laid out in the yard of Court Green a fishing line in the shape of a noose, with a pile of monkey nuts in the middle. An escaped peacock had taken up residence in the garden and was eating Carol's spring flowers. He told the story in a letter to Nick in Alaska: how he got the bird at the first attempt and how an airborne upturned peacock was a remarkable sight. He closed the noose, threw a blanket over his prey and took it to Nethercott, Michael and Clare Morpurgo's farm for city children, where he hoped it would have novelty value. It was soon eaten by a fox.[34] A couple of weeks later he was at the annual dinner of the Salmon and Trout Association. The guest speaker was the actor Michael Hordern. The chairman of the association owned a wonderful 2-mile stretch of the Torridge, which Ted fished on the first day of the season. Such was the life of the countryman.

On 4 June 1987, just over a week before the general election in which Margaret Thatcher coasted to her third successive term as Prime Minister, Hughes published an 'ecological dialogue' in *The Times* newspaper, headed 'First Things First' and subtitled 'An Election Duet, performed in the Womb by foetal Twins'. It blamed man's headlong obsession with economic growth, and more particularly the policies of Western governments and the regulations of the European Economic Community, for a mountain of wasted butter, for contaminated tap water, leukaemia brought on by pesticides sprayed on grain fields, and even the phenomenon of cot death. The price of increasing the Gross National Product was leafless trees, rivers without fish, and human beings suffering from pre-senile dementia. The poem begins in loose iambic pentameter and ends in brisk rhyming trimeter, but contains in the middle the two longest and perhaps least poetic lines of verse that Hughes ever wrote:

> And if the cost of Annual Expansion of the World Chemical
>   Industry taken as a whole over the last two decades is a
>   40% drop in the sperm count of all human males (nor can
>   God alone help the ozone layer or the ovum)
> Then let what can't be sold to your brother and sister be
>   released on the 3rd World and let it return by air and sea
>   to drip down the back of your own throat at night.[35]

He explained to a fellow-poet that pollution was the great theme of the age. He noticed, judging children's poetry competitions, how it was something that even six- and seven-year-olds were worried about. The poem, he explained, was inspired by his reading of John Elkington's book *The Poisoned Womb: Human Reproduction in a Polluted*

World, published the previous year. Elkington was a preacher of eco-apocalypse, speculating that toxins were causing a massive reduction in human fertility. Ted did not have any faith in Mrs Thatcher's willingness to address the question. For one thing, her husband Denis was involved in the waste-disposal trade. For another, she was the sort of woman upon whom nothing could put the frighteners. She resembled an army commander who believed that he could afford a casualty rate of 25 per cent. Her intransigence was ironic, since she had an Oxford degree in Chemistry. But perhaps it was not surprising: as Prime Minister she would listen only to professional consultants with vested interests. Besides, when she had been a practising chemist her job had merely been to research 'the maximum number of bubbles that can be pumped into ice-cream, before it disillusions the customers'.[36]

Ted was worried by bubbles of another kind. His fishing friend Ian Cook, who lived in a house on the Exe, had observed some kind of white foam boiling up on the weir where he fished the river Creedy. There was a sewage works a little way upstream. He would eventually bring a civil case against South West Water. Ted offered his usual support: 'Top Poet in Water Fight' read the headline in the local paper.[37] Inspired by Ted, Cook and his lawyer dramatically invoked the rights enshrined in the Magna Carta. The judge compared the relevant stretch of river to 'the face of a beautiful woman scarred by disease', a metaphor very much up Ted's street. Against expectation, Cook won his case. Ted told the press that it was a historic victory because it had 'reactivated the power of common law in this terrific issue of water quality in rivers'.[38] Instead of seeking damages, Cook asked the water authority to contribute to the research of the Institute of Freshwater Ecology into the polluting effect of detergents in the Exe. This established a connection between Ted and the ecotoxicologist Professor John Sumpter, who was working on the phenomenon of endocrine disruptors causing male fish to change gender.

The 'ecological dialogue' during the election campaign and the South West Water court case are just two of the many instances in which Hughes used his public profile to address environmental concerns. Whether it was ammonia in the Torridge estuary, a proposal to establish a 'Tarka Trail' that risked disrupting the fragile ecosystem of the riverbank and bringing the masses to his sacred territory, an amusement park beside the river at Knaresborough back in Yorkshire, or an international campaign to save the black rhinoceros, he was ready to pen a protest. And he always made it clear that concern for the natural world was also concern for humankind, most forcefully in an interview on the occasion of the publication of his ecological children's fable, *The Iron Woman*. He said that most people tended to 'defend or rationalise the pollution of water'. The general assumption was that environmentalists were merely 'defending fish or insects or flowers'. This missed the point that 'the effects on otters and so on are indicators of what's happening to *us*'. The issue was not so much to look after 'the birds and bees' as to 'ferry human beings through the next century': 'The danger is multiplied through each generation. We don't really know what bomb has already been planted in the human system.'[39] With the Cold War at an end, the old image of the fear of nuclear annihilation was translated into fear of global ecocide. Such was the life of the Poet Laureate as ecowarrior.

He always enjoyed describing his environmental discoveries and interventions in lengthy letters to Nick in Alaska. He was also superb at providing long-distance paternal advice. When Nick broke up with his girlfriend Madeline, whom he had known since Oxford, Ted comforted him with his own story of a life 'oscillating between fierce relationships that become tunnel traps, and sudden escapes into wide freedom when the whole world seems to be just there for the taking'. It is a letter of extraordinary beauty, wisdom and tenderness, telling of the inner child and the paradox that 'the only time most people feel alive is when they're suffering, when something overwhelms their ordinary, careful armour, and the naked child is flung out onto the world'. There is a key to the source of true elegiac and cathartic poetry here: 'That's why the things that are worst to undergo are best to remember.' Father Ted in the role of a very wise agony aunt, this is Hughes at his most humane and compassionate, yet with the necessary touch of self-deprecation: 'And that's how we measure out our real respect for people – by the degree of feeling they can register, the voltage of life they can carry and tolerate – and enjoy. End of sermon. As Buddha says: live like a mighty river.'[40]

★

Countryman, ecowarrior and family man came together in his next collection of poetry for Faber and Faber, which he entitled *Wolfwatching*. Planned by the end of 1987, it was dedicated to Aunt Hilda and published in September 1989. It is a thin volume, in both proportion and poetic development, gathering further elegiac poetry of child-hood memory in the vein of *Remains of Elmet*. The family history is padded out with occasional pieces, such as his polemical lines written for the black rhino campaign. The collection is marred by some of the worst phraseology of the later Hughes, in which the over-vigorous and monotonous hammer-blows of the mother-tongue are combined with a dip into what Philip Larkin scathingly called the myth kitty: 'Oracular spore-breath', 'goblin clump / Of agaric', 'scraggy sheep', 'ectoplasmic pulp', 'Temenos Jaguar mask – a vogue mandala: / Half a Loa, half a drugged Oglala'.[41] Ted himself had doubts about the quality of some of the work that he had included: 'doubting my powers and getting older', he said of the collection. 'Of course both wolves are caged.'[42] He told the critic Keith Sagar, who was by this time tracking his master's every literary move, that it was a funereal volume, a series of 'obsequies over a state of mind that is to me, now, defunct'.[43]

The importance of the book comes from the increasing confidence and directness with which Hughes exposes his personal voice. At its heart are the family poems, most of which he had originally published in fugitive form in the mid-Eighties. Here are tender evocations of his shell-shocked father in the aftermath of the Great War ('Dust As We Are' and 'For the Duration'); of his mother's tears for her husband's damaged soul as she bends over her sewing machine ('Source'); of happier times of early boyhood with Ma walking up Hardcastle Crags ('Leaf Mould'); of Uncle Walt as a young man 'Under High Wood' on the Somme, then as an old man on the clifftop, seeing a peregrine falcon and looking out on the Atlantic towards 'Untrodden, glorious America' ('Walt'). The most telling inclusion is 'Sacrifice', the poem about Uncle Albert's suicide, written just days before Sylvia took her own life in 1963 but only published two decades later, after his father's death.[44]

Wolfwatching was a selection of the Poetry Book Society. In intro-ducing it in the society's *Bulletin*, Ted explained that he had wanted *Remains of Elmet* to focus on the atmosphere of the place, so as to complement Fay Godwin's photographs. He had accordingly excluded more autobiographical poems, to avoid 'hijacking Fay's inclusive vision'.[45] Now the poems of family remembrance were gathered together. Later, he disparaged the collection as 'various pieces that I wished to get out of the way – i.e. published, in order to clear the decks for something different'.[46] The critical response was by and large respectful but muted. The poet Mick Imlah offered the most astute commentary: he saw that the two 'Uncle' poems were the best in the book and that they 'sound like a new start'.[47]

Their true home was in Ted's Yorkshire collection, and that is where they ended up. A year after the re-release of *Remains of Elmet* without photographs as part of *Three Books*, the Elmet poems and Fay Godwin's images were reunited. Faber produced a new edition of the collection, the title now stripped down to a bare *Elmet*. The quality of the paper was much better than that of the 1979 *Remains of Elmet*, so the black-and-white images, many of which had been very murky in the original edition, now looked fresh and sharp. At the end, Ted added in his family poems, implicitly dismembering *Wolfwatching*. 'Sacrifice', 'For the Duration' and 'Anthem for Doomed Youth' are turned into a run of elegies for both place and people, both family and wider community, shadowed by the Great War. Hughes regarded this final version of *Elmet* as the definitive version of his project to memorialise his native valley and its inhabitants, but because the volume was for the most part a reissue, which looked like an expensive coffee-table book (£30 in hardback, £14.99 or $19.99 even for the paperback), it did not have the sales or the impact that it deserved. It remains his most underrated work.

Ted Hughes enjoyed writing Laureate poems. With his belief in the poet as shaman of the tribe and the royal family as embodiment of the land, he took the role more seriously than any of his twentieth-century predecessors. But, for his deeper poetic self, the new role was a new impediment. If in the autumn of 1984 he was on the brink of following Amichai and Heaney into a poetry of raw personal exposure, the Laureateship held him back. The last thing he wanted in his first years as a national figure was renewed attention in the press to the end of his first marriage and Sylvia's death. That would have been the inevitable consequence of publication of any significant part of the long-gestated project that eventually became *Birthday Letters*.

So he kept on approaching his own story indirectly. He acknowledged that among his children's stories one that came especially close to his inner life was *Ffangs the Vampire Bat and the Kiss of Truth*, published in 1986. Ffangs is a vampire bat who doesn't like the sight of blood and only wants to be human. After various adventures including an audience with the Queen in Buckingham Palace – the sort of encounter which a newly crowned Poet Laureate was well qualified to write about – he goes to the moon, where he discovers the Truth when he kisses a girl called Selena who has a snake in her mouth. She is a figuration of the White Goddess, but her bite-kiss which transforms Ffangs into his true self is also that of Sylvia at Falcon Yard. There was more of that true self in this story than in the poetry collections he published at this time. They were *Flowers and Insects*, dedicated to Frieda and the Baskins' daughter Lucretia, a slender volume from Faber containing some very pedestrian writing and few memorable lyrics other than 'Sunstruck Foxglove', and *The Cat and the Cuckoo*, a series of children's poems to accompany colour illustrations of animals by Reg Lloyd. This was dedicated to, among others, 'all the children who visit Farms for City Children'.

There was another reason besides the Laureateship why this was not the moment to write publicly about his relationship with Sylvia. On 6 January 1987, he wrote to János Csokits about the usual sort of literary business: the problems that the shoestring publisher Peter Jay was having over a proposed new selection of János Pilinszky's selected poems, the equally slow progress of a collection of essays on translating poetry that Danny Weissbort was putting together. But these were trifling matters compared to dramatic developments in the lawsuit launched by Jane Anderson in response to the *Bell Jar* film: he was waiting for a phone call that would summon him to an American courtroom.

26

Trial

Ignorant of the tumblers in the lock
Of U.S. Copyright Law
Which your dead fingers so deftly unpicked.

('Costly Speech', in Birthday Letters*)*[1]

When the letter arrived in the spring of 1982, he had no idea who the plaintiff was. A single name: Anderson. He even wondered whether it might be an anagram. The list of co-defendants, an assortment of American INCs and LLCs, was equally baffling. His own name came last. He couldn't work out what Anderson was complaining about. He had never read *The Bell Jar*. He hadn't seen the film, though he had heard that it was very bad. Nor had he read Edward Butscher's biography of Sylvia Plath, which made a single passing reference to the character of Joan Gilling, rival to Esther Greenwood for the love of Buddy Willard, being 'loosely based' on Jane Anderson. Having eventually grasped what it was all about, Ted was puzzled: didn't the fact that the literary character hanged herself cancel the identification? Anderson had not hanged herself. She had lived to sue nineteen years after the novel was published.

The financial stakes were high. Reading the initial correspondence, he discovered that, by some dreadful oversight, there was a clause in the *Bell Jar* film contract making him liable for half the cost of any libel action. This created a 'certain fieriness in the air' for him, 'A certain stress of the blood, a burning, a restlessness'. But the more he thought about the questions raised by Jane Anderson's action, the more intrigued he became. The issues – literary, psychological and biographical as well as legal – were fascinating. The case, he thought,

was going to be a bit like an illness: something that would wholly
preoccupy him until it went away. The good thing about illnesses was
that they activated the immune system. And his deepest creative
immune system, he had to admit, had been dormant for a very long
time. There was 'a certain thrill at the hazard ahead – a certain adren-
alin elation'.[2]

The American legal system moved very, very slowly. Especially
when there were nearly a dozen defendants involved, most of them
corporations. Ted had to work closely with Olwyn, who, as his agent,
had negotiated the film deal for *The Bell Jar* back in the Seventies.
They instructed Jeffrey Jones of Palmer and Dodge, 1 Beacon Street,
Boston. After two and a half years of information-gathering, delay and
negotiation, they made a settlement offer. In October 1984, Ted took
the unusual step of writing a personal letter to Jane Anderson, telling
her how anxious he was about the stress the case was causing her and
giving the reasons why he could not have known about the possible
identification of her with the character of Joan Gilling. He offered to
give Anderson control of the American rights to *The Bell Jar*, in order
to bring the whole thing to an end. He pleaded poverty: the legal costs
had already put his net income for the last financial year into the red.
Just for the record, he reasserted his position that he had no prior
knowledge of Anderson, that he had not read Butscher, and that from
a literary-analytic point of view the identification of her with Joan
Gilling was most unlikely. No settlement was agreed. The case rumbled
on.

So it was that he flew to New York in March 1986, to make his
Deposition. He was worried that the case would be pre-judged in the
court of public opinion, with him being found guilty as a form of
mass revenge on the part of the feminists, with Robin Morgan at their
head. His friends Neil and Susan Schaeffer met him at the airport and
they stopped for a good fish dinner on the way to their home.
Supporters were being rounded up. Neil had rung Norman Mailer,
seeking his assistance. Susan gave him a very helpful essay she had
written about 'The Biographical Fallacy', a parallel to 'The Intentional
Fallacy' that he had learned about as a student of English Literature at
Cambridge. As a literary work should be judged by its own internal
logic, not by the intentions of its author, so no novel should be judged
by its alleged biographical origins. Susan Schaeffer had some experi-

ence of dealing with people who tried to identify themselves as characters in her novels.

When they went into the city the next day, they saw Ted's old friend from Sylvia's day, Ben Sonnenberg, now in a wheelchair. He said that he would try to get Philip Roth to help. Ted jotted down some calculations. He had made $70,000 from the sale of the film rights back in the Seventies. It looked as if the legal case had already cost him £40,000.

Then it was up to Boston to do his homework for the Deposition. He stayed at the Harvard Faculty Club, where he met Seamus Heaney, who now held the prestigious position of Boylston Professor of Rhetoric and Oratory. The helpful development in the case was that the defendants' legal team had obtained an old diary of Jane Anderson's from her student days, in which she wrote 'Today got into bed for first time with [a female name].' If she really did have history as a lesbian, then surely it could not be defamation to have portrayed her as one?

While in Boston, Ted went out to Wellesley to see Aurelia Plath, who seemed shrunken and hunched with age, but still full of spirit. Then on Sunday 24 March, he spent the day at Seamus Heaney's 'jittery electric typewriter' (he still preferred handwriting even to a manual typewriter), preparing his statement.[3] The following day, in ripe Boston light, he met his lawyer, Jeffrey Jones, who suggested that it would be best if Ted were not called as a witness should the case come to trial. So the Deposition was going to be vital. He showed Ted the two pieces of evidence that were going to cause the most difficulty: a letter that he had signed saying that he was happy with the film and his signature beside the statement 'this clause is cancelled', the clause being paragraph 12 of the film contract, where it said that there was to be no reference in any publicity to the movie having autobiographical origins. The cancellation of the clause had licensed the film company to take the biographical line. That was the essence of the problem, and it lay at Ted's door.

His contrary argument, which he had been working out through detailed analysis of the novel, supported by hundreds of pages of summaries, quotations, diagrams and flow charts, was that *The Bell Jar* was a narrative of Sylvia's battle with her own double. This, after all, had been her great literary theme ever since her undergraduate thesis on Dostoevsky. There may have been bits of other people in Joan

Gilling, among them Sylvia's Cambridge housemate Jane Baltzell and her Smith roommate, Nancy Hunter Steiner, who had mentioned the connection, and not objected to it, in an affectionate memoir of Sylvia. So perhaps there was some small element of Jane Anderson. But the most important original for Joan Gilling was Sylvia herself. The trouble was, this was a sophisticated literary and psychological argument. Wouldn't a jury be more likely to take a simplistic view and side with the wronged Dr Anderson?

When Ted became acquainted with the content of Anderson's Deposition, he got three very nasty surprises.[4] The first was a letter from Heinemann, the original English publishers of *The Bell Jar* by 'Victoria Lucas', thanking him for permission to use Sylvia Plath's real name in any republication of the novel. This was dated 13 March 1963, just a month after Sylvia's death. Secondly, there was mention of the letter he had written to Aurelia saying that he wanted to buy a house in North Devon, so he needed money and publication of *The Bell Jar* in the United States would be the best way of getting it. This would not look good for his reputation, especially with the feminists. Thirdly, there was the fact, completely unknown to him until this moment, that Jane Anderson had visited Sylvia in Cambridge, England, in 1956.

Almost a year passed between Deposition and trial. No settlement was reached. The plaintiff was on her third lawyer and Ted himself on his second. He had parted ways from the first with a $60,000 bill, but fortunately his new counsel, Victor Kovner ('the best in New York'), had extracted $90,000 of insurance cover from his co-defendants.[5] The stakes were high. He felt like a student studying for a bizarre examination. He was waiting for Kovner's signal telling him it was time to get on a plane.

The phone call came. Leaving a sealed envelope with Olwyn, he boarded a plane to New York. On 14 January 1987, he spent five hours in Kovner's office, working through every angle on the case. Ted was asked to consider further correspondence with Aurelia Plath that had been obtained from the Lilly Library of Indiana University, which had purchased all the papers pertaining to Sylvia that had been in Aurelia's possession. He was also forced to confront the fact of his not having published *The Bell Jar* at all in the United States. Until, that was, the moment when his hand had been forced by the bizarre twist in US copyright law whereby, because Sylvia was a United States citizen who had died abroad, there was only seven years of American copyright protection for the English text. All the evidence pointed to the fact that he was trying to protect Aurelia from *The Bell Jar*. If he was so keen to protect her, it could only have been because the novel was autobiographical, because she was Esther Greenwood's mother. So the contention that the book did not contain biographical material simply would not wash. Ted's response was his argument about doubles. Sylvia was always creating doubles. 'Lady Lazarus' was her double. 'The Jailor' was her double. So Joan Gilling was Esther Greenwood's, that is Sylvia Plath's, double, not Jane Anderson's.

Ted and Victor also discussed a letter that Sylvia had written from Court Green on 14 November 1961 to her editor at Heinemann, which began, 'Dear James, No, I've not forgotten about the libel issue. In fact, I've thought about little else.'[6] Michie had gently suggested to her that it might be advisable for her heroine to have a different name from the author of the novel. Plath had thought of using 'Victoria Lucas' as both a pseudonym on the title page and the name of the protagonist. This, Michie thought, would be confusing to readers and reviewers. In her letter, Sylvia agreed on a change of name, proposing Esther Greenwood. She then went through various libel risks that Michie had raised. And she told him that most of the characters were based on real people, that the book was all true. 'Jane (I'm changing her name to Joan) is fictitious,' she wrote, 'and so is her suicide.' But if she was fictitious, then why bother to change her name from Jane to Joan? The inference could well be that, yes, the suicide was fictitious, but the character was based on someone called Jane.

The more Ted and Victor talked the case through, the clearer it became that this was 'a precedent case for all fiction'. If the court found for Anderson, could any novelist (any poet, indeed?) ever be entirely safe from legal action of a similar kind? There would be enormous interest in the outcome.

On 20 January 1987, Ted Hughes, Poet Laureate, sat in a Boston courtroom and watched as Dr Jane Anderson arrived wearing a thin grey cardigan draped over a blue dress. The jury was chosen. It was important that none of them had read the novel or seen the film. From Ted's point of view something else was important too, as he scribbled in his black notebook: 'Make sure no Women's Libbers on the Jury.'[7] Then came the opening statement of the plaintiff. The starting point of the case was that everybody knew that *The Bell Jar* was autobiographical. As to the question of why Ted was among the defendants, despite the fact that he had written neither the novel nor the screenplay: it was because 'Mr Hughes took it to Hollywood.'

Sandy Pratt, acting for the co-defendants collectively, made his opening remarks. Ignoring Ted's sophisticated argument about 'doubles', he granted that *The Bell Jar* was autobiographical on Sylvia Plath's part, but this did not necessarily make it biographical about anyone else. The novel was a fiction, not a factual account, and the movie was a further fictionalisation. The jury looked puzzled at some of these fine distinctions. But Pratt scored a palpable hit when he pointed out that Jane Anderson was not able to bring forward any witnesses in the form of friends saying that there were visible signs of mental harm after she had seen the film. The movie had been released in 1979, but she had not filed her suit until 1982. Why had she waited so long before taking legal action? And was it not the case that she had 'called her psychiatrist ahead of time, to tell him she was going to the Movie and how she would be upset'? The implication was that she deliberately embarked on a course of action with a view to winning future legal damages. Pratt then said that there was evidence that Anderson did engage in 'a homosexual act'. Her counsel yelled, 'I object.' The judge called the lawyers to the bar for private words. Ted thought that Pratt had gone too far for this early point in the proceedings. He was right: the judge told the jury to disregard the remark about a homosexual act. For the time being, the point was lost.

As the proceedings unfolded, Ted took detailed notes. Every now and then, sitting in the courtroom, he also began to write poems. Among the first of them was one called 'Beutscher', a doubling of the names of Sylvia's psychoanalyst and the author of the biography that had started the whole sorry saga.

Jane Anderson took the witness stand. Key information was given to the jury. She, as well as Sylvia, had dated Dick Norton, the boy who was the original of 'Buddy Willard'. Indeed, Norton's affair with Sylvia had started while he was still going out with Jane. Anderson had been in the McLean mental hospital at the same time as Plath. There was another boy they had both had affairs with – that was Gordon Lameyer, who had identified Anderson as Joan Gilling in the essay collection *Sylvia Plath: The Woman and the Work*. So, then, had Anderson seen Plath again at any time after all this? Yes, they met again at their graduation from Smith. Victor Kovner got his objection ready. He knew what was coming next: Jane's visit to Cambridge in June 1956, and the conversation about Ted's sadistic tendencies. The judge called over the attorneys. Was this relevant?

It might be, if it could be shown that Sylvia had angry feelings towards Jane which she may then have vented by means of a defamatory portrait of her in the novel. But this was a fragment of a thirty-year-old conversation known only to Anderson, who by her own admission couldn't remember anything else that was said at the time. Might not she have been projecting? There was no firm evidence that Sylvia had said the things she allegedly said on that June day in Cambridge. The judge ruled that the passage about the Cambridge visit in Anderson's diary could be used, but the jury was told to limit its application. It was stressed that the question of Hughes's character was no part of the case. Anderson then described the visit: how Sylvia had spoken of Ted's 'sadistic' tendencies, and how she had advised against Sylvia marrying him, and how this had meant that the encounter ended frostily. The implication was that for this reason Plath had a vendetta against Anderson, a motivation for turning her into a suicidal lesbian.

Anderson was able to quote numerous details from *The Bell Jar* that were clearly based on conversations between the two young women when they were both confined at McLean. Then the offending quotation from the Butscher biography was read out: Joan Gilling alleged to be 'very loosely based' on Jane Anderson. Then an account of the Lameyer essay in the context of the fact that Anderson had dated Lameyer for six to eight months.

The consensus among the defending legal team was that Jane had done very well indeed. The jury was going to have a lot of sympathy for her. Settlement was the only solution, before things got any worse. Victor Kovner pressed Sandy Pratt very hard. The other side was willing to talk, but they wouldn't go below a quarter of a million dollars. That, they said, was what the case had cost Jane Anderson in the five years since she had launched the action. Pratt didn't want to go that high, but he agreed that they should settle. For one thing, it would stop the co-defendants (and their individual lawyers) arguing among themselves as to each party's particular liability.

Ted was very keen to settle. He was horrified at the way that details of his own life were being dragged into the case, for instance a letter to Aurelia in which he had voiced indiscreet feelings about how his parents were burdening his life, and how he wanted them back in Yorkshire, even though his mother was an invalid. The blazing rows between his parents and Assia were not the sort of thing he wanted reported in the press back home. The case was bringing back some very painful memories of his own inward trial in those years. He began to see that the fallout from everything to do with Sylvia had affected his whole life for twenty years, had in many ways led him to suppress his own poetic Muse.

In her final day of testimony, Jane Anderson seemed an even more powerful presence. She swept aside the allegedly homosexual diary entry: it was all a misinterpretation, college 'girlfriends' could cuddle up together in the dorm without there being anything sexual about it. She was not and never had been a lesbian.

On the Wednesday afternoon, terms were agreed: $150,000. As good a result as could be expected, Victor thought. There was a glitch when the California lawyers acting for some of the co-defendants expressed reluctance to settle and a desire to fight on, but they were won round. They all signed in the afternoon: damages awarded for unintentional defamation of character and agreement to the prominent display at all future screenings, and before any future broadcast, that the film was fictitious. Ted spent the evening with Seamus Heaney at Harvard, heartily relieved.

The next day, in snow, he went to see Leonard and Lisa Baskin. They drove him past Smith College and memories came flooding back: how he and Sylvia both felt asphyxiated there, ground down by their teaching jobs. He felt a strange sense of release, even elation. It was as if the case had unlocked everything.

For the most part, the reporting in the British press was fair, concentrating on the interesting question of the relationship between fiction and fact. Only the *Mail on Sunday* published an article blackening his name. Double love-suicides, the Nazi boot in the face from 'Daddy': all the old stuff familiar to him from the writings of the feminist hitwoman Robin Morgan. Should he sue? Victor's advice was always the same: never, ever sue.

They did, however, manage to put one precautionary measure in place. On 31 January 1987, two days after the settlement, the judge's signature was sealed on defendant Hughes's motion to 'exclude from evidence all references to the nature of Hughes' personal relationship with Sylvia Plath' and to exclude the 'sadism' claim. In particular, certain unpublished passages which Jane Anderson had assiduously extracted from holograph letters in the Lilly Library were to be excluded from the record. The harsh words had spilled out when Sylvia was at her angriest and most rejected, between August and October 1962, when Ted was conducting his affair with Assia. She had written: 'a father who is a liar and an adulterer and utterly selfish … Ted has it in him to be kind and true and loving but has chosen not to be'; 'he is a vampire on my life, killing and destroying all'; 'I have no feelings for Ted, except that he is an absolute bastard'; 'he was furious I had not committed suicide'; 'he never has loved or touched little Nicholas'; 'I suppose it is something to have been the first wife of a genius'; 'His family is behind him – the meanest, most material- istic of the English working class'; and 'I think now my creating babies and a novel frightened him – for he wants barren women like his sister and this woman [Assia], who can write nothing, only adore his stuff.'[8]

Ted had come to revere Victor Kovner. And he was deeply bruised, both financially and emotionally, by the *Bell Jar* case. For the rest of his life, he would do his best to follow Kovner's sage advice: he was very reluctant ever to sue, no matter how extreme the provocation. Olwyn was forever riding into battle against the army of Plath biographers, demanding corrections, putting her point of view, threatening action for copyright infringement.

Ted was always much more hesitant, especially on the matter of illustrative quotation from his and Sylvia's poems. He once described a work about him as a 'promotional campaign' for his books, mounted by its author on behalf of his publishers. Books about poets 'can be considered to promote the sale of the books of verse in question', so it was 'obviously in the interest of the publisher of those books that the quotations be liberal, and in this case there is even less occasion to seek payment for the quotes used'. By writing about Hughes and his work, scholars were, he suggested, 'working directly for the publisher, doing an advertising job that would otherwise be costly'.[9]

Olwyn's more effective strategy was not to sue but to commission and take control of a semi-authorised life of Plath (Lois Ames having signally failed to deliver the fully authorised one). 'Dear Ben,' one of Olwyn's characteristically feisty letters to Ben Sonnenberg began, later in the year of the trial,

> You'll no doubt have heard rumours of, seen reviews of, A BIOGRAPHY of SYLVIA PLATH by a person (a Professor, God help us) who started out on the book as Linda Wagner, got herself hyphenated to Wagner-Martin mid-stream, and is on the book cover (completely unfurled at last one hopes) as Linda W. Wagner-Martin. (All this hierarchical donning of names and initials as they hopefully mount fame's ladder in American ladies must have profound implications for their psyches.)
>
> That alas is where L. W. W-M's interest stops. The book is dreary when it is not being nasty (usually, if only archly or by implication, about Ted) or sacchariney (exclusively about Sylvia).

'However,' she continued triumphantly, 'out of it has sprung an infinitely better biography – now on its way to being finished – by Anne Stevenson.'[10] Olwyn was a little optimistic about the timely completion of the biography by poet and scholar Anne Stevenson. Largely because of her own interference, *Bitter Fame: A Life of Sylvia Plath* was not published until 1989. Olwyn's close involvement in the creation of the book – to the author's increasing exasperation, almost to the point of nervous collapse – can be traced in surviving correspondence.[11] The whole story is forensically analysed by Janet Malcolm in her gripping account of Plath and the moral compass of biography, *The Silent Woman* (1994), a book greatly admired by Ted.

Janet Malcolm's book also rehearsed Ted's battle with the literary critic Jacqueline Rose over her reading of Plath's poem 'The Rabbit Catcher' in the psychoanalytic study *The Haunting of Sylvia Plath* (1991). Malcolm was puzzled, as indeed was Rose herself, at what seemed to be the almost pathological vehemence of Ted's objection to her speculative and subtle analysis. At one point, he told Rose that there were cultures in which allegations of the kind she was making were reasonable grounds for murder. The reason for his extreme reaction was not apparent at the time, but with the opening of the archive of the *Bell Jar* case following Jane Anderson's death in 2010, all becomes clear: the two themes at the heart of Rose's reading of 'The Rabbit Catcher' were male sexual sadism and female homosexual desire. These themes came to the very core of the forbidden fruit of the sealed papers associated with the trial. Ted genuinely feared that for him to be seen to endorse in any way a work implying subconscious lesbian tendencies in Plath would have risked breaching the terms of the Anderson settlement and costing him another action, with further vast expense in legal fees and damages. He was still smarting from his six-figure outlay on the *Bell Jar* case – he always said that it cost him his farm.

On the whole, he left it to Olwyn to fight the biographers. He was, however, provoked to intervention in response to matters pertaining directly to Sylvia's death. In the Seventies and Eighties feminists repeatedly defaced her grave in Heptonstall, which bore the name 'Sylvia Plath Hughes' and the inscription 'Even amidst fierce flames the golden lotus can be planted' – words chosen by Ted because he often quoted them to her when she was depressed.[12] The name 'Hughes' was chiselled from the stone by night. It would be reinstated by the stonemason. Then removed another night. After the mason had replaced the letters three times, Ted asked him to keep the stone in his workshop while he 'considered what to do next'. It was during this hiatus that two feminist academics wrote to the *Guardian* newspaper, with supporting signatures from various people in the literary world, among them Al Alvarez and the exiled Russian poet Joseph Brodsky (who had just been awarded the Nobel Prize for Literature). Brodsky told Ted that he had not really known what he was signing: it was a letter, published on 7 April 1989, complaining that Hughes was shamefully neglecting Plath's grave. Ted's dignified retort appeared in the same paper a fortnight later: 'A rational observer might conclude (correctly in my opinion) that the fantasia about Sylvia Plath is more needed than the facts,' he wrote, with magnificent ironic bite. 'Where that leaves respect for the truth of her life (and of mine), or for her memory, or for the literary tradition, I do not know.'[13]

On one subsequent occasion, he did take legal action. Trevor Thomas, an eccentric art historian, had been Sylvia's neighbour in the ground-floor flat at 23 Fitzroy Road. He was the last person to see her alive, when at about midnight on the night of 10–11 February 1963 she went downstairs to ask for some stamps. Years later, in 1989, he cashed in with a privately published memoir called *Sylvia Plath: Last Encounters*, in which he made the scurrilous and groundless allegation that Ted and his friends had a loud party with bongo drums in Sylvia's flat on the night that he returned from her funeral in Heptonstall. Outraged, Ted sued. He got an injunction and an apology in December 1990.[14]

During his time in Boston for the trial, Ted began thinking about the *Bell Jar* case in Shakespearean terms. 'The law's delay': *Hamlet*. The dream of dispossessing himself of everything: *King Lear*. And he thought about the conflicting arguments as a kind of drama. 'The Accusation': *The Bell Jar* as autobiographical text. 'The Defence': *The Bell Jar* as articulation of the myth of the double self.

Autobiography versus myth: was this not his own argument with himself? If there was truth to the analysis of the novel that he had developed in such immense detail – picking up from hints in Lameyer's essay – that 'Esther Greenwood' was Sylvia's autobiographical self and 'Joan Gilling' her mythic double, then what about Ted's own double self? Crow and the demonic double of Nicholas Lumb were his mythic selves. But what about his autobiographical self: was it not time to confront that in poetry?

He began a new poem, in many parts. He called it 'Trial'. It was in the plain, autobiographical voice he had been using in unpublished poems about Sylvia, not the vatic, mythic Crow voice for which he had by this time become known in print.[15] It has now been made available to the public. Section 1 begins with the letter he received about the Anderson action, out of the blue in the spring of 1982. Looked at one way, it was 'only a letter'. But it was also 'The eggshell – from which his next five years had already flown' ('his' replaces the more personal 'your' of his first draft). The letter was, he continues, 'the forensic fragment / Of booby-trap explosion'. The idea is developed in section 2: 'This is what it looked like – / The Letter of the Law. The Letter of the U.S. law.' And section 4: 'The bomb was in the book' – Butscher's biography, that was.

Having begun with the law-case, the poem then flashes back to the origin of the novel. Sylvia, he reveals, wanted *The Bell Jar* to be a mixture of *Crime and Punishment*, *Sons and Lovers*, *The Golden Bowl*, *Light in August*, *The Catcher in the Rye*, and 'It wanted impossibly to be / Ulysses, La Recherche Du Temps Perdu'. Sylvia was nothing if not ambitious. Realistically, the honest comparison was with that other novel of Fifties adolescent angst: 'Isn't it as alive as Salinger?' he quotes her as saying. 'At least, it's as heart-felt.'

He remembers tearful eyes when Sylvia was sitting blocked in front of an empty page and then her thrilled delight with the birth-pangs of creation. He witnesses her creation of a new self in the act of writing. He begins to ask questions about her hatred of her father: 'What was the motive? / What hand or eye framed the plan / You packed such fury into?' ('What immortal hand or eye': she has the Blakean frenzy of the creator of the tiger). In his mind's eye he sees her going down the golden path between her father's salvias and his beehives to McLean. 'Is this the end of a Trail,' he asks ('Trail' playing on 'Trial'), 'Or the beginning / Of a promising line of enquiry?' He wonders where the hatred was born. He could not see it in her smile or her 'platinum / Veronica Lake bang'. No, 'A small girl bore it, crouching in a coffin.' The buried child was resurrected in the art of the adult woman. Writing *The Bell Jar* took Sylvia into confessional mode: 'This was your introduction to yourself.' Her throwing herself into the novel was deeply bound up with her psychoanalysis, with the moment when Dr Ruth Beutscher said, 'I give you / Permission to hate your mother.' This opened the box, the 'bible of Dreams', the terrors and the drowning.

Ted was with Sylvia as she turned the key and released the little girl who was angry because her father had left her, gone off with Lady Death, and not said goodbye and she did not know why. This little girl was buried when Aurelia announced that what was past was past, when she told her daughter not to mourn, to move 'onward', because life was 'for living', the earth was 'beautiful' and one should never be 'unhappy'. Her mother, the poem proposes, should not have denied her the mourning process. The little girl's grief was buried for so many years that when her heart did eventually come out, 'lifting the coffin lid', it took the form of her own vampiric double. The 'Daddy' in the coffin and 'The Jailor': they did not come back to life as the 'man in black', the husband, Ted. No, they came back as Sylvia's own demonic double. Who was Joan Gilling in *The Bell Jar*? Not Jane Anderson, but the ghost of Sylvia's own jailed childhood self, 'the revenant'.

Then he remembers her writing of the novel, in London in 1961. How 'Morning after morning' she worked on it 'In Bill Merwin's study' while he 'patrolled the zoo, introducing / All the creatures to Frieda'. Sylvia would not give him progress reports, would only say 'I am / Having a terrific time.' He remembers recoiling from his own imagining of the novel. Ever the poet, he is suspicious of 'Uneasy, manipulative prose!' He still dislikes the medium of prose fiction, but now, with the trial, he understands it. And the novel could be forgiven because it was helping her poetry. Sylvia was changing fast. In each poem that she wrote alongside the novel, he heard 'a fuller, surer rehearsal' of her voice.

Then he remembers 'The evening of the day the book was published', 23 January 1963 (this is a slip of the pen or the memory – the actual publication date was 13 January). He and Sylvia drank sherry together, they tasted the sensation of her being a published novelist, albeit under the pseudonym Victoria Lucas. He admired the cover:

> The dim, distorted image of a girl
> Dissolving in a Bell Jar. Did I wonder
> 'Now dare I read it? Ought I to read it now?'

This was at 23 Fitzroy Road. 'Trial' provides corroborative evidence for his claim that he did go to see Sylvia night after night in the weeks leading up to her death, that he was more than just the weekly 'apocalyptic Santa Claus'. He summons up every detail of those evenings:

> The electric bars glared in the wall.
> The matting smell of tobacco. The glass-topped table.
> Brightness. Freshness. Novelty.

He was reminded of the way in which she had furnished her room at Whitstead in Cambridge.

The following week, she showed him the reviews: *The Times* from 24 January, the *New Statesman* the following day, the *Sunday Telegraph* and *Observer* on 27 January. 'No pannings. No raves.' Perhaps if there had been a rave she would have had the strength to go on living. He summons:

> Those few evenings,
> All that were left, the evenings of that fortnight
> Between The Bell Jar coming out for the public
> And your death.

And he summons Sylvia's face, coaxing his memory to yield him some 'inkling', some 'little epiphany' that would reveal that she knew what she had done by writing the novel, that what was done 'Could never be undone'.

On those winter nights in Fitzroy Road, they talked about the children as they sipped their sherry. What Ted didn't realise as they sat discussing *The Bell Jar* was that in her head Sylvia was rewriting the suicide attempt described there. She was thinking of doing it again. Of composing a successful sequel. The novel was the map of her journey to the underworld. It was a draft of her Dantesque *Commedia*, her preview of Hamlet's undiscovered country from whose bourn no traveller returns (no traveller except Lady Lazarus, that is):

> The reconnaissance, the summary report
> Of your exploration of that country
> Where your nightmare reigned, the dead land
> Ruled by your buried alter ego.

He did not know at this time that the final edition of her *Commedia* was already written, 'All verses completed, the total song / Inferno, Purgatorio, Paradiso'. It was written in a little book of poems called *Ariel*, which was there in the house along with the ghost of W. B. Yeats. She read him some of the poems on those evenings when they drank sherry and talked about the children. What was she thinking of, he wondered, when she wrote 'Daddy' and 'Medusa', which she declaimed to him 'with a divine malice'? He was appalled, baffled and alarmed: was she aware of what she had done? Surely she didn't really want to hurt her mother so cruelly. Should she not come to her senses, call the novel back in and burn the poems?

Then he turns to the posthumous life of her work. How 'Through the late Sixties', her poems 'crept through America – and / Took hold like an organised addiction'. For womankind, for the 'Libbers':

> Your image in manipulated neons
> Resembling flames was the martyr
> To their centuries of oppression.
> Yourself, would you believe it,
> Their megaphone marching saint.
> Who is she? Who was she?

She became the voice against the patriarchy, but by then it was too late to ask whether or not she had really hated Daddy.

Because of her suicide and because of the explosive content of *Ariel* – 'Ariel's electrocardiograph', he brilliantly calls it, in an allusion to her ECT – *The Bell Jar* was read retrospectively as another anti-Daddy tirade. By the time the novel was published in America, it was too late for the alternative possibility that it was less an autobiographical scream than:

> A sort of metaphor for the tirade
> Many an injured wife would let fly
> At the Daddy of her children if only
> She could find the language.

Sylvia had become a feminist icon because nobody before her, no woman before her,

> Had emptied her whole soul of its rage
> Against all that had suppressed and denied her,
> Against all that had shut her from the life
> She had wanted for herself, from her freedom.

By writing of her father, her mother, her upbringing and her husband ('me'), she became 'the Universal / Hidden, mother hurt of womankind'.

Now he understood about Jane Anderson and Joan Gilling and the meeting in Cambridge. Just as he and Sylvia had been finding each other, her 'old suicide's doppelganger' had arrived on her doorstep to dog her 'new dream'. That is why Jane/Joan had to be destroyed. She was 'the double' of Sylvia's 'old disasters' and that was 'a theme for a novel'. As for Ted himself, he was 'a post-war Englishman' who adopted 'The bereft child in you and the broken girl / Hapless victim of your German nation'. Was she – he is thinking of 'Daddy' again – in some sense 'Hitler's bequest' to him, to the poet whose pike-voice was 'deep as England'?

But then he pulls back and rearticulates the position of the Deposition. A novel is not an autobiography. A work of art is a work of art. It is not life.

> Esther Greenwood is an experiment,
> An extrapolation from the mind-warp nadir
> Of suicidal breakdown. She is not real.

The paradox, though, is that 'Trial', the long poem in which Ted Hughes wrote these words, is about events and feelings that were real: it is a capsule biography of Sylvia Plath and a partial autobiography of Ted Hughes. Its story is real.

A

Fishing was Ted Hughes's recreation of choice, especially in his later years. All the more so if the airfare to Alaska and the rivers of British Columbia could be defrayed by a poetry reading in Vancouver, or the Inland Revenue persuaded that a fishing holiday in Scotland also constituted tax-deductible research for future poems. Another form of both recreation and research was reading. He devoured books throughout his life and after his death a library of 6,000 of them was shipped to Atlanta, Georgia, to join the two and a quarter tonnes of his original manuscripts that were already there. But at various times in his life he dabbled in other hobbies, sometimes in company with his children. At Court Green in 1967 or '68, he bought a potter's wheel. Frieda was already proving herself a talented painter. Now she took to sculpting in clay. She modelled an owl, a bird she would always love (she keeps owls to this day). As Nick matured, he became exceptionally gifted in the art of pottery. He would throw, glaze and fire, creating beautiful animals and other figures. In those early days, Ted had a go himself.

He produced two black jaguars, each about 6 inches long. He knew the anatomy of the beast, and caught every sinew. These were grown-up equivalents of the little plasticine creatures he had made in his boyhood. One of them has its back curved in a smooth arch, its head low, its mouth wide open in a yawn or a roar or a howl of pain. He gave it to Gerald. It survives fully intact.[1] The other is running free, legs curved in motion. He gave it to Olwyn. It survives in a sorry state, three legs gone. The two stances represented, Olwyn thought, the jaguar of his *Hawk in the Rain* poem in and out of the cage. She must be right. But there is another meaning too. Branded on the forehead of Gerald's jaguar is a letter: 'A'.

'A' is for Assia. It is also the Scarlet Letter that Nathaniel Hawthorne's Hester Prynne is forced to wear on her dress as a badge of shame: 'A' is for Adultery.

The release in *Wolfwatching* of 'Sacrifice', the poem about Uncle Albert's suicide, was a readying for confrontation with nearer pain. Still not prepared to release the collection about Sylvia that he had been working on for so many years, Ted turned to the memory of Assia. But he did not want reviews or public attention, so in the spring of 1990 he published an elegiac volume called *Capriccio* in an edition of a mere fifty copies on Leonard Baskin's Gehenna Press. There were engravings by Baskin and ten of the copies were rendered unique (and could thus be sold for more money) by the inclusion of a page of Hughes manuscript and an extra Baskin drawing. A sequence of twenty poems, *Capriccio* seeks to hold together obscure mythographic, sometimes cabbalistic, mumbo-jumbo ('the blood-clepsydra / Limit of Aphrodite's epiphany')[2] and a direct confrontation with Assia's suicide. The imagery is sometimes bold to the point of recklessness, as when Jewish Assia is described knowing exactly how her own death looked: 'It was a long-cold oven / Locked with a swastika.'[3] At other times, the verse is unbearably poignant. Ted writes with still raw emotion of Assia's jealousy of Sylvia's talent ('The Other') and of her all too real threats, for example when she only half jokingly said that she would end her own life once she turned forty. She 'folded' her 'future', he writes, into her 'empty clothes. Which Oxfam took.'[4] He writes, too, of Shura, stripped from life, her little arms 'clinging round' her mother's neck, by the gas oven on the blanket on the cold kitchen floor of the dreary apartment in Clapham.[5]

Capriccio ends with a pair of poems about the end and then the beginning of their relationship. 'Flame' is a record of their house-hunting in the final week of Assia's life, and their final parting at Manchester Central railway station. 'Chlorophyl' is the one about the blade of grass.

The most tender poem in the sequence is entitled 'Snow'. It is a vivid memory, based on Assia's journal, of her lonely walk down the cobbled hill in Haworth just before her suicide. She is seen on an 'unending' walk, down to the Brontë parsonage in which, because it is now a museum (a mausoleum), the oven is empty of fire. But the walk goes on for ever because Assia is following a path down to the underworld by way of another oven empty of fire but full of poison. The blackened Yorkshire stone of the closed cafés and gift-shops is elided with the smoke and fire of war and Holocaust – Assia's Russian-Jewish-German origins are summoned in an image of the faces of her childhood friends 'Beside their snowed-under tanks, locked into the Steppe' where it was so cold that mud froze in the time it took to drink a cup of coffee. Assia in her black coat of ponyskin is going to join those dead. Ted watches her, merging her journal entry with the sight of her when he returned to Haworth to pick her up for the drive further north to Hexham. He feels the touch of the snow that is already burying the print of her feet, 'Drawing its white sheet over everything, / Closing the air behind you'.[6]

As always with Hughes, 'Snow' is a poem as entrenched in literature as in life. Experience is refracted through reading. At the beginning of the poem, snowflakes cling to the black fox fur of Assia's hat and there is an evocation of the 'ghostly wreckage / Of the Moscow Opera'. Ted was meditating deeply on the life and work of Leo Tolstoy. With her beauty and her style, her transgression and her suicide, here Assia is her own favourite literary character: Anna Karenina. Then, as the imagery unfolds, playing the black of the buildings off against the white of the snow, the literary context shifts and the well-versed reader hears the whisper of an allusion to the greatest of all Holocaust poems, Paul Celan's 'Death Fugue', with its 'black milk of daybreak' drunk morning, noon and night in a world where 'Death is a Master from Germany' and the hair of Shulamith is turned to ash.[7] Both a personal elegy for Assia and an elegy for all the Jews who went to the ovens, 'Snow', one of Ted's most moving poems, is in some sense his answer to 'Daddy'. Where Sylvia appropriated the Holocaust into her own private trauma as a reaction against her father's Germanic tendencies, Ted gives Assia back to her people, in recognition of the fact that her perpetual wandering, her inability ever to find a home, had its origin in her father's flight from the Nazis in 1933.

Hardly anyone knew that the fifty copies of *Capriccio* had appeared and of those who did only a handful (Carol and Olwyn most obviously) would have known that it was for Assia, let alone how profoundly autobiographical the content was. Limited release that it was, for Ted to have written openly about Assia was a huge step forward.

The title *Capriccio* suggests a *jeu d'esprit*, a sprightly, lightweight, free-form fantasia. The casualness of the term obscures the fact that this is but a fragment of a much larger and more explicitly autobiographical sequence of Assia poems, which was never completed. In Hughes's private archive at his death, there was a box labelled 'A 4'.[8] This does not refer to the size of the loose sheets of paper and notebooks inside. It means 'for Assia'. Among the densely scrawled and heavily revised manuscripts is an inky-blue Challenge Triplicate Book to the cover of which three small strips of yellow sticky-tape have been attached in the shape of an upside-down 'A'.

'A' is for Assia but now it is also for 'ash'. It is still, too, the Scarlet Letter of Adultery. The inverted 'A' of yellow sticky-tape also resembles a fragment of a star of Zion, thus evoking the yellow star that branded the Jews in Nazi Germany. One of the unifying threads of the material in the box is the recognition that whereas Sylvia wrote 'I think I may well be a Jew,' Assia really was a Jew. Had Dr and Mrs Gutmann not left Germany for Palestine, Assia would have experienced in reality what was for Sylvia a metaphor: 'an engine / Chuffing me off like a Jew. / A Jew to Dachau, Auschwitz, Belsen'.[9]

Had it been completed, 'A' – the sequence of Assia poems – would have been a decisive turning point in Hughes's poetic career. But he could not decide on the content and structure. Or on how explicit the autobiographical references should be. The box 'for Assia' includes several different plans for the work. There is a list of fifteen poems beginning with one that lays out some ground rules: 'So – they – will have clear notion of me – you will not be known, shadowy, a name [–] they will not know how much you were more real than me [–] how much more real than them.' This sounds suitably elusive, and yet the proposed second poem is very explicitly called 'When Dad told Ma': we know that Hughes believed that his father telling his mother of Assia's suicide was the thing that killed her. As for Assia being unknown, the proposed ninth poem was to have been on the subject of her earlier marriage to Dicky Lipsey. But then the closing poem in this plan for the sequence would have faded Assia back into the 'A' of anonymity: '2 months after – evening with Sillitoe, pennicilin [*sic*] allergy, free fall – not a word of you'.

Another plan was for a sequence of thirty poems with an extra-ordinary mix of direct autobiographical recollection and mutation into myth, symbol and a distancing third-person voice. The first of them follows a man as he goes to a pub, leaving his lover in a hotel bedroom. 'He eats sausages drinks beer etc – strolls back through square.' Second is a thunderbolt in the form of a phone call. Poem three: 'The liar – what his lies permit him'. Four: 'The man running along the beach with the girl has 4 children by 3 different women'. Five: 'Goodnight kiss – inventory of its pathos'. Six flicks to the woman's perspective: 'Her dread of what people will say'. Seven goes back to the man: 'He tries to fathom the actual value of copulation.' Eight: 'Bed – the act over – yet round this the torment of every hour, the motive of every action, the slant of every word, the bellow of life that is carrying us towards – what?' The proposed sequence then veers from the aphrodisiac of spring woodlands and old empty houses to the folly of love poetry to the desolation of affairs to a series of ballads on dirty England, a whore-priestess and an existential survivor. Yet another draft outline, meanwhile, is almost entirely mythographic as opposed to personal: an alien passion destroying temple and Goddess, an auto-da-fé, the death-wish and death-recklessness in desire, the coming together of an ascetic and a girl.

The Assia poems, he told himself in a Coleridgean phrase, were to be 'the penetralia of the mystery'. To prepare himself for the writing of 'A', he jotted down his key memories. He disciplined his imagin-ation, told himself to see again Assia at the Beacon, 'sitting in that chair by the phone while Hilda screamed at her, and she helpless to defend herself'. To hear again Assia at Lumb Bank, her horror at its darkness and damp. To remember Assia in her ponyskin coat waiting for a train at Clapham Junction in the last month of her life. To capture the image of her in a pub, wearing a skirt of brown Thai silk and holding an Embassy cigarette. To recapture the energy and freedom of the begin-ning of their affair in London: the newness of everything, the shine of her black handbag, the thick scent of her Dior perfume, the smell of Mayfair in 1962. He even made himself confront the mingling of the hope that always comes at the start of a love affair with his glimmer of suspicion regarding Assia's relationship with Alvarez.

But then there is a later memory, of the continuing dominance of the image of Assia. He recalls another woman 'in her leather skirt, who seemed to me then so identical to A'. If Assia was the catalyst for the escape from Sylvia, he asks, was this other an 'escape from A – as with Susan'? And so, page after page, the memories are gathered, until the last farewell is reached: 'In Haworth – Beethoven's last quartets. The ice on the trees. Walking downhill in the snow alone. The second image.' Assia in the snow alone; Sylvia in the snow alone. 'How these histories repeat', he writes in the margin of his notebook.

The most finished version of the poetry sequence begins with a piece called 'Dream of A'. She appears in the poet's dream, more beautiful than ever before, her beauty more 'Frightening and strange and delicate / Richer with the inaccessible things / That send desire crazy'. The ghost comes with a blackness about her eyes and her hair, a mystery that fevers the imagination and 'makes the prick stand up willy nilly' (one of Hughes's more unfortunate turns of phrase). There is then an attempt to evoke the intensity of their lovemaking, which is never an easy literary task. He imagines faceless people interrupting them. He elevates their lovemaking into a thing that miraculously gives material form to 'An empty space surrounded by the infinity / Of absence and inhumanity and nothingness'. He turns their love-making into a 'masterpiece / Translated from the language of an extinct people / And of some unknown author'. He makes it an 'eternal thing' out of the biblical Song of Songs, an offering of love and beauty so strong that the earth cannot cope with it or allow it, with the result that it is obliterated and Assia destroyed:

> You lost the body to enjoy it
> And the beauty to give to it, and in exchange
> You received death and burning to ashes
> And I lost you.

But because of the dream, he says, he has not wholly lost her. Her image and her voice have returned to him. He, in turn, restores her through his writing. At one level, Assia the super-lover and supreme beauty is being turned into the Goddess of some ancient female-worshipping tribe. At another level, she is the archetypal Jewish beauty out of the Song of Songs. The Jews after Auschwitz are imagined as a near-extinct people and the 'unknown author' is the Yahweh who must not be named.

Throughout the drafts of 'A', Hughes is haunted by the fact that whereas Sylvia lies in her grave in Brontë country, Assia was cremated. This seems to have been Ted's decision, probably made before discovering the will in which she wrote of her desire to be buried in an English country graveyard. Being cremated, there was a double sense in which she lost her body. The sequence of poems in her memory is haunted by the image of both Assia and Shura reduced to ash.[10]

This inevitably draws the narrative back to Nazi Germany. Another attempt to start the story – untitled other than with the number 1 – begins 'When she was eight she started running' (actually she was six when the family fled from Vienna). One line here, 'Her breath puffs like a refugee train,' echoes the Plathian puff of the train on the way to the camps that Assia's 'milky lips shaped to the nipple / Never tasted'. 'But who escapes?' he asks: wherever she went, from America to Russia to Israel to England, Assia lived with the guilt of the survivor. So when she lies on a blanket on the kitchen floor, gassed along with her little girl, she is not one of love's but 'One of Hitler's casualties', albeit a quarter of a century later. The swastika, not his own infidelity, is claimed as the thing that killed her.

Hughes, who believed that all artistic creativity came from a wound, convinces himself – or at least tries to convince himself – that the brief and far from smooth course of their love, and then the poem he is writing in memory of that love, offered Assia respite from the wound inflicted by her origin as a German Jew. He evokes Germany through the image of a black forest and the smell of burning; he writes of touching her hurt, of how everything in Assia rested on a hurt, and of how, as she rested 'in the thick of the forest', she allowed him to 'Touch all her hurts'. He writes tenderly of kissing 'each one', imagines the two of them secretly planting a flower 'Over the buried enmity of our fathers'. But it would have been impossible for Hughes to write publicly of Assia's lifelong wound without the accusation of self-exculpation. His perpetual dilemma with regard to both Sylvia and Assia was that he needed to write his love and grief and guilt into poetry, to expiate in order to move his art forward, but he could not publish.

Remember Alvarez's harsh words about Assia: 'Her only way of outdoing her dead rival was in the manner of her death.'[11] By which Alvarez meant that she took Shura with her, whereas Sylvia tenderly preserved Frieda and Nick. But the other aspect of the outdoing was

that whereby a Jewish woman and a little Jewish girl died in a gas
oven. This was the thought that haunted Ted and that drives many of
the poems in the sequence headed 'A', but that could not be made
public. If critics had castigated Plath for evoking the Holocaust in the
context of her own domestic woes, what would they have said in
response to this line of writing from Hughes?

Without the closure of publication, he endlessly revised, remem-
bered, reconfigured. Without the discipline of print, he was able to
merge verse and prose, little mundane things and potent symbols. One
loose sheet in the box marked 'A 4' outlines memories (or poems)
numbered seven to twelve, beginning from two chestnut horses rolling
in a field of buttercups, their tails exploding upwards like a magnum
of champagne. It then proceeds to a bitter indictment of Assia: 'Who
are you who have come to live with me, you are not my wife. You
pester me worse than any public ... You neglect the children. You
smile bitterly. You are grief.' And then to an equally bitter indictment
of himself: 'My torment is being five ... The merry one is in jail – for
life. He committed a murder. The lustful one is in hell ... The studious
one is in despair ... The holy one waits on a bench ... The reasonable
one spends his whole days and nights arguing with these four.' But it
ends with an immensely tender evocation of Shura's shoes and toys
and clothes, and of how:

> Wherever I go is a little impetuous girl
> Who is not
> And her beautiful mother
> Who wrapped the whole world up
> Put it in the fire of the last day
> And left in all space only her smile
> Where flowers cannot flower, or buds break

There was no atonement for the loss of little Shura.

28

Goddess Revisited

In a letter to a fishing friend written in the summer of 1990, Ted reported that he had no news other than 'strange tales from the depths of the Shakespearean caves, which no man wants to hear'.[1] He had been exploring those caves all his literary life and now a project with a gestation period of more than two decades was coming to a head. It would be his equivalent of Graves's *White Goddess*.[2]

Oscar Wilde remarked that criticism is the only civilised form of autobiography, while Virginia Woolf believed that all Shakespearean criticism is as much about the critic's self as about the dramatist's plays. Shakespeare is a mirror in which serious readers and spectators see sharpened images of themselves and their own worlds. In this respect, the Shakespeare book was also Ted's veiled autobiography.

Shakespeare was the absolute centre of Ted Hughes's sense of the English literary tradition. The plays were a major influence on his own poetry, in both linguistic intensity and thematic preoccupation. The world of Hughes's verse is one in which, as Macbeth puts it, 'light thickens, and the crow / Makes wing to the rooky wood'.[3] More than any other poet, Shakespeare assaulted Hughes – one of the great literary *readers* of the twentieth century – with the shock of the as-if-new. In a long journal note dated 22 January 1998, Ted wrote of reading with amazement ('as if I'd never seen it before') a line of Shakespeare: 'Mine eye hath played the painter and hath stell'd.'[4] This was during the weekend when the news of *Birthday Letters* was released. The line is the opening of Sonnet 24, in which the image of the beloved is held in the poet's heart, as Sylvia's was in Ted. This act of reading at a vital moment was symptomatic of a lifelong passion: all his days, Hughes read Shakespeare with amazement, as if he had never read him before. The key to Shakespearean acting is to speak each line as if it were being spoken for the first time, as if it were new minted from the thought-chamber of the character who utters it. In this regard, Hughes, fascinated as he was by actors and by the process of making theatre, read Shakespeare as if he were an actor playing all the parts. Which is probably how Shakespeare wrote Shakespeare.

Having devoured the whole of Shakespeare as a teenager and studied him at Cambridge, when he moved to America with Sylvia in the summer of 1957 Ted re-read all the plays in what he considered to be their order of composition. He showed particular interest in the late collaborations with Fletcher, *Henry VIII* and *The Two Noble Kinsmen*: 'The Shakespeare in it is incredible in that it seems at first better than Shakespeare – but the rest, a great deal, is Fletcher. "Late Shakespeare" gets the blame for a lot of Fletcher.'[5] In distinguishing between the styles of Shakespeare and Fletcher, he revealed the ear for the movement of Shakespearean verse that went along with his appetite for a big-picture understanding of the plays.

Again and again, Shakespearean characters find their way into Hughes's own creations. A poem in *Lupercal* is written from the point of view of 'Cleopatra to the Asp'. A verse sequence drafted in the Eighties under the title 'Court Cards' offers readings of works ranging from *Venus and Adonis* to *The Tempest*, by way of the major tragedies and the relationship between Hal and Falstaff in *Henry IV*.[6] 'Setebos' in *Birthday Letters* casts Sylvia as Miranda, Ted as Ferdinand, Aurelia Plath as Prospero, Ariel as the aura of creativity shared by the lovers, and Caliban as their dark secret inner life. An unpublished poem among the *Birthday Letters* drafts refracts Plath's anger against her father through Timon of Athens's rage against the world.[7]

Although his responsiveness to Shakespeare in both verse and prose was lifelong, it was only in 1969 that Hughes began to write systematically about the plays. In 1968 he had edited *A Choice of Emily Dickinson's Verse* for a Faber and Faber series. His editor Charles Monteith asked him to undertake a similar volume of Emily Brontë, a poet close to his heart. Hughes replied that he would think about it, but that what he really wanted to do was a selection of Shakespeare's verse for the series. He suggested that it would be novel and interesting to treat Shakespeare as poetry, not as drama. Monteith was extremely enthusiastic, immediately seeing a ready market. He proposed a decent advance (£150 on delivery) and a royalty of 10 per cent on the hardback, 7½ on the paperback. Hughes could do the Brontë as well, but the Shakespeare was infinitely more important.

Ted set to work. But the coming three months, March to May 1969, was the traumatic period of Assia's and Shura's deaths, then his mother's. It was the introduction to his Shakespeare anthology that he was wrestling over, dismayed and disappointed with it, when the phone rang on the morning of 14 May and Olwyn told him that their mother was dead. The gestation of the Shakespeare book was inseparable from the shock of Assia's death and his belief that the terrible news of her suicide had killed his mother.

Despite the anguish of these days, he managed to deliver the type-script of *A Choice of Shakespeare's Verse* to Monteith towards the end of June, explaining in a covering letter that he had written a long intro-duction, but was sending a short one. He was not satisfied. Throughout the summer and autumn, he reworked both the selection and the introduction. In early December, from Lumb Bank, he sent Monteith a new version with a more detailed introduction – and the informa-tion that there were enough rejected drafts of it to fill a small suitcase. He sent the collected *Crow* poems at the same time.

The Shakespeare project, then, had its origins at a time not only of extraordinary personal trauma but also of his first major poetry collec-tion for several years. Hughes sometimes introduced public readings of the *Crow* poems by explaining that Crow's quest was to meet his maker, God. But every time he met Him, it was a Her, a woman, an incarnation of the Goddess. Each time, Crow was unsatisfied and had to move on to another encounter.[8] Hughes read Shakespeare's career in the same way that he read his own *Crow*: the argument that begins to emerge in the introduction to *A Choice of Shakespeare's Verse* and that is articulated at enormous length in *Shakespeare and the Goddess of Complete Being* is that Shakespeare's developing art unfolded through a series of encounters with this same Goddess.

Some time after writing his own *Goddess*, Hughes provided the enquiring enthusiast Nick Gammage with an account of the formative influence of Graves's. Here he recalled that he felt a little resentment on his first reading of *The White Goddess*, since Graves had taken possession of what he considered to be his own 'secret patch'. He recapped the book's argument that the same Goddess who presides over birth, love and death was worshipped under different names in the mythologies of the Greeks and the Egyptians, the Irish and the Welsh, and countless other ancient cultures. Beautiful, fickle, wise and implacable, she later becomes the Ninefold Muse, patroness of the white magic of poetry. Shakespeare, Graves mentions in passing, 'knew and feared her': we see playful elements of the Goddess in Titania, a more serious approach in Lady Macbeth and Cleopatra, her ultimate manifestation in the absent but forceful deity of Sycorax, Caliban's mother in *The Tempest*.[9] Hughes assured Gammage that Graves's syncretic method – his yoking of Middle Eastern material with Celtic – was already familiar to him from his own researches in arcane mythology, which had begun in his early teens. What really struck him in the book were 'those supernatural women. Especially the underworld women'. He reminds his correspondent that he had already begun to work out a relationship to chthonic female deity in 'Song', which he always considered to be his first important poem.

Gammage asked Hughes whether *The White Goddess* had been his first exposure to the religious context in which Shakespeare's imagination was formed. He replied that he was not sure how clearly or consciously he saw the pattern at the time, but that the idea of 'Goddess-centred matriarchy being overthrown by a God-centred patriarchy' was indeed most likely something that he first really grasped in the Graves. 'In giving me that big picture fairly early, yes, The White Goddess had a big part – and it was the Graves maybe that made the link directly to that lineage in English poetry – from the Sycorax figure to La Belle Dame [of Keats] and the Nightmare Life in Death [of Coleridge's 'Ancient Mariner']. Made it conscious and obvious.'[10] Woman and Goddess, sex and death, the underworld and the hidden current of nature worship in opposition to patriarchal monotheism: this was the network of associations that Hughes took from Graves and brought to his reading of Shakespeare.

When he was putting the anthology together in 1969 he knew that such associations would raise the eyebrows of academic Shakespeare experts. On New Year's Day 1970, he explained to Monteith that the argument of his introduction had to be understood as an imaginative rather than a scholarly idea. It wouldn't appeal to the scholars. Disarmingly, Hughes added that he hadn't read any Shakespeare criticism, except for A. C. Bradley long ago.

Because of various complications and delays at Faber, together with anxieties over the timetable for publication of a series of titles in different genres by the ever-prolific Hughes, the Shakespeare anthology did not appear until the autumn of 1971. It was overtaken into print not only by a privately printed text of the introduction accompanied by a quietly self-revelatory poem called 'Crow's Song about Prospero and Sycorax',[11] but also by an American version of the entire book with a variant title, foisted on Hughes by the publisher: *With Fairest Flowers while Summer Lasts*. This was a quotation from *Cymbeline*, one of the lesser-known plays with which he was especially fascinated.

Peter Brook was the Shakespearean whose opinion Hughes valued most highly. It was Brook, he later wrote in the dedication to *Shakespeare and the Goddess of Complete Being*, who 'provided the key to the key'. Tellingly, Hughes made a point of sending Brook the American as opposed to the British version of the anthology. Faber had decided to tuck away most of the introduction, to which he had devoted so much effort through so many difficult months, at the back of the volume. The American version had the virtue of presenting it up front.

The introduction to *With Fairest Flowers while Summer Lasts* remains the most lucid and economic summary of Hughes's hypothesis about the key to Shakespeare's imagination. In reading Shakespeare, he proposes, we periodically come upon passages of white-hot poetic intensity. When he extracted these passages and put them together in an anthology, he discovered that many of them had a structure of feeling in common, a 'strong family resemblance'. They were all hammering at the same thing, 'a particular knot of obsessions'. By reading these passages as short, self-contained lyric poems, we simultaneously 'look through them into our own darkness' and find ourselves 'plucking out Shakespeare's heart' – which, we discover, 'has a black look'.

'The poetry has its taproot', Hughes claims, 'in a sexual dilemma of a peculiarly black and ugly sort.' Belittling as it might seem to boil Shakespeare down to a single idea, if the idea is big enough it can prove itself the key to his imagination. After all, for all his vaunted variety and impersonality, Shakespeare was finally 'stuck with himself'. The works are the expression of his own nature. The greatest passages constitute Shakespeare's recurrent dream. In them, his imagination 'presents the mystery of himself to himself'.[12] Oscar Wilde and Virginia Woolf would no doubt say at this point that the heart, the nature, the dream, the imagination into which Hughes was gazing as he wrote this were not Shakespeare's but his own.

In the early 1590s, during a period when the theatres were closed because of plague, Shakespeare wrote two narrative poems, *Venus and Adonis* (goddess of love attempts to seduce reluctant virginal male youth who is more interested in hunting and ends up being gored to death by a boar) and *The Rape of Lucrece* (royal-blooded Tarquin attempts to seduce, then rapes, virtuous woman Lucrece, who commits suicide, such is her shame). Here, 'where nothing but poetry concerned him', argues Hughes, Shakespeare produced two versions, one light and the other dark, of his core fable. The same structure can, however, be seen in many of the plays, for instance in 'the polar opposition of Falstaff and Prince Hal' in the *Henry IV* plays or the encounter between Angelo and Isabella in *Measure for Measure*.[13] In each case, one figure represents the earth, submission to the body and the forces of desire, while the other stands for the heavens, purity of spirit and the repression of desire. Venus and Falstaff are figures of capacious and celebratory desire, embodiments of the Goddess, while Tarquin and Angelo represent destructive sexual possessiveness turned against the Goddess.

For Hughes, a great poet is, as Ben Jonson said Shakespeare was, the soul of the age. The opposition is accordingly read not only as Shakespeare's personal dilemma, but also as a perfect representation of 'the prevailing psychic conflict of his times in England, the conflict that exploded, eventually, into the Civil War'. The repression of the Goddess by the forces of radical Protestantism took its distinctively English form in the extirpation of the cult of Mary. Though the process was temporarily slowed by the cult of Queen Elizabeth as a kind of substitute Mary, the rise of Puritanism amounted to a dragging into court 'by the young Puritan Jehovah' of 'the Queen of Heaven, who was the goddess of Catholicism, who was the goddess of medieval and pre-Christian England, who was the divinity of the throne, who was the goddess of natural law and of love, who was the goddess of all sensation and organic life – this overwhelmingly powerful, multiple, primeval being'.[14] The forces that drive Hughes's own poetry – the implacable but vital law of nature, woman, sexual desire, sensation, organic life, sacramental royalty – are overwhelmingly those associated with the Goddess.

For Hughes, Shakespeare's distinctive twist on the myth is his imagination of figures who attempt to 'divide nature, and especially love, the creative force of nature, into abstract good and physical evil'. Nature, being unified (the Goddess of *complete* being), will not let them do this, with the result that love returns in the destructive form of rape, murder, madness and the death-wish. An 'occult crossover' occurs, causing a 'mysterious chemical change' in which 'Nature's maddened force' takes over the brain that had rejected her.[15] This was what he called the Tragic Equation. In a single sentence of wild reach and energy, Hughes sketches how the equation operates as the key to the 'powerhouse and torture chamber' of Shakespeare's complete works:

> Hamlet, looking at Ophelia, sees his mother in bed with his uncle and goes mad; Othello, looking at his pure wife, sees Cassio's whore and goes mad; Macbeth, looking at the throne of Scotland and listening to his wife, hears the witches, the three faces of Hecate, and the invitation to hell, and goes mad; Lear, looking at Cordelia, sees Goneril and Regan, and goes mad; Antony, looking at his precious queen, sees the 'ribaudred nag of Egypt' betraying him 'to the very heart of loss', and goes – in a sense – mad; Timon, looking at his loving friends, sees the wolf pack of Athenian creditors and greedy whores, and goes mad; Coriolanus, looking at his wife and mother, sees the Roman mob who want to tear him to pieces, and begins to act like a madman; Leontes, looking at his wife, sees Polixenes' whore, and begins to act like a madman; Posthumus, looking at his bride, who of his 'lawful pleasure oft restrained' him, sees the one Iachimo mounted 'Like a full-acorn'd boar', and begins to act like a madman.[16]

This passage exposes both the strength and the weakness of Hughes's reading of Shakespeare: yes, there is a recurrent pattern of madness or quasi-madness provoked by intensity of sexual and familial relations, but no, this cannot be the key to all of Shakespeare (it underplays comedy, self-conscious theatrical play, and so much more). In trying to reduce all the dramas to a single force, there is inevitably something forced. Hence such giveaways as 'goes – *in a sense* – mad'. Yet the insights offered by the pattern are exceptionally rich. Richard III, Tarquin, Hamlet, Angelo, Othello, Macbeth: each of them is, as Hughes says, a 'strange new being', a 'man of chaos'.[17] And it is the men of chaos ('from Aaron to Caliban') who speak the most memorable poetry, the passages that Hughes extracts and presents in his anthology. His selection has at its centre a great riff of nearly forty sequences of high-voltage poetic madness from Macbeth, Lear and Timon.

At various points in his introduction, Hughes deploys phrases remembered from his undergraduate study of English at Cambridge. 'Dissociation of sensibility' is T. S. Eliot on what happened to English poetry around the time of the Civil War. 'The Shakespearean moment' is Cambridge-influenced critic Patrick Cruttwell's phrase for the historical and cultural forces that came to a head in the 1590s, making it possible for Marlowe, Shakespeare and Donne to write the greatest poetry ever seen in the English language. Hughes redefines Eliot's 'dissociation of sensibility' as a rupture in English culture caused by the banishment of the Goddess from the national psyche. He sees the poetry of Blake, Wordsworth, Keats, Hardy, Hopkins (perhaps), Yeats and Eliot as manifestations of 'Nature's attempt to correct the error, supply the natural body of things and heal the torment'.[18] In this list, he is at once proclaiming a line of succession from Shakespeare to himself and offering a Gravesian reading of the Leavisite canon he studied for the first part of the Cambridge English Tripos, prior to his switch to Archaeology and Anthropology.

The copy of *With Fairest Flowers* that Hughes sent to Peter Brook was accompanied by a letter summarising the argument that had shaped both selection and introduction, together with an outline for a possible dramatisation that would set this argument, and Shakespeare's work, in the religious context of his age: 'Elizabeth and Mary Tudor go straight into the Venus lineage ... Then it could be brought forward, using Milton's Paradise Lost and Samson Agonistes as a continuation of Shakespeare's series.' There could be an epilogue in the style of the ancient Greek satyr play that followed a cycle of tragedies: rival politicians Edward Heath and Harold Wilson would be monkeys in the mask of Adonis and Tarquin, 'Lucrece would be Princess Anne, and Venus would be a schizophrenic female gorilla in Regent's park.'[19]

Though eminently capable of self-parody of this kind, Ted Hughes was deadly serious about his great Shakespearean project. Undeterred by the lukewarm critical response to his anthology, in 1973 he wrote a poem called 'An Alchemy' for a celebration of Shakespeare's birthday.[20] In a letter to fellow-poet Peter Redgrove (who would later visit Gravesian Goddess territory himself in both *The Black Goddess and the Sixth Sense* and *The Wise Wound: Menstruation and Everywoman*, co-written with Penelope Shuttle), Hughes explained that 'An Alchemy' was a compacting of his anthology, in which he had sought to demonstrate how Shakespeare's own personal psychodrama embodied the historical development of the national psyche, even the entire Western tradition: 'Shakespeare recorded, somewhat helplessly, what was actually going on in the English spirit, which was the defamation, subjection and eventual murder of what he first encountered as Venus – the Mary Goddess of the Middle Ages and earlier.' *Venus and Adonis* 'sets up Shakespeare as the crucial record of the real inner story of the whole of Western History. But very abbreviated and in bagatelle style.'[21]

Hughes told Redgrove that he did not want to burden himself with an entire book, which was why he had worked out the idea in the abbreviated form of anthology, introduction and then poem. But he couldn't let go of his desire to unlock the key to the plays. Eventually, in *Shakespeare and the Goddess of Complete Being*, he would tell the same story in unabbreviated form and in a style that was no bagatelle.

In 1978, inspired by Hughes's anthology, a Swedish actor and director called Donya Feuer put together a one-woman show called *Soundings*, which interlinked an array of Shakespearean soliloquies. She started up a correspondence with Hughes, leading him to write a long letter further developing his theory by way of a detailed reading of the play she went on to stage the following year, *Measure for Measure*.[22] They remained in touch, by post and telephone. By now he believed that the fifteen plays of the second half of Shakespeare's career, from *As You Like It* in 1599 to *The Tempest* in 1611, formed a single epic cycle. In 1990, Feuer wrote to suggest that she might create a production that brought extracts from all fifteen together in a single narrative. Beginning on Shakespeare's birthday, 23 April, Hughes sent her in return a steady stream of immensely long letters, which he eventually worked up into the book that was published two years later. Obsessively, he devoted almost all his time to the project. The archives of his papers in Georgia and London contain dozens of drafts, revisions, fragments, proofs, recordings of dictation, amounting to well over 10,000 pages of handwritten and typed material. Hughes later said that writing so much prose had given him shingles, destroyed his immune system, made him ill, almost killed him. To his old friend Terence McCaughey, he described the writing of the book as a two-year sentence in a cage in the walls of the Tower of London.[23] The jaguar confined in the royal menagerie.

Faber agreed, with some scepticism, to publish the book. In the summer of 1991 it was put into the hands of a copy-editor, Gillian Bate. Each of her scrupulous and particular requests for clarification led Hughes to send great screeds of new material. Thus, in answer to a letter about routine copy-editorial matters: 'I'm sorry to be so long returning this, but I wanted to clear up one thing that has been a difficulty from the beginning. The business of Occult Neoplatonism. One can't just refer to this and assume that even Shakespearean scholars will understand and supply the rest. 400 years of cultural suppressive dismissal aren't going to be lifted.'[24] Six weeks later: 'Thank you for the thousand improving suggestions. Don't be alarmed by the enclosed …'[25] The next day: 'Dear Gillian, I've sent you the wrong note – in the text and as a spare copy – for page 344. By wrong I mean an early draft, a little unclear and missing the main opportunity. This is the most important note of all – clarifying every obscurity. Destroy the other one, so it can't creep back in.' A week after this: 'Also, is it possible to have a note to a note. For instance, on this page 18 I would like to add a brief note to "prodigiously virile" – 9th line from the bottom.' The note is then provided:

As the son of an occasional Butcher, and the nephew of several farmers, Shakespeare's familiarity with pigs is not irrelevant to his myth. The imagination's symbols are based on subliminal perception. The male, aphrodisiac, pheromone scent spray, sold in modern sex-shops, is based on a hormone extract from the Wild Boar.[26]

Another letter, the same day: 'How are you getting on? This isn't a new note, though it's new to you. It's an old note that I lost – and have now found. Could you tuck it in? I think it's a Note, don't you? If it were inserted as a para, at that point, it might be just a bit dissonant – in tone, in actual style. How does it appear to you?' Gillian Bate sent a calm postcard in reply: 'Dear Ted, Thank you for all your communications of this week. I am digesting them slowly and hope to be in touch middle of next week with any questions still remaining … I have to return all to Fabers end of next week.'[27]

Before the end of that week, another fat envelope dropped through her letterbox: 'Dear Gillian – "What, will the line stretch out to the crack of doom?" This is a <u>rewritten</u> note – just slightly lengthened. But it struck me that the original was confused and inadequate. Just slot it in.'[28] Then came a desperate plea: 'The last bubbles of the last gasp. I know you are onto other work, that Fagin and Fagin, as my friend Leonard Baskin calls them, have cut off any more payment, and that you are ready to scream if you see that dreaded red–hot iron albatross – the word Shakespeare – ever again, but I am happy to refund you for any time this now costs: and refund you treble … Enclosed below are the last bits of wordage repair.'[29]

In November, Christopher Reid, Hughes's commissioning editor at Faber, put his foot down and said that they simply could not implement the latest set of changes. This did not stop Hughes from making hundreds more corrections in proof, before the typescript was finally sent to the printer at the end of the year.

Various titles were considered: 'The Silence of Cordelia', perhaps, or 'The Boar with the Flower in its Mouth'. Privately, Ted thought of it as his Dark Lady Book, but there was a Gravesian propriety to *Shakespeare and the Goddess of Complete Being*. Published on 9 March 1992, the book was an attempt to read the whole of Shakespeare (though very much weighted towards the second half of his career) through the argument that had been aired in the introduction to the anthology and expanded across Hughes's writings in prose and verse, on poetry and on myth, in the intervening years. 'The idea of nature as a single organism is not new,' he had written in a book review back in 1970, while the anthology was at press. 'It was man's first great thought, the basic intuition of most primitive theologies. Since Christianity hardened into Protestantism, we can follow its underground heretical life, leagued with everything occult, spiritualistic, devilish, over-emotional, bestial, mystical, feminine, crazy, revolutionary, and poetic.'[30] *Shakespeare and the Goddess of Complete Being* presents itself as an excavation of the occult, the underground, Shakespeare. It is an aria upon those aspects of Shakespeare's works that are most spiritualistic, devilish, over-emotional, bestial, mystical, feminine, crazy, revolutionary and poetic. Dipping one moment into cabbala and hermetic occult Neoplatonism, gnostic ritual and alchemy, the next into biographical speculation about Shakespeare's relationship with the Earl of Southampton, and the one after that into the historical clash of Catholic and Protestant – 'Shakespeare was a shaman, a prophet, of the ascendant, revolutionary, Puritan will (in its Elizabethan and Jacobean phase) just as surely as he was a visionary, redemptive shaman of the Catholic defeat'[31] – it maps the Venus/Adonis/boar (sex/will/death) triad across the works, while also sketching a secondary theme of the Rival Brothers (another key Hughesian preoccupation, and one with autobiographical origins).

At several crucial moments, Hughes breaks one of the cardinal rules of twentieth-century Shakespearean criticism: he links the plays directly to the life. It is unimaginable, he suggests, that when Shakespeare came to plot *All's Well that Ends Well* he could have failed to recognise 'just how closely the story tracked his own domestic life, and particularly that most decisive move he ever made – his first flight from his wife (for whatever reason). And his continuing to stay away, except for those visits.'[32] Pursued by an infatuated woman, forced by her powerful guardian to marry her, haunted by her image when he thinks himself in an adulterous liaison with another woman: this is Hughes's reading of both the character of Bertram in the play and William of Stratford in real life. 'When Shakespeare was writing *All's Well that Ends Well* the autobiographical secret sharer must have been breathing down his neck. To avoid it with a different plot, if he had wished to, would have been the simplest thing. But he must have searched out that specific plot for that specific reason – to deal in some way with that heavy breather.'[33]

Wilde and Woolf may assist again: this is Ted Hughes dealing with his own heavy breather, the 'autobiographical secret sharer'. We have no way of knowing whether or not Shakespeare's flight from Stratford and Anne Hathaway some time in the mid- or late 1580s was 'the

Orghast at Persepolis:
Ted in Iran

Second marriage:
Nick, Carol, Frieda
and Ted on the moors

Ted and Carol

Mighty opposites: Philip Larkin and Ted Hughes at a party in June 1977

Jennifer Rankin, Australian poet

Emma Tennant, Scottish novelist

Ted and Jill

Top Withens: the alleged original of Wuthering Heights, to which Ted and Sylvia were driven by Uncle Walt in 1956 (here photographed by Fay Godwin in 1977 for *Remains of Elmet*)

The Fisher King: Ted on the first day of trout-fishing season at Wistland Pond, Devon, April 1986

Frieda and Nicholas Hughes at the unveiling of the blue plaque in memory of their mother at 3 Chalcot Square, Primrose Hill, in 2000

Letter Home: Great War memorial at Paddington railway station, a key influence on 'Black Coat: Opus 131'

With steelhead on the Dean River, British Columbia, 1995

Birthday Letters revealed, January 1998

The memorial stone on Dartmoor, photographed in July 2015

most decisive move he ever made'. But we know for sure that the whole course of Ted Hughes's future life was decided by his flight from Sylvia Plath and Court Green in 1962.

Similarly with his account of the interplay of love and lust in the character of Troilus: 'this new factor, the larval or introductory phase of the hero's idyllic (idealistic) love, enables Shakespeare to connect his Mythic Equation to the impassioned enigma of his own subjectivity (as the *Sonnets* revealed it) in a way that is impossible to ignore ... This helps to give *Troilus and Cressida* its autobiographical feel.'[34] A bomb is exploding here. In short, 'the loved and loathed woman in the one body' is the beautiful, the desired, the unashamedly adulterous Assia Wevill just as much as it is Shakespeare's Cressida.[35] Hughes has thought deeply but above all feelingly, from experience, about heterosexual desire and its relationship to death in this play. He has less to say about the homoerotic dimension of the Greek camp – the question of same-sex desire is a conspicuous absence from nearly all Hughes's work, which cannot be said of Shakespeare's.

From *All's Well*'s Helen, the bold and fatherless traveller who prefigures Sylvia, Hughes's Shakespeare – or rather the Shakespearean Hughes – has proceeded to the dark, complex figure of Cressida/Assia (even the names echo each other), at once seductress and victim, on an inevitable path to a terrible end. Later, with *King Lear*, comfort will be found in the form of a very different woman, younger, de-eroticised and above all discreet. One of the book's epigraphs is a quotation from Ann Pasternak Slater's *Shakespeare the Director*: 'Cordelia is the quiet absolute ... her very silence is the still centre of this turning world.'[36]

Unsurprisingly, *Shakespeare and the Goddess of Complete Being* was condemned by most academic critics as an extended eccentricity. Professor John Carey of Oxford University set the tone in the *Sunday Times*, accusing the book of fundamental self-contradiction, in that the 'goddess-worshipping stance' purported to 'celebrate the female principle, fluid and fertile, as against the logical and scientific male ego', whereas Hughes had adopted a pseudo-logical, pseudo-scientific and very male approach that extended even to his metaphors ('comparing the plays to rockets, space capsules, nuclear power stations etc'). The eccentricities of the Hughesian brain were concoctions at complete odds with 'the anarchic welter of his imagination'. Fortunately, though, his 'poetic dynamism' did at one point 'break free from the rhapsodic muddle of Shakespearean exegesis that mostly entangles him':

> In a long footnote on page 11 he describes a huge matriarchal sow, gross, whiskery, many-breasted, a riot of carnality, with a terrible lolling mouth 'like a Breughelesque nightmare vagina, baggy with overproduction'. Although smuggled in as a hermaphroditic version of the mythic boar, this sow has abso-lutely nothing to do with Shakespeare, and everything to do with Hughes's violently divided feelings about women. A magnificent late-Hughes prose-poem, the footnote is worth all the rest of the book several times over.[37]

Dr Eric Griffiths of Cambridge University was moved to wonder whether Hughes had been rewiring his house, such was the profusion of imagery regarding Shakespeare's voltage, poetic current, flashpoints and the like. As it happens, builders were in Court Green, turning the house upside down as Ted wrestled with the Goddess. Griffiths concluded that there were '28 pages worth reading in this book (beginning at p. 129). In those pages, Hughes pays attention to what Shakespeare wrote. The effect is wonderful.'[38] The pages in question are indeed a masterclass in the close reading of a particular technique of Shakespearean verse, namely the rhetorical figure of doubling known as hendiadys. The analysis of one example from *All's Well*, 'the catastrophe and heel of pastime', is especially brilliant.[39]

Hughes was stung but not deterred. He penned an essay called 'Single Vision and Newton's Sleep in John Carey', which gave him the occasion to set off on his Gravesian mythical-poetic journey once more: 'my Crow is Bran of the Tower Ravens. Bran who was Apollo (a Crow God) plus his son, the Crow demi-god Asclepius the Healer (whose mother was the white Crow Goddess Coronis), was the god-king, a crow god, of early Britain, where he was also the llud who was Llyr who was Lear. More mumbo jumbo to make [Carey] smile.'[40] His reply, and a further counter-blast from Carey, were printed in the *Sunday Times*, which loved a good old literary spat.

As for Griffiths, he was an academic. Hughes did not pretend to be, nor in his worst nightmares could have imagined himself as, such an etiolated creature. He approached the plays, he said in his riposte, 'like an industrial spy, not for the purpose of discursive comment, but with the sole idea of appropriating, somehow, the secrets of what makes them work as fascinating stage events, as big poems, and as language, so that I can adapt them to my own doings in different circumstances'. So it was that 'Griffiths spends his days thinking and talking about scholarship and criticism. I spend my days, as I always have done, inventing and thinking about new poetic fables which, though vastly inferior to Shakespeare's in every way, as I do not need to be told, are nevertheless the same kind of thing.'[41]

The one serious reviewer who seemed genuinely to understand and appreciate the book was Marina Warner, novelist, critic and devotee of myth, cult, folk story and fairy tale. Ted was deeply grateful to her, and struck up a rewarding correspondence.

The American edition, meanwhile, provided an opportunity to add some extra material, including a key sequence that Hughes had unaccountably forgotten to include for Faber, in which he worked out 'The Tragic Equation in *The Two Noble Kinsmen*' – taking him back to his early perception about the power and significance of that last play, written in collaboration with John Fletcher.

Shakespeare and the Goddess of Complete Being remains *sui generis*, and certainly cannot be recommended to students as an introductory critical study of the plays. But it does not now seem quite so eccentric in its entirety. Hughes always regarded the poet as shaman and prophet, and there is indeed something ahead of its time, something prophetic, about several aspects of the book. At the time he was writing, mainstream Shakespearean criticism was almost entirely secular. In subsequent years, there was a huge revival of interest in the playwright's engagement with religious questions and in the possibility of a hidden vein of Catholicism running through his imagination.

Secondly, the proscription against biographical reading of the plays – shaped by Cambridge-style 'new criticism' – began to break down in the early twenty-first century. Hughes's hunches about the possible autobiographical element in such plays as *All's Well* and *Troilus* anticipate a string of subsequent speculations in which critics and biographers have linked details in the plays to everything from Shakespeare's sex life to the social climbing suggested by his pursuit of a coat of arms to his political associations with the circle around the Earl of Essex.

Thirdly, in a remarkable excursion linking the Tragic Equation to the differing impulses of left and right brain,[42] Hughes proves himself to be a John the Baptist heralding the advent of a new and very twenty-first-century genre: neurological literary criticism that benefits from developments in scanning technologies such as functional magnetic resonance imaging in order to ask questions about what exactly might have gone on in Shakespeare's brain as he wrote, and what really happens in our brains as we read or listen to his extraordinary language.

Ultimately, though, on Wildean and Woolfian principles, the spectacle of Hughes reading Shakespeare is less interesting than that of Shakespeare reading Hughes. The 'Tragic Equation' involves AC ('Total Goddess'), 'A(c)' ('The Woman with virtuous, loving aspect dominant'), 'B(d)' ('Tragic Hero: Adonis phase, with puritan censor dominant'), '(a)C' ('The Woman with infernal aspect dominant') and '(b)D' ('Tragic Hero: with Tarquin phase (Boar Madness) dominant'). The use of astrological terms such as 'dominant' and 'aspect' is Hughesian, not Shakespearean. It may or may not be the case that in Shakespeare's narrative poems 'A(c) loves B(d), but B(d) is distancing himself from A(c), actively rejecting her sexual claim with puritan disapproval,' at which point 'Shakespeare intensifies the situation with B(d)'s "double vision" – in which he sees (a)C superimposed on A(c), and rejects both in loathing.'[43] But it is certainly the case that the tangle of love and sexual claim, desire and loathing, possession and rejection, overshadowed by familial 'puritan disapproval', was Ted's own story of A (Assia), B (Brenda) and C (Carol) in the late Sixties.

Shakespeare with his supposed double life, as married country gentleman in the shires but lad about town in London, is Hughes. Shakespeare with his supposed Goddess-worship, and the capacious libido that goes with it, is Hughes. Shakespeare was at once a court poet and a man who knew about 'dark ladies' and sweating tubs for the treatment of sexual disease. Hughes dined privately with members of the royal family (the Queen Mother told him that she was especially fond of *Lupercal*), but he was also intrigued by the London demimonde ('That elegant woman you have just been speaking to', he once said to a friend at a party, 'is the most expensive prostitute in London').[44]

Above all, Shakespeare with his supposed mythic method of composition is Hughes. Shakespeare did not think about boars in the way that Hughes thought about bulls. He wrote many plays about male rivalry but he never thought in terms of the Theme of the Rival Brothers. Shakespeare made frequent allusions to classical mythology, but always in the poetic or dramatic moment, never in an effort to build a system.[45] The systematising belonged to Hughes, under the influence of Graves.

In trying to make sense of Shakespeare, he was really trying to make sense of his own creative life. And in so doing he heard once more the call of Plath. The Goddess is many; one of the many is Plath. Sometimes, then, the manuscript drafts of the Shakespeare book veer away from the ostensible subject. A fragment headed 'A Working Definition of Mythic, in Shakespeare and the Goddess of Complete Being' includes a lengthy excursion concerning 'the role of two obsessive but minatory images (actually two related myths) in Sylvia Plath's basically mythic oeuvre':

> She was obsessed by the story of Phaeton (the earthly son of the Sun-God, who takes the realm of his father's Sun-chariot, loses control and is wrecked) and the story of Icarus (the son of the wizard artificer Daedalus. Escaping from Crete on wings constructed by his father, Icarus flew too near the sun, which melted the fixing wax and plunged him into the sea).[46]

Breughel's painting of the Fall of Icarus, he remembered, was on her wall.

He went on to point out that the title poem of *Ariel* was Plath's version of the Phaeton myth and that 'Sheep in Fog', the poem that he analysed in more detail than any other, was its reverse: they were two opposite poems about riding the same horse over the same moor. In Plath's final corrections of 'Sheep in Fog', he explained, 'the speaker, who in "Ariel" had been a Phaeton urging the flying horse into the sun (triumphant, albeit "suicidal" and doomed to fall), suddenly becomes an Icarus, whose melting world threatens to let her through "into a heaven" not of the sun and freedom, but "starless, fatherless, a dark water"'. The Icarus allusion was no 'pedagogic ornament' or 'dip into the myth-kitty'. The brilliance of Plath was that her finished poems showed no overt signs of the myth: 'nothing in her simple, final correction of the last three lines of "Sheep in Fog" suggests that she was conscious there of the Icarus myth that supplied both verbs, both nouns, and all three adjectives, as well as the situation'. But the deleted drafts were a giveaway: 'the scrapped chariot and the dead man lying on the moor'. Hughes concluded that 'Sheep in Fog' had a quite extraordinary power to move the reader because it was 'obviously drawn from that subjective, visionary, mystical experience', Plath's mythic personality's relationship to her father, which was then 'in crisis'.[47]

That 'obviously' was obvious only to Hughes, because he was more versed than any other human being in Plath's work and its relationship to her life. His method of studying Shakespeare – the search for mythic archetypes buried beneath images and movements of thought that do not overtly allude to myth – yielded him rich rewards as a reader of Plath. He argued that her transformation of Phaeton into Icarus was 'the crucial episode of her soul's myth – in the most literal sense a life and death emergency trying to communicate itself'. With a great author, whether Shakespeare or Plath, the core myth is 'worth searching out' because 'This blood-jet autobiographical truth is what decides the difference in value between a myth (or any other image) as used by the realist and the mythic image as it appears in a truly mythic work.'[48]

In this reading of Plath, as in his reading of Shakespeare, Hughes has found the myth beneath the realism in order to come to the core of the 'evolving struggle' in the artist's 'own psyche'. But really the struggle and the myth are his own. He is supposed to be writing a book about Shakespeare but he cannot stop writing about Plath. And in writing about the crisis in her relationship with her father, he is writing yet once more about her relationship with her husband. He is edging ever closer to his own 'blood-jet autobiographical truth'.

Smiling Public Man

Hughes pondered deeply over the poem 'Among School Children' by his revered W. B. Yeats. It is a meditation on the tension between artists and their work, the dancer and the dance, the exterior life of 'A sixty-year-old smiling public man' – by this time Yeats was a senator of the Irish Free State – and the interior life of the poet as he dreams of a beautiful woman and the loss of a time when 'two natures blent / Into a sphere from youthful sympathy'.[1] These thoughts sounded a persistent echo in the mind of Ted Hughes in the Nineties. Public man, Poet Laureate, famous author, he had much to preoccupy him through his sixties, but his deepest self never ceased to be embroiled with the myth of the Goddess and the loss of Sylvia, the poetic other half of his youthful self.

There were battles to be fought, causes to be taken up, letters to be written to editors and government ministers, lobbying groups to support, whether the campaign to ban the North-East Drift New Salmon Fishery off Northumbria or a local group to prevent the over-development of Devon.[2] There were newspaper articles to be written: defending the hunting of stag and fox on Exmoor because it preserved the delicate ecosystem and the mysterious ancient bond between rural people and indigenous animals or proposing that the interior of the Millennium Dome should be laid out in the shape of a giant human brain.[3] Political decisions to be influenced: in thanking the Prime Minister for a 'Wordsworth evening' at Number 10, he urged John Major, at a time when the national Environment Agency was being restructured, to ensure that responsibility for dealing with pollution was not separated from the National Rivers Authority.[4]

Then there were academic Shakespeareans to be attacked: when a certain Gary Taylor proposed a second-rate little lyric 'Shall I die?

Shall I fly?' as a new addition to the canon of the Bard, Hughes told the *Sunday Times* that it was 'ersatz Taramasalata' whereas true Shakespeare was always caviar, even if sometimes bad caviar. Taylor might *know* everything about Shakespeare but he had never truly *read* him.[5] There was the work of Arvon, for which he tried to get support from first Prince Charles and then the billionaire Paul Getty. And decisions that came with the job of Laureate, such as the award of the Queen's Gold Medal for Poetry. He took particular pleasure in proposing the Scottish poet Sorley MacLean, still more delight when the Queen arranged for her personal piper to lead in the victor with traditional Gaelic tunes. Another year, he was deeply disappointed when Thom Gunn turned the medal down.[6]

In private, he became a more prolific letter-writer than ever before. Letter-writing sustained his deepest friendships, with men from Cambridge days such as McCaughey and Myers, Huws and Weissbort, and with fellow-writers such as Ben Sonnenberg in New York, Yehuda Amichai in Israel and above all Seamus Heaney in Ireland. Heaney, whose great gift, he wrote, was to 'make it easier for people to love each other'.[7] Heaney, who won the Nobel Prize for Literature in 1995, eliciting a magnificent letter of congratulation: 'Well – there it is. And it's there forever. Like a sea-god on a great wave you emerged and inevitably took it, by sovereignty of nature.'[8] Hughes saw that the award was 'perfectly ripe' for the historical moment of Northern Ireland's move towards peace and reconciliation. But there was, Heaney admitted after Hughes's death, just a hint of envy over 'the call from Stockholm'.[9] No English-born poet has ever won the big one. Ted knew that it was almost inconceivable for the Nobel Committee to choose him as the first (imagine the feminist reaction!), but a small part of him found it difficult to see himself surpassed by Heaney, who acknowledged that it was the 'almost magic effect' of Hughes's writing that had made him into a poet.[10] The metaphor of the sea-god emerging on the great wave suggests the death of Hippolytus in a Greek myth to which Hughes kept returning in his later years. Hippolytus is a son-figure and he was famous for his sexual purity. The fertile unconscious of Hughes may be saying something about the metaphoric poetic father being usurped by the son whose hands seem always clean – politically, sexually – even as his work digs in the soil and bogs of rural Ireland.

The argument of *Shakespeare and the Goddess of Complete Being* was rehearsed and refined for the benefit of numerous correspondents. Over several years, Ted exchanged views with the Reverend Moelwyn Merchant – Anglican and scholar – regarding not only Shakespeare but also the reconciliation of Christianity and syncretic mythology. He described himself as a 'radically Pagan soul' who was also in some sense a natural Christian.[11] To the poet Bill Scammell, he wrote at length about the character of Anna Karenina and Tolstoy's fear of sex. To his devoted explicator Keith Sagar and to the gently probing questioner Nick Gammage he wrote about his own work, again and again. His correspondence with another critic, Terry Gifford, is one part poetry, the other part environmental discussion. To others, he enthusiastically recommended the memory-training techniques of Tony Buzan, describing him as a Mental Martial Arts guru.

He was bombarded with invitations – to give readings (two or three requests a week to do free readings for charities, he once explained),[12] to look at people's work, to endorse books, to participate in literary projects, to give away rights. His patience was tried but his appetite for new and unusual ideas never failed him. Nor did his sense of humour. In conversation and in his informal letters, he had deadpan wit. When he met the actress Susannah York at a celebration of Wilfred Owen's poetry in Oswestry, she mentioned that her son was going up to Cambridge to read English. He told her that she should chop off his head to save him from that fate.[13] He was also very good at teasing himself, even making a joke of his erotic dream-life: 'Sophia Loren, teasingly threatening to strip, then, sitting on a steep rock in river, actually being stripped as she slides willy nilly into water. Very vivid comic effects, on her part.'[14]

Often he did agree to write on behalf of writers. On a few occasions he succeeded in persuading Faber to take on a new poet; on many, he failed. He perfected the art of writing endorsements. One of the best was sent to his daughter's American publisher: 'When I think of Frieda Hughes, who is my daughter,' he began, disarmingly, 'I am always reminded of a certain morning, a breakfast of the Devon Beekeepers Association, hearing her talk wildly about various bee-swarms she had extricated from various near-impenetrable fortresses.' This struck him as 'very peculiar', because he knew that 'she had never so much as touched a bee – and was, in fact, allergic to their stings'. He was at the rear of the hall, close to the exit, but he heard her clearly: 'She spoke in her familiar way, very fast and vivaciously, exclaiming and interrupting and cackling, until she had cleared herself enough startled attention to begin orating in earnest. Being Frieda, she did not stop at the savage swarm she had subdued. She had plans for a far grander campaign.'[15] There is a revealing lapse of memory here. Sylvia's beehives stood empty for many years in the garden of Court Green, the wood slowly rotting just as her old car rusted outside the house – Ted could not bear to get rid of them. Then, as a teenager, Nick took up beekeeping, partly in order to get in touch with the heritage of his mother and indeed his grandfather Otto, the bee expert. He, not Frieda, was the one who would get into conversations with old men about bees, tell tales of his adventures, and speak at beekeepers' breakfasts. Ted's memory lapse was part and parcel of the process whereby he saw Frieda as the reincarnation of Sylvia. She was, he said, more German than her mother but also very American, and entirely stultified by England. He was delighted when she found her inner self, and found happiness, in Australia, though of course he missed her even more than he did Gerald. He sent her long letters, filled with good advice about her poems.

In 1990, Frieda published a children's novel called *Waldorf and the Sleeping Granny* about 'a good witch, a bad witch and a girl in her teens taking charge and accepting responsibility for herself, thereby gaining confidence and being able to do wonderful things as a result'. Ted loved the book and its message about self-belief. But, as Frieda remembered it, Carol phoned and said, 'The person you have written about knows what you have done.' Frieda was puzzled, since – like her father in his mythological and folktale mode – she didn't think of her characters as being based on real people. She got the impression that Carol had mistakenly taken the wicked witch to be a portrait of her (Carol says that she was actually referring to Olwyn, and that Frieda was made fully aware of this).[16] The two women were on opposite sides of the world in more ways than one.

Frieda struggled with illness during these years, when she lived in a little house, surrounded by gum trees, in a remote settlement called Wooroloo, about an hour's drive from Perth. Her poetry and her painting pulled her through and in 1996 she married (for the third time). Her union with Hungarian fellow-painter László Lukács, who was also working in Western Australia, inspired one of Ted's loveliest unpublished poems. Written as a wedding present, it is a capsule biography of his daughter that begins, 'The day she was conceived Frieda set off to explore America.'

In the womb she sees the world through her mother's eyes. The grand tour through mountain, forest and prairie, all the way to the California coast, where they stare out at the Pacific, sea-kelp at the water's edge looking like the tails of lions, and she kicks and jumps inside Sylvia just at the moment when her father says 'How far is Australia? O so far, far away!' As energetic before birth as she would be in life, she is born at sunrise on April Fool's Day and her first sight is the mother she would never remember,

> Propped up in the bed, weeping with joy in the first light of
>   the April sun
> Yes, weeping with joy as she held the glowing rosy creature
> That was going to be Frieda.

She then meets her Daddy (she would always call him Daddy), who had stayed awake all night, as giddy as Shakespeare's Troilus, with the expectation of the gift of life, the newborn thing that would sneeze as he first lifted her up 'In the room papered with big roses'.

The poem then gives back to Frieda some of the things she had forgotten: how Sylvia nursed her for more than a year because she wanted to give her everything and more, how she 'shook her cot to pieces / Gripping the bars and shaking the whole thing to pieces / Because she wanted to be off'. How she kept tearing down the 'life-size print of the Great Goddess Isis' that hung over her cot as a talisman. How for hours and hours, by day and night, 'to and fro', her Daddy 'walked with her in his arms' and sang all the old ballads, again and again ('Van Diemen's Land', 'Eppie Morrie', 'Sir Patrick Spens', 'Barnyards of Delgatty', 'The Wearing of the Green', all those songs he had shared with Dan Huws at Cambridge), and little Frieda would suck her thumb but not want to sleep because she did not want to miss 'one minute of the world'. Remember: the album of snapshots in which Frieda is 'Centre of the Universe'. Remember: the little girl as dancing ballerina, with tutu and tiara, whirling round to the music of Handel. Then the creaky boat ride to Ireland and the house by the sea in Connemara. Her love for every living thing – guinea pig, hamster, rat and ferret ('I love them so much they make me shiver, they make me cry!'), even the tick that bit her, because it came from the dog that she loved. And then she is off, impatient with school and teenagerhood. Even the motorbikes are not fast enough for her, so she is off travelling the world, riding, running free, until László catches her in Australia.

She is her father's 'comet made of priceless, blazing jewels', her eyes having blazed from the moment she was born. His 'windfall from heaven', now she must be given to her new husband. He closes by addressing László. The best part of his own life has been 'hidden' in Frieda. Ted trusts that because László is an artist he knows about precious things, about jewels, 'even those that fall out of the blue Australian sky'. So he will know 'how to value / A meteorite of diamonds / Fallen out of heaven'. Frieda will amaze her new husband every bit as much as she has amazed her Daddy. The most important thing for László to know will be 'how to look after Frieda'.[17]

Ted always granted respect to strangers. He patiently responded to questions about his poems. A French graduate student at Oxford asked some good ones and he rewarded her with a letter of more than 5,000 words that amounts to a miniature literary autobiography.[18] Here he acknowledged that his animal poems were the 'dramatisation' of his 'internal psychodrama', while telling of his literary and psychological influences (Jung especially). He granted his interrogator's assumption that he found his own voice through the adoption of 'another persona' (Crow most obviously), that he was not a poet of *ego*, not interested in 'Wordsworthian rumination over my own autobiography'. But he attributed this distancing from the self to the literary–critical climate of his youth, in which 'the secrets of the private life needed total protection'. Later in the letter, he admitted that an autobiographical voice was trying to get out: the farming-diary poems were simply about his own life, 'yes Wordsworthian style'. For all his experiments with mythic systems, this was perhaps his true voice of feeling, his most fertile vein. At the end of the letter, he suggested, to his own surprise, that his work was coming full circle to where he had begun in the little love poem 'Song': to the naked voice, the 'living nerve', of his inner being.

There were bizarreries of the kind that beset him throughout his life: a girl in her thirties who lived in Oxford, called herself Kayak, was obsessed with Lapland and wrote poems in the style of *Crow*, began pushing letters through the door of Court Green, claiming that she was Hughes's daughter. A cease-and-desist letter was dispatched from the lawyers.[19] In another development, his New York lawyer Victor Kovner was put on alert because rumours were emerging of a possible biographical film about the Plath–Hughes marriage – first Madonna was said to be interested and then the actress Molly Ringwald was signed up to play Plath.[20] With the urge to suppress for fear of distortion and vilification came an urge to reveal. Writing to Stephen Spender, who had been wounded by an unauthorised biography, he suggested that the best solution would be to write a detailed autobiography, to tell everything so that interest in the life would be absolutely sated and the past life would no longer belong to the person who had lived it, meaning that they need no longer worry about it. The one thing one should never do, he added, was go to law.[21]

He belatedly surrendered to Wagner, under the influence of the maverick systematiser Dr Iris Gillespie, whose Wagnerian essays with such titles as 'Death-Devoted Heart' he vainly sent to Faber.[22] He praised his friend Josephine Hart for the poetic passion of *Damage*, her novel of obsessive erotic desire.[23] He read as voraciously and eclectically as ever. And over the dinner-table, his appetite still gargantuan despite the vicissitudes of his health, or over bottle upon bottle of good wine, he would talk and talk. Horatio, one of the Morpurgos' children, had vivid memories of Ted's 'table talk'. One evening the Laureate would sound off about abstract art's detachment from real life, another he would turn up with 'a video of two ganglions in a rat's brain actually forming a new connection – the birth of a thought captured on film'.[24] His restless conversation was symptomatic of his deeper restlessness: his desire to live in Ireland rather than England, Devon as 'the graveyard of ambition' – 'drab compared to Alaska, boring compared to London'. 'Are we living in a museum?' he asked one evening, after someone had described the 'picturesque' life of a local smallholder, soon to retire. Perhaps he should have been Jewish instead of 'question-mark Anglican'. In some ways, he would rather have been a doctor than a poet. If only he hadn't wasted so much time running around with women when he was young he 'might have really achieved something'.

By this time, his politics were of the right: 'Mrs Thatcher was a big enthusiasm. Michael Heseltine became a friend. Kenneth Baker – Thatcher's ideologue-in-chief – was also a buddy. He liked Mrs T's belligerent business sense, her militarism, patriotism and all-round impatience with slackers. These were traits he shared and was proud of.' Politically, he was never exactly consistent:'He spoke of how much he owed to the fairness of Butler's 1944 educational reforms – then suddenly Kenneth Baker was coming to dinner and 50% of school-teachers were homosexual. Fact.'

He was at his best with his passions: fishing stories, folklore, the ancient history of his Devon home. Young Morpurgo remembered how Ted loved talking about the Iron Age associations of the area, how the whole locality was a sort of sacred forest – the regional 'Nymet' place-name came from the Celtic word for a 'sacred grove'. The names of fields and rivers were vestiges of 'un-Romanised Celtic populations and culture'. 'Devon rounds' were late Iron Age fortifications. A nearby farmer had turned up 'strange white stones in one of his fields' and Ted was convinced that they were fragments of a pre-Roman temple-floor. As for the Romans' brief occupation of the area, Vespasian set up camp in North Tawton and the garden of Court Green contained the rampart of his military camp, on which fox cubs now played. Morpurgo noted, shrewdly, that Ted had, 'literally on his door-step, and all around him, traces of this tension between a native culture more or less stamped out elsewhere, and an "acquired", wider European one'. He saw rural England as his 'sub-culture' – the place he knew best, the source of his literary voice – but it could 'never be the whole picture': a wider culture had to be integrated, a balance struck. So it was that one moment Ted would insult the French in the tone of a Little England *Spectator* columnist and the next he would translate Racine's *Phèdre*. He would introduce a whole generation to the wonders of Yoruba poetry, then say that Third World aid was a waste of money. There is an odd mix of admiration and scorn in Morpurgo's piece: he recognises himself as an 'earnest young man' who did not fully appreciate Ted's taste for mischief, for the wind-up and the tall story, for deliberate provocation and the opinion that went against the grain of liberal consensus.

That said, there is no doubting the seriousness with which Hughes threw himself into the world of the West Country gentry, which provided him with fishing rights to die for and many a meal at the very upmarket Gidleigh Park Hotel. And the Laureateship had opened the highest doors in the land. A weekend at Windsor with Queen Elizabeth the Queen Mother included a private recital by Sir John Gielgud. Fishing with the Queen Mother in Scotland became a high point of the year. He relished the way that she was interested in everything and everybody, always positive in her outlook on the world.[25] Other well-to-do connections took him beyond the Highlands to the Islands. In August 1991 he stayed at Amhuinnsuidhe Castle on the Isle of Harris in the Hebrides, from where he went deep-sea fishing. The exclusive Grimersta River on the island of Lewis became a Mecca for the Fisher King.

Trips away were a welcome escape from troubles at home – there was a particularly difficult time when Carol's elder sister, whose vitality he loved, died of cancer. Bereavement sent Ted and Carol's shared life into a tunnel from which it was difficult to emerge.[26]

In 1994, he helped Nick get American citizenship, which necessitated a trip to New York and the calling in of some favours. That May he had another week fishing with the Queen Mother on the Dee (this time he caught nothing). Another summer, his thank-you letter for a visit to Birkhall, her Scottish home in Royal Deeside, waxed lyrical about the northern light. The year after that he was at Birkhall again, deerstalking in the company of Prince Charles.[27] The heir to the throne in place of brother Gerald: Ted had come a long way from his childhood hunting ground in the woods and moors above the Calder Valley.

Meanwhile, there was the usual legion of literary projects, though none so all-consuming or important to him as *Shakespeare and the Goddess of Complete Being*. Ever since the publication of *The Rattle Bag*, that highly personal anthology of Hughes and Heaney favourites, Seamus had wanted to produce a 'more decidedly literary-historical' sequel.[28] In January 1990 Ted sent Seamus a list of the greatest English poets from the Middle Ages to the mid-twentieth century, suggesting that there should be no more than two or three works per poet. The focus, he said, should be on those who were 'spiritually great – voices of the whole tribe at a moment of crisis'.[29] Perhaps it should be called 'The Kit Bag': 'a book for the lonely soldier surviving on essentials'.[30]

Heaney told him, more than half in earnest, that he couldn't 'go with the imperial associations of the kit bag', its summoning of 'Brits in cork helmets and shorts, wielding their swagger sticks'.[31]

Other priorities intervened, but the anthology was eventually published in 1997 as *The School Bag*, with a brief preface explaining that it was intended to be 'a kind of listening post, a book where the reader can tune in to the various notes and strains that have gone into the making of the whole score of poetry in English'.[32] Nearly 600 pages long, it is a superb selection from the canon of English and American poetry, inclusive of translations from Irish, Welsh and Scottish Gaelic. The arrangement seems haphazard – neither chronological nor thematic – but nearly all the essential poets from the anthologists' two islands are sampled. An afterword by Ted outlined his method of memorising poems, an art that in his later years he was forever urging upon educators and correspondents. He told Prince Charles that his son Nick had used the memory method for everything from history to science, so perhaps it would be of use to the Princes William and Harry in their studies.[33] In the early Nineties he often visited Highgrove, Prince Charles's country residence in Gloucestershire, and read his stories aloud to the boys. They especially liked extracts from *The Iron Man*.[34]

To mark a visit, Ted would often inscribe a book for his host. There is a noteworthy body of unknown 'occasional verse' of this kind. On the spectrum of his writing, these short pieces lie between the expensive limited editions of fewer than a hundred copies and the unpublished drafts filed away among the writer's own papers. Perhaps such works should never be published: a poem for an individual is a very private thing. But then again, Hughes knew that every scrap of his writing was of potential value and that all his manuscripts had the potential to end up in archive or auction room. Every now and then, one of these little poems-of-the-moment pops up in a sale or is stumbled upon in a library. On other occasions, they become treasured heirlooms. In her apartment in New York City, Jill Barber has what she calls a 'Ted Memorabilia Room', in which she keeps the books that he inscribed for her. At Highgrove, there is a cherished collection of personally inscribed copies of many of his books in the Prince of Wales's private 'sanctuary', where there are also two stained-glass windows dedicated to Ted, who thus lives on as the household shaman. One particular treasure is the copy of *New Selected Poems* that Hughes inscribed for the Prince's grandmother the Queen Mother in 1996, on the occasion of one of his visits to Birkhall. It is a celebration of the hard work undertaken by the royals, but also of their leisure time on Scottish river and moor. To work uncomplainingly is, the poem suggests, a good animal instinct, while the place for rest and recreation is among 'rocks and stones and trees'. The latter phrase is an embedded quotation from Wordsworth's 'Lucy' poem that so haunted Hughes. The poem for the Queen Mother ends with an image of her as an exemplary respondent to the demands of Mother Earth.[35]

Another project, inspired by a brainstorming dinner at Buckingham Palace in which the Duke of Edinburgh tried to elicit ideas for raising public awareness of environmental issues, was for a competition in which schoolchildren would rework material out of myth, religion and folktale into plays that illuminated aspects of our modern ecological crisis. From this emerged the Sacred Earth Drama Trust and the publication by Faber of the competition-winning plays under the title *Sacred Earth Dramas*. When the Sacred Earth Drama Group met in London in 1994, Valerie Eliot donated £10,000 of her earnings from her husband's work.

Early in the decade Ted wrote to the blonde and glamorous Joanna Mackle, a senior figure at Faber and Faber, requesting a reissue of his choice of Shakespeare's verse. No one but specialists would read *The Goddess of Complete Being*, he said, and nobody read Shakespeare's complete works for pleasure any more, but the anthology would give them the essentials. Why not include it in the ticket price for productions at the Royal Shakespeare Company and the National Theatre, sell it at hotels to sit alongside the Gideon Bible or drop it in among the fancy soaps and shampoos in upmarket establishments, give free copies to first-class and Concorde passengers on British Airways and Virgin, offer it to tour groups, negotiate with the Ministry to provide copies for every fifteen-year-old in the land? The reissue duly appeared – with revised introduction and afterword – but nothing came of the grand schemes for distribution.[36]

Ted was not deterred. If they couldn't do it with Shakespeare, then they could try with *The Rattle Bag* – he would write to Lord King at British Airways and Richard Branson at Virgin. Like many of Ted's other bright ideas to promote either his own work or the art of poetry in general, this one blazed for a moment and then fizzled out.

In the summer of 1992, Faber and Faber published his Laureate poems under the title *Rain-Charm for the Duchy*. This consisted of nine poems, eight of which, including two very long ones, had been published in national newspapers to mark various royal occasions.[37] Like the most famous of Faber poetry publications, T. S. Eliot's *The Waste Land*, the book was fleshed out to marketable length by means of prose notes at the back. These are in some ways more readable than the poems themselves. The commentary on 'Rain-Charm for the Duchy' is one of Hughes's most lyrical river essays, telling of how the poem maps the territory that had become his own spiritual home, the 'roughly square "island"' bounded by the Tamar, the Exe, the Torridge and the Taw. Strictly speaking, he explains, this means that he trespasses beyond the bounds of the Duchy itself, the royal lands of the Duke of Cornwall, His Royal Highness Prince Charles. He also explains, with a hint of regret, that since he excluded that part of Devon which lay to the east of the Exe there was no room for Coleridge's 'sweet birthplace', the river Otter. Then he soars into an account of the wonders of the river Mole bringing in the best sea-trout, and of an eighteenth-century diarist attempting to ford the Tamar at a moment when the assembled salmon, coming upstream to spawn, 'had decided to rush the shrunken river': 'His horse refused to approach the water, terrified by the massed fish going up over the gravel, through the ford, backs out, tails churning like propellors [*sic*], moving at their top speed.'[38] At the climax of the note, he evokes the river Torridge 'going over its last weir above the tide – Tarka the Otter's famous Beam Weir', looking like water 'being spilled slowly from a tin bath'. Propeller (wartime bombers and aviator Gerald), Tarka (favourite book) and tin bath (Aspinall Street) are images – homecomings – from his own childhood.

In the note on 'The Dream of the Lion', the first of his poems for his beloved Queen Elizabeth the Queen Mother, he explains further that he had mentally associated her maiden name (Bowes-Lyon) with the 'totem animal of Great Britain' as long ago as his 'boyhood fanatic patriotism'.[39] As for the third lion on the crest, it is Leo, her star sign and his.

The note on 'A Birthday Masque', written for the Queen's sixtieth birthday, veers into the territory of *Shakespeare and the Goddess of Complete Being*. Hughes explains that the poem's three angels, of Water, Earth and Blood, bring, respectively, purity to the polluted waters of modernity, the Taoist Way 'to the world of external bewilderment and empty distraction', and 'Blood's true nature' to 'the lineal unity of mankind, not as an agglomeration of sub-species but as a true family, an orphaned and bereft family, scattered, like the family in Shakespeare's play *The Comedy of Errors*'.[40] Alert to the potentially dark politics of Blood and Soil, here Hughes evokes by contrast the idea of the Queen's Commonwealth as a family. Perhaps, too, he is recalling the scattering of his own family across the globe: Gerald in Australia, Nick in Alaska, Frieda on her travels. The note continues with a brisk tour through the *Goddess* territory of Shakespeare's Lear, 'the Welsh sea-god Llyr, formerly the Irish god Lir, direct heir of an ancient lineage that goes back through Apollo to Ra, the high god of Ancient Egypt, the sun in geological time (flower-time) not that long ago'. And thence to the Sioux shaman Black Elk, the blade of a samurai sword, and 'the Islamic Sufi masterwork, Attar's *Conference of the Birds*'.[41] The note to the most recent of his Laureate poems, 'The Unicorn', first published in the *Daily Telegraph* in February 1992, also becomes a miniature rewrite of the Shakespeare book, replete with references to Prospero, Ariel, Queen Mab, Brutus and Hamlet.

The calmest and most personal note is that to 'A Masque for Three Voices', written for the Queen Mother's ninetieth birthday in August 1990. Ted describes his poem as a miniaturised version of an epic of the twentieth century, coinciding with the Queen Mother's life. She was born in 1900 as the Boer War came to an end, Freud published *The Interpretation of Dreams* and Max Planck began elaborating quantum theory. The main drama of the century was the two world wars, its culmination the collapse of the Soviet system. The Queen Mother lost her beloved brother Fergus in 1915, as Ted's home town lost so many of its sons. He writes, he says, 'from the point of view of the son of an infantryman of the First World War' and explains that one of his earliest recurrent dreams, 'long before 1939, was clouds of German parachutists descending on the Calder Valley' – he fantasised about 'how this or that part of the valley could be defended, where a sniper might best lie, and who would be traitors'.[42] In the age of anxiety leading up to the Second War, he felt that he would have to become a marksman himself. When the war came, the royal family, with the Queen Mother, then Queen, as its public face – encouraging her shy and stuttering husband, staying in London, living through the Blitz with her people – proved itself as a national resource. Now, towards the end of the century, Hughes implies, his role is to be the defensive marksman taking aim at the 'politically correct' who snipe against monarchy and nation. For the Poet Laureate, the nation was like a human soul, which was like a wheel, 'With a Crown at the hub / To keep it whole'.[43] Such imagery of national unity was replicated in his last, and, alas, flattest, Laureate poem, some brief verses for Diana's funeral on 6 September 1997.

When *Rain-Charm* was published, the assault from across the press was merciless. Auberon Waugh was incredulous in the *Sunday Telegraph* and A. L. Rowse scathing in the *Evening Standard*. For Hermione Lee, there was an embarrassing gap between the myth and the actuality of royalty (can the Queen's corgis really stand in for the sleeping British Lion?) and for Hilary Corke it was impossible to read even a few lines 'without emitting several little girlish shrieks of horror'.[44] Poet-critics such as Sean O'Brien, Michael Horovitz and Peter Reading did their best to find something to praise, especially in the river and landscape imagery, but the only unequivocally positive voice was Andrew Motion, always an acolyte, who suggested that the collection revealed Hughes as the best Poet Laureate since Tennyson.[45]

Ted was unlucky in the timing of *Rain-Charm*'s appearance. Nineteen-ninety-two, the Queen said in a speech that November, was not a year on which she would look back with undiluted pleasure: it was indeed her *annus horribilis* of royal scandal and fire in Windsor Castle. The republication of Hughes's worst Laureate poem, written for the marriage of Prince Andrew and Miss Sarah Ferguson, was not exactly timely in the year that 'Fergie' was accused of plagiarising another children's writer in her *Budgie the Helicopter* stories and then snapped sunbathing topless while having her toes sucked by a Texan millionaire. At the end of the year, the *Evening Standard* placed Ted at number eleven among a sorry dozen who had shared an *annus horribilis* with the Queen:

With the Royal Family becoming ever more tawdry, the job of Poet Laureate became intensely embarrassing. His poem 'The Honey Bee and the Thistle', on the Yorks' wedding, came back to haunt him ('A helicopter snatched you up / The pilot it was me'). There were more mutterings about how he treated his first wife, Sylvia Plath [a reference to the Jacqueline Rose book]. The PC lobby attacked his children's story 'How the Polar Bear Became', about a polar bear which dreams of a 'spotless' land where he can be alone with his whiteness. And his book *Shakespeare and the Goddess of Complete Being* was ridiculed for impenetrable mysticism.[46]

★

Nineteen-ninety-three was not only the year in which *Remains of Elmet*, *Cave Birds* and *River* were revised and gathered as *Three Books*. It was also a good vintage for his children's writing. In the spring he published a lovely little limited edition of seaside poems, from a private press in Exeter, inspired and accompanied by the pretty watercolours of local artist R. J. Lloyd. Written mostly in rhyming couplets aimed at children, they show that he had not lost the knack of imagining what it might be like to be a seal or an eel, a crab or a whelk, a bladderwrack or even a sea monster. Entitled *The Mermaid's Purse*, the collection was reissued by Faber the year after Hughes's death, with the additional inclusion of a poem on the graceful flight of seagulls – 'back-flip', 'Wing-waltzing', 'they scissor / Tossed spray' – that had been invisible since its appearance in the *Christian Science Monitor* forty years before.[47]

September saw the publication of *The Iron Woman*, a sequel to *The Iron Man* with a much more overt ecological message. Dedicated once more to Frieda and Nicholas, it tells of how the Iron Woman comes to 'take revenge on mankind for its thoughtless polluting of seas, lakes and rivers'.[48] She emerges from muddy marshland like the sea monster that destroys Hippolytus, is cleansed in a river and, with the assistance of Lucy and Hogarth, destroys the waste-disposal factory, saves the water creatures and is united with the Iron Man.

Two months after the appearance of *The Iron Woman* an adaptation of *The Iron Man* opened at the Young Vic. As a musical. The creator was

Pete Townshend, lead guitarist of The Who. Ted struck up a friendship with him and they hung out at Soho House, an achingly trendy new private members' club for arts and media types. The show received bewildered reviews but garnered full houses. Ted saw it in company with the Sillitoes, the Amichais, the Israeli cultural attaché and Olwyn. The latter was no lover of rock and roll, but found the music 'amazingly likeable and catchy'. She wrote Pete Townshend a fan letter. Ted told the director that he liked the show immensely, though was not sure about the bit where the space-bat–angel came out of the star. He wondered if at the end Josette Bushell-Mingo, who played the angel, could be 'roasted in the sun to a different colour', in order to provide a greater contrast with 'Trevor's engine room grime'. In a postscript he suggested, with no regard for theatrical health-and-safety rules, that the space-bat's approach might be accompanied by 10,000-decibel wingbeats.[49] Young audiences loved the show, which ran through the Christmas holidays, but it failed to find the West End transfer that would have made some serious money.

Two offshoots from *The Goddess of Complete Being* were preoccupying him at this time. In the Shakespeare book, he had been mildly dismissive of Ovid's *Metamorphoses*, the book that was Shakespeare prime source for classical myth. Hughes regarded it as a decadent Roman recension that was insufficiently reverential towards its Greek originals. But when he was invited by the poets Michael Hofmann and James Lasdun to contribute to a book in which some three dozen pre-eminent British poets (and a handful of Americans) would each translate one or two Ovidian tales, he changed his mind. Suddenly in Ovid he found a way of writing myth with a lightness of touch – something that had eluded him in the dark years of *Crow* and *Cave Birds*. Offered a choice of three stories, he did them all. And a fourth.

After Ovid: New Metamorphoses, which appeared from Faber in November 1994, begins with Hughes's version of Ovid's creation story and includes his take on Pentheus being ripped apart by the horde of Bacchic maenads (a return to the territory of *Gaudete*) as well as his sprightly translations of both 'Venus and Adonis' (the obvious one, in the light of the Shakespeare book) and the cognate tale of 'Salmacis and Hermaphroditus'. In the latter he takes particular pleasure in writing about the woman as instigator of a passionate sexual liaison, which ends with a 'dizzy boil' of two bodies melted into one, 'Seamless as water'.[50] To write from the point of view of the male who is the seduced not the seducer afforded him a kind of release. Having started with these four tales, he couldn't stop doing more Ovid. The outcome was his triumphant *Tales from Ovid*, published in 1997.[51]

Salmacis coils herself round Hermaphroditus like a snake and in this she is reminiscent of the witch-like Geraldine seducing the innocent Christabel in Samuel Taylor Coleridge's great poem, which Ted was reading and re-reading and writing about at great length at this time. In 'The Snake in the Oak', a 100-page essay, he sought to find the key to Coleridge's imagination, as he had tried to find the key to Shakespeare's in *Complete Being*. The essay was too long for journal publication but too short to be a book in its own right. By good fortune, while he was working on it the poet and critic William Scammell was putting together a substantial selection of Hughes's prose for Faber and Faber – extracts from *Poetry in the Making*, book reviews, introductions, key essays such as those on Baskin ('The Hanged Man and the Dragonfly') and Plath ('The Evolution of "Sheep in Fog"'). The Coleridge essay could be included, meaning that the book could be marketed as having new material as well as old.

Winter Pollen: Occasional Prose, published in March 1994, is a polished showcase of the best of Hughes's critical writings, in which his muscular and energetic prose, so influenced by Hazlitt and Swift, is shown to fine advantage. There is autobiographical projection in almost every piece, but the long Coleridge essay takes this to an extreme. It is Hughes at his most intense and insightful, and at the same time his most batty and idiosyncratic. In writing of Coleridge's 'two selves' – the Christian and the erotically 'unleavened' – he is also writing of his own battle with the Goddess, the snake-woman, the force of desire. 'Coleridge was besotted with woman,' he begins, matter-of-factly. If time were reversed the poet-critic Coleridge could as well have written 'Hughes was besotted with woman.' 'At the same time,' Hughes continues, not realising that he is writing about himself as much as about Coleridge, 'few can have so specialized in such terrifying nightmares about such terrifying women.'[52] Was it to do with being his mother's favourite, as Coleridge claimed he was? 'Woman is the source of all bliss, all love, all consolation. Then everything went wrong.

Fighting for mother's exclusive love against seven brothers, he lost.' Coleridge became obsessed by William and Dorothy Wordsworth because they presented him with the intense brother–sister bond he craved but lacked: 'his revered Wordsworth and the beloved yet untouchable Dorothy somehow supplied his need'.[53] Ted, who relied so often on both the literary judgement and the business sense of his sister Olwyn, was always intrigued by the symbiosis between the sister's journals and the brother's poems, and by the ineffably profound intimacy between William and Dorothy (in a famous interpretation, the critic Freddie Bateson had wondered whether there was a whiff of incest).

The culmination of Coleridge's woman obsession, Hughes suggests, is the apparition of the Nightmare Life-in-Death in 'The Ancient Mariner'. She has full erotic allure, but she is also 'a Death', 'white as leprosy'. She is Geraldine but she is also Lady Lazarus and she is Assia. But then Coleridge finds a kind of peace – though, with it, a loss of his poetic Muse – in a very different figure from the 'snake in the oak'. This other woman is symbolised by a young birch tree which, though it cannot answer to 'the truth of the heart's passions', does offer 'a substitute happiness', a kind of love free from the dangers of extreme eroticism, a love that is not 'tragic and terrifying' but is rather 'a nostalgia for an idealized love that might have been'. The mother's love is, as it were, recovered through a partner who is desexualised, a 'pure-minded Christian virgin' who appeals to the chaste, devotional aspect of Coleridge's imagination.[54]

But the Goddess would not go away. Hughes was extraordinarily prolific in his sixties. He took on far more commissions than his health could properly stand. Why? Because his curiosity could not resist a challenge. Because he wanted to keep his writing hand in. Because he needed to shield himself from the real necessity, which was to let go of his life with Sylvia. All these are good reasons.

Olwyn had another explanation. In a document now lodged in the Hughes archive in Atlanta, Georgia, she suggests that his prolific volume of work in the mid- to late Nineties was simply intended to raise as much money as possible in order to lead a different life. At some point in 1994 or '95, he told his sister that, much as he had relished the Laureate years and the contacts the post had brought him (all those aristocratic dinner-tables and riparian privileges), he now wanted only to 'please himself'. The language was the same as that in the letter he wrote to Olwyn on the day he parted from Sylvia.

His theatre work, the sale of the farm in the last year of his life, the expensive limited editions: all were part of an effort to buy himself freedom. Naturally, Olwyn concludes, 'he was mindful of posterity', but he was also looking forward to another, happier decade 'of his own life and work'.[55] The thing to which Olwyn here alludes and does not allude is that Ted embarked at this time on a serious affair with a woman in south London. Though not a literary type at all, she was his last great love, a person with whom he relaxed and laughed and let down his guard. A friend tells of a memorable day in May 1997 when he and Ted and the woman went down to the gambler John Aspinall's private zoo in Kent. Ted became like a twelve-year-old boy. He imitated the sound of a wildebeest in order to make a tiger roar and it did. His friend had never seen him so happy.[56]

The following month Ted told János Csokits that his last three years had been 'as great a chaos as any previously', culminating in his getting ill, which came as 'a big shock' causing a 'general revision of priorities'.[57] When Hughes spoke of chaos in his life, he usually meant amorous entanglement. Close friends knew what he was talking about with regard to these last years, but his renewal of a double life between Devon and London was kept secret and did not leak into the public domain until a year after his death when a story appeared in the press about a man in south London coming forward with the information that he had rented a house to Hughes where 'the poet had lived with a woman and the landlord was furious about the mess in which the house had been left' at the time of his death.[58]

The woman in question does not wish to be named. She was from a humble East End background, but had prospered through property development – buying run-down houses in south London, doing them up and selling them on. Ted first met her through one of the well-to-do companions of his Scottish fishing trips. She had ventured north without her husband because he did not like fishing. In August 1995, Ted took her to meet Nick in Alaska. Nick, always loyal to Carol, was uncomfortable. Before going up to Fairbanks, Ted and his new companion joined his British Columbian fishing hosts for a dinner-party in Vancouver and then for an expedition to the wild Dean River.

She was an excellent cook – Olwyn later enthused that 'She made the best bouillabaisse I've ever tasted, and I've eaten in the South of France'[59] – and she worried about the quality of ingredients she might find in Vancouver. Her hosts reassured her that Vancouver was renowned for its food, and she was duly impressed by what she found in the markets. Their first impression of her was not very favourable, largely because her voice seemed affected and posh. When Ted revealed that her origins were as lowly as his own, and that she had remade herself, then reaped the reward of success by joining the elite fishing set, they warmed to her.

Ted was very attentive to her out in the wilderness. 'Even in the midst of storytelling,' one of the group recalled, 'he would spring up from the campfire each night as she called out to him from their tent, slightly annoying the assembly and inspiring us to speculate upon what she had to offer that would make him, a notoriously lingering campfire denizen and scotch nightcapper, abandon us in her favour.' 'It need hardly be said', he added, 'that Ted loved sex in all its variations between man and woman and would sometime seem almost charmingly adolescent in his amazement at how enthusiastic women were about those variations. But he was never disrespectful or crude … It was one of his more endearing qualities, and he had many.' The rugged fishermen were not so impressed when Ted announced that under the influence of his new companion he had taken to frequenting golf courses, which the steelhead fanatics regarded as 'those most artificial of greens, the antithesis of the domain of the savage gods'.[60]

Ted Hughes wrote in the moment. That is why he created such a huge body of poems and left such a vast archive of drafts and notes. Ted Hughes aspired to live in the moment. That is why when he told the woman in south London he would come to live with her permanently, he meant it. And why when he was back at Court Green saying that he would never leave, he meant it.[61] And it is also why he loved writing, fishing and sex, in all of which there is a sense of total absorption, a unity of mind and body, an escape from the shadows of the past and the responsibilities of the future.

*

The volume of late publication was indeed prodigious. There were more fine-press editions, such as *Earth Dances* (1994, 250 copies at £195 each) and *Shakespeare's Ovid* (his translations for Hofmann and Lasdun recycled in an edition of 200 copies, 50 of them signed and with original etchings, selling at £450 each, and the remainder at £100). In 1995 alone, his latest 'Creation Tales' were collected under the title *The Dreamfighter* and his short stories as *Difficulties of a Bridegroom*, his *Collected Animal Poems* were put together in four volumes and there was a printed text of his translation for the Royal Shakespeare Company of the Frank Wedekind play of teenage sexual arousal, *Spring Awakening*.

The Dreamfighter, dedicated to Carol, continues in the vein of *How the Whale Became* and *Tales of the Early World*: surreal folktales and myths of origin, dark revisitings of the territory of the Kipling *Just So Stories* that he had loved as a child. God creates all manner of creatures but demons keep reappearing; bodies are distorted and the reader never knows whether the next twist will be a fight, a kiss, a scream or a conflagration. The stories are a children's version of the *Crow* sequence, slightly watered down but with the injection of humour that is some-times delightful, sometimes bizarre. Every creature comes from the creative head of God. In this sense, God is the writer, Hughes himself. When in the title story God summons a succession of animals to protect him from his nightmares, some of the bad dreams are the same as those recorded in Ted's journals. And every now and then there is a glimpse of his own life, transposed into mythic narrative: 'Suddenly God had a brainwave. If Goka has a baby, he thought, she will calm down. She'll become sensible. And Goku too, he will become serious. Fathers become serious.'[62] But things don't turn out as planned.

A psychoanalyst would have a very interesting time with the last story in the collection, 'The Secret of Man's Wife', in which the wife yearns to escape and the husband believes she is meeting a wolf in the woods. He asks God to capture the wolfiness that is making her strange and to tame it as a pet so that his wife will be normal again. God consults his mother, who tells him that a Demon has got into the wife. So, with the assistance of his mother, God captures the wife, ties her up, gags her, places her by a furnace and drives the Demon out of her through sheer fear. Man then meets the beast that has been driven out. He asks it to come and live with them as a pet: 'Woman pretended to be surprised as he described its red fur, its amber eyes, its slender, jet-black legs, its blazing white chest and chin and its miraculous lovely tail.' She asks whether it agreed to come. Man explains that it did indeed reply, very politely. It said: 'O Man, O husband of glorious and beautiful Woman, it is the fear of being anyone's pet that has turned the tip of my tail quite white.'[63] A wife is not a pet. As this story went into print, Ted was writing and rewriting the poem about his marriage to Sylvia and the fox that he nearly brought home from Chalk Farm Bridge, but did not.

It was also in 1995 that a *New Selected Poems* appeared from Faber. It was partly anticipated by a limited-edition selection the previous year, which was distributed for free to participants in the Struga Poetry Festival in Macedonia, which Ted hugely enjoyed attending. The selection was 'new' not only in that it was different from, and more expansive than, the 1982 *Selected Poems*, but also in that it included a group of confessional poems about Sylvia and Assia, some of which had only previously appeared in occasional publications or in the privately printed *Capriccio*. Others were published for the first time. Equally revealing was a hitherto unpublished poem in memory of his mother. It describes how each year on 13 May, the anniversary of her death, in his imagination he would see her in the company of her sister Miriam. He would look at a 'torn-off diary page' that he had preserved. Gerald had scribbled on it 'Ma died today.' Then the memories would come flooding back: Sunday walks at lark rise, chatter about favourite dresses and shoes.[64] But the memories that push their way to the fore are her recollections of her love for Gerald. It is as if Ted is merely being used to fine-tune Edith's love for her elder son. The younger boy is perpetually in his brother's shadow. The poem ends with a memory of how he once came home across the fields from one of his boyhood moorland walks. His mother watches him all the way. When he comes close, he finds that she is crying because she wanted it to be his brother.

Nearly all the reviews of the *New Selected Poems* took the opportunity to praise the early work and the range of Hughes's achievement:

We've got Ted the exact observer of nature … Ted the social realist (voice a bit squeaky), Ted the wild apocalyptic shaman, Ted the last of the Great War poets, Ted the Ancient Mariner lurking outside the Windsors' doomed weddings, Ted the kiddies' bedtime bard. All these voices, and yet Ted never sounds remotely like anyone else but Hughes.[65]

Leafing through the reviews, which Ted kept and filed, one senses the critics' relief at being able to offer some atonement for the drubbing dished out to *Rain-Charm*. Only a few saw that the book was a 'Trojan horse', that the handful of new poems at the back in a 'new confessional voice' were a testing of the waters that made this 'the most exciting volume of poetry that Hughes has produced in many years'.[66] For the most part, though, the references to Sylvia and Assia went quietly and rather gratifyingly unnoticed.

The quest for money was a constant refrain in his letters in these years. He asked Baskin if he was owed anything from *Capriccio*. Baskin replied that the book had sold twenty-eight copies, which meant that Ted had earned nearly $30,000, of which he was owed just over $2,000, but the Gehenna Press had no money. Still, at least the Royal Shakespeare Company paid well for the Wedekind. He told Heaney that the translation work for the theatre served him as a form of anaesthesia, but was consistently interesting.[67] He explained in the same letter that he needed money because he was looking for a flat in London, but only in private conversation did he tell Seamus why he wanted the flat.

The collaboration inaugurated by the Wedekind translation had its origin at the Young Vic. A dynamic young director called Tim Supple had just taken over the theatre at the time of the Pete Townshend *Iron Man*. Supple wrote to Hughes asking if he would be interested in dramatising some of Grimm's Fairy Tales, a project that would have suited him very well. Having received no reply, Supple asked the poet Carol Ann Duffy instead. Her versions were about to go into rehearsal when Supple received a scrawled note from Ted asking whether the offer was still open. It was too late, but when he saw Supple's show he was impressed. He wrote again, making it clear that he would like to work with him. He reiterated his offer after seeing Supple's revelatory productions of *The Comedy of Errors* and *Twelfth Night*. At this point, the Royal Shakespeare Company asked Supple to direct something different for them, and he chose *Spring Awakening*. He had a gut feeling that 'Ted might be able to express the wildness of the sexual interior shared by the children in the play, and to bring to life the mythic shadow that they feel to be looming over them'.[68]

Spring Awakening, written in 1888, begins with a girl confiding to her mother, during an argument about the length of her skirt, that she sometimes thinks about death and that she might one day wear nothing beneath the skirt. Two boys are tormented by sexual dreams. The girl asks one of the boys, Melchior, to hit her with a switch of wood, then hit her harder, harder. In the second act he rapes her and the other boy kills himself under the pressure of homework and the confusions of puberty. The school authorities blame Melchior for this: he is alleged to have corrupted his friend by writing him a letter explaining the facts of life. He is expelled. In the third act, the girl dies as the result of a botched abortion. Melchior is visited by the ghost of his friend, with his head tucked under his arm and the information that he has been more fulfilled in death than in his miserable life. Melchior is tempted to join his friend in death, but a Masked Gentleman arrives, tells him that death is not to be borne and that all the dead friend wanted was the love of his companion. In a sub-plot two other boys acknowledge their homosexual desire for each other. In another scene, the class of boys indulges in a spree of competitive masturbation. The friends bid farewell and the Masked Man guides Melchior to the future: he must go on living.

It was clear to Supple that as Ted worked he was thinking deeply about sexual awakening and the destruction of love. Repression leads to shame and guilt, tragedy and suicide. Lust and love cannot be denied, whatever social convention tries to dictate. 'He was clearly, as all poets must, mining his own emotional experience,' Supple recalled. 'One of the very few phrases that I remember asking him to change did this too overtly – a character referred to the gas oven. I asked him to change this not because of the personal reference but because it was anachronistic – the play is set in the late 1800s. But it revealed the deep connections he was making.'[69]

Ted went to rehearsals when he could – he listened rather than watched. He would lean back against the steps of the room, cock his head to the ceiling and seem to 'sniff the words in the air'. He struck up a particular rapport with the teenage actors who played the children. Whereas the adult RSC actors were suspicious of his presence (as actors nearly always are when there is an intruder in the rehearsal room), the boys and girls were entirely open: 'not corseted in habit, pride and fear, they loved his observations and he was able to unlock a depth in the way they saw their roles'.[70]

The production opened in August 1995 at the RSC's studio theatre in London, the Barbican Pit. Most of the cast were schoolchildren themselves, lending the performance great credibility. Tim Supple's production won plaudits all round, while Hughes's translation was praised by some critics as 'vivid and robust', indeed 'unobtrusively poetic', but condemned by others as 'stilted and overblown'.[71] The truth is that he was working from a literal crib and both the sinewy strength and the occasional bloating of the language were Wedekind's.

Early in the play's run, Ted went to dinner with Supple and the Morpurgos. Asked what he was doing next, Supple said that he had long wanted to direct Federico García Lorca's *Blood Wedding*. Ted launched into an account of how every great writer had a controlling myth and in Lorca's case it was encapsulated in his essay on *duende*, the demonic spirit of performance in which actor and audience share a kind of Bacchic frenzy. Supple asked him to do the translation, but he shied away from the task. He agreed only when Supple cut a deal: he, in return, would read the latest batch of 'Sacred Earth' environmental plays by children. As with the Wedekind, Ted worked from a literal translation. Supple was thrilled to find him grasping 'the bare, blunt fierceness of the writing', taking 'something essentially Spanish' and hearing in it 'the language of the soil and the folk ritual' and letting that language 're-emerge as something entirely English'.

This time, the translation proved more successful than the production. The directorial and design vision of the production which opened at the Young Vic in September 1996 were, Supple admitted, 'just too complicated, too aesthetic, not direct enough'. Ted was conscious of this. When Supple told him that they were struggling over the design, he replied (still under the influence of Peter Brook), 'Design? what design do you need? A pot for civilisation and a bush for the wild.' In order to promote the show, Ted did a number of press interviews, which he later regretted. 'Never talk about anything before it is finished,' he said. Because he had talked, the production was doomed: 'You see, we cursed it, we said too much and trusted them when we shouldn't.'[72]

The reviews were terrible. 'Laughable Tragedy' was the headline in the *Daily Telegraph*.[73] 'Try to imagine a company of fiery Spanish actors appearing in an adaptation of Jane Austen or Trollope,' said another paper, 'and you will get some idea of the incongruity involved.'[74] 'You know,' said Ted, reflecting on the flop, 'I think that Lorca's theatre was much more simple than we imagine, and more anarchic. A bit like a street pageant or carnival. It would have been much cruder than we think.'[75]

The characters are symbolic types – Mother, Mother-in-Law, Bride and Bridegroom – but Hughes's translation also catches the immediacy of their humanity, as when he evokes the tenderness of love: 'You are so lucky! To wrap your arms around a man, to kiss him, to feel his weight … And the best moment of all, when you wake up and feel him beside you, his breath stroking your shoulder – like a nightingale's feather.'[76] By the end, the language is suffused with death, and the poetry is close to that of *Crow*, as a knife:

> slides in cold
> Through startled flesh
> Till it stops, there,
> In the quivering
> Dark
> Roots
> Of the scream.[77]

Crow itself, meanwhile, had been dramatised in a stunningly successful production at the Tron Theatre in Glasgow by the innovative Ulsterman Michael Boyd, who would later become artistic director of the Royal Shakespeare Company.[78]

The theatre work didn't produce enough money. In March 1997, after two years of careful preparation (organising, editing, weeding), he sold his poetic and epistolary archive to Emory University in Atlanta for a substantial six-figure sum, to be received in staged payments with an option on the purchase of items that were held back (a few things he was still working on, he told Emory – by which he meant anything to do with the *Birthday Letters* project, not to mention nearly all his journals, the poems about Assia, the poems arising from the *Bell Jar* trial and a swathe of other highly intimate material). He told Olwyn that the sale would help with the bills and that he was off to lie low for three weeks.[79]

His unrelenting productivity in these last years also saw the publication in 1997 of *By Heart: 101 Poems to Remember*. The introduction is a guide to ancient 'memory techniques' that use 'strongly visualized imagery'. Even this late in his career, well after the publication of *Shakespeare and the Goddess of Complete Being*, Hughes is still reflecting obsessively on that idea of a rupture in English culture – Eliot's 'dissociation of sensibility' – some time in the mid-seventeenth century. He contrasts the 'unforgettable' remark of Thomas Aquinas, 'the patron saint of memory systems', that 'Man cannot understand without images' against the attempt of the 'Puritan/Protestant ascendancy of the Civil War' to 'eradicate imagery from all aspects of life'. The destruction of images in churches, the banning of stage-plays and the introduction of lifeless 'learning by rote' in schools, displacing the old memory techniques that used 'imagery', are all seen as parts of the same impulse.[80]

The anthology itself, effectively a slimmed-down *School Bag*, compiled without the editorial companionship of Heaney, is Hughes's personal selection of the greatest hits of English poetry. These are the poems that he knew by heart and that lived within him all his days. They may be read as a retrospective gathering of his influences. Here are Alfred Tennyson's 'The Eagle', precursor of 'Hawk Roosting'; Robert Frost's 'The Road not Taken', which always came to his mind when he had to make a big life-choice (for example between two women); Gerard Manley Hopkins's 'The Windhover' (another bird of prey) and 'Inversnaid', which helped to shape Hughes the ecopoet ('What would the world be, once bereft / Of wet and of wildness?'); here is Wordsworth on Westminster Bridge, at Tintern Abbey and with Lucy in the grave; Wilfred Owen in the First World War and Keith Douglas in the Second; here are Edward Thomas, R. S. Thomas and Dylan Thomas; a wealth of Yeats and Eliot, Lawrence's piano, Blake's tiger, Coleridge's 'Kubla Khan' and Keats looking into the classics. Emily Dickinson is represented by five poems, Sylvia Plath by only one – and that is the finely crafted, polished not raw, 'Crossing the Water'. An *Ariel* poem would have been too painful with *Birthday Letters* still not yet published. And the most surprising omission is perhaps unsurprising. There is no Emily Brontë: Hughes cannot bring himself to ask the readers of his anthology to remember by heart the ghost of the beloved ('What I love shall come like visitant of air')[81] or a woman lying in her grave under the snow on the Yorkshire moor.

During these years, Ted was also publishing more personal poetry, though keeping it below the radar of publicity. Especially notable were his three exquisite elegies for Jennifer Rankin, which appeared in a volume of *New Writing* edited by Malcolm Bradbury and Andrew Motion from the school of creative writing at the University of East Anglia, where Ted was glad to give one of his – now infrequent – poetry readings.[82] No one realised how much Jennifer had meant to him.

The elegiac voice was becoming ever more insistent. In June 1997 he told János Csokits that he hadn't written any original poetry for two years. He had been hiding behind his translation work. He was blocked by his failure to get the Plath poems out of his system. Though he informed very few friends, he was also battling with cancer at this time.[83] It was serious enough for Frieda and László to move from Australia to London, and for Ted to write a new will. In July he told the Queen Mother that he was recovering well, following exceptionally good treatment. At the end of August, he confided to Heaney that he had backed himself into a corner but was working his way out of it. He had finished his translation of Aeschylus' *Oresteia*, was working on a version of Euripides' *Alcestis*, and was thinking of doing more Ovid.[84] At the same time he told Leonard Baskin that he had been overwhelmed on all fronts for the last three to five years, but was moving forward by putting together a collection of about a hundred poems about Sylvia.[85]

30

The Sorrows of the Deer

I can't lock myself in behind this glass door one more week

(Ted Hughes)

But I was quite unprepared for the agon(y) of 'Black Coat' and
'The God' – like a 'Prelude' turned inside out

(Seamus Heaney)[1]

On Saturday 17 January 1998 Peter Stothard, the editor of the London *Times*, took the unusual step of writing the front-page story himself. The banner headline shouted 'Revealed – the most tragic literary love story of our time'. The article announced that the Poet Laureate was today breaking his '35-year silence over the life and suicide of his first wife, Sylvia Plath'. In an 'extraordinary verse narrative', copiously sampled in the pages of the paper, 'Hughes gives his account of one of the century's most celebrated and tragic love stories.' The existence of the poems had been 'among the best-kept literary secrets'. Stothard had been in on it since the beginning of December, when he had offered £25,000 for the exclusive, telling Joanna Mackle at Faber and Faber, who was handling the secret sale, how privileged he felt to have been one of the first readers of the collection.[2]

On the leader page, *The Times* opined that this was 'The greatest book by our greatest living writer'. In an op-ed headlined 'A thunderbolt from the blue – this book will live for ever', the poet Andrew Motion exclaimed that the collection was unlike anything else in literature. 'Its power is massive and instant ... Anyone who thought Hughes's reticence was proof of his hard heart will immediately see how stony they have been themselves ... This is a book written by someone obsessed, stricken and deeply loving.' *Birthday Letters* was 'his greatest book', as 'magnetic' as Robert Browning's poems for Elizabeth Barrett and as 'poignant' as Thomas Hardy's elegies of 1912–13 in memory of his dead wife.[3]

News of the poems spread around the world. 'Poet Laureate breaks silence over stormy years with Plath' trumpeted the *Yorkshire Post* from Ted's first home. 'Hughes' amazing love tribute to suicide wife' announced the *Western Morning News* in his adopted county. And on the story went, to New York and Sydney and the *South China Morning Post* ('Secrets of poets' doomed marriage revealed at last').[4] The next day, the *Observer* announced more news: that Plath's unexpurgated journals, less the two lost volumes, would finally be published soon. By the Monday, *The Times* was able to round up endorsements from other poets such as James Fenton and Tom Paulin. On the Tuesday, a backlash began. *The Times* was indulging in hype, overblowing their scoop; the poems were not up to scratch. 'Embarrassing junk' sneered the Glasgow *Herald* under the headline 'A story more soap-operatic than *Brookside*'.[5] The critical consensus which emerged over the following weeks and months was that the poems were of deep sincerity and unique biographical value, but of very variable literary quality, mixing exquisite imagery and memorable phrases with pedestrian and prosaic passages. But nothing could stop the sales.

And what of Ted himself? On the Thursday after publication he wrote a journal entry contemplating flamingoes and clam-dippers, a line in Shakespeare, the need to get back to his translation of the *Alcestis* of Euripides, and his hope of a new life once his chemotherapy was complete. Having loosened himself into his reflective writing mode, he proceeded to an astonishingly detailed account of his feelings and actions upon the appearance of *Birthday Letters*.

On the Friday, as the story was rolling off the press of *The Times*, he had become apprehensive. Was the decision to publish a huge mistake? Still scarred by the Jane Anderson affair, he worried about litigation. Would he be sued by the car-dealer in Rugby Street? Walking to Okehampton Castle, he had felt the trap closing in upon him. He had to vanish. So he and Carol left Court Green and went to stay in the Cotswolds with Matthew Evans, the head of Faber and Faber, and his wife Caroline Michel. Ted worried that Caroline would see the ravages of his chemotherapy – she did not know how ill he had been.

Fearing that the paparazzi would find him with his publisher, they were away before breakfast the next morning. At a motorway service station, he caught a glimpse of himself on the front page of *The Times*: an old photograph beneath the dramatic headline. Then it was back into the fast lane and a great sense of liberation came over him, 'a generally marvelous [*sic*] state of mind' and a determination to hang on to that feeling, to 'make it my new being'.[6]

Freedom from the past was in his grasp; he had to avoid slipping back into the old paralysis. He was ready to live a new life, no longer caring what he revealed about himself. The years of sitting on his version of the story, of fear of public reaction, of dislike of the confessional mode of verse: all had been overturned by his illness. It was as if he had been commanded to speak. Perhaps keeping it all so bottled up had contributed to the sickness.

There were certain things he had to hold on to. Family bonds above all. The stage-like composure of Matthew Evans's little girl had reminded him of Frieda. The two sons in the household made him think of how brothers related to each other, and thus of himself and Gerald. As for work, he was tinkering with his Eighties collection *Flowers and Insects*, and it made him see that for years, decades indeed, his work had been a 'marginalised flora and fauna', 'avoiding the main statement of the major theme'. Reluctance to publish the poetry about his time with Sylvia had crippled him for the better part of his poetic life: 'Only wish now that I'd written a great many more of these B.L. – a thousand would have been few enough.'

And so he goes on, self-castigating: 'Usual error – simply not exploring deeply and tenaciously enough, not writing voluminously and experimentally enough, in the forbidden field. Ironic that I have done this only with the Shakespeare book and the Coleridge essay.' Through the medium of criticism, he had come at Sylvia and the Goddess indirectly. By not 'handling dynamite in a petrol dump', he had opened the way. Now at last he was there. Or almost there: behind the journal entry is the knowledge of certain poems excluded from *Birthday Letters*.

The next day he was at it again, acknowledging that his real poetic work had been blocked since at least 1970. He had excluded and suppressed the main thing. In the early Seventies he had made the disastrous mistake of trying to start again with something simpler – the

A B C of his farming diaries, the lightness of *Season Songs*. He had only got back to the true voice of feeling in the Assia poems, then in the Shakespeare book, the Ovid and *Oresteia* translations. It was too late for remorse, but the price was high: physical wreckage and twenty-five years of second-rate work, the poetic power 'squandered and deflected'. What had become, he asked himself, of the young creature who wrote 'Song' in 1948, of 'the creature that wrote Thought-Fox, Jaguar and Wind – then met S.P.?' He was speculating about the Frostian road not taken and the reasons for not taking it, the difficulty of following the path that maintained the 'true centre of gravity of a talent'. How can an artistic career, the work of a life, take its form as 'a solid city' rather than 'a series of hasty campfires'? That was the question. The answer, he told himself in his journal, was 'to live alone, or as if alone'. And yet how could a man who so loved women live alone?

He remained on the run for nineteen days, staying in luxury hotels, feeling disconnected from the extraordinary public reaction to the book, which went straight to the top of the bestseller list, shifting 50,000 copies in a matter of weeks, a speed and volume of sales unheard of in poetry since the time of Lord Byron.

As well as talking to himself about *Birthday Letters* in his journals, he talked in his letters to friends and family about his feelings on releasing the book. He reiterated his sense of relief, but also his remorse at not having published sooner. He sent copies, often inscribing them with the phrase 'before us stands yesterday'. He had been blocked ever since Sylvia's death, he told the Baskins. The same confession was reiterated in a brave letter to the poet and William Blake scholar Kathleen Raine. This was made public when Frieda Hughes read it out in January 1999 when accepting the Whitbread Prize for *Birthday Letters* on her father's behalf:

I think those letters do release the story that everything I have written since the early nineteen sixties has been evading. It was in a kind of desperation that I finally did publish them – I had always thought them unpublishably raw and unguarded, simply too vulnerable. But then I just could not endure being blocked any longer. How strange that we have to make public declarations of our secrets. But we do. If only I had done the equivalent

30 years ago, I might have had a more fruitful career – certainly a freer psychological life. Even now, the sensation of inner liberation – a huge, sudden possibility of new inner experience.[7]

An enormous burden had been lifted and he cared not a jot for the critics or the circling crocodiles of Plathians. He granted that the poems were 'simple, naïve and unguarded',[8] but that didn't matter: he had written them for himself.

But of course he did value the opinions of his fellow-poets. Heaney above all. Ted had sent him an advance copy. Seamus responded with high praise, saying how overwhelmed he was to read the manuscript and find 'Poetry and wounded power gathering and doing the Cuchullain warp-spasm, the salmon-feat, showing a wild Shakespearean back above their element'. What he most admired was the simultaneous sense of the everyday and the sacred, of the sequence as a narrative of what had really happened and a transformation of what had happened, via a journey 'round the dark side of the mind's moon', into poetry of mythic force. The force of the collection, he suggested, came from the holding together of 'the lens of personal memory and the lens of mythic understanding'. His only anxiety was that the 'up-and-at-them, tell-what-happened' aspect of the poems would prevent critics from seeing the 'gift-myth dimension of it'. But, all in all, the publication of the book would be 'seismic' for both Ted's own being and 'the literary and cultural history of our times'.[9] He was so inspired that he had immediately written a poem in response – his equivalent of Samuel Taylor Coleridge's great meditation on hearing Wordsworth's *Prelude*.

On New Year's Day 1998 Ted replied with some background: how publication was less 'a literary matter' than 'a physical operation' that might 'change the psychic odds' for him and 'clear a route'.[10] He had been wanting to let the poems go for twenty-five years, but had never had the courage. The closest he had come previously was with the *New Selected Poems* of 1995, in which he thought of including some thirty or forty, but because it was such a stressful time in his private life, he backed away, including just the handful (and the few about Assia) that went under the radar. Heaney responded with enormous generosity in both private letters and public pronouncements.

There was also the family reaction to consider. Frieda, who had provided an abstract painting for the jacket, had been prepared. Shortly before publication, she wrote a poem of her own, saluting the collection: 'There it was, born of them both. / Like it or not. Rounded in words, / And cracking open its shell for a voice.'[11] Ted read the poem and laughed and said that it might just as well have been about him and Frieda. She found it hard to understand why her father had not published the *Birthday Letters* before, so great was the love they showed for her mother and so intense the liberation he clearly felt on releasing them.

Nick in Alaska, meanwhile, received one of the most revelatory letters in English literary history, a 4,000-word epistle that stands besides John Keats's heart-opening journal-letters to his brother in America. Dated 20 February 1998, it begins with an account of Ted's involvement with plans for the interior of the Millennium Dome in Greenwich and of his 'runaway' when *Birthday Letters* was published. Then he remembers Yaddo with Nick's mother, his dreams of animals and of the pike in Crookhill Pond, of fishing for salmon when they were living at Doonreagan. Then he explains that his dreams, his fishing and most of his writing were all forms of escape. He was running away from 'the big unmanageable event': the breakdown of his first marriage and its consequences. He kept finding himself unable to write; he would make himself start again, but each time 'the ship of salmon and Jaguars had to sail away again'. The only way he could deal with what he called the 'giant psychological log-jam of your mother and me' was to write private poems, 'simple little attempts to communicate with her about our time together'. Poems for Sylvia's ghost, not for a wider readership – they exposed too much to be publishable. But because he could not publish them, his 'real self' could 'never get on with its life'. It was as if he were living behind a glass door, like one in a dream Nick had once described to his father, in which a glass barrier cut him off from life (as represented by a frog). He could not face the storm that would greet him from the feminists if he went public. He did not want to put Carol through the strain of the publicity that would follow. But he had finally seen that, as with a confession, he had to let it all out. That was his only way of breaking the logjam, moving his life beyond 1963.

Thirty-five years on from that terrible winter, he finally says that the feminists can do whatever they wish, readers can react as they wish, critics can eviscerate, Plathians can rave, Carol can 'go bananas',

Frieda and Nick can dive for shelter. He is doing it for himself. The guard had to come down, the private had to be made public, the simple poems set free into the world: 'I can't care any more, I can't lock myself in behind this glass door one more week.' And when he did let them go, he had the surprise of his life. The heavens did not fall, the critics did not (for the most part) cavil. And his mind was transformed – gigantically, bewilderingly. It was as if he had been presented with a completely new brain. He felt as he had not felt since 1962. The sense of catharsis was complete (except that it wasn't – there were more poems to come). His hope, he added, thinking of the cancer that was in remission but that could not be trusted to stay away, was that 'it wasn't all just a bit too late'.[12] 'Too late': the novelists Noel Streatfeild and Evelyn Waugh said that these were the saddest words in the English language. Eight months after writing this letter to his son, Ted Hughes was dead.

In early March, he noticed that his hair was returning, following the side-effects of chemotherapy. He took this as a good sign. Later in the month, he rewarded himself for both the success of the book and the remission of the cancer with a two-week deep-sea fishing trip in Cuba, where he and his friends encountered bonefish, tarpon and barracuda. Everything seemed all the more exotic because one of the symptoms of his declining health was double vision – he saw not a single new moon but a 'sheaf' of them.[13] Soon afterwards, there was another trip to Birkhall, where he discussed with Prince Charles the difficulty of remembering the Latin names of plants. Later, he offered assistance in the form of a long letter about Eastern memory-training techniques.

Still, though, he could not let Sylvia go. He and Baskin planned another of their expensive limited editions: it would be an opportunity to release, but avoid excessive public examination of, some of the most intimate poems that he had stepped back from including in *Birthday Letters*. In the spring, the volume appeared under the title *Howls and Whispers* ('Cries and Whispers' was the original intention). The print run consisted of a mere hundred copies, with a further ten, especially boxed and hyper-expensive, each containing a unique leaf of Ted's manuscript. Baskin provided colour-printed etchings and additional watercolour drawings exclusively for the tiny de luxe edition.

Despite its status as a supplementary selection from the wealth of unpublished poems, *Howls and Whispers*, luxuriously bound in Easthampton, Massachusetts, has a narrative line of its own. It begins with 'Paris 1954', in which Hughes looks back at his pre-Sylvia self, drinking claret and eating Gruyère before the 'scream' of passion shaped 'like a panther' and like a girl (Sylvia) tracks him down. The second poem ('Religion') turns to her hunger for love and how it became another scream, of hatred for her parents metamorphosed into passion for him. Then there is 'The Hidden Orestes': the Greek idea of tragedy passed from parent to child and more specifically an allusion to Sylvia's claim that the girl who speaks 'Daddy' is suffering from a Freudian Electra complex. The following poem is a jump-cut forward to the afterlife of those laburnum trees, the image of which he and Sylvia had clung on to that day she came to Cleveland Street.[14] There is then a series of poems linking the breakdown of the marriage to Sylvia's breakdown, and finally an exquisitely redemptive encounter with her ghost ('The Offers')[15] and an anticlimactically clumsy poem about the 'Superstitions' of Friday the 13th, the date associated with their first night together (even though it was actually their second).

When *Birthday Letters* was published, most readers and reviewers made two assumptions: that the collection represented a late flowering and that these poems were Hughes's first and last words on the subject of his marriage to Plath. Both assumptions were wrong. *Howls and Whispers* showed that there was more to come. And very few of the Sylvia poems were written late in Hughes's career. As the letters to his friends reveal, he had been gestating the project for more than a quarter of a century.

Explaining the origin of *Birthday Letters*, Ted told many friends that it was in the early Seventies, at the beginning of his second marriage, that he began writing poems about Sylvia – very personal and private pieces to work through his feelings and crystallise his memories, not necessarily intended for publication. In expressing his relief on finally publishing the book in January 1998, he spoke of twenty-five or thirty years of bottled-up emotion. Sometimes, though, he said thirty-five years, the full duration since Sylvia's suicide. Ted's recollection of the dates and locations of the writing of his poems was sometimes exceptionally accurate (especially if there was an astrological conjunction in the case), but he often misremembered, or said different things to different people. And sometimes he shared information that was simply wrong: he not only made Freudian slips, but was also capable of deliberately misleading, laying false trails or covering his tracks. In the absence of a journal entry along the lines of 'today I began writing a sequence of poems in memory of Sylvia', we cannot rule out the possibility that the *Birthday Letters* project was begun before Assia's death in 1969.

One of the notebooks in the British Library archive is especially intriguing in this respect. It is a red, soft-covered, spiral-bound student notebook, with holes punched for filing. Adorned on the cover with the logo of the stationery manufacturer Silvine, reference 140, it could have been bought any time between the late Sixties and the mid-Eighties.[16] Two things are striking about this notebook. Its version of the poem about sleeping with Susan Alliston in 18 Rugby Street on the night of Sylvia's death does not include any reference to the irony of her subsequent residence in the flat and her death. This raises the possibility of a date of composition before 1969. Secondly, the back cover of the notebook is charred brown, suggesting that it may have been rescued from the remnants of the Lumb Bank fire. If that were the case, early 1971 would be the latest possible date of composition.

Those intimate poems about baby Frieda and Uncle Albert's suicide reveal that in early 1963 Ted was moving to a more confessional vein of poetry. But he was halted by Sylvia's suicide. Could it be that, as he brought the *Crow* project towards a conclusion in early 1969, he was again moving into the confessional voice, but that he was then held back by Assia's suicide, then by his mother's and Susan's deaths? That, as before, 'autobiographical things' broke his poetic development into pieces?[17]

The Silvine Notebook: even the manufacturer's name carries an echo of Sylvia. He gave the book a title: 'The Sorrows of the Deer'. In Robert Graves, 'The Roebuck in the Thicket' is a stag that is sacred to the White Goddess. It hides in the undergrowth, keeping a secret.[18] Very late in life, reflecting on the origins of *Birthday Letters*, Hughes wrote of how he was 'pulled inescapably back onto the autobiographical level of S's death' by the 'huge outcry' that 'flushed' him from his 'thicket' in the years 1970 to 1972, 'when Sylvia's poems & novel hit the first militant wave of Feminism as a divine revelation from their

Patron Saint'.[19] By this account, the sorrowful deer is his own inner self. But many of the poems, like many of his best memories, hold his self and Sylvia's together in a single poetic being, so in this sense the deer is also Sylvia. His treasured photograph of a deer taking food from her hand in the Algonquin Provincial Park perhaps served as a private icon, presiding over the project.

The Silvine Notebook begins with a list of twenty-two poems: '59th Bear', 'Fishing Bridge', 'Delivering Frieda', 'Your fingers', 'I brought you to Devon', 'Red', 'Remember the daffodils', 'The morning we set out to drive around America', 'Our happiness', 'Under the laburnums', 'Which part of you liked me rough?', 'What was poured in your ears?', 'The waters off beautiful Nauset', 'Of all that came to drink with you', 'A fragile cutting, tamped into earth', 'I came over the packed snow', 'A film of you skipping', 'We didn't find her – she found us', 'What can I tell you that you do not know / Of the life after death', 'As if you descended in each night's sleep', 'The first time I bought a bottle of wine', and finally, scored through, 'The last I had seen of you was you burning / Your farewell note'. The collection tells, directly and without distraction or attempt at myth-making, the story of his marriage to Sylvia, from Cambridge to America to Devon to parenthood to affair to death to ghostly return. The poems are unified through that vein of natural imagery (daffodils, laburnums, plant-cutting, the green of spring and the white of winter) which for centuries has provided grieving poets with glimmers of comfort as they remember love and loss in the literary genre known as elegy, John Milton's *Lycidas* being the classic example. The Silvine Notebook would have made a slim but splendid volume of elegies, perhaps enabling Ted to move on to some other style.

How different his life might have been if he had had the courage to publish 'The Sorrows of the Deer' some time in the Seventies. A deleted stanza of 'Delivering Frieda' describes his daughter as a 'somnambulist' carrying the memory of her mother.[20] The image of sleepwalking indicates that this was written before he told Frieda of the suicide. How different it would have been if he had shared that knowledge in his own time and his own way, instead of having his hand forced by other people's publications about Sylvia's life and death. Again, he would have been criticised by some for a poem that began by asking Sylvia's ghost 'Which part of you liked me rough?'

But if he had got his story out first – told the truth that some part of Sylvia did like it rough and could give it rough (the bite) – then he would not have been caught in defensive mode by Robin Morgan's allegations of rape and abuse.

Above all, he would have expiated both his grief and his guilt. The Silvine Notebook includes poems of astonishing tenderness and love. Ted and Sylvia's happiness in finding Court Green, a simple house built in the shape of a loaf. Sylvia stooping in the rain to take an armful of daffodils from tiny Frieda. Sylvia's fingers flying over the keyboard of piano and typewriter: 'I remember your fingers. And your daughter's / Fingers remember your fingers / In everything they do.'[21] Late in life, Ted appeared alone on Frieda's doorstep, not having seen her for a long time. 'You can ask me anything you like,' he said to his daughter. The request was so sudden that she did not know where to begin. But she thought of one question: 'What was my mother like?' 'She was just like you,' her father replied. 'Even in the way she moved her hands.'[22]

There is lightness in the Silvine Notebook, but it is also heavy with poems of aching grief. Among them is an early version of what eventually became 'The Inscription' in *Birthday Letters*, the poem about the conversation in Ted's flat in Cleveland Street:

> 'Under the laburnums' – almost your last
> Words to me. But repeated. And again
> 'Tell me we will be together under the laburnums' –
> Which meant summer, the lawn, the children playing.[23]

'The Inscription' omits the most intimate elements: the direct speech and the reference to the children. This early version is fresher, some- how truer. Once the reader discovers that 'under the laburnums' were indeed among Sylvia's last words to Ted, the lovely first part of 'Autumn Nature Notes' in *Season Songs* takes on new meaning: 'The Laburnum top is silent, quite still / In the afternoon yellow September sunlight, / A few leaves yellowing, all its seeds fallen' becomes an elegy for Sylvia's passing: 'She launches away, towards the infinite / And the laburnum subsides to empty.'[24]

'Sorrows' also includes poems of gnawing guilt. The original inten- tion was to end the sequence with 'The first time' and 'The last': the poem about the bottle of wine and the dumping of Shirley, then the one about Sylvia's last letter. The sweet beginning with Sylvia was a bitter end with Shirley; the end with Sylvia was too terrible to contemplate. Ted could not bring himself to publish either poem in his lifetime.

In the same notebook there is a fragmentary poem, on a separate sheet, addressed to Richard Sassoon. How did he manage, Ted wonders, to get away from Sylvia 'without being clobbered / by Ariel'? To escape the 'crashed Phaeton' without being cursed, without the baggage of Sylvia's dark feelings towards her parents. Where did Ted go wrong? 'Show me my mistake.' The project that began as 'The Sorrows of the Deer' was a seemingly never-ending reckoning of mistakes and memories, of good intentions lost and bad moves made worse by circumstance.

Through all the years of writing and rewriting, Ted kept changing his mind about the amount of explicit autobiographical information he should expose, the balance he should create between plain facts and mythic patterns. To the end, he remained guarded about some of the most heart-wrenching details. The beautiful poem called 'Delivering Frieda' in the Silvine Notebook evokes Sylvia's 'cheek-scar' and the 'O-mouth' of her newborn daughter. It ends with an allusion to 'Edge', the poem that concluded *Ariel* in 1965:

> That last poem you ~~wrote~~ designed, modelling your death,
> ~~You planned to take~~ <include> ~~her with you.~~ You wrote
> 'She is taking them with her.'
> Poetic justice ~~crossed it out.~~ cancelled: poetic frenzy.
> You went on alone. Now ~~erase~~ delete
> That line utterly. Reabsorb
> Into unbeing every letter of it –
> Let your last sea-cold kiss evaporate
> From the salt affliction.[25]

Sylvia's own deletion from the draft of 'Edge' of the line about taking her children with her is replicated in Ted's erasure of this terrible thought from a later draft of his poem. His writing hand is shadowed by the fact of Assia making the opposite choice and by the knowledge that in her lowest moment in the final burnt journal Sylvia did indeed contemplate the 'unbeing' of her and Ted's line of inheritance. The image of reabsorption into 'unbeing' is a powerful variant on that of wading into 'underbeing' in that poem of grace, 'Go Fishing'. The double sense of the word 'line', at once genetic and poetic, is one of Hughes's most painfully brilliant strokes. But he felt compelled to spare his children from these dark thoughts – 'Delivering Frieda' was heavily revised before being published in *Birthday Letters* as 'Remission'.

He kept changing his mind about how much and how explicitly to publish. The poem about his honeymoon, 'You Hated Spain', was first slipped unostentatiously into print in a 1979 anthology edited by fellow-poet Douglas Dunn. It reappeared in Hughes's 1982 *Selected Poems* as an addendum to the *Crow* sequence, with which it had no connection – it was Sylvia, not Crow, who hated Spain! 'Portraits' appeared under the title 'An Icon' in the magazine *Grand Street* in autumn 1981. And then there was the trial run of the series of poems in the 1995 *New Selected*. There were times when Ted thought that he was taking a risk even with these murmurs. Perhaps his silence should have been absolute. But there were other times when he thought that he should let everything go.

Among the British Library manuscripts is a Challenge Triplicate Book in which drafts for what will become *Birthday Letters* are written at high speed, copied and reworked, run together, in loose, conversational blank verse, as if the whole thing might become a single autobiographical poem stretching over 5,000 lines, Hughes's equivalent of Wordsworth's *Prelude*. Wordsworth's poem had at its core a meditation on how Nature became his 'mother' as a result of the premature death of both his parents: the scene when he returns from school to hear the news of his father's death is among the most intense of all the 'spots of time' that shape his inner life. So, too, for Hughes the question of parentage, and the influence of fathers in particular, is the key to this station on his journey to poetic autobiography.

On the first page of the notebook there is a title that reads 'Black Coat: Opus 131'.[26] The Black Coat is an unholy trinity, three in one and one in three: the one worn by Otto Plath in Sylvia Plath's nightmare of a fascist father, the one habitually worn at Cambridge by Ted Hughes – the man in black to whom Sylvia said 'I do' on her wedding day – and the one worn by Sylvia herself as he imagines her on that last freezing night walking down to the telephone box at the bottom of St George's Terrace on Primrose Hill with her plait curled up at the back of her head.

As for Opus 131, this was the number of the late Beethoven string quartet that in Ted's mind was the final masterpiece, the breaker of artistic boundaries, the summation of the composer's genius. It had occupied a place of honour in his personal pantheon ever since his youthful discovery of Beethoven. Fellow-poet Peter Redgrove used to tell of his first meeting with Hughes at Pembroke College, Cambridge. As he went up the steep staircase, Redgrove heard a 'strange yowling' coming from Hughes's room. It was not a fox, or even a thought-fox, but Opus 131, in which, Hughes told him, 'the whole of the music is crushed into the first few bars, which are then unravelled'.[27] Ted then took Beethoven's death mask[28] from the wall of his room, put it against his breast and waddled across the room, explaining that this was Beethoven's height and gait. Undergraduate flamboyance this may have been, but there is no doubting the sincerity with which Hughes took Beethoven to heart. The musical key of Opus 131 is C sharp minor, often associated with sorrow and the night (it is also the key of Beethoven's 'Moonlight' sonata). The structural key is its unity: forty minutes long, its seven movements, with recurring adagio tempo, are played without a break. This is why Hughes calls 'Black Coat' his Opus 131: it would have been *Birthday Letters* without any breaks.

It begins with death and the difficulty of death when your own family is a shadow play. Ted's father returns from the Great War, loaded with the memory of the wounded who had died. Day after day and decade after decade he was 'undemobbed', sent back to the Front to search for the place where he could lay down his burden of memory. Death comes to every generation, but you never step into the same river twice. Hughes is schooled by survivors of the Great War but his own growth was shaped by the Second, to which the poem then turns, before reverting to an image of an old soldier, confused on a railway platform, reading a book, not knowing whether he is returning to Flanders or heading for a family holiday on the Cornish Riviera. The train of association clearly links the soldier to his father.

But then there is a Wordsworthian jump-cut from past to present. We are heading for a picnic on the side of Lochnagar in Scotland, in the time when Ted is staying on Deeside in the Queen Mother's beloved home at Birkhall. The air is fresh, the scene is dramatic: a roebuck bounds across the stage (a reminder to the writing hand that 'Black Coat' is a new version of 'The Sorrows of the Deer'). Hughes and his party, in royal company (out of discretion, only the corgis are identified), are both stars and starry-eyed. To the cry of a capercaillie, they sip tea in a log lodge.[29] It is a scene of benediction.

Like Wordsworth in *The Prelude*, the Hughes of 'Black Coat: Opus 131' moves seamlessly from the memory of those 'spots of time' that have shaped his poetic being to reflection on how poetry itself can heal. He describes reading and writing as weight-training for the mind. When he retreated to his writing hut in the garden of Court Green, Hughes undertook a daily mental workout. He went there to tell the tale of Sylvia's tragedy. That was his practice, his toy. Like Beethoven at his keyboard, he played through variation after variation. Practice was the only way 'To wring from life's error / The strange tears of joy'. Poetry, he argued to himself, would eventually enable him to go beyond grief to what Wordsworth called 'Thoughts that do often lie too deep for tears'. But the nagging anxiety for Hughes was that there might be a kind of lie, or at best an evasion, within the truth-telling. Could it ever be right, he asked himself, to make his own 'toy' of Sylvia's tragedy?

This is the point at which Sylvia enters 'Black Coat: Opus 131'. The next variation is a redraft of the soldier on the platform. 'You came to think of him as a sentry cast / In blackening old bronze – probably / Meant to represent forgetfulness.' We are looking not at a real passenger but at the Great Western Railway War Memorial on Platform One of Paddington station. The Tommy is in fact reading a letter from home, not a book. There is then a startling jolt of memory and outside the lost property office Hughes notices banks of snow in the street. Hard cold. Bright, empty light. In the drafting, Hughes becomes the soldier, watched by Plath: 'So you needed me finally … I had promised you everything you asked for.' But Hughes then goes back over the page and turns every 'I' to a 'he', every 'you' to a 'she'. As so often, he is torn between confessional autobiography and the creation of symbolic characters of mythic force. He wants to write about redemptive memory and the resurrection of the dead, but he cannot resolve the question of how much or how little to say about the last week of Sylvia's life. 'What do you want?' he asks the ghost of Sylvia. 'For us to go north together next week, / Yes next week, or for me to vanish off the earth'. That was exactly how he remembered it in his journal record of their final meetings, how one day she would want them to try again and the next never to see him again.

Then the figure of Sylvia sees the book that the bronze soldier is reading on the platform at Paddington. It is Ted's red Oxford Shakespeare that she had ripped to rags in a furious row. She opens it, reads the inscription and closes it again. She begs for reassurance that he will be faithful to her. He gives it to her over and over and over again. The poetry is compacted in such a way that he is giving both the reassurance and the Shakespeare, the token of their shared art. Sylvia's reading of the inscription in the copy of Shakespeare and the words about either going north or vanishing off the earth recur in various guises during the long and complex evolution of *Birthday Letters*. Until shortly before publication, the intention was for them to appear in 'Under the Laburnums', but at the last minute they were moved to 'The Inscription'.

Hughes was proud of the symbolic figure of the soldier reading by Platform One at Paddington, but he could not quite find a way of using him to secure the links between his father and the First War, Sylvia's father and the Second, himself, Sylvia and death. Rather as Wordsworth took the crucial passage about the 'boy of Winander' who blew 'mimic hootings to the silent owls' out of the manuscript of *The Prelude*, turned it from the first person to the third and published it as a freestanding lyric, Hughes stripped all personal association from 'Platform One' and published it in 1995 as his Laureate's contribution to *Freedom: A Commemorative Anthology to Celebrate the 125th Birthday of the British Red Cross*.[30]

The next jump in 'Black Coat: Opus 131' is more awkward. Hughes turns directly to Sylvia's relationship with her parents. First her gratitude to her mother, who 'glued' her 'whole' after she was found in her 'Daddy's tomb in the basement' (the crawl space of her first suicide attempt). But then the rage at her father's death is projected on to her mother. A butterfly in a lump of amber, given to her by her mother, comes to represent the huge tear that she exuded all through her life: the permission to hate. The amber is then transformed into the letter in which Aurelia turns against Ted, gives her daughter permission to hate another man in black, suggests that the lovers try a separation.

None of this is sufficiently worked through to be publishable. The next movement of 'Black Coat: Opus 131' is more fragmented, and some of the fragments did indeed prove salvageable for publication in *Birthday Letters*: here we find a version of the fox cub on the hump of Chalk Farm Bridge, of the Shakespearean fantasia that became 'Setebos' ('Who could play Miranda? / Only you. Ferdinand – Only me'), of 'The Rag Rug' and 'Trophies' and 'Your Paris'. Some of these are marked with asterisks, to indicate that they are worth keeping. Others were too raw, including one that is variously titled 'Generosity', 'Greater Love', 'The Gift' and finally 'The Real Thing', and another, filled with classical allusions, on the reading of Sylvia's dark dreams.

The sequence was beginning to break up. Blank spaces appear between the poems, markers of the realisation that it is not going to work with the unity of Beethoven's Opus 131. At times, there is a journal-like feel, as in a long sequence on the year when Sylvia taught at Smith and Ted was in her shadow. On other pages, there is more of a sense of the poet as psychoanalyst, puzzling over Sylvia's neuroses: 'You were afraid your typewriter / Would fall through the earth … You were afraid all your wedding presents / Would be stolen.' These lines were later worked into 'Apprehensions'. There is a fascination with Sylvia's journal, described as her 'secret hospital', and with the difficulty of mothering, filtered not only through the figure of Aurelia but also through Sylvia and her daughter Frieda. The 'oracle' born by the mother is a 'mighty god' whose name is 'Hurt'.

Later in the notebook, the sense of a Wordsworthian autobiographical unfolding recurs. This becomes 'Visit' in *Birthday Letters*. Hughes remembers a time ten years after his wife's death when, reading her papers, he is hit more strongly than ever before by the shock of memory. Then he retraces their story from her joy when he and Lucas first threw clods of earth at the Whitstead window, to the 'the meltdown of love' (a phrase omitted from the eventual published version), to her despair and her absence. He is haunted by the voice of their daughter as he walks into the silent home: 'Daddy, where's Mummy?' And by the freezing soil he claws in the garden, which symbolically becomes the cold earth of the graveyard at Heptonstall. 'You are ten years dead. I think it is only a story. / Your story. My story.'

It is towards the end of the notebook that the Wordsworthian voice becomes strongest. At the climax of the poem, on seven successive

pages, he wrote seven successive drafts of his memory of the night
when he first slept with Sylvia at her hotel in Fetter Lane. The epiph-
any that Ted experiences when he walks back to Rugby Street across
Holborn, as the dawn chorus washes over the sleeping city, is remem-
bered via Wordsworth. Crows walk the pavement beside him, and then
there is an exquisitely Wordsworthian line-break:

> And I
> Remembering the mighty heart that slept
> For Wordsworth on his September morning
> Heard what was missing from his bliss
> That had now been added to mine –
> The huge awakening of the whole city
> In the robe of throbbing birds in their Eden
> A robe that might have wrapped, for him too,
> The memory of the sleeping foreign woman
> Who had just decided his life.[31]

In some of the drafts 'as for me' replaces 'for him too' and the sleeping
foreign woman is 'a naked woman' or 'the naked body'. The poetic
homage is made explicit by way of an allusion to the sense of grace
and peace that pervades the famous sonnet 'Composed upon
Westminster Bridge, September 3, 1802'.

Wordsworth's poem was actually composed at a quarter past five in
the morning on 31 July 1802, when he and his sister Dorothy were
travelling to visit Annette Vallon, the young French woman with
whom he had fallen passionately in love during his residence in France
at the time of the Revolution, just after he had graduated from
Cambridge. They were going to see not just Annette but also Caroline,
the daughter she had borne him. The purpose of the visit was to make
peace with his foreign lover and child prior to his forthcoming
marriage to Mary Hutchinson. Hughes was fascinated by the relation-
ship between Wordsworth and Annette. In another notebook he wrote
of 'Wordsworth – Annette –Vaudracour & Juliet [he means Julia, but
the Shakespearean echo is apt] – his retreat to the hills – his sister's
imbecility. His human symbols: wild loss – stupefied endurance. His
slow transformation into a rigid scar.'[32]

The identification is clear: like Wordsworth, Hughes is inspired into his poetic vocation by a woman from across the sea, met at a formative moment soon after graduating from Cambridge. But the loss of that woman becomes a scar that marks the full remainder of his life and work. Fatefully, the poet's life is decided by love. Respite from 'stupefied endurance' can come only in the visionary moment of poetry, the recollection of that London dawn in which it was bliss to be alive and very heaven to walk the empty streets, and hear birdsong, having just left the hotel room of a sleeping, beautiful woman to whom one has made love for the first time.

Though the explicit allusion is to the Westminster Bridge sonnet, the tone and style are unmistakably those of Wordsworth writing his memories in blank verse. If Hughes could have sustained the quietly assured voice and loose pentameter rhythm of these lines through a much longer narrative of recollection, he would indeed have written the twentieth century's sequel to *The Prelude*.

On the next page, he turns to the dark words that Sylvia spoke during that night of love. The street lights are still on, and in them he seems to see her face as she told him of her suicide attempts: of jumping off a bridge that was too low, of ice that was too thick for drowning beneath, of a Gillette blade that broke on her wrist. A few pages later there are lines about how Sylvia saw her great love simply standing there on Grand Central station. He resembled her other great love, her equally great love. Who came after her like a ship with searchlights ablaze as she swam under the propeller. The name of that second great love, of that ship, was death. Hughes knew death, but that knowledge did not help him to hold on to Sylvia when he prayed:

> ~~As you screamed for help~~
> For the strength to slip
> From your hands, and fall
> Down the mountain-face.[33]

Over the page, Hughes writes just three words, the notebook turned sidewise: 'The Last Page'.

That was the end of what would have been his *Prelude*. The twin title was later broken up and attached to two short poems. 'Black Coat' is one of the strongest of the *Birthday Letters*. 'Opus 131' is a bitter little piece, first published in *Capriccio*, the Assia volume, and then reprinted in the 1995 *New Selected Poems*. It begins with an image of Assia in a homely hotel room, listening to Beethoven – a memory of that lonely night of hers in Haworth. The poem then tells of foetus, dark insect and wave-particles pronouncing on the unimportance of the meno-pause – Hughes in vatic, crankish mode. The allusion to Beethoven has broken down and what is missing is 'the lifeline music', the very Wordsworthian voice that would have made a finished 'Black Coat: Opus 131' so special: 'consolation, prayer, transcendence', 'the selective disconnecting / Of the pain centre'.[34] Biographically speaking, there is another 'selective disconnecting' in that 'Black Coat' is for Sylvia, 'Opus 131' for Assia. By deliberate contrivance or a slip of the memory, the wrong quartet is cited: it was the previous one, not 'Opus 131 in C Sharp Minor' but Opus 130 in B flat major that she had heard in the dark just up the hill from the Brontë parsonage.

Later, he slipped some loose sheets into the back of the 300-page triplicate book: a fair copy of the poem of the finding of the fox cub on Chalk Farm Bridge in 1960, a note about the price he had paid for putting Sylvia's journals into the public domain in the Seventies ('Maybe the most stupid thing I ever did'), and a summary of the story of Rabbah bar bar Hannah, a Babylonian Jewish Talmudist who, having undergone a series of fantastic adventures through the desert and across the seas, set down his life upon a rock and slept. When he awoke, the rock had gone and he was on a precipice, staring into the abyss.

The thousands of pages of holograph manuscript in the British Library could easily form the basis of a book-length study of the evolution of *Birthday Letters*. As with the Moortown elegies, there is a seamless development from the style of a prose journal to that of blank verse – rather as we can trace a line from Dorothy Wordsworth's journals to her brother William's poetry.

The prose narrative in one of the notebooks is fresh and vivid, making the reader wish that Hughes had published a conventional autobiography. He sets down his first reading of the poem about cary-atids, Daniel Huws's teasing review, Sylvia's reputation before he met her ('The rumour of your height, your slenderness, your hair'). He tells of Shirley, 'so English she was Irish', with her spectacular hair and what he perceived as her dislike of Sylvia. He suggests that the only purpose of the Falcon Yard party was for him to meet Sylvia. He recalls his half-empty brandy bottle, Shirley's rage, Sylvia's drunken daring shining eyes, the kiss, the bite, the 'new world'. Then the first evening in Rugby Street, the explosion of joy, the walk via Holborn to the hotel in Fetter Lane, the story of the scar and the lovemaking, Sylvia's body Americanly firm, slender, fish-like. And so on: walking together in Paris, Sylvia reciting Chaucer's 'Prologue' to the cows on the fen, marrying in the pink wool dress. The dream of Emily Brontë: Walter and the long walk up to Top Withens, 'the whiff of isolation and rain', Sylvia 'smiling your American beach-smile, up that bitter little sycamore, monkeys on the cultural relic'. He created prose sketches, too, for poems subsequently rejected, their titles scored through, among them 'Smashing the table. Misplaced passion', 'The kiss that killed – the dream-kiss, the real', 'Horrors in T.R. Park', and, at the climax of the sequence, 'What happened that night? Did you phone? Why didn't your spirit reach me? I was not there. I was with Susan, in our marriage bed, in Rugby Street – she who also only had 3 years'. Finally, the coda of 'The snow-grave, the funeral', a poem that appears to be lost.[35]

The processes of remembering, composing, decomposing and recomposing were unceasing. Correspondence with editor and copy-editor, revised typescripts and corrected proofs reveal many late changes to the collection.[36] There are changes to the order of the poems. So, for example, 'The Cast' is moved from early to late. And changes to their titles: 'Apprehensions' was originally 'Prophecy and Paranoia', with Sylvia's writing as her fear, held between her fingers in the form of the Schaeffer pen that someone stole after her death. He remained uncertain about the precise contents until a very late stage. '18 Rugby Street', 'A Pink Wool Knitted Dress' and 'Karlsbad Caverns' were sent to the copy-editor as additions.[37] At the very last minute, 'The Laburnum' was taken out and 'The Inscription', a revision of 'Under the Laburnums', inserted instead.[38] There were other late omissions too. Some of them, along with the 'Laburnum' that had been removed, went into the privately published collection *Howls and Whispers*: 'Minotaur 2', 'The Hidden Orestes', 'The Difference', 'The Offers', 'Cries and Whispers' (the title poem, with 'howls' revised from 'cries'). Others remain unpublished: a poem alluding to Shakespeare's *Timon of Athens*, another about a near-drowning incident with a girl when he was in Australia, and the lovely story of the jaguar-skin rug told by the ex-colonial beekeeper in North Tawton. There are, in short, as many unpublished poems about Sylvia as published ones. But the reading public was not aware of this.

Her suicide presented Ted with his most difficult decision as to what he should publish and what he should not. In the original plan for 'The Sorrows of the Deer', and many intermediate versions, the intention was to end the sequence with a poem about the night of her suicide. Having begun as 'The last I had seen of you was you burning / Your farewell note', it was much revised over the years under the titles 'What did happen that Sunday night?' and 'That Sunday Night'.[39] It reached its final form as 'Last Letter'. It would have been the obvious climax, allowing *Birthday Letters* to end with Dr Horder's words 'Your wife is dead.' Why did he exclude it? Surely not because it was simply too painful to remember: so much about his life with Sylvia was painful to remember, and the whole point of publishing was catharsis for the pain. No, the reason was that he did not want journalists crawling all over the fact that he spent that last night not with Assia, as had been generally assumed by Sylvia's biographers, but with Susan Alliston. He wanted to protect her name, not least to shield her sister from intrusion.

His dilemma was that he needed the sense of symmetry provided by his return to 18 Rugby Street that last weekend. Over time, parts of 'That Sunday Night' had evolved into the poem about the ill-fated house. So he decided, late in the production process, to include '18 Rugby Street' in a version that did not mention the business about the last letter, but did bring the wheel full circle back to the flat. His hope was that by burying the mention of Sue mid-poem, its full significance would not become apparent to critics and journalists. On the first night with Sylvia, he writes, he was not thinking of the 'Belgian girl' in the flat below, who eventually gassed herself: 'She was nothing to do with me.' Then he moves seamlessly to Sue:

> Nor was Susan
> Who still had to be caught in the labyrinth,
> And who would meet the Minotaur there,
> And would be holding me from my telephone
> Those nights you would most need me.[40]

This is the moment when he acknowledges in print Sue's part in the fateful last weekend. The apportionment of blame is deliberately ambiguous: was it Sue or simply his own desire for Sue that held him from the phone? Before pursuing this awkward question any further, he cuts back to his first night with Sylvia: 'Nothing could make me think I would ever be needed / By anybody.' But then Sue returns as he tells of how a decade darkened prior to the moment when she paced the floorboards overhead, 'night after night', tearful, alone, facing death in the very room 'Where you and I, the new rings big on our fingers, / Had warmed our wedding night in the single bed'.[41] Like the Belgian (or German) girl, Susan indeed had 'nothing to do with' Ted and 18 Rugby Street in 1956, the time the poem is set in the story of *Birthday Letters*. But she had a great deal to do with him and the house in 1963 and again when she returned to it after her travels among the Bedouin. The memory of her tears on his last visits to her in University College Hospital is subsumed into the last line of the sequence, but lymphoma is changed to leukaemia to help with the disguise. Ted's gamble paid off. The reviewers did not probe at the reference to Sue holding him from the telephone on those last nights when Sylvia so needed him; the journalistic pack did not start sniffing around for traces of 'Susan'.

Just as Wordsworth at some level repressed the autobiographical actuality of 'Upon Westminster Bridge' by getting the date wrong, so Hughes in '18 Rugby Street' deliberately or unconsciously misdated this first night of love with Sylvia to Friday 13 April, which was actually the night on which she returned to him after her trip to Paris and Rome. The poem needs that later date for the sake not only of the astrologically ominous portent of Friday the 13th, but also because Sylvia Plath's father Otto, so crucial to Hughes's account of her life and the failure of his own marriage, was born on 13 April 1885. Equally, in remembering the girl downstairs, Hughes deliberately or unconsciously changes the nationality and miscounts the years: the poem dates her death to 1963, the year of Sylvia's suicide in Fitzroy Road, whereas in reality the Belgian/German girl, whose name was Helen, had gassed herself in Rugby Street a couple of years earlier. Indeed, in the memory of another resident of the house, she was English and did not own an Alsatian.[42] Here, and in 'Last Letter', there is also a fusion or confusion of the two flats, one above the other, which were owned by Dan Huws's father. The poem is not to be read as a literal memory, but rather as the conversion of 18 Rugby Street into an ill-fated House of Atreus.

Birthday Letters was published without its 'Last Letter'. In the absence of that key poem, and a few other equally important ones, such as 'The first time I brought a bottle of wine', 'The Grouse', 'Soho Square' and 'The Offers', the book did not give the whole story. But critics, journalists and readers, not knowing the manuscript history, assumed that it did. Ted, it appeared, had finally told his version of the story and, by and large, he was forgiven. Without question, he was financially rewarded. By the end of 1998, *Birthday Letters* had sold more than 100,000 copies in hardback, making it the fastest-selling volume of verse in the history of English poetry. More than fifty writers chose it among their 'Books of the Year', its poignancy heightened by the proximity of its release to Hughes's death.

The Return of Alcestis

Uncle Albert's suicide, Sylvia's suicide, Assia's suicide and the filicide of Shura, Susan's painful death, 18 Rugby Street as a House of Atreus, the Lumb Bank fire, the Plathian maenads, the *Bell Jar* lawsuit, the cancers (Jack Orchard, Jennifer Rankin, Carol's sister), the years of blockage, the realisation that the release into *Birthday Letters* might have come too late: Ted Hughes's life was, in the vulgar sense, 'like a Greek tragedy'. But his fascination with mythology and the resonance of the recurring tragic idea of the sins of the fathers being visited upon the children meant that reading and translating Greek tragedy was also a way of coming to terms with that life.

In March 1995, Leonard Baskin sent him a collection of skulls in the hope that they might inspire some poetry. Ted replied that he was busy on translation work. He had been deep in Ovid, had been working on Euripides' *Alcestis* and had been commissioned by the Northcott Theatre in Exeter to do a new version of the foundation text of Western tragedy, Aeschylus' *Oresteia*, from which he hoped to make some money. He feared that he was becoming a hack, but on the other hand he reckoned that he had found a technical solution to one of the main difficulties of the action and that, for the actor, his version would be much easier to speak than other recent attempts. His aim was 'to release the howl in every line' of the verse.[1]

At the end of the year he reported back that he had not managed to work up any skull poems, indeed had not written any original verse for over a year, his longest fallow period since the age of sixteen. He was too busy with commissions for much-needed cash. Besides, he did not want to write anything that was not central to his own concerns – it was too late to be messing around in the foothills. The following autumn, he told Baskin that it had now been two years since he had written 'a connected page' of his own verse.[2] He sent him a great slab of the completed *Oresteia* translation instead.

His recurring complaint was that the translations were distracting him from his own work. They had been intended to get him going, but had gone on too long. They did, however, have the virtue of distracting from what he described to Baskin as the other confusions and crises in his own life, by which he meant his double life in Devon and London, as well as his health problems. His painful shingles kept recurring.

Then the plans for a production at the Northcott collapsed for financial reasons, leaving the *Oresteia* high and dry. The Ovid progressed more happily. His 'Twenty-four Passages from the *Metamorphoses*' were completed by the summer of 1996 and published under the unassuming title *Tales from Ovid* the following May. Neither Ted nor Faber had especially high hopes for sales, but the reviews passed all expectations. Michael Hofmann set the tone in *The Times*, where he also explained his own part in the origin of the collection, telling of how when he received Ted's contributions to *After Ovid* he experienced the kind of awe that Keats described in his sonnet 'On First Looking into Chapman's Homer'. Standing by the telephone to appease his sense of urgency, he read the thirty or forty pages straight through and scribbled a note to Ted urging him to 'go on and do an Ovid book all of his own'. Now that the master had done so, it was the most beautiful match: he had created a modern masterpiece out of a series of 2,000-year-old stories of dried-up rivers, hunting dogs and mutinous sailors, both broad and subtle, violent and erotic, elegant and folksy.[3]

The influential Professor John Carey in the *Sunday Times* described it as a 'breathtaking' book that should be given to every school in the land. He explained incisively how Hughes had fulfilled the task of the creative poetic translator by simultaneously being true to the original and making the work his own. Each alteration from the Latin was an awe-inspiring revelation of 'the range and ingenuity of his poetic intelligence'. He 'slims and strengthens', 'makes Latin's swift, filmic effects available in uninflected English', 'puts throat-drying narrative suspense back into stories – such as Atalanta's race – as familiar as the hare and the tortoise'. Of course it is not an 'accurate' translation. Hughes has done what great poet-translators have always done: he 'commandeers and ransacks his original'. He has intensified the violence: passages such as Jupiter electrocuting Lycaon and 'the nymph Thetis trussed by her ravisher' ('Her feet and hands were a single squirming cluster') have been elaborated not out of 'sadistic self-indulgence', but in the spirit of the original, where people are indeed 'dismembered, raped, impaled, mutilated, incinerated, cooked, eaten' as 'Ovid accommodates the whole gamut of perversity from incest to genocide'. 'Writing in Augustan Rome', Carey concludes, Ovid 'anticipated centuries of crime-reporting, acres of newsprint. Hughes's cruelty is entirely in key with his source.'[4]

Carey was far from alone. There was hardly a dissenting voice to the acclaim. The book's reception was a huge boost for Ted as he underwent surgery and chemotherapy following his diagnosis with cancer of the colon the previous month. Before long, the book was appearing on summer reading recommendations and then in July it was short-listed for the prestigious Forward Poetry Prize. There was a small flurry of controversy over its eligibility, given that it was a translation, but the judges deemed it sufficiently free to count as original poetry. Sales were brisk because of the good reviews.

On 27 January 1998, just a week after the revelation of *Birthday Letters*, the Ovid book won Britain's biggest literary award apart from the Booker (which was only for novels): the Whitbread Prize, worth over £20,000. Ted was too ill to attend the award ceremony, so his friend the broadcaster and novelist Melvyn Bragg collected it on his behalf. A month earlier, in a column in *The Times*, Bragg had described the book as 'the most exciting, addictive collection of poems in English written in recent and not so recent times', perhaps the masterpiece of 'a poet whose profligacy and magnificent unfashionability have made him the object of sneers by some etiolated critics whose swotted degrees make them think of themselves as the arbiters of good writing':

Hughes is a great poet. He can be bad, he can be poor, like all great poets. But at his best he can be called in with the very greatest – even with Wordsworth, our third poet, and sometimes with Milton, our second. Here, through Ovid, he challenges Shakespeare. Read Hughes's Ovid and know the depths of our inheritance. I am not a pundit, but for my last column of this year let me push out the boat and guarantee that, like me, you will be awash with awe and newly alert understanding about the deep springs of our culture.[5]

The prize propelled *Tales from Ovid* into the paperback bestseller list, a rather extraordinary place for a translated volume of Latin verse.

In his introduction to the translation Hughes suggested that the reason for Ovid's enormous influence on the history of Western art and literature was the thing he shared with Shakespeare: a fascination with the extremities of human passion, with the psychology of what passion feels like to someone who has been 'possessed by it'. Thus in 'Venus and Adonis' Ovid stripped away all the encumbrances of previous versions of the tale and zeroed in on 'the story of hopelessly besotted and doomed love in the most intense form imaginable'.[6]

Ted's selection of tales begins with Ovid's narrative of cosmological and human origins – always a primary Hughesian theme as he ranged across cultures and mythologies. Characteristically, he gives it a modern twist with apocalyptic references to nuclear catastrophe. He then provides an exceptionally energetic telling of the Phaethon story that he believed was so important to Plath's poetry. Thereafter, the emphasis is on the human passions, especially extreme sexual desire: the rapes of Callisto, Proserpina and Philomel; Myrrha's horrifying incestuous desire for her father; and the sculptor Pygmalion's obsessive love for the statue he has made. The old stories are brought back to life through a combination of vivid Hughesian phrases – a screech owl described as a bird with a 'sewn-up face', Achilles smiting the helmet off an enemy 'in shards / Like the shell of a boiled egg'[7] – and occasional touches that have a personal feel. Arachne hangs herself, dangling and jerking at the rope's end in an echo of Hughes's recurring image of the hanged man, who was both a figure in the Tarot and his own Uncle Albert. And when the Arcadian beauty Callisto runs with 'Her ponytail in a white ribbon'[8] she seems for a moment to become the youthful Sylvia, whose long, sandy-coloured ponytail, bound with a white ribbon, is preserved in a box in the Lilly Library in Bloomington, Indiana.[9] When the disguised Jupiter takes Callisto by force, the language has a momentary (probably subconscious) hint of Plath's 'Rabbit Catcher'. The voracious lover stretches out beside the girl and kisses her with a kiss that roughens, 'A kiss that, as she tried to answer him, / Gagged her voice, while his arms tightened around her, // Straitjacketing her body'.[10] The girl is metamorphosed into a bear, a beast which always made Ted think back to the fifty-ninth bear on his American road trip with Sylvia.

The triumph of *Tales from Ovid* showed Ted that it was possible to write a full-length volume of verse in a series of self-contained but linked narratives. This encouraged him in the preparation of *Birthday Letters*, which has a similar form. It also made him want to resume his unfinished engagements with the classics. The *Oresteia* project was revived, with a view to a production at the National Theatre in London, which was eventually realised a year after Ted's death. The translation had a mixed response, but it includes many lines of great ingenuity, some of them influenced by Hughes's favourite poets: 'Do not massage me in public with oiled praise,' Agamemnon says Shakespeareanly to Clytemnestra. 'Words can do no more ... / Nothing remains but the act / Everything waits for the act ... Quickly. Now,' the Chorus of Libation-Bearers recite Eliotically in the second play of the trilogy. The Furies of *The Eumenides*, 'Black, like the rags of soot that hang in a chimney, / Like bats, yet wingless', are pure Hughes.[11]

As in *Tales from Ovid*, there are occasional intrusions from Ted's contemporaneous wrestling with his memories of Sylvia and the force of her poetry. The most startling of these is the account of Iphigenia going to her death, as her father Agamemnon sacrifices her in order to appease the gods and set the Greek ships sailing for Troy:

> The wind presses her long dress to her body
> And flutters the skirt, and tugs at her tangled hair –
> 'Daddy!' she screams. 'Daddy!' –
> Her voice is snatched away by the boom of the surf.
> Her father turns aside, with a word
> She cannot hear. She chokes –
> Hands are cramming a gag into her mouth.[12]

Given the Plathian cry 'Daddy', there can be no mistaking the echo of 'The wind gagging my mouth with my own blown hair', that line in 'The Rabbit Catcher' analysed by Jacqueline Rose in a way that raised Ted's furies.

Translating the *Oresteia* was part of his process of expiating guilt and sorrow by turning strong emotion into myth. Though there is nothing so crude as a direct correspondence, his immersion in the imagined emotional lives of Electra and Orestes, children of a tragic household, was a way of coping with the burden that had fallen on Frieda and Nick. There was also a personal subtext to his version of Jean Racine's *Phèdre*, a commission of the Almeida Theatre for a production by its artistic director Jonathan Kent, which opened in Malvern in August 1998 and transferred to the Albery Theatre in London's West End the following month. Like Ovid's tales, this play is a forensic examination of the psychology of extreme, transgressive passion: in this case, the subject is a woman's burning sexual desire for her own stepson.

Ted was also thinking at this time about the process of releasing Plath's journals in full. The particular autobiographical significance in his acceptance of the *Phèdre* commission was his knowledge, via those journals, that on the night of the Falcon Yard party a page of Sylvia's essay on the poetic imagery of Racine's *Phèdre* was rolled into her Smith Corona typewriter on her desk at Newnham College. And he never forgot that two days later, when she wrote 'Pursuit', her first poem about him, she took as its epigraph Racine's line '*Dans le fond des forêts votre image me suit,*' which Ted now translated into 'Everywhere in the woods your image hunts me.'[13] Racine had given her the black panther of desire and death, which she imagined embodied in him and his jaguar spirit.

Sylvia is an even more vivid presence in his other translation from the classics. Surprisingly, *Shakespeare and the Goddess of Complete Being* did not contain a detailed discussion of the beautiful, redemptive scene in *The Winter's Tale*, where the statue of Hermione seems to come back to life and the beloved lost wife returns after sixteen years' supposed death. Perhaps Ted could not bear to confront his own dearest wish, because he knew it would never come true. But as he moved ever closer to the publication of *Birthday Letters* he became more and more determined to make it true for himself. Through the power of words he would bring Sylvia back to life, as Paulina restores Hermione in Shakespeare. In 1993 and 1994, he worked – simply for his own satisfaction, without a formal commission – on a version of Euripides' *Alcestis*, which, along with Ovid's tale of Pygmalion, was the shadow story behind *The Winter's Tale*: a play about the return of a beloved wife from the grave.

In his first draft, scrawled at speed in one of his Challenge Triplicate Books, there are lines that did not make it into the final version, perhaps because they were too painful:

> ~~She has gone. She cannot hear us.~~
> ~~Your mother has gone.~~
> Is this why we were given our life?
> ~~So that we would have to bear this?~~
> ~~The unbearable.~~
> So that we ~~would~~ could each of us be tested
> By the unbearable?[14]

Through the act of translation, Hughes comes to terms with the fact of his own destiny: that he was given life so as to be tested by the unbearable.

The *Alcestis* was set aside while he busied himself on paid commissions from 1995 to 1997, but in January 1998 on the very weekend when the existence of *Birthday Letters* was made public he exhorted himself in his journal to get back into it. The following week, he wrote to fellow-Yorkshireman, actor and director Barrie Rutter. Ted spoke of his 'tuning fork' being in the Calder Valley.[15] It occurred to him that Rutter was a kindred spirit and that his company Northern Broadsides, which performed classic plays in the broad accents of the North as opposed to the smooth sounds of southern received pronunciation, might give a home to the *Alcestis*. He completed his version, including an expansion of a sequence in which the demi-god Heracles gets drunk, and offered it to Rutter. Two years after Hughes's death Northern Broadsides staged it, to strong reviews, in their Viaduct Theatre in the cellar of the former Dean Clough Mills in Halifax.

Alcestis is Ted Hughes's last major completed work. That status gives it a special poignancy. The echoes of his own life are all too clear. The action is driven by a choice: either the husband or the wife must die. When Ted wrote to Olwyn on the day in 1962 when he split from Sylvia, he said that the strain of living with her volatility was such that it was 'her or me'. He would die if he stayed.

The wife is taken, but she ensures that the children, a son and a daughter, are safe. Her last injunction to her husband is not to remarry. Hughes greatly expands Euripides' original at this moment, spelling out the image of another woman in Admetos' bed after Alcestis' death. Sometimes, though, he does not need to expand in order for there to be resonances. 'I shall mourn you, Alcestis, not for a year / But for my entire life.' 'But what of the girl – / A stepmother will tear her to pieces / One way or another.' 'We should never have married.'[16] A dream in which the wife returns, only to be lost again on waking. All these are in the original.

Again and again Hughes nudges the text close to his own life. Death as a fall through 'a hole in the air, / A hole in the earth, endlessly falling'[17] is Euripides' descent to the underworld rewritten in the imagery of the first Plath elegy in Gaudete. Heracles' 'you have lost a good wife' becomes 'you have lost an extraordinary woman'.[18] Euripides' Alcestis is praised for her courage and virtue in dying on behalf of her husband, but in the Hughes version her death is a transfiguration into fame:

> And when you died
> Your death astonished the living …
> Your death
> Was your greatest opportunity
> And magnificently you took it.[19]

And the fame is universalised: Heracles' 'I know the story' in the original becomes 'The whole world knows the story.'[20] Most striking of all is an exchange within the Chorus:

> Chorus 1: She is dead.
> Chorus 2: Alcestis is dead. Your wife is dead.[21]

The draft of the working manuscript is in biro, but the latter phrase is in ink, darker black.[22] It is clearly an afterthought, a late insertion of the very words spoken by Dr Horder on the telephone in his 'voice like a selected weapon / Or a measured injection', those four coolly delivered words that never left Ted's ear: 'Your wife is dead.'[23]

After his wife's death, Admetos shows hospitality to a visitor, who turns out to be Heracles. There is drunkenness that some consider inappropriate at such a time – shadows of the bongo-drum accusation. And then there is castigation, as if from Robin Morgan and the radical feminists: 'You killed her. You. You. You.'[24]

Contrary to his wife's injunction, Admetos agrees to remarry, as Ted did. But by an act of grace, the second bride turns out to be Alcestis herself, brought up from the underworld by Heracles in gratitude for the hospitality that Admetos showed at his darkest hour. One of Hughes's expansions of the original text is a long sequence about Orpheus and the fatal glance that sends Eurydice back to Hades. With the return of Alcestis, the backward glance is redeemed. She lives. The final word of the play is 'hope', a raising of the heart akin to 'spring', the final word of the original manuscript of *Ariel* that lay on Sylvia's desk in Fitzroy Road in February 1963.

If in one sense the memory of Sylvia lives through the redemptive power of literary art, in another Ted joins her in the imagination of death. The manuscript draft of *Alcestis* has a long and somewhat over-blown passage about the vacuum and silence of the empty house after the loss of the mother. In the final version, this is replaced by some much more powerful lines in which Hughes develops Euripides' image of Admetos envying the dead into something very personal:

> I think of cool soil
> A mask over my face,
> A weight of stillness over my body,
> A darkness
> In which she lies next to me – her lips
> Maybe only an inch from my lips.
> Forever.[25]

This is Hughescliff, imagining himself in the moorland graveyard at Heptonstall:

> 'You were very wicked, Mr Heathcliff!' I exclaimed; 'were you not ashamed to disturb the dead?'
>
> 'I disturbed nobody, Nelly,' he replied; 'and I gave some ease to myself. I shall be a great deal more comfortable now; and

you'll have a better chance of keeping me underground, when I get there. Disturbed her? No! she has disturbed me, night and day, through eighteen years – incessantly – remorselessly – till yesternight; and yesternight I was tranquil. I dreamt I was sleeping the last sleep by that sleeper, with my heart stopped and my cheek frozen against hers.'[26]

Why did Ted bury Sylvia in Heptonstall rather than north London or Devon? (The churchyard with the yew trees beside Court Green had been closed to new burials for years, so was not an option.) Of course it was to place her near his family. But in a deeper and more literary sense, it was because of *Wuthering Heights*. 'Haworth and graves', Sylvia had once written in her notebook.[27] She wanted to be Cathy. And for the rest of his life, until the completion of *Alcestis*, he was Heathcliff, the brooding figure, tall, dark and handsome, who wanders the moors in search of his lost love.

In September 1998, not long after putting the finishing touches to *Alcestis*, Ted wrote to Dan Huws, hinting that his life was in a state of upheaval – and not just for health reasons. It had been another strange summer and he was spending part of his time in London – seeing his oncologist, undergoing treatment and tests, attending rehearsals for *Phèdre*, and settling in to the flat he and Carol had bought in July.

At three o'clock in the afternoon on Thursday 17 September, the Poet Laureate sat in the left-hand corner of the lounge of the Connaught Hotel in Mayfair. The man he had arranged to meet was a few minutes late. When his friend arrived, Ted put away the copy of his translation of Racine's *Phèdre* in which, obsessive reviser that he was, he had been making post-publication alterations. He looked 'haggard but undefeated', unaffected by the new celebrity brought to him by the success of *Tales from Ovid* and *Birthday Letters*. He complained of the recurrence of his shingles. There were sores on his forehead, itches on his scalp and he was almost blind in his formerly strong right eye. As always, he talked fast, ranging widely, ending on the subject of the importance of wine to keep the heart of an old man ticking (never less than two glasses at a time). His friend, a former Faber poet who had fallen out of favour since the retirement of Charles Monteith, asked him whether he should let the northern press

Bloodaxe publish his collected poems. 'Going to Bloodaxe from Faber', said Ted, 'would be like leaving the Brigade of Guards to join a Territorial regiment.' So what about joining the poetry list of Oxford University Press? Ted paused, then answered, 'Salvation Army.' As they were leaving, after three hours of laughter and reminiscence, he explained why he had chosen the Connaught for the rendezvous. It was to do with birthdays and remembering and Sylvia:

> 'I sat in this chair in this corner on my thirty-second birthday.'
>   'Was that in August 1962?'
>   'August 17th. Sylvia was sitting where you are, with her mother next to her, and a woman who was a mentor of Sylvia's on the other side. The woman sensed there was something troubling us, and said, to brush it aside, "In thirty years' time, none of us will remember that we were sitting here in this corner of the Connaught Hotel."'[28]

The two men embraced and parted as Ted got into a taxi. They would not meet again.

The friend whom he had summoned was Richard Murphy. The meeting at the Connaught in 1962 had taken place during the summer of crisis that came to a head when Ted and Sylvia arrived at his cottage in Cleggan, in the hope of saving their marriage, but with the disastrous outcome of Ted going off to Assia and Sylvia making a pass at Murphy. Once again, a circle was being closed. That night, Murphy went to the Almeida production of Ted's version of *Phèdre*. He had with him the emended copy of the text that Ted had pressed into his hands as they parted, inscribed with the words 'Love as ever' and a north-country proverb: 'bout's bare, but it's easy'. Murphy found this cryptic, but Hughes, as always, knew what he was doing. 'Bout' means 'without': without is bare (empty) but not troubling. This was the proverb that he added as epigraph to the poem 'Climbing into Heptonstall' when it was published for the third time.[29] Without Sylvia: bare, but easier than being with her. Climbing into Heptonstall was synonymous with the return to her grave and the poem's closing words were Hughes's signature for his own sense of being trapped in the past of which Murphy had been such an important part: 'Before us − / Stands yesterday'.

October was a momentous month. Frieda's first volume of poetry was published. Dame Diana Rigg was burning up the London stage in Jonathan Kent's production of the *Phèdre* translation. On the 7th, *Birthday Letters* won the £10,000 Forward Prize for Poetry. Four days later, Seamus Heaney published his tribute to the collection, 'On a new work in the English tongue'. The poem praises Hughes's 'language that can still knock language sideways' and compares his 'stunt and stress / Of hurt-in-hiding' to the best of *Beowulf*, which Heaney was translating from Old to modern English at the time.[30]

At the end of July, Ted had heard from Buckingham Palace that he was to be awarded the Order of Merit, the highest honour in the land, personal gift of the Queen, limited to the nation's twenty-four most distinguished individuals in the arts and sciences. The presentation was on 16 October. Three days afterwards he wrote to his Aunt Hilda, telling her of his pride. He drew a picture of the medal and told of his private meeting with the Queen – there is an official photograph of the moment of presentation, in which he looks very ill – and of how he gave her a copy of *Birthday Letters* and explained to her how he came to write and publish it, and she was fascinated. Talking about the poems, he was able to open his heart to her as never before, 'and so she responded in kind'.[31] Then they had lunch with the Queen's private secretary. Carol was a great hit.

To Hilda, he sounded cheerful. There was no mention of his cancer. Future projects were still very much on his mind that autumn. On his long desk in the writing hut in the garden of Court Green lay his abandoned translation into modern English of *Sir Gawain and the Green Knight*, that wonderful anonymous poem he had studied at Cambridge and that infused his own verse with the Middle English alliterative idiom: should he perhaps pick it up again? (Reg Lloyd was keen to offer illustrations.) He was also preparing for the staging of a selection of the *Tales from Ovid*, to be directed by Tim Supple for the Royal Shakespeare Company, and sketching out a dramatisation of the ancient Epic of Gilgamesh, also for Supple. Other clouds were lifting, too: he made peace with the critic John Carey, who had so savaged the Shakespeare book, sending him a first edition of *Ariel* and 'a cut-out from a newspaper showing one of those psychological puzzles made of thousands of multicoloured dots, which different viewers will see different shapes in'. They had seen different things in the multi-tudinous world of Shakespeare, that was all.[32]

It is impossible to tell in what direction Ted's original poetry would have gone had he lived. The mythic vein was mined through and the elegiac voice almost expiated – though there was a degree of unfinished family business, in that his exceptionally close relationship with Olwyn was rarely turned into poetry and the theme of the Rival Brothers was still on his mind with regard to Gerald. A pair of late uncollected poems, one about Gerald's boyhood love of comics and the other about his mother's possessiveness, which subtly fuses into Olwyn's, might have been the beginnings of a sequence about sibling relations.[33] He would certainly have gone on writing for young people and for his own children. Among his late uncollected poems, published in the angling magazine *Waterlog* opposite a drawing of Ted's head in the form of a cluster of fishhooks, was 'Some Pike for Nicholas', in which memory is 'rocked' by the tail of a huge jumping pike on Lough Allen, swinging Ted into the past 'like a hurricane lantern', igniting the memory of camping with his son by the water all those years ago.[34]

In addition, his work would almost certainly have focused more on the public role of the poet, not as royal encomiast but as dark prophet in dark times, a voice akin to the later work of Geoffrey Hill, who some said should have succeeded him as Laureate. Probably Ted's last poem was a translation of Pushkin's 'The Prophet', an archetypal early nineteenth-century Romantic lyric in which the language of the Old Testament prophet Isaiah is transposed to the secular domain and the poet becomes the shaman, the conscience of his tribe, the hierophant of an unapprehended inspiration, the mirror of the gigantic shadow which futurity casts upon the present, the unacknowledged legislator of the world: 'God's voice' comes to him, tells the poet-prophet to be his 'witness' all across the earth, to speak 'the Word' that will 'Burn the hearts of the people'.[35]

Ted died nine days after writing the letter to Aunt Hilda. He and Carol had travelled by train from their Devon home back up to London, where he was admitted on Tuesday 20 October to the private London Bridge Hospital, just along the Thames from Shakespeare's reconstructed Globe. The hospital had been recommended by his consultant, Dr Peter Harper, for the specialist treatment he now required. After various tests, the poet underwent surgery on the Friday but insisted that Carol must not tell Olwyn and his children until the operation was underway.

Frieda and Olwyn visited over the weekend. Ted was moved back onto the ward on Monday – a room overlooking the river. Carol asked the doctors if she could take her husband back to Devon but was told very gently that he was too weak to make the journey. By now she was staying overnight in his room. Tuesday passed quietly and that night Ted slipped into unconsciousness.

The next day, Wednesday 28 October, Olwyn recalled that when she went back to the hospital her brother was in a coma. Nick had arrived just in time on the red-eye flight from Alaska. He was holding one of his father's hands. Olwyn took the other. Then she passed that hand over to Frieda. Carol was also there – as she had been since Ted was moved up to the ward. Olwyn's recollection is that her brother then seemed to wake; his doctor called this a 'startle response' where Ted seemed to wake up and mouth some sounds. Soon after that, he finally faded away.[36]

The jaguar was at rest in his cage.

Epilogue

The Legacy

The body was returned to Devon, accompanied by Nicholas and Carol. Frieda filed and signed her father's death certificate. Place: London Bridge Hospital, Tooley Street. Date: 28 October 1998. Cause: Metastatic Colon Cancer and LVF (Left Ventricular Failure).[1] Faber and Faber announced the death the next day. The Queen sent her condolences and the news made the front pages. Tributes and obituaries appeared with headlines such as 'The god of granite who could shatter stones with plain words'.[2]

At Court Green, Frieda would spend an evening sitting by his open coffin. She wrote a poem called 'Conversation with Death', in which Death boasts:

> 'To take him at the peak of his
> Perfection, when he was at his
> Escaping most cleverest, meant
> I really got to achieve something.'[3]

The funeral took place the following Tuesday, 3 November, in the rain-lashed church of St Peter in North Tawton, crammed with 200 mourners. Friends came down from London and convened in the kitchen of Court Green before going across to the church. For some, it was an uncanny experience to see Frieda, the image of her mother, open the door to the house.

The massive coffin was not shouldered but carried by its handles. 'As though', Heaney said later, 'on a river of light and air'.[4] The Nobel Laureate spoke in honour of his dear friend and inspiration the Poet Laureate. His passing, said Seamus, was 'a rent in the veil of poetry'. Heaney read Dylan Thomas's 'Do not go gentle into that good night' (ironically, a poem that Ted had come to detest), together with two of Ted's later poems. One was 'The day he died', from the sequence of Moortown elegies for Jack Orchard: in this context, the son-in-law stands in for the widow's father. The other was a Heaney favourite, 'Go Fishing'. An extract was quoted in the BBC News report: the poet joining water, wading 'in underbeing', letting 'brain mist into moist earth', gulping 'river and gravity', losing 'words' and ceasing, as a shade floats towards the sea that is eternity.[5] Dante to Hughes's Virgil, Heaney was summoning the national poet's spirit downstream, to meet the 'Ophelia' of *River*, who was Sylvia. The Shaman and the 'Darkfish' with 'finger to her lips', reunited as they go Lethe-wards, 'into the afterworld'.[6]

The Bible reading was from St Paul's first letter to the Corinthians: love does not keep a score of wrongs but rather it enables us to bear all things, believe all things, hope all things, endure all things. And then the Reverend Terence McCaughey, friend since Cambridge days, spoke of Ted's kindness and loyalty, of how he would say things that made the familiar seem beautiful and strange, how he would encourage his friends when they floundered, would share his schemes and plans. Of the power of his speaking but also of his silence: 'for it would be my sense that this craftsman with words, this "makar" (to use the Scottish lowland word for "poet" which I remember, he loved) this makar – for all his own vitality and exuberance with words – well recognized that there are times to be reticent in the use of them'. The only words in which Ted Hughes believed were those wrung from the way things are, 'in all their vitality; their terrible harshness; their vividness; their funniness or sheer silliness; and sometimes in their almost unbearable gentleness'.[7] The coffin and the family departed for a private cremation in Exeter in the November rain. Court Green was reopened later for close friends and family.

In the weeks following the funeral, there were reported sightings of a big cat on the loose on Dartmoor.[8] Emma Tennant recalled that 'Ted's face keeps appearing in flashes at the end of programmes, on TV. Film of swollen rivers – the rivers he loved – in a dark landscape. Weirdly, the main story is of an escaped lion in Devon; children are interviewed saying they're "not really frightened". No-one knows where the lion came from, and the story is dropped after a couple of days.'[9] A cast of a paw print was taken and police marksmen were alerted, but the mysterious beast was never seen again.

The following May, the great and the good of the nation, including Ted's fishing companion Queen Elizabeth the Queen Mother, together with the Prince who regarded him as a guru, gathered in Westminster Abbey to give thanks for his life. His Iranian friend Shusha Guppy sang a poem that Ted had adapted for her from the thirteenth-century Scottish ballad-writer Thomas the Rhymer, accompanying herself on the guitar: 'When you are old enough to love / You'll be taken prisoner / By the blossom of apple and pear, / In the pink shade of the cherry.'[10] Friends such as Michael Baldwin and Grey Gowrie read from the works, Alfred Brendel played the adagio from Beethoven's 17th piano sonata. Heaney delivered another silken eulogy, comparing Hughes to Caedmon, father of English poetry, and to Wilfred Owen, to Gerard Manley Hopkins and to Shakespeare. The Prince of Wales privately described his poet as the incarnation of England, taking a special relish in Heaney's words of Avalon and of King Arthur on the ship of death. The entire congregation joined in a rousing rendition of Blake's 'Jerusalem' and the Dean of Westminster pronounced the blessing. Silence fell and then a Yorkshire voice, deep as England, was heard. Members of the congregation craned their necks from behind pillars. No one could see who was speaking. Then it dawned that the voice was coming over the public address system:

> Fear no more the heat o' the sun,
> Nor the furious winter's rages;
> Thou thy worldly task hast done,
> Home art gone, and ta'en thy wages;
> Golden lads and girls all must,
> As chimney-sweepers, come to dust.[11]

Ted himself conjuring his beloved Shakespeare from beyond the grave.

After this *coup de théâtre*, the Tallis Scholars sang the haunting *Spem in alium*, chosen by Carol as a special favourite of Ted's, a piece of music the couple had spent many evenings listening to in the last year of his life. This glorious forty-part motet from the Tudor age – that time when, Hughes had always believed, the Goddess was still alive within the national consciousness – was also loved by the Prince of Wales. Then, the royals and the literati, the 'fishermen and fine-printers, old socialites and new socialists, Devonians, Yorkshiremen, friends and family'[12] departed to the sound of Bach's Prelude and Fugue in G major.

When a prolific poet fears or even knows that he is dying, there must be significance in his choice of the final poems published in his lifetime. In the last two months of his life, Ted Hughes submitted two poems to the *Sunday Times*. The first was a revised and retitled version of a piece originally written as part of a series of poems about Shakespeare published in a limited edition in aid of the actor Sam Wanamaker's plan to rebuild the Globe Theatre.[13] In its self-contained end-of-life form, the poem is called 'Shakespeare, drafting his will in 1605, plots an autobiographical play for 1606'.

Published seven weeks before Hughes's death, it is prefaced with an explanatory note by Hughes, telling of how 'Shakespeare is imagined dividing his estate into three, like King Lear.' One third goes to his wife Anne and another to each of his daughters, Susanna and Judith, the twin of Hamnet, Shakespeare's only son, who would have come of age in 1606 had he not died aged eleven in 1596. Hughes also explains that the coat of arms to which he alludes in the final verse of his poem is the one that Shakespeare obtained on behalf of his father, as part of his effort to restore the family name after John Shakespeare fell into debt and disgrace, and that 'In 1606, the only heir to it was Edmund (or Edward), the illegitimate son of Shakespeare's youngest brother, Edmund – who died just before his father in 1607.'[14]

In the poem, Hughes's imaginary Shakespeare says that his will will be as he has planned. His treasure (a term suggesting the value of his work) and his land (the impressive property portfolio built up by the business-canny poet) will be split into three. One third will be to help his wife Anne in her old age to 'Put her youth's rage / And hate away'. 'Hate away' is Ted's borrowing of Shakespeare's own apparent pun on 'Hathaway' in Sonnet 145. The reference to Anne's youth is slightly curious, since she was – very unusually for marriage customs in the age of the first Elizabeth – nearly a decade older than Will Shakespeare. Whether in Hughes's version of events the wife's rage and hate have anything to do with the well-attested anecdotes of her husband's philandering in London is a matter for speculation.

As the prefatory note indicates, Hughes – still unable to let go of his Shakespearean obsession, even though several years had passed since the publication of *The Goddess of Complete Being* – was intrigued by the fact that at the time when Shakespeare was writing *King Lear* the consequence of young Hamnet's death was that the potential heir to the Shakespeare name and the honour of the family crest was Edmund, son of Shakespeare's youngest brother Edmund, the only member of the family who followed him into the theatrical profession in London. But Edmund's son Edmund – to whom Edward James Hughes, on the scantest of scholarly warrant, gives the alternative name Edward – was illegitimate. For Hughes, it was not a coincidence that the name of the illegitimate son whose plotting is so central to the familial disintegration of *King Lear* is Edmund.

'The man running along the beach with the girl has 4 children by 3 different women,' he had written in the outline for the deeply auto-biographical poem sequence 'A'.[15] Four children by three women? That is not quite Shakespeare, even if Poet Laureate William Davenant was telling the truth when he claimed that he was the greater William's illegitimate son. In his self-identification with Shakespeare, Ted Hughes merges the Lear-thought of three daughters, the Hamnet-thought of a child who died, and the Edmund Shakespeare/William Davenant-thought of illegitimate offspring. He was thinking very hard. Thinking about his own place in the lineage of English literature: Ted as both William Hughes's son and that greatest of Williams' metaphoric heir. Thinking, too, about the future of his bloodline and his name. Nick was unmarried, Frieda childless. Only in the work would the name endure. Perhaps, too, he was thinking of a shadow story that may one day be revealed.

Most pressingly, he was, like Lear and Shakespeare, thinking about the division of his own estate. When he went to America for his court appearance in the *Bell Jar* case back in the Eighties, Ted had left with Olwyn a sealed envelope to be opened only in the event of his death. She wondered what he was going to do: he was afraid of losing everything. Olwyn genuinely thought that he might not come back. When she eventually opened the envelope, she found a simple state-ment, unwitnessed, saying that he wanted all his earthly goods to be divided equally in four parts between her, Frieda, Nicholas and Carol.

In April 1997, his cancer having been diagnosed, Ted Hughes wrote a will. It is not, however, the usual kind of document drawn up by a solicitor with elaborate legal phrasing concerning the revoking of former testamentary dispositions, the appointment of executors and trustees, residuary estate and alternative provisions in the event of the predecease of a legatee.

It is a single sheet of hand-scrawled paper, with just three clauses. In the first he left 'everything' to his wife Carol Hughes. In the second he said that he wanted his remains to be cremated and his ashes kept by Carol Hughes his wife, until such time as she decided to scatter them 'on Dartmoor at a point between the sources of the River Taw and the East Okement'. The point was to be chosen by his fishing friend Ian Cook. 'If a point roughly equidistant to the sources of the Teign, the Dart, the Taw and the East Okemont can be found, that would be ideal.' Subsequently, his name should be 'cut in a long slab of granite, near that place, if that is possible'. Finally, his funeral was to be in the North Tawton village church, 'public and open'. The cremation was to be private.[16]

River, moor, stone, carefully plotted symbolic spot of English earth: one would have expected the fishing poet whose words were solid as Yorkshire granite to think of such things as he imagined his own mortal remains. In due time, his wish was carried out to the letter. With Cook's assistance, the spot was found. A remote corner of Dartmoor, it can be reached only by crossing bog, stream and army firing range.

By serendipity (or fate, Hughes would have said), the land belonged to the Duchy of Cornwall. Prince Charles, who keeps a private shrine to Ted Hughes at Highgrove, was happy to break the custom of not allowing such things as memorial stones on Duchy land. Approval was obtained from English Nature and the Dartmoor National Park Authority. A granite slab was taken from an area to the east of nearby Beardown Woods. It was carved with a simple inscription, 'TED HUGHES OM 1930–1998'. In November 2001, it was flown in by helicopter. There would be no Yorkshire grave for Plath obsessives to deface. It would take a very determined proponent of the Plath fantasia to find the spot and chip into the stone.

One would not, however, have expected the will to be so preoccupied with river source, ash and stone as to make no mention of Frieda, Nick and Olwyn. The likeliest explanation of this omission is that Ted Hughes had a long history of worrying about tax. An estate passed between husband and wife has no liability to inheritance tax, whereas a division into four would have incurred a considerable and immediate obligation, which would almost certainly have necessitated the sale of Ted's copyright. The gross value of the estate was £1,417,560, the net value £1,196,737, so the financial stakes were high. That the gross sum was less than the million and a half pounds Hughes's assets were said to be worth back in the Seventies was partly because of the passing of the valuable Plath estate to Frieda and Nick at Carol's suggestion, but also a mark of Ted's ability to spend money rather than save it. Estimated future royalties are included in the calculation of probate for a writer, so Hughes's literary legacy formed a considerable portion of his estate: in this sense, the success of *Birthday Letters* had posthumous consequences.

In order to ensure that his sister and his children were well provided for, Ted wrote a 'Letter of Wishes' alongside the will. Here he expressed his desire for an equal division of his copyrights into four parts, as in the earlier informal testament. The language and rhythm of the letter are uncannily similar to those of the poem about Shakespeare writing his will. There is one-quarter for each of the two children, one-quarter for Olwyn, and the fourth for Carol, until she decides to pass it to Frieda and Nick, or until her death, when it would pass to them.[17] Four years after Hughes's death, a bitter family dispute over the will was reported in the press.[18] The solicitor for the Ted Hughes Estate responded with a robust press release, pointing out that a 'Letter of Wishes' does not have force in English law and that Carol had told Ted that 'she could not implement this ambiguous and confusing letter as it stood'.[19] The statement also laid out the Estate's handling of royalties as of 2002. Ted's sister and children shared between them 50 per cent of all his net copyright income every year from the time he had died, and this continued right up to the end of 2015. Ted's close friend János Csokits heard rumours of the dispute. He was not satisfied by the Estate's response:

> Whatever the four of you do now or in the near future, once all those involved are gone forever, the details of this painful affair will be dug up, analysed and commented upon by academics, biographers, journalists and housewives: the jury of posterity. I for one have no doubt what the long term verdict will be … To be generous is always a nobler way than the one laws and judges can offer us.[20]

*

The lesson of Hughes's life was that you never knew what twist fate would throw at you next. The lesson of Plath's afterlife was that a spouse cannot control the public legacy of a famous writer. The shade of Ted Hughes would have wanted the year 2003 to be remembered for the publication of his *Collected Poems* by Faber and Faber, a great 1,300-page slab of a book that gathered together almost all his published poetry, including private-press and fugitive work (though, oddly, excluding the main body of *Gaudete*). The book was reviewed with high praise from the literary establishment, but for the wider public 2003 was memorable as the year in which Ted Hughes was played on screen, gruffly and sympathetically, by Daniel Craig (a future James Bond) opposite Gwyneth Paltrow's Plath in Christine Jeffs's film *Sylvia*. The project did not have the support of Hughes's family – though Elizabeth Sigmund (Compton), dedicatee of *The Bell Jar*, was eager to help.

One of the legacies of a great artist is indeed to become the subject of later artworks. Shakespeare and Byron, Beethoven and Pushkin have become characters in novels and films as well as the objects of numerous biographies. Emma Tennant recreated Ted Hughes biographically in her memoir *Burnt Diaries* (1999) and then fictionally in her novel *The Ballad of Sylvia and Ted* (2001). Some would say that the fictional representation was truer to his inner life than the supposedly factual one.

Four years after the dispute over the will entered the public domain, a 600-page work of fiction entitled *Poison* was published by W. W. Norton in New York. It was the fourteenth novel of Susan Fromberg Schaeffer, poet and Professor of English at the University of Chicago, where she had moved after spending the bulk of her career teaching at the small college in Brooklyn where Ted had read for her. The novel, which has never been published in Britain, carries the usual disclaimer: 'This is a work of fiction. The characters in this book are products of the author's imagination and any resemblance to real living or dead persons or any similarities to actual historical events are purely coincidental.' The *Kirkus Review* offered a lively summary of the narrative:

> The epic saga of a landmark British poet and his three wives, two of whom committed suicide … this vast, overwhelming vortex of a novel [is] built on the life of promiscuous Peter Grosvenor,

'a man with an immeasurable weakness for women' and a gargantuan gift for poetry. Less a narrative, more a spreading ink blot of reminiscence and reflection, the story, which always keeps Peter's death at its center, shifts its point-of-view between the perspectives of a range of family members and literary friends while also moving back and forth in time. Peter's first wife, Evelyn, was a manic and gifted American poet who gave birth to two children, Sophie and Andrew. Her decision to gas herself was subsequently copied by Peter's second wife, Elfie, who killed their daughter as well as herself. Needing a mother for Sophie and Andrew, Peter made a third – calculated, loveless – marriage to Meena, who bestrides the novel as gothically as any wicked stepmother.[21]

As we have seen, Susan Schaeffer first met Ted Hughes when he was in New York in early 1971 for the American publication of *Crow*. She and her husband Neil, also an English professor, remained good friends with him. Ted stayed with them on several occasions when he returned to America, including at the time of the *Bell Jar* lawsuit. He also wrote Susan some of his more candid letters. After his death, she engaged in lengthy conversations with Olwyn and others. These raw materials were then transmuted into fiction, rather as Plath had transmuted her pre-Ted life into the narrative of *The Bell Jar* and her relationship with Ted into 'Falcon Yard' and the lost 'Double Exposure'.

The biographer is bound by fact, whereas the novelist can penetrate to the heart of a story through selective dramatisation and invention. In the *Bell Jar* trial, and in his many dealings with Plath's biographers, Ted Hughes complained again and again about the tendency to treat Sylvia's work as autobiographical rather than symbolic. Because she used the form of fiction, Susan Schaeffer was able to do the opposite: instead of writing a biography of Ted, she turned his life into myth and the people in his story into symbolic figures.

The character of Sigrid is a representation not of Olwyn but of a great writer's sister acting as agent, gatekeeper and guardian, possessor and interpreter of her beloved brother's life and work. Clare is a representation not of the woman in south London with whom Ted Hughes shared a house (she was not, as Clare is, a chandelier-designer), but of a complicated man's last great love. She is a symbolic bringer of grace through *lightness* found in a brief interlude of serenity before death. 'Peter' tells her, laughingly, that he will cut himself loose, 'come back as a spirit, an unmarried spirit': 'laughing, both of them, laughing, Peter long ago having noted her indifference to what was said about his first two wives, even incurious about what he wrote, completely heedless of things like "reputation," "ambition," "a place in the canon".'[22] Peter and Clare share a romantic love of the ocean, of crashing wave and windy clifftop, something that has more symbolic force than the mundane reality of the shared love of fishing and cooking that brought Ted close to his last love.

Ted Hughes discovered during his cross-examination for the *Bell Jar* Deposition that the problem with a fiction based on fact is that the presence of any element of biography or autobiography is sufficient to make the reader wonder precisely which elements are factual and which are invented. *Poison* begins with a sensitively realised scene that is manifestly an imagining of the occasion when Ted took the children home from school and told them the true circumstances of their mother's death. By beginning the novel in this way, Schaeffer inevitably makes her readers wonder what sort of truth lies behind her treatment of the funeral of Peter, the dispute over his will, the attitude of the family to his first biography, and so on.

The real-life parallels range from the famous photograph of Ted and Sylvia in newly married bliss, to the cowbell at the door of Court Green, to the near-quotation of Ted's phrase in the most public of his spats with the Plath fantasia ('I hope everyone is entitled to his own life'),[23] to the reading of *Crow* at the New York 92nd Street Y and the handsome poet's flirtation with a character who is manifestly Erica Jong, to the visits to Highgrove, to the voicing of Shakespeare's 'Fear no more' from beyond the grave in the memorial service, to the telephonic intimacy of brother and sister ('She knew everything, on the phone to Peter almost daily for more than forty years, and if she did not ring him, he rang her, or worse, got on the train and stayed in her little house overnight, or sometimes more than overnight'). Even, boldly, to Olwyn's theory about the reason for the publication of *Birthday Letters*: 'That long affair of Peter's. He would never have published that book of poems about Evelyn if he hadn't needed the money ... Of course he didn't count on the cancer coming back.'[24]

Schaeffer knew that Ted wrote at length about Sylvia in his unpublished journals: this before it was widely known that he even kept a journal. Olwyn claims that she was never aware that he did so.[25] Remarkably, the novel even offers an accurate account of the contents of Sylvia's final note to Ted: how did Schaeffer know about this, given that she was writing several years before the poem 'Last Letter' entered the public domain?

Anyone acquainted with the real Olwyn will smile in recognition upon reading of the sister-agent's taste for Ouija boards and horoscopes, or at the account of Sigrid slamming the phone down so hard that she hurts her wrist, or of her sitting in the fug of her little London house 'on her overstuffed chair which she long ago covered with an indigo kilim to hide the cigarette holes in the chair's fabric, but now there are so many cigarette holes in the kilim, they are even more obvious than the holes in the chair were before, if only because the kilim itself is so beautiful and draws attention'.[26] The long stub of ash on the cigarette in hand is familiar to all who have sat listening to Olwyn reminisce with love for Ted and hatred – in more recent years modified by pity[27] – for Sylvia. In 2013, as if in a miniature recreation of the Lumb Bunk conflagration, the ash fell on the chaise and set fire to the house in Chetwynd Road, nearly killing Olwyn and destroying some of the remnants of her collection of Hughesiana. Fortunately for her brother's literary legacy, she had previously sold her most important manuscripts to the British Library, where they joined the huge and immeasurably rich archive of poetic and prose drafts, letters, journals, autobiographical meditations and other materials that his widow sold to the nation in the autumn of 2008 for half a million pounds.

Meena is a monster of the imagination and not a representation of Carol Hughes. Sigrid is another monster, a grotesque exaggeration in her possessiveness towards her brother and his work. Olwyn felt an entirely understandable sense of betrayal when the novel was published. Of Susan Schaeffer she said, 'I thought she was my friend. She isn't now.'[28] Yet in many of its particular details, *Poison* is every bit as much a *roman-à-clef* as *The Bell Jar*. The reader is accordingly forced to ask some painful questions akin to those with which Ted was confronted when interrogated by Jane Anderson's attorney. A single example will suffice. The character of Penelope is manifestly inspired by Dido Merwin, who knew Sylvia and Ted exceptionally well but who had very complicated feelings about them both. So what credence may be given to Schaeffer's sentence, 'Penelope, hugging her secret, the only one still alive who knew that Peter had struck Evelyn and caused her to miscarry'?[29] Sylvia's tender journal entries following her miscarriage almost certainly give the lie to the claim of Penelope. But the casual reader of the novel is not to know this. The accusation feeds the myth of Ted himself as the monster. That is the pernicious aspect of the book. At times, *Poison* is itself a kind of poison.

Poisonous she may have been, but Susan Schaeffer's own close familiarity with Ted gives an authority to her account of his magnetic effect upon women. In meditating upon the source of his power, Julia, the novel's projection of Schaeffer herself, concludes astutely and persuasively that it was to do with the way that 'he turned you back into a child':

> Something about the way he stared at you, as if he'd forgotten there was anyone else in the world. Well, everyone mentions that. Though that wasn't the important thing. What was important was how safe he made you feel. And that laughter of his, barely hidden, no matter what you were talking about, so you didn't carry on feeling serious for very long. And that voice, completely soothing, as if you'd known it once before, nothing to do with his accent, or its pitch, nor anything like that, but its essence of soothingness, if there's such a phrase for it. A mischievousness, completely incorrigible, and a way of drawing you into it, as if the two of you were children together, but he was still the safe and protecting one; he was both things at once, the parent and the child.[30]

These are the words of a woman who loved and understood Ted Hughes, though in the knowledge that her looks meant that he would never look at her as a lover rather than a friend.

Horrified that American readers would take the autobiographical projections of *The Bell Jar* as the whole truth about Sylvia, Aurelia Plath set about preparing her daughter's letters for publication as a way of setting the record straight and creating a more rounded picture, a more nuanced legacy. She hoped that the 'real' relationship between mother and daughter revealed in *Letters Home* would displace the fictionalised dynamic of the novel.

By the time that *Poison* was published in America, Christopher Reid, Ted's last editor at Faber and Faber, was well advanced with the editorial work of preparing a selection of Hughes's letters for publication. Carol Hughes was collaborating with him, providing contacts, photocopies and explanations, and doing her best to facilitate his task, while offering Reid what he called 'unimpaired editorial freedom'. She chose, though, not to offer any letters Ted had written to her for inclusion in the book – deciding, instead, to adopt a Cordelia-like silence on the matter of her own marriage.

This decision meant that when the 750 pages of selected letters were published in 2007, the volume was curiously lopsided. The first half, reaching from National Service and Cambridge through the Sylvia and the Assia years, is as full of Ted's emotional life as his literary meditations. There are glorious and poignant love letters to both Sylvia and Assia. The second half, by contrast, offers rich insights into the writer and the public man, into his preoccupations (fishing, pollution, royalty) and his idiosyncrasies (the perpetual casting of horoscopes, the fascination with faith-healer Ted Cornish), but little sense of the complicated personal life of the later Hughes.

Though the editor's introduction denied that the book was 'a biography in disguise',[31] *Letters of Ted Hughes* was in effect the authorised autobiography. Stitched together with brief but informative biographical headnotes and footnotes by Christopher Reid, it amounts to a brilliantly constructed and astonishingly well-written 'literary life', a posthumous Coleridgean *Biographia Literaria*. Each letter is a brightly coloured snapshot of the poet in the act of writing, thinking, reacting, remembering.

The reader of the letters meets undergraduate Ted getting up at six o'clock in the morning to read Shakespeare. Wide-eyed Ted wondering at cellophane-wrapped America. Ted full one moment of bizarre ideas. Early summer 1962: 'I think of the gall-bladder as one of the vital centres, along with the prostate gland & the cerebellum – inside all Defences.'[32] And the next bursting with energy for some new scheme. Late summer 1962: 'I am rapidly becoming editor of a Magazine of translation ... publishing modern poetry only, from other languages – destroy Larkin's affable familiar.'[33] Ted on people: 'The bloke directing this play "Oedipus" is one of the best most imaginative directors in the world, and we get on very well together.'[34] Ted opinionating: 'What an odd thing to think of "modern" English literature. I can see why Americans aren't very interested. It's a collection of eccentrics – English Parson style, like Larkin, and ever shallower whiz kids ... Did you see the Rozewicz, and the Celan? Both lovely books.'[35] Ted being kind to schoolgirl enquirers: 'Dear Miss Clement and Miss George, Thank you for your letter. If I answered your question, it might stop you worrying, but it would not help you. You know that when you answer a problem, you kill it. And it might be a fruitful problem. Best wishes, Ted Hughes.'[36] Ted becoming an environmentalist: 'I do think a good deal about the whole complication of the re-alignment of human life to the natural world which created him [humankind], and on which he depends.'[37] Ted looking deeply into his wounded inner self: 'Almost all art is an attempt by somebody unusually badly hit (but almost everybody is badly hit), who is also unusually ill-equipped to defend themselves internally against the wound, to improvise some sort of modus vivendi with their internal haemophilia etc. In other words, all art is trying to become an anaesthetic and at the same time a healing session drawing up the magical healing electrics.'[38]

Reviewing the volume in the *Sunday Times*, John Carey more than atoned for his scathing review of *Shakespeare and the Goddess of Complete Being* by judging that 'No other English poet's letters, not even Keats's, unparalleled as they are, take us so intimately into the wellsprings of his own art.'[39] This point is so true and so momentous that it is worth reiterating: for a century and a half, Keats's letters had held a unique place in English literature as the greatest example of a poet's intensely self-aware reflections on his own art. In 2007, those of Hughes joined them. And we have barely begun to absorb their riches. The Reid selection offers but a small proportion of his monumental correspondence.

Many of Hughes's letters are prose poems, magnificent works of art in their own right. He often spent hours drafting and honing a single letter. He kept copies of many of them and eventually sold them to Emory University in Atlanta, without restrictions on the availability of most of them. Though not composed expressly for publication, Hughes's letters, from a surprisingly early stage in his literary career, were written in the knowledge that posthumous publication was highly probable. When, to take the supreme example, the correspondence between Hughes and Heaney is published in full, as one fervently hopes it will be, it will come to be regarded as a literary monument akin to the letters that passed between Wordsworth and Coleridge or T. S. Eliot and Ezra Pound.

But the published letters are not sufficient to constitute a full biographical record.

Ted Hughes made a point of explicating his poems at length when scholars enquired about them. In the latter part of his life, he wrote extensively about the biographical origins of his work. There is an even greater wealth of biographical gold dust in his extensive but fragmented journals and in the 100,000 pages of unpublished drafts of his poems, plays and prose works. He died in 1998 in the full knowledge that he had left the raw material for years of scholarly investigation into the circumstances in which his works came into being and the ways in which they transformed his life into literature.

He burnt Sylvia Plath's last journal, but did not burn his own. He carefully preserved a huge archive. Two archives, rather: the one sold to Emory before he died and another, containing more intimate material, held back by his widow for a decade but then sold to the British Library in London. Unlike his rival Philip Larkin, who told his literary executors to burn his manuscripts, Ted Hughes deliberately left trails and clues, tantalising invitations to future critics and biographers. What he preserved, he manifestly intended to be read and discussed.

But how fully, how candidly? Besides making the comparison with Keats, Carey's review of the published selection of letters pointed out that more scandal is attached to the life of Ted Hughes than to that of any English poet since Lord Byron. He might have added that in her last days Plath herself implicitly reflected on the Byronic parallel in her final book review. The series of unfortunate events in Ted Hughes's life – and indeed his afterlife – includes not just the fame, bed-hopping and quarrels over bad reviews that are the usual stuff of high-profile literary life, but several suicides, a mother taking her child with her to death, arson, the royal family, a repeatedly defaced grave, exhortation to lynching, toxic allusions to Nazism and the death camps, and a very unusual will. One can see why he did not appoint a literary executor to pave the way for the writing of an authorised biography. How could he not have been ambivalent about the idea of anyone writing his life?

His view of biographers was made clear in a letter to Stephen and Natasha Spender, written in 1992 upon the publication of a book that dredged up Spender's homosexual liaisons. He suggested that the oppressed victims of biography should form themselves into a 'solidarity' pack that, with the assistance of the Royal Society of Literature, could serve as a kind of 'vigilante commando' that would 'form an effective superego for the literary world'. He granted that this sounded a bit 'Ku Klux Clannish', but said that there were times when he felt distinctly Clannish.[40] His sister Olwyn was equally forthright:

> Dear Natasha Spender,
> Just a note to wish you and Sir Stephen well and to congratulate you warmly on your splendid TLS piece on vampire biographies. The dilemma of their victims has never been so well expressed. The wonder to me is how otherwise fairly serious reviewers treat these hacks seriously. Their only reviews should read 'Another inhuman, inaccurate and impertinent junk biography.' Or they should simply be shot.
>
> The deafness to the moral issues is astounding in most people who have not been actually clobbered by them.[41]

After his death, for entirely understandable reasons, the message 'no biographies' went out loud and clear from the Estate of Ted Hughes and his publishers, Faber and Faber.

And yet in the last months of his life each time he visited Olwyn in Tufnell Park, he silently left a literary biography on the table: Gibson's Lorca, Foster's Yeats, and others. 'He had never done that sort of thing before,' Olwyn recalled. 'Never shown any interest in biography.'[42] She thought that this was a quiet message.

Once the collected poems and selected letters were published, and the British Library archive made available to the public in 2010, the time was manifestly ripe for a literary biography.[43] Hughes would not have wanted all those archival resources to go to waste or for large portions of his work to stop being read because of the absence of an explanatory apparatus that could help to keep it alive. At the same time, he systematically weeded his archives. Again and again, burrowing through his papers, one comes across a ripped-out page, a heavily deleted paragraph, a missing poem known only from its title. Some of the pages torn from the notebooks in the Emory archive are to be found as loose sheets among the British Library materials, but even the more intimate second archive has tantalising gaps. There were some things that he did not want revealed, even beyond the grave. Should these silences and mysteries be respected? To tell the truth, the whole truth and nothing but the truth about the mighty dead while maintaining the privacy of the living is a delicate task.

The biographies of writers that Ted admired were not those that came branded as the 'authorised version' of a literary estate. They were those that honoured, though not uncritically, their subject, the craft of poetry, and the complicated relationship between art and life. Hughes disciplined himself into complete literary honesty. 'What is the Truth?' he asked in the title of that children's book which he said came to the core of his writerly being. As a writer, he saw it as his primary duty to tell the truth about how he saw the world. As an autobiographer in his journals, he examined the deepest truths of his own self: 'And that's the use of this writing to myself,' he wrote in a journal entry about journal-keeping. 'It does bring me closer to my self. It does lock me in close conversation with my most conscientious self – and so it gives me energy, and ties me to my real feelings.'[44] To examine Hughes's life with an honesty answerable to his own requires the biographer to explore that 'most conscientious self', to expose those 'real feelings', and in so doing to fill in some of the gaps left by the weeding of the archive. At the same time, it must be acknowledged that no biographer can tell the whole truth and that what Hughes says about the writing of the natural world in *What is the Truth?* is equally applicable to human subjects: 'the truth about them could never be more than provisional, distorted by human interpretation'.[45]

'I hope each of us owns the facts of his or her own life,' wrote Ted at the time of the dispute over the state of Sylvia's grave.[46] But every life intersects with other lives. Hughes's family and friends had the right to tell the facts of his place in their lives, and books such as Lucas Myers's exceptionally insightful *Crow Steered, Bergs Appeared* (2001), Daniel Huws's brief but touching *Memories of Ted Hughes* (2010) and Ehor Boyanowsky's flamboyant if occasionally unreliable *Savage Gods, Silver Ghosts* (2009) truly bring aspects of Ted back to life. Gerald's *Ted and I* (2012) is an important family record. Olwyn's reluctance to publish an autobiography of her own, instead of correcting the biographies of others, will always be a matter for regret. And Frieda Hughes, a writer and an artist in her own right as well as the daughter of two great poets, perhaps has more right than anyone else to tell her version of the story.

On her fortieth birthday, 1 April 2000, she began work on what might be described as her own version of *Birthday Letters*, a sequence of poems and accompanying abstract paintings, one for each year of her life. The aftermath of her father's death was the obvious time for such a reckoning. Her abstract oils of this period, some of her best work, embody her emotions at this difficult time. One of them, *Man Thinking*, executed in 1999, includes the head of a pike that she did not realise she was painting.[47]

The autobiographical project took five years of thinking, feeling and creating, so by the time it was finished there were *Forty-Five* poems and paintings and that became the title of the book. As her friend the broadcaster Libby Purves explained in a foreword, this was not a 'plodding autobiography' but 'the internal story', a series of snapshot memories revealing 'the way it felt to her at each time'.[48]

For the first four years, there were no direct memories. She sees herself in the garden of Court Green among the creepy-crawlies, but that is a back projection or an image from a photograph or a family tradition. She believes that the trauma of her mother's death caused a period of complete amnesia. Only in her fifth year does sentience of her family emerge: her troubled father, her little brother, and the woman she had thought was her mother but who she is now told is really her aunt, Olwyn, sacrificing the glamour of Paris for the sake of Ted and the children.

Then the snapshots become real. The search for a new life in Ireland with Assia and Shura; first school surrounded by Irish accents and a statue of the Virgin on top of the stationery cupboard. Back in Devon, a sense of being the outsider, looking on as Ted teaches Nick how to tie flies for fishing while Assia and Shura make wings for imaginary angels with paper feathers. Like her father before her, she makes models of clay and plasticine – flowers and dragons where his were zoo and farm animals. Again as he had done as a boy, she brings home wounded animals. In the tiny, gossip-filled Devon town she feels self-conscious when wearing the American clothes sent over for Christmas by Grandmother Aurelia. At her Hughes grandmother's funeral, she throws shells on the coffin and they clatter so loudly that she cringes in shame.

That was in the terrible year of 1969. Next she is in Yorkshire with a new mother and new hope. While the family is on the bonding holiday by Loch Ness, 'Collecting ticks from an adopted dog … In a mildewed tent at the lake's edge',[49] Lumb Bank smoulders. In Frieda's memory, the arsonist takes only one thing from the house: the tin box in which she kept her special treasures and the tokens from her baptism, a silver house-fly on a shirt stud of bone, a silver mug embossed with a teddy bear and the square-shaped pearly beads that had belonged to Granny Hughes.

Then in 1971, with the *Orghast* actors in Persia, she witnesses a world at once exotic and bloody, sees the mutilated body of a criminal with 'Hands chopped off at wrists, / Mouth open, tongue-slit and earless'.[50] Later that same year, as the result of Alvarez's article, Ted took his children home for a week and told them that their mother had not in fact died of pneumonia. Later, Frieda asked her father why he had kept it from her for so long. He said, 'What do you tell a three-year-old who doesn't understand?' And then he said, 'Once having told a three-year-old something that they could cope with at the time, how do you determine the age at which you tell them the truth? Every year would go by and I'd say, could I tell them now? It was because of the pain that I put it off and put it off.'[51]

The poem sequence goes on to tell of how as a teenager she struggled with bulimia and fell in love with a dangerous man on a fast motorcycle. In 1981 when her grandfather Bill Hughes lay dying in the nursing home run by Carol's sister, she arrived twenty minutes too late to say goodbye to him. She had clerical jobs in the tax office and the bureaucracy of the Ministry of Defence. Then she sold greeting cards and split from her husband. A second partner proved to be a fraudster. She studied art in London, then went off and sailed the world with a shipboard engineer, her Flying Dutchman. She wrote,

she painted, she ran through more relationships, she lived in Australia
– welcomed by Gerald and Joan – and published children's stories. She
tells of how she dealt with ill health – anorexia, endometriosis, chronic
fatigue syndrome – and how she coped with her Australian home
being burnt in a bushfire, but also of how she found happiness, for a
long time, with fellow-artist László.

And then in her father's last year she publishes *Wooroloo*, filled with
Australian light. He died in the knowledge that she was a published
poet who had finally found a happy marriage. She comforted herself
with the knowledge of her father's love, reiterated in almost daily
phone calls:

> His voice on the telephone telling me
> Over and over how he loved me
> As if I must learn it, and
> Might not have heard him the first, second,
> Or third time.[52]

For all its pain, *Forty-Five* achieves a sense of requital, of making peace
with tumultuous history, by means of the honesty of that kind of
confessional poetry which Frieda's mother had pioneered in the *Ariel*
poems and her father had turned to in *Birthday Letters*. In this, the slim
volume stands in sharp contrast to *Waxworks*, the collection Frieda
completed and published halfway along the journey to *Forty-Five*,
which – in the manner of her father's other poetic mode – comes at
her personal story indirectly through symbolic figures, many of them
monstrous, out of classical mythology.[53]

Nick, by contrast, chose not to tell his own story. After his father's
death, he remained in Fairbanks, immersed in his academic work on
stream salmonid ecology, conducting research in the Alaskan interior
and in New Zealand. He resigned from his university position at the
end of 2006 and devoted more time to his work as a potter. But he
continued his research on king salmon and he supervised graduate
students. One of them remembers staying out with him on fieldwork
until 3 a.m. on the night of the summer solstice in 2008, 'just watching
fish'. Another recalled 'his passion for everything he did', his encyclo-
paedic command of piscean natural history, his brilliance and creativ-

ity and patience and kindness, and his gift of always making time 'to sit down with a cup of tea and help with anything: questions about class, working out a study design, writing computer code, building sampling equipment, chatting about fish or life'.[54]

Joe Saxton, a friend since Bedales, told of a darker turn in the aftermath of Ted's passing. In a moving newspaper article he explained that until the death of his beloved father in 1998, Nick had been 'a man in whom a zest for life and a thirst for learning welled over': 'Whether it was investigating Nile perch in Kenya for his undergraduate dissertation, working out how to make the perfect glaze for his pottery, discovering the ecology of grayling or trout, or "calibrating" (his term, not mine) how to only just lose at football in the garden against his godchild, my youngest son, his lust for learning was undimmed.' Ted was Nick's 'soulmate', his sharer in the world of water and fish. 'Hey Sag,' Nick would say to his friend as the two of them retraced the steps that father and son had trodden in Alaska. 'This is the branch where dad's line snagged when he had a big salmon.' The death of Ted, Saxton wrote, meant that Nick lost 'the most important relationship in his life': 'Worse still were the repercussions: disagreements of the sort that many grieving families have when the family linchpin dies. Nick was in his late thirties then and his mental health began to suffer.'[55]

On 16 March 2009, in his small wooden house on a steep, snow-covered Alaskan hillside reached through a dense forest of silver birch and spruce, Nicholas Farrar Hughes, aged forty-seven, took his own life. Frieda and Olwyn had to bear the anguish of flying all the way to Alaska to make the necessary arrangements. Ted Hughes endured great sorrow. It is a mercy that he did not have to endure this. Ted's sister Olwyn believed it is the one thing that would have destroyed him.

When a prolific poet fears or even knows that he is dying, there must be significance in his choice of the last lines of verse published in his lifetime. The second of the two poems Ted submitted to the *Sunday Times* in the last months of his life was published on 18 October 1998, in honour of the award of the Order of Merit. Much longer than 'Shakespeare, drafting his will', it was called 'The Offers'. It had previously appeared only in the privately printed *Howls and Whispers*.

This was, from the point of view of his public self, Ted Hughes's final poetic testament.

It tells of how a few months after Plath's suicide he met her ghost on a Northern Line tube train to Chalk Farm: Orpheus in the underground, glimpsing but not recovering Eurydice. These are some of the most poignant lines Ted ever wrote, not least because of the quiet echo, with light turned to darkness, of his Wordsworthian epiphany on the threshold of 'London's waking life' in the sequence of 'Black Coat: Opus 131' that describes his walk home after their first night of love: 'Chalk Farm came. I got up. You stayed.' It is 'the testing moment'. He lifts her face from her and takes it with him to the platform, in a dream which is 'the whole of London's waking life'. Then he watches the train and Sylvia 'move away, carried away / Northwards, back into the abyss'. Her 'real new face' is 'unaltered, lit, unwitting'. It remains in sight for a moment before vanishing to leave Ted his 'original emptiness / Of where you had been and abruptly were not'.[56]

The poem then tells of how the ghost appeared a second time, in her own home. He is sitting talking to another woman and before his eyes, in hallucinatory fashion, she seems to transform into Sylvia. He allows himself to be 'covertly'[57] wooed a second time. By two of those extraordinary coincidences, or synchronicities, that made Ted feel that his life was being controlled by some mysterious supernatural force of fate, the woman happened to share a birthday with Sylvia and a name with Sylvia's 'oldest rival': her name was Shirley Smith. A friend of Olwyn's, she did indeed, as the poem says, subsequently send Ted an annual postcard from Honolulu.[58] This section of the poem includes the superbly formed phrase 'Death had repossessed your talent' and a bold image of Sylvia courting Ted anew as he breathes 'a bewildering air – the gas / Of the underworld in which you moved so easily / And had your new being'. It took enormous courage to use the word 'gas' in this context.

And then, because offers and immortal intimations tend to come in threes, the ghost of Sylvia appears a third time, as he is stepping into the bath:

> But suddenly – the third time – you were there.
> Younger than I had ever known you. You
> As if new made, half a wild roe, half

A flawless thing, priceless, faceted
Like a cobalt jewel. You came behind me
(At my helpless movement, as I lowered
A testing foot into the running bath)
And spoke – peremptory, as a familiar voice
Will startle out of a river's uproar, urgent,
Close: 'This is the last. This one. This time
Don't fail me.'[59]

As in the London-dawn sequence of 'Black Coat: Opus 131', Hughes is here writing in the classic Wordsworthian vein of memory: the 'wild roe' mimics the memorial recovery of a happier past in 'Tintern Abbey' ('when like a roe / I bounded o'er the mountains'), while the delicate enjambment of the verse is learned from *The Prelude* ('half / A flawless thing'; 'a familiar voice / Will startle out of a river's uproar').

Whereas Clytemnestra kills unfaithful Agamemnon in his bath, Sylvia gives Ted one last chance as he is entering his. This is the Alcestis moment, the second chance. He takes it. He honours Sylvia's ghost, the sorrow of the deer and the jewels that were her eyes. He does not fail her memory. It is a poem of longed-for redemption.

Like so many of the *Birthday Letters* and *Howls and Whispers* poems, Ted worked and reworked 'The Offers' over many years. In successive manuscripts, it has various titles, including 'Resemblances', 'Mind-warp' and 'Three Chances'. The earliest draft, written in a red school exercise book when the Sylvia project was still called 'The Sorrows of the Deer', was entitled 'Your after image', then revised to 'After image'. It is longer and more directly autobiographical than the final published version. The opening conceit is that the mask of Sylvia's face distorts Ted's retina: he keeps seeing her face in that of other women.

First, on the Underground, in the spring, just after Sylvia's death. A girl with full shopping bags gets on to a Northern Line train at Tottenham Court Road, just after the rush hour. Her face seems to his sorrowful eyes to be identical to Sylvia's. She gets off at Chalk Farm, and he follows her. It is as if Sylvia is back and they are going home together. This is the biographical origin of the incident. In the more polished version, the girl stays on the train as Ted gets off at Chalk Farm. She becomes the ghost of Sylvia, being driven into the underworld.

The second encounter, with Olwyn's friend Shirley Smith, is dated to the autumn of 1963, at Court Green. Olwyn is living with him there and her Parisian 'fellow-campaigner' has come for a visit. Again, the face becomes Sylvia's. As in the published version, Ted mentions the coincidence of birthdays, but in this first draft he also includes the autobiographical detail, discreetly dropped in later drafts, that Shirley made a pass at him, which he rejected. It would have been too strange to go to bed in Court Green, so soon after Sylvia's death, with a woman who was in more than one respect her after-image.

The third chance in 'After image' is completely different from that in the eventual published text. There is no reference to the bath and the ghostly voice. Ted sees Sylvia not in a fleeting after-image, but in the whole demeanour of a woman he knows very well indeed. She is his 'third' love, long known to him but 'still a riddle'. She is a 'creature so unlike' Sylvia, a 'thesis' to her 'antithesis', and yet 'as surely my wife'. 'Her profile' is 'identical but made perfect' in 'every feature'. She has a kind of 'Apache' look and in her 'phase of dark beauty' she is somehow associated with the moon. He is 'fixed', trapped 'like a fly in amber' in her 'occult brightness'.[60] There can be little doubt as to the identity of this imagined figure. Ted always said that his second bride had a face and hair that seemed vaguely Red Indian. Such features went with the whiff of gypsy origin that he found romantic in her. This is one of the very few poems that he wrote about his second wife. She is a 'survivor' and an enigma. She is the opposite of Sylvia and yet there are times when she looks to him like another Sylvia, though more beautiful.

But these lines are scored through, marked as a false start. He rejects the idea that finding a resemblance in another wife is the way to bring back Sylvia. In subsequent drafts, the third chance becomes that of the dream he recorded when Assia moved out of Court Green in the summer of 1967: 'dreamed: in bath – feeling somebody behind me, stunning shock, it was Sylvia, very young and happy'.[61] Whereas the first two offers turn on momentary resemblances, this is an encounter with the true ghost. No woman belongs here other than Sylvia herself.

In making this revision, and putting into ghost-Sylvia's mouth the demand that this time he should not fail her, Ted was probably influenced by one of the elegies of the Roman poet Sextus Propertius. Here, the ghost of the poet's dead beloved comes to his bedside and chides him for his infidelity. This model was familiar to Ted from a well-known free translation by Robert Lowell, entitled 'The Ghost'. 'I will not hound you, much as you have earned / It, Sextus,' says the woman. Instead, 'I shall reign in your four books.' As Sylvia reigns in Ted's late elegies. 'Propertius, I kept faith,' says the ghost.[62] Hughes revises the tone by having Sylvia's ghost offer forgiveness and ask him to be the one to keep faith. He does so by writing the poem and publishing it from his deathbed.

The Propertius elegy also mentions 'Agamemnon's wife', perhaps contributing to the bath scenario in Hughes's response – but, as throughout his career, the literary allusiveness in no way diminishes the reality of the apparition, the dream, the memory. It is fitting that this last poem is also a homage to Robert Lowell, at whose feet Ted and Sylvia sat in Boston, and whose personal voice in *Life Studies* did so much to liberate and shape their work. Lowell was on Ted's mind at this time because he had also published a translation of Racine's *Phèdre*: Ted's version was, among other things, an outdoing of the master-translator of modern poetry.

Sylvia Plath's death was the central fact of Ted Hughes's life. However he tried to get away from it, he could not; however the biographer broadens the picture, it is her image that returns. In the letters of his final months, even after the expiation that came with *Birthday Letters*, Plath remains the most vivid presence in his mental world. So, for example, in a single sentence of luminous poetic prose in a long letter to his German translators who had sought advice on the meaning of various phrases in such poems as 'The Bee God', Ted explains how the image 'Your page a dark swarm':

> brings together SP bending over the bees (bending over the beehive with its roof off), SP bending over her page (where the letters as she composed writhed and twisted, superimposed on each other, displacing each other), her page, as a seething mass and depth and compound ball of living ideas – carrying, some-where in the heart of it, in the heart of the words, of the phrases, of the poetic whole struggling to form itself, the vital nuclei of her poetic operation – her 'self' and her 'Daddy' – and finally, her poem (in process of composition there on her page as she bends over it) as a swarm of bees clinging under a blossoming bough.

'The lit blossom', he writes, 'is also SP's face.'[63] It is as if Sylvia instead of the thought-fox has entered the room and is bending over Ted as he writes. Her face is radiant. Her ghost has returned in recognition of the knowledge that he loved her until the day he died. Before him stands yesterday.

Notes

Place of publication is London unless otherwise stated.

Abbreviations

BL – British Library

CP – Ted Hughes, *Collected Poems*, ed. Paul Keegan (Faber & Faber; New York: Farrar, Straus & Giroux, 2003)

CPSP – Sylvia Plath, *Collected Poems*, ed. with an introduction by Ted Hughes (New York: Harper & Row, 1981)

Emory – Manuscript, Archives, and Rare Book Library, Emory University, Atlanta, Georgia

JSP – *The Unabridged Journals of Sylvia Plath 1950–1962*, ed. Karen V. Kukil (New York: Anchor, 2000)

L – *Letters of Ted Hughes*, selected by and ed. Christopher Reid (Faber & Faber, 2007; New York: Farrar, Straus & Giroux, 2008)

SGCB – Ted Hughes, *Shakespeare and the Goddess of Complete Being* (Faber & Faber; New York: Farrar, Straus & Giroux, 1992)

SPLH – Sylvia Plath, *Letters Home*, selected and ed. with commentary by Aurelia Schober Plath (New York: Harper & Row, 1975; repr. Bantam Books, 1977)

WP – Ted Hughes, *Winter Pollen: Occasional Prose*, ed. William Scammell (Faber & Faber, 1994; New York: Picador USA, 1995)

All Sylvia Plath quotations are from American editions published by Harper & Row (now HarperCollins).

Prologue: The Deposition

1. 'Deposition of Edward James Hughes', before the United States Federal District Court, District of Massachusetts, copy now held in the Jane V. Anderson Papers, Mortimer Rare Book Room, Neilson Library, Smith College. Public-domain document quoted under the United States Right of Public Access to Judicial Proceedings and Records.

2. '9 Willow Street', in Ted Hughes, *Birthday Letters* (Faber & Faber, 1998), pp. 71–4. Hughes was a habitual reviser. Many of his poems have minor variations as they move through periodical publication, limited private-press edition and trade-book form. Normally, I quote from the version in the first published text, though revisions are sometimes noted. For convenience, I give page references to CP. Thus '9 Willow Street', CP 1087.

3. 'That Morning' was Hughes's contribution to *A Garland for the Laureate* (1981), a privately printed volume presented to Sir John Betjeman on his seventy-fifth birthday; it then appeared in the *London Review of Books* on 3 December 1981 and in *New Selected Poems* (New York: Harper & Row, 1982) and *Selected Poems 1957–1981* (Faber & Faber, 1982), before finding its true home in *River* (Faber & Faber, 1983).

4. Quoted from the memorial stone in Westminster Abbey, a monument in the public domain.

5. L 514. Where possible, letters cited from this edition have been checked against their holograph originals and, where appropriate, omitted passages have been restored.

6. A meeting noted by Plath in her appointments diary, but unnoticed by her biographers prior to the opening of the Anderson Papers in 2012.

7. 'Deposition of Jane V. Anderson', before the United States Federal District Court, District of Massachusetts, copy now held in the Anderson Papers. Public-domain document quoted under the United States Right of Public Access to Judicial Proceedings and Records.

8. Victor A. Kovner, in 'Libel in Fiction: The Sylvia Plath Case and its Aftermath', *Columbia-VLA Journal of Law and the Arts*, 11 (1987), p. 473.

9. *New York Times*, 21 Jan 1987.

10. In Chapter 26, 'Trial', below.

11. Lois Ames, 'Sylvia Plath: A Biographical Note', in Sylvia Plath, *The Bell Jar* (New York: Harper & Row, 1971), p. 203.

12. Opening paragraph of *The Bell Jar*.

13. Hughes Deposition, p. 67.

14. Sylvia Plath, *Ariel* (Faber & Faber, 1965).

15. 'Ted Hughes/Sylvia Plath: The Bell Jar legal case', BL Add. MS 88993.

16. To Victor Kovner, 7 Feb 1987, quoted, Roy Davids, 'The Making of Birthday Letters', roydavids.com/birthday.htm (accessed 12 Jan 2014).

17. 'Voices and Visions: Sylvia Plath', broadcast on American PBS, 21 April 1988, available (in 2014) at youtube.com/watch?v=wmamNSa3sP8.

18. Quotations from 'They are crawling all over the church', unpublished fragment of long poem among *Birthday Letters* drafts (BL Add. MS 88918/1).

19. Roy Davids, 'Memories, Reflections, Gratitudes', in Nick Gammage, ed., *The Epic Poise: A Celebration of Ted Hughes* (Faber & Faber, 1999), p. 188.

20. Lecture at the Dartington Way with Words Festival, July 2007, published as 'Suffering and Decision', in Mark Wormald, Neil Roberts and Terry Gifford, eds, *Ted Hughes: From Cambridge to Collected* (Basingstoke: Palgrave Macmillan, 2013), pp. 221–37.

21. After hearing the lecture, I put the Wordsworth parallel to Heaney: he immediately acknowledged it, but said that he had not seen it.

22. Heaney, 'Suffering and Decision', p. 233.

23. Wendy Cope, *Making Cocoa for Kingsley Amis* (Faber & Faber, 1986), p. 47.

24. Philip Larkin, *Selected Letters* (Faber & Faber, 1993), p. 581.

25. Ted Hughes Papers 1940–1997, Emory 644/4 (Incoming Correspondence, 13 June 1975, 8 Nov 1982).

26. 'The Jaguar', 'Pike', 'The Thought-Fox', 'Hawk Roosting', 'Last Letter'.

27. Written in 1958; Olwyn Hughes Papers (BL Add. MS 88948/1).

28. Lucas Myers, *Crow Steered, Bergs Appeared: A Memoir of Ted Hughes and Sylvia Plath* (Sewanee, Tenn.: Proctor's Hall Press, 2001), p. 2.

29. 'Money my enemy', Olwyn Hughes Papers (Emory 980/2/2).

30. Robert Graves, a key influence, was a precedent for a life of writing and nothing but writing, but he resorted to novels and potboilers in a way that Hughes did not. The other, though short-lived, exemplar was a Welshman, Dylan Thomas.

31. In the light of this, I refer throughout this book to the contents of this particular box file as Hughes's 'journal'. See further, Roy Davids, 'Ted Hughes Archive, The Final Portion: Papers of Ted Hughes mostly arranged in standard filing boxes, folders and cardboard boxes still in his possession at his death', ted-hughes.info/uploads/media/The_Ted_Hughes_Archive_at_The_British_Library.pdf, from which the examples listed here are taken. This was Davids's catalogue for the sale of the (second) archive to the British Library. The collection is now catalogued rather differently, with much of the journal-style material having been rearranged.

32. The centrality of fishing to Hughes's life and work, together with the revelatory quality of his unpublished fishing diaries, is the subject of a major forthcoming book by Mark Wormald of Pembroke College, Cambridge.

33. The exception is Andrew Wilson's excellent *Mad Girl's Love Song* (Simon & Schuster, 2013), which self-consciously breaks the mould by focusing exclusively on Plath's 'Life before Ted'.

34. Philip Davis, *Bernard Malamud: A Writer's Life* (Oxford: Oxford University Press, 2007), p. vii.

35. Heaney, interviewed at the Bloomsbury Hotel, London, 27 Oct 2009.

36. BL Add. MS 88918/129.

37. Yeats's essay 'At Stratford-on-Avon', quoted, SGCB xvii.

38. Personal communication.

39. 'Child's Park', CP 1087.

Chapter 1: 'fastened into place'

1. When the film *Sylvia* (2003) was shown at the Picture House 2 miles down the road in Hebden Bridge, there was a 'sharp and reproachful' intake of collective audience breath when Daniel Craig, playing the part of Ted Hughes opposite Gwyneth Paltrow's Sylvia Plath, said that he was from 'myth-olm-royd': John Billingsley, *A Laureate's Landscape: Walks around Ted Hughes' Mytholmroyd* (Hebden Bridge: Northern Earth Books, 2007), p. 41.

2. Opening of 'The Rock', BBC radio talk, printed in Geoffrey Summerfield, ed., *Worlds: Seven Modern Poets* (Harmondsworth: Penguin, 1974), pp. 122–7. This publication was accompanied by Fay Godwin photographs. For original broadcast and publication, see note 5, below.

3. Ibid., p. 123.

4. Ibid., p. 124. Olwyn Hughes has no memory of this story and denies that Ted knew it, despite his explicit account in 'The Rock'.

5. Broadcast 11 Sept 1963; published in the *Listener*, 19 Sept, then collected in *Writers on Themselves* (BBC Books, 1964).

6. Plath's working title was 'Landscape of a Childhood'. See Gail Crowther and Peter K. Steinberg, 'These Ghostly Archives' in the online journal *Plath Profiles*, 2, scholarworks.iu.edu/journals/index.php/plath/article/view/4745/4380.

7. BBC radio talk, 'Ocean 1212-W', repr. in Sylvia Plath, *Johnny Panic and the Bible of Dreams and Other Prose Writings* (Faber & Faber, 1977, 2nd edn 1979; New York: Harper & Row, 1980), pp. 117–24. Hughes's note in this edition misdates the broadcast to 1962: perhaps it was too painful to remember that it went out posthumously.

8. William Wordsworth, *The Prelude* (1805 version), 2.232.

9. 'Wild Rock', in *Remains of Elmet: A Pennine Sequence* (Faber & Faber, 1979; New York: Harper & Row, 1979) (CP 464).

10. 'Climbing into Heptonstall', in *Wolfwatching* (Faber & Faber, 1989; New York: Farrar, Straus & Giroux, 1991) (CP 750). First published in *London Review of Books*, 19 June 1986.

11. 'Mount Zion', in *Remains of Elmet* (CP 480). First published in *Encounter*, Dec 1977.

12. Edith (Farrar) Hughes, 'Past and Present' (1965), unfinished holograph manuscript, Olwyn Hughes Papers (Emory 980/2), quoted by kind permission of Olwyn Hughes.

13. Or did it really? At eighty-five, Olwyn was more sceptical: 'That we believed astrology is ridiculous. We are not stupid. But it was a charming old craze and as material to indulge in – the planets all given meanings and so on – we were charmed with it and interested to see what it showed (if anything). Just a game really' (Olwyn Hughes to Jonathan Bate, 22 Jan 2014). Despite such protestations, Olwyn insisted on casting this biographer's horoscope before agreeing to co-operate.

14. To Leonard Clark, letter of 1974, Berg Collection, New York Public Library. Cited by Diane Middlebrook, *Her Husband: Hughes and Plath – A*

Marriage (Little, Brown, 2004), p. 51. My interpretation is derived from Olwyn Hughes, 'Corrections of Diane Middlebrook's Her Husband', Olwyn Hughes Papers (Emory 980/2).

15. 'Superstitions', book review of 1964 (WP 51).

16. Ibid.

17. He was Willie to the family, Billie or Billy to his wife Edith, Bill in later years.

18. To Keith Sagar, 18 July 1998 (L 724).

19. Included in *Lupercal* (CP 84). First published in the *Spectator* on 4 July 1958 and read in the BBC Third Programme on 27 Aug 1958.

20. To Sagar (L 724).

21. Epigraph to 'The Martyrdom of Bishop Farrar', read in the BBC Third Programme series *The Poet's Voice*; published as closing poem of *The Hawk in the Rain* (Faber & Faber, 1957).

22. 'Little Gidding', in T. S. Eliot, *Four Quartets* (Faber & Faber, 1944). Hughes's 'Nicholas Ferrer' was in his second collection, *Lupercal* (CP 69–70).

23. Olwyn remembers the story vividly; Ted records it in his short story 'The Deadfall'.

24. Reminiscences from a series of interviews with Olwyn Hughes, 2010–14.

25. Edith remembered her sister's age of death as eighteen, but Miriam was born in July 1896.

26. Note to *Three Books* (Faber & Faber, 1993) version of *Remains of Elmet* (p. 183).

27. 'Sacrifice', CP 759. Ted's cousin Vicky still remembers hers.

28. His daughter's phrase: Vicky Watling (interviewed 31 March 2010), who also provided some of the other details in the remainder of this chapter.

29. Edith's memoir, 'Past and Present'.

Chapter 2: Capturing Animals

1. 'Dumpy' is Seamus Heaney's recollection of her (interview at Bloomsbury Hotel). He could not understand how Sylvia Plath could have been jealous of Moira (see Chapter 11, 'Famous Poet', below).

2. Hughes's radio plays *The Coming of the Kings* (Nov–Dec 1964) and *The Tiger's Bones* (Nov 1965) were also broadcast under the banner of *Listening and Writing*.

3. Initial print run of 4,000 in December 1967; reprint of 6,250 copies in 1968; paperback initial run of 6,000 copies in 1969, reprint of 8,000 copies in 1970, 10,000 in 1973, over 10,000 in 1975; subsequent reprints every three or four years through the Eighties. The omitted talk, about birds (including Hughes's own 'Hawk Roosting', Edward Thomas's 'The Owl' and Yeats's 'Wild Swans at Coole'), was called 'Creatures of the Air'.

4. Ted Hughes, *Poetry in the Making: An Anthology of Poems and Programmes from 'Listening and Writing'* (Faber & Faber, 1967), pp. 11–13. Revised American edition: *Poetry Is* (New York: Doubleday, 1970).

5. Ibid., p. 15.

6. Gerald Hughes, *Ted and I: A Brother's Memoir* (Robson Press, 2012), p. 20.

7. See 'The Ancient Briton Lay under his Rock', in *Remains of Elmet* (CP 481).

8. This paragraph is based on Olwyn's reminiscences.

9. Letter to Donald Crossley, 21 Jan 1985, private collection.

10. Gerald Hughes to Donald Crossley, 21 April 2005, private collection.

11. Gerald Hughes, *Ted and I*, p. 56.

12. Michael Morpurgo, ed., *Ghostly Haunts* (Pavilion Books, in association with the National Trust, 1994). 'The Deadfall' repr. in Ted Hughes, *Difficulties of a Bridegroom: Collected Short Stories* (Faber & Faber, 1995), pp. 1–19.

13. Ibid., p. ix. Ted to Keith Sagar, 19 Oct 1995: 'Yes, I have the ivory fox. Let you see it some day.' In Keith Sagar, ed., *Poet and Critic: The Letters of Ted Hughes and Keith Sagar* (British Library, 2012), p. 249. Is this a tease or has Ted genuinely convinced himself of the story of the fox's origin?

14. *Difficulties of a Bridegroom*, p. ix.

15. *Poetry in the Making*, p. 33.

16. Wordsworth, *The Prelude* (1805 version), 11.258–79.

17. *Poetry in the Making*, p. 57.

18. In his collected short stories, Hughes describes 'The Head' (1978) as 'the finale' of the sequence to which 'The Deadfall' was overture. 'These nine pieces', he says, 'hang together, in my own mind, as an accompaniment to my poems' (*Difficulties of a Bridegroom*, pp. vii–ix).

19. *Poetry in the Making*, p. 17.

20. Ibid., p. 17.

21. Ibid., p. 81.

22. Ibid., p. 104. Poems from *Meet My Folks!* quoted in *Poetry in the Making*.

23. Ibid., p. 102. Poems from *Meet My Folks!* quoted in *Poetry in the Making*.

24. 'The Thought-Fox', in ibid., pp. 19–20 (CP 21). First published in the *New Yorker*, 31 Aug 1957.

Chapter 3: Tarka, Rain Horse, Pike

1. L 692–3.

2. Emory 980/2.

3. Ted Hughes, 'Tarka the Otter, by Henry Williamson', *Sunday Times Colour Supplement*, 16 Sept 1962, p. 18. One of a series of introductions to children's classics, or rather classics suitable for children, especially boys. The others were Antoine de Saint-Exupéry's *The Little Prince*, Kenneth Grahame's *The Wind in the Willows*, Apsley Cherry-Garrard's *The Worst Journey in the World*, and H. G. Wells's *The War of the Worlds* (the copy of another Wells story, *The Time Machine*, that Hughes borrowed from the Mexborough school library when in 'Form 3A' has recently turned up, mylifeinknitwear.com/ted-hughes-lives-here/).

4. Henry Williamson, *Tarka the Otter* (1927; repr. Penguin Modern Classics, 2009), ch. 9.

5. Brenda Hedden, the girlfriend who sometimes accompanied him, recalls that Williamson took the senior role and often read from his works at great length.

6. Ted Hughes, *Henry Williamson: A Tribute by Ted Hughes Given at the Service of Thanksgiving at the Royal Parish Church of St Martin-in-the-Fields 1 December 1977* (Rainbow Press, 1979); repr. as 'Address Given at the Memorial Service', in *Henry Williamson: The Man, the Writings: A Symposium* (Padstow: Tabb House, 1980), pp. 159–65.

7 L 686.

8. Henry Williamson, *The Patriot's Progress* (1930; repr. Stroud: Sutton, 2004), 'Third Phase', p. 86.

9. Hughes, 'Address Given at the Memorial Service', pp. 161–2. See further, Yvonne Reddick's excellent essay, 'Henry Williamson and Ted Hughes: Politics, Nationhood, and Nature Writing', *English*, 62:213 (Winter 2013), pp. 353–74.

10. Hughes, 'Address Given at the Memorial Service', p. 162.

11. See further my *The Song of the Earth* (Picador, 2000; Cambridge, Mass.: Harvard University Press, 2000), especially its final chapter.

12. L 624–5.

13. Ted Hughes, interviewed by Drue Heinz, 'The Art of Poetry: LXXI', *Paris Review*, 37:134 (Spring 1995), p. 60. This key interview is available at theparisreview.org/interviews/1669/the-art-of-poetry-no-71-ted-hughes.

14. Gerald Hughes, *Ted and I*, p. 111.

15. David Smart, 'John Fisher at Mexborough Grammar School: A Memoir', Mexborough and District Heritage Society website, June 2011, joseflocke.co.uk/heritage/MGS02.htm.

16. Alan Johnson, a close friend in the sixth form, quoted in Steve Ely's excellent 'Ted Hughes's South Yorkshire', *Ted Hughes Society Journal*, 3:1 (2013), pp. 26–36.

17. L 625.

18. Ely, 'Ted Hughes's South Yorkshire', p. 35, citing an interview with fellow-pupil Geoffrey Griffiths.

19. Hughes passed this at 'subsidiary standard' in June 1949, a year after his other Higher exams.

20. Donald Crossley (also a neighbour), personal communication.

21. 'Sacrifice', CP 760.

22. *Paris Review* interview, p. 58.

23. 'Notes on Published Works', March 1992 (Emory 644/115).

24. To Keith Sagar, 4 April 1990, in Keith Sagar, ed., *Poet and Critic: The Letters of Ted Hughes and Keith Sagar* (British Library, 2012), p. 181.

25. Donald Crossley, personal communication.

26. 'Ted and Crookhill', handwritten memoir by Edna Wholey, 30 July 2000 ('Ted Hughes Letters to Edna Wholey', Emory 870/1), to which I also owe much of the detail in this section.

27. *Paris Review* interview, pp. 60–1.

28. L 3.

29. Ted Hughes, *Poetry in the Making: An Anthology of Poems and Programmes from 'Listening and Writing'* (Faber & Faber, 1967), p. 21.

30. 'So Quickly It's Over', interview with Ted Hughes, *Wild Steelhead and Salmon*, Winter 1999, p. 50.
31. Published by the Appledore Press, Devon (1982) in an edition of just twenty-six copies (price £300), in the form of six sheets, each being a facsimile of Hughes's holograph of a single stanza of the poem with accompanying lithograph by his Irish fishing companion Barrie Cooke. Text reprinted in *London Review of Books*, Dec 1982.
32. L 287.

Chapter 4: Goddess

1. See Colin Wilcockson, 'Ted Hughes' Undergraduate Years at Pembroke College, Cambridge: Some Myths Demystified', *Agenda*, 44:4/45:1 (Winter 2009), pp. 147–53, and Neil Roberts, 'Ted Hughes and Cambridge', in Mark Wormald, Neil Roberts and Terry Gifford, eds, *Ted Hughes: From Cambridge to Collected* (Basingstoke: Palgrave Macmillan, 2013), pp. 17–18.
2. Recollection of another local girl, Enid Wilkinson, quoted in Olivia Cole, 'Found after 50 years: first love poems of Ted Hughes', *Sunday Times*, 13 Aug 2006.
3. To Tom Paulin, 17 May 1994 (Emory 880/3).
4. See especially the manuscript poem 'Summer she goes' (Emory 644/84).
5. Loose leaf dating *Hawk in the Rain* poems, with Jean Findlay identified as 'J.F.' (BL Add. MS 88918/7); Hughes wrote 'June 13th 59' but clearly meant either '49' or '50'; a transcription of the datings in a copy of *Hawk* now at Worcester Polytechnic Institute, Massachusetts, gives 16 June 1949; see also L 617–18. His memories of dates of composition are an odd mix of precision and error. Assuming the poem genuinely was written during National Service, it must have been June 1950, not 1949, since he did not join up until October 1949.
6. 'Song', in *The Hawk in the Rain* (CP 24).
7. Christmas 1946, Olwyn Hughes Papers (BL Add. MS 88948/4).
8. L 204, explicitly citing Jung.
9. E. J. Hughes's RAF Discharge (Emory 644/180).
10. Inscribed: 'Edward J. Hughes, to celebrate "going up." October 1951, with all good wishes, John Fisher' (Emory University, PR6013.R35 W58 1948 HUGHES).
11. Robert Graves, *The White Goddess: A Historical Grammar of Poetic Myth* (Faber & Faber, 1948); all above quotations from ch. 1, 'Poets and Gleemen'.
12. Hughes to Graves, 20 July 1967 (L 273), on thanking him for taking part in the Poetry International Festival. Canellun Collection of Robert Graves Manuscripts, St John's College Library, Oxford, CC-0234-001.
13. Graves, *The White Goddess*, ch. 22, 'The Triple Muse'.

Chapter 5: Burnt Fox

1. Glen Fallows, 'Reminiscences', *Martlet* (alumni magazine of Pembroke College, Cambridge, 1999), p. 8; Philip Hobsbaum, 'Ted Hughes at Cambridge', *The Dark Horse*, 8 (1999), pp. 6–12.

2. Hughes had a story of their one meeting: he was walking along a London street wearing his trademark greatcoat when a drunken and dyspeptic Waugh staggered out of his club, looked him up and down, took him for some sort of radical, said 'I don't like the cut of your jib,' and spat at him. This may be apocryphal. Years later, shortly after the publication of *Birthday Letters*, Waugh's son Auberon, a familiar figure on the London literary scene, thundered from his pulpit in the *Literary Review* to the effect that Hughes was a 'rotten poet' who wrote 'pretentious drivel' in abhorrent free verse. Hughes sent him a graceful postcard and a photocopy of an essay on verse form in *Winter Pollen*, together with the comment that he was a Tyndale man whereas Auberon was a Thomas More man. Auberon responded by thanking him for his 'extraordinarily good-natured response to my unmannerly tirade' and expressing the hope that they might one day meet again and sink their differences over some good wine. I am most grateful to Alexander Waugh for sight of this unpublished exchange.

3. Unpublished memoir of Hughes by Terence McCaughey, read publicly by Carol Hughes, Pembroke College, Cambridge, 17 Sept 2010.

4. Brian Cox, 'Ted Hughes (1930–1998): A Personal Retrospect', *Hudson Review*, 52:1 (Spring 1999), pp. 29–43 (pp. 30–1). Cox was two years ahead of Hughes, but stayed on at Pembroke to do graduate work.

5. To Olwyn (L 20).

6. During his second term as a freshman (L 12).

7. He told his Australian friend Jennifer Rankin that he was often mistaken for Dexter (draft manuscript of a radio talk about Ted, Jennifer Rankin Papers, University of New South Wales, Australian Defence Force Academy Library, MS 348). But Dexter, 'Lord Ted', as he was known, went up to Cambridge the year after Hughes went down, so if the encounter(s) did take place, this would have been when Hughes was back in Cambridge after graduating.

8. 'Words and Experience', in Ted Hughes, *Poetry in the Making: An Anthology of Poems and Programmes from 'Listening and Writing'* (Faber & Faber, 1967), p. 121.

9. Olwyn Hughes Papers (Emory 980/1).

10. Daniel Huws, *Memories of Ted Hughes 1952–1963* (Nottingham: Richard Hollis, 2010), p. 13.

11. Accounts of the burnt-fox dream from letter to Keith Sagar, 16 July 1979 (Keith Sagar, ed., *Poet and Critic: The Letters of Ted Hughes and Keith Sagar* (British Library, 2012), pp. 74–6, the fullest version); letter to Seamus Heaney, Emory 960/40; 'The Burnt Fox', WP 8–9; and Cox, 'Ted Hughes (1930–1998)', pp. 33–4.

12. Syllabus for Archaeology and Anthropology Part I, in *Student's Handbook to Cambridge 1953–4* (Cambridge: Cambridge University Press, 1953), pp. 148–9.

13. Huws, *Memories of Ted Hughes*, p. 18, adding, 'The two splayed wings of the building, the vaginal entrance and the phallic tower had some complementary suggestiveness.' Many students over the years have been struck by the phallic mass of the UL tower, which allegedly held pornographic materials in a closed stack at the top.

14. Part 6 of Bronisław Malinowski, *Coral Gardens and their Magic: A Study of the Methods of Tilling the Soil and of Agricultural Rites in the Trobriand Islands* (George Allen & Unwin, 1935).

15. Hobsbaum, 'Ted Hughes at Cambridge', p. 7.

16. *delta*, 5:12 (Spring 1955) (CP 11).

17. Huws, *Memories of Ted Hughes*, p. 20.

18. *Chequer*, 7.2 (Nov 1954) (CP 10).

19. Hughes's file in the Pembroke College Archive. 'The Tutor' at Pembroke was the Senior Tutor, responsible both for discipline and for the overall progress of all undergraduates.

20. Cox, 'Ted Hughes (1930–1998)', p. 32.

21. Huws, *Memories of Ted Hughes*, p. 16.

22. L 25.

Chapter 6: 'a compact index of everything to follow'

1. 'Paris 1954', in *Howls and Whispers* (Northampton, Mass.: Gehenna Press, 1998) (CP 1173).

2. See letter from Ted to Olwyn (BL Add. MS 88948/1).

3. BL Add. MS 88918/129.

4. To Gerald and his family, 16 Oct 1954 (L 26).

5. Lucas Myers Papers at Emory 865/1.

6. Boddy's reminiscences are recorded in Elaine Feinstein, *Ted Hughes: The Life of a Poet* (Weidenfeld & Nicolson, 2001), pp. 41–4. This book, as much memoir as biography, is at its best on Hughes's Cambridge friendships.

7. Lucas Myers, *An Essential Self: Ted Hughes and Sylvia Plath* (Nottingham: Richard Hollis, 2011), pp. 19–20.

8. May/June 1955 (L 28).

9. See Nicholas Wroe, 'Speaking of foreign tongues' (interview with Weissbort), *Guardian*, 30 June 2001.

10. Myers, *Essential Self*, p. 16.

11. Ibid., p. 24.

12. See Neil Roberts, *A Lucid Dreamer: The Life of Peter Redgrove* (Jonathan Cape, 2012), p. 89.

13. Philip Hobsbaum, 'Ted Hughes at Cambridge', *The Dark Horse*, 8 (1999), p. 10, misquoting 'dark' as 'darkness'.

14. Helen Melody, 'Rediscovered: the earliest recording of Ted Hughes?', britishlibrary.typepad.co.uk/english-and-drama/2013/10/rediscovered-the-earliest-recording-of-ted-hughes.html. The tape was discovered by Peter Redgrove's wife, Penelope Shuttle. It may well be that the readings were rehearsals for Redgrove's and Hughes's BBC radio auditions in September 1956. The Hughes poems on the recording were included in *Hawk in the*

Rain, save that the first half of one called 'Lust and Desire' was omitted. It remains unpublished, while the second half was renamed 'Incompatibilities'.

15. *A Group Anthology*, ed. Edward Lucie-Smith and Philip Hobsbaum (Oxford University Press, 1963), p. 47.

16. CP 25.

17. Untitled insert in the long poetic sequence of BL Add. MS 88918/1.

18. *Saint Botolph's Review*, Feb 1956, repr. in *Hawk in the Rain* (CP 29).

19. 27 June 1955 (BL Add. MS 88918/129).

20. Ted Hughes, *A Dancer to God: Tributes to T. S. Eliot* (Faber & Faber, 1992; New York: Farrar, Straus & Giroux, 1993), p. 20.

21. Ibid., pp. 5, 20–4.

22. Ibid., pp. 21, 44, 36.

23. Ibid., pp. 21, 44, 36.

24. Ibid., pp. 30–3.

25. *Poetry*, 88 (Aug 1956), pp. 295–7 (sent to the editor by Sylvia) (CP 13–15). Described by Dan Huws as the product of a challenge concocted by Luke Myers and Ted to write a poem with this title, and as Ted's 'first professional piece of work … his existential celebration of his relationship with Sylvia, but written for his friends' (Daniel Huws, *Memories of Ted Hughes 1952–1963* (Nottingham: Richard Hollis, 2010), p. 36).

26. Loose notebook leaves listing circumstances and dates of composition of early poems (BL Add. MS 88918/7).

27. Ted Hughes MS 1, Lilly Library, Indiana University, Bloomington (CP 19–20).

28. He often told the story, most fully in a 1990 letter to Sonnenberg, responding to the latter's memory of an earlier telling (L 586–7).

29. Ben Sonnenberg, *Lost Property: Memoirs and Confessions of a Bad Boy* (New York: Summit Books, 1991), p. 131.

30. The story is recounted in Jung's 1952 essay 'Synchronicity: An Acausal Connecting Principle'.

31. *Hawk in the Rain* version of 'The Jaguar' (CP 19).

32. BL Add. MS 88918/7.

Chapter 7: Falcon Yard

1. BL Add. MS 88918/129.

2. To McCaughey (L 35).

3. The above account is based on private reminiscences (telephone interview, 2 May 2015, and subsequent emails).

4. 'Stone Boy with Dolphin', in Sylvia Plath, *Johnny Panic and the Bible of Dreams and Other Prose Writings* (Faber & Faber, 1977, 2nd edn 1979; New York: Harper & Row, 1980), p. 297. This story is a chapter from her incomplete, and now lost, autobiographical novel 'Falcon Yard'.

5. Bertram Wyatt-Brown, 'Reuben Davis, Sylvia Plath and Other American Writers: The Perils of Emotional Struggle', in Peter Stearns and Jan Lewis, eds, *An Emotional History of the United States* (New York: New York University Press, 1998), p. 446.

6. Lucas Myers, *An Essential Self: Ted Hughes and Sylvia Plath* (Nottingham: Richard Hollis, 2011), p. 27.

7. The essay survives, with supervisor's comments, in the Lilly Library, Indiana University, Bloomington (Plath MSS II.13.2).

8. Plath, 'Stone Boy', p. 299.

9. JSP 211. Myers's poem was in *Saint Botolph's Review* (1956), p. 8.

10. Plath, 'Stone Boy', p. 297.

11. Ibid., p. 305.

12. JSP 211.

13. JSP 212.

14. JSP 212.

15. Plath, 'Stone Boy', p. 308.

16. Ibid., p. 309.

17. Ibid., p. 311.

18. Email from Jean Gooder to Jonathan Bate, 3 May 2015.

19. 'St Botolph's', in *Birthday Letters* (CP 1052).

20. JSP 44.

21. William Carlos Williams, in his poem 'To Elsie'.

22. Plath, 'Stone Boy', p. 309.

23. CP 1169–70.

24. Both poems were reprinted in *The Hawk in the Rain* (CP 41, 43).

25. *The Hawk in the Rain* (CP 42–7). This war sequence is, strictly speaking, not quite the ending of the collection. One further poem follows as a kind of epilogue: 'The Martyrdom of Bishop Farrar', which simultaneously invokes the old religious civil wars of the sixteenth century and Hughes's own maternal Farrar heritage.

26. The fullest and best account of Plath's 'life before Ted' is Andrew Wilson, *Mad Girl's Love Song: Sylvia Plath and Life before Ted* (Simon & Schuster, 2013).

27. JSP 212–14.

28. JSP 214.

29. To Aurelia Plath, 9 March 1956 (SPLH 249).

30. 'Pursuit', CPSP 22.

31. SPLH 249, 247.

32. 6 March 1956 (JSP 225).

33. L 37.

34. JSP 232–5; Lucas Myers, *Crow Steered, Bergs Appeared: A Memoir of Ted Hughes and Sylvia Plath* (Seewanee, Tenn.: Proctor's Hall Press, 2001), p. 35, and *Essential Self*, p. 28; 'Visit' in *Birthday Letters* is Hughes's version, recording his shock ten years after her death upon reading for the first time her journal account of her feelings that weekend.

35. Jane Baltzell Kopp, who also lodged at Whitstead, in '"Gone, Very Gone Youth": Sylvia Plath at Cambridge, 1955–1957', in Edward Butscher, ed., *Sylvia Plath: The Woman and the Work* (New York: Dodd, Mead, 1977; repr. Peter Owen, 1979), p. 63.

Chapter 8: 18 Rugby Street

1. Daniel Huws, *Memories of Ted Hughes 1952–1963* (Nottingham: Richard Hollis, 2010), p. 26.
2. JSP 552.
3. JSP 554.
4. JSP 563.
5. JSP 567.
6. '18 Rugby Street', CP 1055–8.
7. These lines were first published in their original verse form in Jonathan Bate, 'Sorrow in a Black Coat', *Times Literary Supplement*, 5 Feb 2014 (extract from 'Black Coat: Opus 131', BL Add. MS 88918/1).
8. L 37.
9. JSP 217.
10. JSP 553.
11. Sassoon's autobiographical story 'The Diagram', *Chicago Review*, 17:4 (1965), p. 111, quoted, Andrew Wilson, *Mad Girl's Love Song: Sylvia Plath and Life before Ted* (Simon & Schuster, 2013), much the fullest and best account of the relationship between Plath and Sassoon.
12. 9 April 1956 (L 38).
13. Emory 644/139.
14. 'Venus in the Seventh', draft chapter for 'Falcon Yard' (Emory 644/130/12).
15. JSP 570 (16 April 1956); SPLH 263 (19 April 1956).
16. JSP 570.
17. 'The first time I bought a bottle of wine' (BL Add. MS 88918/1).
18. 'Fidelity', in *Birthday Letters* (CP 1060).
19. Jane Baltzell Kopp, '"Gone, Very Gone Youth": Sylvia Plath at Cambridge 1955–1957', in Edward Butscher, ed., Sylvia Plath: The Woman and the Work (New York: Dodd, Mead, 1977; repr. Peter Owen, 1979)', p. 74.
20. Lucas Myers, *Crow Steered, Bergs Appeared: A Memoir of Ted Hughes and Sylvia Plath* (Seewanee, Tenn.: Proctor's Hall Press, 2001), p. 148.
21. SPLH 264, 265, 266.
22. SPLH 272.
23. SPLH 274.
24. SPLH 288.
25. 'I didn't even ask her to marry me. She suggested it as a good idea and I said OK, why not?' (to Aurelia Plath, Emory 644/18).
26. 'So Quickly It's Over', interview with Ted Hughes, *Wild Steelhead and Salmon*, Winter 1999, p. 51.
27. Emory 644/180.
28. 'A Pink Wool Knitted Dress', in *Birthday Letters* (CP 1064).
29. L 39.
30. SPLH 292–3.

Chapter 9: 'Marriage is my medium'

1. As noted in the Prologue, the story of Ted and Sylvia's years together has been told many times, most accurately, though not without errors of fact, in Anne Stevenson, *Bitter Fame: A Life of Sylvia Plath* (Viking, 1989; repr. Penguin, 1998), written with assistance from Olwyn and checked by Ted. In the following chapters, I am indebted to Stevenson, but have based my narrative on primary sources, in particular Sylvia Plath, *Letters Home* (SPLH), *The Unabridged Journals of Sylvia Plath 1950–1962* (JSP), Sylvia's unpublished letters, Ted's published and unpublished letters, and his unpublished journal entries, notebooks and pocket diaries, as well as his poetically reshaped memories in *Birthday Letters* and related poems. Specific references are given for all quotations.
2. 'Your Paris', CP 1065–7.
3. SPLH 298.
4. L 44.
5. JSP 240.
6. L 46.
7. 'Moonwalk', CP 1070.
8. Notes on *How the Whale Became* (Emory 744/115/6).
9. There are three fine drawings of Ted by Sylvia on the honeymoon. One is now in the National Portrait Gallery, one in the possession of Warren Plath, and the third (drawn in Paris, on the return journey) in the possession of Frieda Hughes, reproduced in her *Sylvia Plath: Drawings* (Faber & Faber, 2013), p. 25.
10. SPLH 298–9.
11. SPLH 300.
12. L 46.
13. JSP 259.
14. 'You Hated Spain', CP 1068. Plath's discomfort is apparent in her poems 'The Goring' and 'The Beggars'.
15. JSP 250.
16. Paul Alexander, *Rough Magic: A Biography of Sylvia Plath* (New York: Viking, 1991, repr. 1999), p. 194. The friend of Plath's from whom Alexander derived this story is not an entirely reliable source.
17. SPLH 304–5.
18. SPLH 305.
19. SPLH 306. In terms of the chronological run in the narrative of *Birthday Letters*, the poem 'Wuthering Heights' is misplaced insofar as it occurs after the poems about the following year in Cambridge ('55 Eltisley', 'Chaucer').
20. 'Wuthering Heights', CP 1080–2.
21. CPSP 71–2, 167–8.
22. SPLH 311.
23. 10 Oct 1956 (Plath MSS II, Lilly Library, Indiana University, Bloomington); 5 Oct 1956 (L 57–60).
24. Sylvia's letters to Ted remain in private hands. This one (7–8 Oct 1956) was published in *Sylvia Plath: Drawings*, pp. 2–4.

25. Olwyn Hughes, in Stevenson, *Bitter Fame*, p. 99.

26. SPLH 329.

27. Notes on *The Hawk in the Rain* (Emory 644/11).

28. SPLH (21 Nov 1956).

29. Plath to Marcia Brown Plumer, 4 Feb 1963 (Sylvia Plath Collection, Mortimer Rare Book Room, Smith College, MS 45, 16/3/13).

30. '55 Eltisley', CP 1073–4.

31. Plath to Marcia Brown Plumer, 9 April 1957 (Smith College MS 45, 16/3/15).

32. 23 Feb 1957 (L 94).

33. 24 Feb 1957 (SPLH 340).

34. L 98.

35. 'Chaucer', CP 1075–6.

36. Letter to Gerald and Joan Hughes, May 1957 (Emory 854/1).

37. L 97–8.

38. Olwyn Hughes, in Stevenson, *Bitter Fame*, p. 110.

39. To Olwyn, 20–3 June 1957, from on board ship (L 99–104).

40. JSP 302.

41. JSP 289.

42. L 104.

43. 'The Chipmunk', CP 1082–3.

44. To Gerald and Joan from Wellesley, late June 1957 (L 103).

45. 22 Aug 1957 (L 106).

46. To Gerald and Joan from Wellesley, late June 1957 (L 104).

47. JSP 296, inspiring Plath's 'Mussel Hunter at Rock Harbor' and Hughes's *Birthday Letters* poem 'Flounders'.

48. JSP 284.

49. JSP 285.

50. 20 July 1957 (JSP 289).

51. Ibid.

52. 'The Prism', CP 1162–3.

Chapter 10: 'So this is America'

1. JSP 305.

2. '18 Rugby Street', CP 1058.

3. JSP 302.

4. To Myers, Oct 1957 (L 110).

5. Ibid.

6. See 'Child's Park' in *Birthday Letters*.

7. It was reprinted in 1960, though not all copies of the first edition had sold by this time, so they were recycled bearing the dust wrapper of the second.

8. Sylvia to Ted's parents, 5 Nov 1957 (Emory 980/1).

9. Notes on *The Hawk in the Rain* (Emory 644/11).

10. L 111–12.

11. *New Statesman*, 28 Sept 1957.

12. To Myers, Oct 1957 (L 110).

13. nytimes.com/books/98/03/01/home/plath-hawk.html.
14. Sylvia to Olwyn, quoted, Anne Stevenson, *Bitter Fame: A Life of Sylvia Plath* (Viking, 1989, repr. Penguin, 1998), p. 117; Ted to Olwyn (BL Add. MS 88948/1).
15. L 112.
16. *Observer*, 6 Oct 1957.
17. CP 36.
18. CP 45–6.
19. Draft for 'The Hawk in the Rain', unbound notebook page (Emory 644/57). < > indicates an arrowed insertion.
20. Drafts for 'The Thought-Fox', in drafts, notes and corrected page proof of *The Hawk in the Rain*, in the Ted Hughes Papers MS 1, Lilly Library, Indiana University, Bloomington.
21. It is now in the Hughes Archive at Emory. On Ted's syllabus, see further Amanda Golden's excellent article 'Ted Hughes and the Midcentury American Academy', *Ted Hughes Society Journal*, 3:1 (2013), pp. 47–52.
22. To Huws, late Feb 1958 (L 120–1).
23. To Olwyn, late March 1958 (L 123).
24. Peter Davison, *The Fading Smile: Poets in Boston from Robert Frost to Robert Lowell to Sylvia Plath, 1955–1960* (New York: Alfred A. Knopf, 1994), p. 166.
25. 20 May 1959 (JSP 484–5).
26. 5 March 1958 (JSP 345–6).
27. 29 March 1958 (JSP 360–1).
28. JSP 388 (the performance was on 21 May 1958).
29. Amanda Golden, 'Ted Hughes, Isaac Bashevis Singer, and an Interview with Jules Chametzky', *Ted Hughes Society Journal*, 3:1 (2013), pp. 59–66, records the following memory of Chametzky, who arrived to teach at UMass Amherst the semester after Ted: 'I was visited by two senior students, officers in the then Literary Club ... [who] had studied with Ted Hughes the year before, when he had occupied the very office I was in. They both seemed to have a crush on Hughes. The older one named Susan Goldstein, about six feet tall, gave me a copy of Ted's first book – *The Hawk in the Rain*' (p. 64). Susan Goldstein is deceased.
30. 22 May 1958 (JSP 391).
31. BL Add. MS 88918/128.
32. 11 June 1958 (JSP 392). Plath biographers are not averse to turning the glass into Ted: 'He hit her hard enough that she saw stars' (Carl Rollyson, *American Isis: The Life and Art of Sylvia Plath* (New York: St Martin's Press, 2013), p. 155).
33. 11 June 1958 (JSP 392).
34. 27 Dec 1958 (JSP 447).
35. 7 July 1958 (JSP 401).
36. 9 July 1958 (JSP 403).
37. '9 Willow Street', CP 1087–90.

38. CP 1090–4.
39. 31 Dec 1958 (JSP 454).
40. 14 Sept 1958 (JSP 420).
41. 12 Dec 1958 (JSP 434).
42. Eliot to Hughes, 30 Oct 1958 (pasted by Sylvia into a blue scrapbook of memorabilia, Emory 644/OP103).
43. Early 1959 (L 139).
44. To Davison, 27 April 1959, in Davison, *The Fading Smile*, p. 166 (where the year is incorrectly remembered as 1958).
45. L 142.
46. John Summers, Obituary of Rollie McKenna, *Guardian*, 21 July 2003.
47. Robert Lowell, *Life Studies* (New York: Farrar, Straus & Giroux, 1959, repr. 1964), pp. 81–2.
48. To Weissbort, 21 March 1959 (L 140).
49. To Myers, 19 May 1959 (L 145).
50. To Myers, 19 June 1959 (L 146).
51. D. H. Lawrence, 'Figs', in *Birds, Beasts and Flowers* (Martin Secker, 1923).
52. To Baskin, July 1959 (L 147).
53. See Peter K. Steinberg, 'Did You Know … Sylvia Plath at Yaddo', Sylvia Plath Info Blog, 19 Nov 2014, sylviaplathinfo.blogspot.co. uk/2014_11_01_archive.html.
54. 'The Badlands', in *Birthday Letters* (CP 1095–8).
55. To his parents, from Yellowstone (Emory 980/1/18).
56. Ibid.
57. Sylvia to Aurelia and Warren Plath, 28 July 1959, from California, describing what she called the 'Bear Incident' in a long letter composed on the new typewriter that they took with them on their travels (Lilly Library, only partially printed in SPLH 402–4). Some details also taken from Ted's Yellowstone letter to his parents (partially printed in L 150–1).
58. Quoted phrase from Hughes, 'The 59th Bear', CP 1100–4.
59. Letter in Lilly Library, postscript not in SPLH extract.
60. Ibid.
61. 'Yogi Bear's Big Break', his debut episode, aired on the ABC network on 2 Oct 1958. Ted and Sylvia's television habits during their American residence are hard to reconstruct, but Sylvia was sufficiently in tune with popular culture to write in her journal on 31 May 1959, 'Last night I sent off my application from here for a TV writing grant … Money, money. I like CBS, too. They are more attentive than most stations' (JSP 487). Characteristically (and depressingly), Plath biographers tend to read the name of Norton in 'The Fifty-Ninth Bear' as the articulation of a murderous impulse towards either her ex-boyfriend Dick Norton or Ted (or both), rather than a jokey allusion to Yogi Bear.
62. Sylvia Plath, 'The Fifty-Ninth Bear' (1959), in *Johnny Panic and the Bible of Dreams and Other Prose Writings* (Faber & Faber, 1977, rev. edn 1979; New York: Harper & Row, 1980), p. 98.
63. CP 1103.

64. Sylvia to Aurelia and Warren Plath, 28 July 1959 (Plath MSS II, Lilly Library).

65. Sylvia to her mother and brother (ibid.); Ted to his parents (Emory 980/1).

66. Draft in red exercise book (BL Add. MS 88918/1).

67. To his parents (Emory 980/1).

68. 'Grand Canyon', CP 1104–6.

69. yaddo.org/yaddo/history.shtml.

70. 10 Sept 1959 (SPLH 407).

71. 'Portraits', in *Birthday Letters* (CP 1109–11).

72. See further, Jeremy Treglown's fine article 'Howard's Way: Painting Sylvia Plath', *Times Literary Supplement*, 30 Aug 2013, p. 13.

73. Ted's working draft is preserved in BL Add. MS 88918/9.

74. 7 Oct 1959 (SPLH 409).

75. JSP 207.

76. JSP 516, 517, 520.

77. JSP 514, 518.

78. SPLH 411.

79. L 153.

80. 9 March 1959 (JSP 473).

81. Ibid.

82. CPSP 119–20.

83. 'Black Coat', in *Birthday Letters* (CP 1108–9).

Chapter 11: Famous Poet

1. L 170–7.

2. 4 Oct 1959 (JSP 513–14).

3. Olwyn Hughes, in Anne Stevenson, *Bitter Fame: A Life of Sylvia Plath* (Viking, 1989; repr. Penguin, 1998), pp. 176–7.

4. SPLH 416–17.

5. SPLH 423.

6. 'Isis', in *Birthday Letters* (CP 1114).

7. Lucas Myers, *Crow Steered, Bergs Appeared: A Memoir of Ted Hughes and Sylvia Plath* (Seewanee, Tenn.: Proctor's Hall Press, 2001), p. 77.

8. SPLH 424.

9. Stevenson, *Bitter Fame*, pp. 185–7; letter from Janet Crosbie-Hill to *New Review*, June 1976; unpublished letter from Olwyn Hughes to Jonathan Bate, 2 Jan 2014.

10. To Myers, 22 Apr 1960 (L 158–9). Ted remembered the birth in a lovely poem called 'Delivering Frieda', later revised as 'Remission' in *Birthday Letters* (CP 1113–14).

11. Ted and Sylvia to Olwyn, 2 April 1960 (Emory 980/1).

12. SPLH 440.

13. L 148.

14. Loose-leaf listing of dates and places of composition (BL Add. MS 88918/7). 'Crag Jack's Apostasy' was the one poem written (on the guest-room bed) in Aurelia Plath's house in Elmwood Road, Wellesley.

It is neat that a poem inspired by a Hughes ancestor was written in the Plath house.

15. Ted Hughes MS 1, Lilly Library, Indiana University, Bloomington. The manuscript actually combines pages from 'The Feast of Lupercal' with some from the collection that Sylvia was putting together at the time, which, the manuscript reveals, she titled 'New Poems 1958', then 'The Bull of Bendylaw', then 'The Devil of the Stairs'. The sheaf of paper thus has one page reading simply 'To Sylvia' (his dedication) and another reading simply 'For Ted' (hers).
16. CP 82–3; Emory 644/59.
17. Samuel Johnson, 'Life of Cowley', in *Lives of the Most Eminent English Poets* (1779–81); Hughes, 'Notes on Lupercal' (Ted Hughes MS 1, Lilly Library).
18. CP 84–5.
19. Ibid.
20. CP 68–9; 'Notes on Lupercal' (Lilly Library).
21. L 244 (programme transmitted 3 Sept 1965).
22. Interviewed by Ekbert Faas, in *Ted Hughes: The Unaccommodated Universe* (Santa Barbara, Calif.: Black Sparrow Press, 1980), p. 199.
23. *Queen*, 15 March 1960, p. 140.
24. 'Poetic force refined by deep thought', Halifax *Daily Courier and Guardian*, 18 March 1960.
25. *Observer*, 27 March 1960.
26. *Times Literary Supplement*, 15 April 1960, unsigned review by G. S. Fraser.
27. *Spectator*, 22 April 1960.
28. Kenneth Young, 'Poet from the Pennines', *Daily Telegraph*, 14 April 1960.
29. Philip Booth, 'The instinct to survive', *New York Times*, 14 Aug 1960.
30. *Harper's Magazine*, Sept 1960, p. 103.
31. *Observer*, 18 Dec 1960. Ted kept his review clippings. Those for *Lupercal* are gathered at Emory 644/175.
32. To Olwyn, May 1960 (L 159–60).
33. To the Merwins, June 1960 (L 162–3).
34. To Olwyn (Emory 980/1).
35. L 165–6; SPLH 448–9.
36. Olwyn Hughes to Jonathan Bate, 2 Jan 2014.
37. The other two were Ted and Assia Wevill. Susan Alliston was just possibly a fourth.
38. Sylvia's version of the Christmas row is in a letter to her mother: Sylvia to Aurelia, 1 Jan 1961 (unpublished passages of letter in Lilly Library). Olwyn's is in Stevenson, *Bitter Fame*, pp. 203–4 (supplemented by personal communication). Both women had fierce tempers and were capable of exaggerating slights, so neither's version can necessarily be trusted in every particular.
39. BL Add. MS 88918/128. Journal entries on torn notebook sheets.
40. Ibid., 26 Dec 1960.
41. Ibid., 3 Jan 1961.
42. Ibid., 2 April 1962.

43. Plath, 'Tulips', 18 March 1961; Hughes journal, 12 April 1961.

44. Broadcast 31 Jan 1961. Available on CD, *The Spoken Word: Sylvia Plath* (BBC/British Library, 2010).

45. Letter from Frances to David McCullough, 7 July 1974 (Frances McCullough Papers, University of Maryland, hdl.handle.net/1903.1/4603).

46. 28 Feb 1961 (JSP 601).

47. 5 March 1961 (JSP 605).

48. Plath to Dorothy Benotti, 29 March 1961 (Sylvia Plath Collection, Mortimer Rare Book Room, Smith College, MS 45, 16/2).

49. Mentioned in a letter to John Fisher and family, April 1961.

50. 'The Gypsy', in *Birthday Letters* (CP 117–18).

51. Myers, *Crow Steered*, p. 78.

52. Olwyn Hughes to Jonathan Bate, 2 Jan 2014.

53. Ibid.

Chapter 12: The Grass Blade

1. Emory 980/1.

2. 'The Table', CP 1132–4.

3. Hughes journal, 11 Sept 1961.

4. 'Notes on the Chronological Order of Sylvia Plath's Poems', in *The Art of Sylvia Plath: A Symposium* (Bloomington: Indiana University Press, 1970), pp. 187–95 (pp. 193–4).

5. SPLH 521.

6. Emory 980/1.

7. SPLH 520.

8. SPLH 529.

9. *The New Poetry: An Anthology Selected and Introduced by A. Alvarez* (Harmondsworth: Penguin, 1962), p. 15.

10. A. Alvarez, 'The New Poetry', in ibid., pp. 17–28.

11. Jan–May 1962 (JSP 630–43).

12. To Dan and Helga Huws, 9 June 1962 (Emory 644/4).

13. JSP 641.

14. See further, 'Secret life of Sylvia Plath', *Daily Mail*, 5 Feb 2004.

15. The novel was lost around 1970, according to Ted, so perhaps it was a victim of the 1971 fire at his Yorkshire home, discussed below.

16. 10 June 1962 (JSP 659).

17. 'The Jaguar Skin', quoted from BL Add. MM 88918/1, the typescript of *Birthday Letters* as originally submitted to Faber & Faber.

18. Ibid., though the poem exists in multiple drafts. Ted told the story in attenuated form in a letter to Gerald and Joan, 2 July 1962 (Emory 854/1).

19. Ruth Fainlight, 'Sylvia and Jane', *Times Literary Supplement*, 12 Dec 2003.

20. Plath to Leonard Baskin, 16 April 1962 (BL Add. MS 83684).

21. David Wevill, interview quoted in Yehuda Koren and Eilat Negev, *A Lover of Unreason: The Life and Tragic Death of Assia Wevill, Ted Hughes' Doomed Love* (Robson Books, 2006), p. 90.

22. Macedo, interviewed twenty-five years after the event, quoted in Anne Stevenson, *Bitter Fame: A Life of Sylvia Plath* (Viking, 1989; repr. Penguin, 1998), p. 243. In a more elaborate (embroidered?) interview given a further decade later, Macedo has Assia telling her that what Ted said in the kitchen was 'You know what's happened to us, don't you?', to which Assia allegedly said, 'Yes' (Elaine Feinstein, *Ted Hughes: The Life of a Poet* (Weidenfeld & Nicolson, 2001), p. 140).

23. Nathaniel Tarn Papers, Department of Special Collections, Stanford University Libraries.

24. Angela Landels, interview quoted in Koren and Negev, *Lover of Unreason*, p. 86.

25. 'Dreamers', in *Birthday Letters* (CP 1145–6).

26. 'The Rabbit Catcher', in *Birthday Letters* (CP 1136–8).

27. CPSP 193–4.

28. 'Event', CPSP 194–5.

29. Suzette Macedo, who claimed that Assia showed her the note, interviewed in Feinstein, *Ted Hughes: The Life of a Poet*, p. 141.

30. Nathaniel Tarn Papers, Stanford. Tarn, a minor writer from 'the Group', was in the extraordinary position of being (a) the intimate confidant of both David and Assia Wevill, separately, and (b) a psychoanalyst. He kept detailed notes on these events, which he heard about (from both points of view) over a series of lunch dates.

31. William Trevor, *Excursions in the Real World: Memoirs* (Hutchinson, 1993), p. 117.

32. Hughes, 'Chlorophyl', in *Capriccio* (Lurley: Gehenna Press, 1990) (CP 799). In their biography of Assia, the touchingly literalistic Koren and Negev quote the next two lines of the poem, 'Inside it, / The witchy doll, soaked in Dior', and proceed to the assumption that 'the blade of grass had been dipped in Dior perfume' (*Lover of Unreason*, p. 95). But the poem says that it was a doll, not the grass, which was perfumed. 'Chlorophyl' proceeds like a Russian doll, with a series of things inside each other, the next being a gravestone and the one after that a sample of Assia's ashes. One may assume that these were not also contained in the envelope with the blade of grass: Hughes is collapsing different memories, ending the *Capriccio* cycle by yoking the beginning and the end of his relationship with Assia.

33. CPSP 202–3.

34. CPSP 224.

35. CP 585–6, first published in *Ploughshares* (1980), repr. in 1982 and 1995 *Selected Poems*. Omitted lines: CP 1281.

36. CP 1195, where it is also printed as the closing poem.

37. 'Lily', CP 587.

38. CPSP 204–5.

39. Nathaniel Tarn Papers, Stanford.

40. Draft notes for *Capriccio* poem sequence (BL Add. MS 88918/1).

41. CP 783, with clear references to Sylvia and Assia. The third, who 'sank without a cry', may be Susan Alliston, in the light of her link to 18 Rugby Street, the house of Ted's Friday the 13th night with Sylvia.

42. Nathaniel Tarn Papers, Stanford.
43. Ibid.
44. Richard Murphy, *The Kick: A Life among Writers* (Granta, 2002), p. 222.
45. Ibid., p. 223.
46. Ibid., p. 225.
47. Plath to Murphy, 7 Oct 1962 (Richard Murphy Papers, Department of Special Collections, McFarlin Library, University of Tulsa).
48. Late Sept 1962 (L 208).
49. Nathaniel Tarn Papers, Stanford.

Chapter 13: 'That Sunday Night'

1. To Gerald and family, 2 July 1962 (Emory 854/1).
2. SPLH 542, 554.
3. Olwyn Hughes Papers (BL Add. MS 88948/1). Subsequent quotations and paraphrase from the same crucial letter.
4. Lines from 'The Grouse' (BL Add. MS 88918/1).
5. Lines from 'By day it was teaching in college' (BL Add. MS 88918/1).
6. 'Epiphany', CP 1115–17.
7. Plath and Hughes to Davidow, Christmas 1960 (Sylvia Plath Collection, Mortimer Rare Book Room, Smith College, MS 45, 16/5/20).
8. 'Error', CP 1121–3.
9. Coleridge, 'Frost at Midnight' (1798).
10. 'Error', CP 1121–3.
11. To Marcia Brown Plumer, 4 Feb 1963 (Smith College MS 45, 16/3/20).
12. Ibid., 2 Jan 1963 (Smith College MS 45, 16/3/21).
13. To Clarissa Roche, 19 Oct 1962 (Smith College MS 45, 17/17/3), continuing, in more bitter but still witty vein: 'The fact that he left the week after I almost died of influenza last month, and that his family does not want him to support us in any way, is just one step, I guess, in the path of poetic genius.'
14. To Aurelia Plath, 12 Oct 1962 (SPLH 551).
15. CPSP 223–4.
16. CPSP 226–7.
17. CPSP 231–2.
18. CPSP 233–4.
19. CPSP 240–2.
20. 7 Nov 1962 (SPLH 567).
21. To Olwyn, pre-Christmas 1962 (Emory 980/1/10).
22. 26 Oct 1962 (Nathaniel Tarn Papers, Department of Special Collections, Stanford University Libraries).
23. 5 Jan 1963 (ibid.).
24. Quoted, Preface by Richard Hollis, in Susan Alliston, *Poems and Journals 1960–1969*, introduction by Ted Hughes (Nottingham: Richard Hollis, 2010), p. 9.
25. I owe this information to Gail Crowther, in Elizabeth Sigmund and Gail Crowther, *Sylvia Plath in Devon: A Year's Turning* (Stroud: Fonthill Media, 2014), p. 117.

26. *Nation*, 14 May 1960, p. 426.

27. Hughes, 'Susan Alliston', in Alliston, *Poems and Journals*, p. 13.

28. Ibid., p. 15.

29. 'Samurai', in Alliston, *Poems and Journals*, p. 19.

30. Hughes, 'Susan Alliston', p. 15.

31. Alliston, *Poems and Journals*, p. 82.

32. 'Soho Square' (BL Add. MS 88918/1).

33. Ibid. If only at the level of metaphor, the language is orgasmic: 'came / At the top of your voice. Volcanic'.

34. 'Robbing Myself', in *Birthday Letters* (CP 1150–1).

35. To Marty Brown, 4 Feb 1963 (Smith College MS 45, 16/3/20).

36. Quoted and paraphrased from BL Add. MS 88918/129.

37. 'The Inscription', CP 1154–5.

38. Susan Alliston, unpublished journal entry for 12 Feb 1963, quoted by kind permission of her sister.

39. Ibid.

40. Ibid.

41. Nathaniel Minton, *A Memoir of Ted Hughes* (Westmoreland Press, 2015), p. 27.

42. Ibid.

43. 'That Sunday Night', manuscript draft in BL Add. MS 88918/1. 'Of guilt' is scored through in the holograph. The three epithets for the voice are from another draft.

44. L 213.

45. Dr John Horder, interviewed in Jane Feinmann, 'Rhyme, reason and depression', *Guardian*, 16 Feb 1993.

46. Emory 644/180.

47. Barbara Blackman, personal communication.

48. *Observer*, 17 Feb 1963.

49. Jillian Becker, *Giving Up: The Last Days of Sylvia Plath* (Ferrington, 2002), p. 26.

50. Ibid.

51. Ibid.

52. BL Add. MS 88918/1.

53. End of 'Last Letter', in a special edition of the *New Statesman*, edited by Ted's friend Melvyn Bragg (11 Oct 2010), p. 44.

54. 'Walking in the Snow Alone', in 'That Sunday Night' exercise book (BL Add. MS 88918/1).

55. The haunting thought of the phone calls was best expressed in the version of 'What did happen that Sunday night?' in the same exercise book, in which he asks himself 'How often the phone rang' in his 'empty room', with Sylvia 'hearing it' in her 'receiver' as if she were 'already a fading memory / Of a telephone ringing in a brain / That was already dead'.

56. 'They're doing "Difficulties of a Bridegroom" this week': it was broadcast on Monday 21 Jan 1963, so the (undated) letter was probably written the previous day, 20 Jan 1963 (Emory 980/1).

57. There are extensive drafts of both this poem and 'Uncle Albert's Suicide' in Emory 644/58.
58. 'Full Moon and Little Frieda', CP 182–3.
59. 'Uncle A', in Jan 1963 letter to Olwyn, much revised into 'Sacrifice' in *Wolfwatching* (CP 758–60).

Chapter 14: The Custodian

1. 21 April 1967 (L 272).
2. 15 March 1963 (L 215–16).
3. Hughes to Lowell, 15 May 1963 (Houghton Library, Harvard University).
4. 12 March 1963 (Nathaniel Tarn Papers, Department of Special Collections, Stanford University Libraries).
5. Ibid.
6. Postcard supplied by Peter Porter to Yehuda Koren and Eilat Negev for *A Lover of Unreason: The Life and Tragic Death of Assia Wevill, Ted Hughes' Doomed Love* (Robson Books, 2006).
7. Elizabeth Compton Sigmund, interviewed in the *Guardian*, 18 Jan 2013 (theguardian.com/books/2013/jan/18/elizabeth-sigmund-bell-jar-sylvia-plath). See also her co-written memoir (with Gail Crowther), *Sylvia Plath in Devon: A Year's Turning* (Stroud: Fonthill Media, 2014). Her memory is not always reliable, but it does seem that in his darker moments Ted did make the 'murder a genius' remark (Alvarez reports hearing it at a party, about a year after Sylvia's death).
8. Assia Wevill journal, quoted, Koren and Negev, *Lover of Unreason*, pp. 122–4.
9. Susan Alliston, *Poems and Journals 1960–1969*, introduction by Ted Hughes (Nottingham: Richard Hollis, 2010), p. 87.
10. Hughes to Elizabeth Compton (BL Add. MS 88612).
11. Double airmail letter, 22 July 1963 (Emory 854/1).
12. Hughes journal, Aug 1963.
13. Ibid., 27 Sept 1963.
14. Ibid., Aug 1963.
15. Ibid., 4 Feb 1965.
16. Now with the other books from Ted's library at Emory.
17. Hilda to Aurelia, 12 Oct 1963 (Plath MS II, Lilly Library, Indiana University, Bloomington).
18. 24 Nov 1963, 'Ted Hughes: Letters to Assia Wevill' (Emory 1058/1).
19. Olwyn Hughes, personal communication.
20. Ted to Gerald, 4 Dec 1963 (Emory 854/1).
21. Assia to Ted, 22 Jan 1964 (Emory 1058/1).
22. Ted to Assia, 15 Jan 1964 (Emory 1058/1).
23. Alliston, *Poems and Journals*, p. 87, supplemented by unpublished passages.
24. 28 Aug 1963 (Emory 865/1).
25. See first draft at Emory 644/59.
26. CP 172; see also Diane Middlebrook, *Her Husband: Hughes and Plath – A Marriage* (Little, Brown, 2004), p. 213, where it is asserted that Hughes also

wrote the *Wodwo* poem 'Ballad from a Fairy Tale' at this time as another 'incoherent elegy for Sylvia'. This claim is based on Ted's remark to the critic Ann Skea some twenty years later that the 'fringed square of satin' in this poem (CP 172) was a piece of 'funerary furnishing' (Ann Skea, *Ted Hughes: The Poetic Quest* (Armidale, NSW: University of New England Press, 1994), p. 254), which Middlebrook assumes 'he had seen under Plath's head as she lay in her casket'. But this seems unlikely, since the poem was written on a train as Ted travelled from Court Green to London one morning long before Sylvia's death – though the image may well have taken on new meaning after her death.

27. 'Life after Death', CP 1160–1.

28. *New York Times Book Review*, 8 Nov 1964, p. 28.

29. *British Book News*, Feb 1964, p. 141.

30. *Guardian*, 10 July 1964; *Daily Telegraph*, 23 July 1964.

31. Hughes journal, Aug 1963.

32. *Wodwo*, discussed below, and a selection of poems that he did not consider good enough to include in his Faber volume, gathered as *Recklings*, his first limited-edition fine-press project (150 copies for Turret Books of Kensington, with 1966 on the title page but actually published in January 1967, at five guineas a copy).

33. *Saturday Night*, 78:10 (Nov 1963), pp. 21–7.

34. Audio books: *T. S. Eliot Reads* (Caedmon, 2000); *T. S. Eliot: Four Quartets*, read by Ted Hughes (Faber/Penguin, 1996).

35. To 'Gerald & Joan & infantry', 10 May 1964 (Emory 854/1).

36. Hughes journal, 16–17 Aug 1964, with insertion written later in the year.

37. Ibid., 2 Sept 1964.

38. Ibid., 15 Sept 1964.

39. Ibid., 9 Oct 1964.

40. See ibid., 29 Sept 1964.

41. Produced by Ted's friend Douglas Cleverdon. Cast listed at genome.ch.bbc.co.uk/72a24606054a46b5a37b2ee27fa4318b.

42. Account book for March 1964 to January 1967, its corners charred from the Lumb Bank fire (Emory 644/180/7).

43. Unsigned editorial, *Modern Poetry in Translation*, 1:1 (Autumn 1965). See further Daniel Weissbort, *Ted Hughes and Translation* (Nottingham: Richard Hollis, 2011).

44. Reviewed together with Idries Shah's *The Sufis* under the title 'Secret Ecstasies', *Listener*, 29 Oct 1964.

45. Mircea Eliade, *Shamanism: Archaic Techniques of Ecstasy*, trans. Willard Trask (1964, repr. Penguin, 1989), pp. 466–7.

46. Introduction to Keith Douglas, *Selected Poems* (Faber & Faber, 1964), repr. in WP 212–15.

47. 'NOTES from Olwyn Hughes relating to Ted Hughes's handling of Sylvia Plath publications and placing of ARIEL after her death' (Emory 980/1/25).

48. 'The Crime of Fools Exposed', *New York Times Book Review*, 12 April 1964 (WP 42–4).

49. *Encounter*, 21:4 (Oct 1963), p. 45.
50. L 240.
51. Sylvia Plath, *Ariel: The Restored Edition: A Facsimile of Plath's Manuscript, Reinstating her Original Selection and Arrangement*, foreword by Frieda Hughes (Faber & Faber, 2004), p. 43.
52. Sylvia Plath, *Ariel* (Faber & Faber, 1965), pp. 84–5.
53. Restored edition, pp. 7, 23.
54. The case for the prosecution was first made by Marjorie Perloff, 'The Two Ariels: The (Re)Making of the Sylvia Plath Canon', *American Poetry Review*, 13 (Nov–Dec 1984), pp. 10–18. The defence case is well articulated by Stephen Enniss, 'Sylvia Plath, Ted Hughes, and the Myth of Textual Betrayal', *Papers of the Bibliographical Society of America*, 101:1 (March 2007), pp. 63–71.
55. Interview with John Horder, 'Desk poet', *Guardian*, 23 March 1965, p. 9.
56. 'Sylvia Plath', *Poetry Book Society Bulletin*, 44 (Feb 1965) (WP 161–2).
57. Undated letter, 1965. Quotation missing but story by Nick present in extract in L 239.
58. *Observer*, 14 March 1965.
59. The talk was published in October 1963, in a special issue of the magazine *The Review* devoted to Plath (9, pp. 20–6).
60. *Spectator*, 19 March 1965.
61. *Reporter*, 33 (7 Oct 1963), pp. 51–4.
62. Lowell, foreword to Plath, *Ariel* (New York: Harper & Row, 1966). The American edition contained a slightly different selection of poems.
63. 'Russian Roulette', *Newsweek*, 20 June 1966; 'The Blood Jet is Poetry', *Time*, 10 June 1966 (content.time.com/time/magazine/ article/0,9171,942057,00.html). There is a helpful overview of the evolution of Plath's posthumous reception in Marianne Egeland, *Claiming Sylvia Plath: The Poet as Exemplary Figure* (Cambridge Scholars Publishing, 2013).
64. Assia was always an erratic speller. In a letter to Luke Myers (13 March 1965) announcing her daughter's birth, she used the spellings 'Tatianna' and 'Schura' ('to rhyme with Jura').

Chapter 15: The Iron Man

1. Hughes journal, 15 Feb 1965.
2. To Murphy, 14 Sept 1965 (Richard Murphy Papers, Department of Special Collections, McFarlin Library, University of Tulsa).
3. Gerald Hughes, *Ted and I: A Brother's Memoir* (Robson Press, 2012), p. 165.
4. Susan Alliston, *Poems and Journals 1960–1969*, introduction by Ted Hughes (Nottingham: Richard Hollis, 2010), p. 89 (24 Jan 1965).
5. Ibid., p. 87.
6. Emory 1058/1.
7. CP 731–6.
8. Introduction to *A Choice of Emily Dickinson's Verse* (Faber & Faber, 1968) (WP 158).

9. Assia to Luke Myers, 15 July 1965 (Emory 865/1/11).

10. To Charles Tomlinson, fellow-poet and great friend of Ted (L 247).

11. To Assia, 31 Aug 1965 (Emory 865/1/35).

12. Plath MS II, Lilly Library, Indiana University, Bloomington.

13. 'So Quickly It's Over', interview with Ted Hughes, *Wild Steelhead and Salmon*, Winter 1999, p. 51.

14. L 254.

15. I owe this, and much other information in this chapter, to Brenda Hedden.

16. Hughes journal, summer 1966 (BL Add. MS 88918/128).

17. End of Nov 1966 (Emory 1058/1).

18. Yehuda Koren and Eilat Negev, *A Lover of Unreason: The Life and Tragic Death of Assia Wevill, Ted Hughes' Doomed Love* (Robson Books, 2006), p. 164.

19. End of Nov 1966 (Emory 1058/1).

20. *Wodwo* (Faber & Faber, 1967), p. 9.

21. CP 183.

22. Since 'The Rain Horse' was written in 1958, this doesn't quite fit with the link to his own life after 1961. Ted was never averse to a little rewriting of history for the sake of an aesthetic or mythic pattern.

23. To Csokits, 6 Aug 1967 (L 273–4).

24. Mircea Eliade, *Shamanism: Archaic Techniques of Ecstasy*, trans. Willard Trask (1964, repr. Penguin, 1989), p. 53.

25. 'The Howling of Wolves', 'Full Moon and Little Frieda', 'Out', CP 180, 182, 165.

26. Epithets from 'On the Shelf: Sean O'Brien recalls the inspirational example of Ted Hughes's *Wodwo*', *Sunday Times* (London), 3 April 1994.

27. *Times Literary Supplement*, 6 July 1967.

28. *The Times* (London), 13 July 1967.

29. C.B. Cox, 'New Beasts for Old', *Spectator*, 28 July 1967.

30. *Critical Survey*, Summer 1967.

31. Jeremy Robson, *Tribune*, 30 June 1967; Thwaite, *Times Literary Supplement*, 6 July 1967; Alvarez, *Observer*, 21 May 1967.

32. *Guardian*, 19 May 1967.

33. To Murphy, quoted, independent.co.uk/arts-entertainment/classical/features/the-diary-london-symphony-orchestra-poetry-international-festival-morrissey-harry-hill-richard-curtis-2100679.html.

34. See further Jack Malvern, 'Beat it, British audience told drunk Ginsberg', *The Times* (London), 10 April 2015.

35. To Spender, 21 July 1967 (Emory 644/8).

36. Film-maker Mira Hamermesh, quoted, Koren and Negev, *Lover of Unreason*, p. 167.

37. Hughes journal, 14 Aug 1967.

38. Ibid., undated, but immediately above entry of 18 Aug 1967.

39. Ibid., 11 Sept 1967.

40. BL Add. MS 88918/128.

41. To Myers, 10 Dec 1967 (Emory 865/1).

42. The evolution of his version can be traced in the manuscript drafts, which are now in the small Ted Hughes Archive in the library of Liverpool University – see especially his heavily corrected working draft, MS 24.55(2).

43. Peter Brook Archive, Victoria and Albert Museum, THM/452.

44. Introduction to *Seneca's Oedipus*, adapted by Ted Hughes (Faber & Faber, 1969), pp. 7–8.

45. Irene Worth, reminiscence to Nick Gammage.

46. Charles Marowitz, review in the *Village Voice*, March 1968, repr. in his *Confessions of a Counterfeit Critic: London Theatre Notebook, 1958–71* (Methuen, 1973), pp. 135–6, to which the whole of this paragraph (apart from my Crow allusion) is indebted.

47. *Seneca's Oedipus*, p. 35.

48. Ibid., p.47.

49. Hughes, notes on *Oedipus* (Emory 644/115).

50. Peter Brook Archive, THM/452.

51. *Seneca's Oedipus*, p. 41.

52. Ibid., p. 55.

53. Koren and Negev, *Lover of Unreason*, p. 174.

54. *Observer*, 24 March 1968.

55. Marowitz, *Confessions of a Counterfeit Critic*, pp. 137–9.

56. Their collaborations are selectively documented in the Peter Brook Archive acquired by the Victoria and Albert Museum in September 2014 and made available to the public in summer 2015.

57. 15 May 1968 (L 281–2).

58. BL Add. MS 88918/10.

59. Interviews on BBC Radio 4 with Nigel Forde (22 March 1992) and Radio 3 with Clive Wilmer (5 April 1992), on the publication of *Shakespeare and the Goddess of Complete Being*, explaining (or fantastically elaborating) the project's genesis. He did write to John Fisher in December 1968, saying that he had given up on the Brook plan because the task was giving him bad dreams. *Mahabharata* comparison: Peter Brook Archive, THM/452. Ted told Brook that his production of the *Mahabharata* was 'the most stiring [*sic*] and enthralling performance of any kind I've ever experienced' (Peter Brook Archive, THM/452).

60. Notes on *The Iron Man* (Emory 644/115).

Chapter 16: 'Then autobiographical things knocked it all to bits, as before'

1. Emory 1058/1/71.

2. March 1968 (Emory 1058/1/66).

3. Emory 1058/1.

4. I owe this information, and other material in this chapter, to Brenda Hedden.

5. Personal communication.

6. Nevertheless, she uncrumpled the poem and preserved it over five decades

7. This paragraph is based on Baldwin's somewhat tongue-in-cheek 'Ted Hughes and Shamanism', ann.skea.com/MichaelBaldwinMemoir1.htm.

8. Pat Kavanagh, 'An Awkward Shyness', *Guardian*, 12 July 1968.

9. Broadcast 12 Dec 1968.

10. Emory 644/57.

11. Journal note, 15 Aug 1968, quoted, Stephen Enniss and Karen Kukil, *'No Other Appetite': Sylvia Plath, Ted Hughes, and the Blood Jet of Poetry* (New York: Grolier Club, 2005), p. 59.

12. Journal note, 15 Aug 1968 (Emory 644/57).

13. First published in *Word in the Desert*, the tenth-anniversary volume of *Critical Quarterly*, the journal of Ted's friends C. B. Cox and A. E. Dyson, 25 July 1968.

14. Brenda Hedden, quoted, Yehuda Koren and Eilat Negev, *A Lover of Unreason: The Life and Tragic Death of Assia Wevill, Ted Hughes' Doomed Love* (Robson Books, 2006), pp. 189–90.

15. Brenda Hedden, personal communication.

16. Emory 644/57.

17. Emory 644/58.

18. Interview with Heaney, London, 27 Oct 2009.

19. Dennis O'Driscoll, *Stepping Stones: Interviews with Seamus Heaney* (Faber & Faber, 2008), p. 116.

20. Emory 1058/1.

21. To Anne-Lorraine Bujon, 16 Dec 1992 (L 632).

22. Assia's journal entry, dated 20 March 1969, but it was actually 19 March (correct dates reconstructed from information in BBC Archive).

23. Assia's journal entry dated 'March 21st', but it was actually 20 March 1969. Koren and Negev, *Lover of Unreason* is inaccurate at this point, missing the Haworth location.

24. BL Add. MS 88918/1.

25. Information from Olwyn Hughes, not known to Koren and Negev.

26. Ted to Assia's sister, Celia Chaikin, 14 April 1969 (L 290).

27. This was her constant complaint to friends such as Edward Lucie-Smith (personal communication).

28. Private collection.

29. This paragraph is based on Koren and Negev, *Lover of Unreason*, p. 202. I am much indebted to this piece of research by the book's authors.

30. Hughes, statement to Det. Sgt J. Loakman, Clapham Police Station, quoted, ibid., p. 203.

31. Porter, 'Ted Hughes and Sylvia Plath: A Bystander's Recollections', in Peter Craven, ed., *The Best Australian Essays 2001* (Melbourne: Black Inc., 2001), p. 411.

32. 'Requiem pro duabus filiis Israel', in Nathaniel Tarn, *Selected Poems 1950–2002* (Middletown, Conn.: Wesleyan University Press, 2002), pp. 62–4.

33. L 292.

34. L 290.

35. Jottings in spiral shorthand notebook, in Ireland, April to early May 1969 (Emory 644/57).

36. Letter of early May 1969, Peter Brook Archive, Victoria and Albert Museum, THM/452. One of the wretched coincidences was presumably the unfortunate fact of Olwyn's friend being the person who picked up the phone when Assia made her last call to Court Green.

37. BL Add. MS 88918/128.

38. Ibid.

39. To Aurelia, 10 July 1969 (Plath MS II, Lilly Library, Indiana University, Bloomington).

40. BL Add. MS 88918/128.

41. Ibid.

42. Ibid.

43. Ted Hughes, 'Susan Alliston', in her *Poems and Journals 1960–1969* (Nottingham: Richard Hollis, 2010), p. 16.

44. Hughes to Herbert, 9 May 1967 (Emory 644/182).

45. BL Add. MS 88918/128.

46. 30 July 1969 (ibid.).

47. To Murphy, 10 Oct 1969 (L 295).

48. Vasko Popa, *Selected Poems*, trans. Anne Pennington, with an introduction by Ted Hughes (Penguin, 1969) (WP 220–7). The introduction was adapted from a radio talk recorded for the Third Programme in June 1966, broadcast that October, and published in *Critical Survey*, Summer 1966.

49. To Baskin, 1 Dec 1969 (L 300).

50. Introduction to Vasko Popa, *Collected Poems 1943–1976* (Manchester: Carcanet, 1978) (WP 228).

51. L 298–9.

Chapter 17: The Crow

1. Quotations from 'Words and Experience', BBC radio talk, 24 Jan 1967, repr. in Ted Hughes, *Poetry in the Making: An Anthology of Poems and Programmes from 'Listening and Writing'* (Faber & Faber, 1967), pp. 118–24.

2. Letter to Celia Chaikin (Emory 1058/1/1).

3. Emory 854/1/58.

4. Plath MS II, Lilly Library, Indiana University, Bloomington.

5. '59 poems – out of about 90', he put it to Peter Redgrove (L 306), but that was to count the 'Two Eskimo Songs' as one.

6. L 304.

7. Leonard Baskin, quoted, Leonard Scigaj, *The Poetry of Ted Hughes: Form and Imagination* (Iowa City: University of Iowa Press, 1986), p. 144.

8. 1977 interview with Ekbert Faas, in Faas, *Ted Hughes: The Unaccommodated Universe* (Santa Barbara, Calif.: Black Sparrow Press, 1980), p. 212.

9. *Critical Quarterly*, 8 (Autumn 1966), pp. 200–2.

10. On Crow and the Trickster, see further Keith Sagar, *The Laughter of Foxes: A Study of Ted Hughes* (Liverpool: Liverpool University Press, 2006), pp. 170–81, and Ann Skea, 'Ted Hughes and Crow', ann.skea.com/Trickstr.htm.

11. 'Crow on the Beach', in Alberta Turner, ed., *45 Contemporary Poems: The Creative Process* (Longman, 1985) (WP 240–1).

12. 'Notes on Published Works' (Emory 644/115).

13. 'Crow Goes Hunting', CP 236.

14. 'In Laughter', CP 233.

15. 'Lovesong', CP 255.

16. Quotations from March 1976 interview on Radio 3AW Adelaide, Australia.

17. 'Crow's First Lesson', CP 211.

18. CP 213, 228, 252.

19. Unidentified fragment re *Crow* (Emory 644/115).

20. 'Black Bird', *Observer*, 11 Oct 1970.

21. 'Books of the Day', unknown paper, undated (Emory 644/175).

22. Stephen Spender, 'The Last Ditch', *New York Review of Books*, 17:1 (22 July 1971), pp. 3–4.

23. Patrick Cosgrove, *Spectator*, 6 March 1971.

24. Jack Kroll, 'The Tree and the Bird', *Newsweek*, 12 April 1971.

25. Daniel Hoffman, 'Plain Songs for an Apocalypse', *New York Times Book Review*, 18 April 1971.

26. Victor Howes, 'Supercrow as a Black Rainbow', *Christian Science Monitor*, 29 April 1971.

27. Nicola Barker, *Sunday Times* (London), 1 Oct 1995.

28. Reviews of *Crow* (Emory 644/175).

29. Keith Sagar and Stephen Tabor, *Ted Hughes: A Bibliography 1946–1995* (London and New York: Mansell, 1998), p. 52. I am much indebted to this work.

30. Ibid., p. 58.

31. 1971, 300 copies at £18.

32. Lexham Press, 1971. The Shakespeare project is discussed in Chapter 28, 'Goddess Revisited', below.

33. CP 269.

34. CP 231–2.

35. CP 255. For a brilliant account of the hidden presence of Plath in 'Lovesong', and indeed elsewhere in *Crow*, see ch. 9 of Heather Clark's admirable study, *The Grief of Influence: Sylvia Plath and Ted Hughes* (Oxford University Press, 2011).

36. 'Littleblood' (the title being a figuration of the wounded self), CP 258.

37. 'Crow Wakes', CP 258; also in *Eat Crow* (not in CP).

38. Letter to Keith Sagar, 18–19 July 1998, acknowledging that *Crow* was an 'oblique' creative response to Plath's death (Keith Sagar, ed., *Poet and Critic: The Letters of Ted Hughes and Keith Sagar* (British Library, 2012), p. 269).

Chapter 18: The Savage God

1. 'The Environmental Revolution', *Spectator*, 21 March 1970 (edited version); repr. in full in *Your Environment*, 1:3 (Summer 1970), pp. 81–3 (WP 128–35).

2. WP 130.

3. Frieda Hughes, 'Father dear father', *Daily Telegraph*, 29 Oct 2002.

4. Personal communication.

5. 20 April 1970 (BL Add. MS 88918/128).

6. Letter in the possession of Brenda Hedden.

7. Personal communication.

8. Personal communication.

9. This section is based on conversations with Brenda Hedden, Olwyn Hughes and others, and a chronology compiled by Hughes in BL Add. MS 88993.

10. BL Add. MS 88918/128/1.

11. Erica Jong, *Seducing the Demon: Writing for My Life* (New York: Jeremy P. Tarcher, 2006), p. 40. Subsequent quotations from the same source.

12. Hughes journal, 17 Sept 1964.

13. Personal communication.

14. To Redgrove, 27 Oct 1971 (Redgrove Archive, Sheffield University Library).

15. Aurelia Plath, in 'Sylvia Plath: A Biographical Note' by Lois Ames, in *The Bell Jar* (New York: Harper & Row, 1971), pp. 214–15.

16. Fran McCullough, foreword to twenty-fifth anniversary reissue of *The Bell Jar* (1996), p. xiv.

17. To Redgrove, spring 1971 (Peter Redgrove Papers, Emory MS 867, redacted from L).

18. To Redgrove, spring 1971 (L 311).

19. Peter Brook, *The Empty Space* (MacGibbon & Kee, 1968), p. 49.

20. A. C. H. Smith, *Orghast at Persepolis: An International Experiment in Theatre* (Eyre Methuen, 1972; New York: Viking, 1973), p. 43. This eyewitness account, with notes and interviews taken at the time, is an essential resource, to which the following paragraphs are deeply indebted. I have also drawn on the drafts and production materials in the Peter Brook Archive, Victoria and Albert Museum, THM 452/8/45.

21. 'Orghast', *Times Literary Supplement*, 1 Oct 1971, p. 1174, incorporating interview with Hughes by Stoppard (who visited the ensemble in Persepolis).

22. Smith, *Orghast at Persepolis*, p. 50.

23. Ibid., p. 91.

24. Ibid., p. 97.

25. Ibid., p. 104.

26. Confusingly, Hughes gave the same title to the collection of his short stories that was published in 1995.

27. Peter Brook Archive, THM/452/8.

28. Smith, *Orghast at Persepolis*, p. 200.

29. Opening of *Orghast* in Ted Hughes, *Selected Translations*, ed. Daniel Weissbort (Faber & Faber, 2006), pp. 74–5. There is also a wealth of draft material now in the Emory archive (644/120). Sample translations, for example: GRADOB: bombs. PULLUTTU: bird. NARGA: of darkness.

OPPA BLAV: on the wall. OPPA CLAUN: on the door. KHERN
SHEER: words of steel. TAP TAP DUTTU: tap tap of the leaden. TAP
TAP TAPUN: tap tap tapping (Brook always likes tapping because his
actors often come on stage bearing wooden sticks or poles). Sample
passages, too: 'Unkher brida kher udda khern sludda kher avokka dotta
khern ... grafot gleblot balugvablot'.

30. Smith, *Orghast at Persepolis*, pp. 209–10.
31. L 317.
32. Hughes journal, 13 Nov 1971.
33. L 323.
34. BL Add. MS 88918/128.
35. Olwyn referred to the passage in a letter to Alvarez, 9 June 1988 (Alvarez
    Papers, BL Add. MS 88603.3036c). In reply, rather than denying it, he
    asked what else Sylvia had said about him in her last journal. Olwyn told
    him that Sylvia confided in no one, that her journal was the only witness
    to their brief liaison, but that at least one other person was aware of it.
36. Fragment in BL Add. MS 88918/1.
37. BL Add. MS 88603.3036c.
38. Ibid.
39. According to Olwyn's recollection of Sylvia's last journal, in January she
    set her sights on another poet-friend, Bill Merwin, and was rejected a third
    time. There is no corroborative evidence for this.
40. Al Alvarez, *Where Did It All Go Right? A Memoir* (Richard Cohen Books,
    1999; New York: William Morrow, 2000), p. 209.
41. Nathaniel Tarn Papers, Department of Special Collections, Stanford
    University Libraries.
42. Alvarez, *Where Did It All Go Right?*, p. 209.
43. Nathaniel Tarn Papers, Stanford.

Chapter 19: Farmer Ted

1. Emory 854/1.
2. Peter Brook Archive, Victoria and Albert Museum, production material for
   The Conference of the Birds, THM/452/8.
3. To Luke Myers, summer 1972 (L 331).
4. To Leonard Baskin, Nov 1972 (L 333).
5. Preface to *Moortown Diary* (Faber & Faber, 1989) (CP 1203).
6. Hughes journal, 12 June 1973.
7. 'Roe-deer', CP 513.
8. Hughes journal, 29 Aug 1973: a random choice from among scores of such
   entries.
9. Ibid., undated pages, *circa* 1974.
10. Introduction to János Pilinszky's *Selected Poems*, trans. Ted Hughes and János
    Csokits (Carcanet, 1976) (WP 229–36).
11. Ibid.
12. Radio broadcast, BBC World Service, 18 Sept 1976.
13. All János Pilinszky poems quoted from his *Selected Poems*.

14. CP 288, 290, 291, 293, 295–6.
15. 'The Scream', 'The Summoner', 'The Interrogator', 'The Scapegoat', CP 419, 420, 421, 433. The initial sequence matched each poem to the Baskin drawing that inspired it (thus 'The Summoner' went with 'A Hercules-in-the-Underworld Bird' and 'The Interrogator' with 'A Titled Vulturess'), while the expanded Faber text of 1978 included extra poems originating from Hughes (e.g. 'The Scream'), for some of which Baskin then created drawings.
16. Endnote to reprint in 1982 *Selected Poems* (CP 1271).
17. L 356–7.
18. See John Moat, *The Founding of Arvon: A Memoir of the Early Years of the Arvon Foundation* (Frances Lincoln, 2005).
19. 'Ted Hughes Introduces and Reads *Season Songs*', BBC Radio 3, 6 Sept 1977.
20. CP 307.
21. 'April Birthday' (addressed (without saying so) to Frieda, who was born on 1 April), 'Swifts', 'The Harvest Moon', 'Autumn Nature Notes', CP 312, 315, 323, 327.
22. 'Spring Nature Notes', 'Autumn Nature Notes', CP 311, 329.
23. Michael Harris, *Montreal Star*, 4 March 1978; Adam Thorpe, *Observer*, 5 March 1995.
24. To Daniel Weissbort (Emory 644/10/5).
25. L 361–2.
26. L 367.
27. To Charles Tomlinson, 22 Jan 1976, projecting his own trajectory on to that of his fellow-poet.
28. To Frieda, 7 Feb 1976 (Emory 1014/1).
29. L 376.

Chapter 20: The Elegiac Turn

1. L 632.
2. 13 July 1969 (BL Add. MS 88918/128).
3. L 204.
4. To Aurelia and Warren Plath, Dec 1960 (L 173).
5. 'The House of Aries Part I' appeared in print in the spring 1961 issue of a quarterly magazine called *Audience*, published in Cambridge, Mass. Part II seems never to have been published, save in the form of a few fragments spoken by a military captain (*Two Cities*, Summer 1961, pp. 12–13; *Texas Quarterly*, Autumn 1961, pp. 146–7).
6. To Assia, 31 Jan 1964 (Emory 1058/1/6).
7. To Baskin, 29 July 1974 (Emory 644/1).
8. Keith Sagar, ed., *Poet and Critic: The Letters of Ted Hughes and Keith Sagar* (British Library, 2012), p. 58.
9. Heaney praising *Gaudete*, 22 May 1977: he has read it twice and been 'deeply pleasured' by it (a phrase that may unconsciously echo the poem's sexual language). He thought that the shape of the story ploughed deep into the soil of Hughes's genius. (Emory 644/9.)

10. L 376–7.

11. Martin Dodsworth, *Guardian*, 19 May 1977.

12. Conrad, 'In the Safari Park', *New Statesman*, 27 May 1977.

13. Symons, 'The case of the lecherous cleric', *Sunday Times* (London), 29 May 1977.

14. Donald Hall, *Washington Post Book World*, 18 Dec 1977; Joan Joffe Hall, 'A bloody, violent poem', *Houston Post*, 5 March 1978; Mark Halliday, 'Ted Hughes's new poem: rural sex and violence', *Providence Sunday Journal*, 5 March 1978. Collected, with other reviews, in Emory 644/175/14.

15. *Gaudete* (Faber & Faber, 1977), pp. 140–1 (not in CP).

16. Ibid., p. 155.

17. 'On the Shelf: Simon Armitage on why Ted Hughes's *Gaudete* made him forget the laundry', *Sunday Times* (London), 17 March 1996.

18. 'Ted Hughes and *Gaudete*', 1977 interview in Ekbert Faas, *Ted Hughes: The Unaccommodated Universe* (Santa Barbara, Calif.: Black Sparrow Press, 1980), p. 214.

19. Ibid.

20. Ibid., p. 137, citing Ramanujan's *Speaking of Siva*.

21. *Speaking of Siva*, trans. A. K. Ramanujan (Penguin Classics, 1973), pp. 48–53.

22. Faas, *Ted Hughes*, p. 138.

23. Influencing 'The viper fell from the sun', *Gaudete*, p. 188; quoted, Faas, *Ted Hughes*, p. 122.

24. 30 May 1977, in Sagar, ed., *Poet and Critic*, p. 57; BL Add. MS 88918/128.

25. Personal communication; see also Dennis O'Driscoll, *Stepping Stones: Interviews with Seamus Heaney* (Faber & Faber, 2008), p. 392.

26. William Scammell, 'The fox thinks twice' (Cheltenham lecture), edited version published as 'Burst Open Under a Blue-Black Pressure', *Poetry Review*, Hughes and Plath Special (1998), pp. 82–7.

27. BL Add. MS 88918/35.

28. *Gaudete*, p. 182.

29. BL Add. MS 88918/128.

30. *Gaudete*, p. 191.

31. Emory 644/65 and 644/58.

32. *Orts* (Rainbow Press, 1978), poems 9, 22, 4, 11, 13, 19, 32, 36, 48, 52, 53.

33. Emory 644/57/10, Notebook 11.

34. Adapting Paul Keegan's phrase (CP 1277).

35. 'The day he died', 'A monument', 'The formal auctioneer', 'A memory', 'Now you have to push', 'Hands', CP 533–7. 'Aloof' was emended to 'estranged' in the trade printings.

36. *Remains of Elmet* (Rainbow Press, April 1979; Faber & Faber, May 1979).

Chapter 21: The Arraignment

1. 28 Aug 1968, repr. in *Sisterhood is Powerful* and at redstockings.org/index. php?option=com_content&view=article&id=65&Itemid=103.

2. 'Lesbos', CPSP 228.

3. Al Alvarez, *The Savage God: A Study of Suicide* (Weidenfeld & Nicolson, 1971), p. 19.

4. 'Publishing Sylvia Plath', WP 168.

5. See further, Ann Skea, 'Ted Hughes and Small Press Publication', ann.skea. com/RainbowPress.htm. *Fiesta Melons by Sylvia Plath with an Introduction by Ted Hughes* (Exeter: Rougemont Press, May 1971) was an analogous production (not mentioned by Skea).

6. Original version of 'Arraignment' published in *Feminist Art Journal* (New York), Oct 1972.

7. 'Arraignment', in *Monster* (New York: Random House, 1972).

8. Quoted by Robin Morgan on her website, robinmorgan.us.

9. C.G. Jung et al., *Man and his Symbols* (Picador, 1964), p. 169.

10. See Judith Kroll, *Chapters in a Mythology: The Poetry of Sylvia Plath* (New York: Harper & Row, 1976), especially p. 177.

11. BL Add. MS 88918/128. Correspondence regarding this and other projects is preserved in the Frances McCullough Papers at the University of Maryland, hdl.handle.net/1903.1/4603.

12. To Aurelia Plath, 12 Jan 1975 (Plath MS II, Lilly Library, Indiana University, Bloomington).

13. Mary Folliet, 'Reviewing Sylvia Plath', *New York Review of Books*, 30 Sept 1976.

14. Olwyn Hughes, *New York Review of Books*, 30 Sept 1976.

15. 22 Dec 1976, passage excluded from text in L 380–2.

16. To Ben Sonnenberg (L 451).

17. 'Sylvia Plath and her Journals', WP 177–90, repr. from *Grand Street*, 1:3 (Spring 1982).

18. *The Journals of Sylvia Plath* (New York: Dial Press, 1982), p. xiii. As Janet Malcolm points out in the opening pages of her superb *The Silent Woman: Sylvia Plath and Ted Hughes* (New York: Alfred A. Knopf, 1993), in the *Grand Street* version Ted changed 'I destroyed' to 'her husband destroyed' and 'disappeared' to 'disappeared more recently (and may, presumably, still turn up)'. The latter phrase has led to much speculation and fantasy.

19. Preface to Edward Butscher, ed., *Sylvia Plath: The Woman and the Work* (New York: Dodd, Mead, 1977; repr. Peter Owen, 1979), p. vii. Like Butscher's biography, this was a book whose gestation involved a difficult history with Ted and Olwyn, as is clear from a publisher's note on the first page of the introductory essay, 'In Search of Sylvia': 'Mr Butscher wishes it known that changes were made in his Introduction by hands other than his own.'

20. Lameyer, in ibid., p. 143.

21. Ibid., p. 164.

22. Ibid., p. 165.

Chapter 22: Sunstruck Foxglove

1. Hughes journal (BL Add. MS 88918/128). The phrasing belongs to the unthinking racism of Hughes's generation; subsequent quotations are from

the same source, illustrative of his great gifts of observation and phrasing in his travel journals.

2. Gerald Hughes, *Ted and I: A Brother's Memoir* (Robson Press, 2012), p. 184.

3. My account of the relationship with Jill Barber is based on her articles in the *Mail on Sunday*, 13 and 20 May 2001 ('Ted Hughes, my secret lover'), her unpublished memoir, and conversations by email and at her home in New York.

4. BL Add. MS 88918/128.

5. Interview for Radio 3AW Adelaide, produced by Julie Copeland. There is a transcription by Ann Skea at ann.skea.com/Adelaide3.htm.

6. Ibid.

7. Ted Hughes at the Adelaide Festival Writers' Week: A transcription of Ted Hughes own commentary, ann.skea.com/adelaide.htm

8. Personal communication.

9. To Murphy, 31 March 1976; the whole sequence about Jennifer Rankin is suppressed from the text in L.

10. To János Csokits, May 1976 (L 376).

11. BL Add. MS 88918/128.

12. Barber, 'Ted Hughes, my secret lover'.

13. First published 1983, collected in *Flowers and Insects* (Faber & Faber, 1986) (CP 723–4).

14. Jennifer Rankin, draft manuscript of a radio talk about Ted, University of New South Wales, Australian Defence Force Academy Library, MS 348.

15. Back cover of Jennifer J. Rankin, *Earth Hold* (Secker & Warburg, 1978).

16. Jennifer Rankin, *Collected Poems*, ed. Judith Rodriguez (St Lucia: University of Queensland Press, 1990), p. 195. My account of Rankin is indebted to Rodriguez and her husband, the poet Tom Shapcott, who was at the Adelaide Festival and visited the Rankins in Devon. The Toronto lift story, below, is quoted, by permission, from an email from Rodriguez.

17. Now in the archive of her papers in the library of the Australian Defence Force Academy.

18. 'Three Poems for J.R.', published in 1985, 1986, 1993 (CP 838–40).

19. Emory 644/82.

20. Emma Tennant, *Burnt Diaries* (Edinburgh: Canongate, 1999), p. 45. Subsequent Tennant quotations are all from this memoir.

21. The Emory archive includes Harry Fainlight letters written from prison and from 'a Scottish madhouse' (644/2/23).

22. Elaine Feinstein, *It Goes with the Territory: Memoirs of a Poet* (Chicago: Alma Books, 2013), p. 156.

23. Tennant, *Burnt Diaries*, p. 96.

24. Edna O'Brien, *Country Girl: A Memoir* (Faber & Faber, 2012), pp. 136–40, 210–15. One might compare and contrast 'I will know you for a long time' with Emma Tennant's 'I want you for no more than a year': affirmations almost too Hughescliffian to have been truly uttered?

25. Barber, 'Ted Hughes, my secret lover'.

26. For example: the astonishingly beautiful and charismatic feminist, memoirist and political activist Sally Belfrage went to dinner with Ted and Sylvia in Chalcot Square with her then partner Ben Sonnenberg. Before he died, Sonnenberg said that he did not know whether Ted later had an affair with Sally after Sylvia's death, but he suspected that they might have become close. Sally died of cancer in Middlesex Hospital, just at the time when Ted's own cancer was first diagnosed. Her private papers in the Tamiment Library and Robert F. Wagner Labor Archive, New York University, remain closed until 2021.

27. Personal communication.

28. BL Add. MS 88918/128.

29. Syed Muhammad Hussain, 'Remembering Ted Hughes', *Financial Express* (Dhaka), 14 April 2012, thefinancialexpress-bd.com/old/more. php?newsid=126732&date=2012-04-14.

30. Amzed Hossein, 'An Interview with Ted Hughes', 18–20 Nov 1989, transcribed at ann.skea.com/AsiaFestivalInterview.html.

31. Quoted, Hussain, 'Remembering Ted Hughes'.

32. This and preceding quotations from Carolyne Wright, 'What Happens in the Heart: An Encounter with Ted Hughes', *Poetry Review*, 89:3 (Autumn 1999), pp. 3–9.

33. BL Add. MS 88919/128.

34. Ibid.

Chapter 23: Remembrance of Elmet

1. Emma Tennant, *Burnt Diaries* (Edinburgh: Canongate, 1999), pp. 178–9.

2. Letter of Feb 1977 (Emory 865/1).

3. Letters to Gerald (Emory 854/1).

4. Robert Graves, *The White Goddess: A Historical Grammar of Poetic Myth* (Faber & Faber, 1948), p. 143.

5. By the time of his father's death, Nicholas Hughes had built an impressive academic curriculum vitae: sfos.uaf.edu/memorial/hughes/hughes_ cv-99.pdf.

6. Hughes journal fragment, 20 Feb 1980.

7. Hull University Archives, DPL(2)3/8/9.

8. John Moat, *The Founding of Arvon: A Memoir of the Early Years of the Arvon Foundation* (Frances Lincoln, 2005), p. 26.

9. L 476.

10. 'Comments' by Larkin, 2 Jan 1981 (Emory 644/4).

11. Letter to Lucas Myers, Dec 1980 (Emory 865/1).

12. Heaney on *The Rattle Bag* in a 'Memo to Joanna Mackle re The School Bag: 6 January 1997' (BL Add. MS 88918/16).

13. Review by Christopher Reid (clipping in Emory 645/176/3).

14. *Moon Whales and Other Moon Poems* is conveniently reprinted in Ted Hughes, *Collected Poems for Children*, illustrated by Raymond Briggs (Faber & Faber, 2005, paperback 2008), pp. 67–107.

15. To Monteith, 21 May 1976 (L 377).

16. Hughes's copy is now among his library books at Emory.

17. Glyn Hughes, *Millstone Grit* (Victor Gollancz, 1975), p. 12. Subsequent quotations from pp. 17, 28, 29, 139.

18. Ted Hughes, 'Introduction', in Glyn Hughes, *Where I Used to Play on the Green* (Victor Gollancz, 1982; repr. Penguin, 1984), pp. 5–6.

19. *Remains of Elmet: A Pennine Sequence – Poems by Ted Hughes, Photographs by Fay Godwin* (Faber & Faber, 1979), p. 7.

20. CP 483.

21. Plath: 'Now, in valleys narrow / And black as purses, the house lights / Gleam like small change' (CPSP 167–8); Hughes: 'Rain / Crashes the black taut glass, // Lights in floundering valleys, in the gulf, / Splinter from their sockets' (CP 485).

22. Included in both *Three Books: Remains of Elmet, Cave Birds, River* (unillustrated, Faber & Faber, 1993) and *Elmet* (illustrated, Faber & Faber, 1994).

23. CP 486. Assia's diary entry noted the blackness of the buildings in Haworth, contrasting with the white of the snow on the ground.

24. CP 492.

25. CP 470–1.

26. CP 473.

27. Peter Porter, 'Landscape with poems', *Observer*, 15 July 1979.

28. To Joanna Mackle, 4 Jan 1992 (Emory 644/14). On the origins of *River*, see Chapter 24, 'The Fisher King', below.

29. Blurb for *Three Books*.

30. *Three Books*, p. 183.

31. CP 462–3.

32. CP 840.

Chapter 24: The Fisher King

1. 'So Quickly It's Over', interview with Ted Hughes, *Wild Steelhead and Salmon*, Winter 1999, p. 57.

2. To Gerald, 21 Dec 1979 (Emory 854/1); to Murphy, 20 Dec 1979 (Richard Murphy Papers, Department of Special Collections, McFarlin Library, University of Tulsa).

3. To Gerald, Feb 1981 (Emory 854/1).

4. To Gerald (Emory 854/1).

5. To Gerald (Emory 854/1).

6. Nathaniel Minton, *A Memoir of Ted Hughes* (Westmoreland Press, 2015), pp. 28, 40. The request for anti-depressants came in the early Nineties.

7. BL Add. MS 88918/128.

8. 'Portraits' (BL Add. MS 88918/7).

9. Ibid.

10. BL Add. MS 88918/128.

11. For a particularly good example, see the verse journal of an Irish fishing expedition with Barrie Cooke, dated 29 Feb 1980 (BL Add. MS 88918/128/3, fos. 6–14).

12. BL Add. MS 88918/128.

13. 29 June 1983.

14. BL Add. MS 88918/128.

15. Ibid.

16. L 433.

17. L 434.

18. To Danny Weissbort, 23 Oct 1983 (L 472).

19. To Barrie Cooke, 23 Oct 1983 (L 468).

20. 10 Nov 1982 (Emory 644/5).

21. To Myers, 29 Sept 1984 (Emory 865/1).

22. See the facsimile of this wonderful 1976 letter, with sketch maps, in Simon Armitage, 'Dear Peter', *Granta*, 26 June 2012, granta.com/New-Writing/Dear-Peter.

23. To Gerald, 26 Aug 1980 (Emory 854/1). The genesis of the project is well documented in BL Add. MS 88614, Letters etc., to Peter Keen from Ted Hughes (1976–1985). Mark Wormald's fine essay 'Fishing for Ted' has an especially strong account of the gestation and context of the project, in Mark Wormald, Neil Roberts and Terry Gifford, eds, *Ted Hughes: From Cambridge to Collected* (Basingstoke: Palgrave Macmillan, 2013), pp. 112–29.

24. BL Add. MS 88614.

25. Ibid.

26. *River: Poems by Ted Hughes, Photographs by Peter Keen* (Faber & Faber, 1983), pp. 127–8.

27. Report to Coroner's Inquest on death of Assia Wevill, cited in Yehuda Koren and Eilat Negev, *A Lover of Unreason: The Life and Tragic Death of Assia Wevill, Ted Hughes' Doomed Love* (Robson Books, 2006), p. 203.

28. CP 643 (first published in the *Listener*, 13 Jan 1983).

29. CP 681 (first published in *Grand Street*, Autumn 1981).

30. 'So Quickly It's Over', p. 57.

31. Though not published until 1999, the interview was conducted on a sunny August morning in 1995, on Ehor Boyanowsky's deck overlooking Horseshoe Bay, British Columbia, under huge cedar trees, the morning after Ted gave a rousing reading of 'The Bear' at a fundraiser for the Steelhead Society of British Columbia (personal communication from the interviewer, Tom Pero). He gave very few interviews thereafter, largely because of his illness.

32. CP 679 (originally published as 'An October Salmon', *London Review of Books*, 16 April 1981; included among *Remains of Elmet* poems in 1982 *Selected Poems*, a placing that makes the link to the poems of family memory).

33. CP 655.

34. *Sunday Times* (London), 23 Oct 1983.

35. To Keith Sagar, 14 Dec 1983, in Keith Sagar, ed., *Poet and Critic: The Letters of Ted Hughes and Keith Sagar* (British Library, 2012), p. 132.

36. 'Torridge Action Group – Summary of Issues' (Emory 644/170).

37. CP 740 (originally published in the short-lived *Sunday Correspondent* newspaper, 17 Sept 1989).

Chapter 25: The Laureate

1. 28 Dec 1981 (L 450).
2. 'A Swallow', CP 604.
3. 'Evening Thrush', CP 607.
4. Ann Skea, in her excellent piece, 'A Creative Collaboration: R. J. Lloyd and Ted Hughes', ann.skea.com/ArtisticCollaboration1.htm.
5. Ted Hughes, *Collected Poems for Children*, illustrated by Raymond Briggs (Faber & Faber, 2005; paperback 2008), pp. 157–8.
6. *West Country Fly Fishing* was edited by his friend Anne Voss Bark (1983); the pamphlet for the Frances Horovitz Benefit (to assist her only son) was called *Tenfold* (1983); Ted's contribution was, interestingly, 'Sunstruck Foxglove' (that poem's first publication).
7. WP 88.
8. To Leonard and Lisa Baskin, May 1984 (L 484).
9. To Myers, 29 Sept 1984 (L 489; the published version omits the parts of the letter concerning Nick and Frieda).
10. Dream diary, 15 May 1983 (BL Add. MS 88918/1).
11. L 464.
12. To Heaney, autumn 1984 (L 488).
13. Hughes's sense that Heaney had beaten him to the achievement of the Wordsworthian voice became explicit in his response to the subsequent autobiographical sequence, 'Squarings' (1989, in pamphlet form, reprinted at the core of Heaney's next Faber volume, *Seeing Things*, 1991): 'Made me think of The Prelude, in the ranging self-reassessment, the lifting of sacred moments … and in the way the whole thing is a self-rededication, a realigning of yourself' (Hughes to Heaney, L 564).
14. To Martin Booth, 12 June 1984 (Emory 644/2).
15. Mistranscribed as 'Warrener' in L 495.
16. CP 803–5.
17. L 495.
18. To Larkin, Emory 644/4.
19. To Sagar, 21 Jan 1985, in Keith Sagar, ed., *Poet and Critic: The Letters of Ted Hughes and Keith Sagar* (British Library, 2012), p. 142.
20. L 497. 'The Zodiac in the Shape of a Crown', for Prince William, was eventually published in 1987 in the form of a facsimile of the manuscript in a limited-edition charity volume in aid of St Magnus' Cathedral in Kirkwall on the Orkneys, together with poems by Seamus Heaney, Christopher Fry and local poet George Mackay Brown. Hughes never reprinted it, and it is not in CP.
21. Ehor Boyanowsky, *Savage Gods, Silver Ghosts: In the Wild with Ted Hughes* (Vancouver: Douglas & McIntyre, 2010). Information and quotations in this section are derived from this vivid and powerfully written memoir,

supplemented by additional points provided privately by Boyanowsky, to whom I am most grateful.

22. CP 669. See Nick Gammage's fine account of the poem, in Nick Gammage, ed., *The Epic Poise: A Celebration of Ted Hughes* (Faber & Faber, 1999), pp. 86–91.

23. Boyanowsky, *Savage Gods*, p. 23.

24. Ibid., pp. 26–7. As with all the verbatim quotations in *Savage Gods*, these are Ted's words as remembered by Boyanowsky, and to some degree as embellished for literary effect, not necessarily as spoken in the moment.

25. CP 847.

26. Boyanowsky, *Savage Gods*, p. 89.

27. Ibid., p. 73.

28. Ibid., p. 48.

29. Ted was introduced to Carol and her sister by Michael Dyton, a local antiques dealer.

30. Ibid., pp. 108–9.

31. Ibid., pp. 141–3.

32. Ibid., p. 127.

33. Ibid., p. 174. Boyanowsky misremembers: it was, of course, the RAF.

34. L 510–11.

35. CP 730. Never reprinted by Hughes, but included in *Save the Earth*, ed. Jonathon Porritt, with a foreword by the Prince of Wales and an introduction by David Attenborough, for the environmental campaigning organisation Friends of the Earth, Sept 1991.

36. To the poet Michael Hamburger (L 538), with further comments on the dangers of the nuclear industry (Hamburger lived in Suffolk, near the Sizewell B power station).

37. Quoted, Ed Douglas, 'Portrait of a poet as eco warrior', *Observer*, 4 Nov 2007, an excellent article which includes an interview with Ian Cook. There are further valuable interviews in Simon Armitage's 2009 BBC Radio 4 documentary 'Ted Hughes: Eco Warrior'. See further the admirable work of Terry Gifford: 'Rivers and Water Quality in the Work of Brian Clarke and Ted Hughes', *Concentric: Literary and Cultural Studies*, 34:1 (March 2008), pp. 75–91, revised and reprinted as 'Hughes's Social Ecology', in Terry Gifford, ed., *The Cambridge Companion to Ted Hughes* (Cambridge: Cambridge University Press, 2011), pp. 81–93; also the review of eco-critical treatments in Gifford, *Ted Hughes* (Routledge Guides to Literature, 2009), pp. 139–47.

38. *Guardian*, 16 April 1992.

39. Blake Morrison, 'Man of mettle', interview with Hughes in *Independent on Sunday*, 5 Sept 1993.

40. Undated, 1986 (L 512–14).

41. 'Slump Sundays', 'Macaw' (a far cry from the 'Macaw and Little Miss' of *The Hawk in the Rain*), 'On the Reservations: III The Ghost Dancer', CP 750, 752, 779.

42. Conversation with Ann Skea, quoted in her online chronology, ann.skea. com/timeline.htm.

43. Sagar, ed., *Poet and Critic*, p. 165 (14 Nov 1987).

44. *London Review of Books*, 24 Jan 1985.

45. *The Poetry Book Society Bulletin*, 142 (Autumn 1989), pp. 1–3.

46. Emory 644/115.

47. 'Not with a bang but a hum', *Observer*, 17 Sept 1989.

Chapter 26: Trial

1. CP 1153–4.

2. Diary entry, 4 April 1982, in purple exercise book (BL Add. MS 88993/3). All papers relating to the *Bell Jar* trial were embargoed until Jane Anderson's death in 2010, but they have now been made available to the public in two sources: BL Add. MS 88993: 'Ted Hughes/Sylvia Plath: *The Bell Jar* legal case: archive of poetry, diary entries, correspondence and other papers relating to the legal case brought by Dr Jane Anderson against the Plath Estate (then managed by Plath's widower, Ted Hughes), Avco Embassy Pictures Corporation and others for defamation of character, invasion of privacy and intentional infliction of emotional damage following the release of *The Bell Jar* film in 1979'; and Jane V. Anderson Papers, Mortimer Rare Book Room, Smith College (grateful thanks to Karen Kukil for the provision of extensive photocopies of this material).

3. BL Add. MS 88993/3.

4. Ibid.

5. L 529.

6. Plath to James Michie (Sylvia Plath Collection, Mortimer Rare Book Room, Smith College, MS 45/5/46).

7. BL Add. MS 88993/3.

8. BL Add. MS 88993/3, quoting letters to Aurelia Plath and Olive Higgins Prouty, dated 27 Aug, 26 Sept, 18 Oct, 21 Oct 1962.

9. Hughes to Leonard Scigaj and to his editors at Faber & Faber, Viking Penguin and HarperCollins, 9 March 1992. By the same account, one of the principal aims of this book is to explicate, celebrate and immortalise the writings of Ted Hughes, both published and unpublished, so as to bring him new readers.

10. 5 Oct 1987 (Emory 644/7).

11. Correspondence relating to *Bitter Fame*, in Literary Papers and Correspondence of Anne Stevenson, Cambridge University Library, MS Add. 9451/19.

12. He ascribed them to the *Bhagavad-Gita*, but the quotation is actually from *Journey to the West* by the classical Chinese author Wu Cheng'en.

13. *Guardian*, 20 April 1989.

14. Trevor Thomas's archive of papers arising from the case was acquired by the bookseller Richard Ford in 2009, and is now in the Lilly Library, Indiana University, Bloomington, sylviaplathinfo.blogspot.co. uk/2009_04_01_archive.html.

15. 'Trial' Draft 1 and Draft 2, in BL Add. MS 88993/1. All subsequent quotations in this chapter are from this draft poem, which is nearly two thousand lines in length (subdivided into forty-six sections).

Chapter 27: A

1. He put it up for sale in 2011: see Dalya Alberge, 'Ted Hughes's jaguar sculpture hints at poet's demons', *Observer*, 31 Jan 2011, theguardian.com/books/2011/dec/31/ted-hughes-jaguar-sculpture-sale. Further information derived from Olwyn Hughes, letter to Jonathan Bate, 7 Feb 2012.
2. 'Fanaticism', CP 789.
3. 'The Locket', CP 784.
4. 'Fanaticism', CP 789.
5. 'Descent', CP 787.
6. CP 789–90.
7. Paul Celan, 'Todesfuge', in his *Der Sand aus den Urnen* (1948), my translation.
8. Now in the British Library archive, split into two folders within BL Add. MS 88918/1. Unless otherwise stated, all subsequent quotations in this chapter are from these manuscripts.
9. 'Daddy', CPSP 223.
10. For Shura as ash, see especially the end of the tender lyric 'You found a magic path, your little girl'.
11. Al Alvarez, *Where Did It All Go Right? A Memoir* (Richard Cohen Books, 1999; New York: William Morrow, 2000), p. 209.

Chapter 28: Goddess Revisited

1. To Dermot Wilson (L 574).
2. Earlier versions of this chapter were essayed as 'Hughes on Shakespeare', in Terry Gifford, ed., *The Cambridge Companion to Ted Hughes* (Cambridge: Cambridge University Press, 2011), and, with actors reading relevant passages from the plays, as the 2014 Sam Wanamaker Fellowship Lecture on the stage of the Sam Wanamaker Theatre at Shakespeare's Globe, London.
3. *Macbeth*, Act 3, scene 2, quoted in the editorial version corresponding to that of the old red Oxford edition owned by Hughes.
4. BL Add. MS 88918/1.
5. L 105.
6. Partially published in 1987 as *A Full House* (CP 731–6).
7. BL Add. MS 88918/1.
8. Personal recollections by John Billingsley of a reading in 1976 and Jonathan Bate of a reading at the Hobson Gallery, Cambridge, 27 February 1978.
9. Robert Graves, *The White Goddess: A Historical Grammar of Poetic Myth* (Faber & Faber, 1948), p. 426.
10. L 679–81.
11. CP 576.

12. *With Fairest Flowers while Summer Lasts: Poems from Shakespeare*, ed. and introduced by Ted Hughes (New York: Doubleday, 1971), pp. v–ix.
13. Ibid., p. ix.
14. Ibid., pp. xi, xiii.
15. Ibid., p. xvii.
16. Ibid.
17. Ibid.
18. L 336.
19. L 329.
20. CP 279–82.
21. L 336.
22. L 405–19.
23. Letter of 9 Sept 1991 (Emory 644/4).
24. 21 July 1991 (L 596).
25. This and subsequent quotations from Emory 844/105, first published in Gifford, ed., *The Cambridge Companion to Ted Hughes*, pp. 135–49.
26. SGCB 11.
27. Quoted, Gifford, ed., *The Cambridge Companion to Ted Hughes*, p. 143.
28. Ibid., 16 Sept 1991.
29. Ibid., 3 Nov 1991.
30. WP 132.
31. SGCB 91.
32. SGCB 116. 'Those visits' refers to Shakespeare's (presumably regular) returns to Stratford-upon-Avon to see his family and conduct business.
33. Ibid.
34. SGCB 179.
35. SGCB 183.
36. SGCB xix.
37. *Sunday Times* (London), 5 April 1992.
38. *The Times* (London), 9 April 1992.
39. SGCB 142–5.
40. BL Add. MS 88918/6.
41. Ibid.
42. SGCB 157–61.
43. 'A Brief Guide' to *Shakespeare and the Goddess of Complete Being*, sent to the theatre director Michael Kustow on 2 Dec 1993 (Emory 644/55).
44. Personal communication.
45. See my *Shakespeare and Ovid* (Oxford: Clarendon Press, 1993) and my forthcoming *Shakespeare and the Classical Imagination* (Princeton, NJ: Princeton University Press).
46. Add. MS 88918/6.
47. Ibid.
48. Ibid.

Chapter 29: Smiling Public Man

1. Yeats, 'Among School Children', in *The Tower* (1928).
2. Letters to Bernard Jenkin MP, 3 Feb 1990, to John Gummer MP, Minister in the Department of Agriculture, Farming and Fisheries, 10 Sept 1991, and to Emma Nicholson MP, 22 March 1990 (Emory 644/53).
3. 'The hart of the mystery', *Guardian*, 5 July 1997; 'A brainy idea for the Domeheads', *The Times* (London), 18 Feb 1998.
4. Letter of 28 Jan 1992 (Emory 644/53).
5. Letter to *Sunday Times* (London), book review section, 20 Jan 1990.
6. L 652–4.
7. To Heaney, 29 Sept 1990 (Heaney Papers, Emory 960/40/16).
8. L 683.
9. My interview with Heaney.
10. Dennis O'Driscoll, *Stepping Stones: Interviews with Seamus Heaney* (Faber & Faber, 2008), p. 189. 'View of a Pig' was a particularly strong influence, shaping 'Turkeys', the earliest poem in Heaney's first collection (p. 79). *Stepping Stones* also includes valuable material on the creation of *The Rattle Bag* and *The School Bag* and on Heaney's response to *Birthday Letters* (see especially pp. 390–7).
11. To Martin Palmer, 26 Aug 1992 (Emory 644/38).
12. To Nicki Clinton, 28 Nov 1994 (Emory 644/55).
13. To William Scammell, 31 March 1993 (Emory 644/7).
14. BL Add. MS 88918/129.
15. 17 Aug 1993 (Emory 1014/1).
16. Frieda Hughes, 'Father dear father', *Daily Telegraph*, 29 Oct 2002.
17. Emory 1014/1. 'Windfall from heaven' is a lovely improvement on the banal 'treasure' in an earlier draft. Ted considered the piece more of a 'rambling rhapsody' (ibid.) than a poem.
18. To Anne-Lorraine Bujon, 16 Dec 1992, L 621–36.
19. To Baskin, 15 Aug 1991 (Emory 644/1).
20. The film was supposedly to be based on the Paul Alexander biography *Rough Magic*; Kovner sent a warning letter to Columbia Pictures and to Ringwald. Columbia backed away (letter to Hughes from New York libel lawyer David Ellenhorn, 7 April 1992; Emory 644/37).
21. To Spender, 27 July 1992 (Emory 644/8).
22. L 638.
23. Letter of 7 Oct 1991 (Emory 644/3).
24. This and subsequent quotations from Horatio Morpurgo, 'The Table Talk of Ted Hughes', *Areté*, 6 (Autumn 2001), aretemagazine.co.uk/06-autumn-2001/the-table-talk-of-ted-hughes/.
25. For the Gielgud evening, there is a fulsome thank-you letter dated 12 March 1990 in the Royal Archives at Windsor (RA/QEQM/PRIV/CSP/PAL), together with a poem. The fishing visit is described in a long letter to Gerald and Joan, 18 May 1991 (Emory 854/1/95).
26. 16 Feb 1994, Ted Hughes, 'Letters to János Csokits' (Emory 895/1).
27. Unpublished letters of June 1996 and April 1997 (Emory 644/55).

28. O'Driscoll, *Stepping Stones*, p. 397.

29. L 574.

30. L 576.

31. O'Driscoll, *Stepping Stones*, p. 397.

32. Seamus Heaney and Ted Hughes, eds, *The School Bag* (Faber & Faber, 1997), p. xvii.

33. To HRH the Prince of Wales, 9 Oct 1997 (Emory 644/55).

34. 'Tell us princes another story, poet Ted', *Sunday Times* (London), 20 Feb 2011.

35. It is inappropriate to cite anything other than the Wordsworth quotation from this private poem, but I am most grateful to HRH Prince Charles for allowing Ian Skelly of the Temenos Academy to transcribe it and show it to me.

36. To Joanna Mackle, 4 Jan 1992 (Emory 644/14).

37. Some of those written in the Eighties were discussed in Chapter 24, 'The Fisher King', above. Along with the trade printing there was a two-volume limited edition (280 signed copies at £75, a nice little earner), with 'The Unicorn' standing alone in the second volume.

38. CP 1215.

39. CP 1216.

40. CP 1216–17.

41. Ibid.

42. CP 1219.

43. Epigraph to *Rain-Charm*, also quoted at climax of note to 'A Birthday Masque' (CP 1218) and inscribed by hand on books presented personally to members of the royal family (personal communication).

44. Hermione Lee, 'Sacred myths and fishing lines', *Independent on Sunday*, 21 June 1992; Hilary Corke, 'Sunny Side up for the Laureate', *Spectator*, 20 June 1992.

45. 'The crow vs the teddy bear', *Observer*, 14 June 1992.

46. Peter Bradshaw, 'The dismal dozen', *Evening Standard*, 30 Dec 1992.

47. CP 55.

48. Blurb for *The Iron Woman: A Sequel to The Iron Man* (Faber & Faber, 1993).

49. To David Thacker, 30 Nov 1993 (Emory 644/54).

50. CP 1024.

51. Discussed in Chapter 31, 'The Return of Alcestis', below.

52. WP 377.

53. WP 378, 383.

54. WP 446–7.

55. 'Corrections by Olwyn Hughes of Diane Middlebrook's Her Husband' (Emory 980/2/20).

56. Personal communication.

57. Csokits Letters (Emory 895/1).

58. Phyllis Grosskurth, 'Ted Hughes undone', *Globe and Mail* (Toronto), 13 Nov 1999.

59. Olwyn Hughes in conversation, March 2010.

60. Personal communication.

61. I owe this astute observation to Roy Davids (conversation of 10 Aug 2011).

62. 'Goku', in Ted Hughes, *The Dreamfighter and Other Creation Tales* (Faber & Faber, 2003), pp. 200–1. This posthumous collection is a gathering of *How the Whale Became* (1963), *Tales of the Early World* (1988) and – borrowing its title – *The Dreamfighter and Other Creation Tales* (1995).

63. Ibid., p. 320.

64. 'Anniversary', CP 854.

65. Gordon Wardman, 'They Do the Ted in Different Voices', *Poetry Quarterly Review*, Spring 1995, p. 5.

66. Brian Hinton, *Tears in the Fence*, 16 (Oct 1995), pp. 56–8. 'New confessional voice' is Wardman's phrase.

67. To Heaney, 18 April 1995 (Emory 644/55).

68. Tim Supple, 'Ted Hughes and the Theatre', ann.skea.com/TimSupple.html.

69. Ibid.

70. Ibid.

71. Benedict Nightingale, *The Times* (London), 10 Aug 1995; Robert Hanks, unidentified clipping, Emory 644/176/27; Charles Spencer, *Daily Telegraph*, 10 Aug 1995. The process of tightening the translation can be traced in the rehearsal typescript, now at Emory (644/121/7).

72. Supple, 'Ted Hughes and the Theatre'.

73. *Daily Telegraph*, 30 Sept 1996.

74. *Sunday Telegraph*, 6 Oct 1996.

75. Supple, 'Ted Hughes and the Theatre'.

76. Act 2, scene 1, in Lorca, *Blood Wedding*, in a version by Ted Hughes (Faber & Faber, 1996), p. 23.

77. End of Act 3, scene 2, ibid., p. 72.

78. April 1990, to rave reviews. Licensed but not seen by Hughes. This was not the first Hughes dramatisation to attract the eyes of the critics: in 1986 a company called dereck Productions pulled off an extraordinary epic version of *Gaudete* at the Almeida in Islington ('Contains some of the most stunning images one is likely to see in the theatre,' raved the *Financial Times*) – see reviews in Emory 644/176/24.

79. To Olwyn, 6 March 1997 (BL Add. MS 88948/1).

80. *By Heart: 101 Poems to Remember*, ed. with an introduction by Ted Hughes (Faber & Faber, 1997), pp. xv–xvi.

81. 'Silent is the house', which is included in *The School Bag*, p. 449.

82. He charged £1,000, with his bookkeeper reminding him to add on the VAT (sales tax).

83. Frieda's poem 'The Last Secret', written at this time and later published in her collection *Stonepicker* (Hexham: Bloodaxe, 2001), is about her father's desire for the family not to share the news of his cancer.

84. To Heaney, 26 Aug 1997 (Heaney Archive, Emory 960/40/16/2).

85. To Baskin, 15 Aug 1997 (BL Add. MS 83685).

Chapter 30: The Sorrows of the Deer

1. Comment on reading the Sylvia poems in the 1995 *New Selected*, so referring to the short 'Black Coat' lyric, not the full epic version discussed below. Heaney to Hughes, from Glanmore Cottage, 14 March 1995 (Emory 644/55).
2. BL Add. MS 88918/1.
3. *The Times* (London), 17 Jan 1998.
4. All quotations from 19 Jan 1998.
5. *Herald* (Glasgow), 20 Jan 1998. The reference is to a popular British television soap opera.
6. BL Add. MS 88918/1. Subsequent quotations from same source.
7. To Raine, 31 Jan 1998 (Emory 644/5); read in public by Frieda Hughes, and broadcast on BBC Television, 26 Jan 1999.
8. To Baskins, 5 Feb 1998, quoted, John Ezard, 'Hughes in hiding over *Birthday Letters*', *Guardian*, 14 April 2004.
9. Heaney to Hughes, 14 Dec 1997 (BL Add. MS 88918/8).
10. L 703.
11. Published in her debut poetry collection, *Wooroloo* (HarperCollins, 1998).
12. L 712–13.
13. To Caroline Tisdall and her partner Paul van Vlissingen, 8 April 1998 (BL Add. MS 88918/8). There is a wonderfully vivid journal of this adventurous holiday in BL Add. MS 88918/128.
14. 'The Laburnum', CP 1176.
15. Discussed at the end of the Epilogue, below.
16. I am most grateful to Andrew Howard, Chairman and Managing Director of Sinclairs Products, for this information (email of 12 Oct 2010).
17. Alternatively, the notebook might have been charred in the Lumb Bank fire before anything was written in it, or there may have been some other minor conflagration.
18. Robert Graves, *The White Goddess: A Historical Grammar of Poetic Myth* (Faber & Faber, 1948), ch. 14, 'The Roebuck in the Thicket'. Ann Skea helpfully suggests other resonances in her article 'Notes on the British Library's *Birthday Letters* Archive', ann.skea.com/BLArchiveLists.html. In the summer of 1978, when gathering poems for *The Rattle Bag*, Hughes asked Terence McCaughey 'what is "The Sorrows of the Deer"?' (L 394), an apparent reference to St Patrick's hymn ('The Deer's Cry'). This may suggest that the title was not applied to the Sylvia sequence until the late Seventies. Another source seems to be a poem by the Hungarian Ferenc Juhász called 'The boy changed into a stag cries out at the gate of secrets', which Hughes retranslated on reading what he regarded as an unsatisfactory translation in an anthology of Hungarian poems that was published in 1963 (Ted Hughes, *Selected Translations*, ed. Daniel Weissbort (Faber & Faber, 2006), p. 24). To complicate matters further, David Wevill also translated this poem, for a Penguin anthology published shortly after Assia's death.
19. To Sagar, 18 July 1998 (Keith Sagar, ed., *Poet and Critic: The Letters of Ted Hughes and Keith Sagar* (British Library, 2012), p. 269).

20. The only occasions on which he used the word 'somnambulist' in his published poems were with regard to his father and fellow-soldiers going over the top on the Western Front ('For the Duration') and to Sylvia on the beach in their first days in Devon ('The Beach', where the Hartland peninsula becomes 'the reverse of beautiful Nauset').

21. 'Your fingers' in Silvine Notebook, BL Add. MS 88918/1, revised as 'Fingers' in *Birthday Letters* (CP 1167–8).

22. Personal communication.

23. 'Under the Laburnums', in Silvine Notebook.

24. CP 326.

25. BL Add. MS 88918/1.

26. BL Add. MS 88918/1. It is unclear whether 'Black Coat' and 'Opus 131' represent alternative titles or title and subtitle. Probably the latter.

27. Quoted, Neil Roberts, *A Lucid Dreamer: The Life of Peter Redgrove* (Jonathan Cape, 2012), p. 80.

28. In Redgrove's version, but in the *Two of a Kind: Poets in Partnership* radio interview of Jan 1961 (available on *The Spoken Word: Sylvia Plath* (BBC/British Library, 2010, CD)), Ted corrects Sylvia and describes it as a 'life mask'.

29. I am grateful to Professor Norman Hammond for the information that Hughes is topographically imprecise here: the log cabin (a gift of the Norwegian government) where the royal family like to barbecue amid the midges is actually on one of the branches of the Garbh Allt, south of the Dee, some considerable distance from the proud cone of Lochnagar itself, and a considerable drive from Birkhall, perhaps in the Queen's Land Rover.

30. *Freedom: A Commemorative Anthology to Celebrate the 125th Birthday of the British Red Cross* (Little, Brown, 1995)

31. Extract from 'Black Coat: Opus 131', first published in 'Sorrow in a Black Coat', *Times Literary Supplement*, 5 Feb 2014.

32. BL Add. MS 88918/129. In 1963, shortly after Sylvia's death, Hughes had submitted to *Poetry* magazine in Chicago a modern 'angry young man' reworking of Wordsworth's 'Upon Westminster Bridge', with a polluted Thames and the nation becoming a sewer (CP 104).

33. Extract from 'Black Coat: Opus 131', first published in 'Sorrow in a Black Coat'.

34. CP 797.

35. This paragraph describes the contents of one of the old school exercise books in BL Add. MS 88918/1. Hughes gathered many more of these exercise books together, numbering them from 'S1' ('S' for Sylvia) to 'S9', as he built up the sequence of 'The Sorrows of the Deer' before alighting on the new title *Birthday Letters* (in the assemblage of the sequence into a rough chronological order of events – not, that is to say, chronological order of composition – the original Silvine Notebook is numbered S6). The distribution of the published poems among these draft notebooks is helpfully tabulated by Ann Skea, 'Notes on the British Library's *Birthday Letters* Archive'.

36. See especially BL Add. MS 88918/1/12, a photocopy of the typescript as submitted to Faber & Faber. This includes a dedication of 'Caryatids' to Daniel Huws, which editor Christopher Reid thought ill advised given that the entire collection was dedicated formally to his children and implicitly to Sylvia's memory. 'The Tender Place', 'Chaucer' and 'The God' take the form of photocopies of previously published versions.
37. 1 Oct 1997 (BL Add. MS 88918/1/13).
38. BL Add. MS 88918/1/11, a revised proof.
39. The latter is the title written on the front of another of the school exercise books in BL Add. MS 88918/1/6.
40. '18 Rugby Street', CP 1055.
41. Ibid.
42. Richard Hollis, personal communication.

Chapter 31: The Return of Alcestis

1. To Baskin, 25 March 1995 (BL Add. MS 83685).
2. To Baskin, 13 Oct 1996 (BL Add. MS 83685).
3. *The Times* (London), 8 May 1997.
4. *Sunday Times* (London), 11 May 1997.
5. Melvyn Bragg, 'Two Poets Laureate joined by 2,000 years', *The Times* (London), 29 Dec 1997.
6. Ted Hughes, *Tales from Ovid* (Faber & Faber, 1997), pp. ix–x.
7. Ibid., pp. 124, 171.
8. Ibid., p. 46.
9. Sylvia Plath Collection, Lilly Library, Indiana University, Bloomington, Lilly II/14/5, hair.
10. *Tales from Ovid*, p. 47.
11. Aeschylus, *The Oresteia: A New Translation by Ted Hughes* (Faber & Faber, 1999; quoted here from the American paperback edition, New York: Farrar, Straus and Giroux, 2000), pp. 44, 117, 152.
12. Ibid., p. 16. The Plathian parallel is discussed in Michael Silk's superb essay 'Ted Hughes: Allusion and Poetic Language', in the admirable collection Roger Rees, ed., *Ted Hughes and the Classics* (Oxford: Oxford University Press, 2009).
13. Hughes's translation, in Jean Racine, *Phèdre: A Version by Ted Hughes* (Faber & Faber, 1998), p. 28.
14. BL Add. MS 88918/4.
15. Personal communication from Barrie Rutter.
16. Euripides, *Alcestis, in a New Version by Ted Hughes* (Faber & Faber, 1999), pp. 22, 21, 67.
17. Ibid., p. 26.
18. Ibid., p. 77.
19. Ibid., pp. 26–7.
20. Ibid., p. 33.
21. Ibid., p. 25.
22. BL Add. MS 88918/4.

23. 'Last Letter', *New Statesman*, 11 Oct 2010.

24. *Alcestis*, p. 45.

25. Ibid., p. 66.

26. Emily Brontë, *Wuthering Heights* (1847), ch. 29, with thanks to Alistair Heys for pointing out the centrality of this passage.

27. JSP 594.

28. Richard Murphy, *The Kick: A Life among Writers* (Granta, 2002), pp. 378–9. Ted's memory plays him false: Aurelia had returned home by this point, so the meeting must have been some weeks earlier.

29. The texts in *London Review of Books* (19 June 1986) and *Wolfwatching* (1989) have no epigraph; the proverb was introduced into the *Elmet* text (1994).

30. Seamus Heaney, 'On a new work in the English tongue', *Sunday Times* (London), 11 Oct 1998.

31. In possession of Hilda's daughter Vicky Watling (L 738). Postmarked 19 Oct and the line 'Recovering ever since' indicates written then, but the date on the letter itself is that of the royal audience, 16 Oct.

32. 6 Oct 1998 (L 733). For the enclosures, see John Carey, *The Unexpected Professor: An Oxford Life in Books* (Faber & Faber, 2014), p. 309. Humbled, Carey sent an apologetic reply to Court Green, but since Hughes was in London he did not open it before his death.

33. 'Comics' (in a 1997 pamphlet from the Prospero Press), 'Mother-Tongue' (*Sunday Times* (London), 12 Oct 1997).

34. *Waterlog*, 7 (Dec/Jan 1997/8), p. 10 (CP 1191).

35. *Daily Telegraph*, 9 Jan 1999 (CP 1194).

36. Olwyn Hughes, personal communication.

Epilogue: The Legacy

1. Emory 1014/2/2.

2. Boyd Tonkin, *Independent*, 30 Oct 1998, p. 3.

3. Frieda Hughes, *Stonepicker* (Hexham: Bloodaxe, 2001), p. 80.

4. Memorial address in Westminster Abbey, quoted, Peter Stothard, 'The moment that changed a memorial', *The Times* (London), 14 May 1999.

5. news.bbc.co.uk/1/hi/uk/207169.stm, misquoting 'in underbeing' as 'into underbeing' and, ironically, 'Loose words' for 'Lose words' (CP 652).

6. CP 655.

7. Terence McCaughey, 'A Light Gone Out – A Tribute to Ted Hughes at his Funeral Service in St Peter's Church, North Tawton, 3rd November, 1998', *Céide: A Review from the Margins*, 2:6 (July/Aug 1999), pp. 12–13.

8. 'Hunters Try to Bag Dartmoor Lion', BBC News, 20 Nov 1998, news.bbc.co.uk/1/hi/uk/218650.stm.

9. Emma Tennant, *Burnt Diaries* (Edinburgh: Canongate, 1999), p. 228.

10. 'Thomas the Rhymer's Song', from Guppy's album *Durable Fire* (Linnet Records, 1982) (CP 628).

11. Song over the headless body, supposed to be Fidele/Imogen, in *Cymbeline*. A Hughesian favourite, included in his 1971 Shakespeare anthology, as well as in both *The Rattle Bag* and *By Heart*.

12. Stothard, 'The moment that changed a memorial'.

13. *Poems for Shakespeare*, ed. Charles Osborne, July 1987.

14. *Sunday Times* (London), 6 Sept 1998 (CP 1303).

15. BL Add. MS 88918/1.

16. Proved 'In the High Court of Justice: The District Probate Registry at Bristol', 25 March 1999. Now in the public domain, as are all wills proven in English law.

17. Copy of 'Letter of Wishes' in the possession of Olwyn Hughes.

18. telegraph.co.uk/news/uknews/1411415/Dying-wish-of-Ted-Hughes-splits-family.html (originally published 27 Oct 2002).

19. Emory 895/23. 'For the Duration', CP 760, and 'The Beach', CP 1143.

20. 17 Nov 2002 (Emory, 895/2).

21. kirkusreviews.com/book-reviews/susan-fromberg-schaeffer/poison-5/ (review originally published 24 April 2006).

22. Susan Fromberg Schaeffer, *Poison* (New York: W. W. Norton, 2006), pp. 244–5.

23. Ibid., p. 249.

24. Ibid., pp. 236, 571.

25. Olwyn Hughes, personal communication.

26. Schaeffer, *Poison*.

27. I detected a striking change in Olwyn's language about Sylvia in the immediate aftermath of Nick's suicide. Before, she spoke of Sylvia as being bad; afterwards, of her as being ill. It was as if the heart-rending loss of little Nicky – whom she had loved from his infancy and who so resembled Ted – made her finally believe that depression is real. The Yorkshire 'pull your socks up' attitude dissolved, at least for a while, into sorrow and compassion.

28. Personal communication, 2010, the year before Schaeffer's death.

29. Schaeffer, *Poison*, p. 182.

30. Ibid., p. 279.

31. *Letters of Ted Hughes*, selected by and ed. Christopher Reid (Faber & Faber, 2007), p. xi.

32. To Bill and Dido Merwin (L 198).

33. To Olwyn (L 204). 'Affable familiar' alludes to Shakespeare on the 'rival poet' of his sonnets as an 'affable familiar ghost' (Sonnet 86).

34. To Gerald, March 1968, on first meeting Peter Brook (L 281).

35. To Daniel Weissbort, April 1982 (L 453).

36. July 1985, to two thirteen-year-old schoolgirls who had written asking him to interpret his work for them (L 500).

37. To Nick Gammage, Nov 1989 (L 570).

38. To Leonard and Lisa Baskin, May 1984 (L 484).

39. *Sunday Times* (London), 21 Oct 2007.

40. 17 Dec 1992 (BL Add. MS 88918/123).

41. Unpublished letter, 12 Dec 1992 (BL Add. MS 88948).

42. Olwyn Hughes, personal communication.

43. Elaine Feinstein, a literary acquaintance, got Ted Hughes biography off to a personally inflected start with *Ted Hughes: The Life of a Poet* (Weidenfeld &

Nicolson, 2001): written prior to the availability of many archival materials and without the co-operation of the Estate, it animated some of the key friendships but was inevitably cursory in its treatment of the writings. Diane Middlebrook's *Her Husband: Hughes and Plath – A Marriage* (New York:Viking, 2003) offers much more on the poetic partnership with Plath, but did not have the benefit of the vital second archive. Neil Roberts's *Ted Hughes: A Literary Life* (Basingstoke: Palgrave Macmillan, 2006) skilfully surveys the development of the literary career, but is sparing in biographical detail.

44. Hughes journal, 31 May 1979.
45. Emory 644/115.
46. Letters page, *Independent*, 22 April 1989.
47. Personal communication. The painting is now owned by Dr Paula Byrne.
48. Foreword by Libby Purves, in Frieda Hughes, *Forty-Five: Poems* (HarperCollins, 2006), p. ix.
49. Frieda Hughes, *Forty-Five*, p. 18. In fact, her memory is playing her slightly false: the borrowed dog and the tick belonged to the loughs, not the lochs: see Ted's account of a family fishing trip in Ireland (hosted by Richard Murphy) later that summer (L 314).
50. Frieda Hughes, *Forty-Five*, p. 19.
51. Quoted, Andrea Sachs, 'Q & A with Frieda Hughes', *Time*, 13 March 2007.
52. Frieda Hughes, *Forty-Five*, p. 89.
53. Frieda Hughes, *Waxworks: Poems* (HarperCollins, 2003), especially 'Medea', 'Job', 'Hera' and 'Honos'. 'Hippolytus' is also especially intriguing, in relation both to Nick and to Ted's late return to the *Phèdre* story. But these are matters for Frieda's future biographer, as are the vicissitudes of her relationship with Olwyn, which are hinted at by indirection in her clever and funny children's story *Getting Rid of Aunt Edna* (New York: Harper & Row, 1986).
54. Jason Neuswanger and Bessie Green, quoted, 'Remembering Dr Nicholas Hughes' on the website of the School of Fisheries and Ocean Sciences, University of Alaska Fairbanks, sfos.uaf.edu/memorial/hughes/.
55. Joe Saxton, 'What suicide gene? My friend Nick was brilliant, passionate and fun', *Sunday Times* (London), 29 March 2009.
56. In *Howls and Whispers* (CP 1182).
57. The only time this word occurs in his *Collected Poems*.
58. Personal communication.
59. CP 1180. There are good pages on 'The Offers' in Middlebrook, *Her Husband*, pp. 280–2, and Edward Hadley, *The Elegies of Ted Hughes* (Basingstoke and New York: Palgrave Macmillan, 2010), pp. 138–40 (where it is compared to Thomas Hardy's 'The Voice'), though these accounts were written without the benefit of the draft manuscripts.
60. BL Add. MS 88918/1.
61. BL Add. MS 88918/128.
62. Propertius, *Elegies*, 4.7; 'The Ghost (after Sextus Propertius)', in Robert Lowell, *Collected Poems* (New York: Farrar, Straus & Giroux, 2003), pp. 52–4

(originally published in *Lord Weary's Castle* (1946), a book which Sylvia gave Ted for his birthday when they were living in America). John Donne's wonderful 'The Apparition' is in the same Propertian tradition of lover–ghost poem.

63. 16 June 1998, to Andrea Paluch and Robert Habeck, in Keith Sagar, ed., *Poet and Critic: The Letters of Ted Hughes and Keith Sagar* (British Library, 2012), p. 324.

Picture Credits

p.3: © Ann Davidow-Goodman (Mrs Hayes) (top); © Siv Arb/
Writer Pictures (middle); © Jane Bown/Camera Press (bottom)

p.4: © David Wevill (top); © Richard Hollis (middle); © Celia
Chaikin (bottom)

p.5: © Jonathan Bate

p.6: © Eddie Jacob Photography (top); © David Willis McCullough,
courtesy of University of Maryland (bottom)

p.7: © Zoë Dominic

p.8: © Estate of Trevor Hedden, courtesy of Brenda Hedden (top);
© Alex Lentati/Associated Newspapers/REX (bottom)

Section Three

p.1: © Henri Cartier-Bresson/Magnum, via National Portrait
Gallery, London

p.2: © Stuart Clarke/Writer Pictures (top); © Stuart Clarke/Writer
Pictures (bottom)

p.3: © Bill Brandt Archive (top); © Mark Gerson/Bridgeman Images
(bottom)

p.4: © Hazel de Berg Collection of Photographs, National Library
of Australia (top left); © Jane Bown/*The Observer*/TopFoto (top
right); courtesy of Jill Petchesky © Estate of Barbara Trentham
(bottom)

p.5: © British Library Board/Fay Godwin Archive (top); © Nick
Rogers/REX (bottom)

p.6: © Dr Renate Latimer, courtesy of Mortimer Rare Book Room,
Smith College (top); © Robin McMorran (bottom)

p.7: © Ehor Boyanowsky (top); © News UK, photographed by Tom
Bate (bottom)

p. 8: © Tom Bate

The Principal Works
of Ted Hughes

The Hawk in the Rain (London: Faber & Faber, 1957; New York: Harper & Brothers, 1957)

Lupercal (London: Faber & Faber, 1960; New York: Harper & Row, 1960)

Meet My Folks! (Illustrated by George Adamson. London: Faber & Faber, 1961; Illustrated by Mila Lazarevich. New York: Bobbs-Merrill, 1973)

Selected Poems by Thom Gunn and Ted Hughes (London: Faber & Faber, 1962)

How the Whale Became and Other Stories (Illustrated by George Adamson. London: Faber & Faber, 1963; Illustrated by Rick Schreiter. New York: Atheneon, 1964)

The Earth-Owl and Other Moon People (Illustrated by R. A. Brandt. London: Faber & Faber, 1963)

Nessie the Mannerless Monster (Illustrated by Gerald Rose. London: Faber & Faber, 1964; Illustrated by Jan Pyk. New York: Bobbs-Merrill, 1974, as *Nessie the Monster*)

Recklings (London: Turret Books, 1966)

Wodwo (London: Faber & Faber, 1967; New York: Harper & Row, 1967)

Animal Poems (Crediton, Devon: Richard Gilbertson, 1967)

Poetry in the Making: An Anthology of Poems and Programmes from 'Listening and Writing' (London: Faber & Faber, 1967; New York: Doubleday, 1970, as *Poetry Is*)

Gravestones (Linocuts by Gavin Robbins. Exeter: Bartholomew Books/Exeter College of Art, ?1968)

The Iron Man: A Story in Five Nights (Illustrated by George Adamson. London: Faber & Faber, 1968; Illustrated by Robert Nadler. New York: Harper & Row, 1968, as *The Iron Giant*)

Seneca's Oedipus Adapted by Ted Hughes (London: Faber & Faber, 1969; New York: Doubleday, 1972)

The Coming of the Kings and Other Plays (London: Faber & Faber, 1970; Illustrated by Alan E. Cober. New York: Viking, 1974, as *The Tiger's Bones*, including additional play *Orpheus*)

A Few Crows (Illustrated by Reiner Burger. Exeter: Rougemont Press, 1970)

Crow: From the Life and the Songs of the Crow (Illustrated by Leonard Baskin. London: Faber & Faber, 1970; augmented edition 1972; New York: Harper & Row, 1971)

Crow Wakes (Woodford Green, Essex: Poet & Printer, 1971)

Poems: Ruth Fainlight, Ted Hughes, Alan Sillitoe (London: Rainbow Press, 1971)

Shakespeare's Poem (London: Lexham Press, 1971)

Eat Crow (London: Rainbow Press, 1971)

Selected Poems 1957–1967 (London: Faber & Faber, 1972; New York: Harper & Row, 1973)

Orghast at Persepolis: An Account of the Experiment in Theatre Directed by Peter Brook and Written by Ted Hughes, by A. C. H. Smith (London: Eyre Methuen, 1972; New York: Viking, 1973; including excerpts, summaries and explanations of the play, which was never published)

Prometheus on his Crag (London: Rainbow Press, 1973)

The Story of Vasco: Opera in Three Acts, Music by Gordon Crosse, Libretto Based on an English Version by Ted Hughes of the Play (London: Oxford University Press, 1974)

Season Songs (Illustrated by Leonard Baskin. New York: Viking, 1975; London: Faber & Faber, 1976, though first published privately as *Spring Summer Autumn Winter*. London: Rainbow Press, 1974; expanded edition, London: Faber & Faber, 1985)

Earth-Moon (Illustrated by the author. London: Rainbow Press, 1976)

Moon-Whales and Other Moon Poems (Illustrated by Leonard Baskin. New York: Viking, 1976; including poems from *The Earth-Owl and Other Moon People* and *Earth-Moon*; later UK edition, as *Moon-Whales*, illustrated by Chris Riddell, London: Faber & Faber, 1988)

Gaudete (London: Faber & Faber, 1977; New York: Harper & Row, 1977)

Moon-Bells and Other Poems (London: Chatto & Windus, 1978; expanded edition illustrated by Felicity Roma Bowers, London: Bodley Head, 1986)

Cave Birds: An Alchemical Cave Drama (Illustrated by Leonard Baskin. London: Faber & Faber, 1978; New York: Viking, 1979; greatly revised and expanded from *Cave Birds*, London: Scolar Press, 1975)

Orts (London: Rainbow Press, 1978)

Moortown Elegies (London: Rainbow Press, 1978)

Adam and the Sacred Nine (London: Rainbow Press, 1979)

Remains of Elmet (Photographs by Fay Godwin. London: Rainbow Press, 1979; as *Remains of Elmet: A Pennine Sequence*, London: Faber & Faber, 1979; New York: Harper & Row, 1979)

Moortown (London: Faber & Faber, 1979; New York: Harper & Row, 1980; collects *Moortown Elegies*, revised version of *Prometheus on his Crag*, *Earth-Numb* (sequence including poems from *Orts*, occasional and broadside publications and some unpublished poems), and revised version of *Adam and the Sacred Nine*)

Henry Williamson: A Tribute (London: Rainbow Press, 1979)

Under the North Star (Illustrated by Leonard Baskin. New York: Viking, 1981; London: Faber & Faber, 1981)

A Primer of Birds (Woodcuts by Leonard Baskin. Lurley, Devon: Gehenna Press, 1981)

New Selected Poems (New York: Harper & Row, 1982; UK edition as *Selected Poems 1957–1981*, London: Faber & Faber, 1982)

The Achievement of Ted Hughes, edited by Keith Sagar (Manchester: Manchester University Press, 1983; a collection of critical pieces on Hughes, with thirty uncollected or unpublished poems)

River (Photographs by Peter Keen. London: Faber & Faber in association with James & James, 1983; New York: Harper & Row, 1984, without photographs)

What is the Truth? A Farmyard Fable for the Young (Illustrated by R. J. Lloyd. London: Faber & Faber, 1984; New York: Harper & Row, 1984)

Ffangs the Vampire Bat and the Kiss of Truth (Illustrated by Chris Riddell. London: Faber & Faber, 1986)

Flowers and Insects: Some Birds and a Pair of Spiders (Illustrated by Leonard Baskin. London: Faber & Faber, 1986; New York: Alfred A. Knopf, 1986)

The Cat and the Cuckoo (Illustrated by R. J. Lloyd. Bideford: Sunstone Press, 1987. Illustrated by Flora McDonnell. London: Faber & Faber, 2002)

Tales of the Early World (Illustrated by Andrew Davidson. London: Faber & Faber, 1988; New York: Farrar, Straus & Giroux, 1991)

Wolfwatching (London: Faber & Faber, 1989; New York: Farrar, Straus & Giroux, 1991)

Moortown Diary (London and Boston, Mass.: Faber & Faber, 1989; revised and expanded trade reprint of *Moortown Elegies*)

Capriccio (Illustrated by Leonard Baskin. Lurley, Devon: Gehenna Press, 1990)

Shakespeare and the Goddess of Complete Being (London: Faber & Faber, 1992; New York: Farrar, Straus & Giroux, 1992, corrected and expanded)

Rain-Charm for the Duchy and Other Laureate Poems (London: Faber & Faber, 1992; also in a limited Faber & Faber edition with a second volume called *The Unicorn*)

A Dancer to God: Tributes to T. S. Eliot (London: Faber & Faber, 1992; New York: Farrar, Straus & Giroux, 1993; incorporating *T. S. Eliot: A Tribute*, London: Faber & Faber, printed privately, 1987)

The Mermaid's Purse (Illustrated by R. J. Lloyd. Bideford: Sunstone Press, 1993; revised trade edition, illustrated by Flora McDonnell, London: Faber & Faber, 1999)

Three Books: Remains of Elmet, Cave Birds, River (London: Faber & Faber, 1993; collecting poems from these earlier collections, without photographs and with various additions, omissions and revisions)

The Iron Woman: A Sequel to The Iron Man (Illustrated by Andrew Davidson. London: Faber & Faber, 1993; Engravings by Barry Moser. New York: Dial Books, 1995)

Elmet (Photography by Fay Godwin. London: Faber & Faber, 1994; expanded and revised from *Remains of Elmet*)

Winter Pollen: Occasional Prose, edited by William Scammell (London: Faber & Faber, 1994; New York: Picador USA, 1995)

Earth Dances (Illustrated by R. J. Lloyd. Llandogo, Monmouth: Old Stile Press, 1994)

New Selected Poems: 1957–1994 (London: Faber & Faber, 1995; including 'Uncollected' poems from *Capriccio / Birthday Letters*)

The Dreamfighter and Other Creation Tales (London: Faber & Faber, 1995)

Frank Wedekind: Spring Awakening in a New Version by Ted Hughes (London: Faber & Faber, 1995)

Shakespeare's Ovid (Illustrated by Christopher Le Brun. London: Enitharmon Press, 1995)

Difficulties of a Bridegroom: Collected Short Stories (London: Faber & Faber, 1995; New York: Picador USA, 1995)

Collected Animal Poems, 4 vols, entitled *The Iron Wolf* (Illustrated by Chris Riddell), *What is the Truth?* (Illustrated by Lisa Flather), *A March Calf* and *The Thought-Fox* (London: Faber & Faber, 1995)

Federico García Lorca: Blood Wedding. In a New Version by Ted Hughes (London: Faber & Faber, 1996)

Tales from Ovid (London: Faber & Faber, 1997; New York: Farrar, Straus & Giroux, 1997; four of the tales first translated for *After Ovid: New Metamorphoses*, edited by Michael Hofmann and James Lasdun, London: Faber & Faber, 1994, and then published separately as *Shakespeare's Ovid*)

Shaggy and Spotty (Illustrated by David Lucas. London: Faber & Faber, 1997)

Birthday Letters (London: Faber & Faber, 1998; New York: Farrar, Straus & Giroux, 1998)

Howls and Whispers (Illustrated by Leonard Baskin. Northampton, Mass.: Gehenna Press, 1998)

Jean Racine: Phèdre. A New Version by Ted Hughes (London: Faber & Faber, 1998; New York: Farrar, Straus & Giroux, 1999)

The Oresteia of Aeschylus: A New Translation by Ted Hughes (London: Faber & Faber, 1999; New York: Farrar, Straus & Giroux, 1999)

Euripides: Alcestis. In a Version by Ted Hughes (London: Faber & Faber, 1999; New York: Farrar, Straus & Giroux, 1999)

Ted Hughes: Poems Selected by Simon Armitage (London: Faber & Faber, 2000)

Collected Plays for Children (Illustrated by Quentin Blake. London: Faber & Faber 2001; republishes the plays from *The Coming of the Kings / The Tiger's Bones* with previously uncollected *The Pig Organ*)

Collected Poems, edited by Paul Keegan (London: Faber & Faber, 2003; New York: Farrar, Straus & Giroux, 2003; excludes children's poems, main sequence of *Gaudete* and some other material)

The Dreamfighter and Other Creation Tales (London: Faber & Faber, 2003)

Collected Poems for Children (Illustrated by Raymond Briggs. London: Faber & Faber, 2005)

Selected Translations, edited by Daniel Weissbort (London: Faber & Faber, 2006)

Letters of Ted Hughes, selected and edited by Christopher Reid (London: Faber & Faber, 2007; New York: Farrar, Straus & Giroux, 2008)

Timmy the Tug: A Story in Colour by Jim Downer; a Story in Rhyme by Ted Hughes (London: Thames & Hudson, 2009)

Poet and Critic: The Letters of Ted Hughes and Keith Sagar, edited by Keith Sagar (London: British Library, 2012)

As Editor

Keith Douglas: Selected Poems (London: Faber & Faber, 1964; New York: Chilmark Press, 1965)

Sylvia Plath: Ariel (London: Faber & Faber, 1965; New York: Harper & Row, 1966)

A Choice of Emily Dickinson's Verse (London: Faber & Faber, 1968)

Yehuda Amichai: Selected Poems Translated by Assia Gutmann (London: Cape Goliard, 1968; New York: Harper & Row, 1969; expanded reprint, London: Penguin, 1971, acknowledges 'the collaboration of Ted Hughes')

A Choice of Shakespeare's Verse (London: Faber & Faber, 1971; New York: Doubleday, 1971, as *With Fairest Flowers while Summer Lasts: Poems from Shakespeare*)

Sylvia Plath: Crossing the Water (London: Faber & Faber, 1971; New York: Harper & Row, 1971)

Sylvia Plath: Winter Trees (London: Faber & Faber, 1971; New York: Harper & Row, 1972)

János Pilinszky: Selected Poems Translated by Ted Hughes & János Csokits (Manchester: Carcanet, 1976; revised and enlarged edition, London: Anvil, 1989, as *The Desert of Love*)

Sylvia Plath: Johnny Panic and the Bible of Dreams (London: Faber & Faber, 1977; New York: Harper & Row, 1979)

Sylvia Plath: Collected Poems (London: Faber & Faber, 1981; New York: Harper & Row, 1981)

The Journals of Sylvia Plath, Ted Hughes, consulting editor, and
  Frances McCullough, editor (New York: Dial Press, 1982)
Arvon Foundation Poetry Competition: 1980 Anthology, edited by Ted
  Hughes and Seamus Heaney (NP [Todmorden, Lancashire]:
  Kilnhurst Publishing, 1982)
The Rattle Bag: An Anthology of Poetry, selected by Seamus Heaney
  and Ted Hughes (London: Faber & Faber, 1982)
Sylvia Plath's Selected Poems, chosen by Ted Hughes (London: Faber
  & Faber, 1985)
A Choice of Coleridge's Verse (London: Faber & Faber, 1996)
The School Bag, edited by Seamus Heaney and Ted Hughes (London:
  Faber & Faber, 1997)
By Heart: 101 Poems to Remember, with an introduction by Ted
  Hughes (London: Faber & Faber, 1997)

This bibliography excludes broadside and pamphlet publications of
single poems, contributions to multi-authored volumes and periodicals,
occasional works, individual essays, articles and reviews. For a full listing,
see *Ted Hughes: A Bibliography 1946–1995* by Keith Sagar and Stephen
Tabor (London and New York: Mansell, 1998). An online supplement
by Sagar listing post-1995 publications is, at the time of writing, avail-
able at keithsagar.co.uk/Downloads/Hughes/Supplement.pdf.

Hughes's prolific career reading his work and talking about poetry
on the radio can be traced by typing his name into the invaluable
'BBC Genome' that reproduces the *Radio Times* listings for every one
of his more than 300 broadcasts (genome.ch.bbc.co.uk). The British
Library has nearly 500 recordings of his voice, listed in its Sound and
Moving Image Catalogue (cadensa.bl.uk/uhtbin/cgisirsi/?ps=wiRqg-
So17g/WORKS-FILE/0/49).

A selection of audio recordings of him reading his poems and
stories, and of the original broadcasts of *Poetry in the Making*, is avail-
able on two sets of two compact discs under the title *Ted Hughes: The
Spoken Word* (BBC/British Library, 2008). The companion *Spoken
Word* CD for Sylvia Plath (BBC/British Library, 2010) includes *Two
of a Kind: Poets in Partnership*, the joint interview with Sylvia Plath and
Ted Hughes recorded on 18 January 1961. 'The Artist and the Poet:
Leonard Baskin and Ted Hughes in Conversation', recorded in 1983,
is available on DVD (Noel Chanan, 2009).

The richest and most revealing interview of Hughes is that by Drue
  Heinz, 'The Art of Poetry: LXXI', *The Paris Review*, 37 (Spring
  1995), http://www.theparisreview.org/interviews/1669/
  the-art-of-poetry-no-71-ted-hughes

The following websites are of great value:

Earth–Moon: Information about Ted Hughes: ted-hughes.info/
  home.html
The Poetry Archive (examples of Ted Hughes reading his own
  poems): poetryarchive.org/poet/ted-hughes
The Ted Hughes Homepage: ann.skea.com/THHome.htm
THOR: Ted Hughes Online Resources: thetedhughessociety.org/
  apps/links/

The Ted Hughes Society is well worth joining; its online journal
contains a wealth of recent research on both the life and the work.

Suggestions for Further Reading

Readers coming to Ted Hughes for the first time should begin with either the *Selected Poems* edited by Simon Armitage for Faber & Faber in 2000 or, more ambitiously, Hughes's own choice in *New Selected Poems: 1957–1994* supplemented by *Tales from Ovid* and *Birthday Letters*. The Faber edition of selected *Letters* is the best introduction to his prose, followed by the essays gathered in *Winter Pollen*.

Selected Memoirs

Alliston, Susan, *Poems and Journals 1960–1969*, introduction by Ted Hughes (2010)

Boyanowsky, Ehor, *Savage Gods, Silver Ghosts: In the Wild with Ted Hughes* (2009)

Feinstein, Elaine, *Ted Hughes: The Life of a Poet* (2001)

Gammage, Nick, ed., *The Epic Poise: A Celebration of Ted Hughes* (1999)

Hughes, Gerald, *Ted and I: A Brother's Memoir* (2012)

Huws, Daniel, *Memories of Ted Hughes 1952–1963* (2010)

Koren, Yehuda, and Eilat Negev, *A Lover of Unreason: The Life and Tragic Death of Assia Wevill, Ted Hughes' Doomed Love* (2006)

Malcolm, Janet, *The Silent Woman: Sylvia Plath and Ted Hughes* (1993)

Murphy, Richard, *The Kick: A Life among Writers* (2002)

Myers, Lucas, *Crow Steered, Bergs Appeared: A Memoir of Ted Hughes and Sylvia Plath* (2001)

Sigmund, Elizabeth, and Gail Crowther, *Sylvia Plath in Devon: A Year's Turning* (2014)

Sonnenberg, Ben, *Lost Property: Memoirs and Confessions of a Bad Boy* (1991)

Tennant, Emma, *Burnt Diaries* (1999)

Selected Criticism

Ely, Steve, *Ted Hughes and South Yorkshire: Made in Mexborough* (2015)

Faas, Ekbert, *Ted Hughes: The Unaccommodated Universe* (1980)

Gifford, Terry, *Ted Hughes* (2009)

Gifford, Terry, ed., *The Cambridge Companion to Ted Hughes* (2011)

Hadley, Edward, *The Elegies of Ted Hughes* (2010)

Heaney, Seamus, 'Englands of the Mind', in his *Preoccupations: Selected Prose 1968–1978* (1980)

Paulin, Tom, 'Laureate of the Free Market? Ted Hughes', in his *Minotaur: Poetry and the Nation State* (1992)

Rees, Roger, ed., *Ted Hughes and the Classics* (2009)

Roberts, Neil, *Ted Hughes: A Literary Life* (2006)

Sagar, Keith, *The Laughter of Foxes: A Study of Ted Hughes* (2000, rev. edn 2006)

——, *Ted Hughes and Nature: Terror and Exultation* (2010)

Scigaj, Leonard, *The Poetry of Ted Hughes: Form and Imagination* (1986)

Skea, Ann, *Ted Hughes: The Poetic Quest* (1994)

Weissbort, Daniel, *Ted Hughes and Translation* (2011)

Wormald, Mark, Neil Roberts, and Terry Gifford, eds, *Ted Hughes: From Cambridge to Collected* (2013)

Hughes and Plath

Clark, Heather, *The Grief of Influence: Sylvia Plath and Ted Hughes* (2011)

Kukil, Karen, ed., *The Journals of Sylvia Plath 1950–1962* (2000)

Kukil, Karen, and Peter K. Steinberg, eds, *The Letters of Sylvia Plath* (forthcoming from Faber & Faber)

Middlebrook, Diane, *Her Husband: Hughes and Plath – A Marriage* (2003)

Stevenson, Anne, with assistance from Olwyn Hughes and additional material by Lucas Myers, Dido Merwin and Richard Murphy, *Bitter Fame: A Life of Sylvia Plath* (1989, repr. 1998)

Wagner, Erica, *Ariel's Gift: Ted Hughes, Sylvia Plath and the Story of Birthday Letters* (2000)

Acknowledgements

This book offers a preliminary report from the richest personal archive in the history of English poetry. For the purposes of research over a period of five years, I read and took notes on nearly 100,000 pages of Ted Hughes manuscripts. I also benefited immeasurably from conversations and correspondence with the late Olwyn Hughes, Frieda Hughes, Jill Barber, Barbara Blackman, Ehor Boyanowsky, Melvyn Bragg, His Royal Highness Prince Charles, Roy Davids, Anne Donovan, Jean Gooder, Grey and Neiti Gowrie, the late Seamus Heaney, Brenda Hedden, Richard Hollis, Edward Lucie-Smith, Janet Malcolm, Robin Morgan, Lucas Myers, Tom Paulin, Tom Pero, Roger Pringle, Craig Raine, David Rankin, Christopher Reid, Annie Robinson, Judith Rodriguez, Jacqueline Rose, Elizabeth Sigmund (formerly Compton), Ann Pasternak Slater, the late Ben Sonnenberg, Sir Peter Stothard, Marina Warner, Vicky Watling, the late Daniel Weissbort, Carolyne Wright and others who prefer not to be named. Several people, including David Wevill, wished the project well but declined to be interviewed.

I had the privilege, very rare for a biographer, of writing the childhood chapters of this book in the very house where Ted Hughes was born and spent the first eight years of his life. Through the good offices of the Elmet Trust, 1 Aspinall Street, now known as 'Ted's House', is available as a holiday let. I am grateful to John Billingsley and the late Donald Crossley for being my guides to the moors above Mytholmroyd, which were so formative of Hughes's imagination. I am also grateful to Marion Allen and Julia Ashby of the Mexborough District Heritage Society.

My deep gratitude goes to the librarians and archivists who made the work possible, especially Steve Enniss (now of the Harry Ransom

Center at the University of Texas, Austin) and Kathy Shoemaker at the Manuscript and Rare Book Library, Emory University; Jamie Andrews and Helen Melody at the British Library; David Frasier at the Lilly Library, University of Indiana, Bloomington; Karen Kukil (who went far beyond the call of duty) at the Mortimer Rare Books Room, Smith College; Wilgha Edwards at the Australian Defence Force Academy; Marc Carlson and Kristen Leatherwood at the McFarlin Library, University of Tulsa. Manuscripts that are now in the following collections were also consulted, either as originals or as copies: BBC Written Archives Centre, Caversham; Peter Brook Archive, Victoria and Albert Museum; Cambridge University Library; Special Collections, University of Exeter; Special Collections, University of Liverpool; Special Collections, University of Maryland Libraries; the archive of Pembroke College, Cambridge; Sheffield University Library.

For insights into Hughes at Cambridge University, thanks to Jayne Ringrose, Colin Wilcockson and especially Mark Wormald. Into his dealings with Faber and Faber: Gillian Bate, Joanna Mackle and others. Thanks, too, to theatre workers, especially Michael Boyd, Peter Brook, Barrie Rutter, Tim Supple and Oliver Taplin. And to poets, especially Simon Armitage and Sir Andrew Motion. To Hughes scholars: Terry Gifford, Claas Kazzer (special thanks for recordings of interviews with Ted's childhood friends), Neil Roberts, the late Keith Sagar, Ann Skea, Carrie Smith, Stephen Tabor (for his indispensable bibliographic acumen), Mark Wormald and others. To Warren Plath's neighbour, Richard Larschan. And to my doctoral student Yvonne Reddick, for invaluable research assistance in the archive at Emory. To the great Plath scholar Peter K. Steinberg, who provided valuable information and corrected several errors when he read a draft through Plathian eyes. And for a reading with a novelist's eye for narrative and character, to my dear friend Candida Crewe. Most of all, to two Hughes scholars, who were also Ted's friends: Christopher Reid for making available the letters, and Nick Gammage for an astute and scrupulous reading of the entire typescript, as well as copies of manuscripts in his possession.

The early research phase of the project in 2010–11, my final year as a professor at the University of Warwick, was made possible by a generous Research Fellowship from the Leverhulme Trust, matched by study leave from the Department of English. A Visiting Fellowship at Harris Manchester College, Oxford, gave me a room in a quiet tower where I could read through the hundred books written or edited by Ted Hughes; thanks to the Principal, Ralph Waller, and the Fellows of Harris Manchester for making this possible (and to Eric Anderson for suggesting it). The Fellows of Worcester College, Oxford, were generous in allowing me to retain my life as a scholar and writer while also becoming their Provost.

I am deeply grateful to several senior members of the legal profession who gave informal advice, and especially to Richard Hooper for explaining the background to the important changes in copyright that were implemented in 2014, following the Hooper Review of 2012. It was a pleasure to work with Ross Wilson of Matchlight, Liz Hartford, Lucy Evans and especially the visionary Richard Curson Smith on a documentary about Hughes's life and work, for broadcast on BBC2 television at the time of this book's publication.

Andrew Wylie and his team, notably Tracy Bohan, looked after me as no other agency could – especially at the difficult moments. At HarperCollins, Arabella Pike in London and Terry Karten in New York stepped into the breach with courage and passion. I am proud to have joined them. The whole publishing team was superb: special thanks to Joseph Zigmond, Stephen Guise, Jo Walker, copy-editor Peter James and proof-reader Philip Parr for their hawk eyes, and Tom Jarvis for his legal expertise.

Tom Bate's photography was on the button. Assistance in sorting vast piles of photocopies was provided by Vicky Ironmonger in the early stages and Hester Styles towards the end. My personal assistants in the Provost's Lodgings at Worcester, first Corinna Hilton and then Ilaria Gualino, served as gatekeepers when I needed to be free from other business. Barrie and Deedee Wigmore gave me the place by the college lake where the book was written in the dawn company of kingfisher and heron. Tom, Ellie and Harry showed their habitual grace and good humour in putting up with their father's distraction and absence. Paula Byrne read it all, shared it all, argued about it, understood Ted and Sylvia and marriage better than I do.

Index